lañ/ guage

introductory readings

lañ/guage

introductory readings

Virginia P. Clark,
Paul A. Eschholz,
Alfred F. Rosa,
Editors
University of Vermont

St. Martin's Press, New York

ACKNOWLEDGMENTS

Part One   Language, Thought, and Culture

p. 3   "Language, Thought, and Culture," by Peter Woolfson. St. Martin's Press, Inc., 1972. Copyright © 1972 by Peter Woolfson.

p. 12   "Work with the Wolof," by Patricia M. Greenfield and Jerome S. Bruner. Reprinted from *The Relevance of Education* by Jerome S. Bruner, edited by Anita Gil. By permission of W. W. Norton & Company, Inc. Copyright © 1971 by Jerome S. Bruner.

p. 27   "Language and Animal Signals," by Claire Russell and W. M. S. Russell. From *Linguistics at Large*, edited by Noel Minnis. New York: The Viking Press, 1971, pp. 159–194. Reprinted by permission of Dr. W. M. S. Russell and David Higham Associates, Ltd.

p. 56   "Feral and Isolated Man," by Roger Brown. Reprinted with permission of The Macmillan Company from *Words and Things* by Roger Brown. © by The Free Press, 1958.

p. 62   "The Linguistic Development of Children," by M. M. Lewis. From *Linguistics at Large*, edited by Noel Minnis. New York: The Viking Press, 1971, pp. 197–208. Reprinted by permission of Mrs. H. Lewis.

p. 72   "Conditioning the Uncommitted Cortex for Language Learning," by Wilder Penfield. In *Brain*, Vol. 88, Part 4 (November 1965). Reprinted by permission.

p. 84   "Bilingualism and Information Processing," by Paul A. Kolers. Copyright © 1968 by Scientific American, Inc. All rights reserved. Reprinted by permission.

p. 97   "Speech Is More Than Language," by Peter Woolfson. St. Martin's Press, Inc., 1972. Copyright © 1972 by Peter Woolfson.

Part Two   The Systems of Grammar

p. 107   "Trouble in Linguistic Paradise," by Charlton Laird. From Charlton Laird's *And Gladly Teche: Notes on Instructing the Natives in the Native Tongue*, © 1970. Reprinted by permission of Prentice-Hall, Inc., Englewood Cliffs, N.J.

p. 111   "Revolution in Grammar," by W. Nelson Francis, is reprinted from *Quarterly Journal of Speech*, 40 (1954), 299–312, by permission of the Speech Communication Association and the author.

p. 129   "The Scholarly Dispute over the Meaning of Linguistics." Reprinted by permission from *Time*, The Weekly Newsmagazine; Copyright Time Inc., 1968.

p. 132   "The Psycholinguists: On the New Scientists of Language," by George A. Miller, is reprinted from *Encounter*, 23 (1964), 29–37, by permission of *Encounter* and the author.

p. 149   "Transformational Grammar: An Introduction," by Paul M. Postal. Reprinted by permission of the publisher, from "The Epilogue" by Paul M. Postal in Jacobs/Rosenbaum: *English Transformational Grammar*, Copyright © in 1968 by Roderick A. Jacobs and Peter S. Rosenbaum and published by Xerox Corporation through Xerox College Publishing, successor in interest to Blaisdell Publishing Company, 1968, Waltham, Mass.

p. 172   "Language and the Mind," by Noam Chomsky. Reprinted from *Psychology Today* Magazine, February, 1968. Copyright © Communications/Research/ Machines, Inc.

p. 185   "Stratificational Grammar: A New Theory of Language," by John White, from the October 1969 *College Composition and Communication*. Copyright © 1969 by the National Council of Teachers of English. Reprinted by permission of the publisher and John White.

p. 194   "Tagmemics," by Peter H. Fries. St. Martin's Press, Inc., 1972. Copyright © 1972 by Peter H. Fries.

p. 209   "The Problem of Describing Syntactic Complexity," by Sven Jacobson, from *Studia Neophilologica*, 40 (1968), 114–129. Reprinted by permission of Swets & Zeitlinger, who hold the right to reprint volumes 1-40 of *Studia Neophilologica*.

Part Three   Words, Meanings, and the Dictionary

p. 229   "Dictionaries and the English Language," by Albert H. Marckwardt, from the May 1963 *English Journal*. Copyright © 1963 by the National Council of Teachers of English. Reprinted by permission of the publisher and Albert H. Marckwardt.

p. 242   "The English Language Is My Enemy!" by Ossie Davis. Copyright © by the Association for the Study of Negro Life and History, Inc. Reprinted by permission.

p. 243   "How 'White' Is Your Dictionary?" by William Walter Duncan, is reprinted from *ETC: A Review of General Semantics*, 27, No. 1, 89–91, by permission of the International Society for General Semantics.

p. 246   "Profile of a Best Seller," by B. L. Trippett, is reprinted from *Technical Communications*, 3rd Quarter of the 1970 issue, by permission of the Society for Technical Communication.

p. 254   "Computers in Language Analysis and in Lexicography," by Henry Kučera. From *The American Heritage Dictionary of the English Language*, © Copyright 1969, 1970, 1971 by American Heritage Publishing Co., Inc. Reprinted by permission.

p. 260   "Word-Making: Some Sources of New Words," by W. Nelson Francis. Reprinted from *The English Language, An Introduction*, by W. Nelson Francis. By permission of W. W. Norton & Company, Inc. Copyright © 1963, 1965 by W. W. Norton & Company, Inc.

p. 272   "Preface to the Dictionary of American Slang," by Stuart Berg Flexner. From *Dictionary of American Slang*, compiled and edited by Harold Wentworth and Stuart Berg Flexner, Copyright © 1967, 1960 by Thomas Y. Crowell Company, Inc., New York and reprinted with their permission.

p. 288   "Collegiate Slang: Aspects of Word Formation and Semantic Change," by Richard K. Seymour, is reprinted from *Publication of the American Dialect Society*, No. 51 (April 1969), 13–22, by permission of the University of Alabama Press.

p. 297   "The Agonies of Acronymania." Reprinted by permission from *Time*, The Weekly Newsmagazine; Copyright Time Inc., 1970.

p. 299   "Speaking of Space," by David McNeill, is reprinted from *Science*, 152 (May 13, 1966), 875–880. Copyright 1966 by the American Association for the Advancement of Science.

p. 312   "American Euphemisms for Dying, Death, and Burial: An Anthology," by Louise Pound, is reprinted from *American Speech*, 11, No. 3 (October 1936), 195–202, by permission of Columbia University Press.

p. 320   A corrected version of "Cobweb and Spider Web," by Gary N. Underwood. By permission. From the April issue of *Word Watching* © 1970 by G. & C. Merriam Co., Publishers of the Merriam-Webster Dictionaries.

p. 324   "Existential: Sixties' Cinderella Word," by Benjamin DeMott. From the book *Supergrow: Essays and Reports on Imagination in America* by Benjamin

Part Four Americans Speaking

Part Five Space and the Language of the Body

p. 478 "Other Ways of Packaging Information," by Randall P. Harrison. In *Communication-Spectrum* '7, Lawrence, Kansas: International Communication Association, 1968, pp. 121–136. Reprinted by permission of the author and the International Communication Association.

p. 492 "Kinesics and Communication," by Ray L. Birdwhistell, is reprinted from *Explorations in Communication*, ed. Edmund Carpenter and Marshall McLuhan. Copyright © 1960 by the Beacon Press. Reprinted by permission of Beacon Press.

p. 501 "Winking, Blinking and Nods," by Julius Fast. From *Body Language* by Julius Fast. Copyright © 1970 by Julius Fast. Published by M. Evans and Company, Inc., New York.

p. 511 "Communication by Gesture in the Middle East," by Leo Hamalian, is reprinted from *ETC: A Review of General Semantics*, 22 (1965), 43–49, by permission of the International Society for General Semantics.

p. 516 "Space Speaks," by Edward T. Hall, Chapter 10 of *The Silent Language* by Edward T. Hall. Copyright © 1959 by Edward T. Hall. Reprinted by permission of Doubleday & Co., Inc.

p. 531 "When Space Is Invaded," by Julius Fast. From *Body Language* by Julius Fast. Copyright © 1970 by Julius Fast. Published by M. Evans and Company, Inc., New York.

p. 544 "Teacher's Desk," in *Psychology Today*, Vol. 5 (September 1971), 12. Copyright © Communications/Research/Machines, Inc.

p. 547 from *The American Speaker for Boys and Girls*, by Benjamin Walter. Chicago: Homewood Publishing Company, 1902.

p. 551 from *Secrets of Charm*, by John Robert Powers and Mary Sue Miller. Copyright 1954 by John F. Dille Company. Reprinted by permission of Holt, Rinehart and Winston, Inc.

p. 552 from *How to Read a Person Like a Book*, by Gerard I. Nierenberg and Henry H. Calero. Copyright © 1971 by Gerard I. Nierenberg and Henry H. Calero. By permission of Hawthorn Books, Inc.

PICTURE CREDITS

p. 472 photograph by St. Hilaire. Copyright © 1963 by Columbia Pictures Corp. All Rights Reserved.

p. 473 *top left:* Copyright © 1963 Columbia Pictures Corp. All Rights Reserved. *bottom left:* Copyright © 1965 by Columbia Pictures Corp. All Rights Reserved. *right:* Rizzoli Film Distributors, Inc.

p. 474 *top left:* photograph by Leonard Freed, MAGNUM PHOTOS. *top right:* photograph by Sergio Larrain © 1963 MAGNUM PHOTOS. *bottom:* photograph by Ron Benvenisti, MAGNUM PHOTOS.

p. 475 *top:* photograph by Rene Burri © 1965 MAGNUM PHOTOS. *center:* photograph by Leonard Freed © 1970 MAGNUM PHOTOS. *bottom:* photograph by Charles Harbutt © 1970 MAGNUM PHOTOS.

p. 476 *top:* photograph by Burk Uzzle © 1970 MAGNUM PHOTOS. *bottom:* photograph by David Margolin, from BLACK STAR.

To Harry, Eva, and Maggie

PREFACE

"The limits of my language mean
the limits of my world."
—*Ludwig Wittgenstein*

Man's language is central to everything he does. Since man
cannot transcend his linguistic boundaries, the tremendous
changes that have taken place in language study within
the past fifty years have had profound implications for his
view of himself and his place in society. This collection of
introductory readings reflects these changing attitudes toward
language through its treatment of five major topics:
1) animal communication, the human mind, and language
and culture; 2) the systems of grammar; 3) words and how
they are used; 4) regional, functional, and social dialect
variations; and 5) the gestures and spatial relationships
that complement verbal language. These five sections provide
a basis for a meaningful study of language.

Our emphasis on nonverbal communication is new to
introductory anthologies. Recent work in kinesics and
proxemics and their interrelationships with verbal
communication makes it clear that no consideration of
language is complete that does not recognize this important
area. Since nonverbal communication is in large part
visual, we have included photographic materials as

illustrations of the principles discussed in the text.

In selecting the articles for each of these sections, we have sought to achieve an evenness of sophistication. Furthermore, we have tried to include articles that are informative, in line with current thinking about language, and comprehensive in their coverage. We have prized readability and therefore have not hesitated to go beyond the standard linguistic authors and journals for the kind of material that not only challenges the student but also stimulates his interest. Although there is a rationale for the arrangement of the sections, the order is by no means inflexible and the instructor may wish to establish his own sequence.

In addition to questions at the end of each article which serve to focus the student's attention on specific issues in his reading, we have included a series of projects at the end of each section. These projects are designed to encourage the student to go beyond his reading and to apply what he has learned. The annotated bibliographies that conclude each section are designed to aid the student in working with these projects.

We are grateful to J. R. Bashore, Jr., Robert Palmatier, and Louis Milic for their helpful suggestions and comments on the manuscript. We would also like to thank Thomas V. Broadbent, Judy Green, and Jonathan Latimer at St. Martin's. The book is better for their guidance, and they have made our task all the more enjoyable. Frank Manchel generously made available his extensive collection of movie stills. We appreciate the advice of our colleague Littleton Long and the assistance of Mrs. Evelyn C. Kyle. Special thanks go to Verne Reaves, who edited the manuscript, and to our students at the University of Vermont whose enthusiasm for language study and responses to materials included in this book were most helpful.

Virginia P. Clark
Paul A. Eschholz
Alfred F. Rosa

CONTENTS

PART THREE
Words, Meanings, and the Dictionary

PART FOUR
Americans Speaking

PART FIVE
Space and the Language of the Body

PART ONE

Language, Thought, and Culture

Recent studies of language have shown an increasing reliance upon the research of sociologists, anthropologists, psychologists, ethologists, and neurosurgeons. Clearly this reliance is the product of an awareness by linguists that language is a part of the total behavior of man and that his behavior, in turn, influences his language. Questions concerning the interrelationships of language and culture, the functions of the brain, the mental processes of the bilingual, the extent to which speech is necessary for thought, the child's acquisition of language, and what the communication systems of animals can tell us about language are only some of the questions which these new studies are attempting to answer.

The readings that follow, most of which have been published recently, will give the student both a basic understanding of a central issue—the Sapir-Whorf hypothesis that language is culture-bound and shapes reality—and a sample of recent studies involving such a thesis. Other selections show how the findings of the brain surgeon can influence foreign language teaching and how the language of small children can give us insights into the nature of grammar. There is diversity in these readings because man's behavior is complex. There is also a sense of unity because a greater knowledge of language and how it is acquired and used is a central theme.

1
Language, Thought, and Culture

Peter Woolfson

As far back as 1836, Wilhelm von Humboldt, in *Linguistic Variability and Intellectual Development*, looked at language as a tool man uses to represent ideas in sentences. His work prefigured the emphasis on the relationship between language and thought later developed by Edward Sapir in *Language* (1921) and popularized by Benjamin Lee Whorf. The so-called Sapir-Whorf hypothesis that language shapes reality is probably one of the most controversial hypotheses in linguistic anthropology and psycholinguistics. In the following article, Peter Woolfson examines the limitations and potentialities of Whorf's linguistic relativity hypothesis.

PSYCHOLINGUISTS and linguistic anthropologists share a common concern with the relationship between language and thought. Several questions have been raised about this relationship, but the dominant one can be stated very simply: does the language we speak determine the way we think? One well-known attempt to answer the question is the *linguistic relativity hypothesis* (also called the Sapir-Whorf hypothesis or the Whorfian hypothesis).[1] In essence, the hypothesis suggests that a given language, especially in its grammar, provides its speakers with habitual grooves of expression which predispose these speakers to see the world in ready-made patterns. Since grammars vary from language to language, it is likely that the habitual patterns of thought vary from language to language. If so, the world view of a speaker of a particular language will be different from the world view of a speaker of a different language. Although the hypothesis seems to affirm the view that language determines thought, one

---

[1] Benjamin L. Whorf, *Language, Thought, and Reality*, ed. J. B. Carroll (New York: John Wiley & Sons, 1964).

should remember that it concentrates on habitual patterns; and habitual patterns may be ignored or circumvented. What is necessary is that we become aware of these patterns by conscious introspection, scientific study, or cross-cultural comparison.

Why are habitual patterns of expression so important? We all have approximately the same set of physical organs for perceiving reality— eyes to see, ears to hear, noses to smell, tongues to taste, and skins to feel. Reality should be the same for us all. Our nervous systems, however, are being bombarded by a continual flow of sensations of different kinds, intensities, and durations. It is obvious that all of these sensations do not reach our consciousness; some kind of filtering system reduces them to manageable proportions. The Whorfian hypothesis suggests that the filtering system is one's language. Our language, in effect, provides us with a special pair of glasses that heightens certain perceptions and dims others. Thus, while all sensations are received by the nervous system, only some are brought to the level of consciousness. One of Whorf's classic examples, *snow*, illustrates the role of language in this process:

> We have the same word for falling snow, snow on the ground, snow packed hard like ice, slushy snow, wind-driven flying snow—whatever the situation may be. To an Eskimo, this all-inclusive word would be almost unthinkable; he would say that falling snow, slushy snow, and so on, are sensually and operationally different, different things to contend with; he uses different words for them and for other kinds of snow. The Aztecs go even farther than we in the opposite direction with "cold," "ice," and "snow" all represented by the same basic word. . . .[2]

Although Whorf demonstrated that different languages use words differently to classify reality, he also indicated by his techniques of illustration that these concepts can be expressed, in a language that lacks them, by other means. Thus, the different types of snow may be described by adjectival words and phrases. Using these alternatives in English grammar, he makes it possible for us to visualize the different types of snow and to perceive the differences among them. Because the differences are specifically labeled, we become conscious of them. The important point to remember is that we are not *habitually conscious* of these distinctions. But if it becomes necessary for us to perceive these distinctions, as a skier might with snow, then they would become conscious, and the vocabulary or descriptive items would follow. In the case of the skier, he borrows his terms for snow from the more specialized vocabulary of the Austrians.

2 Whorf, p. 216.

Snow, however, is an example of a word with obvious cultural and environmental emphases. In many instances the relationship between cultural emphasis and vocabulary is much less apparent. For example, Americans are a mobile people and transportation plays an extremely important role culturally in our society. And yet we use the word *go* whether we are going by foot, car, train, or plane. Germans, on the other hand, use *gehen* when they go by foot, and *fahren* when they go by vehicle. The Navaho, according to Kluckholn and Leighton, make an even more complex set of distinctions:

> When a Navaho says that he went somewhere he never fails to specify whether it was afoot, astride, by wagon, auto, train, or airplane. This is done partly by using different verb stems which indicate whether the traveler moved under his own steam or was transported, partly by naming the actual means. . . .
>
> Moreover the Navaho language insists upon another type of splitting of the generic idea of "going" to which German is as indifferent as English. The Navaho always differentiates between starting to go, going along, arriving at, returning from a point. . . .[3]

And so, although transportation is a major cultural emphasis in American society, our word *go* is certainly considerably less precise than the terms used by the Navaho for this activity. It becomes apparent, then, that even when an activity has considerable cultural emphasis, certain perceptions may be heightened by the language while others may remain dim.

Does having separate words for different aspects of a thing or an event really make a difference in our consciousness, our awareness? For example, we commonly make distinctions between the colors *purple,* *blue, green, yellow, orange,* and *red.* If we have special interests like painting or dress designing, we may have a much wider vocabulary which includes distinctions between shades such as "cerise," "burgundy," or "magenta." These distinctions, however, are not part of the ordinary vocabulary of the American male, for instance. Investigations show that other languages are more restricted in their color vocabulary than English. The Shona of Rhodesia have only three major terms: *cips^{w}uka* (orange, red, purple and some blue); *citema* (blue and some green); and *cicena* (green and yellow). The Bassa of Liberia have only two major color terms: *hui* which represents purple, blue, and green; and *zīza* which represents yellow, orange, and red.[4] In one sense, these more restricted vocabularies do not affect consciousness. If the speaker

---

[3] Clyde Kluckhohn and Dorothea Leighton, *The Navaho* (New York: Doubleday & Company, 1962), pp. 274–75.

[4] H. A. Gleason, Jr., *An Introduction to Descriptive Linguistics,* rev. ed. (New York: Holt, Rinehart and Winston, 1961), pp. 4–5.

of one of these languages finds it necessary to make color distinctions not indicated by his color terms, he can still express the distinction by using the objects in the environment—"that's leaf *citema*" or "that's sky *citema*," for example. On the other hand, psycholinguists like Lantz, Brown, and Lenneberg have shown that having a number of terms for color distinctions is particularly useful for remembering colors that have been seen at an earlier time.[5] The more color terms the subjects in these experiments had, the better their memories were for sorting out the colors they had seen. These examples show that there is a relationship between vocabulary, cultural emphasis, and habitual consciousness.

But does the language of a speaker provide him with a structure for seeing the world in ready-made patterns? In other words, is the Whorfian hypothesis valid? It should be obvious that the Whorfian hypothesis is just that, a hypothesis: an idea to be tested, an informed guess. In spite of numerous attempts at verification, it has never been satisfactorily proved or disproved. But it remains plausible. For example, the grammatical categories of singular and plural are important ones in English grammar, so important that they are expressed redundantly:

One boy goes outside.
Two boys go outside.

Plurality, in these examples, is reiterated by the use of a number word, a noun suffix, and a specific verbal form. Singular and plural are categories that can hardly be ignored. A speaker of English finds it natural to divide his universe into things that are either singular or plural. To a speaker of Taos, an American Indian language, however, this view would represent a gross oversimplification. According to Trager:

> . . . In the Taos linguistic universe there is no such simple distinction: some things are indeed unitary, and others are multiple, but some unitary things can be multiple only in sets, while others are multiple as aggregates: moreover, a set can be unitary, if it is inanimate, or it can be multiple—but then only if it is animate. . . .[6]

Thus, the Taos Indian classifies the objects in his universe differently from a native speaker of English. The Whorfian hypothesis suggests that because of this difference in classification, the Taos Indian actually sees the world differently from a native speaker of English.

The apparent relationship between grammar and world view can be seen in the basic types of sentence structures. Probably the most typical kind of sentence in English is the declarative sentence made up of a

---

[5] Joseph DeVito, *The Psychology of Speech and Language* (New York: Random House, 1970), p. 200.

[6] George L. Trager, *Languages of the World* (Buffalo, New York: unpublished manuscript), IV, 17.

subject, verb, and direct object and associated with our conceptual focus of an actor, an action, and the object of an action. For example, the answer to the question "What happened?" could be either

John	*dropped*	*the ball*
Subject	Verb	Direct Object
Actor	Action	Object of Action

or

The car	*hit*	*the bridge*
Subject	Verb	Direct Object
Actor	Action	Object of Action

This sentence form is so common in English that we use the form metaphorically without being the least bit conscious of imposing the form "actor, action, object of action" where it does not literally apply. As a result, English commonly produces sentences such as:

Communism	*threatens*	*Southeast Asia*
Subject	Verb	Direct Object
Actor	Action	Object of Action

Northern Chinese, however, does not ordinarily use this kind of sentence structure. If one asked a speaker of Chinese the equivalent of the question "What happened?" he would probably get the answer in the form of *topic* and *comment*. In other words, where the American would say, "John dropped the ball," the Chinese would say, "Ball-particle (type of object)-dropping." It is not necessary for the Chinese to indicate the actor or the time of the action. Speakers of English, in contrast, specify whether the action was in the past or not. However, they do have a sentence form where the actor is not specified: subject and passive verb: "The ball was dropped." Nevertheless, many speakers of English feel uneasy about this construction; it does not appear complete. Since only two of the three habitual components are present, they feel compelled to ask, "Dropped by whom?" In short, Americans and Chinese have different basic sentence structures which focus on different aspects of a situation.[7]

In order to deal systematically with the question of the validity of the Whorfian hypothesis, it is necessary to ask several other questions. First, is thought possible without speech? If it is, then at least some perceptions are possible without the mediation of language. Studies of animal behavior suggest some answers. W. H. Thorpe, an ethologist, maintains that all animals perceive—that is, anticipate and recognize.

[7] Charles F. Hockett, *A Course in Modern Linguistics* (New York: The Macmillan Company, 1958), pp. 201–03.

He writes, "Some essential ability to deal with events in time as in space is, by definition, to be expected throughout the world of living things."[8] For example, when a cat runs up a tree after seeing a dog, he exhibits this ability. The cat sees the dog (perception); it identifies the dog as dangerous (cognition); it foresees trouble (anticipation); it quickly checks its environment (evaluation); and it runs up the nearest tree (resolution). The cat does all this without the aid of language, and therefore it seems reasonable to assume that we are capable of some processes of thought without the mediation of language.

Second, are the grammars of various languages really different? Do not all languages possess features in common? Is there not a universal grammar, a general grammar of human languages? Are not the differences between languages, in reality, superficial, of little consequence in determining man's perceptions of reality? Let us look at the kinds of language universals that have been identified by Charles Hockett and Joseph Greenberg. Hockett[9] outlines thirteen design features of language, such as *semanticity* (shared associations), *arbitrariness* (non-iconicity), and *productivity* (open-endedness). Greenberg[10] discusses such universals as *multi-modality: indicative mode* (statement) and *imperative mode* (command), for example. There are, to be sure, very broad and general, universal statements about language that can be made to which no exceptions can be found. However, it is equally true that the grammars of the languages of the world show considerable variety in the devices they employ to classify reality. It is this level of classification, dissection, and organization, the level of diversity rather than universality, with which Whorf's linguistic relativity hypothesis is concerned.

Third, what effect does culture—learned and shared behavior patterns—have on the way we perceive the world? Although language is our principal means of transmitting culture from generation to generation, much of our learning, especially while we are young, takes place without explicit verbalizations: that is, much of our behavior is learned informally through observation and imitation. All kinds of sensory data may be used to recognize, classify, anticipate, and evaluate experiences. For example, a child whose first experiences of life take place within a single-roomed structure such as an igloo, tipi, or tent develops a sense of reality which is quite different from the child whose early experiences take place in a multi-partitioned structure in which his own place, the nursery, is safely insulated from the adult experiences around him. The different settings, themselves, affect the child's image of self, his rela-

8 W. H. Thorpe, *Learning and Instinct in Animals* (Cambridge, Mass.: Harvard Univ. Press, 1958), p. 4.
9 Charles Hockett, "The Origin of Speech," *American Scientist*, 203 (1960), 89–96.
10 Joseph Greenberg, *Anthropological Linguistics* (New York: Random House, 1968).

tionship to others, to events, and to things. Thus culture provides many avenues for developing our perception of reality.

In spite of these questions, social scientists have attempted to devise tests for verifying the Whorfian hypothesis. One major consideration in such testing has been the nature of Whorf's evidence. Frequently, he named a grammatical device in one language and a different device for handling a similar situation in another language, and assumed that the difference demonstrated a difference in perception. This assumption is not necessarily valid. For example, French classifies all nouns as either masculine or feminine—*le soleil*, "the sun," is masculine, but *la lune*, "the moon," is feminine. Despite this classification, the Frenchman does not actually perceive these gender distinctions as real; they are simply grammatical devices. Whatever relationships these classifications once had with reality are now very remote.

In an attempt to provide a more defensible way of verifying the hypothesis, social scientists began to look for non-verbal behavioral concomitants for linguistic categories. One test, given by John Carroll, involved showing English and Hopi subjects three pictures from which they were to select the two that they felt were most alike. The pictures were based on differences in the way objects are handled. For example, one series of pictures showed three men, one unloading a carton of fruit, one spilling milk, and one dropping a coin. English subjects most often grouped the accidental actions, whereas the Hopi grouped the first two because words in their language for these actions are similar.[11]

Another experiment, conducted by Joseph Casagrande, involved Navaho and English-speaking children:

> Navaho and English-speaking children were presented with two objects which differed from each other in both form and color, for example, a blue stick and a yellow rope. They were then shown a third object which matched one of the original objects in color and the other in form, for example, a blue rope. They were asked to select one of the two original objects which best matched this third object. A number of such sets were used and the results confirmed the hypothesis. Navaho children, in the example cited above, selected the yellow rope, whereas English-speaking children selected the blue stick.[12]

When middle-class English-speaking children in metropolitan Boston were given the same test, however, there were unexpected results.[13] They made choices similar to those of the Navaho children. Apparently,

---

11 DeVito, p. 205.

12 DeVito, p. 206.

13 John B. Carroll and Joseph B. Casagrande, "The Function of Language Classifications in Behavior," *Communication and Culture*, ed. Alfred Smith (New York: Holt, Rinehart & Winston, 1966), pp. 503–04.

the Boston children were accustomed to having "creative" toys to play with, toys that involve the child in manipulating objects. Certainly the results achieved in Boston weaken the conclusiveness of the original experiment. An additional problem with the validity of these tests is that they are designed to show relationships between language and behavior on a relatively concrete level, and the selection of a yellow rope or a blue stick hardly qualifies as an example of philosophical orientation. In reality, the Whorfian hypothesis has most relevance in the areas that are most difficult to pin down: philosophy, religion, ethics, and values. Behavioral concomitants on this level are difficult to find and test.

Another difficulty in testing the Whorfian hypothesis is that of controlling variables. Ideally, tests should be conducted on subjects whose backgrounds include a unilingual-unicultural environment. Unfortunately, the kind of geographic and cultural isolation necessary for this kind of environment is very rare. The modern world is one that fosters cultures which are multilingual and languages which are multicultural.

In the final analysis, Whorf's linguistic relativity hypothesis will probably remain only a hypothesis. But this does not mean that we should abandon it as a useful tool. On the contrary, by comparing patterns of grammatical usage—becoming conscious of them, studying them, and evaluating them—we will gain insights into the categories our language forces us to pay attention to, the ideas that are easy for us to express, and the ideas that are difficult to voice. We can, as Whorf put it, turn background into foreground. Thus, both science and man are served.

Bibliography

Brown, Roger. *Social Psychology.* New York: The Free Press, 1965.

Carroll, John B. *Language and Thought.* Englewood Cliffs, New Jersey: Prentice-Hall, 1964.

————, and Joseph B. Casagrande. "The Function of Language Classifications in Behavior." *Communication and Culture.* Ed. Alfred Smith. New York: Holt, Rinehart & Winston, 1966.

Chomsky, Noam. *Language and Mind.* New York: Harcourt, Brace & World, 1968.

DeVito, Joseph. *The Psychology of Speech and Language.* New York: Random House, 1970.

Fishman, Joshua. "A Systematization of the Whorfian Hypothesis." *Behavioral Science,* 5 (1960), 323–39.

Gleason, H. A., Jr., *An Introduction to Descriptive Linguistics.* Rev. ed. New York: Holt, Rinehart & Winston, 1961.

Greenberg, Joseph. *Anthropological Linguistics.* New York: Random House, 1968.

Hockett, Charles F. *A Course in Modern Linguistics.* New York: The Macmillan Company, 1958.

————. "The Origin of Speech." *American Scientist,* 203 (1960), 89–96.

Hoijer, Harry, ed. *Language in Culture.* Chicago: University of Chicago Press, 1954.

Hymes, Dell, ed. *Language in Culture and Society.* New York: Harper, 1964.

Kluckhohn, Clyde, and Dorothea Leighton. *The Navaho.* New York: Doubleday & Company, 1962.

Sapir, Edward. *Culture, Language, and Personality.* Ed. David B. Mandelbaum. Berkeley and Los Angeles: University of California Press, 1949.

———, *Language.* New York: Harcourt, Brace, 1921.

Thorpe, W. H. *Learning and Instinct in Animals.* Cambridge, Mass.: Harvard University Press, 1958.

Trager, George L. *Languages of the World.* Buffalo, New York: Unpublished manuscript.

Whorf, Benjamin L. *Language, Thought, and Reality.* Ed. J. B. Carroll. New York: John Wiley & Sons, 1964.

Woolfson, Peter, "Sapir's Theory of Language." *Language Sciences*, No. 11 (August 1970), 8–10.

FOR DISCUSSION AND REVIEW

1 In brief, what is the *linguistic relativity hypothesis* (or *Whorfian hypothesis*)?

2 What are "habitual patterns"? According to Woolfson, why are they important to the Whorfian hypothesis?

3 At the lexical level, how does language shape perception? What evidence does the author provide on this point?

4 Is there a relationship between vocabulary, cultural emphasis, and habitual consciousness? If so, explain what the relationship is.

5 In what ways can the grammar of a language affect the way a person perceives his environment?

6 On the basis of a cat's behavior in the presence of a dog, Woolfson believes that it is "reasonable to assume that we are capable of some processes of thought without the mediation of language." Do you agree? Why or why not?

7 In what ways can culture, according to Woolfson, shape one's perception of reality? Can you think of any examples from your own experiences that show how culture influences perception? Explain.

8 Even though the Whorfian hypothesis is likely to remain a hypothesis, why does it continue to be interesting and valuable?

2

Work with the Wolof

In the course of their attempts to determine how and to what extent different cultures lead to different ways of thinking and perceiving, anthropologists, linguists, and psychologists have carried out various kinds of experiments. One such recent study is that conducted by Patricia M. Greenfield during 1963 and 1964 in Senegal. Whereas Woolfson, in the preceding article, discusses the ways in which language may affect culture, Greenfield and Bruner point to the effects that culture, and particularly education, have on cognitive processes.

Patricia M. Greenfield
and Jerome S. Bruner

THE IDEA that different cultures produce different modes of thought is not new. Anthropologists and psychologists have long investigated cultural influences on cognitive development. However, their methods rarely have been equal to the task.

One of the most interesting and oldest lines of cross-cultural work in this area is the study of sensation and perception. More than one intelligence tester noted that performance tests often put foreigners at as much disadvantage as verbal tests did, and they concluded that perceptual as well as verbal habits could vary radically from culture to culture.

The classical work on perception was done when the Cambridge Anthropological Expedition to the Torres Straits in 1901 to 1905 found that Murray Islanders were less susceptible than Europeans to the Müller-Lyer illusion. Anthropologists found this same lack of susceptibility

among the Todas of India. But as soon as researchers used three-dimensional materials with the Todas, cultural differences disappeared. Perhaps the Todas were less subject to the illusion because they were not accustomed to inferring three-dimensions from two-dimensional displays.

This work suggests that particular cultural conditions such as the absence of pictures affect perception, and later studies have confirmed this theory. Members of different cultures apparently differ in the inferences they draw from perceptual cues, not in the cues they can distinguish. Given complex input, the principles of selectivity can also vary from culture to culture.

Anthropological linguists like Benjamin Whorf suggest that language differences may reflect cognitive differences. More to the point than Whorf's theory that vocabulary structure influences the perception of reality is the question of how cultures differ in their use of language as a tool of thought.

Psychologists who work on development are strongly influenced by Jean Piaget. But although Piaget has given us our richest picture of cognitive development, it is a view based almost entirely on experiments in which age alone is varied. While Piaget recognizes that environmental influences play a role, his classic experiments were confined to Western-European children, usually from the middle class. Today, many psychologists are doing Piagetian experiments in non-Western settings.

At the Harvard Center for Cognitive Studies, we have attempted to discover what kinds of cultural differences make intellectual differences at what points in development. By comparing children of different ages in extremely different cultures, we can ask the developmental question in its most radical form. And we have found that value orientation and language are two cultural constraints that affect the children's development.

In her studies of basic value orientation, Florence Kluckhohn points out the cognitive implications of collective and of individualistic orientation, both for individual coping and for social solidarity. This value contrast represents more than alternate ways of seeing how things ought to be. It reflects a contrast in how things *are*—a matter of world view and origins and existence.

In 1963 through 1964, Patricia Greenfield did a series of studies in Senegal, the westernmost tip of former French West Africa. She explored two main areas of cognitive development: concept formation and conservation in the classic Piagetian sense—i.e., in the realization that the mass of an object remains constant, no matter how much its shape changes.

Piaget demonstrated that if you give a five-year-old two tumblers, each half-full of water, he will say that there is the same amount of water in each. But if, before his eyes, you pour the water from one glass into a tall, narrow container, he will say that there is more water in this glass than in the other one. The five-year-old has a different concept of the conservation of substance, but—among the middle-class Swiss children that Piaget studied—by the time the child is seven, he will understand that the amount of water in each glass remains the same.

The subjects in Greenfield's experiments were all Wolof, members of the country's dominant ethnic group. She divided the children into nine groups, according to three degrees of urbanization and education, with three age levels in each category.

The members of the first group had never left the bush. Although their traditional Wolof village had an elementary school, they had never attended it. She divided these rural, unschooled Wolof among three age groups: six- and seven-year-olds, eight- and nine-year-olds, and 11- to 13-year-olds. There also was a group of adults.

The second major group—the bush school children—attended school in the same village or in a nearby village. She divided this group among first-graders, third-graders and sixth-graders, corresponding as closely as possible to the three age levels of the unschooled groups. City school children made up the third major group. These children lived in Dakar, Senegal's cosmopolitan capital, and—like the second group—included first-, third- and sixth-graders. All the children were questioned in Wolof, although French was the official language of instruction.

In both the conservation and the concept experiments, the children gave reasons for their answers. With both American and European children, one generally evokes the reason by asking: "Why do you say (or think) that thus and such is true?" Specifically, in a conservation problem, one might ask: "Why do you say that this glass has more water than this one?" Unschooled children met this type of question with uncomprehending silence. When, however, we changed the question to "Why *is* thus and such true?" unschooled children often answered it quite easily.

Unschooled Wolof children appear to lack Western self-consciousness: they do not distinguish between their own thought or statement about a thing and the thing itself. Thought and the object of thought seem to be one. Consequently, the idea of explaining a *statement* is meaningless; one can only explain the external event. From all this we might conclude that our relativistic notion that events can vary according to point of view is not prevalent among the Wolof. Greenfield's concept-formation studies confirm this expectation, for the unschooled children can group a given set of objects or pictures according to only one attribute, although there are several other possible ways to classify them.

Let it be noted that Wolof school children do not differ essentially from Western children in this respect. It appears that school tends to give Wolof children something akin to Western self-consciousness, for school children can answer questions implying a distinction between their own psychological reactions and external events; and, as they advance in school, they become increasingly capable of grouping the same items according to several different points of view.

Piaget has proposed that intellectual growth begins with an egocentric stage, based on the inability to distinguish between internal and external. A more developed egocentrism then follows, in which the child can distinguish between inner and outer but still confuses the two. When one attributes inner psychological phenomena, such as emotion, to inanimate features of the world, we have *animism*; when one gives characteristics of the inanimate, external world to one's psychological processes, we speak of *realism*. These two tendencies are supposed to be complementary and universal forms of childish thought. Their mutual presence indicates the child's preliminary distinction between inner and outer.

Animism often has been considered the characteristic of primitive thought par excellence. But our findings contradict this opinion. Quite possibly, only the powerful, well-cared-for, competent child sees the world in the pattern of his own feelings, and the child of traditional subsistence cultures like that of the Wolof never passes through the animistic stage. Abram Kardiner has noted that only when the child's every whim is satisfied is he led to believe that his thought is omnipotent. Our claim here is more severe. It is that where the culture gives no support for individualistic orientation, animism does not develop. The world stays on one level of reality—the realistic level.

Other studies support this point. In an experiment done in the United States, Rose Olver and Joan Hornsby showed children an assortment of pictures and asked them to put the similar ones together. Very young children often put things together because they fit into the same story, or whatnot. As they grow older, children increasingly form groups by placing those things together that share a common attribute. This is called superordinate grouping.

In this country, the transition from the earlier to the later mode of grouping is handled by egocentrism. That is, things are alike by virtue of the relationship that "I" or "you" have to them, or the action "I" or "you" take toward them. But, using parallel techniques in Anchorage, Alaska, Lee Reich found that Eskimo children do not express the function of things in terms of personal interaction with them nearly so often as do American children of European descent. The Eskimo value system puts emphasis on self-reliance but it strongly suppresses any expression of individualism. The Eskimos have a subsistence culture that depends for survival upon group action in hunting seal and caribou and communal stone-weir fishing. Eskimo children develop their superordinate structures without the kind of egocentrism that we observe in European children. Thus, such egocentrism cannot be a universal stage. Instead, it appears to be clearly relative to cultural conditions and values.

It should be clear by now that the kind of implicit egocentrism in which one cannot distinguish different personal viewpoints—the kind that we have been calling realism—is strikingly different from the type that explicitly relates everything to oneself. To use Piaget's terminology, one could say that the egocentrism that ends in realism is diametrically opposed to the kind that ends in "artificialism," or the tendency to see all physical phenomena as made by and for men. This tendency is closely related to animism. It is the artificialistic type of egocentrism that appears in Rose Olver and Joan Hornsby's experiments and that is probably typical of individualistically oriented industrial societies.

In the Senegalese experiments, unselfconscious realism was clear at yet another point. Here, too, one sensed its origins in the indigenous society's lack of control over the inanimate world. As in the classic experiment on the conservation of liquids, Greenfield showed Wolof children two identical beakers, one of them filled with water to a certain level. The Wolof child poured an equal amount in the second beaker. Then the experimenter poured the water from one beaker into a longer, thinner beaker, in which the water level was higher. She then asked the child if the two beakers contained the same amount of water, or if one beaker held more water than the other. The child gave a reason for his answer.

Wolof children tended to support non-conservation judgments with a reason that we had not encountered among American children (although Piaget reports one example in a Swiss four-year-old). The child would say, "It's not the same" because "you poured it," explaining a natural phenomenon by attributing special "magical" powers to the experimenter. That is, faced with the change in the water, the child bases his causal inference on the experimenter's handling of the water —a not unreasonable assumption. But this explanation mingles contiguous physical events with contiguous social events—a causal chain unacceptable in our society. This kind of magical causation is possible only in a realism in which animate and inanimate phenomena occupy a single plane of reality.

Note well that school suppresses this mode of thinking with astonishing absoluteness. There is not one instance of such reasoning among either bush or city Senegalese children who have been in school seven months or longer. School seems to promote the self-consciousness born of a distinction between the human processes and the physical phenomena.

One can argue that just as soon as the child has control of the situation, his realism and magical reasoning will disappear, for a child might be willing to attribute powers to an authority figure like the experimenter that he would not claim for himself. And so it was. We repeated the experiment with one exception: this time the child did *all* the pouring himself.

Among the younger children, two thirds of the group who transferred the water themselves achieved conservation, in contrast to only one quarter of the children who had only watched the experimenter pour. Among the older children the contrast was equally dramatic: eight in 10 of those who did the pouring themselves—as compared with slightly less than half of those who watched the experimenter—achieved conservation. When the child did his own pouring, the reasons he gave were dramatically different from those he gave when an adult was pouring. Magical action virtually disappears among the unschooled children and they justify conservation by saying, "They were equal at the beginning."

Douglass Price-Williams' study of conservation among Tiv children in Nigeria supports our study. He found that all Tiv children achieve conservation by age eight, in sharp contrast to only half of the much older Senegalese children. But Tiv culture is quite different from Wolof, for it promotes an active, manipulative approach to the physical world. Price-Williams describes the children as spontaneously pouring the earth he used in the experiment, and as reversing the experiment on their own initiative. Unschooled Wolof children never showed such initiative during the experiments, and this single factor may well be the key to the great disparity between the two cultures in their response to conservation tests.

It may be that a collective value orientation develops when the individual lacks power over the physical world. Lacking personal power, he has no notion of personal importance. He will be less likely to set himself apart from others and from the physical world; he will be less self-conscious; and he will place less value on himself. The very same Wolof children who lack self-consciousness when they are questioned about their "thoughts" also seem, in the conservation experiment, to be hindered by a lack of experience in manipulating the physical world. Thus, mastery over the physical world and individualistic self-consciousness should appear together in a culture.

Is there, however, developmental reason for this dichotomy between individual mastery and a collective or social-value orientation? Is there a point in child rearing at which a choice is made? Jacqueline Rabain-Zempléni studied the Wolof child in his traditional bush setting from the time of his weaning (age two) to his integration into a peer group (age four). Her findings confirm our interpretation of later intellectual development among the Wolof children and show how Wolof child-training practice and infant experience dramatically foreshadow these developments.

Her work shows that adult members of a Wolof family evaluate and interpret the child's motor activity in terms of the relation of this activity to the people around him. That is, the Wolof child's first steps are not treated as beginning mastery of the walking process, but as evidence of the child's desire to move nearer to another person. In such a culture one would expect less mastery of physical acts and less differentiation of the physical from the social.

A social interpretation of an act not only relates the actor to the group, but also relates the group—including the actor—to physical events. When, on the other hand, adults interpret the child's early actions in terms of motor competence, other people are irrelevant, and the act becomes separated from the motivations, intentions and desires of the actor himself. It would appear that there is a developmental reason for the dichotomy between physical mastery and a collective orientation and that it appears at the very beginning of life.

Rabain-Zempléni confirms our hypothesis that Wolof children lack manipulatory experience, for she notes that manipulation of objects is an occasional and secondary activity for the child from two to four and that, furthermore, the Wolof child's "self-image does not have to rest in the same way as in Europe on the power which he has over objects but rather on that which he has over other bodies." She also notes that children and adults often talk about relations between people but they rarely discuss natural phenomena.

At the same time, the Wolof culture discourages personal desires and intentions that would isolate the Wolof child from the group. Thus, the collective orientation is systematically encouraged as socialization progresses. Western society recognizes individual intention and desire as a positive function of age. But, according to Rabain-Zempléni, Wolof society does the reverse. The Wolof treat the newborn child as a person full of personal desire and intention; after he reaches the age of two, adults increasingly subordinate his desires to the ends of the group. He becomes less and less an individual and more and more a member of a collectivity.

On a broader cultural level, this very same quality has been recognized by the poets of *negritude* or the African Personality as setting off black from white. In her book on Aimé Césaire, originator of the negritude concept, Lilyan Kesteloff contrasts negritude with the values of Western civilization. In opposition to the individualism of European cultures she places "solidarity born of the cohesion of the primitive clan." This strong element of collective or social values is particularly clear in the modern concept of African socialism, which—unlike Western socialism—is supposed to be a modernization of existing ideals and social conditions rather than a radical revolution.

These world views and ideologies are strongly reflected in cognitive growth. Bear in mind, however, that the distinctions we propose are not all-or-none. We do not know to what extent this social or collective orientation may be typical of nonindustrial, traditional, or perhaps, oral cultures. Although our evidence comes from Africa, it may not be a valid description for every African society. Finally, we do not really know what causes what in the whole complex of features that we have discussed.

Our second cultural constraint is language. We presented pictures in sets of three to Wolof children and asked them to choose the two out of each three that were alike. In each set, two pictures were similar in color, two were similar in form, and two were similar in the function of the pictured object.

The children spoke either French or Wolof. It is impossible to verbalize the three possible color groupings in Wolof without the aid of French words. Specifically, in one set of three pictures, the French word *bleu* must be used to describe the basis of grouping, for there is no single word for blue in Wolof. In another set, color-grouping involves two orange pictures and a red one. The Wolof language has a single word (*honka*) for both orange and red, so that unless the children use the French word *orange*, they cannot contrast the red pair with the third member of the set. For the first set of three pictures, Wolof codes the relevant colors almost as well as French.

On lexical grounds, then, one would at very least expect that children who speak only Wolof would be less color-oriented and more functionally oriented in their groupings than children who speak two languages, and that, in a forced-choice situation, both of these groups would form fewer color and more functional groups than do children who speak only French.

The results, however, were unambiguously contrary to our expectations. The unschooled bush Wolofs could use nothing but color as a grouping principle, even when they had a chance to make second-choice groupings. In sharp contrast, the other groups of children used color less and less with age; increasingly they turned to shape or function to make their groupings. Obviously, the lack of color words does not stop monolingual Wolofs from grouping by color.

But does it make their color discrimination less accurate? Recall that one set of pictures consists of two predominantly orange pictures and one predominantly red one. We counted it an error when a child who claimed to be grouping by color selected one orange and one red picture as being most similar. If such errors of discrimination are due to language coding, Wolof monolinguals should make them most frequently, Wolof bilinguals next most frequently, and French monolinguals not at all. The results are exactly as predicted. At every age, bilinguals make fewer errors of this kind than Wolof monolinguals, and French monolingual children make no such errors at all.

But even among children who speak only Wolof, mistakes are relatively rare—we never found more than three color errors in a group of 20 children. We begin to wonder whether the lexical features of language should be assigned as large a role in thought as has been claimed by Benjamin Whorf and others.

These perceptual errors decrease with age until at last they are completely eliminated in all groups. It appears that age brings increasingly accurate perceptual discriminations. This would appear to be a universal trend, even when the lexicon of a culture hinders such discrimination. One may conclude that, with age, reality increasingly overcomes the oppositions of language.

David McNeill suggests that such findings prove merely that people learn to see, that language influences memory but does not affect perception. Some research reinforces this view. In a classic experiment, John Carroll and Joseph Casagrande asked children which of two objects (for example, a yellow block and a blue rope) would go best with a third item that was like one of the pair in color and like the other in shape. The subjects were Navaho-dominant and English-dominant Navaho children and white children from three to 10 years. The experimenters expected the Navaho-dominant children to be more sensitive to form than the other groups, because in Navaho the form of an object dictates the verb of handling. The Navaho-dominant Indian children did indeed classify by form more frequently than did the English-dominant ones, but, alas, the white children who knew no Navaho used form most frequently of all!

But language does influence perception, at least during childhood. As early as 1915, W. Peters experimentally produced color-matching errors by teaching children an artificial vocabulary in which certain colors were indistinguishable. Later, when the children learned different words for the different colors, the corresponding perceptual discriminations appeared. Eric Lenneberg, on the other hand, confirms the notion that this influence of language on perception diminishes with age, for he finds that the absence of certain color terms, which impairs color memory in Zuni adults and present color perception in Wolof children, does not affect present color perception in Zuni adults.

McNeill's hypothesis about language's affecting only the memory pattern plainly is false. Yet his notions of a linguistic label plus a correct visual image may still hold. In fact, Howard Ranken shows that linguistic coding in the form of labels can help when it is a matter of ordering shapes relative to one another, when it is not necessary to remember exact forms, but such labeling can hinder performance when the task requires a precise image of the same stimuli (as in a mental jigsaw puzzle).

Perhaps different cultures vary in their tendency to use linguistic coding. Unschooled Wolof children, for instance, tend to explain their grouping choices by pointing to the common pictorial elements. This method may counteract the detrimental effects of an inexact vocabulary by bypassing language altogether. In assessing cross-cultural studies, we do well to remember that most cultures are nontechnical, traditional, and less verbally oriented than our own.

It appears from this and other work that the presence of labels in a language encoding can affect the ordering of stimuli by providing a way to relate them across time or space. The potential influence of linguistic encoding becomes stronger as cognitive conditions become more difficult. But actual linguistic influence depends upon whether labels are available to a given person and are activated in a particular situation.

There has been much controversy about the role of superordinate words in conceptual thought. In contrast to French—and to English— the Wolof language has neither the word "color" nor the word "shape." It is clear from the results of our experiments that the lack of the word "color" does not hinder the Wolof from forming color groupings. Does the absence of the general word, however, mean that the Wolof have no general concept of color?

One set of pictures used with the Wolof consisted of a yellow clock, a banana and an orange. Suppose we represent the hierarchical structure of the three pictures in this way:

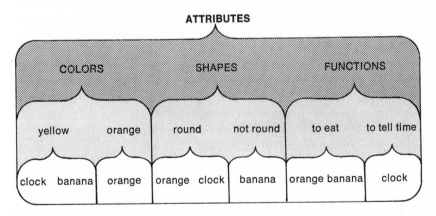

If a person uses the superordinate words "color" or "shape" to deal with his arrangement of the pictures, he is operating at the top of the hierarchy and has access to the entire hierarchy. If he is pressed, he should be able to supply more than one kind of attribute. For he is plainly contrasting, say, color with shape or with use. By the same reasoning, his exclusive use of names like "round" or "yellow" would mean that he was operating one level lower in the hierarchy. He would be cut off from the top of the hierarchy and would therefore be less likely to operate in branches other than the one in which he found himself.

If this reasoning is correct, then one would expect that, if a subject ever used an abstract word like "color" or "shape," he could vary his method of grouping when he was asked to make a first and second choice of pairs for each of the three sets of pictures. But if he used only a concrete word like "red," then he would form nothing but color groupings in all six tasks.

Our results do indeed indicate that there is a significant association between use of superordinate words like "color" and "shape" and the number of attributes used for grouping. And this relationship holds when all other factors such as knowledge of French and school level are held constant. Thus, if a Wolof child uses a superordinate word, his chances of grouping by a variety of attributes are twice as great as those of a child who uses no superordinate vocabulary. Recall that when a Wolof child uses the word "color," he is introducing a French word into a Wolof linguistic context.

We also carried out the experiment in French with French sixth-grade children. If a French child uses an abstract "top-of-the-hierarchy" label, he is almost certain to vary his basis of grouping at least once. But when Wolof children are questioned in French, there is little relationship between use of superordinate terms and variety of grouping attributes. So we must conclude that abstract terms indicate a child's access to the conceptual hierarchy only if he has thoroughly mastered the semantic implications of the terms. Such apparently is the case under normal conditions of spontaneous use in the context of one's native language.

Superordinate class words are not just a luxury for people who do not have to deal with concrete phenomena, as Roger Brown hypothesizes. In a way quite different from that envisaged by Whorf, we seem to have found an important correspondence between linguistic and conceptual structure. But it relates not to words in isolation but to their depth of hierarchical imbedding both in the language and in thought. This correspondence has to do with the presence or absence of higher-order words that can be used to integrate different domains of words and objects into structures. No matter how rich the vocabulary, it is of limited use as an instrument of thought if it is not organized into a hierarchy that can be activated.

Consider the grammatical aspect of language. Superordinate structure is different from the use of a general word like color or shape, just as the grammar of a language is different from its vocabulary. To indicate a superordinate group, one must explicitly state that the attribute is shared by every member of the group. Thus, "they are all the same color" would have the same structural status as "they are all red." Previous work has shown that one's structure of such groupings becomes increasingly superordinate with age.

Senegalese children conform to the usual developmental trend. Although the grouping choices of the unschooled Wolof group got increasingly systematic with age, their explanations showed a somewhat different form. Instead of explicitly connecting the common attribute to every member of their groupings by saying, "they are all the same color," or "they are all red," unschooled Wolof children said nothing more than "red."

Consider the matter purely in grammatical terms. Let us assume three stages of symbolic reference. The first is the mere pointing at an object. The second consists of nothing more than a verbal tag, which replaces or accompanies the pointing. In the third stage, this label is integrated into a complete sentence.

Among French monolinguals, not even first-graders point. Pointing, however, occupies a definite position in the reasoning of all the youngest Wolof groups, especially the unschooled, but disappears in all groups with advancing age. Other differences set the unschooled children apart from all the school children. In the unschooled groups, labeling increases with age. But the use of sentences remains at a constantly low level. In all the school groups, both Wolof-French bilingual and French monolingual, sentence placement ("they are all red") becomes the rule with age and increased schooling.

There is, let it be noted, virtually no difference on any measure between the oldest French monolinguals and the oldest Wolof-French bilinguals when the experiment is run in French. When we carry out the experiment in the native language of each group, the superiority is slightly on the side of the French. The contrast is most dramatic between Wolof school children questioned in French and unschooled children questioned in Wolof. Some 97 percent of the 11- to 13-year-old Wolof monolinguals indicate grouping with labels; 90 percent of the Wolof sixth graders doing the experiment in French use sentences.

Is there any direct relation between grammatical and conceptual structure? A child can frame an explicit superordinate structure with either labels or sentences. Using labels, he says, "These . . . round"; he can express the same structure in sentence form by adding a form of the verb to be; "These (or "they") are round." Among Wolof children, a particular mode of reference is strongly associated with a particular conceptual structure. When a school child frames a reason in sentence form, the probability that he will form a superordinate structure is on the average almost three times as great as when he uses simple labeling.

For an unschooled child, this same probability of a superordinate structure is almost six times as great when his reasons are sentences rather than labels.

We are led to the hypothesis that school affects grouping operations through the training embodied in the written language. This hypothesis has a good theoretical basis. The written language, as Lev S. Vygotskii points out, forces one to use language out of the immediate context of reference. The writer cannot use simple pointing, nor can he count on labeling that depends on the present context. Writing, then, is training in the use of linguistic contexts that are independent of immediate referents. Indeed, the linguistic independence of context achieved by certain grammatical modes appears to favor the development of the more self-contained superordinate structure used by the school children.

Note the recurrent theme that has been running through all our results: it is always schooling that makes qualitative differences in directions of growth. Wolof children who have been to school are more different intellectually from unschooled children living in the same bush village than they are from city children in Mexico City or Brookline, Massachusetts. Similar results demonstrating the huge impact of school have emerged from the Belgian Congo and from South Africa.

How, then, do school and language interrelate? We may hypothesize that French is a powerful factor in the cognitive growth of the children we have studied because it is a written language. All the language features that we have discussed in relation to concept formation become necessary when one must communicate away from the context of immediate reference. And it is precisely in this respect that written language differs from spoken. But school itself provides the same opportunity to use language out of context—even spoken language—for, to a very high degree, what one talks about are things not immediately present.

How exactly does the school process relate to the decline of a "realistic" world view and the rise in self-consciousness discussed earlier? When a word is considered to be as "real" as the thing for which it stands, the psychological attitude (and philosophical position) is called nominal or verbal realism. School separates word and thing and destroys verbal realism by presenting a situation in which words are systematically and continually "there" without their referents.

When names—or symbols in general—no longer inhere in their referents, they must go somewhere; and the logical place is the psyche of the language user. Thus, the separation of word and thing demands a notion that words are in a person's head, not in his referents. Meaning varies with the particular speaker, and the notion of psychological relativity is born. Implicit in this notion is the distinctness of oneself and one's own point of view. Thus, the individual must conceptually separate himself from the group; he must become self-conscious, aware of having a particular slant on things, a certain individuality.

The destruction of nominal or verbal realism may thus be the wedge that ultimately fragments the unitary solidarity of a "realistic" world view. Once thought has been dissociated from its objects, the stage is set for symbolic processes to run ahead of concrete fact, for thought to be in terms of possibility rather than actuality. At this point, symbolic reference can go beyond the capacities of visual images, and the way is opened for Piaget's stage of formal operations. So school and the written language may have a privileged position in the shift from a collective to an individualistic orientation.

None of this supports a complete cultural determinism. Species-specific behavior does not appear out of the blue. It has an evolutionary history, and that history reflects itself in the early growth of the young. We are primates, and our primate heritage affects our growth. All cultures must work on the stuff of the biological organism, specifically on man's primate constraints.

One of the huge discontinuities in man's evolution was his capacity for language and symbolism, and this only gradually achieves realization through training. Edward Sapir may have been quite right in pointing out that no human language can be shown to be more sophisticated than any other and that the speech used by the member of the Academy is no more complex than that of a Hottentot. But again it was Sapir who pointed out that peoples differ from each other precisely in extracting the powerful tools for organizing thought from their use of language. Intellectual nurturing that fully develops language as a tool of thought requires years and complex training.

As Heinz Werner pointed out, "Development among primitive people is characterized on the one hand by precocity and, on the other, by a relatively early arrest of the process of intellectual growth." His remark is telling with respect to the difference we find between school children and those who have not been to school. The unschooled stabilize earlier and do not go on to new levels of operation.

In short, some environments push a certain form of cognitive growth better, earlier, and longer than others. But different cultures do not produce completely divergent and unrelated modes of thought. The reason for this must be the constraint of our biological heritage. That heritage makes it possible for man to reach a form of intellectual maturity that can elaborate a highly technical, industrial society. Less technical societies do not produce so much symbolic embedding nor so many ways of looking and thinking. Whether one wishes to judge these differences on some universal human scale as favoring industrial man is a matter of one's values. But, however one judges, let it be clear that a decision *not* to intervene in the intellectual development of those who live in less technically developed societies cannot be based on the careless claim that it makes little difference.

FOR DISCUSSION AND REVIEW

1 What are some of the cultural factors that influence perception?

2 What were some of the deficiencies in Jean Piaget's methods, as far as psychologists and anthropologists are concerned?

3 What major differences did Greenfield find between the unschooled and the schooled Wolof children in testing for concept formation?

4 What do *animism* and *realism* have to do with egocentrism and concept formation? According to Greenfield and Bruner, is egocentrism culturally related? Explain.

5 What did the Piaget conservation experiment reveal about Wolof children of the bush? What effect does attendance at school have?

6 Does manipulative experience with physical objects have anything to do with individualistic self-consciousness? Discuss.

7 Greenfield and Bruner say that there is one recurrent theme running through all their results. What is that theme and why is it important?

8 Is Greenfield's characterization of the Whorfian hypothesis as dealing with the semantic level of language a fair one in light of Woolfson's discussion (pp. 3–11)?

9 Although cognitive growth differs from environment to environment, what finally limits that cognitive growth?

10 What does the last sentence of this article imply?

3

Language and Animal Signals

Claire Russell and W. M. S. Russell

Is it language that separates man from the rest of the animal kingdom? Is man the only symbol-making animal? These questions have attracted the attention and study of noted linguists and ethologists. Lengthy and detailed studies have been carried out with "talking" horses, dolphins, bees, whales, monkeys, birds, and chimpanzees. In this essay, the Russells discuss the meaning of language, survey the important work that has been done with the communication systems of the bee, the dolphin, and the monkey, and speculate about the origin of human language as we know it. As you read the selection, consider carefully the distinction the Russells draw between "true language" and "automatic signal codes."

THE IDEA that animals have their own language or languages is an old one. Folklore teems with examples, and the subject is allotted several pages in Stith Thompson's enormous *Motif-Index of Folk Literature*. Methods of learning animal languages vary widely. You can do it by wearing a magic ring, like King Solomon, or by taking a cocktail of dragon's blood, like Siegfried. But there are much simpler ways, such as having your ears cleaned out, or carrying churchyard mould in your hat. Several people have published dictionaries of animal languages. The Abbé Guillaume-Hyacinthe Bougeant, a Jesuit Professor, published a glossary for several bird and mammal species in 1739, and got into serious trouble with his superiors. The French aristocrat Dupont de Nemours is famous for founding in America a firm that is one of the biggest in the world today (partly thanks to developing and making nylon). He had other interests, and in 1807 he compiled Crow-French and Nightingale-French dictionaries. In recent times, an English-Ape and Ape-English dictionary has been produced by a former assistant director of Washington Zoo called Schwidetsky. The chimpanzee word for "food," according to Schwidetsky, is *ngahk*; it is related to the German word for "nutcracking," which is *knacken*.

Language and Signal Codes

We need not really worry unduly about the linguistic relations of German and Chimpanzee. But the idea that some animals may be capable of language is far from ridiculous. As we shall see, it is a matter of serious scientific study in the later 20th century. At first sight, indeed, there seems to be a lot in common between human spoken language and the calls used by a great variety of animals. A human language can be broken down into units of sound called *phonemes*, which include consonants, vowels and certain double consonants and double vowels such as *ch* [tʃ] and *ou* [au] (as in *house*). In terms of patterns of sound waves of different frequencies, a given phoneme is by no means always identical. Thus the *p* sounds in the words *pin, spin* and *nip* are somewhat different from each other in physical properties. But an English-speaker will recognize all of them as the *p* phoneme. English has between 35 and 45 of these phonemes, according to whether certain double vowels are counted as one or two units each. Italian has 27 phonemes, which must be a satisfactory number from the musical point of view, since Italian sounds so good when it is sung. The different human languages vary widely in number of phonemes, from 11 to 67. Any of us can make far more different sounds than this, and hence can learn other languages; but we rely on the basic number of phonemes when speaking our own language. Now animal call systems can similarly be broken down into basic signal units or calls, and the numbers of such units for different species of mammals and even birds fall roughly into the same range as do the numbers of phonemes of human languages, as is clear from the Table.

Animal Species	Number of Identified Basic Vocal Signals
Birds	
Chaffinch	12
Domestic chicken	20
European finch	20
White-throated warbler	25
Lower Mammals	
Coati	7
Brown lemur	7

Tree-shrew	8
Domestic and wild cow	8
Prairie dog	10
Pig	23
Fox	36

Dolphins

Amazon freshwater dolphin, pulsed sounds (e.g. "squawk")	7
Pilot whale, whistles	7
Pacific bottlenose dolphin, whistles	16
Pacific common dolphin, whistles	19
Atlantic bottlenose dolphin, whistles	17
Atlantic bottlenose dolphin, pulsed sounds	11

Monkey and Apes

Gray langur	10
Night monkey	10
Patas monkey	11
Cynocephalus baboons	15
Gibbon	15
Rhesus monkey	17
Howler monkey	20
Gorilla	23
Chimpanzee	25
Squirrel monkey	26
Vervet monkey	36
Japanese monkey	37

Human Languages   11–67

On this basis alone, we might be tempted to regard human languages and animal call systems as quite comparable. But the number of vocal units is not everything, and we need not suppose that Japanese monkeys, with 37 units, must be more sophisticated than human speakers of Hawaiian, who make do with 13. About 2300 years ago, Aristotle put his finger on the crucial point. "The articulated signs of human language," he declared, "are not like the expression of emotions of children or animals. Animal noises cannot be combined to form syllables." It is the principle of combination that makes all the difference.

Aristotle was, however, being rather dogmatic. If we are seriously to consider whether any animals have languages, we must begin by considering some properties of languages and automatic signal codes. To begin with, human spoken language is generally conveyed by sound; and, as we've just seen, many animal signals are also calls. But this is not an essential feature of either language or animal signals. There are several different types of true sign or gesture language, evolved for communication between the deaf and dumb and between monks of religious orders forbidden to talk. These sign or gesture languages are perceived through the eyes instead of the ears. Animal signal codes too are often predominantly gestures or postures to be seen by the recipient. In teaching severely handicapped children such as Helen Keller, use has been made of communication by touch, and touch signals are also widely used by animals. Human language is not normally conveyed by smell or taste, though it could conceivably be coded in this way, but elaborate chemical signals are quite common among animals and simpler ones are involved in the human perfume industry. So the use of a particular physical medium or sense is not a crucial feature of language.

Another distinction we can make also cuts across the distinction between true language and automatic signal codes. Both can convey messages about two different kinds of things, which we can sum up as *emotion* and *economics*. We can talk about how we feel about somebody else; we can also talk about natural surroundings, things, techniques and technical aspects of our life in society. In the same way an animal's signals may convey, for instance, a readiness to groom another animal's coat (emotion) or the presence of food or danger (economics). This is an important distinction, but it is no help in deciding what is or is not true language.

The use of symbols or symbolization used to be regarded as unique to human language. This is now known to be nonsense. Symbolization simply means that a set of things or events can be translated into a set of signals, with one signal for each, and that the individual who receives the signals can translate them back into the things symbolized. There is no doubt at all that animals can symbolize in this sense, both as signallers and receivers, as we shall see most clearly in the case of honeybees. A more interesting contrast is that between two kinds of symbols, *representative* and *arbitrary*. A representative symbol has something structurally in common with the thing symbolized. When a herring gull lifts his wrist joints as if about to unfold his wings, and holds his head up straight with beak pointing downwards, this actually *looks like* the beginning of a fighting attack, in which the gull would raise his wings to beat his opponent, and raise his head to peck downwards from above. The raising of the wrist joints and the position of the head are examples of *intention movements*; they symbolize attack, and act as a threat: a gull so threatened will often retreat. On the other hand, an arbitrary symbol bears no particular formal resemblance to the thing it symbolizes. Herring gulls in a conflict between the urges to attack and flee may resolve their problem by doing a third, irrelevant thing derived from some other behaviour context—a *displacement activity*, as it is called. They may, for instance, pluck at the grass as if gathering material for a nest. This does not look at all like a real attack, but it also comes to symbolize attack, and acts as a threat which may cause another gull to retreat. Niko Tinbergen has shown that intention movements and displacement activities are the basic units of signal codes in many animal species: animals thus use both representative and arbitrary symbols.

Human language relies heavily on arbitrary symbols. The sound of the word *sun*, for instance, has nothing structurally in common with the sun itself. It is true that we sometimes use representational symbols in language. In spoken language, words that symbolize sounds often resemble the sounds themselves: words such as *thunder* and *hiss* really represent what they symbolize. In American Sign Language, used by the deaf in North America, many signs are arbitrary, but the symbol for *flower* is touching the two nostrils in turn with the tip of the tapered hand, which clearly suggests smelling a flower. Representational effects of a subtler kind are important in poetry, as Pope observed in his *Essay on Criticism.*

> 'Tis not enough no harshness gives offence,
> The sound must seem an Echo to the sense:
> Soft is the strain when Zephyr gently blows,
> And the smooth stream in smoother numbers flows;
> But when loud surges lash the sounding shore,
> The hoarse, rough verse should like the torrent roar.

But, on the whole, the lavish use of arbitrary symbols is a great advantage. Only by arbitrary symbols can we represent such complicated or abstract conceptions as *Institute, Contemporary* or *Arts.* We can see this well in the special case of written language, which advanced from simple picture signs as representational symbols to arbitrary symbols for the sound units of spoken language, and hence for the things which are symbolized in turn by the patterns of sound units making up words.

In the long run, too, arbitrary symbols lend themselves most readily to the formation of many combinations and recombinations. And here we do come to a crucial feature of true language. The signal units of many animals can be put together in many different combinations. Thus the calls and facial expressions of monkeys consist of units which can be combined in many ways. For instance, rhesus monkeys, observed at Whipsnade Zoo by Vernon Reynolds, had a number of different signal units for threat, such as bobbing the head up and down, raising the eyebrows, drooping the eyelids, opening the mouth without showing the teeth, and making a low-pitched noise described as *hough*. A number of different combinations of these units could be observed, according to the intensity of aggression expressed.[1] Even the threat postures of gulls can show a number of different combinations of units signalling various in-

[1] V. Reynolds: Dissertation (University of London, 1961).

tensities of the urges to attack and flee, as Niko Tinbergen and his colleagues have shown.

But these animal signal combinations are both governed and limited by the close relation here between emotion and its expression in vocal and postural and facial symbols. Each signal is tied to a particular emotional state, and signal combinations reflect only combinations of emotions. Some combinations, for instance of units expressing extreme fear with units expressing extreme sexual desire, are simply impossible. Now any symbol units of true language can be uttered in any emotional state. Hence many new combinations become possible, and emotional rules of combination are replaced by logical ones, which we call grammar and syntax. In this way it becomes possible to form at any time totally new combinations of symbols, which the speaker may never have used before, and even combinations which no member of his language-group has ever used before. Human languages vary in their vocabularies or terms of reference, but they all have this potential flexibility. During World War II, when young East Africans were being trained for the Bantu Rifles, a problem arose because there were no words for "red" or "green" in the local language. The problem was easily solved by using the phrases *colour of blood* and *colour of leaves*. By similar means, totally new situations can be described, or totally new possibilities envisaged. This power of producing new combinations is crucial to true language.

R. J. Pumphrey has noted another advantage of detaching symbols from the direct expression of immediate emotion. An alarm call indicating the presence of a lion is given only when the calling animal is feeling the special fear associated with seeing or hearing or smelling a lion. The word *lion*, on the other hand, can be used when no lions are about. "Whereas an emotive lion is necessarily in the present, an intelligible lion could be discussed in the future or in the past; and so tradition and forward planning about lions became possible."

True language, therefore, involves the free combination of symbols limited only by logical rules of grammar and syntax, which themselves express *relations between* symbols and hence symbolize *relations between* things and individuals and events. In addition, true language must involve true communication. Compulsive utterance of signals in the absence of other individuals is not true communication. And signalling which produces automatic effects on other individuals is mere interaction. In true communication the signaller transmits information which enables the recipient to behave more freely, to have a greater range of choice and decision; so whereas interaction reduces, communication increases the variability of the recipient's behaviour. No doubt the combination of all these qualities is necessary before we can speak of true language, as opposed to an automatic code of signals.

An Animal Without True Language

Equipped with these general ideas, we can consider more exactly whether any animals have true languages. To begin with, it is worth glancing at the signal code of an animal which certainly cannot talk, namely the human infant—the word *infant* is simply the Latin root meaning "speechless." Infants have, in fact, a very simple signalling system with at most 8 sound units. These are said to correspond to phonemes, 5 vowels and 3 consonants, but they are certainly not used as elements to be combined in a language. Four kinds of infant cries have been studied in 351 infants in Sweden and Finland, by means of sound spectrographs, which display on a sort of graph called a sonagram the amount of energy produced at different sound frequencies over the time-course of a cry. Birth cries were produced only at birth. Pain cries were produced when the baby was vaccinated. Hunger cries were produced about 4 hours 20 minutes after a feed. Pleasure cries were produced when the infant, after being fed and changed, was lying comfortably in bed or in the mother's or nurse's arms. The sonagrams showed that each kind of cry varied considerably but always differed in definite ways from the other 3 kinds of cry. Each cry was uttered only in its appropriate situation, so there was no question of combining them to produce, say, a sentence like *I was hungry, now I am comfortable*, still less to describe something unusual and new. All this, perhaps, is a bit obvious. But it shows rather clearly what we mean by a simple signal code as opposed to a true language. Adults have to interpret the signals much as they try to interpret the signals of a cat or a dog.

High-fidelity tape recordings of 6 of each of the 4 kinds of cries were played to 483 adults under 50, including 349 women, and these people were asked to identify the cries as birth, pain, hunger or pleasure cries. They were far from perfectly accurate in their interpretations. Pleasure cries were easiest to recognize, with 85% correct interpretations; then came hunger cries, 68%; pain cries, 63%; and birth cries, which most people hear very rarely, with only 48% correct interpretations. Experience naturally helps in such matters. Children's nurses were better at recognizing pain and hunger cries than mothers who had only had one child each; and, not surprisingly, the top score for recognizing birth cries was obtained by midwives.

If the signals of babies are so relatively difficult to interpret, it will be clear that it takes much work and skill to understand animal signals. The great decoders of animal signal codes, such as Karl von Frisch, Konrad Lorenz and Niko Tinbergen, have had to use as much ingenuity as those of Cretan Linear B or the script of the Mayas. If we are to consider whether any animals have true languages, we shall naturally focus our attention on the most promising candidates, whose signalling is enormously more elaborate than that of human babies. These animals fall into three groups, which we shall consider in turn, beginning with the extraordinary code of the honeybees. It is simplest to describe this as a language; whether it deserves to be called a true language will appear when we have seen what it does.

The Dance of the Honeybee

In 1788, Pastor Ernst Spitzner reported a surprising fact. When a honeybee finds a good supply of honey, she returns to the hive and there performs a curious circular dance. Spitzner put out some honey, brought 2 bees to it, watched them dance on their return to the hive, and saw that many of their fellow-bees came to the honey-place. He concluded that the returning bees had somehow told their colleagues about the honey. It was a beautiful observation and a true inference, but Spitzner went no further, and it was left to Karl von Frisch, in our own age, to interpret the language of the honeybees. How he made his discoveries can be read in his books. Here we will simply summarize some of what he and Martin Lindauer and their colleagues discovered, beginning with the language of the Carniolan honeybee.[2]

When a honeybee of this race discovers a new source of honey within about 10 m. of the hive, she returns to the hive and regurgitates drops of honey which are eagerly drunk by other bees. Then she begins to dance round in a circle; first she goes one way round, then she reverses and goes the other way round, then another reverse, and so on. This is called the *round dance*. Other bees follow her about, holding their antennae against her abdomen. After dancing, she "refuels" by taking a drop or two of honey back from some other bee, and flies back to the food source, which in natural conditions is a flower or group of flowers. The other bees who followed the dance do not fly after her. They fly out in all directions. But, fairly soon, a lot of them find the new food source. They do so because they have smelt the scent of the flower that clung to the dancer's body, and so look for the right kind of flower. In one experiment, bees informed by a dancer found the right flowers in a section of the Munich Botanical Garden where 700 different plant species were blooming at once. The round dance, therefore, tells the other bees to go out and search the near neighbourhood of the hive; the scent on the dancer's body tells them what flowers to look for.

But honeybees can forage for food at far greater distances than 10 m. They have been known to fly more than 13 km. in search of honey. A honeybee is only about 13 mm. long, so 13 km. for a bee is the equivalent of about 1000 miles for a human being—not a bad commut-

2 *Apis mellifera carnica.*

ing trip. But of course, even at much smaller distances, a round dance would not be much use. If the discoverer of new food told her colleagues to go out and search in all directions for several km., she might just as well save her energy. They would never find the flowers. So when a Carniolan honeybee finds food at a considerable distance from the hive, say between 100 m. and 10 km., she returns to the hive, offers the honey she has found, and then performs a different kind of number, called a *tail-wagging dance,* which is somewhat reminiscent of the Charleston or Black Bottom. She dances along in a straight line for a certain distance, wagging her tail for all she is worth and buzzing away by means of slight vibrations of the muscles that flap her wings in flight. It is as if she was, so to speak, flying on the spot. At the end of this *waggling run,* she stops buzzing and wagging her tail, circles round to one side back to where she started, does another waggling run, circles round to the opposite side, does a third waggling run, circles to the first side, and so on. A number of other bees follow her around, showing special interest in the waggling runs. Bees cannot hear sounds in air, but they can feel the buzzing vibrations through the surface on which the dance is done. Like the round dance, the tail-wagging dance tells the bees who follow it that there is food available, and what flowers to look for, from the smell. But it tells them much more than this. It tells them exactly how far away the flowers are, and in exactly what direction. And so, even at distances of km., the bees who study the dance can fly with precision to the spot indicated and find the honey-bearing flowers.

The distance to the food is conveyed by the tempo of the dance. A quickstep tempo means a relatively nearby food source, a slow foxtrot tempo a more distant one. To be exact, as the distance increases so does the duration of each waggling run. A single waggling run may be inaccurate, but Von Frisch and his colleagues have shown that the bees who follow the dance study several waggling runs and calculate the average duration, which they then translate into distance by a mathematical rule.

The tail-wagging dance is sometimes done on a horizontal surface just outside the hive. When this happens, the dancer indicates the direction of the food by aiming her waggling run in exactly this direction. She can only do this if she can see the sun (or the polarized light of the blue sky, which indicates the position of the sun to bees, though not to us). So actually she is taking up a position in which she sees the sun at the same angle as during her flight to the honey source. The waggling run makes the same angle with the sun as her outward flight did.

But the dance is normally performed in the dark inside the hive, on the *vertical* surface of the comb. Here the angle between the flight path and the sun is translated into the angle between the waggling run and the vertical direction straight upwards. Thus if the flight path was, say, 30° to the right of the sun's position, the waggling run will be 30° to the right of the vertical. This symbolism is remarkable enough, but the dancing bee's achievements go even further. If on the flight there is a sidewind, the bee corrects for the tendency to drift sideways by flying with her body at an oblique angle to the flight path. So the angle at which she sees the sun is not the same as the angle between sun and flight path. Nevertheless, in the dance, she makes the necessary correction, and tells the other bees the true angle between sun and flight path. More remarkable still, if she has reached her goal (and returned from it) by an L-shaped detour, she uses the angles and lengths of the 2 segments of the flight to calculate the true direction of the goal by straight-line flight, and this is the direction she conveys in her dance, although she has never flown this direct route herself. One critic objected to the idea of a bee calculating, and proposed instead "a kind of 'mixture' of the neuronal learning effects during the segments." As Von Frisch observes, this is "a statement that simply clothes the phenomena in other words."

As for the bees who are following the dance, they are working literally in the dark and can only use touch to find out the angle of the dancer's waggling run with the vertical. They translate this back into a visual angle with the sun, fly off in this direction (allowing for any bending *they* have to do to oppose a sidewind) for the distance signalled by the waggling run tempo, and look for flowers of the scent they smelled on the dancer. Many experiments by Von Frisch and his colleagues show that they duly find the food.

On 14 August 1946, Von Frisch returned from a trip in the mountains to his field base. His daughters told him they had set up a new station with sugar-water for the bees in his experimental hive, but they would not tell him where it was. He must ask the bees! Von Frisch did ask the bees (by observing their dances), and he found the feeding station. On 22 September 1951, while doing some experiments, Von Frisch noticed lively dancing going on in a hive. He decoded the dances, entered the spot indicated on a map, and found it was a place (600 m. away) where a local dealer kept his bees. An assistant went over and found the dealer had just spun down honey from some combs, and then put them out in the sun for his own bees to gather back the remaining traces of honey. The assistant told the dealer Von Frisch's bees were stealing this honey and had told Von Frisch where it was. The dealer told the assistant he had to be joking, and never did believe this story, which, however, is perfectly true.

Even all this does not exhaust the symbolism of the honeybee dances. They can also vary in liveliness and total duration. They are livelier and longer the sweeter the food, the easier it is gathered, the better the weather. When honey is short in the hive, any returning bee will be eagerly badgered for honey drops, and this stimulates her to longer and livelier dances; when there is plenty of honey in the hive, the returning bee will have to search hard for customers, and this makes for shorter and less lively dances. If, of two food sources, one is richer, fewer customers are left for bees returning from the other, so even the relative attractions of different sources are represented. All this makes for flexibility and economy of labour and a readiness to exploit a variety of flowers as each ripens. The dances do not compel a reaction from every bee that the dancer meets; as Von Frisch nicely puts it, there is a most subtle regulation of "supply and demand on the flower market."

So far we have described the language of the Carniolan race of the honeybee. Other races have different dialects. German, North African, Caucasian, Italian and Egyptian honeybees[3] all begin to indicate distance and direction at much shorter distances than the Carniolan race. Italian honeybees, for instance, start indicating these data by a modified tail-wagging dance at about 10 m., as opposed to about 85 m. in the Carniolan bees. All the races indicate distance by dance tempo, but on different scales. Thus Italian honeybees dance slower than Carniolan ones for any distance of the food source. When a colony was made up of Italian and Carniolan bees, misunderstandings arose. When Italian bees danced, Carniolan ones flew too far; when Carniolan bees danced, Italian ones did not fly far enough. Each race was using their own scale to interpret the other's dances. Bees of different species, living in India and Ceylon, the Indian honeybee, dwarf honeybee and giant honeybee,[4] show similar but more extreme differences in tempo scales. The dwarf honeybee dances in the open on top of its comb, which is unprotected from the weather, and thus on a horizontal surface; unlike all the other honeybees, she cannot translate the angle with the sun into the angle with the vertical.

Wonderful as the bee language is in its precise and elaborate symbolism, there are many indications that it is really a matter of automatic signalling and not a true language after all. One experiment will perhaps make this clear. We have mentioned that the Italian bee uses a modified tail-wagging dance at 10 m. At smaller distances, this bee uses round dances in the usual way. On one occasion Von Frisch and his colleagues put a hive of these bees on the concrete foundation of a radio tower, and brought 10 bees a distance of 50 m. straight *up* the inside of the tower to a station with rich sugar water. The 10 bees flew

[3] A. m. *mellifera, intermissa, caucasica, ligustica* and *fasciata*, respectively.
[4] A. *indica, florea, dorsata.*

down to the hive and danced "most vigorously" for 4 hours. But the honeybee languages contain no symbols for "up" or "down." All the dancers could do was to perform round dances (indicating that the food source was not far away *horizontally*). Consequently their colleagues all set out and scoured round the neighbourhood of the hive at ground level. Not one of them found her way up to the feeding station high up in the tower right over the hive. In Von Frisch's words, the dancers "sent their hivemates astray—their ability to communicate broke down when faced with the unaccustomed task." Thus the bee language, unlike human languages (such as the East African one we mentioned) cannot generate new combinations of symbols to describe a completely unusual event. We are bound to conclude it is not a true language. Studies of other insects suggest origins for both the round and the tail-wagging dances in automatic circling and wagging movements performed by flies and moths, respectively, without any communicative function. The moths even wag their bodies more the further they have just flown. Even the marvellous translation of sun angle into vertical angle can be seen to have developed from a widespread automatic tendency of insects to translate responses to light into responses to gravity in darkness. This arises from the simple fact that an insect can generally move upwards either by going towards the light or, of course, by going against gravity. What the honeybees have evolved from these elements is marvellous indeed, but it is not a true language.[5]

The Voice of the Dolphin

For our next candidates, we can choose animals much more like ourselves—individualistic mammals: the whales, dolphins and porpoises, notably dolphins and above all the best studied and so far the most

[5] The honeybee signal code introduces us to yet another distinction. The signalling of distance by waggling run duration, and the signalling of angle of flight path with sun by angle of waggling run with vertical, are both examples of *continuous* signalling. Distance and direction vary continuously, and so do the signals for them. In human languages, signalling is normally done by separate or *discrete* signal *units*, such as phonemes, combined in various ways. As we have seen, many animal signal codes are also based on combinations of discrete units, and the whole science of animal behaviour study is based on the description and observation of such units of social behaviour. Signal units may be arbitrary or representational, as we have seen in the case of human words (*sun* and *hiss*, respectively). Continuous signals could in theory be arbitrary—for instance, bees could signal a flight angle of 40° by a dance angle of 10°, an angle of 60° by 11°, 80° by 9°, and so on. But, as Stuart A. Altmann has pointed out, in such a system any slight error in signalling would lead to serious mistakes, so continuous signalling must in practice be representational, as it is in honeybees, with a real formal relationship between signals and events.

remarkable species, the Atlantic bottlenose dolphin.[6] Dolphins are, so to speak, the monkeys of the sea: they have evolved many similar aspects of behaviour. Both groups of animals show prolonged and intense parental care for their young, and with this go very long-term relationships between mother and offspring. Amicable relations between 3 generations—grandmother, mother and daughter—have been seen among chimpanzees and in bottlenose dolphins. Male Japanese monkeys and bottlenose dolphins "baby-sit" for the females when these are otherwise occupied; on one occasion, a bottle-fed baby dolphin, suffering from wind due to a badly composed formula, had his buoyancy relations upset and could not stay upright: he was cured in a rough but effective way by an adult male, who gave him a bang on the belly to empty out the wind. In both groups, mothers become so attached to their babies that they cannot be parted from them even after the baby has died of some illness. A rhesus monkey mother will carry a dead infant around till it is completely decomposed, and the same is observed in dolphin mothers, for instance one observed at sea "supporting the partially decomposed head of a dolphin young with its own head"; it "withdrew support only long enough to surface and breathe, then returned to its burden." Live dolphin infants are normally held at the surface after birth to enable them to take their first breath—for of course dolphins are mammals and need to surface regularly for air.

The prolonged parental care gives young dolphins, like young monkeys, the opportunity for a great deal of play and exploration. They make up a great variety of games. For instance, in captivity in a tank, one young dolphin will put an object over an intake jet and let it go, allowing the current of water to whirl it up towards the surface, where another youngster catches it, and immediately returns it to the jet while the first player goes up to catch it in his turn. Even as adults, dolphins, like monkeys, are highly exploratory animals.

The powerful parental urge is also extended, in both groups, to a care for the welfare and survival of other adults. In the wild, adult monkeys will remove thorns and clean wounds for each other, and a band of monkeys will rush into danger to rescue one of their number who has fallen down a well or been captured by human beings. In the open sea, adult dolphins and also many species of large whales will stand by a wounded comrade; 19th-century whalers knew this well, and would regularly wound a whale without killing it so that they could easily kill his comrades, who would not leave while he was alive; the procedure was risky, because sometimes the comrades managed to release the first victim or even attacked the whale-boats. Dolphins have extended to sick or injured adults the practice of holding the patient's head above water to let him breathe, just as they do with babies. When

6 *Tursiops truncatus.*

dynamite is exploded at sea near a school of dolphins, they will all leave the area at once. But on one occasion one dolphin was stunned by the explosion. Two comrades at once came and held the victim's head out of water; when they had to surface to breathe themselves, two others relieved them; the whole school stayed around till the stunned dolphin recovered completely, whereupon all left at once.

In captivity, under crowding stress, monkeys and dolphins can be as cruel as human beings under such pressures. Monkeys will cruelly wound and kill each other, including females and young. Dolphin adult males and females have been observed to bite juveniles and bash them against the tank wall, and one adult male bottlenose dolphin bit and bashed a small female so viciously, drawing much blood, that she had to be separated from him to save her life. But even in captivity, the care for others in distress can also be seen. J. C. Lilly found that sick dolphins often recover without treatment provided they are left with other dolphins, who support them at the surface. He found that dolphins will instantly help sick or stunned *strangers*, even of different species. On one memorable occasion, reported by D. H. Brown, a female Pacific Common Dolphin[7] was giving birth to a stillborn baby, whose fin stuck in the birth canal. Two females of *other* species acted as midwives. One of them[8] pulled out the foetus, and helped the mother to hold the stillborn baby at the surface (in vain, unfortunately). The other female[9] pulled out the afterbirth. On another occasion, Lilly reports that two bottlenose dolphins, male and female, supported a conscious adult female with a back injury at the surface for 48 hours till she recovered. They worked out 10 different methods of keeping her head out of water, the simplest being to hold her tail on the bottom in such a way that she was pushed upright. During this and similar occasions, Lilly has noted prolonged and complicated exchange of calls between the patient and his or her helpers, and it is hard to resist the suggestion that they may be exchanging requests and information in true language, or even discussing what to do.

The dolphin brain resembles the human brain in being very large and having its cerebral cortex (surface layer) very wrinkled, and in certain other respects.[10] But some say the cortex is so wrinkled only for

---

[7] *Delphinus bairdi.*

[8] *Lagenorhynchus* species.

[9] *Pseudorca* species.

[10] Nearly all of the dolphin cerebral cortex, like that of man, is made up of the most recently evolved kind of structures (neocortex); but this may only be because the older structures are related to the sense of smell, which is much reduced in these sea animals. It is also said that large areas of the dolphin cortex, as of the human cortex, are not directly concerned with control of muscular activity.

mechanical reasons, because it is very thin, and that in fine structure of layering it is simpler and cruder, and has a lower density of nerve cells, than that of a rabbit. So if we seek for evidence from the dolphin brain about the dolphin's capabilities, we are back where we started. The behaviour observations, however, are so suggestive that in the past two decades people have been seriously studying the calls of the dolphins to find out whether they are a true language.

Dolphins are extremely vocal animals. As Gregory Bateson has put it, "adaptation to life in the ocean has stripped the whales of facial expression." Their heads and bodies are naked, rigid and streamlined, and anyway visibility under water is probably usually not good enough to recognize subtle facial expressions or bodily postures. So nearly all their signalling is by sound. It seems likely from records of their calls that they produce discrete vocal signal units in more elaborate sequences or combinations than any other animals, though this leaves open the question whether the rules of combination are emotional or truly logical, with grammar and syntax.

Dolphin calls are of three kinds. They produce sequences of clicks. These are probably used mainly for echolocation ("sound radar") but to some extent for signalling also—among sperm whales, where click sequences are the only calls, they are almost certainly used for signalling. The two other kinds of dolphin calls are pulsed sounds (such as squawks and mews) and whistles, and both these are certainly signals. The pulsed sounds are easily recognized as different-sounding unit calls. The analysis of the whistles can be done by exactly the methods used to analyse certain human languages.

A number of human languages, in North America, East Asia, and Africa south of the Sahara, are said to be *tonal*. That is, much of the meaning of the words is carried by the relative *pitch* at which they are uttered. There are a varying number of pitch levels or *registers*, higher or lower. The voice goes up or down so that syllables are *relatively* higher or lower, and it is the difference or contrast and not the absolute pitch that matters; hence women and boys can talk on average at a higher pitch than men without misunderstandings. Tone may be so important that a language can be almost completely intelligible without hearing vowels and consonants at all. Hence many African tribes construct drums with the same number of registers (pitch levels) as their languages, and can transmit long conversations over long distances by drumming. The distinguishable units of tone languages are often *glides*, in which the voice goes up, down, up and down, down and up, starting and ending at different levels, changing pitch faster or slower, and so on. These units can be represented on paper as *contours*, in which a line goes up and down to represent rising and falling pitch; a contour in the shape of the letter V, for instance, would mean that the voice gets lower and then suddenly rises again in pitch by the same amount; and all other variations can be represented in this sort of way. A similar method was used for writing down music in Georgia in the 8th to 11th centuries A.D.

Some peoples speaking tonal languages have also evolved actual whistling languages which they use in addition. Whistling languages have been studied on Gomera Island in the Canaries, in the village of Aas in the French Pyrenees, and among the Mazatecos, Zapotecos and Tlapanecos of Mexico. Among the Mexican peoples, only the men whistle. It is considered bad form to raise the male voice, so the men began to communicate over the mountain trails by whistling. Women do not normally whistle, but they understand the language and can demonstrate it (with a certain embarrassment). G. M. Cowan heard a young man whistle to a girl for several minutes. It was far more detailed than a wolf whistle, and she understood every word he whistled—finally she answered him back furiously in ordinary words. These whistling languages can also be represented as sets of contours.

John J. Dreher and René-Guy Busnel have tried to study dolphin whistling as if it were a human tonal or whistled language (respectively). The idea is to represent each different whistle unit by a contour, and then try to decipher whole sequences of contours as if one were deciphering sequences of hieroglyphs from some ancient script, or, for that matter, the Georgian medieval musical contour notation, which actually has been deciphered from Georgian musical documents preserved in the monasteries of Mount Athos and Mount Sinai. Such decoding methods depend on analysing the frequency of different units and how they combine together. In addition, of course, since this is a living language, or at least a living signalling system, the occurrence of each different sound unit and each combination can be related first to what is happening to the signalling dolphin, and second to what other dolphins do in response. Both whistles and pulsed sounds have been studied in this way in Atlantic bottlenose dolphins, and Dreher has also played different whistle units back to dolphins and obtained different complicated responses in the form of actions and long sequences of calls. So far a number of units have been related to simple emotional situations, such as the distress call, a whistle of falling pitch, and the sex yelp of the male. But these are quite on a par with the simple automatic signal codes of many animals. Little progress has yet been made in deciphering long sequences of calls. J. C. Lilly, and later T. G. Lang and H. A. P. Smith, have recorded long exchanges of calls between pairs of dolphins who could not see each other. But many animals will exchange vocal signals, and there is no certain evidence that these are real conversations, though there is some indication that a dolphin can distinguish the naturally changing calls of another dolphin from repeated playback of a standard dolphin call recording.

It was against this background of uncertainty that Jarvis Bastian, in 1966, reported on a highly imaginative experiment. Two Atlantic bottlenose dolphins, a male and a female, were kept in a large tank and trained to work together in pressing paddles to be rewarded by an automat which disgorged fish when the proper paddles were pressed. At a certain stage in the complicated sequence of training procedures, the tank was divided by an opaque partition, with the male on one side and the female on the other. The arrangement was then as follows. Both the male and the female were warned by lamps being switched on that the game was ready to begin. Then another lamp was switched on to give *either* a continuous *or* a flashing light. In the former case, the right-hand paddle must be pressed, in the latter case the left-hand paddle. Now the female could see this signal lamp, but the male *could not see either the lamp or her*. Both dolphins got fish if, and only if, the *male first* pressed the correct paddle on his side of the tank, and *then the female* pressed the correct paddle on her side, there being a pair of paddles for each of them. So the male had to press the correct paddle without seeing the lamp that signalled which paddle to press.[11] On the face of it, he could only do this if *the female told him, by her calls, which paddle to press, when she saw whether the lamp was flashing or steady*. Nevertheless, over many thousands of runs, the male pressed the correct paddle and the dolphins succeeded in earning their reward on more than 90% of the tests. Analysis of the female's calls indicated that she made different pulsed sounds when her lamp was flashing and steady, responding sooner, longer and at faster pulse rate to the steady light; it is quite possible the male, hearing her, could tell the difference between the two kinds of call. The dolphins' success was only prevented if *either* the female was not rewarded with fish (as happened accidentally in two test series through a defect of her automat), *or* her signal light was hidden from her as well as from the male, *or* the barrier between male and female was made sound-proof. It seems certain from this amazing experiment that *in some sense* the female was telling the male whether the light was flashing or steady, so that he could press the correct paddle in response.

Was this true language? The dolphins were surely presented with a most unusual and novel situation and problem, and, unlike the honeybees, they solved it. Were they using a new combination of symbols to

11 Very elaborate control experiments ensured that the male could not be guided by noises from the lamps or even by echolocation to find which paddle the female was nearest to, for putting the paddles far apart or side by side made no difference to the results.

deal with this problem in communication? In 1966, the answer was uncertain. But alas! in 1969 Bastian published further findings. It now seemed all too clear that true language was not involved after all. Apparently the female went on giving her different calls in response to flashing and steady light when the barrier was taken down, the male could see the light himself, and the calls were quite superfluous. And she went on doing it after this even after the male had been taken out of the tank before her very eyes and she was "talking" all by herself. This and other detailed evidence made it extremely likely that the female had become conditioned to giving different calls in response to the different light signals, because this *worked* in getting her fish, without realizing that it worked by telling the male what to do; and that the male had become conditioned to pressing different paddles in response to the two different calls of the female, because this also *worked* for him, without realizing why she gave these calls. This is pretty remarkable in itself, and the male did make a very quick transfer from using visual clues (when he could see the signal lamp) to using sound clues (when he could only hear the female's calls); people have said in the past that this easy juggling between the senses was necessary for human language and not present in animals. But, after all, we cannot speak of true language where both signalling and reaction were conditioned and compulsive and not a true communication between individuals. So the dolphins, so far, like the bees, cannot be said to have a true language. There have been other indications that these enigmatic animals may not be quite so bright as they sometimes appear. One female bottlenose dolphin had a 5-foot leopard shark[12] in a tank with her. She apparently mistook it for a baby dolphin, and held its head repeatedly above water. Dolphins breathe in air, but sharks are fishes and breathe in water, and within a day the wretched shark had suffocated and died. So far this could have been the intelligent use for killing a shark of a technique evolved for saving baby dolphins. But the dolphin really was making a mistake, it seems, for she carried the dead shark about for 8 days as if it were a dead infant, fed little as if in mourning, and would not let divers take the carcass away till it was decomposed. It seems inescapable that this particular dolphin was not very bright, unless she was as short-sighted as Mr. McGoo.[13]

The Monkey's Paw

After honeybees and dolphins, it is natural to turn back to what have always seemed the most hopeful candidates for true animal lan-

[12] *Triakis semifasciatum.*

[13] But before dismissing dolphin capabilities altogether, we must make one reservation. As Dreher and Evans have pointed out, not all the work being done on

guage, the monkeys and apes (for convenience, we refer to both as *monkeys*). Though, as we have seen, monkeys have much in common with dolphins, they differ from them strikingly in at least one respect. They have agile bodies and mobile faces. Most species have considerable repertoires of calls, and some species living in dense forest rely heavily on these. But many species live partly on the ground and/or in relatively open country, where visibility is good; and these include the species we know most about. Among these monkeys, visual signals, made by gesture, posture and facial expression, are far more important than vocal signals made by calls. Thus in the rhesus monkey[14] colony studied by Vernon Reynolds at Whipsnade Zoo, 73 signal units could be distinguished. Of these 63 were visual signals, and only 10 were calls. In another rhesus community, Stuart A. Altmann recorded a total of 5504 signalling events. Only 5.1% of these social signals involved calls (with or without accompanying gestures), and only 3% consisted of calls alone. Comparable counts have not been made for chimpanzees, among whom the richness and sensitivity of facial expression are considerably greater than among rhesus monkeys.

Unlike the honeybee code, which concerns itself entirely with information about economics—whereabouts of food, weather conditions, state of the hive's food reserves, and so on—monkey signalling is mainly concerned with emotional states and events and interpersonal relationships. Thus 36 vocal units have been distinguished in vervet monkeys[15] by Thomas T. Struhsaker, working in the Amboseli Reserve of Kenya. Only 7 of these refer to events in the natural surroundings (sighting, approach or sudden movement of various kinds of predatory animals); 3 are not really signals (coughing, sneezing, vomiting); the other 26 all refer to different social situations (such as a subordinate monkey appeasing a dominant one nearby, a female protesting she is not in the mood for sex, or several monkeys warning of the approach of a "foreign" group of the same species).

In Struhsaker's study of the vervet monkeys, he found that the calls occurred in at least 21 different situations, and produced at least 22

---

dolphins is being published: much of it is enveloped in military secrecy. Already in 1963, L. Harrison Matthews, then Director of the London Zoo, remarked that "some people are proposing to prostitute their biological work on the Cetacea and involve the animals in human international strife by training them as underwater watch-dogs to guard naval installations from frogmen, or to act as unmanned submarines. Intelligent as the animals may be, they are, unfortunately, not sufficiently intelligent to refuse cooperation and treat their trainers to some of those characteristic underwater noises which, if produced in the air, would be regarded as gestures of contempt."

[14] *Macaca mulatta.*

[15] *Cercopithecus aethiops.*

different responses in the monkeys who heard them. As with the dolphins, studies of the situations evoking different signals and their effects on other individuals have been made in many monkey species, in this case for visual as well as vocal signals. One result of great interest has been the finding that different communities of the *same species* may have different signal codes. This is a special case of the fact that different communities of the same monkey species differ in many aspects of their behaviour, including diet, way of getting food, and even mating taboos. Thus among Japanese monkeys[16] one community scratches up edible roots, another invades rice-fields, others do neither. It appears that young monkeys acquire the customs of their band by imitation and because some of their actions are encouraged, others discouraged, by mothers and leaders. Occasionally a new habit is adopted by a young monkey and accepted by his or her mother, and gradually spreads through the kinship group in the mother's line, and eventually to the whole band (except some of the older monkeys who, like old dogs, will not learn new tricks), being afterwards transmitted to subsequent generations. This has happened, for instance, in a band on Kōshima Island, with the practices of washing sweet potatoes before eating them and separating wheat grains (supplied by human observers) from the sand on which they have fallen by washing out a handful of grain and sand in water. In this way each band has its own *culture*, and this includes its own signal units. The Kōshima monkeys have acquired a completely new gesture for asking for food. A rhesus monkey community in Regent's Park Zoo used regularly to smack their lips as a friendly gesture and to execute a kind of press-up by bending and stretching their arms as a form of threat; neither gesture was ever seen in the rhesus community at Whipsnade.

Monkey signal codes have been much more studied than those of dolphins, and we know enough about them to be quite sure that they are simply automatic codes of signals which, as we saw earlier, are combined only according to emotional and not according to logical rules. Monkeys certainly have not evolved true languages. But so many combinations are at least possible, and monkey behaviour is so variable and exploratory, that several scientists have tried seriously to teach a *human* language to chimpanzees, the most variable and exploratory of them all. It has long been known that chimpanzees can respond separately to as many as 60 different human words. But then even a seal can do so to 35 words, and an elephant to 20. The real test is whether chimpanzees can be taught to use human words themselves, and to combine them, in appropriate ways. A very intensive attempt to teach a chimpanzee to talk was made some years ago by a married couple, both

---

[16] *Macaca fuscata.*

scientists, K. J. and Cathy Hayes. They adopted a baby chimp called Viki, and brought her up in their house exactly as if she were a human child, but using in addition the most sophisticated methods of teaching available. The result was disappointing. After 6 years of great effort and ingenuity, Viki had learned to utter only 4 sounds resembling English words. From this and other studies, it looked as if chimpanzees cannot be taught a human language.

So matters stood until June 1966, when another scientist couple, R. A. and Beatrice T. Gardner, began work at the University of Nevada with a female chimpanzee between 8 and 14 months old, whom they named Washoe after the county where the University is situated. Benefiting from the Hayes' experience, the Gardners had had an imaginative new idea. We have seen that most monkeys rely more on visual than on vocal signals. Even the actual vocal apparatus of chimpanzees is very different from man's. So instead of trying to teach *spoken* English, the Gardners decided to teach Washoe American Sign Language, as used by the deaf in North America, in which English words or concepts are represented by signs made with the hands; some of these symbols are representational, others are arbitrary, and all can be combined according to principles of English grammar and syntax. The Gardners and their colleagues brought up Washoe in shifts so that she never lacked for affectionate human company. They played all sorts of games with her and seem to have given her a very good time. All the time they were chattering among themselves in Sign Language, for it is known that simply being exposed to adults talking helps human children to learn to talk. They encouraged Washoe to imitate them, prompted her to get a sign right by repeating it themselves or by placing her hands in the right position, introduced plenty of toys and other objects to increase her vocabulary, encouraged her to "babble" with her hands, as a child does with his voice, and rewarded her for correct usage by tickling her, which she greatly enjoyed.

The results of all this were as follows. After 22 months of teaching, Washoe could use 34 words correctly in the appropriate circumstances. (She was only counted as knowing a word if three observers independently saw her use it correctly and without prompting). Whenever Washoe learned a new word, she very soon and quite spontaneously transferred it from a particular object, such as the key of a cupboard, to a whole class of objects, such as all keys. She would spontaneously call the humans' attention to objects by making the correct signs. She used the sign for "dog" when she saw a picture of a dog or even heard a dog bark without seeing it; evidently, like the dolphins, she had the capacity, previously supposed to be unique to man, of transposing patterns from one sense to another.

All this is remarkable, but Washoe did more. Without any prompting and apparently quite spontaneously, as soon as she had about 10 signs in her repertoire, Washoe began to *invent combinations* of signs and use them in a perfectly appropriate way. Among combinations which she invented are:—*open food drink*, for opening the refrigerator; *go sweet*, for being carried to a raspberry bush; *open flower*, to be let through the gate to a flower garden; and *listen eat*, at the sound of an alarm clock signalling meal-time. Just before the Gardners published their first results (in August 1969), Washoe had learned the pronouns *I-me* and *you*, "so that combinations that resemble short sentences have begun to appear." It only remains to add that Washoe's learning was accelerating—she had learned 4 signs in the first 7 months, 9 in the next, and 21 in the last 7 months.

Since Washoe unmistakably combines and recombines signs to describe objects and situations new to her in perfectly appropriate ways, this wonderful experiment seems to have established beyond doubt that a chimpanzee is capable of learning true language. True, at 3 years of age, she only has 34 words; at the equivalent age in terms of development, namely 5 years old, the average human child has a vocabulary of hundreds of words and makes sentences averaging 4.6 words in length. Sheer numerical differences of this kind may be important for the potentialities of human language. But the Gardners' achievement remains epoch-making. An animal has been taught to use true language, to communicate with human teachers.

The Origin of Language

So far, however, we have no evidence of any animals spontaneously evolving true language without anybody to teach them. Man *did*. How, and when, did this happen? What are the origins of human language? Our study of animal signals may help in some ways towards answering these questions.

How old is human language? Obviously it is at least as old as writing. The art of writing evolved rapidly in ancient Iraq between 3500 and 2900 B.C. A series of tablets from Erech, Jamdat Nasr, Ur and Fara tell the story of a transition from pictured objects and numbers to true writing with conventional signs for the syllables of the spoken language. But of course, even the first stage presupposes language itself, which must therefore be older than 3500 B.C. Much earlier than this, some time between 9000 and 6500 B.C., there lived at Ishango, on the shores of Lake Edward in the Congo, a people, apparently Negro, of great technological achievement for their time. The excellent bone harpoons they manufactured were exported as far as the Upper Nile and almost to the coast of West Africa. A bone tool-handle found at Ishango is marked with 3 series of notches grouped together in sets.

One series has 11, 13, 17 and 19 notches—the 4 prime numbers between 10 and 20. Another has groups suggesting multiplication—3 and 6, 4 and 8, 10 and 5 and 5. The third series has 11 (10 + 1), 21 (20 + 1), 19 (20 − 1) and 9 (10 − 1), suggesting a decimal system. If these people really had a number system, they certainly must have talked, and we can put the age of language back to at latest 6500 B.C.

Now let us go back to the other end of man's story. Man-like beings who made and kept stone tools seem to have been at Olduvai Gorge in Tanzania 1,750,000 years ago, to judge from potassium dating. Now human language is connected with another peculiarity of man: his brain functions in an asymmetrical way. Language is controlled by the left side of the brain in 97% of human adults. The asymmetry also appears in the fact that most people are right-handed, whereas in monkeys right- and left-handedness appear to be about equally common. E. H. Lenneberg has suggested, for complicated reasons, that there is a *necessary* connection between the two things, language and an asymmetrical brain. Washoe has, perhaps, proved him wrong in one way; but the idea may still be relevant for the *initial spontaneous evolution* of language, as opposed to the capacity to learn it. It is said that the earliest human stone tools show evidence of a predominance of right-handed tool-makers; so if Lenneberg is right, man had the potentiality of developing language from his earliest beginnings.

But did he develop it at once? For nearly all of his 1,750,000 years, man continued to make simple hand-axes and flake tools. All these crude stone implements look virtually alike to those of us who are not experts in prehistoric archaeology; there is scarcely any obvious difference between hand-axes hundreds of thousands of years apart. Then, suddenly, in the last Ice Age, about 100,000 years ago, there was a breakthrough: people began to manufacture more and more elaborate stone and bone tools in greater and greater diversity. To us, the conclusion has seemed inescapable that this efflorescence was made possible by the emergence of true language.

We reached this conclusion a few years ago, and have since found we are not the first to reach it. In 1951, in his Inaugural Lecture as Derby Professor of Zoology in the University of Liverpool, R. J. Pumphrey presented just this hypothesis. Throughout those hundreds of thousands of years, he wrote, "the hand-axe and flake cultures show an extraordinary conservatism of type and an improvement in the technique of manufacture so gradual as to make the intervention of what we should call 'reason' unlikely in the extreme. . . . And then in the last Ice Age the picture changes . . . with dramatic suddenness." Pumphrey had already stressed the relationship between true language and planning for the future ("forward planning about lions"). He noted that in the last Ice Age a wide range of stone tools began to be designed and made *to make other tools* by boring, scraping, cutting and polishing bone and antler, "clear evidence of an objective reached through a planned and orderly succession of *different* operations." And so, he suggested, "characteristically human speech" appeared about 100,000 years ago in the last Ice Age.

A similar idea had apparently suggested itself independently to the Australian archaeologist V. Gordon Childe. In an article published in 1953, he too noted the enormous acceleration of technical progress in the last Ice Age, and concluded that this "apparent change in tempo might reasonably be attributed to the increasing use of a more flexible system of symbols with which to 'operate in the head' as a substitute for physical trial-and-error processes."

Suppose that true language did originate in or just before the last Ice Age: we have still to consider what stimulated this momentous development. Now we have seen that monkey bands are regulated by automatic codes of signals, and that these signal codes *vary* between bands of the same species. This creates no new problems of communication, for when monkey bands meet they do not normally mix, interacting only by a set of common threat signals, simpler than those used within the band. When bands of howler monkeys meet, for instance, each band sets up a howl, and the louder band must be the larger; the smaller and less noisy band discreetly withdraws. Human beings originally moved about in similar small groups, and there was probably comparatively little contact between these groups. While still living under these conditions, they developed the manufacture of durable tools. They could very well manage to continue to function thus, tools and all, on the basis of automatic monkey-like codes of signals. Chimpanzees are known to shape sticks and straws to size, for fighting leopards and for luring termites out of their nests, respectively.

But about 300,000–400,000 years ago, man achieved control of fire, gathered on lavafields or from lightning brush fires and carefully kept burning, and some time between then and the last Ice Age he discovered how to *light* fires himself. These tremendous advances gave him a new control over his environment, notably in defence against predators and protection from the cold; the world human population increased considerably, and spread out over the continents, invading temperate and even colder regions for the first time. Now there were many more small groups, and more likelihood of their meeting frequently. Moreover, tools at last began to become gradually more elaborate and diversified from group to group. With this frequent contact between groups, and this incentive to borrow and copy each other's tools, a new development began. The old automatic signal codes would not work *between* groups (compare the Carniolan and Italian honeybees). The automatic noises and gestures that had formerly sufficed would eventually have to be replaced by *words*—overriding and controlling automatic moods—intelligible and intelligent between groups with different cultures. In this way man was stimulated to break the link between signal and automatic mood, and begin the logical combination of signals, or true language. Claire Russell has shown that a connection between the dawn of language and contact between culturally different groups can be detected in myths from several parts of the world. Gordon Childe has summarized the considerable evidence for trade and technical influence, and hence for communication, between culturally different groups great distances apart in the last Ice Age. So we may plausibly suppose that increasing contact between culturally separate groups was the stimulus for the evolution of true language. Even today, intercultural relations can stimulate new combinations of words—as in the case cited earlier of East African recruits and the phrases *colour of blood* and *colour of leaves*.

It remains to ask, why vocal rather than sign language, especially since chimpanzees and other advanced monkeys are, as we have seen, so geared to visual signals? Now we have also seen that where visibility is poor, calls predominate, as in dolphins or monkeys of dense forest. Martin Moynihan studied a Central American monkey active at night —the night monkey.[17] Though this species has only 10 calls, it has even fewer visual signals, and uses the calls far more. Now human eyes are not much use at night, and one of the results of man's control of fire was a new ability to continue his activities after sundown. Kenneth Oakley has suggested that "the lighting aspect of fire was probably almost as important as its heating aspect in extending man's range northwards." But visibility is *far from perfect* on a dark night around a flickering fire, and we may suppose that, as man became active at night, the value of vocal signals would greatly increase. So, we may conjecture, when true language appeared, it was conveyed by voice and not by gesture, until the deaf and their teachers, and certain monks, evolved sign languages to translate existing spoken ones.

The Future of Language

Finally, let us return to our contrast of economic and emotional information. We have seen that monkey signalling is heavily biased towards emotion. With the coming of true language in man, the balance tipped towards economics. For purposes of handling tools, techniques, science, our natural surroundings, language has come a long way since the last Ice Age, and made possible the achievement of many marvels, from bone harpoons to moon-walks. But for purposes of com-

[17] *Aotus trivirgatus.*

municative mood, for conveying subtle and sophisticated aspects of emotion and human relationship, language was, and still is, only developed to a rudimentary degree. We continue to convey emotion by crude, often unconscious, automatic signal codes, carried by "calls"— our *tone of voice* when speaking—or by the posture changes, gestures and facial expressions with which we are interacting all the time—as you can easily see by turning off the sound on your television set during an interview, discussion or documentary. These signals vary from group to group, transmitted as a crude and automatic culture in the monkey way, while true language is transmitting its creative culture of accumulated knowledge. The gesture we call beckoning means a summons in Britain, a dismissal in Italy, a deadly insult in Malawi—such variation is an obvious source of cross-purposes. In an isolated Scandinavian village, a scientist noticed that everyone bowed to a certain whitewashed wall. They did not know why—they did not even know they were doing it till he asked. He removed the whitewash, and found a religious ikon, *centuries* old. How is such a pattern transmitted? We once saw, on documentary film, a Japanese mother in traditional dress with her baby on her back, bowing to a Shinto shrine. As she bowed, she put her hand behind her own head and *pushed the baby's head down.*

Language itself is involved in this automatic signalling, through tone of voice and also accent, which differs from group to group like other patterns, and forms the basis for crude stress behaviour of a highly automatic kind. At worst, it directs violence: the ancient Israelites are said to have massacred, on one occasion, all who could not pronounce the word *shibboleth*; the medieval Sicilians, rising against the French, killed all who could not pronounce the word *ciceri*. At mildest, such signal differences may affect cultural cross-mating, as neatly indicated in the Ira Gershwin lyric—"You say potartoes and I say potaytoes, You say tomartoes and I say tomaytoes, Potartoes, potaytoes, Tomartoes, tomaytoes, Let's call the whole thing off."

Our very talking may be as compulsive and conditioned as that of Bastian's female dolphin: humans, too, are liable to talk when alone, and often when two apparently converse, neither is listening to the other or really concerned whether the other listens to them. We may also be conditioned by words—and conditioning is the reduction of variability of behaviour, whereas learning is the increase of variability. Russian scientists have "trained" human individuals to blink in reaction to spoken sentences. The sentences worked as a conditioning signal even if the word order was reversed, just as the song of a robin has been recorded, reversed and played back (by the French scientists Bremond and Busnel) to another robin, who reacted exactly as to the usual song. Language is here debased to the level of a crude signalling system. And all these many indications of deficiency and degradation of language appear far more when we discuss emotion than when we discuss technical matters. Indeed language has so far been of little help in relieving the sense of emotional isolation from which humans have always suffered. "What are the sorrows of other men to us" wrote Daniel Defoe, "and what their joy? . . . Our passions are all exercised in retirement; we love, we hate, we covet, we enjoy, all in privacy and solitude. All that we communicate of those things to any other is but for their assistance in the pursuit of our desires; the end is at home . . . it is for ourselves we enjoy, and for ourselves we suffer."

Mankind, then, has achieved technical wonders by means of his true language such as no animal could begin to achieve. It is now time— and high time, for we live in an age of emotional turmoil under the stress of population pressure—for man to begin to achieve wonders of emotional relationship and social harmony. Perhaps, to emancipate signals from immediate emotional impulse, the stimulus of discussing technical matters was necessary. But now we may hope to use the subtlety and power of language for true *communication* about our emotions. Art, and above all poetry, has been man's chief effort so far in this direction, and it is fitting that this series of lectures is launched by the Institute of Contemporary Arts. It is fitting, too, to end our story with a poem (by Claire Russell) about language.

> Words, like pebbles galore
> At the mouth of the sea,
> Litter the shore
> Of society.
> Worn into every shape and size
> Their hard reality defies
> The sea's speechless agitated tongue
> That lives and cries
> Upon the wind, unsung.

> I wonder what these words are for
> That I pick up along the shore;
> I wander restlessly to seek
> For pebbles of reality,
> I wander restlessly along the shore to speak
> Against the stormy agitated feelings of society.
> But the storm defies
> The pebbly scientific tongue
> And a voice that dies
> Upon the wind, unsung.

Pebbly words galore
Litter the shore,
While speechless feelings seek
To speak;
And a voice that lives and cries
With an agitated tongue
Echoes a voice that ever lives and dies,
As waves upon the wind, a far off magic legend that is sung.

Further Reading

1. Babies

Irwin, O. C.: *Infant Speech, Scientific American Reprint* 417 (San Francisco, 1949).

Wasz-Höckert, O.; Lind, J.; Vuorenkoski, V.; Partanen, T.; Valanné, E.: *The Infant Cry* (London, 1968), with 45 rpm record.

2. Bees

Von Frisch, K.: *The Dance Language and Orientation of Bees*, translated by L. E. Chadwick (London, 1967).

3. Whales, Dolphins and Porpoises

Andersen, H. T. (Ed.): *The Biology of Marine Mammals* (New York and London, 1969).

Busnel, R. H. G. (Ed.): *Animal Sonar Systems: Biology and Bionics*, Vol. 2 (Jouy-en-Josas, France, 1966).

Norris, K. S. (Ed.): *Whales, Dolphins and Porpoises* (Berkeley and Los Angeles, 1966).

Tavolga, W. N. (Ed.): *Marine Bio-Acoustics* (Oxford, London and New York, 1964).

4. Monkeys and Apes

Altmann, S. A. (Ed.): *Social Communication among Primates* (Chicago and London, 1967).

Devore, I. (Ed.): *Primate Behavior* (New York and London, 1965).

Gardner, R. A. and Gardner, B. T.: "Teaching Sign Language to a Chimpanzee," *Science* 165, pp. 664–72 (15th August, 1969).

Morris, D.: *The Naked Ape* (London, 1967).

Moynihan, M.: *Some Behaviour Patterns of Platyrrhine Monkeys. 1. The Night Monkey* (Aotus trivirgatus) (Washington, 1964).

Russell, C. and Russell, W. M. S.: *Violence, Monkeys and Man* (London, 1968).

Southwick, C. J. (Ed.): *Primate Social Behaviour* (Princeton and London, 1963).

5. Language and Animal Signals: General

Cornwall, I. V.: *The World of Ancient Man* (London, 1964).

Count, E. W.: "An Essay on Phasia: on the Phylogenesis of Man's Speech Function," *Homo* 19, pp. 170–227 (1969).

Gerard, R. W.; Kluckhohn, C. and Rapoport, A.: "Biological and Cultural Evolution: Some Analogies and Explorations," *Behavioral Science* 1, pp. 6–34 (1956).

Hastings, H. (Ed.): *Abbé Bougeant: Amusement Philosophique sur le Language des Bêtes* (Geneva and Lille, 1954).

Heinzelin, J. de: "Ishango," *Scientific American Reprint* 613 (San Francisco, 1962).

Hockett, C. D.: "The Origin of Speech," *Scientific American Reprint* 603 (San Francisco, 1960).

Kalmus, H.: "Ethnic Differences in Sensory Perception," *Journal of Biosocial Science* Supplement 1, pp. 81–90 (1969).

Lenneberg, E. H.: *Biological Foundations of Language* (New York and London, 1967).

Métraux, G. S. and Crouzet, F.: *The Evolution of Science* (London, 1963).

Oakley, K.: "Fire as Palaeolithic Tool and Weapon," *Proceeding of the Prehistoric Society* 21, pp. 36–48 (1955).

Pike, K. L.: *Tone Languages* (Ann Arbor, 1948).

Pumphrey, R. J.: *The Origin of Language* (Liverpool, 1951).

Russell, C.: *Forbidden Fruit* (Stockholm, in press).

—— and Russell, W. M. S.: *Human Behaviour: a New Approach* (London, 1961).

Russell, W. M. S.: "Animals, Robots and Man; Signals and Shibboleths," *The Listener* 68, pp. 169–70, 207–8, 213 (2nd and 9th August, 1962).

——: *Man, Nature and History* (London, 1967).

Smith, F. and Miller, G. A. (Ed.): *The Genesis of Language* (Cambridge, Mass., and London, 1966).

Thompson, S.: *Motif-Index of Folk-Literature* Volume 1 (Helsinki, 1932).

Tinbergen, N.: *The Herring Gull's World* (London, 1953).

——: *Social Behaviour in Animals* (London, 1953).

Woolley, Sir Leonard: *The Beginnings of Civilization* (London, 1963).

FOR DISCUSSION AND REVIEW

1 According to the Russells, what do human spoken language and the calls used by a great variety of animals have in common?

2 What is a *phoneme*?

3 The Russells refer to two categories of symbols, *representative symbols* and *arbitrary symbols*. What distinctions are made between them? In what way are these concepts useful or valuable?

4 The Russells state that the "power of producing new combinations is crucial to true language." Explain this statement by using several examples or illustrations.

5 What do the Russells mean by "true language"? How do they differentiate it from "automatic signal codes"? Do you agree with their distinction? Explain.

6 Discuss the symbolism involved in the bee's "round dance" and "tail-wagging dance." Why do the Russells say these dances are not true language?

7 What is your opinion of the Russells' theory concerning "the origin of language"? Explain.

8 Why, according to the Russells, have man's messages tended to be "economic" and not "emotional"? Do the Russells offer a solution for this probelm? Discuss.

4

Feral and Isolated Man

Roger Brown

There is for "civilized" man an aura of exoticism and fascination surrounding humans who are wild or "uncivilized." We measure ourselves against such individuals and hope to see revealed in them some of the reasons for our own behavior. Studies of feral and isolated man also hope to tell us something about the acquisition of language. However, one of the major problems in the studies of such individuals is the determination of those factors which are hereditarily linked and those which are the product of environment. In the following article, Roger Brown reviews nine of the major specimens of feral and isolated man found to date in the light of those forces most influential on behavior.

IN THE TENTH edition of his *Systemae Naturae*, published in 1758, Linnaeus listed *Homo Ferus* (L. wild man) as a subdivision of the genus *Homo Sapiens*. The defining characteristics of feral man, succinctly listed by Linnaeus, were *tetrapus, mutus, hursutus*. There were nine historical records of wild men available to the great taxonomist. These included the Hessian wolf-boy of 1349, the Lithuanian bear-boy of 1661, and Wild Peter of Hanover of 1724. Since Linnaeus' time about thirty additional cases have accumulated. These cases have generally conformed to two of Linnaeus' specifications: They have lacked speech and have gone on all fours. The majority have not been especially hirsute and that characteristic does not help define feral man. An attribute not mentioned by Linnaeus, but reliably found in these cases, is the depression of sexuality. It appears, like speech, to be a function that a society must develop. Within the class of feral men a distinction should be made between those known to have been nurtured by wild animals and those who lived on their own in the wilds.

It must be assumed that these latter cases lived in human society until they were old enough to wander off and look after themselves. They fall between true feral man and cases of extreme isolation. It has sometimes happened that a child has been shut away from human society except for routine feeding. These cases, living with minimal human aid, are called isolated man.

Feral and isolated man interest the psychologist, philosopher, and sociologist because they provide an important natural experiment on the relative importance of genetic and environmental factors in the determination of all aspects of human behavior. The importance of feral man to the science of man was perceived long ago. Lord Monboddo proclaimed the discovery of Wild Peter of Hanover to be more important than the discovery of 30,000 new stars. Wild Peter was brought from Hanover to England by King George so that he might be used to test the doctrine of innate ideas. The king presented Peter to the enlightened princess of Wales and she placed him in charge of Dr. Arbuthnot, that good friend of Pope and Swift.

While Peter began the tradition of scientific interest in feral man, he also, unfortunately, began an equally hardy tradition of scientific difficulty in interpreting the data so obtained. There was, first of all, the problem of determining the exact circumstances of Peter's earlier life. From a number of sources it seems clear that he had lived for some time in human society. He was probably the child of a certain widower whose second wife drove Peter from the house. There was, secondly, the problem of estimating Peter's native intelligence. The behavior of feral man somewhat resembles that of the ament living in human society. If one cannot decide whether or not these cases are congenitally deficient, the results obtained are all open to the following directly opposed interpretations.

The extreme environmentalists, like Rousseau, have found in feral man proof of the infinite plasticity of man. The feral cases violate all parochial notions of human nature and prove that human nature is created in society and may take any form that society dictates. However, the extreme environmentalist cannot deny the importance of genetic factors since, as Zingg remarks, there is something lacking to make this case complete—a wolf or dog who has been trained to human behavior. He can acknowledge that the character of the species sets limits on behavioral development but that, within these limits, environment is the principal factor.

The student who is inclined to give more importance to heredity will interpret the cases of feral man quite differently. He believes them all to be congenitally feeble-minded; their behavior simply demonstrates the strong determining power of innate intelligence. Aments, whether in human or wolf society, are much alike. To be sure some

feral cases have recovered and demonstrated considerable learning ability, but these cases cannot have been true aments, in the opinion of
the men backing heredity. Their recovery proves that when there is no
genetic deficiency the most unfavorable environment has only a
temporary handicapping effect. With this uncertainty about native
intelligence the environmentalist cannot prove that genetically normal human specimens are rendered permanently inhuman by the
lack of society in their early years. Those that remain *mutus* and
tetrapus may be feeble-minded. Those that recover have not remained
inhuman. The environmentalist points out, with irritation, the improb-
ability that all feral cases would be feeble-minded. The heredity-man
counters that the feeble-minded child is just the one to be driven out
of his home or exposed to wild beasts and furthermore, not all feral
men are assumed to be feeble-minded—only those who do not recover.
In the opinion of the environmentalist, anyone who thinks that a
child who has survived in the wilds on his own initiative could possibly
be feeble-minded . . . —the man who thinks that must himself be
suspected of feeble-mindedness. We tiptoe out and softly close the
door behind us. Let us look at several of the best documented cases
to see if they do not teach something more modest than the truth
about human nature, perhaps something about the nature of language.

   The Wild Boy of Aveyron. The case of Victor, the wild boy of
Aveyron, [is described in the Introduction to Brown's book]. Victor
was about twelve years old when he was captured in the Caune Woods
and Dr. Itard tried for five years to teach him to speak and read. Victor
succeeded in understanding a large number of words and phrases but
he could produce no speech except the two exclamations: *"Oh, Dieu!"*
and *"Lait!"* These came out, in very imperfect form, quite early in
training. The discrepancy between the boy's achievements in reading
and in speech production requires some explanation.

   It is conceivable that Victor's mentality was adequate to the full
use of language and that he was simply held back by inability to master
the business of articulation and phonation. Perhaps the impulse to
babble which is so evident in infants operates on a maturational time-
table such that it must receive social support when the readiness is
there or the impulse will die. The pecking response in chicks is an
example of this kind of timed skill. A bright spot elicits the pecking
response in newborn chicks. When chicks were raised in the dark and
fed by dropper for fourteen days it was found that they would not
peck though exposed to daylight. The original study includes a dramatic photograph of a starving chick standing in the midst of a pile of
grain—not pecking! Itard's experience with Victor suggests that speech
in man, like pecking in chicks, may require social reinforcement at the
crucial age when the impulse is ripe or else it will not develop at all. To

evaluate this proposal we will look at other cases of feral and isolated man.

Kamala and Amala. Since 1850, at least, there have been constant reports of wolf-children in India. Some of the Indian people have a superstitious reluctance to kill wolves and there has also been a practice of exposing unwanted children. Most of those carried off have certainly been killed but occasionally the child is taken to the wolf den and survives for a time as an extra cub.

In 1920 the Rev. A. L. Singh was told of a *manushbhaga,* a man ghost, haunting a certain Indian village. The ghost had been seen in the company of wolves going in and out of a giant dead ant hill which the animals presumably used as a den. Singh had a shooting platform built over the hill. He and some natives watched there one night and saw a procession of mother wolf and cubs, two of which looked human though they went on all fours and had long matted hair. The local natives would not dig out the hill but Singh brought in some more willing workers. The mother darted out to attack the invaders, and was killed. In the den itself they found a monkey ball of four little creatures clinging together—two cubs and two little girls.

Kamala was about eight years old and Amala only one and one-half. They were thoroughly wolfish in appearance and behavior: Hard callus had developed on their knees and palms from going on all fours. Their teeth were sharp edged. They moved their nostrils sniffing food. Eating and drinking were accomplished by lowering their mouths to the plate. They ate raw meat and, on one occasion, killed and devoured a whole chicken. At night they prowled and sometimes howled. They shunned other children but followed the dog and cat. They slept rolled up together on the floor.

Amala died within a year but Kamala lived to be eighteen. Both children's bodies were covered with sores when they were captured. Mrs. Singh healed these and softened their skins with oils and massage. She fed and bathed and caressed Kamala and evidently was the means of her socialization. The first sign that Kamala had become "involved" with a human being appeared when Mrs. Singh returned from a trip and Kamala ran to her with evident affection. In time Kamala learned to walk erect, to wear clothing and even to speak a few words.

Because Amala learned to talk a little, and promised to learn more, we cannot believe that continuous social support of infantile babbling is an essential pre-requisite to speech. Vocalization survived in her as an operant response while it did not for Victor. It is, of course, possible that Kamala lived for a longer time with adults than did Victor and so received more reinforcement for vocalizing. The situation, however, was the reverse. Victor was not found in the care of animals but was living alone. A child could survive outside of human society at an earlier age if it was in the society of some animal than would be possible if it had to shift for itself in the wilds. Victor is likely to have remained longer at home. It seems that speech is possible even when left dormant for many childhood years. Victor's failure was probably due to some specific impairment—probably of hearing. The facts on several cases of extreme social isolation will reinforce these conclusions.

Cases of Extreme Social Isolation. In 1937, in Illinois, the child Anna was discovered tied to a chair in a second floor attic-like room. She was nearly six years of age, emaciated, and speechless. She had received absolutely minimal attention since her birth, had been fed almost exclusively on cow's milk, seldom moved from her chair, and never instructed in anything. Anna was an illegitimate child whose mother had hidden her away to avoid the anger of the child's grand-father.

The child was taken to a county home for retarded children and, after a year and a half there, removed to a private home. Anna lived for only four more years. In that time she learned to walk, to dress herself, to play simple games with other children, and to speak a little. She could call attendants by name and had a few sentences to express her desires. The school report on Anna expressed the opinion that she was probably congenitally feeble-minded. This diagnosis is strengthened by the fact that Anna's mother proved to be a middle-grade moron with an IQ of 50 on the Stanford revision of the Binet-Simon scale. The probability that feral and isolated children who have learned little or no speech were feeble-minded is increased by the remarkable achievements of another isolated child—Isabelle.

Isabelle was found in Ohio at about the same time as Anna. Isabelle was also nearly of an age with Anna, being six and one-half at the time of her discovery. She was the illegitimate child of a deaf mute, and mother and child had lived most of the time in a darkened room away from the rest of the family. Isabelle behaved in many ways like a wild animal. She was fearful and hostile. She had no speech and made only a croaking noise. At first she seemed deaf, so unused were her senses.

Isabelle was taken away and given excellent care by doctors and clinical psychologists. Although her first score on the Stanford-Binet was nineteen months, practically at the zero point of the scale, a program of speech training was, nevertheless, undertaken. A week of intensive work was required to elicit even a first vocalization. Yet a little more than two months later she was beginning to put sentences together. Nine months after that, she could identify words and sentences on the printed page and write very well. Isabelle passed through the usual stages of linguistic development at a greatly accelerated rate. She covered in two years the learning that ordinarily occupies six years. By the age of eight and one-half Isabelle had a normal IQ and was not easily distinguished from ordinary children of her age. In this case speech behaved like many other human and animal performances; the delayed subject progressed at an accelerated rate, presumably because of her maturity.

The case of Isabelle strongly suggests that a child with good congenital intelligence can overcome the mutism caused by social isolation. It is possible that Anna would have done as well with equally expert tutelage but it seems likely that Anna was not Isabelle's equal in congenital intelligence. We do not yet know how many years of social isolation it is possible to overcome with speech training. The excellent results with Isabelle indicate that as many as six and one-half years of isolation can be made up. The moderate success with Kamala (carried on by less expert teachers) suggests that much may be done to offset even eight years of isolation from the human community.

Neither feral nor isolated man creates his own language these days, but must not such a man have done so once in some prehistoric time and so got language started? Actually the circumstances in which language must have begun represent a combination for which we can provide no instances. We have animals among themselves, animals in linguistic communities, and humans among animals, and in none of these cases does language develop. We have humans raised in linguistic communities and, in these circumstances, language does develop. What about a human born into a human society that has no language? We don't know of any such societies and so we don't know of any such individuals. But these must have been the circumstances of language origination. We shall be better able to guess what happened in these circumstances, intermediate between the primate community and the linguistic community, when we are clearer about the lines of phyletic advance that lead toward language function.

FOR DISCUSSION AND REVIEW

1 What three characteristics did Linnaeus use to differentiate *Homo Ferus* and *Homo Sapiens*? Which characteristic is not helpful in defining feral man? Is there a characteristic Linnaeus fails to mention? Explain.

2 What is the difference between feral and isolated man?

3 Man is a social creature. What problems or complications arise because of this fact when we attempt to determine how language is acquired?

4 Brown says, "We have animals among themselves, animals in linguistic communities, and humans among animals, and in none of these cases does language develop." Is it the linguist's conclusion that language is human? Explain.

5 Discuss the pros and cons of the heredity-environment issue as posed in Brown's essay.

5

The Linguistic Development of Children

The complex process of language acquisition has long been of interest to scholars in many fields. The connection between the noises of a baby—his cries, coos, and babblings—and the language of an adult is crucial to an understanding of this process. In a lecture presented to the Institute of Contemporary Arts, M. M. Lewis first gives a brief background sketch of the history of the study of language acquisition, and theories of reinforcement and conditioning developed by scientists like Ivan Pavlov and B. F. Skinner, and then discusses the revolutionary ideas of Noam Chomsky.

M. M. Lewis

The Roots of Language

WHAT ARE we talking about this evening? This: . . . the infant, mewling and puking in his nurse's arms. I don't know about puking; what I can say is that there is nothing more important for a child than his mewling. His crying is the beginning of his language. On his very first day, as soon as he cries and his mother comes to him, we have the basic pattern of language between people—one person utters sounds and another responds.

It is on his first day also that a child often shows that he is already aware of sounds. Recent investigations have demonstrated, as early as this, an "auditory orienting reflex"—a movement of the child's head towards the source of a sound.[1] Within a couple of weeks this has usually become more specific: the child responds more readily and more regularly to a high-pitched human voice than to any other auditory stimulus.[2] And of course the most frequent high-pitched human voice is his mother's.

[1] R. H. Walters and R. D. Parke: "The Role of the Distance Receptors in the Development of Social Responsiveness," in L. P. Lipsitt and C. S. Spiker: *Advances in Child Development and Behaviour* (1965), p. 75.

[2] *Ibid*, p. 65.

During these early days a child not only cries; he coos. When he is hungry or uncomfortable he cries; when he is content and comfortable he coos.[3]

The next new thing to come from the child—different from his crying and his cooing—is his babbling. Often as early as his sixth week he will be heard uttering strings of sounds, repeating them with a rhythm and intonation, apparently for the pleasure of making them; playing with sounds.[4]

He cries or coos or babbles; to each of these his mother is likely to respond in a specific way. He cries and she attempts to alleviate his discomfort; he coos and she comes and smiles and perhaps pets him; he babbles and she may well encourage him by joining in, imitating him in fun, so that in turn he imitates her.

The simple pattern of interchange is enlarged as the child begins to respond to speech in its situation. These are the rudiments of comprehension; how far back in his history they begin it is impossible to say. His earliest response to *Baby, Milk!* may be to his mother's voice as an auditory stimulus specific to him as a human infant. From this there will be a transition to the time when he responds to the phonemic form of *milk* in the situation in which he hears it, the context of circumstances, even when he can see neither the speaker nor the milk.

While these are the rudiments of meaning in what a child hears, there are also rudiments of meaning in what he utters. From the beginning, his crying and his cooing have each of them its own context of situation in the child himself—discomfort, distress when he cries, contentment when he coos. This, of course, is not to say that at the beginning he himself is aware of the connection between his crying and discomfort, or his cooing and contentment. But we who are with him have to recognize, from a very early moment, the rudimentary semantic content of his crying or his cooing. His babbling has another place in his development: he plays, practises, experiments.[5]

Advance in Early Childhood

The speed of linguistic development is phenomenal. By the end of the third year most children have a working command of a good many of the phonemic and syntactical structures of the mother tongue and of their use and comprehension in communication. Five years later this has normally extended to the whole range of the structures of the lan-

[3] M. M. Lewis: *Language, Thought and Personality in Infancy and Childhood* (1963), pp. 16–19.
[4] *Ibid*, p. 20.
[5] *Ibid*, pp. 20–22.

guage; what has yet to come is an increase in the size and scope of vocabulary and in the complexity of syntax; above all, in the development of the complex relationships between the structural and the semantic systems of the language.[6]

All this has been seen by mothers and others from time immemorial; seen, but rarely observed. Not the least remarkable thing about children's linguistic development is that we know so little about it. Today we have barely reached the centenary of the first systematic studies. One of the pioneers is Darwin, who made a record of his son as early as 1840, though he refrained from publishing it until 1877.[7]

During the greater part of the present century, while there has been a stream of sporadic attempts at description and interpretation, gaps have remained unfilled. But now, suddenly, in the last few years, there has burst upon us an explosion of concern, thought and observation. This is one of the major products of modern psycholinguistics, from which the name of Noam Chomsky is now inseparable.

Chomsky has been hailed as the herald of revolution in the study of language, as the Einstein of modern psycholinguistics. Here we ask what he has to say to us about the development of language in children.

Half-a-Century of Study

Chomsky offers hypotheses which have injected fresh vigour into observation and experiment by a variety of workers. What is new in these hypotheses is best seen in the perspective of the ideas current before he arrived.

We go back to the beginning of the century, to the pioneers, William and Clara Stern, whose book *Die Kindersprache* first appeared in 1908. They take as the fundamental explanation of linguistic development the principle of "convergence": the interaction between what comes from the child—the drive in him to use language (Sprachdrang) —and what comes to him from his linguistic environment.[8] This would no doubt seem to many even today irrefutable if innocuous. But it soon proved to be altogether too broad a formulation to satisfy the growing demand in psychology for precision; least palatable was the somewhat mystical hypothesis of an inborn "drive."

During the following half-century the main line of thought about linguistic development took a different course. In the U.S.A., under the influence of studies of the processes of learning; in the U.S.S.R.,

---

[6] M. C. Templin: *Certain Language Skills in Children* (1957), p. 141.
[7] C. Darwin: "The Biography of an Infant," *Mind*, II (1877).
[8] C. and W. Stern: *Die Kindersprache* (1908), p. 123.

under the influence of Pavlov; in both, the balance of "convergence" shifted to a heavier emphasis on the outside forces acting upon the child. In the U.S.A. the development of language was seen by many as the reinforcement of a child's responses to others. There was a solid movement of thought in this direction, among philosophers, sociologists and linguists no less than among psychologists. Of these we may name Skinner as one of the latest as well as one of the most thoroughgoing exponents of the function of reinforcement in linguistic development.[9]

The parallel with work in the U.S.S.R. on conditioning is too obvious to need more than a mention. The genesis of language was one of the main preoccupations of Pavlov because of its far-reaching relationships with every aspect of human behaviour. Pavlov envisaged language as the "second signal system," established by the conditioning of primary conditioned reflexes.[10] The fertility of this concept of linguistic development is attested by the quantity and quality of the work carried out under its influence by such men as Vigotsky and Luria.

The Chomsky Revolution

Reinforcement or conditioning; these were as strongly entrenched explanatory concepts as any in the history of psychology. But in 1957, five decades after *Die Kindersprache,* there appeared a treatise with an innocent title-page: *Syntactic Structures,* by N. Chomsky. Apparently addressed to professional linguists, it dealt with problems which might be regarded as of limited interest even to them: the syntactic structures of a language could be shown to be logically "generated in accordance with the rules, the grammar of the language."[11]

If this was new in linguistics, it was not obviously a revolution in psycholinguistics. But although Chomsky was careful to point out that his description of the generation of structures must not be taken as an account of actual genesis, its implications for the understanding of linguistic development soon appeared. The cat among the pigeons was seen to have sharp claws.

The pigeons were Skinner's. In a series of elegant experiments he had demonstrated that by selecting some more or less random movements of a pigeon and reinforcing a succession of these by appropriate "rewards," a complex pattern of behaviour could be set up. The behaviour of the pigeon was determined by what we did to him.

When Skinner applied the same principles to verbal behaviour in

---

9 B. F. Skinner: *Verbal Behaviour* (1957).
10 I. P. Pavlov: *Conditioned Reflexes,* trans. G. V. Anrep (1927).
11 N. Chomsky: *Syntactic Structures* (1957).

his book of that name, his treatment seemed to many to be vitiated by a serious limitation: the suggestion that a child's linguistic development is mainly determined by what we do to him. Chomsky was roused to a ferocious polemic, reminiscent of the cut-and-thrust of seventeenth-century philosophers' battles. In a slashing review he set about clawing Skinner's book into shreds, not without some glee.[12] Not merely by negative strictures, but by positive refutations Chomsky expounded his ideas on language and linguistic development. As subsequently elaborated by him and his colleagues, they are revolutionary to this degree, that they have given a new direction to thought about language and a new stimulus to the examination of the linguistic development of children.

Back to the Past

Like many another revolutionary, Chomsky takes a step backward in order to take two forward. There was already in the U.S.A. something of an uneasy movement back to the past. It is startling to find a modern psychologist of the calibre of J. McV. Hunt "revisiting" McDougall for his insistence on primary drives as factors in development; still more, recalling one Montessori for her recognition of children's initiative and creativeness.[13]

Chomsky takes a wider sweep, back to a golden age, long before the philosophy of language was polluted by Behaviorism and S–R learning theory. He invokes a line of honourable ancestry for his ideas: Descartes and Leibniz and the seventeenth-century thinkers about language, Goethe and von Humboldt in the following century.[14] He turns to them for support as he expounds his hypotheses. From the logical genesis of language by generative processes he goes on to suggest implications for the linguistic development of children, still denying that he can offer a factual account of what actually happens.

Chomsky on Linguistic Development

Chomsky's exposition consists of six main statements:

There is an innate predisposition to achieve the mastery of language

The structures of a language are generated from primary deep structures

---

[12] N. Chomsky: Review of Skinner's "Verbal Behaviour," *Language*, 35 (1959).

[13] J. McV. Hunt: "The Importance of Pre-verbal Experience," in M. Deutsch *et al*: *Social Class, Race and Psychological Development* (1968).

[14] N. Chomsky: *Cartesian Linguistics* (1966).

The linguistic development of children is a process of maturation
In the process of development the child is essentially creative
Imitation is a subsidiary factor in the acquisition of a language
Analogy is a complex factor in this development.
We look at these in turn.

The most fundamental and at the same time the most controversial
of Chomsky's hypotheses is that we are born with a disposition to acquire language. This he regards as peculiar to man; or, in Lenneberg's
terms, it is "species-specific."[15] In Chomsky's terms, children are born
with a potential knowledge of grammar. Nonsense? But as Chomsky
uses them, "knowledge" and "grammar" are pickwickian terms. By
knowledge he means what he also calls "competence" in language, to
be sharply distinguished from "performance." And the meaning of
"grammar" he extends to include the whole system of rules covering
the relationships of the phonemic, syntactic and semantic components
of a language. Chomsky is maintaining that we are born with an apti-
tude to acquire these rules, and that as linguistic development goes on
there is "a grammar which each individual has somehow and in some
form internalized."[16]

Thus "competence" is the grasp, more or less conscious, of the rules
of a language; "performance," actual linguistic behaviour which will be
—more or less—in accordance with these rules. By the systematic study
of children's performance we can infer the nature and degree of their
competence.

One of Chomsky's chief grounds for postulating innate competence
is the speed with which a child attains the mastery of the complex
system of skills that constitute a language, "on the basis of a fairly
restricted amount of evidence."[17] In passing, it may be pointed out that
Chomsky is underestimating the richness of a child's linguistic experience. A child with normal hearing, born into a society of speakers, is
surrounded by language from the moment of his birth. In his first three
years, say his first one thousand days, he must hear some millions of
words.

Is there anything new in Chomsky's insistence on the innate bases
of language? This: while it has always been recognized that there are
innate roots of *speech*, Chomsky postulates an innate competence in

[15] E. H. Lenneberg: *Biological Foundations of Language* (1967), p. 296.

[16] N. Chomsky: "Methodological Preliminaries," in L. A. Jakobovitz and M. S.
Miron: *Readings in the Psychology of Language* (1967), p. 89; N. Chomsky:
"The Formal Nature of Language," in E. H. Lenneberg: *Biological Foundations
of Language* (1967), p. 408; N. Chomsky: Review of Skinner's "Verbal Behaviour," *Language*, 35 (1959), p. 170.

[17] N. Chomsky: "The Formal Nature of Language," in E. H. Lenneberg: *Biological
Foundations of Language* (1967), p. 437.

language. Indeed, as Lenneberg has shown, language may develop in the absence of speech, even comprehension of spoken language in the absence of articulation.[18] To say that there is an innate basis of competence means that it is natural for a child growing up in a linguistic society to become linguistic.

The second main idea of Chomsky's is that competence develops out of basic innate deep structures, through a succession of transformations. The genesis of a language for a child, as Chomsky sees it, is this:

Deep structures . . . kernel sentences . . . infantile structures . . . structures of the mother tongue.

Deep structures are the hypothetical capacities inferred from a child's overt language later. It is not surprising therefore if different readers of Chomsky's exposition do not agree in their ideas of deep structures.

Chomsky would seem to suggest that while deep structures are dispositions to acquire language, they are not themselves linguistic. They are pre-linguistic; cognitive, but in forms that lend themselves to language. Chomsky concurs with Descartes' description of them as "a simple reflection of the form of thought"; and with von Humboldt's conclusion "that the force that generates language is indistinguishable from that which generates thought."[19]

To test our interpretation of Chomsky we may attempt an example of a basic deep structure and its subsequent progressive transformations into a structure of English. The argument would run on something like the following lines.

We may reasonably suppose that when an infant, even in his earliest days, sees the movement of a bird across the sky, his perception is already different from that of a dog, however intelligent. While the dog, we may suppose, has a single integral perception of the bird in flight, the child is born with more advanced cognitive capacities. His perception, we would assume, soon has the rudiments of two components—the bird and its movement. He begins to see the *bird* . . . *fly*-ing, and the *flying* . . . as performed by the bird. If all this is highly hypothetical, it is what is implied by saying that a child, by contrast with a dog, begins with deep structures which will lend themselves to language.

As a child acquires words, he may begin to use them to symbolize his perception. *Bird!* he announces—more probably, *Birdie!*—later perhaps, *Bird flying!* This is a kernel sentence; so too was *Bird!* earlier; it has long been recognized that many of a child's single early words are

[18] E. H. Lenneberg: "Speech as a Motor Skill," *Child Development Monograph* (1964), p. 127.

[19] F. Smith and G. A. Miller: *The Genesis of Language* (1966), p. 6; N. Chomsky: *Cartesian Linguistics* (1966), pp. 30 and 35.

semantically sentences. From a kernal sentence there is a transformation or a series of transformations to a structure of current English: *The bird is flying*. A French child, beginning with the same basic deep structure, ends up with *l'oiseau qui vole*—not with the English schoolboy's *l'oiseau est volant*.

Chomsky's third main idea is that the linguistic development of a child is a process of *maturation*, not the imposition upon him of the forms of the mother tongue by authority from above, through conditioning, reinforcement or any other means.

This is a very important tenet in Chomsky's system and he and his colleagues have taken a great deal of trouble to demonstrate the validity of this principle of development. For support, Chomsky again goes back to von Humboldt, citing him to the effect that language grows by the maturation of relatively fixed capacities under appropriate external conditions.[20] Among Chomsky's colleagues a principal exponent of this view is Lenneberg, who adduces evidence to show that, like progress in walking, talking develops by the unrolling of tendencies already present in the child. Environment may, of course, be more or less favourable—but it is a condition, not the source, of linguistic development.[21]

The last three of Chomsky's general hypotheses expound a most important implication of the first three: that a child is creative in his linguistic development.

For Chomsky this is indeed an indispensable concept for the understanding of all human behaviour. He brings in the support of Descartes for the doctrine that "a fully adequate psychology of man requires the postulation of a 'creative principle.'" This has become so intrinsic in Chomsky's view of language that one of his exponents, McNeill, heads a paper with a title that is surely meant to be provocative: "The Creation of Language by Children."[22] This sets itself to counter the line of thought which so long had seen the development of language as a process of social influence upon the child, whether by reinforcement or conditioning or example.

What then immediately becomes unavoidable is the crucial question of the function of imitation. Nothing could be more obvious than that the linguistic differences between English and French children must be due to imitation. Chomsky asks, How far due to imitation? And he brings forward two lines of argument to show that imitation is much less important than would appear at first sight: first, the nature

[20] N. Chomsky: *Cartesian Linguistics* (1966), p. 64.
[21] E. H. Lenneberg: *Biological Foundations of Language* (1967), pp. 136, 142.
[22] N. Chomsky: *Cartesian Linguistics* (1966), p. 6; D. McNeill: "The Creation of Language by Children," in J. Lyons and R. J. Wales: *Psycholinguistic Papers* (1966).

of imitation itself as a psychological process; and secondly the relation between imitation and other factors in linguistic development.

Imitation, Chomsky points out, is not only a means by which we learn; imitation itself has to be learnt. Lenneberg enjoins us to remember "that imitation implies the learning of analytic tools, namely grammatical and phonemic rules."[23] Imitation in language thus goes far beyond mere mimicry; the child is active in that he forms for himself systems of rules and applies them. When a child has encountered a particular usage of language, his imitation consists of similar usages in similar circumstances.

More than this: the rôle, of imitation, though powerful, is limited. How else can we explain some of the mistakes children make? *I taked; I eated.* These, and so many others, can only be due to a process that we must call reasoning by analogy, even though in saying this we realize that a good deal of the time the "reasoning" is unconscious.

The more closely we observe children the clearer does it become that in their linguistic development both imitation and analogy are at work. It is found, for instance, that some children, at a time when they are saying *I breaked,* are also saying *I broke.*[24] It is worth noticing that each of these owes something to imitation, something to analogy. *Breaked* is by analogy with such a form as *walked,* which directly or indirectly comes from imitation. *Broke* is imitated, but then used, analogically, in a new situation.

Chomsky is so anxious to stress the function of creation that he maintains that even "analogy" may be misleading; that it would be truer to say that the child behaves as though he were reasoning by analogy when in fact he is acting creatively in a new situation.[25]

Throughout Chomsky's exposition there runs this thought: to say that a child acquires language is misleading if it is taken to mean that he gathers and enlarges a stock of structures which he learns to understand and utter. It is rather that the child extends his competence over the rules of the language as he generates structures in accordance with these rules.

Language is Creation

Chomsky's six hypotheses are likely to have important influences on our knowledge of children's linguistic development. As hypotheses some are open to direct verification, others not.

[23] E. H. Lenneberg: "Speech as a Motor Skill," *Child Development Monograph* (1964), p. 122.

[24] S. M. Ervin: "Imitation and Structural Change in Children's Language," in E. H. Lenneberg: *Biological Foundations of Language* (1964), p. 179.

[25] N. Chomsky: *Cartesian Linguistics* (1966), p. 12.

The first—the innate basis of competence—can be tested only indirectly, by inference from the observed facts of children's development. The second hypothesis—the generation of the structures of a language —lends itself somewhat more readily to verification, but only through careful and even subtle experiment and controlled observation.

The hypothesis of maturation as the process of development is rather better supported by available data, particularly of the kind presented by Lenneberg; and it gains some additional force from its agreement with Piaget's principle of the biological adaptation of the child to his society.

The last three hypotheses of Chomsky's are of a different kind. The creativeness of the child and the functions of imitation and analogy in his linguistic development—these are descriptive of actual "performance," so that their validity rests on the systematic observation of children, supplemented where possible by experiment. Both observation and experiment have been given a powerful impetus by the discussions of Chomsky and his colleagues; and it is to the work in the field that we look for the closure of the gaps in our knowledge of the linguistic development of children. We may hazard the prediction that more will be found to depend on a child's linguistic environment than Chomsky seems inclined to allow.

In the meantime let us record a new outlook on the nature of language itself. There is a new creed. Its major tenets have nowhere been stated so clearly as by Miller who, among the disciples of Chomsky, may rank as the apostle of common sense. In an admonitory epistle to the psychologists he announces a revelation: "Language is exceedingly complicated." And he makes his confession of faith: "I now believe that mind is something more than an Anglo-Saxon four-letter word; human minds exist."[26]

FOR DISCUSSION AND REVIEW

1   Why, according to Lewis, is there "nothing more important for a child than his mewling"?

2   What are the three early stages of linguistic development in a child, as seen by Lewis? Explain the importance of each.

3   What are Noam Chomsky's six main hypotheses concerning linguistic development in a child? In what ways are they "revolutionary"?

4   Chomsky says that "imitation is a subsidiary factor in the acquisition of a language." How would B. F. Skinner and other behaviorists react to this statement? Does Brown's dis-

---

[26] G. A. Miller: "Some Preliminaries to Psycholinguistics" in R. C. Oldfield and J. C. Marshall: *Language* (1968), p. 212; G. A. Miller: "Some Psychological Studies of Grammar" in L. A. Jakobovitz and M. S. Miron: *Readings in the Psychology of Language* (1967), p. 217.

cussion of feral and isolated man (pp. 56–61) provide any insights? Discuss.

5 People have a tendency to demean imitation. Is imitation as simple a process as has been supposed? Explain.

6 What does Chomsky mean when he says "man is born with a disposition to acquire language"? What distinctions does Chomsky make between *knowledge* and *grammar,* and between *competence* and *performance?*

6

Conditioning the Uncommitted Cortex for Language Learning[1]

Wilder Penfield

We are now beginning to realize in this country that the best time to learn a language is when we are young. This conclusion would appear to be common sense, since we know that children of every language community learn their own language with no difficulty. The reasons we have given for learning languages when we are young have not, however, been empirical or very logical. In the following article, Wilder Penfield, a neurosurgeon, gives physiologically sound evidence for the belief that languages should be taught before the age of twelve. His research on the uncommitted cortex of the brain, that area of the brain that develops as a speech and perception center, reveals that it must be developed early and that its proper development may, in fact, influence performance on intelligence tests.

I N THIS changing modern world, it is most urgent for a "well-educated" man to master one or more secondary languages. Once it was

---

[1] A part of this communication was published in different form in *The Atlantic Monthly,* Boston, July 1964, vol. 214, p. 77, entitled *The Uncommitted Cortex.*

the dead languages. Now it is the living languages that are important. This calls for change in the plan of education. The following discussion of the neurophysiology of speech and its relation to language-learning was prepared for this volume of *Brain*, which honours a neurologist, F. M. R. Walshe. But it is not written for neurologists. It is intended for educators and parents, in the hope that it may help them to adjust school curricula and home instruction to the changing physiology of the brain of childhood.

The human brain is not a previously programmed calculator. It is a living, growing, changing organ. It can even carry out its own repairs to some extent. But it is subject to an inexorable evolution of its functional aptitudes. No one can alter the time schedule of the human brain, not even a psychiatrist, or an educator. The built-in biological clock tells the passage of learning aptitudes and the teacher's opportunity.

When I was in India in 1957, visiting some of the universities under the Commonwealth Colombo Plan, I received a startling invitation from the Department of Education—to give a series of two broadcasts over the All-India Radio on the teaching of secondary languages. Some educator, I reflected, must indeed be desperate! It might well have been so, for the Government of India had laid at the door of the Ministry of Education the task of teaching the people Hindustani and English, although the mother-tongue of the majority was something else. The request was startling to me, not because the problem was new but because an educator had turned to a neurosurgeon.

My wife tried to reassure me by pointing out that our own children had gained a satisfactory command of two added languages. We had done no more than to have them hear German and French well-spoken in their early childhood. Was it, after all, as simple as that? I gave the broadcast and the Department of Education had 10,000 copies of it printed and distributed to the teachers of India. This seemed to leave me with no avenue for retreat. But fortunately this has not been necessary.

For my own part, I had heard no foreign tongue before the age of 16. After that, I studied three modern languages for professional purposes but spoke none well. Before beginning the study of medicine, I even spent a whole year teaching German and was paid for it in an otherwise efficient boys' school. It was, I fear, very poor language teaching. I handed on, as best I could, the words and the grammar I had learned at Princeton to boys who were between 15 and 18 years of age.

On the other hand, my own children learned to use German and French without apparent effort, without foreign accent, and without the long hours of toil that I had sacrificed to language study. They did well what I did badly. There must be a physiological explanation for the difference (unless these children were vastly more intelligent than their father!).

Before saying anything more about the children or the broadcast in India, perhaps the reader will follow me in a short detour. I have had a remarkable opportunity to study speech mechanisms, language learning and bilingualism. Most of my clinical career has been passed in Montreal where my patients were, half of them, French-speaking and half English-speaking. I have seen children, below the age of 10 or 12, lose the power of speech when the speech convolutions in the left hemisphere of the brain had been destroyed by a head injury or a brain tumour. I have seen them recover after a year of dumbness and aphasia. In time, they spoke as well as ever because the young child's brain is functionally flexible for the start of a language. They began all over again. Occasionally when such children had become epileptic because of the brain injury, we were able to study what had happened, while we were trying to cure them. In every case, we found they had established a speech centre located on the other side of the brain in what is called the non-dominant hemisphere. (In a right-handed person, the left hemisphere is normally dominant for speech. That is, it contains the whole specialized speech mechanism.)

When the major speech centre is severely injured in adult life, the adult cannot do what he might have done as a child. He may improve but he is apt to be using the remaining uninjured cortex on the side of the injury. He can never establish a completely new centre on the non-dominant side, as far as our experience goes. That is not because he is senile. It is because he has, by that time, taken over the initially uncommitted convolutions on the non-dominant side of his brain for other uses.

Grey matter is made up of many millions of living nerve cells that are capable of receiving and sending electrical impulses. The cerebral cortex, which is the thick layer of grey matter covering the outer surface of the brain, has been called "new" since it is found to be more and more voluminous as one ascends the philogenetic scale from fish to man. It covers the convolutions and dips down into the fissures between them. The underlying white matter is made up of the branching connexions of the nerve cells. They are capable of transmitting electric potentials like insulated wires. Some of the connexions pass inward from cortex into the "old" grey matter of the brain-stem (the old brain); some unite cortex and brain-stem with the eyes and ears; some pass up and down the spinal cord and along the nerves to the muscles and the skin.

Certain parts of the cerebral cortex are functionally committed from the start. The so-called "sensory cortex" and "motor cortex" can only be used for sensory and motor purposes because these parts seem to have fixed functional connexions from birth onward.

But there is a large area of cortex covering a given, large part of each of the two temporal lobes that is uncommitted at birth. This uncommitted cortex will in time be used for language and for perception. For language, it will make possible the remembrance and use of words. For perception, it will play a part in the recall of the past and the interpretation of present experience. As the child begins to perceive and to speak, electrical currents must be passing in corresponding patterns through this cortex and underlying brain. After each time of passage, it is easier for the passage of later currents along the same trail. This tendency to facilitation of electrical passage results in man's amazingly permanent records of the auditory and visual stream of his conscious life.

Now, if the posterior half of the left uncommitted cortex is used by the child for speech, as it usually is, it becomes the major speech area, or speech cortex.[2] Then the remaining three-quarters is used for interpretation of experience (interpretive cortex). Functional connexions are gradually established by the child and by the time he enters the teens the general uses of the uncommitted areas are apparently fixed for life.

Much of this information about mechanisms of speech and perception has come to us from the well-known work of others. Some has come to us unexpectedly during long operations on conscious alert patients who were kept from pain by local novocain injection into the scalp while a trap door opening was made in the skull. In the attempt to relieve each patient of his attacks of focal epilepsy, a preliminary survey of the brain was made after the exposure was completed.

A gentle electrical stimulus was applied by touching the cortex here and there with an electrode. This served to map the sensory cortex by causing sensation (visual auditory or bodily, according to which of the different areas was touched) and the motor cortex by producing crude movement of the face or tongue or limb. When an abnormality in a certain area of brain was suspected of being the cause of fits, the electrode might produce by stimulation there the characteristic beginning of the attack from which the patient sought relief. (Surgical excision of areas of bad cortex is a worth-while

2 There are also two secondary speech areas, both of them in the frontal lobe of the dominant hemisphere: Broca's area in the third frontal convolution, and the supplementary speech area in the supplementary motor area. An adult can recover speech after aphasia of varying lengths of time when either one is destroyed. The posterior speech area (Wernicke's), established in the uncommitted temporal cortex, is the major one.

method of treatment in case conservative medical therapy has failed in the hands of experienced neurologists.)

The most precious and indispensable portion of the adult's cortex is the major speech area. It might be worth while to forfeit other areas and so lose other functions in order to gain a cure of epilepsy, but never the speech area. Thus the need of a method to map out the exact territory devoted to speech was urgent.

When the electrode was applied to the speech cortex, it did not cause a man to speak. It seemed at first to have no effect. But if the patient tried to speak while the electrode was in place, he discovered to his astonishment (and to ours at first) that he could not find his words. If shown a pencil, he knew what it was and could make appropriate movements with the hand, but he had lost the power of speaking. He was aphasic. The gentle electric current was blocking the action of the speech cortex, with its underlying connexion, without disturbing the function of the adjacent areas. When the patient was shown an object and was asked to name it, he perceived its nature, and he must have dispatched electric potentials along the brain's integrating circuits to the speech mechanism. But, to his surprise, he "drew a blank."

Normally, when the appropriately patterned potentials reach the speech mechanism, the word, by instant reflex action, is made available to consciousness—its sound, how to write it, how to speak it and how to recognize the written word. As long as the electrode continued to paralyse the action of the speech unit, none of these was possible. But as the electrode was lifted, the patient, not knowing what had been done, would exclaim, "Now I can speak! That was a pencil."

So we had a much-needed method of mapping out the major speech area exactly (and the minor ones as well). And we could remove less useful cortex right up to the speech frontier without fear of losing speech function. We mapped out the cortical area thus in hundreds of cases and acquired precise knowledge of the demarcation in each case. This took the place of anatomical conjecture. But what about the similar area in the non-dominant hemisphere and the uncommitted temporal cortex farther forward on both sides? So far, neurologists had found no clear indication of function for these areas.

Stimulation in them never produced aphasia. What were they used for? One day I stumbled on a clue. I applied the electrode to the right temporal cortex (non-dominant). The patient, a woman of middle age, exclaimed suddenly, "I seem to be the way I was when I was giving birth to my baby girl." I did not recognize this as a clue. But I could not help feeling that the suddenness of her exclamation was strange and so I made a note of it.

Several years later during a similar operation, the electrode caused a young girl to describe, with considerable emotion, a specific experience she had when running through a meadow. There is no sensation in the cortex and she could not know when I had touched the electrode to her right temporal lobe but, each time I did so, she described the experience again, and stopped when the electrode was removed. Since that day we have been on the alert and have gathered more and more cases which could be studied critically. We have now published all of them in complete summary.[3]

The conclusion is as follows: There is within the adult human brain a remarkable record of the stream of each individual's awareness. It is as though the electrode cuts in, at random, on the record of that stream. The patient sees and hears what he saw and heard in some earlier strip of time and he feels the same accompanying emotions. The stream of consciousness flows for him again, exactly as before, stopping instantly on removal of the electrode. He is aware of those things to which he paid attention in this earlier period, even twenty years ago. He is not aware of the things that were ignored. The experience evidently moves forward at the original pace. This was demonstrated by the fact that when, for example, the music of an orchestra, or song or piano, is heard and the patient is asked to hum in accompaniment, the tempo of his humming is what one would expect. He is still aware of being in the operating room but he can describe this other run of consciousness at the same time.

The patient recognizes the experience as having been his own, although usually he could not have recalled it if he had tried. The complete record of his auditory and visual experience is not subject to conscious recall, but it is evidently used in the subconscious brain-transaction that results in perception. By means of it, a man in normal life compares each succeeding experience with his own past experience. He knows at once whether it is familiar or not. If it is familiar, he interprets the present stream of consciousness in the light of the past.

Careful comparison of all the brain maps we have made shows no overlap of the boundaries that separate speech cortex (which endows a man with memory of words) and the interpretive cortex which gives him access to the memory of past similar experience and thus enables him to understand the present.

Before the child begins to speak and to perceive, the uncommitted

[3] W. Penfield and Ph. Perot—Brain (1963), 86, 595–696.

cortex is a blank slate on which nothing has been written. In the ensuing years much is written, and the writing is normally never erased. After the age of 10 or 12, the general functional connexions have been established and fixed for the speech cortex. After that the speech centre cannot be transferred to the cortex of the lesser side and set up all over again. This "non-dominant" area that might have been used for speech is now fully occupied with the business of perception.

The brain of the 12 year old, you may say, is prepared for rapid expansion of the vocabulary of the mother tongue and of the other languages he may have heard in the formative period. If he has heard these other languages, he has developed also a remarkable *switch mechanism* that enables him to turn from one language to another without confusion, without translation, without a mother-tongue accent.

In my broadcast to the teachers of India, I could only reason as follows: Do not turn without question to the West for your model of teaching secondary languages. Consider first the changing functional capacities of the child's brain. Most of our schools in the West begin the teaching of foreign languages by the dead-language technique. It was designed for adults learning Greek and Latin by means of word-lists and grammar. Your hope that the people of India will speak English and Hindustani as living-languages is doomed to failure if you follow this technique. The dead-language technique has its place, no doubt, but it cannot be used in the years when the child is a genius at language initiation.

But there is another method of beginning a language—the direct method that mothers use. It was used to teach foreign languages as well as the mother-tongue, in the families of ancient Ur and during the Roman Empire. It is used by some parents in the West and in the East today. Even a child's nurse or the least experienced tutor can use the mother's method for a second language. The mother does her teaching when the child's brain is ready for it. In three or four years she may only give the child a few hundred words, perhaps. But he gets the set, acquires the units, creates the functional connexions of the speech cortex. In unilingual countries the mother conducts the first stage of language learning by the direct method and the school carries on easily with the second stage—vocabulary expansion. If a nation is to be bilingual or trilingual, or multilingual, the nation's schools should adopt the mother's direct method for the first stage of foreign language teaching.

In retrospect, I am not sure whether, when I presumed to offer a solution to the teachers of India, I was speaking from scientific evidence, or as a man who had tried unsuccessfully to master secondary languages by the classical methods, or as a teacher of German who had employed the classical method, or, finally, as a father whose children had approached two second languages successfully by the mother's method. In any case, I ventured an opinion:

India's problem is not insuperable. Use the mother's method at the very beginning of formal education with teachers who can speak either English or Hindustani well and who understand kindergarten techniques. Following that, I outlined, in a rather confused manner (my thinking was less clear in this regard then than now) what is described below as *parallel bilingualism* (one language in the morning, the other in the afternoon).

But India, with her most important task of language-teaching, is far away. In other nations of the world the problem of second-language teaching is hardly less urgent, although it presents itself in varying patterns. The urgency of the problem will, I hope, excuse a parent and a clinical neurophysiologist if he addresses school teachers and parents nearer home than India.

There is a good deal of evidence to suggest that when a young child is allowed to hear a second language and learns to use only a few hundred words of that language—he becomes a better potential linguist; his uncommitted cortex is conditioned to further second-language learning. It is difficult or impossible to condition it thus later in life because the functional connexions tend to become fixed.

This would explain the reputed genius of the Swiss, the Poles and the Belgians as linguists. Most of them hear a second language in early childhood in the streets and the playgrounds, if not at home. On the contrary, the average so-called Anglo-Saxon, in Great Britain or the United States, hears only English until possibly he is taught a modern language in his teens at school.

J. B. Conant (former President of Harvard), in his recent studies of American high schools, concluded that in the best schools of today the work is satisfactory, except in one department: the teaching of foreign languages. The classical method, with its grammar and word lists designed to teach dead languages, is the indirect method of the high school. A little child cannot use it. He would only laugh at it, and yet the little child is the genius in our society for starting languages. The brain of the 12 year old is already senescent in that regard. He is ready for vocabulary expansion.

Education, to be scientific, must consider the physiology of a child's brain. When the classical method is used to start a unilingual teenage pupil or adult in the learning of second languages, the procedure is unscientific and not in accordance with the dictates of neurophysiology. With hard work, it may serve the purpose as a second-best method.

The teaching of additional living languages, as intelligent parents have managed it, ever since the society of ancient Ur became bilingual, is in accordance with the modern findings of speech physiology.

The mother's method of initiating the learning of the mother tongue is scientifically correct and successful. This is the original direct method. It conditions the child's uncommitted cortex to the set and the style of the language. Second languages can be started by the same direct method without confusion.

There are examples of early language teaching by the direct method in schools in many parts of the world. But these are still sporadic. It may serve my purpose best to describe a school in Montreal in which the mother's direct method is being well used. The school is available to children from French-speaking homes or English-speaking homes and also to children from Polish or Ukrainian-speaking families.

This is a day-school in which the method of *parallel bilingualism* is used by teachers speaking their native tongue (English or French). They are the teaching nuns of Notre Dame de Sion, 4701 Dornal Avenue, Montreal. The procedure is not at all complicated. Their school has two years of kindergarten and one of first grade. In the morning the children, aged 4 to 6, are received by English-speaking teachers and in the afternoon by French-speaking teachers or vice versa. No time is wasted teaching language as such. The children play and sing and study in one language in the morning and the other in the afternoon. They begin to read and write in two languages. If there is any difficulty in spelling, it disappears spontaneously after the manner of vanishing baby-talk. Every evening the children return to their homes to speak the mother tongue and to receive whatever home religious instruction is desired by their parents.

After two years of bilingual kindergarten and one in the first grade, children of this school have started reading and writing. They are ready to carry on in either language smoothly and without accent or confusion in some other elementary school. They could, of course, transfer to a school that used a third language. Vocabulary expansion could be provided for by reading and conversation almost any time in the first and second decades of life. When they enter middle school, high school or university, these children should be able to study the literature of second languages instead of struggling with grammar.

The child is the genius in our society when it comes to acquiring the early set, the units or the patterns of a language. The enlargement of vocabulary is another story. The 10 year old expands vocabulary as he expands his knowledge miraculously in the direction of his interests.

The secret of the child's freedom from confusion lies in the action of a conditioned reflex that works in his brain automatically from the beginning. It is what might be called the *switch mechanism*. When the English child (or adult) hears a French word or meets a French person or enters a French school, he unconsciously switches on his French "network" with its vocabulary, however meagre it may be. What he proceeds to learn is then added to the French network. In the brain, French, English and Chinese, if learned, seem to utilize the same general area of speech cortex without demonstrable separation into different areas. Every adult who speaks secondary languages is aware of this subconscious reflex which brings the word *bleistift* to his mind instead of "pencil" as he turns to a German companion, or *crayon* as he enters the class conducted in French.

It is preferable in my opinion that, in the early stages, a bilingual adult, charged with the care of a young child, should not switch back and forth too often from one language to another in conversation. But it works well to do what a bilingual mother of my acquaintance has done: establish "upstairs" in the home as a French-speaking area and "downstairs" for English. Her little children accepted it as no problem at all. Language to them is only a way of getting what is wanted or expressing constructive (or destructive!) ideas.

The first stage of language learning is always in the home. During the first two years of life, imitation of words comes only after months of hearing them.[4] Baby talk shows that the set of the brain for language is not established immediately. It takes time, and the baby's accent and the formal phrasing and organization of sentences alters gradually to that of the adult (without the need of lectures on grammar).

In our own home the two younger children heard German in the nursery from a governess who could speak nothing else. When she took them to French nursery school (aged 3 and 4) they switched to French as they entered the door and switched back again when they found her waiting outside the door at the close of the school. Our two older children, aged 8 and 9, first heard German spoken for a few months in Germany. After that they spoke German to their younger brother and sister and, on occasion, to the governess, but they were never taught the language formally. In spite of that, both older children had excellent command of the language, one for a year of university work in Munich, the other for wireless intelligence in the Second World War.

A unilingual adult, who begins the learning of a second language late, speaks it with a mother-tongue accent and tends to learn by translation. However, the adult who has previously learned some other language in childhood is apt to learn a later third and fourth language faster and probably better than a unilingual adult. It may be suggested that this greater facility of the bilingual adult is due, at least in part, to

---

[4] According to W. E. Leopold's careful study, there is a lag of two to seven months after the child first hears a word in the second year of life before he uses it in a meaningful manner. (Northwestern University Press, 4 vols., 1939–1949.)

the well developed "switch mechanism" which he acquired in childhood. He is able to switch off the mother tongue more easily and, thus, to learn directly.

It follows, for example, that in a school district where the only foreign native-born teachers available are Swedish or Spanish, it would be the part of wisdom to have beginning years taught in Swedish (or on a bilingual basis—Swedish in the mornings and Spanish in the afternoons). Those children who continue their schooling in English and eventually go on to college and into professional schools will be better prepared to learn the Russian and Chinese which intelligent English-speaking adults of the future will want to understand. The bilingual child, prepared for formal education by the mother and the child's nurse, or mother and a second language kindergarten, has undoubted advantage over other children whatever the second languages may have been and whatever the eventual work of the individual may prove to be.

The experience of many parents has, of course, been similar to our own, past and present. It is a common experience that when families immigrate, the children learn the new language by the direct method (without confusion) and unilingual parents learn it less well and more slowly by translation and with a mother-tongue accent. This is the supporting evidence of common sense and common experience. And yet there are those who argue that it is better for a child to establish the mother-tongue well before confusing him by exposure to a second language! The child seems to be protected from confusion by rapidly acquired conditioned reflexes and by the action of the switch mechanism which is a conditioned reflex.

There is other good evidence that even a limited familiarity with additional languages in the first decade endows the normal child with a more efficient and useful brain. In a study supported by the Carnegie Foundation and conducted under W. E. Lambert, Professor of Psychology at McGill University, it was concluded recently that bilingual children, at the 10-year level in Montreal, showed greater intelligence than unilingual children of the same age. They were examined by non-verbal as well as verbal tests.[5]

A second study has been carried out in the same department.[6] In this study, an equal number of bilingual university students was compared with a similar selection of unilingual students. The bilingual students scored higher in intelligence tests when those tests were verbal and also when they were non-verbal. In the bilingual society of the

---

[5] Peel, Elizabeth and Lambert, W.: The Relation of Bilingualism to Intelligence, Psychological Monographs, General and Applied, vol. 76, 27, Amer. Psychol. Ass'n. Washington, D.C., 1962.

[6] Anisfeld, Elizabeth Peel: The Cognitive Aspects of Bilingualism. McGill University, Ph.D. thesis.

Province of Quebec, those who were bilingual before entering university would have heard the second language early.

In conclusion, man (to a far greater extent than other mammals) is endowed with extensive areas of cerebral cortex which, at birth, are not committed to sensory or motor function. Much of the uncommitted areas covering the temporal lobes that are not used as "speech cortex" will, in time, be used as "interpretive cortex" and so play a rôle in the process of perception. While the mother is teaching the child to understand and to use a few hundred words and teaching the child to perceive the meanings of words and experiences, she is "programming" the brain. Part of the uncommitted cortex is being conditioned or "programmed" for speech, the remaining uncommitted cortex is used as a part of the mechanism of perception. In the second decade of life, functional connexions seem to have become fixed. Vocabulary expansion and multiplication of perceptions then proceed rapidly.

The mother's method of direct language teaching can be used for second languages but this should *begin* before the age of 6 or 8 if possible. When the uncommitted cortex is thus conditioned early, the individual becomes a better linguist; the child is better prepared for the long educational climb. In the years of life that follow, the man or woman will more easily become the "well-educated" adult for which the future calls so urgently.

Teachers and parents must always share responsibility for the education of each new generation. This includes the conditioning of each child's brain. How and when it is conditioned, prepares the man for great achievement or limits him to mediocrity. A neurophysiologist can only suggest that the human brain is capable of far more than is demanded of it today. Adjust the time and the manner of teaching to the aptitudes of the growing, changing master-organ. Then, double your demands and your reasonable expectations.

FOR DISCUSSION AND REVIEW

1 What is "the uncommitted cortex of the brain"?

2 How exactly have the functions of particular areas of the brain been determined?

3 If an adult receives damage in the speech center, why is that damage usually permanent?

4 Penfield refers to a "switch mechanism" that allows a bilingual speaker to interchange languages. Does he say how this mechanism

works? Explain.

5 On the basis of limited research, Penfield claims that bilingual children perform better on I.Q. tests than unilingual children do. Can you offer an explanation for this from what you have learned from this article? Discuss.

6 Why does Penfield say that the West is not, or traditionally has not been, a good model for language teaching?

7

Bilingualism and Information Processing

Paul Kolers, like Wilder Penfield (p. 72), is interested in how the human mind functions. In a set of experiments designed to obtain information about the mental operations involved in the acquisition, storage, and retrieval of information, Kolers selected bilingual subjects because they have two sets of symbols operative in their minds. In essence, Kolers' experiments provide valuable insights into three important questions: What exactly is the mental "switch mechanism" that characterizes the successful use of different languages? How does language limit access to information stored in the memory? How does the set of rules a person learns for employing a language affect his linguistic performance?

Paul A. Kolers

IS THE HUMAN mind too complex to be a profitable object of study? Many investigators have felt that it is, and yet one approach to it has always seemed promising. One of the principal activities of the human mind is the manipulation of symbols; might not an investigation of the way people use symbols yield some insights into the workings of the mind?

If so, a person who can speak two languages with reasonable fluency is of particular interest, because he works with two distinct sets of symbols. By presenting a bilingual subject with information in one language and then testing him in the other, the investigator should be able to learn much about the mental operations involved in the acquisition, storage and retrieval of the information. This has been the objective of experiments my colleagues and I have conducted with bilingual subjects in the Research Laboratory of Electronics at the Massachusetts Institute of Technology and in the Center for Cognitive Studies at Harvard University.

At the outset a qualification is in order. The experiments were concerned only with words, whereas the mind also receives and manipulates information in many other forms. One can remember the appearance of an object, the tonal quality of a musical instrument, the texture of a surface or the smell of a flower without being able to describe them precisely in words. The reader can remind himself of this fact by trying to find words for the smell of a rose. Nonetheless, much of a human being's thinking is expressed in words; they are clearly his principal means of receiving, storing, manipulating and transmitting information. The question of how words are involved in these processes is now the subject of intensive inquiry.

Let me proceed to our own work with an anecdote. Once when I was visiting Belgrade I set out with a colleague to buy a certain kind of decorated shoe—a part of the national costume of Yugoslavia—that had caught his eye. We tried several shops, where, with a combination of German, French, guidebook Serbian and gestures, he tried to get what he wanted. Finally we found a shop that had the shoes, but not in the right size.

As we started to leave, two other men came into the store speaking Italian. My friend listened and then said in Spanish, "They don't have that size; I just asked." One of the newcomers said, "Why do you speak Spanish to us? We're speaking Italian." "I know," said my friend in Spanish, "but I don't speak Italian. Can't you understand me? I understand you." "Well then," said the other man in French, "it is not so good. How is your French?" My friend answered in French, "I don't understand why you don't understand Spanish when you know Italian. My French is poor. Do you speak German?" "But yes, all right, let us speak German. Where do you come from?" My friend replied in German, "The United States. And where are you from?" The reply—in English—was "We're from New York," and everyone laughed. The entire exchange, involving the use of five languages, lasted for less than a minute.

I tell this story not only because it illustrates a number of aspects of the skilled use of languages but also because it was in thinking about the implications of the episode that I became interested in bilingualism. One point the story makes about the skilled user of two or more languages is that he can switch readily from one language to another. A second point is that the changeover is usually total: the people in the episode did not speak a mixture of Italian, Spanish, French, German and English; they spoke one or another exclusively.

Let us consider what such switching entails. In some languages, such as English and French, the meaning of a sentence is strongly dependent on the sequence of the words. The point is well made by the contrast between "The dog bit the man" and "The man bit the dog."

The individual words are identical; the meanings are not. In other languages, such as German and Latin, meaning is less dependent on word order because the subjects and objects of sentences are indicated by case endings and the declension of articles. The difference in German between "Der Hund biss den Mann" and "Den Mann biss der Hund" is more one of emphasis than of meaning. Even though the order of words is different, both sentences translate as "The dog bit the man," although the second sentence might be taken to indicate a particular man.

There are of course many rules that characterize the use of a language. The body of rules is the grammar of the language; the individual words are its lexicon. The two men speaking in the Belgrade store did at least three things when they switched languages. They selected words from five different lexicons. They used words in different order, that is, they used different grammatical rules to generate meaningful sequences of words. They also made sounds in different ways, that is, they used a German accent for German, a French accent for French and so on. Moreover, although they were performing a complicated psychological task in switching among linguistic codes, they did not really have to think about the process.

One of our experiments was aimed at assessing the psychological cost of such code-switching. We were interested not only in the mental processes of a bilingual person when he hears or reads either of his languages but also in what is involved when he speaks or writes either of them. Our approach made use of passages of connected discourse, some of which violated normal grammatical rules. In one session bilingual subjects read such passages silently and then were tested for comprehension of what they had read. In a second session they read the passages aloud.

Four abbreviated passages are shown in the chart on the right. Two of them are wholly unilingual—one in English and one in French. The other two are mixed; both are made up of some English words and some French ones, but in the first the word order is English and in the second it is French. All four passages convey the same message.

Before testing our subjects we had established how much time other subjects needed to read unilingual passages of the same length as the experimental passages and get a score of 75 percent correct on a comprehension test. Our experimental subjects were then asked to read the various unilingual and mixed passages in exactly that length of time. One might think that in order to understand a mixed passage a subject would have to translate all the words into one language or to switch between linguistic codes in some other way. If so, one might expect that the subjects would be so busy translating and switching that they would have less time to consider the meaning of the passage. Hence they

His horse, followed by two hounds, made the earth resound under its even tread. Drops of ice stuck to his
cloak. A strong wind was blowing. One side of the horizon lighted up, and in the whiteness of the early morning
light, he saw rabbits hopping at the edge of their burrows.

Son cheval, suivi de deux bassets, en marchant d'un pas
égal faisait résonner la terre. Des gouttes de verglas se
collaient à son manteau. Une brise violente soufflait. Un
côté de l'horizon s'éclaircit; et, dans la blancheur du
crépuscule, il aperçut des lapins sautillant au bord de
leurs terriers.

His horse, followed de deux bassets, faisait la terre résonner under its even tread. Des gouttes de verglas
stuck to his manteau. Une violente brise was blowing.
One side de l'horizon lighted up, and dans la blancheur
of the early morning light, il aperçut rabbits hopping at
the bord de leurs terriers.

Son cheval, suivi by two hounds, en marchant d'un pas
égal, made resound the earth. Drops of ice se collaient à
son cloak. A wind strong soufflait. Un côté of the horizon
s'éclaircit; et, in the whiteness du crépuscule, he saw
des lapins sautillant au edge of their burrows.

would get a lower score on a comprehension test of a mixed passage than on one of a unilingual passage.

Our findings, however, were that the subjects had almost identical scores on comprehension tests following the silent reading of unilingual and mixed passages. I concluded that a skilled reader of two languages can—in reading silently—comprehend a passage readily no matter to what extent words from either language are mixed in the passage. He apparently does not have to do any switching between linguistic codes when the passages are read. (We have not yet done the experiment to test if the same ease of comprehension is evident when a bilingual person listens to a message in which words from his two languages are mixed.)

The results were markedly different when we had our subjects read various passages aloud instead of silently. They needed more time to read the mixed passages than to read the unilingual ones. Evidently reading aloud entailed some kind of code-switching between languages; the reader could not move as smoothly through "his horse, followed de deux bassets" as he could through "his horse, followed by two hounds."

We had constructed the passages in such a way that the unilingual ones contained an average of 110 words of English or French. The mixed passages contained 55 words from each language. We therefore were in a position to measure the amount of time required for code-switching by seeing how long it took a subject to read one passage in English and one in French and then subtracting the average of those times from the amount of time it took to read a mixed passage. Dividing the difference by the number of linguistic transitions in a mixed passage—the number of times a switch occurred between English and French—we determined that the average amount of time required for each switch in code was a third of a second. That is, it took a subject a third of a second longer, on the average, to read something like "his horse, followed de deux bassets" than to read "his horse, followed by two hounds."

Doubtless some of the difference is attributable to mechanical effects: the subject must physically adjust his vocal apparatus in switching from the sounds of one language to the sounds of another. We are not sure how much of the difference is due to such adjustments, but from control experiments involving code-switching in English alone we have concluded that a significant portion of the code-switching interval is occupied by a mental operation. The operation can be described as a "call time," meaning the amount of time the mind needs to organize a set of procedures for handling a piece of information. The length of call time probably varies from person to person. It may vary also with the procedure being called. In reading a science textbook, for example, one

sees words, pictures, formulas and other kinds of symbols and uses different procedures for each of them. The length of time required to call
the appropriate procedures may also differ.

The experiments with mixed passages involved the important matter
of context. Clearly the fact that each of the passages had a context—a
thematic continuity—made it easier for the subjects to comprehend the
passages. In some instances context is created by the system of symbols
itself, as when a writer uses words to tell the reader what topic he is
discussing. Other systems of symbols are different. Computer program-
mers and engineers, for example, cannot usually understand each other's
programs or circuit drawings until they are told separately what the
program or the drawing is designed to do—what its context is. (How
subtle one's dependence on context can be is illustrated by a recent
newspaper story that described the bewilderment of a foreign visitor to
New York when he saw a sign saying, "BUS STOP. NO STANDING." Lacking the context that would be familiar to any New Yorker driving a
car, he at first took the sign to mean that he was supposed to sit down
while waiting for the bus.)

Words and other symbols, however, are not always embedded in a
context. I wanted to investigate how the mind dealt with words that
were isolated from context. To that end I undertook two other experiments. Before I describe them I need to supply some context.

Many bilingual people say that they think differently and respond
with different emotions to the same experience in their two languages.
For example, reading a poem or a play in French and reading its translation in English are said to create markedly different feelings and impressions. It is difficult to assess these introspective statements, if only
because emotive texts are notoriously difficult to translate well. As
Robert Frost once remarked, when a poem is translated, the poetry is
often lost.

Nonetheless, if one accepts the premise that such statements reflect
a genuine mental experience, one wonders about its nature. In particular we wondered whether the difference in impression arises from the
difficulty of translating words accurately or from some overall property
of languages and the contexts in which they are used. To put the question another way, we wondered how verbal symbols are stored in the
mind.

Perhaps a metaphor will help to clarify the issue. Regard the mind
as a storage tank and languages as taps. Is all the information that
words represent stored in some central tank in the mind, so that if a
person is bilingual he has access to the same information even though
he is using two different taps? If so, one could expect a variety of taps:
some could be large and some small; some could release the contents of
the tank as a spray and some as a stream. That is, the taps might be

regarded as the rules of grammar that affect the translation of information in the mind into sentences. The information being tapped would always be the same, but its appearance and form would differ (according to the grammar being used) in such characteristics as word order, tense agreement and the like.

Another possibility is that the information in the mind of a bilingual person depends fundamentally on the language that was used to put it there. To continue the metaphor, such a person would have two tanks in his mind, each with its own tap. The tanks would reflect a situation in which the rules for using a language are indelibly stamped on the information stored, so that the bilingual person has access to different information when he uses the different taps.

The first of the two alternatives can be described as common storage of information. The second entails separate storage. The alternatives define two extreme ways of characterizing the issue. If common storage were the case, the differences in reading a poem in two languages would be due entirely to the difficulty of translation. If separate storage were the case, the difference would be due to other kinds of experience. The fact is, as I shall show with a description of the experiments, that neither extreme alternative correctly describes the mental storage of information. A third arrangement that combines features of the other two seems to be required.

The method I chose for examining the extreme alternatives was a word-association test in which the subject is required to say the first word that comes to mind in response to a stimulus word. For example, a large percentage of English-speaking adults respond to "table" with "chair" and to "black" with "white." My subjects were students whose native languages were German, Spanish or Thai but who were also fluent in English. In my tests the subjects responded in their native language to a list of words in that language; they responded in English to the same list in English, and they responded in one language to stimulus words presented in the other. A typical selection of words is shown in all four languages in the illustration on the right.

Consider the German words *Haus* (house) and *Tisch* (table). Suppose a person fluent in German and English who was taking the German-German association test responded to *Tisch* with *Haus*. Would he respond to *table* with *house* or with some other word, such as *chair*? And how would he respond when the stimulus was in one language and he was asked to react in the other?

If the hypothesis of a common store of information were correct, one would expect a large percentage of responses to be similar in all the tests, since the concepts with which the subject was dealing would be essentially the same regardless of the language he was speaking. On the other hand, if information were stored according to language, one

	ENGLISH	GERMAN	SPANISH	THAI
EVOCATIVE	man	Mann	hombre	poo chai
	table	Tisch	mesa	dto
	bread	Brot	pan	ka-nom bpung
	boy	Junge	muchacho	dek poo chai
	blossom	Blüte	flor	dauk mai barn
	girl	Mädchen	niña	dek poo ying
	butter	Butter	mantequilla	nur-ie
	scissors	Schere	tijeras	gkan gkrai
ABSTRACTIONS	freedom	Freiheit	libertad	say-ree parp
	justice	Gerechtigkeit	justicia	yoo-dti tum
	law	Gesetz	ley	gkot mai
	honor	Ehre	honor	gkee-at-dti
	patience	Geduld	paciéncia	kwam ot-ton
	wisdom	Weisheit	sabiduria	kwam raub roo
	duty	Pflicht	el deber	nah tee
	civilization	Zivilisation	civilisación	ah-ra-ya tum
THINGS	lamb	Lamm	ovejito	look gkaa
	thorn	Dorn	espina	nam
	butterfly	Schmetterling	mariposa	pee sur-ah
	worm	Wurm	gusano	naun
	smoke	Rauch	humo	kwan
	castle	Schloss	castillo	bprah-sart
	tree	Baum	árbol	dton mai
	Norway	Norwegen	Noruega	nor-way
FEELINGS	pain	Schmerz	dolor	chjep bpoo-at
	hate	Hass	odio	kwam gklee-at
	jealousy	Eifersucht	celos	heung
	fear	Furcht	miedo	kwam gklau
	love	Liebe	amor	kwam ruk
	guilt	Schuld	culpa	kwam pit
	sadness	Traurigkeit	tristeza	kwam sow
	pity	Mitleid	piedad	song sarn

would expect the percentage of such direct translations to be low; for example, the subject might respond to *Tisch* with *Haus* in the German-German test and to *table* with *chair* in the English-English test.

Our finding was that about a fifth of the responses were the same in a bilingual subject's two languages. That is too large a percentage to warrant the belief that the meanings of words were stored completely in linguistically separate tanks. On the other hand, the large number of responses (about a quarter of the total) confined to one language or another enabled us to reject the idea that the meanings existed in a single tank for which the languages were merely taps. The bilingual person does not have a single store of meanings in his mind that he taps with his two languages. What it comes down to is that access to the information one has in one's mind is in some cases restricted to the language by which—or, more broadly, the context in which—it was encoded.

What are these cases? An indication is provided by the different responses we received to different categories of words. Some of the words we used referred to concrete objects; examples are *lamb, thorn, tree*. Other words were more abstract: *freedom, justice, wisdom, materialism*. Still other words—*hate, jealousy, love, guilt*—referred to feelings.

Our results revealed that words referring to concrete, manipulable objects were more likely to elicit similar responses in the bilingual person's two languages than abstract words. The abstract words in turn elicited a larger number of similar responses than the words referring to feelings. To put the matter another way, *love* and *Liebe* or *democracy* and *Demokratie* do not mean the same thing to someone familiar with English and German, even though they are dictionary translations of one another. He has different contexts and different expectations for each of the two words in the pairs. In contrast, words that refer to objects that people in various countries manipulate in similar ways—objects such as pencils, books and desks—have very similar meanings in the two languages. The idea that there are operational definitions of terms, as many philosophers of science put it, seems to have some psychological reality as one basis of meaning.

Our work showed that some information can be stored in such a way that it is readily accessible in either of two languages. Other information is, in terms of its accessibility, closely bound to the language by which it was stored in the mind. In another set of experiments we explored the way in which words are stored and retrieved. The question was: Are words perceived and then stored in the memory as individual items or does the process take place in terms of their meanings?

Our experiment was based on a phenomenon first studied in detail by Nancy C. Waugh, a former colleague of mine who is now at the

Harvard Medical School. She found that if a subject was presented with a unilingual list of words, some of which were repeated, his ability to recall a given word was directly proportional to the number of times it had been repeated. If a subject is shown, say, 120 words one at a time for about a second each, and if a few of the words are repeated on the list, he is twice as likely to recall a word presented four times as one presented twice.

My colleagues and I wondered what the result would be if a list were presented with some words appearing in two languages. Taking as an example the English word *fold* and its French translation *pli*, would a bilingual subject seeing each of them two or three times in a long list of words presented singly recall *fold* and *pli* according to the frequency with which each appeared or would his recall reflect the frequency of occurrence of the common meaning of the two words? An English-French list typical of the ones we used [follows]; the reader must remember that the subject saw the words one at a time and not in a complete array as in the illustration. Among the words that translate each other are *fold* and *pli* and *ten* and *dix*; among the words that are not translated are *herd* and *fonds* (funds).

The results showed that the percentage of recall increased linearly with the frequency of occurrence of meaning. Presenting *fold* twice and *pli* twice produces the same effect on the recall of either word as presenting either one four times. Since *fold* and *pli* neither look alike nor sound alike, it cannot be the words themselves that interact in perception and memory. Our subjects did not see and store the words individually as visual or phonetic objects; they stored them in terms of their meaning.

The implication is clear that the subjects were able to code and store verbal items in some form other than the language in which the items appeared. A further implication is that information repeated in different languages (different symbol systems) is as well retained as information repeated in a single language. The amount of information that can be retained, however, is not increased by using different symbol systems for storing it, but access to the information is increased.

To put the point more concretely, suppose one wanted to give a student two lessons in geography. If the student knew two languages, he would retain as much geography from one lesson in each language as from two lessons in one of them. Moreover, he would be able to talk about geography readily in both languages. On the other hand, teaching him geography in one language and also teaching him a second language would not necessarily enable him to express his knowledge of geography in the second language without some kind of additional instruction. The information one has and the mechanisms or rules used to acquire it are clearly separate aspects of memory.

ten	nerve	rız	tique
herd	truffe	isthme	preux
fold	paste	dix	fouet
soul	ice	glace	game
spout	gust	riz	clash
fonds	soul	âme	deux
jeu	truffe	fonds	game
tain	dix	crook	leaf
deux	preux	pli	bulk
pli	seing	bonne	golf
stub	ten	pli	bonne
bonne	nerf	spout	rampe
herd	rampe	golf	seing
âme	maid	two	gust
fold	maid	whip	clash
tain	jig	pâte	two
fold	truffe	psaume	whip
pli	gust	maid	âme
gust	preux	leaf	maid
bulk	cook	bonne	rampe
fouet	preux	clash	soul
fold	bulk	leaf	tain
riz	ice	glace	deux
riz	jeu	leaf	golf
two	juge	whip	fouet

Storage of words was tested with lists in which a subject saw, one at a time, words in both his languages. Some were repeated in the same language, others in both languages by means of translations; for example, *ten* and *dix* translate into each other. Recall is improved by repetition. The question was whether recall of translated words would reflect the frequency with which their common meaning appeared or only the frequency with which the words themselves appeared. The results showed that words are stored in terms of their meanings.

I have so far described two aspects of the use of verbal symbol systems: the mental switching that characterizes the successful use of different languages and one of the ways language limits access to information stored in the memory. A third aspect involves the set of rules a person learns for employing a language. In some of our experiments we found that such rules affect his linguistic performance in subtle ways.

Earlier I described how our bilingual subjects switched between their languages. Such switching is not always perfect, particularly in the daily use of language. Linguists use the word calque, which is the French word for "imitation," to describe the interference of one linguistic system with another. Examples of calques appear in the semi-Germanic sentences "Throw the baby out the window a bottle" and "Throw mama from the train a kiss." I have heard Hebrew-speaking people (Israeli students in the U.S.) inadvertently say "spoontea" for "teaspoon" and "cuptea" for "teacup." (In Hebrew the adjective always follows the noun.) Once I heard such a student say "washdisher" for "dishwasher." The last example is of particular linguistic interest because the Hebrew for "dishwasher" translates literally as "washerdish"; the speaker, however, combined the Hebrew word order with the English sequence of syllables.

In sum, speakers of a language develop linguistic habits, or characteristic ways of ordering words. One effect of these habits was revealed when our bilingual subjects were asked to read aloud linguistically mixed passages of the kind described at the beginning of this article. The rules we had used for constructing the passages gave rise to many cases in which the normal word order of English or French was violated. Two examples in the illustration are "made resound the earth" and "une violente brise."

Subjects reading the passages aloud sometimes said "made the earth resound" and "une brise violente." Thus they showed that their experience with the normal syntactic forms affected their way of speaking words presented visually. In effect, the students were producing calques, but in a direction opposite to the normal one. Usually a calque distorts a verbal expression by applying a syntactic form of one language to words in another. In our experiment the subjects' ingrained skills in using the rules of English and French induced them to rectify word sequences that had been distorted deliberately.

The various experiments I have described embody some significant implications for both education and the study of the mind. Education entails the acquisition of information and the use of mental skills. Languages, as I have shown, can train one's mind in the way it orders and uses information. The phenomenon of bilingualism enables us to give people information or teach people a skill in one language and find out if the information or the skill can be expressed in another language. In this way we can separate for study the mental processes used in acquiring or manipulating information from the information itself.

One example of the difference between mental skills and information is found in mathematics. Nearly all our bilingual subjects remarked during interviews that they did mathematical operations in the language in which they were taught the operations. They could always tell us the results of their operations in either language, and they could even describe what operations they had performed and how they had performed them, but the operations could be performed in only one way. Indeed, a bilingual colleague once told me that, having moved from France to the U.S. at the age of 12, he does his arithmetic in French and his calculus in English.

The point to be made is that mental activities and information learned in one context are not necessarily available for use in another. They often have to be learned anew in the second context, although perhaps with less time and effort. The fact is, however, that relatively little is known about how the activities of the mind affect one another. The study of bilingualism, being a study of the interaction of symbol systems and the way they affect one's acquisition and use of information, promises to provide valuable information on these questions.

FOR DISCUSSION AND REVIEW

1   What are the two hypotheses proposed by Kolers to account for the way a bilingual person handles information? Is either of these hypotheses satisfactory? How does Kolers explain the mental storage of information? Describe the experiment that enabled him to arrive at this conclusion.

2   What are some of the problems encountered by a person switching from one language to another?

3   Do Kolers' experiments help to explain the "switch mechanism" referred to by Wilder Penfield (pp. 80–81)? Explain.

4   Kolers makes the statement that "mental activities and information learned in one context are not necessarily available for use in another." Can you support this generalization from your own experiences? Discuss.

5   Kolers quotes Robert Frost as having said that when a poem is translated, the poetry is often lost. What did Frost mean? Do you think that the information in a poem is closely bound to the language by which it was stored in the mind? How does the information in poems differ from other types of information?

8
Speech Is More Than Language

Peter Woolfson

Although language is man's primary means of communication, it is not, as is commonly supposed, man's only means of communicating. Language is, as Peter Woolfson suggests, only one part of a large network of communication systems which humans use to interact with each other. It is speech that facilitates communication among men and, while speech is usually associated only with language, it is actually composed of three communication systems. Woolfson discusses the interdependent nature of language, paralanguage, and kinesics in human communication.

When we think of communication among humans, we automatically think of language: the intricate system of sounds that differentiates between words that fit into a grammatical framework that makes sense. Yet human communication is multi-dimensional, occurring within the setting of human interaction and functioning within that complex blueprint of life's activities called *culture*. Culture, itself, can be considered "an interacting set of communications."[1] It is made up of a network of communication systems in which humans interact and participate. We can see on an obvious level how all aspects of culture communicate when we walk into a doctor's office, a barbershop, a supermarket, a library, or a schoolroom. Each place has a special character that indicates its function immediately to the senses.

E. T. Hall in a classic work, *The Silent Language*,[2] effectively illustrates the concept of culture as communication, especially in terms of systems of time and space (*proxemics*). By examining the idea of lateness, Hall argues that there is an informal system of expectations,

---

1 George L. Trager, "Paralanguage: A First Approximation," in *Language in Culture and Society*, ed. Dell Hymes (New York: Harper & Row, 1964), p. 275.
2 Edward T. Hall, *The Silent Language* (Garden City, N.Y.: Doubleday & Company, 1959).

varying from culture to culture, that requires different responses. In America, significant units of lateness are: mumble-something periods (after five minutes); mild apology periods (after fifteen minutes); and full apology periods (after a half hour). By examining the concepts of space in different cultures, he argues that the distance between men in talking to one another and in behaving with each other provides significant information. For example, in America if a man approaches another man more closely than one arm-length—approximately two feet—the former becomes uneasy, because the violation of his territory could be interpreted as aggressiveness.

Although all culture communicates, the communication complex designed to carry the weight of interaction and participation is speech. *Speech* is a complex network of three interdependent communication systems: *language, paralanguage,* and *kinesics. Language* is the central and apparently most highly developed of the three communication systems, yet in actual speech it is always accompanied by the other two. *Paralanguage,* the system of extra-linguistic noises, is often thought of as "tone of voice." *Kinesics,* the system of postures, facial expressions, and bodily motions, is thought of as "body language." The three systems make an interlocking and interpenetrating communication set.

Paralanguage, as a system, was developed principally by George Trager along lines analogous to those he established for the analysis of language. One of the difficulties of paralinguistic analysis is distinguishing between language sounds and paralinguistic noises. Language sounds fall into distinctive and contrastive classes called *phonemes* that identify and distinguish among the various grammatical units of the language. Paralinguistic noises, by definition, are excluded from these classes. They function in a complementary capacity—they accompany, interpenetrate, or even substitute for language, but they are not part of it.

There are apparently two main classes of paralinguistic noises: *voice qualities* and *vocalizations. Voice qualities* operate as background characteristics of a person's voice: his pitch range, his articulation control, his tempo, and his rhythm. Much information is conveyed—usually without much conscious notice—by the voice qualities: an overhigh pitch can indicate nervous excitement; sloppy articulation can indicate a "high" on drugs or alcohol; a jerky rhythm can indicate insecurity. *Vocalizations* are classified into three groups: *vocal characterizers, vocal qualifiers,* and *vocal segregates. Vocal characterizers* represent such phenomena as laughing, crying, groaning, moaning, giggling, whispering, yelling. They are useful, of course, for indicating attitude. If you say the sentence "John went to the bank" using each of the characterizers listed above, you will convey a different message each time. It is this level that is meant when someone says, "It was not *what* he said that bothered me, but the *way* that he said it!" V*ocal qualifiers* represent modifications of utterances in terms of intensity (loud or soft), pitch height (high or low), and extent (drawl or clipping). They, too, indicate attitude, but not overall attitude; rather they indicate attitudes to specific lexical items. If you say the phrase "Get out" with loudness, high pitch, and clipping, you will probably be demonstrating agitated anger; however, if you say it with softness, low pitch, and drawl, you will probably be demonstrating controlled, dangerous anger. V*ocal segregates* represent such phenomena as *uh-uh, shh, tsk*, and *brr*. Vocal segregates substitute for language; for example, you can express disgust or contempt by extending the tip of your tongue and trilling your lips —an excellent way to make a "Bronx cheer."

Kinesics, as a science, was developed by Ray Birdwhistell along the lines he found in linguistics. Thus, *kines* are parallel to *phones*, *kinemes* to *phonemes*, *kinemorphs* to *morphs*, and *kinemorphemes* to *morphemes*. Kinesic messages are expressed through a variety of gestures. Doubt, for example, can be expressed in a number of ways: scratching the scalp, biting the lip, knitting the brows, pulling the ear, pulling the nose, scratching the chin, and scratching the cheek. There are all kinds of movements which have message potentials from crossing your legs to curling your toes. The kinesicist has a relatively complex system of *kinegraphs* for describing body motion within each of eight basic sections of the body: the total head, the face, the neck, the trunk, the shoulder (including arm and wrist), the hand (including finger activity), the hip (including leg and ankle), and the foot.

Kinesic markers are particularly interesting gestures because, in addition to communicating in themselves, they also complement language. In their complementary function they usually reinforce the verbal message; occasionally, however, they contradict it. For example, consider a woman who says "But I love him" while shaking her head in a negative manner. Kinesic markers are of various types. There are *pronominal markers* where the hand is directed toward an object or event and accompanies a word like *he, she, it, any*, and *some*. There are *pluralization markers* indicated by a slight sweep of the hand or head accompanying a word like *we, us, they, these*, and *our*. There are *verboid markers* which involve movement of the body forward or backward accompanying references to future or past time. There are *area markers* signaled by a movement of the body and accompanying words like *on, over, under, by, through*, and *behind*. And there are *manner markers* involving jerky or smooth motions which accompany words like *slowly, smoothly*, and *quickly*.

In summary, the act of speech requires a speaker and a hearer; both are members of society and participants in a culture. The communication interaction between them is very complex—they act according to

Language, Thought, and Culture

the expectations of their social roles by a blueprint provided by their culture. They speak to each other not only in words, their language, but with space, gestures, facial expressions, and body movements; with extralinguistic noises, changes in pitch, loudness, and length; accompanied by giggling, laughing, crying, moaning, groaning, whispering, and yelling. Although we are not consciously aware of many of these activities, they are a necessary part of the communication act. Speech is more than language: it is a complex network of interpenetrating communication systems.

Bibliography

Birdwhistell, Ray L. *Kinesics and Context.* Philadelphia: University of Pennsylvania Press, 1970.

Hall, Edward T. *The Silent Language.* Garden City, N.Y.: Doubleday & Company, 1959.

Trager, George L. "Paralanguage: A First Approximation." *Language in Culture and Society.* Ed. Dell Hymes. New York: Harper & Row, 1964.

———. "The Typology of Paralanguage." *Anthropological Linguistics,* 3, No. 1 (1961), 17–21.

FOR DISCUSSION AND REVIEW

1 According to Woolfson, how does "culture communicate"?

2 As Woolfson indicates, speech is a complex network of three interdependent communication systems: *language, paralanguage,* and *kinesics.* Define each of these communication systems.

3 What are *voice qualities* and *vocalizations*? Give an example of each so that the difference between the two is clear.

4 Say the sentence "Mary is beautiful" using the seven vocal characterizers presented by Woolfson. What are the various messages indicated?

5 How do gestures reinforce verbal messages?

6 What are *kinesic markers*? Are you conscious of using any of them yourself? Explain.

7 What does Woolfson mean when he says that communication between two people "is very complex—they act according to the expectations of their social roles by a blueprint provided by their culture"? (You may find it helpful to consult the first article in this section, also by Woolfson, "Language, Thought, and Culture," on pp. 3–11.)

8 Explain the paradox in Woolfson's title, "Speech Is More Than Language." Can you provide evidence from your own experiences to support this generalization? Discuss.

PROJECTS FOR "LANGUAGE, THOUGHT, AND CULTURE"

1 *Man, for the most part, inhabits a verbal environment. According to Edward Sapir,*

Language . . . completely interpenetrates . . . direct experience. For most persons every experience, real or potential, is saturated with verbalism. This explains why so many lovers of nature, for instance, do not feel that they are truly in touch with it until they have mastered the names of a great many flowers and trees, as though the primary world of reality were a verbal one and as though one could not get close to nature unless one first mastered the terminology which somehow magically expresses it. It is this constant interplay between language and experience which removes language from the cold status of such purely and simply symbolic systems as mathematical symbolism or flag signalling.[1]

Have you ever had an experience similar to that of Sapir's "nature lover"? What does Sapir's discussion of language tell you about your experience? Write a paper in which you explore the implications of Sapir's statement.

2   *Try the "conservation" experiment with water tumblers and/or the "shape-color" experiment related by Greenfield and Bruner (pp. 13 and 20) on a group of selected children. What are your results? Write a report in which you compare your conclusions with those of Greenfield and Bruner.*

3   *Much fascinating work has been done with animals and their systems of communication. Using items included in the bibliography for this section, write a paper in which you review the research that has been done with either bees, birds, dolphins, or chimpanzees. You can supplement your research materials by looking in the* Reader's Guide to Periodical Literature *or* The International Index for the Social Sciences and Humanities.

4   *Examine the following conversation between Eve, a 24-month-old child, and her mother:*

Eve: Have that?
Mother: No, you may not have it.
Eve: Mom, where my tapioca?
Mother: It's getting cool. You'll have it in just a minute.
Eve: Let me have it.
Mother: Would you like to have your lunch right now?
Eve: Yeah. My tapioca cool?
Mother: Yes, it's cool.
Eve: You gonna watch me eat my lunch?
Mother: Yeah, I'm gonna watch you eat your lunch.
Eve: I eating it.
Mother: I know you are.
Eve: It time Sarah take a nap.
Mother: It's time for Sarah to have some milk, yeah. And then she's gonna take a nap and you're gonna take a nap.
Eve: And you?
Mother: And me too, yeah.[2]

---

[1] Edward Sapir, "Language," *Encyclopaedia of the Social Sciences* (New York: The Macmillan Company, 1933), IX, 157.

[2] A transcription of a taped conversation from Ursula Bellugi, "Learning the Language," *Psychology Today,* 4 (December 1970), 33.

Compare the grammar of the child's speech with that of her mother.
What elements are systematically missing from the child's speech?
Now, look at Eve's speech in a conversation with her mother that was
taped only three months later:

Mother: Come and sit over here.
Eve: You can sit down by me. That will make me happy. Ready to turn it.
Mother: We're not quite ready to turn the page.
Eve: Yep, we are.
Mother: Shut the door, we won't hear her then.
Eve: Then Fraser won't hear her too. Where he's going? Did you make a
    great big hole there?
Mother: Yes, we made a great big hole in here; we have to get a new one.
Eve: Could I get some other piece of paper?
Mother: You ask Fraser.
Eve: Could I use this one?
Mother: I suppose so.
Eve: Is Fraser goin take his pencil home when he goes?
Mother: Yes, he is.[3]

What startling changes do you note in Eve's speech? Try to describe
the "grammatical rules" that govern her speech in each passage. Al-
though Eve could not tell us of the rules she learned during the three-
month interval, what rules, as evidenced implicitly by her speech, has
she internalized? What conclusions can you draw about the process
of language learning among children? Write a short paper dealing
with these questions.

5 *It is fascinating to watch children learn language. Try taping conver-*
  sations with a child at two-week intervals for several months. Share
  the tapes with other members of the class. Note the child's develop-
  ment. On the basis of one tape, plan a strategy (leading questions,
  etc.) for the next session with the child. Write a report in which you
  summarize and interpret your data.

6 *Any discussion of language is bound to arrive at the question: What is*
  the origin of language? A great number of interesting hypotheses have
  been put forward in addition to the one proposed by the Russells (pp.
  48–51). Using items included in the bibliography for this section,
  write a paper in which you discuss the various theories about the origin
  of language. Do any seem more plausible than others? Why are they
  all only hypotheses?

SELECTED BIBLIOGRAPHY

Barnett, Lincoln. *The Treasure of Our Tongue: The Story of English from Its Ob-*
    scure Beginnings to Its Present Eminence as the Most Widely Spoken Lan-

[3] *Ibid.,* 33–34.

guage. New York: Alfred A. Knopf, 1964. (See pp. 39–78 for an interesting discussion of the theories of the origin of language.)

Bellugi, Ursula. "Learning the Language." *Psychology Today,* 4 (December 1970), 32–35, 66. (A study of language acquisition and the grammar of children.)

Bolinger, Dwight. "Mind in the Grip of Language." *Aspects of Language.* New York: Harcourt, Brace & World, 1968. (A brief analysis and discussion of the Whorfian hypothesis.)

Bronowski, J., and Ursula Bellugi. "Language, Name, and Concept." *Science,* 168 (May 8, 1970), 669–73. (A comparative study of the linguistic capabilities of children and chimpanzees.)

Brown, Roger. "How Shall A Thing Be Called?" *Psychological Review,* 85 (1958), 145–54. (A discussion of how adults teach children the names of objects.)
————. "The Comparative Psychology of Linguistic Reference." *Words and Things.* New York: The Free Press, 1958. (An historical review of research on animal communication.)

Carroll, John B. *The Study of Language: A Survey of Linguistics and Related Disciplines in America.* Cambridge, Mass.: Harvard University Press, 1963. (Contains interesting chapters on linguistics and psychology, and on linguistics and the social sciences.)

Chase, Stuart. "How Language Shapes Our Thoughts." *Harper's Magazine,* April 1954, pp. 76–82. (A discussion of language as a shaper of thought with examples drawn from many different cultures.)

Dinneen, Francis P. *An Introduction to General Linguistics.* New York: Holt, Rinehart & Winston, 1967. (See pp. 213–98, 355–99 for discussions of the contributions made to linguistics by Franz Boas, Edward Sapir, Leonard Bloomfield, and Noam Chomsky.)

Fishman, Joshua, ed. *Readings in the Sociology of Language.* The Hague: Mouton & Company, 1968. (A standard collection of sociolinguistic readings.)

Ford, Barbara. "How They Taught a Chimp to Talk." *Science Digest,* 67 (May 1970), 10–17. (A discussion of the chimpanzee Washoe's sign language, with illustrations.)

Francis, W. Nelson. *The English Language: An Introduction.* New York: W. W. Norton & Company, 1963. (See pp. 118–20 for a discussion of the Whorfian hypothesis and the perception of colors.)

Gardner, Allen, and Beatrice T. Gardner. "Teaching Sign Language to a Chimpanzee." *Science,* 165 (August 15, 1969), 664–72. (Teaching the infant chimpanzee Washoe the gestural langauge of the deaf.)

Hayes, Catherine. *The Ape in Our House.* New York: Harper & Brothers, 1951. (The story of the Hayes family's experiences with the chimpanzee Viki.)

Hymes, Dell, ed. *Language in Culture and Society: A Reader in Linguistics and Anthropology.* New York: Harper & Row, 1964. (A standard anthology.)

Jakobovits, Leon A., and Murray S. Miron, eds. *Readings in the Psychology of Language.* Englewood Cliffs, New Jersey: Prentice-Hall, 1967. (Includes essays by Katz, Miller, Mowrer, Skinner, and others.)

Kluckhohn, Clyde. "The Gift of Tongues." *Mirror for Man: The Relation of Anthropology to Modern Life.* New York: Whittlesey House, 1949. (An anthropologist's view of language, culture, and the Whorfian hypothesis.)

Krough, August. "The Language of the Bees." *Scientific American Reader.* New York: Simon & Schuster, 1953. (A summary of Karl von Frisch's classic study of communication among bees.)

Langacker, Ronald W. "Language and Thought." *Language and Its Structure: Some Fundamental Linguistic Concepts.* New York: Harcourt, Brace & World, 1967. (An assessment of the influence of language on thought.)

Lenneberg, Eric H. *Biological Foundations of Language*. New York: John Wiley & Sons, 1967. (An interesting but technical investigation of the biological aspects of language.)

Lilly, John C. *Man and Dolphin*. New York: Pyramid Publications, 1969. (The story of man's attempt to communicate with another species.)

————. *The Mind of the Dolphin: A Nonhuman Intelligence*. New York: Avon Books, 1969. (An introduction to the controversial world of communication among dolphins.)

McNeill, David. *The Acquisition of Language: The Study of Developmental Psycholinguistics*. New York: Harper & Row, 1970. (Brief but technical discussion of language acquisition.)

Malmstrom, Jean. *Language in Society*. New York: Hayden Book Company, 1965. (A general discussion of language and society which draws upon findings from many cross-disciplinary studies.)

Miller, George A. *The Psychology of Communication*. New York: Basic Books, 1967. (A collection of seven essays dealing with the psychology of language.)

Myers, L. M. *The Roots of Modern English*. Boston: Little, Brown and Company, 1966. (An historical approach to modern English with an interesting chapter on the nature of language.)

Osgood, Charles E., and Thomas A. Sebeok, eds. *Psycholinguistics: A Survey of Theory and Research Problems*. Bloomington, Indiana: Indiana University Press, 1965. (A standard but technical collection of readings.)

Premack, David. "The Education of Sarah: A Chimp Learns the Language." *Psychology Today*, 4 (September 1970), 54–58. (Teaching a chimpanzee a nonvocal language.)

Riopelle, A. J., ed. *Animal Problem Solving*. Baltimore: Penguin Books, 1967. (A collection of reports on problem-solving experiments with animals.)

Robertson, Stuart, and Frederic G. Cassidy. *The Development of Modern English*. 2nd edition. Englewood Cliffs, New Jersey: Prentice-Hall, 1954. (See pp. 1–14 for a discussion of theories about the nature and origin of language.)

Sapir, Edward. *Language: An Introduction to the Study of Speech*. New York: Harcourt, Brace & World, 1949. (A classic book which explores the relationship between speech and culture.)

Saporta, Sol, ed. *Psycholinguistics: A Book of Readings*. New York: Holt, Rinehart & Winston, 1961. (A standard collection of introductory readings.)

Sebeok, Thomas A., and Alexandra Ramsay, eds. *Approaches to Animal Communication*. The Hague: Mouton & Company, 1969. (A collection of essays resulting from a symposium on animal communication, or zoosemiotics.)

Smith, Frank, and George A. Miller, eds. *The Genesis of Language: A Psycholinguistic Approach*. Cambridge, Mass.: The M.I.T. Press, 1966. (Essays dealing with language development in children.)

Sturtevant, E. H. *An Introduction to Linguistic Science*. New Haven: Yale University Press, 1947. (A provocative discussion of the origin of language in the fifth chapter.)

Vetter, Harold J. "Sign Language of the Deaf." *Language Behavior and Communication: An Introduction*. Itasca, Illinois: F. E. Peacock Publishers, 1969. (A discussion of communication by a system of gestures.)

Whorf, Benjamin Lee. *Language, Thought, and Reality*. Ed. John B. Carroll. Cambridge, Mass.: The M.I.T. Press, 1956. (A classic and essential work.)

PART TWO

The Systems of Grammar

Investigation of language and its structure has always interested some scholars, but the last thirty years have brought an amazing growth of that interest. Linguistics has experienced an explosion of knowledge similar to that which has occurred in many other fields. Stimulated by the work of anthropologists with the American Indian and also by the need for language-study programs during World War II, scholars began a still uncompleted re-examination of the nature of language and of particular languages. In America, this re-examination involved new analyses of English quite unlike the traditional grammar that had been accepted almost without question. And it led eventually to the introduction into the public schools of several "new grammars" and to the growth in many universities of departments of linguistics.

The articles in this section illustrate the development of linguistics in America since World War II, a development remarkable for the diversity of approaches to language analysis. Structural linguistics, the earliest approach described, aroused misgivings in many Americans who still like their grammar prescriptive, as we were reminded again in 1961 by the controversy about *Webster's Third New International Dictionary*. Then, in the late 1950's, another grammatical theory, transformational generative, began to gain increasing acceptance. The emphasis that it placed on cognitive processes and on linguistic universals seemed wholly new, although in fact it had its roots in centuries-old ideas. Today, even as work continues on transformational generative grammar—which now reaches about one-fifth of the school children in the United States—still other grammatical theories are being developed. Two of these, stratificational grammar and tagmemics, are also discussed in this section.

Linguists do not yet fully understand human language and how it works, nor do they agree about what form a grammatical description should take. They all share, however, in the excitement and challenge involved in the study of the marvelous phenomenon that is human language.

1
Trouble
in Linguistic
Paradise

Charlton Laird

An allegory, like Bunyan's *Pilgrim's Progress* or Spenser's *The Faerie Queene,* arouses our interest both in the characters and events that are actually described and also in what lies behind them, what they represent. In this short allegorical piece, Professor Charlton Laird describes the feelings of many people in the United States in the mid 1950's as they became aware of the differences between structural linguistics, by then taught in many schools, and the traditional grammar which they had accepted since childhood. Especially disturbing to many was the apparent erosion of standards.

O NCE UPON a time the User of English dwelt in a paradise known as the Eden of Linguistic Authority, which the Gods of Prescriptive Grammar had made to wall him from the sins of Doubt, Thought, and Unsanctioned Innovation. The plants in the garden were neatly trimmed, freed of all weedy vulgarisms which might suggest the Vulgus, a many-headed beast, who was to be kept out of the garden. Furthermore, the Great I-Decide of Prescriptive Grammar had provided a Rulebook for the Policing of English, and a Usage Ukase Unifier to enforce it, so that there would never be any uncertainty or irregularity about anything, and the garden would retain its beauty and order forever. The Usage Unifier had put labels on the plants identifying them as they had come from the Celestial Inflectional Syntactical Lexicographical Nursery.

There was, for example, the Lexicographical Tree, which bore all the words in the world. True, these words did not grow quite on the tree itself, but they were in the dictionaries, and the dictionaries hung from the boughs of the tree, and in these works the irrefragable facts about the words were culled and recorded, forever to remain unchanged, *saecula saeculorum.* Each of these words the Gods of Prescriptive Grammar had made in their own images, and the user of English could trust the words because once they had been hung from the boughs of the Lexicographical Tree, that was all he knew and all he would ever need to know.

There was also the Trellis of the Authoritarian Decalogue, a rambling vine draped on a series of handsome signs: "Thou shalt not say 'Ain't,'" "Thou shalt not end a sentence with a preposition," "Thou shalt not use the gauche word *get*, which is inelegant," "Thou shalt not say 'It's me,' which is illogical," and many more. By its name the trellis should have had only ten signs, but time out of mind there seemed to have been an infinity of them, and every time the User of English looked at the trellis he noticed some new ones: "Thou shalt not say 'I will' when 'I shall' is correct"; "Thou shalt not confuse *like* and *as* or say 'Everybody took their hats.'"

Then there were the Hedges of Preferred Usage, which were perhaps the most wonderful plants in the garden, for they surrounded everything. True, they seemed to get nowhere but they kept the more circumspect dwellers in the garden from straying into inelegant locutions. They bore few flowers of poetry, and even the fruits of prose might wither on the durable redundancies that proliferated like suckers from the hedges, but they had a consistency that would cry out strumpet-tongued against the deep damnation of their digging up. The User of English was occasionally irked with them since they got in his way, but he hesitated to root any of them out lest he thereby disrupt some ancient symmetry which the Great I-Decide would feel was very real, although not to the vulgar eye.

Now, there were in the Garden creeping and crawling things, which would skitter under the Hedges of Preferred Usage and go where they pleased, or they would stray outside the walls of the Garden and bring back ways of saying things which were not in the dictionaries on the Lexicographical Tree, and what concourse they had with these Lilith-like locutions of dubious virtue, it were perhaps best not to inquire. One of the cleverest of these creatures was a serpent known as the Modern Linguist, a pernicious fellow, always up to mischief. He would entice the Termites of Research to riddle the signs in the Trellis of the Authoritarian Decalogue, and would whisper slyly to the fat, well-dressed words in the dictionaries, "Did you know, my dear, that your occasional linguistic slips are showing?"

Naturally, the conduct of this serpent troubled the User of English, and one day when he caught the reptile slithering out of a sort of den he had concocted out of multigraphed monographs, linguistic institutes, and rejected allophones, the User accosted him, saying "Look here. I want a conference with you."

"You mean you wish to transform a few morphemes?" the serpent asked slyly, knowing full well that the words *phoneme* and *morpheme* always made the User of English blush for shame.

But the User was not abashed. Recalling his course in English Minus 1, The Principles and Practice of Approved Jargon, he said firmly, "You are featuring a position of maintaining an uncooperative attitude toward certain aspects of the circumstances involving conditions not approved in the regulations, and accordingly I am about to emphasize taking under consideration the expediting of a report."

During this speech the serpent had had plenty of time to twist himself up the Tree of Knowledge of Good and Evil Speech. "The trouble with you, my friend," he said, "is that you have too little poetry in your soul. Even a bit of doggerel would do you no harm. For whatever good it may do, here is a jingle I have been puttering with." Then he recited as follows:

> Oh, purist with zeal thermostatic,
> Devoted to forms hieratic,
>   Degoggle your eyes
>   And try on for size,
> Something morphophonematic.

The serpent disappeared among the leaves, but the User of English could still hear him muttering, as though to himself,

> A pedagogue aptly called Domsky,
> Never got loose from his Momsky,
>   He approached his demise
>   With Carpenter Fries,
> But wait till he hears about Chomsky!

The User of English was outraged. He assumed that these limericks were not intended for him, but there was that crack about the goggles. He was outraged, but he was also intrigued. True, he was wearing goggles, and the Great I-Decide had strictly forbidden him to remove them. Still, I-Decide did not come around as often as he used to, and accordingly the User slipped the goggles sideways for just a peep. Then in amazement he took them off and stared.

The Garden was no longer there. Or it was so changed that at first it seemed not to be there. He could stroll through the Hedges of Preferred Usage, which were full of holes. Even the neat little Parts of Speech were lopping every which way, having little to stand on. The dictionaries still dangled from the Lexicographical Tree, but the definitions in them no longer looked like the codification of eternal truth. And now the User of English was taken with a staggering surmise. Suppose there were no Gods of Prescriptive Grammar, and the Great I-Decide himself a quack or a hoax? Suppose that language had not been made in the images of the Gods of anything, but that he himself, the User of English, had made his language in his own image, not even in his best image, but had blundered into much of it, as it were accidentally, when he was not thinking at all, so that it reflected, along with other things, that little unselfconscious self of dubious repute with Freudian overtones—and the Lord knew what undertones—which another serpent, the Modern Psychologist, had been telling him about?

By the time such questions had been asked, the User of English found himself well outside anything which could any longer be called an Eden of Linguistic Authority. Like Milton's Adam and Eve, "some natural tears he shed, but wiped them soon; the world was all before him." If he could discover nowhere the order and symmetry which he had once supposed existed in the garden of his mother tongue, he found that the more human his language appeared to be, the more interesting it became. It was a bit like a charming baby, his own offspring, which he could chuck under the chin, while listening to it gurgle. Accordingly, he set to examining it, and in the last half century he has discovered a good bit. Meanwhile, he found that his old enemy, the Modern Linguist, was quite a chummy fellow, and what they found together has considerable importance for teachers of English. Let us have a look at some of it.

FOR DISCUSSION AND REVIEW

1 Prepare a brief, non-allegorical summary of Professor Laird's tale. Try to describe very specifically as many beliefs and reactions of the "User of English" as you can.

2 Throughout this essay, allustons are made to the story of the Garden of Eden. How do they work? Explain.

2
Revolution in Grammar

1954

"Revolution" is not too strong a word to describe the effects that structural linguistics had on language analysis and teaching. Writing in 1954, Professor W. Nelson Francis sets forth the basic premises of the structuralists concerning the characteristics of human language and the appropriate methods of analyzing it. Since the structuralists objected to the inadequacies of traditional grammar, Francis discusses these and briefly traces the history of this grammar; he concludes that "It is now as unrealistic to teach 'traditional' grammar of English as it is to teach 'traditional' (i.e. pre-Darwinian) biology or 'traditional' (i.e. four-element) chemistry." Three years after the original publication of this article, the arrival of another grammatical revolution, that of the transformationalists, was signaled by the appearance of Noam Chomsky's *Syntactic Structures*.

W. Nelson Francis

(Chomsky Syntactic Structures = 1957)

I

A LONG overdue revolution is at present taking place in the study of English grammar—a revolution as sweeping in its consequences as the Darwinian revolution in biology. It is the result of the application to English of methods of descriptive analysis originally developed for use with languages of primitive peoples. To anyone at all interested in language, it is challenging; to those concerned with the teaching of English (including parents), it presents the necessity of radically revising both the substance and the methods of their teaching.

A curious paradox exists in regard to grammar. On the one hand it is felt to be the dullest and driest of academic subjects, fit only for those in whose veins the red blood of life has long since turned to ink.

On the other, it is a subject upon which people who would scorn to be professional grammarians hold very dogmatic opinions, which they will defend with considerable emotion. Much of this prejudice stems from the usual sources of prejudice—ignorance and confusion. Even highly educated people seldom have a clear idea of what grammarians do, and there is an unfortunate confusion about the meaning of the term "grammar" itself.

Hence it would be well to begin with definitions. What do people mean when they use the word "grammar"? Actually the word is used to refer to three different things, and much of the emotional thinking about matters grammatical arises from confusion among these different meanings.

The first thing we mean by "grammar" is "the set of formal patterns in which the words of a language are arranged in order to convey larger meanings." It is not necessary that we be able to discuss these patterns self-consciously in order to be able to use them. In fact, all speakers of a language above the age of five or six know how to use its complex forms of organization with considerable skill; in this sense of the word—call it "Grammar 1"—they are thoroughly familiar with its grammar.

The second meaning of "grammar"—call it "Grammar 2"—is "the branch of linguistic science which is concerned with the description, analysis, and formulization of formal language patterns." Just as gravity was in full operation before Newton's apple fell, so grammar in the first sense was in full operation before anyone formulated the first rule that began the history of grammar as a study.

The third sense in which people use the word "grammar" is "linguistic etiquette." This we may call "Grammar 3." The word in this sense is often coupled with a derogatory adjective: we say that the expression "he ain't here" is "bad grammar." What we mean is that such an expression is bad linguistic manners in certain circles. From the point of view of "Grammar 1" it is faultless; it conforms just as completely to the structural patterns of English as does "he isn't here." The trouble with it is like the trouble with Prince Hal in Shakespeare's play—it is "bad," not in itself, but in the company it keeps.

As has already been suggested, much confusion arises from mixing these meanings. One hears a good deal of criticism of teachers of English couched in such terms as "they don't teach grammar any more." Criticism of this sort is based on the wholly unproved assumption that teaching Grammar 2 will increase the student's proficiency in Grammar 1 or improve his manners in Grammar 3. Actually, the form of Grammar 2 which is usually taught is a very inaccurate and misleading analysis of the facts of Grammar 1; and it therefore is of highly questionable value in improving a person's ability to handle the structural patterns of his language. It is hardly reasonable to expect that teaching a person some inaccurate grammatical analysis will either improve the effectiveness of his assertions or teach him what expressions are acceptable to use in a given social context.

These, then, are the three meanings of "grammar": Grammar 1, a form of behavior; Grammar 2, a field of study, a science; and Grammar 3, a branch of etiquette.

II (basic principles of linguistic science)

Grammarians have arrived at some basic principles of their science, three of which are fundamental to this discussion. The first is that a language constitutes a set of behavior patterns common to the members of a given community. It is a part of what the anthropologists call the culture of the community. Actually it has complex and intimate relationships with other phases of culture such as myth and ritual. But for purposes of study it may be dealt with as a separate set of phenomena that can be objectively described and analyzed like any other universe of facts. Specifically, its phenomena can be observed, recorded, classified, and compared; and general laws of their behavior can be made by the same inductive process that is used to produce the "laws" of physics, chemistry, and the other sciences.

A second important principle of linguistic science is that each language or dialect has its own unique system of behavior patterns. Parts of this system may show similarities to parts of the systems of other languages, particularly if those languages are genetically related. But different languages solve the problems of expression and communication in different ways, just as the problems of movement through water are solved in different ways by lobsters, fish, seals, and penguins. A couple of corollaries of this principle are important. The first is that there is no such thing as "universal grammar," or at least if there is, it is so general and abstract as to be of little use. The second corollary is that the grammar of each language must be made up on the basis of a study of that particular language—a study that is free from preconceived notions of what a language should contain and how it should operate. The marine biologist does not criticize the octopus for using jet-propulsion to get him through the water instead of the methods of self-respecting fish. Neither does the linguistic scientist express alarm or distress when he finds a language that seems to get along quite well without any words that correspond to what in English we call verbs.

A third principle on which linguistic science is based is that the analysis and description of a given language must conform to the requirements laid down for any satisfactory scientific theory. These are (1) simplicity, (2) consistency, (3) completeness, and (4) usefulness for predicting the behavior of phenomena not brought under immediate observation when the theory was formed. Linguistic scientists who have recently turned their attention to English have found that, judged by these criteria, the traditional grammar of English is unsatisfactory. It falls down badly on the first two requirements, being unduly complex and glaringly inconsistent within itself. It can be made to work, just as the Ptolemaic earth-centered astronomy can be, but at the cost of great elaboration and complication. The new grammar, like the Copernican sun-centered astronomy, solves the same problems with greater elegance, which is the scientist's word for the simplicity, compactness, and tidiness that characterize a satisfactory theory.

III

A brief look at the history of the traditional grammar of English will make apparent the reasons for its inadequacy. The study of English grammar is actually an outgrowth of the linguistic interest of the Renaissance. It was during the later Middle Ages and early Renaissance that the various vernacular languages of Europe came into their own. They began to be used for many kinds of writing which had previously always been done in Latin. As the vernaculars, in the hands of great writers like Dante and Chaucer, came of age as members of the linguistic family, a concomitant interest in their grammars arose. The earliest important English grammar was written by Shakespeare's contemporary, Ben Jonson.

It is important to observe that not only Ben Jonson himself but also those who followed him in the study of English grammar were men deeply learned in Latin and sometimes in Greek. For all their interest in English, they were conditioned from earliest school days to conceive of the classical languages as superior to the vernaculars. We still sometimes call the elementary school the "grammar school"; historically the term means the school where Latin grammar was taught. By the time the Renaissance or eighteenth-century scholar took his university degree, he was accustomed to use Latin as the normal means of communication with his fellow scholars. Dr. Samuel Johnson, for instance, who had only three years at the university and did not take a degree, wrote poetry in both Latin and Greek. Hence it was natural for these men to take Latin grammar as the norm, and to analyze English in terms of Latin. The grammarians of the seventeenth and eighteenth centuries who formulated the traditional grammar of English looked for the devices and distinctions of Latin grammar in English, and where they did not actually find them they imagined or created them. Of course, since English is a member of the Indo-European family of languages, to which Latin and Greek also belong, it did have many grammatical elements in common with them. But many of these had been obscured or wholly lost as a result of the extensive changes that had taken place in English—changes that the early grammarians inevitably conceived of as degeneration. They felt that it was their function to resist further change, if not to repair the damage already done. So preoccupied were they with the grammar of Latin as the ideal that they overlooked in large part the exceedingly complex and delicate system that English had substituted for the Indo-European grammar it had abandoned. Instead they stretched unhappy English on the Procrustean bed of Latin. It is no wonder that we commonly hear people say, "I didn't really understand grammar until I began to study Latin." This is eloquent testimony to the fact that the grammar "rules" of our present-day textbooks are largely an inheritance from the Latin-based grammar of the eighteenth century.

Meanwhile the extension of linguistic study beyond the Indo-European and Semitic families began to reveal that there are many different ways in which linguistic phenomena are organized—in other words, many different kinds of grammar. The tone-languages of the Orient and of North America, and the complex agglutinative languages of Africa, among others, forced grammarians to abandon the idea of a universal or ideal grammar and to direct their attention more closely to the individual systems employed by the multifarious languages of mankind. With the growth and refinement of the scientific method and its application to the field of anthropology, language came under more rigorous scientific scrutiny. As with anthropology in general, linguistic science at first concerned itself with the primitive. Finally, again following the lead of anthropology, linguistics began to apply its techniques to the old familiar tongues, among them English. Accelerated by the practical need during World War II of teaching languages, including English, to large numbers in a short time, research into the nature of English grammar has moved rapidly in the last fifteen years. The definitive grammar of English is yet to be written, but the results so far achieved are spectacular. It is now as unrealistic to teach "traditional" grammar of English as it is to teach "traditional" (i.e. pre-Darwinian) biology or "traditional" (i.e. four-element) chemistry. Yet nearly all certified teachers of English on all levels are doing so. Here is a cultural lag of major proportions.

IV

Before we can proceed to a sketch of what the new grammar of English looks like, we must take account of a few more of the premises of linguistic science. They must be understood and accepted by anyone who wishes to understand the new grammar.

First, the spoken language is primary, at least for the original study of a language. In many of the primitive languages,[1] of course, where writing is unknown, the spoken language is the *only* form. This is in many ways an advantage to the linguist, because the written language may use conventions that obscure its basic structure. The reason for the primary importance of the spoken language is that language originates as speech, and most of the changes and innovations that occur in the history of a given language begin in the spoken tongue.

Secondly, we must take account of the concept of dialect. I suppose most laymen would define a dialect as "a corrupt form of language spoken in a given region by people who don't know any better." This introduces moral judgments which are repulsive to the linguistic scholar. Let us approach the definition of a dialect from the more objective end, through the notion of a speech community. A speech community is merely a group of people who are in pretty constant intercommunication. There are various types of speech communities: local ones, like "the people who live in Tidewater Virginia"; class ones, like "the white-collar class"; occupational ones, like "doctors, nurses, and other people who work in hospitals"; social ones, like "clubwomen." In a sense, each of these has its own dialect. Each family may be said to have its own dialect; in fact, in so far as each of us has his own vocabulary and particular quirks of speech, each individual has his own dialect. Also, of course, in so far as he is a member of many speech communities, each individual is more or less master of many dialects and shifts easily and almost unconsciously from one to another as he shifts from one social environment to another.

In the light of this concept of dialects, a language can be defined as a group of dialects which have enough of their sound-system, vocabulary, and grammar (Grammar 1, that is) in common to permit their speakers to be mutually intelligible in the ordinary affairs of life. It usually happens that one of the many dialects that make up a language comes to have more prestige than the others; in modern times it has usually been the dialect of the middle-class residents of the capital, like Parisian French and London English, which is so distinguished. This comes to be thought of as the standard dialect; in fact, its speakers become snobbish and succeed in establishing the belief that it is not a dialect at all, but the only proper form of the language. This causes

---

[1] "Primitive languages" here is really an abbreviated statement for "languages used by peoples of relatively primitive culture"; it is not to be taken as implying anything simple or rudimentary about the languages themselves. Many languages included under the term, such as native languages of Africa and Mexico, exhibit grammatical complexities unknown to more "civilized" languages.

the speakers of other dialects to become self-conscious and ashamed of their speech, or else aggressive and jingoistic about it—either of which is an acknowledgment of their feelings of inferiority. Thus one of the duties of the educational system comes to be that of teaching the standard dialect to all so as to relieve them of feelings of inferiority, and thus relieve society of linguistic neurotics. This is where Grammar 3, linguistic etiquette, comes into the picture.

A third premise arising from the two just discussed is that the difference between the way educated people talk and the way they write is a dialectical difference. The spread between these two dialects may be very narrow, as in present-day America, or very wide, as in Norway, where people often speak local Norwegian dialects but write in the Dano-Norwegian *Riksmaal*. The extreme is the use by writers of an entirely different language, or at least an ancient and no longer spoken form of the language—like Sanskrit in northern India or Latin in western Europe during the later Middle Ages. A corollary of this premise is that anyone setting out to write a grammar must know and make clear whether he is dealing with the spoken or the written dialect. Virtually all current English grammars deal with the written language only; evidence for this is that their rules for the plurals of nouns, for instance, are really spelling rules, which say nothing about pronunciation.

This is not the place to go into any sort of detail about the methods of analysis the linguistic scientist uses. Suffice it to say that he begins by breaking up the flow of speech into minimum sound-units, or phones, which he then groups into families called phonemes, the minimum significant sound-units. Most languages have from twenty to sixty of these. American English has forty-one: nine vowels, twenty-four consonants, four degrees of stress, and four levels of pitch. These phonemes group themselves into minimum meaningful units, called morphemes. These fall into two groups: free morphemes, those that can enter freely into many combinations with other free morphemes to make phrases and sentences; and bound morphemes, which are always found tied in a close and often indissoluble relationship with other bound or free morphemes. An example of a free morpheme is "dog"; an example of a bound morpheme is "un-" or "ex-". The linguist usually avoids talking about "words" because the term is very inexact. Is "instead of," for instance, to be considered one, two, or three words? This is purely a matter of opinion; but it is a matter of fact that it is made up of three morphemes.

In any case, our analysis has now brought the linguist to the point where he has some notion of the word-stock (he would call it the "lexicon") of his language. He must then go into the question of how the morphemes are grouped into meaningful utterances, which is the field of grammar proper. At this point in the analysis of English, as of many other languages, it becomes apparent that there are three bases upon which classification and analysis may be built: form, function, and meaning. For illustration let us take the word "boys" in the utterance "the boys are here." From the point of view of form, "boys" is a noun with the plural ending "s" (pronounced like "z"), preceded by the noun-determiner "the," and tied by concord to the verb "are," which it precedes. From the point of view of function, "boys" is the subject of the verb "are" and of the sentence. From the point of view of meaning, "boys" points out or names more than one of the male young of the human species, about whom an assertion is being made.

Of these three bases of classification, the one most amenable to objective description and analysis of a rigorously scientific sort is form. In fact, many conclusions about form can be drawn by a person unable to understand or speak the language. Next comes function. But except as it is revealed by form, function is dependent on knowing the meaning. In a telegraphic sentence like "ship sails today"[2] no one can say whether "ship" is the subject of "sails" or an imperative verb with "sails" as its object until he knows what the sentence means. Most shaky of all bases for grammatical analysis is meaning. Attempts have been made to reduce the phenomena of meaning to objective description, but so far they have not succeeded very well. Meaning is such a subjective quality that it is usually omitted entirely from scientific description. The botanist can describe the forms of plants and the functions of their various parts, but he refuses to concern himself with their meaning. It is left to the poet to find symbolic meaning in roses, violets, and lilies.

At this point it is interesting to note that the traditional grammar of English bases some of its key concepts and definitions on this very subjective and shaky foundation of meaning. A recent English grammar defines a sentence as "a group of words which expresses a complete thought through the use of a verb, called its predicate, and a subject, consisting of a noun or pronoun about which the verb has something to say."[3] But what is a complete thought? Actually we do not identify sentences this way at all. If someone says, "I don't know what to do," dropping his voice at the end, and pauses, the hearer will know that it is quite safe for him to make a comment without running the risk of interrupting an unfinished sentence. But if the speaker says the same words and maintains a level pitch at the end, the polite listener will wait for him to finish his sentence. The words are the same, the meaning is the same; the only difference is a slight one in the pitch of the

[2] This example is taken from C. C. Fries, *The Structure of English* (New York, 1952), p. 62. This important book will be discussed below.
[3] Ralph B. Allen, *English Grammar* (New York, 1950), p. 187.

final syllable—a purely formal distinction, which signals that the first utterance is complete, a sentence, while the second is incomplete. In writing we would translate these signals into punctuation: a period or exclamation point at the end of the first, a comma or dash at the end of the second. It is the form of the utterance, not the completeness of the thought, that tells us whether it is a whole sentence or only part of one.

Another favorite definition of the traditional grammar, also based on meaning, is that of "noun" as "the name of a person, place, or thing"; or, as the grammar just quoted has it, "the name of anybody or anything, with or without life, and with or without substance or form."[4] Yet we identify nouns, not by asking if they name something, but by their positions in expressions and by the formal marks they carry. In the sentence, "The slithy toves did gyre and gimble in the wabe," any speaker of English knows that "toves" and "wabe" are nouns, though he cannot tell what they name, if indeed they name anything. How does he know? Actually because they have certain formal marks, like their position in relation to "the" as well as the whole arrangement of the sentence. We know from our practical knowledge of English grammar (Grammar 1), which we have had since before we went to school, that if we were to put meaningful words into this sentence, we would have to put nouns in place of "toves" and "wabe," giving something like "The slithy snakes did gyre and gimble in the wood." The pattern of the sentence simply will not allow us to say "The slithy arounds did gyre and gimble in the wooden."

One trouble with the traditional grammar, then, is that it relies heavily on the most subjective element in language, meaning. Another is that it shifts the ground of its classification and produces the elementary logical error of cross-division. A zoologist who divided animals into invertebrates, mammals, and beasts of burden would not get very far before running into trouble. Yet the traditional grammar is guilty of the same error when it defines three parts of speech on the basis of meaning (noun, verb, and interjection), four more on the basis of function (adjective, adverb, pronoun, conjunction), and one partly on function and partly on form (preposition). The result is that in such an expression as "a dog's life" there can be endless futile argument about whether "dog's" is a noun or an adjective. It is, of course, a noun from the point of view of form and an adjective from the point of view of function, and hence falls into both classes, just as a horse is both a mammal and a beast of burden. No wonder students are bewildered in their attempts to master the traditional grammar. Their natural clear-

4 Ibid., p. 1.

ness of mind tells them that it is a crazy patchwork violating the elementary principles of logical thought.

V

If the traditional grammar is so bad, what does the new grammar offer in its place?

It offers a description, analysis, and set of definitions and formulas —rules, if you will—based firmly and consistently on the easiest, or at least the most objective, aspect of language, form. Experts can quibble over whether "dog's" in "a dog's life" is a noun or an adjective, but anyone can see that it is spelled with "s" and hear that it ends with a "z" sound; likewise anyone can tell that it comes in the middle between "a" and "life." Furthermore he can tell that something important has happened if the expression is changed to "the dog's alive," "the live dogs," or "the dogs lived," even if he doesn't know what the words mean and has never heard of such functions as modifier, subject, or attributive genitive. He cannot, of course, get very far into his analysis without either a knowledge of the language or access to someone with such knowledge. He will also need a minimum technical vocabulary describing grammatical functions. Just so the anatomist is better off for knowing physiology. But the grammarian, like the anatomist, must beware of allowing his preconceived notions to lead him into the error of interpreting before he describes—an error which often results in his finding only what he is looking for.

When the grammarian looks at English objectively, he finds that it conveys its meanings by two broad devices: the denotations and connotations of words separately considered, which the linguist calls "lexical meaning," and the significance of word-forms, word-groups, and arrangements apart from the lexical meanings of the words, which the linguist calls "structural meaning." The first of these is the domain of the lexicographer and the semanticist, and hence is not our present concern. The second, the structural meaning, is the business of the structural linguist, or grammarian. The importance of this second kind of meaning must be emphasized because it is often overlooked. The man in the street tends to think of the meaning of a sentence as being the aggregate of the dictionary meanings of the words that make it up; hence the widespread fallacy of literal translation—the feeling that if you take a French sentence and a French-English dictionary and write down the English equivalent of each French word you will come out with an intelligible English sentence. How ludicrous the results can be, anyone knows who is familiar with Mark Twain's retranslation from the French of his jumping frog story. One sentence reads, "Eh bien! I no saw not that that frog has nothing of better than each frog." Upon which Mark's comment is, "if that isn't grammar gone to seed, then I count myself no judge."[5]

The second point brought out by a formal analysis of English is that it uses four principal devices of form to signal structural meanings:

1. Word order—the sequence in which words and word-groups are arranged.

2. Function-words—words devoid of lexical meaning which indicate relationships among the meaningful words with which they appear.

3. Inflections—alterations in the forms of words themselves to signal changes in meaning and relationship.

4. Formal contrasts—contrasts in the forms of words signaling greater differences in function and meaning. These could also be considered inflections, but it is more convenient for both the lexicographer and the grammarian to consider them separately.

Usually several of these are present in any utterance, but they can be separately illustrated by means of contrasting expressions involving minimum variation—the kind of controlled experiment used in the scientific laboratory.

To illustrate the structural meaning of word order, let us compare the two sentences "man bites dog" and "dog bites man." The words are identical in lexical meaning and in form; the only difference is in sequence. It is interesting to note that Latin expresses the difference between these two by changes in the form of the words, without necessarily altering the order: "homo canem mordet" or "hominem canis mordet." Latin grammar is worse than useless in understanding this point of English grammar.

Next, compare the sentences "the dog is the friend of man" and "any dog is a friend of that man." Here the words having lexical meaning are "dog," "is," "friend," and "man," which appear in the same form and the same order in both sentences. The formal differences between them are in the substitution of "any" and "a" for "the," and in the insertion of "that." These little words are function-words; they make quite a difference in the meanings of the two sentences, though it is virtually impossible to say what they mean in isolation.

Third, compare the sentences "the dog loves the man" and "the dogs loved the men." Here the words are the same, in the same order, with the same function-words in the same positions. But the forms of the three words having lexical meaning have been changed: "dog" to "dogs," "loves" to "loved," and "man" to "men." These changes are inflections. English has very few of them as compared with Greek,

---

[5] Mark Twain, "The Jumping Frog; the Original Story in English; the Retranslation Clawed Back from the French, into a Civilized Language Once More, by Patient and Unremunerated Toil," 1601 . . . and Sketches Old and New (n.p., 1933), p. 50.

Latin, Russian, or even German. But it still uses them; about one word in four in an ordinary English sentence is inflected.

Fourth, consider the difference between "the dog's friend arrived" and "the dog's friendly arrival." Here the difference lies in the change of "friend" to "friendly," a formal alteration signaling a change of function from subject to modifier, and the change of "arrived" to "arrival," signaling a change of function from predicate to head-word in a noun-modifier group. These changes are of the same formal nature as inflections, but because they produce words of different lexical meaning, classifiable as different parts of speech, it is better to call them formal contrasts than inflections. In other words, it is logically quite defensible to consider "love," "loves," "loving," and "loved" as the same word in differing aspects and to consider "friend," "friendly," "friendliness," "friendship," and "befriend" as different words related by formal and semantic similarities. But this is only a matter of convenience of analysis, which permits a more accurate description of English structure. In another language we might find that this kind of distinction is unnecessary but that some other distinction, unnecessary in English, is required. The categories of grammatical description are not sacrosanct; they are as much a part of man's organization of his observations as they are of the nature of things.

If we are considering the spoken variety of English, we must add a fifth device for indicating structural meaning—the various musical and rhythmic patterns which the linguist classifies under juncture, stress, and intonation. Consider the following pair of sentences:

Alfred, the alligator is sick!
Alfred the alligator is sick.

These are identical in the four respects discussed above—word order, function-words, inflections, and word-form. Yet they have markedly different meanings, as would be revealed by the intonation if they were spoken aloud. These differences in intonation are to a certain extent indicated in the written language by punctuation—that is, in fact, the primary function of punctuation.

VI

The examples so far given were chosen to illustrate in isolation the various kinds of structural devices in English grammar. Much more commonly the structural meaning of a given sentence is indicated by a combination of two or more of these devices: a sort of margin of safety which permits some of the devices to be missed or done away with without obscuring the structural meaning of the sentence, as indeed anyone knows who has ever written a telegram or a newspaper headline. On the other hand, sentences which do not have enough of these formal devices are inevitably ambiguous. Take the example already given, Fries's "ship sails today." This is ambiguous because there is nothing to indicate which of the first two words is performing a noun function and which a verb function. If we mark the noun by putting the noun-determining function-word "the" in front of it, the ambiguity disappears; we have either "the ship sails today" or "ship the sails today." The ambiguity could just as well be resolved by using other devices: consider "ship sailed today," "ship to sail today," "ship sail today," "shipping sails today," "shipment of sails today," and so on. It is simply a question of having enough formal devices in the sentence to indicate its structural meaning clearly.

How powerful the structural meanings of English are is illustrated by so-called "nonsense." In English, nonsense as a literary form often consists of utterances that have a clear structural meaning but use words that either have no lexical meaning, or whose lexical meanings are inconsistent one with another. This will become apparent if we subject a rather famous bit of English nonsense to formal grammatical analysis:

All mimsy were the borogoves
And the mome raths outgrabe.

This passage consists of ten words, five of them words that should have lexical meaning but don't, one standard verb, and four function-words. In so far as it is possible to indicate its abstract structure, it would be this:

All . . . . y were the . . . . .s
And the . . .   . . .s   . . . .

Although this is a relatively simple formal organization, it signals some rather complicated meanings. The first thing we observe is that the first line presents a conflict: word order seems to signal one thing, and inflections and function-words something else. Specifically, "mimsy" is in the position normally occupied by the subject, but we know that it is not the subject and that "borogoves" is. We know this because there is an inflectional tie between the form "were" and the "s" ending of "borogoves," because there is the noun-determiner "the" before it, and because the alternative candidate for the subject, "mimsy," lacks both of these. It is true that "mimsy" does have the function-word "all" before it, which may indicate a noun; but when it does, the noun is either plural (in which case "mimsy" would most likely end in "s"), or else the noun is what grammarians call a mass-word (like "sugar," "coal," "snow"), in which case the verb would have to be "was," not "were." All these formal considerations are sufficient to counteract the effect of word order and show that the sentence is of the type that may be represented thus:

All gloomy were the Democrats.

Actually there is one other possibility. If "mimsy" belongs to the small group of nouns which don't use "s" to make the plural, and if "borogoves" has been so implied (but not specifically mentioned) in the context as to justify its appearing with the determiner "the," the sentence would then belong to the following type:

[In the campaign for funds] all alumni were the canvassers.
[In the drought last summer] all cattle were the sufferers.

But the odds are so much against this that most of us would be prepared to fight for our belief that "borogoves" are things that can be named, and that at the time referred to they were in a complete state of "mimsyness."

Moving on to the second line, "And the mome raths outgrabe," the first thing we note is that the "And" signals another parallel assertion to follow. We are thus prepared to recognize from the noun-determiner "the," the plural inflection "s," and the particular positions of "mome" and "outgrabe," as well as the continuing influence of the "were" of the preceding line, that we are dealing with a sentence of this pattern:

And the lone rats agreed.

The influence of the "were" is particularly important here; it guides us in selecting among several interpretations of the sentence. Specifically, it requires us to identify "outgrabe" as a verb in the past tense, and thus a "strong" or "irregular" verb, since it lacks the characteristic past-tense ending "d" or "ed." We do this in spite of the fact that there is another strong candidate for the position of verb: that is, "raths," which bears a regular verb inflection and could be tied with "mome" as its subject in the normal noun-verb relationship. In such a case we should have to recognize "outgrabe" as either an adverb of the kind not marked by the form-contrast ending "ly," an adjective, or the past participle of a strong verb. The sentence would then belong to one of the following types:

And the moon shines above.
And the man stays aloof.
And the fool seems outdone.

But we reject all of these—probably they don't even occur to us—because they all have verbs in the present tense, whereas the "were" of the first line combines with the "And" at the beginning of the second to set the whole in the past.

We might recognize one further possibility for the structural meaning of this second line, particularly in the verse context, since we are used to certain patterns in verse that do not often appear in speech or prose. The "were" of the first line could be understood as doing double duty, its ghost or echo appearing between "raths" and "outgrabe." Then we would have something like this:

> All gloomy were the Democrats
> And the home folks outraged.

But again the odds are pretty heavy against this. I for one am so sure that "outgrabe" is the past tense of a strong verb that I can give its present. In my dialect, at least, it is "outgribe."

The reader may not realize it, but in the last four paragraphs I have been discussing grammar from a purely formal point of view. I have not once called a word a noun because it names something (that is, I have not once resorted to meaning), nor have I called any word an adjective because it modifies a noun (that is, resorted to function). Instead I have been working in the opposite direction, from form toward function and meaning. I have used only criteria which are objectively observable, and I have assumed only a working knowledge of certain structural patterns and devices known to all speakers of English over the age of six. I did use some technical terms like "noun," "verb," and "tense," but only to save time; I could have got along without them.

If one clears his mind of the inconsistencies of the traditional grammar (not so easy a process as it might be), he can proceed with a similarly rigorous formal analysis of a sufficient number of representative utterances in English and come out with a descriptive grammar. This is just what Professor Fries did in gathering and studying the material for the analysis he presents in the remarkable book to which I have already referred, *The Structure of English*. What he actually did was to put a tape recorder into action and record about fifty hours of telephone conversation among the good citizens of Ann Arbor, Michigan. When this material was transcribed, it constituted about a quarter of a million words of perfectly natural speech by educated middle-class Americans. The details of his conclusions cannot be presented here, but they are sufficiently different from the usual grammar to be revolutionary. For instance, he recognizes only four parts of speech among the words with lexical meaning, roughly corresponding to what the traditional grammar calls substantives, verbs, adjectives, and adverbs, though to avoid preconceived notions from the traditional grammar Fries calls them Class 1, Class 2, Class 3, and Class 4 words. To these he adds a relatively small group of function-words, 154 in his materials, which he divides into fifteen groups. These must be memorized by anyone learning the language; they are not subject to the same kind of general rules that govern the four parts of speech. Undoubtedly his conclusions will be developed and modified by himself and by other linguistic scholars, but for the present his book remains the most complete treatment extant of English grammar from the point of view of linguistic science.

VII

Two vital questions are raised by this revolution in grammar. The first is, "What is the value of this new system?" In the minds of many who ask it, the implication of this question is, "We have been getting along all these years with traditional grammar, so it can't be so very bad. Why should we go through the painful process of unlearning and relearning grammar just because linguistic scientists have concocted some new theories?"

The first answer to this question is the bravest and most honest. It is that the superseding of vague and sloppy thinking by clear and precise thinking is an exciting experience in and for itself. To acquire insight into the workings of a language, and to recognize the infinitely delicate system of relationship, balance, and interplay that constitutes its grammar, is to become closely acquainted with one of man's most miraculous creations, not unworthy to be set beside the equally beautiful organization of the physical universe. And to find that its most complex effects are produced by the multi-layered organization of relatively simple materials is to bring our thinking about language into accord with modern thought in other fields, which is more and more coming to emphasize the importance of organization—the fact that an organized whole is truly greater than the sum of all its parts.

There are other answers, more practical if less philosophically valid. It is too early to tell, but it seems probable that a realistic, scientific grammar should vastly facilitate the teaching of English, especially as a foreign language. Already results are showing here; it has been found that if intonation contours and other structural patterns are taught quite early, the student has a confidence that allows him to attempt to speak the language much sooner than he otherwise would.

The new grammar can also be of use in improving the native speaker's proficiency in handling the structural devices of his own language. In other words, Grammar 2, if it is accurate and consistent, can be of use in improving skill in Grammar 1. An illustration is that famous bugaboo, the dangling participle. Consider a specific instance of it, which once appeared on a college freshman's theme, to the mingled delight and despair of the instructor:

Having eaten our lunch, the steamboat departed.

What is the trouble with this sentence? Clearly there must be something wrong with it, because it makes people laugh, although it was not the intent of the writer to make them laugh. In other words, it produces a completely wrong response, resulting in total breakdown of communication. It is, in fact, "bad grammar" in a much more serious way than are mere dialectical divergences like "he ain't here" or "he never seen none," which produce social reactions but communicate effectively. In the light of the new grammar, the trouble with our dangling participle is that the form, instead of leading to the meaning, is in conflict with it. Into the position which, in this pattern, is reserved for the word naming the eater of the lunch, the writer has inserted the word "steamboat." The resulting tug-of-war between form and meaning is only momentary; meaning quickly wins out, simply because our common sense tells us that steamboats don't eat lunches. But if the pull of the lexical meaning is not given a good deal of help from common sense, the form will conquer the meaning, or the two will remain in ambiguous equilibrium—as, for instance, in "Having eaten our lunch, the passengers boarded the steamboat." Writers will find it easier to avoid such troubles if they know about the forms of English and are taught to use the form to convey the meaning, instead of setting up tensions between form and meaning. This, of course, is what English teachers are already trying to do. The new grammar should be a better weapon in their arsenal than the traditional grammar, since it is based on a clear understanding of the realities.

The second and more difficult question is, "How can the change from one grammar to the other be effected?" Here we face obstacles of a formidable nature. When we remember the controversies attending on revolutionary changes in biology and astronomy, we realize what a tenacious hold the race can maintain on anything it has once learned, and the resistance it can offer to new ideas. And remember that neither astronomy nor biology was taught in the elementary schools. They were, in fact, rather specialized subjects in advanced education. How then change grammar, which is taught to everybody, from the fifth grade up through college? The vested interest represented by thousands upon thousands of English and Speech teachers who have learned the traditional grammar and taught it for many years is a conservative force comparable to those which keep us still using the chaotic system of English spelling and the unwieldy measuring system of inches and feet, pounds and ounces, quarts, bushels, and acres. Moreover, this army is constantly receiving new recruits. It is possible in my state to become certified to teach English in high school if one has had eighteen credit hours of college English—let us say two semesters of freshman composition (almost all of which is taught by people unfamiliar with the new grammar), two semesters of a survey course in English literature, one semester of Shakespeare, and one semester of the contemporary novel. And since hard-pressed school administrators feel that anyone who can speak English can in a pinch teach it, the result is that many people are called upon to teach grammar whose knowledge of the subject is totally inadequate.

There is, in other words, a battle ahead of the new grammar. It will have to fight not only the apathy of the general public but the ignorance and inertia of those who count themselves competent in the field of grammar. The battle is already on, in fact. Those who try to get the concepts of the new grammar introduced into the curriculum are tagged as "liberal" grammarians—the implication being, I suppose, that one has a free choice between "liberal" and "conservative" grammar, and that the liberals are a bit dangerous, perhaps even a touch subversive. They are accused of undermining standards, of holding that "any way of saying something is just as good as any other," of not teaching the fundamentals of good English. I trust that the readers of this article will see how unfounded these charges are. But the smear campaign is on. So far as I know, neither religion nor patriotism has yet been brought into it. When they are, Professor Fries will have to say to Socrates, Galileo, Darwin, Freud, and the other members of the honorable fraternity of the misunderstood, "Move over, gentlemen, and make room for me."

FOR DISCUSSION AND REVIEW

1 According to Francis, what meanings may the word *grammar* have?

2 List five or six basic premises underlying the "new grammar."

3 What objections does the structuralist have to traditional grammar?

4 What devices does English use to signal structural meaning?

5 Of what value does Professor Francis find the new grammar? What obstacles did it face in 1954?

6 What do your reactions to Francis' statements suggest about your own attitudes toward language and "correctness"?

3
The Scholarly Dispute over the Meaning of Linguistics

Time Magazine

In the preceding article, Professor W. Nelson Francis argued that "obstacles of a formidable nature" faced the new grammar in its struggle for acceptance. It is true that, as the study of linguistics flourished during the 1950's and 1960's, the ideas of the structural linguists did gain widespread acceptance; for a few years they in large part dominated the teaching of linguistics in the United States. But in spite of the urgings of several enthusiastic supporters, the new grammar received at best only modified acceptance from the great majority of English teachers. The structuralists were soon challenged in their turn by the transformational linguists. A number of philosophical and methodological differences between the two groups exist. Some of the most important of these, discussed in this article from *Time*, deal with the acquisition and use of language.

FASHIONS IN academe may be a bit more durable than those of Paris couturiers, but, like hemlines, the popularity of disciplines rises and falls. Much in vogue at the moment, right up there with particle physics and computer technology, is the study of linguistics. Its new popularity, contends Princeton Linguist William Moulton, stems from a growing recognition that it is "the most scientific of the humanities and the most humanistic of the sciences."

In the U.S. today, at least 30 universities now offer a Ph.D. in linguistics, compared with only four just 20 years ago. Ten years ago, the offering of an undergraduate major in linguistics was a rarity; now it is an option at some 30 universities. The field is growing so fast that the nation's 4,000 or so fully qualified linguists (roughly one for each of the world's languages) cannot keep up with the research and teaching load

—and the shortage of scholars makes them highly mobile, gradually pushes up their salaries.

Basically, linguistics is the study of the underlying principles of language. The discipline concerns itself with dissecting the grammar and logic of the world's languages, tracing their shifting patterns and distribution, studying their impact on individuals, groups and institutions. Ultimately, it seeks to explain the ages-old mystery of precisely how and why man developed the unique facility of speech as an expression of thought, which, more than any other activity, separates him from animals.

In tackling his topic, today's linguistics scholar often must command one or more of such diverse fields of expertise as psychology, biology, mathematics, even electrical engineering or analytic philosophy. As it develops, the discipline has spawned such hybrids or specialties as computational linguistics, sociolinguistics, psycholinguistics, even biological linguistics. All of which has led to a far higher standing in academe than universities traditionally accorded their linguists, who until recently were normally employed as mere appendages to anthropology or foreign-language departments.

As an academic discipline, the study of linguistics can probably be traced back to 400 B.C., when the Indian scholar Panini worked out the first systematic description of Sanskrit. Its recent recognition, however, stems largely from the spirited intellectual battle now going on between two opposing schools: structural linguistics, led by Yale's Leonard Bloomfield in the 1930s and today defended most vigorously by Charles Hockett of Cornell, and the newer transformational linguistics, which was conceived and developed by Noam Chomsky of the Massachusetts Institute of Technology.

The argument between the schools is extremely complex; in essence it revolves around the fundamental question of how man learns and uses language. The long-dominant structuralists claim that language is a habit man acquires by imitating other men, and thus should be studied by analyzing sounds and how they are manipulated to create sentences. Generally, structural linguists tend to reject the idea that there is any "right" or "correct" grammar; its permissive principles influenced the word selection of Webster's *Third New International Dictionary*. By contrast, the school of transformationalists contends that language is an innate, instinctively acquired facility; the study of it should start with sentences, then try to discern the rules by which a sentence conveys its meaning.

Chomsky concedes that an individual must hear someone speak before he can speak meaningfully himself, but says that listening only triggers an intrinsic linguistic competence man already has. If this were not so, asks Chomsky, why is it that man can construct an infinite variety of sentences that he has never heard before, and always in grammatical patterns that are predictable? The transformational linguists thus theorize that a spoken sentence must be analyzed on two different levels—a "surface" level consisting of what one actually hears and an inner "deep" level, predictable but as yet unexplainable, that provides the basic meaning.

Esoteric as it may seem, the transformational argument threatens the validity of the behaviorist approach in social sciences, which rejects as meaningless anything that cannot be objectively measured and observed. For that reason, Structuralist Hockett argues that the followers of Chomsky have abandoned "scientific linguistics" in favor of "the speculations of a neo-medieval philosopher." Others in the field, however, compare Chomsky with Galileo and Freud in his impact on a scientific discipline.

Despite its all but impenetrable jargon, linguistics has practical applications that reach well beyond the university lecture hall. Linguists helped produce the mathematically based language that computers digest and transmit—and computers, in turn, have been a powerful tool in linguistic analysis. The U.S. Government used the knowledge of the linguists to develop highly effective language-teaching techniques in World War II, and even before Sputnik it made linguistic studies one of the main interests of the National Science Foundation. It is a charter concern for the new National Foundation on the Arts and the Humanities. Other uses are being explored by the Center for Applied Linguistics in Washington, financed mainly with federal funds. A whole "new English" grammar, based on transformational linguistics, is spreading through the nation's public schools, reaches nearly 20% of all students.

The Chomsky school, as it happens, is not much interested in whether linguistics is much of a help in teaching grammar. It is, says his M.I.T. colleague Jerry A. Fodor, "like teaching the driver of a car the theory of the internal-combustion engine before letting him drive." Chomsky's own goal is far grander than grammar: to refine a philosophy of language and to fathom the workings of the mind. But he is not arrogant about his task. "It may be beyond the limits of human intelligence," he sighs, "to understand how human intelligence works."

FOR DISCUSSION AND REVIEW

1 How does the *Time* article account for the "higher standing in academe" now offered linguists?

2 In the popular mind, a linguist is sometimes considered someone who knows a number of languages, a polyglot. Not so, according to *Time*.

What is the subject matter of linguistics?

3 How adequately does the phrase "innate vs. imitative" summarize the differences described here between the transformational linguists and the structuralists? Explain.

4
The Psycholinguists:
On the New Scientists of Language

George A. Miller

The interest of transformationalists in the human mind and their belief that "language is an innate, instinctively acquired facility," mentioned in the preceding article, point to some of the differences between them and the structuralists. Exploring these ideas more fully, Professor George A. Miller discusses the kinds of psycholinguistic processes underlying the production and comprehension of speech and argues that conditioning and imitation can not account for language acquisition, as some structuralists suppose. Central to this discussion is the ability of human beings to combine elements in completely novel ways and to be understood when they do so. Miller refers to this puzzling ability as "our combinatorial productivity." The puzzle is solved by realizing that we have learned, not lists of acceptable utterances, but rather rules that will generate grammatical sentences.

PSYCHOLOGISTS have long recognized that human minds feed on linguistic symbols. Linguists have always admitted that some kind of psycho-social motor must move the machinery of grammar and lexicon. Sooner or later they were certain to examine their intersection self-consciously. Perhaps it was also inevitable that the result would be called "psycholinguistics."

In fact, although the enterprise itself has slowly been gathering strength at least since the invention of the telephone, the name, in its unhyphenated form, is only about ten years old. Few seem pleased with the term, but the field has grown so rapidly and stirred so much interest in recent years that some way of referring to it is urgently needed.

Psycholinguistics is as descriptive a term as any, and shorter than most.

Among psychologists it was principally the behaviourists who wished to take a closer look at language. Behaviourists generally try to replace anything subjective by its most tangible, physical manifestation, so they have had a long tradition of confusing thought with speech—or with "verbal behaviour," as many prefer to call it. Among linguists it was principally those with an anthropological sideline who were most willing to collaborate, perhaps because as anthropologists they were sensitive to all those social and psychological processes that support our linguistic practices. By working together they managed to call attention to an important field of scientific research and to integrate it, or at least to acquaint its various parts with one another, under this new rubric.[1]

Interest in psycholinguistics, however, is not confined to psychologists and linguists. Many people have been stirred by splendid visions of its practical possibilities. One thinks of medical applications to the diagnosis and treatment of a heterogeneous variety of language disorders ranging from simple stammering to the overwhelming complexities of aphasia.[2] One thinks too of pedagogical applications, of potential improvements in our methods for teaching reading and writing, or for teaching second languages. If psycholinguistic principles were made sufficiently explicit, they could be imparted to those technological miracles of the twentieth century, the computing machines, which would bring into view a whole spectrum of cybernetic possibilities.[3] We could exploit our electrical channels for voice communications more efficiently. We might improve and automate our dictionaries, using them for mechanical translation from one language to another. Perhaps computers could print what we say, or even say what we print, thus making speech visible for the deaf and printing audible for the blind. We might, in short, learn to adapt computers to dozens of our human purposes if only they could interpret our languages. Little wonder that assorted physicians, educators, philosophers, logicians, and engineers have been intrigued by this new adventure.

Of course, the realisation of practical benefits must await the success of the scientific effort; there is some danger that enthusiasm may colour our estimate of what can be accomplished. Not a few sceptics remain

---

[1] A representative sample of research papers in this field can be found in *Psycholinguistics, a Book of Readings*, edited by S. Saporta (Holt, Rinehart & Winston, New York, 1962). R. Brown provides a readable survey from a psychologist's point of view in *Words and Things* (Free Press, Glencoe, Illinois, 1957).

[2] The CIBA Foundation Symposium, *Disorders of Language* (J. & A. Churchill, London, 1964) provides an excellent sample of the current status of medical psycholinguistics.

[3] *Natural Language and the Computer*, edited by P. L. Garvin (McGraw-Hill, New York, 1963).

unconvinced; some can even be found who argue that success is impossible in principle. "Science," they say, "can go only so far. . . ."

The integration of psycholinguistic studies has occurred so recently that there is still some confusion concerning its scope and purpose; efforts to clarify it necessarily have something of the character of personal opinion.[4] In my own version, the central task of this new science is to describe the psychological processes that go on when people use sentences. The real crux of the psycholinguistic problem does not appear until one tries to deal with sentences, for only then does the importance of productivity become completely obvious. It is true that productivity can also appear with individual words, but there it is not overwhelming. With sentences, productivity is literally unlimited.

Before considering this somewhat technical problem, however, it might be well to illustrate the variety of processes that psycholinguists hope to explain. This can best be done if we ask what a listener can do about a spoken utterance, and consider his alternatives in order from the superficial to the inscrutable.

The simplest thing one can do in the presence of a spoken utterance is to listen. Even if the language is incomprehensible, one can still *hear* an utterance as an auditory stimulus and respond to it in terms of some discriminative set: how loud, how fast, how long, from which direction, etc.

Given that an utterance is heard, the next level involves *matching* it as a phonemic pattern in terms of phonological skills acquired as a user of the language. The ability to match an input can be tested in psychological experiments by asking listeners to echo what they hear; a wide variety of experimental situations—experiments on the perception of speech and on the rote memorisation of verbal materials—can be summarised as tests of a person's ability to repeat the speech he hears under various conditions of audibility or delay.

If a listener can hear and match an utterance, the next question to ask is whether he will *accept* it as a sentence in terms of his knowledge of grammar. At this level we encounter processes difficult to study experimentally, and one is forced to rely most heavily on linguistic analyses of the structure of sentences. Some experiments are possible, however, for we can measure how much a listener's ability to accept the utterance as a sentence facilitates his ability to hear and match it; grammatical sentences are much easier to hear, utter or remember than are ungrammatical strings of words, and even nonsense (*pirot, karol, elat,*

---

[4] My own opinions have been strongly influenced by Noam Chomsky. A rather technical exposition of this work can be found in Chapters 11–13 of the second volume of the *Handbook of Mathematical Psychology*, edited by R. D. Luce, R. R. Bush, and E. Galanter (Wiley, New York, 1963), from which many of the ideas discussed here have been drawn.

etc.) is easier to deal with if it looks grammatical (*pirots karolise elati-cally*, etc.).[5] Needless to say, the grammatical knowledge we wish to study does not concern those explicit rules drilled into us by teachers of traditional grammar, but rather the implicit generative knowledge that we all must acquire in order to use a language appropriately.

Beyond grammatical acceptance comes semantic interpretation: we can ask how listeners *interpret* an utterance as meaningful in terms of their semantic system. Interpretation is not merely a matter of assigning meanings to individual words; we must also consider how these component meanings combine in grammatical sentences. Compare the sentences: *Healthy young babies sleep soundly* and *Colourless green ideas sleep furiously*. Although they are syntactically similar, the second is far harder to perceive and remember correctly—because it cannot be interpreted by the usual semantic rules for combining the senses of adjacent English words.[6] The interpretation of each word is affected by the company it keeps; a central problem is to systematise the interactions of words and phrases with their linguistic contexts. The lexicographer makes his major contribution at this point, but psychological studies of our ability to paraphrase an utterance also have their place.

At the next level it seems essential to make some distinction between interpreting an utterance and understanding it, for understanding frequently goes well beyond the linguistic context provided by the utterance itself. A husband greeted at the door by "I bought some electric light bulbs to-day" must do more than interpret its literal reference; he must understand that he should go to the kitchen and replace that burned-out lamp. Such contextual information lies well outside any grammar or lexicon. The listener can *understand* the function of an utterance in terms of contextual knowledge of the most diverse sort.

Finally, at a level now almost invisible through the clouds, a listener may *believe* that an utterance is valid in terms of its relevance to his own conduct. The child who says "I saw five lions in the garden" may be heard, matched, accepted, interpreted, and understood, but in few parts of the world will he be believed.

The boundaries between successive levels are not sharp and distinct. One shades off gradually into the next. Still the hierarchy is real enough and important to keep in mind. Simpler types of psycholinguistic processes can be studied rather intensively; already we know much about hearing and matching. Accepting and interpreting are just now coming

---

[5] W. Epstein, "The Influence of Syntactical Structure on Learning," *American Journal of Psychology* (1961), vol. 74, pp. 80–85.

[6] G. A. Miller and S. Isard, "Some Perceptual Consequences of Linguistic Rules," *Journal of Verbal Learning and Verbal Behaviour* (1963), vol. 2, pp. 217–228. J. J. Katz and J. A. Fodor have recently contributed a thoughtful discussion of "The Structure of Semantic Theory," *Language* (1963), vol. 39, pp. 170–210.

into scientific focus. Understanding is still over the horizon, and pragmatic questions involving belief systems are presently so vague as to be hardly worth asking. But the whole range of processes must be included in any adequate definition of psycholinguistics.

I phrased the description of these various psycholinguistic processes in terms of a listener; the question inevitably arises as to whether a different hierarchy is required to describe the speaker. One problem a psycholinguist faces is to decide whether speaking and listening are two separate abilities, co-ordinate but distinct, or whether they are merely different manifestations of a single linguistic faculty.

The mouth and ear are different organs; at the simplest levels we must distinguish hearing and matching from vocalising and speaking. At more complex levels it is less easy to decide whether the two abilities are distinct. At some point they must converge, if only to explain why it is so difficult to speak and listen simultaneously. The question is where.

It is easy to demonstrate how important to a speaker is the sound of his own voice. If his speech is delayed a fifth of a second, amplified, and fed back into his own ears, the voice-ear asynchrony can be devastating to the motor skills of articulate speech. It is more difficult, however, to demonstrate that the same linguistic competence required for speaking is also involved in processing the speech of others.

Recently Morris Halle and Kenneth Stevens of the Massachusetts Institute of Technology revived a suggestion made by Wilhelm von Humboldt over a century ago.[7] Suppose we accept the notion that a listener recognises what he hears by comparing it with some internal representation. To the extent that a match can be obtained, the input is accepted and interpreted. One trouble with this hypothesis, however, is that a listener must be ready to recognise any one of an enormous number of different sentences. It is inconceivable that a separate internal representation for each of them could be stored in his memory in advance. Halle and Stevens suggest that these internal representations must be generated as they are needed by following the same generative rules that are normally used in producing speech. In this way the rules of the language are incorporated into the theory only once, in a generative form; they need not be learned once by the ear and again by the tongue. This is a theory of a language-user, not of a speaker or a listener alone.

The listener begins with a guess about the input. On that basis he generates an internal matching signal. The first attempt will probably

[7] M. Halle and K. N. Stevens, "Speech Recognition: A Model and a Program for Research," IRE Transactions on Information Theory (1962), vol. IT-8, pp. 155–159.

be in error; if so, the mismatch is reported and used as a basis for a next guess, which should be closer. This cycle repeats (unconsciously, almost certainly) until a satisfactory (not necessarily a correct) match is obtained, at which point the next segment of speech is scanned and matched, etc. The output is not a transformed version of the input; it is the programme that was followed to generate the matching representation.

The perceptual categories available to such a system are defined by the generative rules at its disposal. It is also reasonably obvious that its efficiency is critically dependent on the quality of the initial guess. If this guess is close, an iterative process can converge rapidly; if not, the listener will be unable to keep pace with the rapid flow of conversational speech.

A listener's first guess probably derives in part from syntactic markers in the form of intonation, inflection, suffixes, etc., and in part from his general knowledge of the semantic and situational context. Syntactic cues indicate how the input is to be grouped and which words function together; semantic and contextual contributions are more difficult to characterise, but must somehow enable him to limit the range of possible words that he can expect to hear.

How he is able to do this is an utter mystery, but the fact that he can do it is easily demonstrated.

The English psychologist David Bruce recorded a set of ordinary sentences and played them in the presence of noise so intense that the voice was just audible, but not intelligible.[8] He told his listeners that these were sentences on some general topic—sports, say—and asked them to repeat what they heard. He then told them they would hear more sentences on a different topic, which they were also to repeat. This was done several times. Each time the listeners repeated sentences appropriate to the topic announced in advance. When at the end of the experiment Bruce told them they had heard the same recording every time—all he had changed was the topic they were given—most listeners were unable to believe it.

With an advance hypothesis about what the message will be we can tune our perceptual system to favour certain interpretations and reject others. This fact is no proof of a generative process in speech perception, but it does emphasise the important role of context. For most theories of speech perception the facilitation provided by context is merely a fortunate though rather complicated fact. For a generative theory it is essential.

Note that generative theories do not assume that a listener must be

[8] "Effects of Context upon the Intelligibility of Heard Speech," in *Information Theory*, edited by Colin Cherry (Butterworths, London, 1956, pp. 245–252).

able to articulate the sounds he recognises, but merely that he be able to generate some internal representation to match the input. In this respect a generative theory differs from a motor theory (such as that of Sir Richard Paget) which assumes that we can identify only those utterances we are capable of producing ourselves. There is some rather compelling evidence against a motor theory. The American psychologist Eric Lenneberg has described the case of an eight-year-old boy with congenital anarthria; despite his complete inability to speak, the boy acquired an excellent ability to understand language.[9] Moreover, it is a common observation that utterances can be understood by young children before they are able to produce them. A motor theory of speech-perception draws too close a parallel between our two capacities as users of language. Even so, the two are more closely integrated than most people realise.

I have already offered the opinion that productivity sets the central problem for the psycholinguist and have even referred to it indirectly by arguing that we can produce too many different sentences to store them all in memory. The issue can be postponed no longer.

To make the problem plain, consider an example on the level of individual words. For several days I carried in my pocket a small white card on which was typed UNDERSTANDER. On suitable occasions I would hand it to someone. "How do you pronounce this?" I asked.

He pronounced it.

"Is it an English word?"

He hesitated. "I haven't seen it used very much. I'm not sure."

"Do you know what it means?"

"I suppose it means 'one who understands.' "

I thanked him and changed the subject.

Of course, understander *is* an English word, but to find it you must look in a large dictionary where you will probably read that it is "now rare." Rare enough, I think, for none of my respondents to have seen it before. Nevertheless, they all answered in the same way. Nobody seemed surprised. Nobody wondered how he could understand and pronounce a word without knowing whether it was a word. Everybody put the main stress on the third syllable and constructed a meaning from the verb "to understand" and the agentive suffix "*er*." Familiar morphological rules of English were applied as a matter of course, even though the combination was completely novel.

Probably no one but a psycholinguist captured by the ingenuous behaviouristic theory that words are vocal responses conditioned to occur in the presence of appropriate stimuli would find anything exceptional

[9] "Understanding Language without Ability to Speak: A Case Report," *Journal of Abnormal and Social Psychology* (1962), vol. 63, pp. 419–425.

in this. Since none of my friends had seen the word before, and so could not have been "conditioned" to give the responses they did, how would this theory account for their "verbal behaviour"? Advocates of a conditioning theory of meaning—and there are several distinguished scientists among them—would probably explain linguistic productivity in terms of "conditioned generalisations."[10] They could argue that my respondents had been conditioned to the word understand and to the suffix—*er*; responses to their union could conceivably be counted as instances of stimulus generalisation. In this way, novel responses could occur without special training.

Although a surprising amount of psychological ingenuity has been invested in this kind of argument, it is difficult to estimate its value. No one has carried the theory through for all the related combinations that must be explained simultaneously. One can speculate, however, that there would have to be many different kinds of generalisation, each with a carefully defined range of applicability. For example, it would be necessary to explain why "understander" is acceptable, whereas "erunderstand" is not. Worked out in detail, such a theory would become a sort of Pavlovian paraphrase of a linguistic description. Of course, if one believes there is some essential difference between behaviour governed by conditioned habits and behaviour governed by rules, the paraphrase could never be more than a vast intellectual pun.

Original combinations of elements are the life blood of language. It is our ability to produce and comprehend such novelties that makes language so ubiquitously useful. As psychologists have become more seriously interested in the cognitive processes that language entails, they have been forced to recognise that the fundamental puzzle is not our ability to associate vocal noises with perceptual objects, but rather our combinatorial productivity—our ability to understand an unlimited diversity of utterances never heard before and to produce an equal variety of utterances similarly intelligible to other members of our speech community. Faced with this problem, concepts borrowed from conditioning theory seem not so much invalid as totally inadequate.

Some idea of the relative magnitudes of what we might call the productive as opposed to the reproductive components of any psycholinguistic theory is provided by statistical studies of language. A few numbers can reinforce the point. If you interrupt a speaker at some randomly chosen instant, there will be, on the average, about ten words that form grammatical and meaningful continuations. Often only one word is admissible and sometimes there are thousands, but on the aver-

---

[10] A dog conditioned to salivate at the sound of a tone will also salivate, though less copiously, at the sound of similar tones, the magnitude declining as the new tones become less similar to the original. This phenomenon is called "stimulus generalisation."

age it works out to about ten. (If you think this estimate too low, I will not object; larger estimates strengthen the argument.) A simple English sentence can easily run to a length of twenty words, so elementary arithmetic tells us that there must be at least 10^{20} such sentences that a person who knows English must know how to deal with. Compare this productive potential with the 10^4 or 10^5 individual words we know—the reproductive component of our theory—and the discrepancy is dramatically illustrated. Putting it differently, it would take 100,000,000,000 centuries (one thousand times the estimated age of the earth) to utter all the admissible twenty-word sentences of English. Thus, the probability that you might have heard any particular twenty-word sentence before is negligible. Unless it is a cliché, every sentence must come to you as a novel combination of morphemes. Yet you can interpret it at once if you know the English language.

With these facts in mind it is impossible to argue that we learn to understand sentences from teachers who have pronounced each one and explained what it meant. What we have learned are not particular strings of words, but *rules* for generating admissible strings of words.

Consider what it means to follow a rule; this consideration shifts the discussion of psycholinguistics into very difficult territory. The nature of rules has been a central concern of modern philosophy and perhaps no analysis has been more influential than Ludwig Wittgenstein's. Wittgenstein remarked that the most characteristic thing we can say about "rule-governed behaviour" is that the person who knows the rules knows whether he is proceeding correctly or incorrectly. Although he may not be able to formulate the rules explicitly, he knows what it is to make a mistake. If this remark is accepted, we must ask ourselves whether an animal that has been conditioned is privy to any such knowledge about the correctness of what he is doing. Perhaps such a degree of insight could be achieved by the great apes, but surely not by all the various species that can acquire conditioned reflexes. On this basis alone it would seem necessary to preserve a distinction between conditioning and learning rules.

As psychologists have learned to appreciate the complexities of language, the prospect of reducing it to the laws of behaviour so carefully studied in lower animals has grown increasingly remote. We have been forced more and more into a position that non-psychologists probably take for granted, namely, that language is rule-governed behaviour characterised by enormous flexibility and freedom of choice.

Obvious as this conclusion may seem, it has important implications for any scientific theory of language. If rules involve the concepts of right and wrong, they introduce a normative aspect that has always been avoided in the natural sciences. One hears repeatedly that the scientist's ability to suppress normative judgments about his subject-matter enables him to see the world objectively, as it really is. To admit that language follows rules seems to put it outside the range of phenomena accessible to scientific investigation.

At this point a psycholinguist who wishes to preserve his standing as a natural scientist faces an old but always difficult decision. Should he withdraw and leave the study of language to others? Or should he give up all pretence of being a "natural scientist," searching for causal explanations, and embrace a more phenomenological approach? Or should he push blindly ahead with his empirical methods, hoping to find a causal basis for normative practices, but running the risk that all his efforts will be wasted because rule-governed behaviour in principle lies beyond the scope of natural science?

To withdraw means to abandon hope of understanding scientifically all those human mental processes that involve language in any important degree. To persevere means to face the enormously difficult, if not actually impossible task of finding a place for normative rules in a descriptive science.

Difficult, yes. Still one wonders whether these alternatives are really as mutually exclusive as they seem.

The first thing we notice when we survey the languages of the world is how few we can understand and how diverse they all seem. Not until one looks for some time does an even more significant observation emerge concerning the pervasive similarities in the midst of all this diversity.

Every human group that anthropologists have studied has spoken a language. The language always has a lexicon and a grammar. The lexicon is not a haphazard collection of vocalisations, but is highly organised; it always has pronouns, means for dealing with time, space, and number, words to represent true and false, the basic concepts necessary for propositional logic. The grammar has distinguishable levels of structure, some phonological, some syntactic. The phonology always contains both vowels and consonants, and the phonemes can always be described in terms of distinctive features drawn from a limited set of possibilities. The syntax always specifies rules for grouping elements sequentially into phrases and sentences, rules governing normal intonation, rules for transforming some types of sentences into other types.

The nature and importance of these common properties, called "linguistic universals," are only beginning to emerge as our knowledge of the world's languages grows more systematic.[11] These universals appear even in languages that developed with a minimum of interaction. One is forced to assume, therefore, either that (a) no other kind of

11 *Universals of Language*, edited by J. Greenberg (M.I.T. Technology Press, Cambridge, Mass., 1963).

linguistic practices are conceivable, or that (*b*) something in the biological makeup of human beings favours languages having these similarities. Only a moment's reflection is needed to reject (*a*). When one
considers the variety of artificial languages developed in mathematics,
in the communication sciences, in the use of computers, in symbolic
logic, and elsewhere, it soon becomes apparent that the universal features of natural languages are not the only ones possible. Natural
languages are, in fact, rather special and often seem unnecessarily
complicated.

A popular belief regards human language as a more or less free creation of the human intellect, as if its elements were chosen arbitrarily
and could be combined into meaningful utterances by any rules that
strike our collective fancy. The assumption is implicit, for example, in
Wittgenstein's well-known conception of "the language game." This
metaphor, which casts valuable light on many aspects of language, can,
if followed blindly, lead one to think that all linguistic rules are just as
arbitrary as, say, the rules of chess or football. As Lenneberg has pointed
out, however, it makes a great deal of sense to inquire into the biological basis for language, but very little to ask about the biological foundations of card games.[12]

Man is the only animal to have a combinatorially productive language. In the jargon of biology, language is "a species-specific form of
behaviour." Other animals have signalling systems of various kinds and
for various purposes—but only man has evolved this particular and
highly improbable form of communication. Those who think of language as a free and spontaneous intellectual invention are also likely
to believe that any animal with a brain sufficiently large to support a
high level of intelligence can acquire a language. This asumption is
demonstrably false. The human brain is not just an ape brain enlarged;
its extra size is less important than its different structure. Moreover,
Lenneberg has pointed out that nanocephalic dwarfs, with brains half
the normal size but grown on the human blueprint, can use language
reasonably well, and even mongoloids, not intelligent enough to perform the simplest functions for themselves, can acquire the rudiments.[13]
Talking and understanding language do not depend on being intelligent
or having a large brain. They depend on "being human."

Serious attempts have been made to teach animals to speak. If
words were conditioned responses, animals as intelligent as chimpanzees

---

[12] E. Lenneberg, "Language, Evolution, and Purposive Behavior," in *Culture in History: Essays in Honor of Paul Radin* (Columbia University Press, New York, 1960).

[13] E. Lenneberg, I. A. Nichols, and E. R. Rosenberger, "Primitive Stages of Language Development in Mongolism," in the *Proceedings* of the 42nd. Annual Meeting (1962) of the *Association for Research in Nervous and Mental Diseases*.

or porpoises should be able to learn them. These attempts have uniformly failed in the past and, if the argument here is correct, they will always fail in the future—for just the same reason that attempts to teach fish to walk or dogs to fly would fail. Such efforts misconstrue the basis for our linguistic competence: they fly in the face of biological facts.[14]

Human language must be such that a child can acquire it. He acquires it, moreover, from parents who have no idea how to explain it to him. No careful schedule of rewards for correct or punishments for incorrect utterances is necessary. It is sufficient that the child be allowed to grow up naturally in an environment where language is used.

The child's achievement seems all the more remarkable when we recall the speed with which he accomplishes it and the limitations of his intelligence in other respects. It is difficult to avoid an impression that infants are little machines specially designed by nature to perform this particular learning task.

I believe this analogy with machines is worth pursuing. If we could imagine what a language-learning automaton would have to do, it would dramatise—and perhaps even clarify—what a child can do. The linguist and logician Noam Chomsky has argued that the description of such an automaton would comprise our hypothesis about the child's innate ability to learn languages or (to borrow a term from Ferdinand de Saussure) his innate *faculté de langage*.[15]

Consider what information a language-learning automaton would be

14 The belief that animals have, or could have, languages is as old as man's interest in the evolution of his special talent, but the truth of the matter has long been known. Listen, for example, to Max Müller (*Three Lectures on the Science of Language*) in 1889: "It is easy enough to show that animals communicate, but this is a fact which has never been doubted. Dogs who growl and bark leave no doubt in the minds of other dogs or cats, or even of man, of what they mean, but growling and barking are not language, nor do they even contain the elements of language."

Unfortunately, Müller's authority, great as it was, did not suffice, and in 1890 we hear Samuel Butler ("Thought and Language," in his *Collected Essays*) reply that although "growling and barking cannot be called very highly specialised language," still there is "a sayer, a sayee, and a covenanted symbol designedly applied. Our own speech is vertebrated and articulated by means of nouns, verbs, and the rules of grammar. A dog's speech is invertebrate, but I do not see how it is possible to deny that it possesses all the essential elements of language."

Müller and Butler did not argue about the facts of animal behaviour which Darwin had described. Their disagreement arose more directly from differences of opinion about the correct definition of the term "language." To-day our definitions of human language are more precise, so we can say with correspondingly more precision why Butler was wrong.

15 N. Chomsky, "Explanatory Models in Linguistics," in *Logic, Methodology, and Philosophy of Science*, edited by E. Wagel, P. Suppes, and A. Tarski (Stanford Univ. Press, Stanford, 1962, pp. 528–550).

given to work with. Inputs to the machine would include a finite set of sentences, a finite set of non-sentences accompanied by some signal that they were incorrect, some way to indicate that one item is a repetition or elaboration or transformation of another, and some access to a universe of perceptual objects and events associated with the sentences. Inside the machine there would be a computer so programmed as to extract from these inputs the nature of the language, *i.e.*, the particular syntactic rules by which sentences are generated, and the rules that associate with each syntactic structure a particular phonetic representation and semantic interpretation. The important question, of course, is what programme of instructions would have to be given to the computer.

We could instruct the computer to discover any imaginable set of rules that might, in some formal sense of the term, constitute a grammar. This approach—the natural one if we believe that human languages can be infinitely diverse and various—is doomed from the start. The computer would have to evaluate an infinitude of possible grammars; with only a finite corpus of evidence it would be impossible, even if sufficient time were available for computation, to arrive at any unique solution.

A language-learning automaton could not possibly discover a suitable grammar unless some strong *a priori* assumptions were built into it from the start. These assumptions would limit the alternatives that the automaton considered—limit them presumably to the range defined by linguistic universals. The automaton would test various grammars of the appropriate form to see if they would generate all of the sentences and none of the non-sentences. Certain aspects would be tested before others; those found acceptable would be preserved for further evaluation. If we wished the automaton to replicate a child's performance, the order in which these aspects would be evaluated could only be decided after careful analysis of the successive stages of language acquisition in human children.

The actual construction of such an automaton is, of course, far beyond our reach at the present time. That is not the point. The lesson to learn from such speculations is that the whole project would be impossible unless the automaton—and so, presumably, a child—knew in advance to look for particular kinds of regularities and correspondences, to discover rules of a rather special kind uniquely characteristic of human language in general.

The features that human infants are prepared to notice sharply limit the structure of any human language. Even if one imagines creating by decree a Newspeak in which this generalisation were false, within one generation it would have become true again.

Psycholinguistics does not deal with social practices determined arbitrarily either by caprice or intelligent design, but with practices that grow organically out of the biological nature of man and the linguistic capacities of human infants. To that extent, at least, it is possible to define an area of empirical fact well within the reach of our scientific methods.

Another line of scientific investigation is opened up by the observation that we do not always follow our own rules. If this were not so, of course, we would not speak of rules, but of the laws of language. The fact that we make mistakes, and that we can know we made mistakes, is central to the psycholinguistic problem. Before we can see the empirical issue this entails, however, we should first draw a crucial distinction between theories of language and theories of the users of language.

There is nothing in the linguistic description of a language to indicate what mistakes will occur. Mistakes result from the psychological limitations of people who use the language, not from the language itself. It would be meaningless to state rules for making mistakes.

A formal characterisation of a natural language in terms of a set of elements and rules for combining those elements must inevitably generate an infinitude of possible sentences that will never occur in actual use. Most of these sentences are too complicated for us. There is nothing mysterious about this. It is very similar to the situation in arithmetic where a student may understand perfectly the rules for multiplication, yet find that some multiplication problems are too difficult for him to do "in his head," i.e., without extending his memory capacity by the use of pencil and paper.

There is no longest grammatical sentence. There is no limit to the number of different grammatical sentences. Moreover, since the number of elements and rules is finite, there must be some rules and elements that can recur any number of times in a grammatical sentence. Chomsky has even managed to pinpoint a kind of recursive operation in language that, in principle, lies beyond the power of any finite device to perform indefinitely often. Compare these sentences:

(R) Remarkable is the rapidity of the motion of the wing of the hummingbird.
(L) The hummingbird's wing's motion's rapidity is remarkable.
(E) The rapidity that the motion that the wing that the hummingbird has has has is remarkable.

When you parse these sentences you find that the phrase structure of (R) dangles off to the right; each prepositional phrase hangs to the noun in the prepositional phrase preceding it. In (R), therefore, we see a type of recurring construction that has been called right-branching. Sentence (L), on the other hand, is left-branching; each possessive modifies the possessive immediately following. Finally, (E) is an onion;

it grows by embedding sentences within sentences. Inside "The rapidity is remarkable" we first insert "the motion is rapid" by a syntactic transformation that permits us to construct relative clauses, and so we obtain "The rapidity that the motion has is remarkable." Then we repeat the transformation, this time inserting "the wing has motion" to obtain "The rapidity that the motion that the wing has has is remarkable." Repeating the transformation once more gives (E).

It is intuitively obvious that, of these three types of recursive operations, self-embedding (E) is psychologically the most difficult. Although they seem grammatical by any reasonable standard of grammar, such sentences never occur in ordinary usage because they exceed our cognitive capacities. Chomsky's achievement was to prove rigorously that any language that does *not* restrict this kind of recursive embedding contains sentences that cannot be spoken or understood by devices, human or mechanical, with finite memories. Any device that uses these rules must remember each left portion until it can be related to its corresponding right portion; if the memory of the user is limited, but the number of admissible left portions is not, it is inevitable that some admissible sentences will exceed the capacity of the user to process them correctly.[16]

It is necessary, therefore, to distinguish between a description of the language in terms of the rules that a person *knows* and uses and a description of that person's *performance* as a user of the rules. The distinction is sometimes criticised as "psycholatry" by strict adherents of behaviourism; "knowing" is considered too mentalistic and subjective, therefore unscientific. The objection cannot be taken seriously. Our conception of the rules that a language-user knows is indeed a hypothetical construct, not something observed directly in his behaviour. But if such hypotheses were to be forbidden, science in general would become an empty pursuit.

Given a reasonable hypothesis about the rules that a language-user knows, the exploration of his limitations in following those rules is proper work for an experimental psychologist. "Psychology should assist us," a great linguist once said, "in understanding what is going on in the mind of speakers, and more particularly how they are led to deviate from previously existing rules in consequence of conflicting tendencies." Otto Jespersen made this request of psychology in 1924; now at last the work is beginning.[17]

One example. Stephen Isard and I asked Harvard undergraduates to memorise several sentences that differed in degree of self-embedding. For instance, the twenty-two words in the right-branching sentence,

---

[16] N. Chomsky, *Syntactic Structures* (Mouton, The Hague, 1957).
[17] *The Philosophy of Grammar* (Allen and Unwin, London, 1924, p. 344).

"We cheered the football squad that played the team that brought the mascot that chased the girls that were in the park," can be re-arranged to give one, two, three, or four self-embeddings; with four it becomes, "The girls (that the mascot (that the team (that the football squad (that we cheered) played) brought) chased) were in the park." One self-embedding caused no difficulty; it was almost as easy to memorise as the sentence with none. Three or four embeddings were most difficult. When the sentence had two self-embeddings—"The team (that the football squad (that we cheered) played) brought the mascot that chased the girls that were in the park"—some subjects found it as easy to memorise as sentences with zero or one embedding, others found it as difficult as sentences with three or four. That is to say, everybody can manage one embedding, some people can manage two, but everybody has trouble with three or more.

Records of eye movements while people are reading such sentences show that the trouble begins with the long string of verbs, "cheered played brought," at which point all grasp of the sentence structure crumbles and they are left with a random list of verbs. This is just what would be expected from a computer executing a programme that did not make provision for a sub-routine to refer to itself, *i.e.*, that was not recursive. If our ability to handle this type of self-embedded recursion is really as limited as the experiment indicates, it places a strong limitation on the kinds of theories we can propose to explain our human capacities for processing information.

On the simpler levels of our psycholinguistic hierarchy the pessimists are wrong; much remains there to be explored and systematised by scientific methods. How far these methods can carry us remains an open question. Although syntax seems well within our grasp and techniques for studying semantic systems are now beginning to emerge, understanding and belief raise problems well beyond the scope of linguistics. Perhaps it is there that scientific progress will be forced to halt.

No psychological process is more important or difficult to understand than understanding, and nowhere has scientific psychology proved more disappointing to those who have turned to it for help. The complaint is as old as scientific psychology itself. It was probably first seen clearly by Wilhelm Dilthey, who called for a new kind of psychology—a kind to which Karl Jaspers later gave the name "*verstehende Psychologie*"—and in one form or another the division has plagued psychologists ever since. Obviously a tremendous gulf separates the interpretation of a sentence from the understanding of a personality, a society, a historical epoch. But the gap is narrowing. Indeed, one can even pretend to see certain similarities between the generative theory of speech perception discussed above and the reconstructive intellectual processes that have been labelled *verstehende*. The analogy may some day prove helpful, but how optimistic one dares feel at the present time is not easily decided.

Meanwhile, the psycholinguists will undoubtedly continue to advance as far as they can. It should prove interesting to see how far that will be.

FOR DISCUSSION AND REVIEW

1   What does Miller mean by the statement, "With sentences, productivity is literally unlimited"?

2   Explain what is involved in Miller's hierarchy for a listener of "heard, matched, accepted, understood, believed."

3   Define *cybernetics, recursive,* and *phonological.* What importance does Miller attach to each of these terms?

4   Why does Miller conclude that "language is rule-governed behaviour"? In what sense is "rule" being used?

5   Give some examples of "linguistic universals." How does Miller explain their occurrence? What is the connection between them and the concept of infants as "little machines specially designed by nature" to acquire language?

6   Explain the importance of *right-branching, left-branching,* and *self-embedding sentences* to the theory of transformational grammar.

7   Compare Miller's assertion that "Man is the only animal to have a combinatorially productive language" with the conclusions drawn by Lewis (p. 62) and the Russells (p. 29).

what is IC — ol Immediate Constituent grammar (do Christensen usesthe term)?

5

Transformational Grammar:

An Introduction

Paul M. Postal

The "happy unanimity" of linguists in the 1950's, to borrow the late Paul Roberts' felicitous phrase, was shattered by the appearance in 1957 of Noam Chomsky's *Syntactic Structures*. This book started what Roberts called "the revolt of the transformationalists." Transformational generative grammar was a revolt partly because it asks very different questions about language than did earlier grammars; it is no wonder, therefore, that it arrives at different answers. Paul M. Postal states that the central problem for grammatical description is to account for the ability of people to create and understand novel utterances. An adequate description of a language, he says, must provide "a finite grammar which generates the infinite number of sentences in a language." As yet this goal has not been reached for any language; but *English Transformational Grammar*, in which this selection appeared as the "Epilogue," is a significant contribution.

I. Linguistic Novelty and the Problem of Grammar

GRAMMAR IS something that we are all apparently familiar with by the time we graduate from high school; indeed, a lot of time has been spent studying matters which are normally referred to as "grammar." The assumption behind this book [*English Transformational Grammar*] is not that you have somehow done a bad job or failed to learn what was taught in your study of English "grammar" from primary school to the present. Rather, this book is based on the fact that there is a real, very complex and little known field of study rightfully called "grammar" which is only very indirectly related to what you have studied in previous years. Let us briefly contrast this new field of study with that which is usually called "grammar."

The purpose of this book has been to provide the basis for an explanation of an almost miraculous and easily overlooked fact: Any speaker of a human language, like English, French, or Chinese, can produce and understand utterances which are completely *novel* to him. "Completely novel" means that, as whole, single sentences, these utterances have never been produced or heard by the person who makes use of them, and in most cases they have not been produced or heard by anyone else either. Although there are a large number of familiar expressions which are used again and again (such as "Hello!" "How are you?" or "What time is it?"), these expressions make up only a tiny portion of normal linguistic behavior. The vast majority of utterances used from day to day are completely novel.

As an illustration of this novelty, you will observe that the sentences that follow are completely new to you; that is, you have never seen exactly these sentences before. Perhaps the easiest way to convince yourself that normal use of language involves completely novel expressions is to try to find in a book or a newspaper some sentences which you can reasonably claim to have experienced before in their entirety. A search of this sort will reveal an interesting fact: Even in a long book it is unlikely that you can find a repetition of the same sentence.

In another sense, however, all of these sentences are somehow not totally novel; that is, they are composed of parts which are completely *familiar*. The subject of familiarity will be discussed later. First, let us explore some of the implications of novelty in the normal use of language.

Why is this element of novelty in linguistic behavior so important? The reason is this: Since people typically operate with novel expressions, it must be the case that what we learn when learning a language is something more than a list of sentences. Learning Chinese, for example, is not a matter of memorizing an enormous list of Chinese sentences. The number of sentences used in normal communication in any language is so large that it would be impossible to learn all of them directly. In English, for example, the number of possible sentences consisting of twenty words or less is estimated at 10^{30}. There are about 3×10^9 seconds in a century, so you can gauge how titanically large that number of sentences is.

But finally, it is clear that even this enormous number of expressions does not exhaust those that can *in principle* be used. In reality there is no end to the number of sentences in any human language. That is, as is usually said, the number of sentences is infinite. The reason for this is that there is *no longest sentence*. So for example there is no arbitrary termination for a series of the form:

(1) a. I saw Joe and Carl
     b. I saw Joe, Carl, and my mother's brother
     c. I saw Joe, Carl, my mother's brother, and the boy whom you don't like
     d. I saw Joe, Carl, my mother's brother, the boy whom you don't like, and a horse . . . .

That is, there is no maximum number of elements which can be conjoined to form an English sentence.

An objection may come to mind at this point. It could be pointed out that in fact, because of human limitations, we can only produce and understand a finite number of utterances; namely, those which are not too long or complex. For example, no one would be able to produce or understand a sentence which was so long that its production time was eleven and a half weeks. This perfectly true observation might then lead to the view that languages must be finite in scope even if enormously large. But this view ignores a fundamental distinction, namely, that between knowledge and behavior or, more exactly, between linguistic *competence* and linguistic *performance*. It is quite true that the performance of any finite organism, humans included, must necessarily be finite; that is, any performance is limited by various physical, neural, and temporal factors inherent in all biological creatures. This does not mean, however, that the knowledge or competence is finite. Rather, it is simply that performance limitations impose a constraint on our ability to use the infinite language we know.

A description of actual behavior must account for the finite and highly restricted character of that behavior. But this does not require the assumption that the underlying system of knowledge, or language, is finite. Quite the contrary: The finite character of performance is determined by a variety of other factors besides linguistic knowledge, that is, besides *language*. Memory limitations, for instance, severely constrain linguistic performance, for demands are made on memory in speaking and hearing. But it would be a mistake to assume that these memory limitations define the language. They only determine (in part) that portion of the language that can be used. The distinction between the language known and that portion of the language which is usable makes it possible to account for otherwise inexplicable facts. For example, it is well known that *written* performances may use longer sentences on the average than spoken performances. The reason is that with the written medium, the use of language makes fewer demands on memory, and more of the total number of sentences can be used. The following sentence is barely understandable when written, but when spoken it is beyond comprehensibility because of the excessive demands it makes on our perceptual apparatus:

(2) The rat which the cat which the dog chased ate was black.

The distinction between a language, which is an infinite system of sentences, and linguistic performance, which can use only a finite portion of those sentences, is quite analogous to the distinction between the knowledge and performance of simple mathematics. We have all learned the rules for multiplication. This system of knowledge guarantees that we can multiply any two whole numbers. But any single person, or even everyone together, can make and has made only a finite number of such computations. This does not mean that arithmetic deals only with a finite set of numbers. It is simply a consequence of memory and other grosser limitations, such as a finite life span. Quite analogously, the finite character of our linguistic performance does not mean that the language we know contains only a finite number of sentences. Since there is no longest sentence, the number of sentences is, in fact, infinite. It is not surprising, therefore, that the majority of sentences encountered or used from day to day are completely novel.

II. Infinite Knowledge in a Finite Organism

The fact that there are an infinite number of sentences in a language is crucial and very closely related to one of the most basic differences between the grammar you have studied in this book and "grammar" as the word is normally used. Consider these facts: Each human being is a finite organism that can learn and store within itself only a finite amount of information, even if a very large amount; still, it has been determined that each speaker of a language in some sense knows an infinite number of expressions. This appears to be a paradox or contradiction. It is neither, however, since there are kinds of finite systems which, in a clear sense, define and characterize, or, as we shall technically say, *generate*, infinite collections of objects. Rather than discuss this abstractly, let us consider an elementary example of such a system and examine how it works.

Consider an artificial "language" which is made up of strings consisting of just the two letters *a* and *b* and in which "sentences" are defined as those strings which contain a certain number of *a*'s followed by an equal number of *b*'s. In this language, (3)–(5) are well-formed sentences, but (6)–(8) are not:

(3) ab
(4) aabb
(5) aaaaabbbbb
(6) abb

(7) bbaa
(8) bbba

It is clear that this "language" will contain an infinite number of "sentences," since there is no limit to the number of *a*'s which may begin a well-formed expression. The problem, however, is to show how some finite system can represent the infinite number of sentences in the language.

Imagine a very simple machine which can carry out elementary instructions—a computing device of a very restricted kind. The machine is based on a finite system consisting of three symbols: *Sentence*, *a*, and *b*. The machine is subject to two kinds of instructions, General Instructions (GI) and Particular Instructions (PI). The Particular Instructions are:

(PI 1) Replace the symbol *Sentence* by the string of symbols *a b*.
(PI 2) Replace the symbol *Sentence* by the string of symbols *a Sentence b*.

The General Instructions are:

(GI a) The PI will be used to construct a sequence of symbols. Each string in the sequence will be formed by the application of one and only one of the PI to the preceding string.
(GI b) Each sequence will begin with the string consisting of the single symbol *Sentence*.
(GI c) The PI may be used in any order.
(GI d) Any PI may be used any number of times.
(GI e) A sequence of strings formed by the PI may be terminated after any number of uses of one of the PI providing only that the last string in the sequence is formed by the use of PI 1.

Each single operation (in accord with the GI) of the simple computer is called a *run*, and each sequence of strings produced by a run is called a *derivation*. A possible run would look like this:

(9) | Line | Symbol String on Line | Origin of String |
|---|---|---|
| 1 | *Sentence* | GI b |
| 2 | *a Sentence b* | PI 2 |
| 3 | *a a Sentence b b* | PI 2 |
| 4 | *a a a Sentence b b b* | PI 2 |
| 5 | *a a a a b b b b* | PI 1 |

In this run, the derivation consists of the sequence of strings *Sentence*, *a Sentence b*, *a a Sentence b b*, *a a a Sentence b b b*, and *a a a a b b b b*. This derivation is well formed in accordance with the Particular and the General Instructions, and a proper run through the system did, in fact, produce a well-formed sentence of the language which consists of the symbols *a* and *b* and in which a well-formed sentence is defined as a number of *a*'s followed by an equal number of *b*'s.

The number of well-formed sentences which the computer can generate is infinite, since, according to General Instruction d, any Particular Instruction can be used any number of times. Each use of PI 2 yields a derivation whose last line is one *a* and one *b* longer than the preceding line. If there is no occurrence of PI 2 in the run, the derivation will consist of only two lines: *Sentence* (per GI b) and *a b* (per PI 1 and GI e). If there is one occurrence of PI 2, a sentence consisting of four symbols (*a a b b*) will result; if, as in the sample run above, there are three occurrences of PI 2, eight symbols will result. Any proper run— that is, any run which is in accord with the General and the Particular Instructions—will by necessity produce a derivation the last line of which will be a string of a certain number of *a*'s followed by an equal number of *b*'s. In other words, the computer can not only produce an infinite number of sentences in the *a b* "language," but also, when operating properly, it will produce *only* well-formed sentences in that language.

Obviously the system containing five General Instructions and two Particular Instructions is a finite system; it can be represented in some physical apparatus (such as a computer) or can be learned by a human being. But a physical apparatus which contains this finite system is capable of operating with the infinite number of "sentences" which it describes, subject to finite performance limitations such as memory. Similarly, a human being who "knows" this finite system is capable of using the infinite number of sentences described by the system, subject to such finite limitations as life span and memory.

There is consequently no paradox at all involved in the idea of learning a finite system which describes an infinite set of elements. Human languages are infinite sets, and human beings are finite physical objects with finite storage and learning capacities. It follows that we must assume that a human language is, in another and more interesting sense, some finite system which can describe the infinite set of sentences of that language in a way analogous to that in which our simple system describes the infinite "language" of strings "$a^n b^n$" (an indefinite number of *a*'s followed by the same number of *b*'s). We need a term for finite systems which describe infinite sets, and with respect to sets of sentences in human languages, the term *grammar* has come into use.

By the *grammar of English*, therefore, is meant that finite system which generates the infinite number of possible English sentences. Each of us must have such a grammar represented in us. It is the possession of this grammar which makes it possible for us to produce and understand an infinite number of sentences, the vast majority of which are completely *novel* to us. For although a particular sentence is novel to us in the sense that we have not uttered or heard it before, it is *familiar* in the sense that it is fully described by a system which we have learned and which is consequently part of us.

III. Knowledge and Behavior

When discussing almost any aspect of human affairs, we must consider two separate, though intimately related, domains: the domain of knowledge, competence and ability, on the one hand; and, on the other, the domain of behavior, performance and action. The latter consists of observable activities and affairs which we can see and hear; the former, however, is not nearly so accessible. The distinction between these two domains can be clarified by reference to music; it is quite normal to distinguish between a certain piece of music and various performances of that music.

In linguistic affairs, although the same distinction is crucial, it is seldom made. In the discussion of the infinite character of human languages, we distinguished between knowledge-competence, on the one hand, and behavior-performance, on the other. It cannot be too strongly emphasized that grammar is a description of part of what people *know*, not of what they *do*.

The discussion can be further clarified by considering the distinction between such notions as *sentence, language, grammar* and the notions *utterance, linguistic behavior*. *Sentence* is a notion which belongs to the world of abstract elements, analogous to *concerto* in music. *Utterance* is a term relating to the world of behavior or performance. Though it may at first seem a bit odd, it can be said that utterances are *performances of sentences*. Clearly, the abstract structure of the sentence is the primary determinant of the performance. But many other factors enter into any particular performance. Thus the actual behavioral event is controlled by such factors as the physical structure of the particular speech apparatus involved, by the presence of food in the mouth, by the presence of noise in the environment, or by the emotional state of the speaker. But all of these factors are irrelevant linguistically; that is, they are all irrelevant to the study of linguistic *knowledge*.

Grammar, now in a second sense as the name for a field of study, is concerned with linguistic knowledge—that is, with the primary but by no means only factor which must be taken into account in the study of linguistic performance.

Sentences and grammar, therefore, are abstract objects. Many different kinds of abstract objects are familiar in daily life: numbers, laws, symphonies, driving regulations, jokes. All of these objects have the negative property of not being physically located in time and space. That is, one cannot sensibly ask "Where is the law against embezzlement?" or "Where is Mozart's 40th Symphony?" or "Where is English?" But all of these abstract objects can be represented in physical objects or can be performed in space and time; and one can sensibly ask where the representations or performances can be found or where they took place. There is another class of words in English which refers, sometimes ambiguously, both to the abstract object and to the physical object in or by which the abstract object is represented. The words "book," "magazine," "newspaper," "manuscript," and "diary" are examples of this class. When we say, "Where is my book?" or "That book is ripped," we are speaking of "book" as a physical object located in space and time. But when we say "That book is poorly written," or "The book *Gone With The Wind* was a best-seller," we are speaking of "book" as an abstract object not located in space and time.

Languages are abstract objects, but from the point of view of ordinary acquaintance with such things, languages are unusual abstract objects in a sense already considered. That is, languages are *infinite*, while most of the abstract objects encountered in daily life, outside of the study of mathematics, tend to be *finite*.

Sentence, therefore, is the concept which refers to the individual elements of which languages contain an infinite number. *Grammar* is the concept which refers to the finite systems which specify and generate these infinite numbers of sentences. Since languages are infinite abstract objects, they can be viewed in two different, but equivalent, ways. It can be said, for instance, that the English language is simply the infinite collection of English sentences, or it can be said that the English language is exactly that finite system which generates this infinite collection of sentences.

Although both sentences and grammars are abstract objects, it must be emphasized that grammar is a much more abstract notion. We can gather information rather directly about sentences by considering performances of them and by specifying our intuitive knowledge of the properties of some of the sentences of a language we know. The character of grammars is much more obscure and difficult to determine. This fact is related to a connotation which our use of the term "linguistic knowledge" may have, a connotation which is quite undesirable. When thinking about knowledge, we may accept only something which is or can be explicit. If I know how to multiply, I can tell you how to multiply. In this sense, then, knowing English grammar would mean being able to describe it explicitly. It is evident that this is not the case. We cannot readily make explicit our knowledge of the principles of grammar. This knowledge is evidently below the level of direct awareness or access. If this were not so, one could simply write down all of the grammar of any language one knew and grammatical investigation would be easy and trivial, instead of being the difficult pursuit it is.

One might say, therefore, that linguistic knowledge is typically largely unconscious, although this term is not very clear. In fact, however, inexplicit knowledge is quite familiar and common. For example, a familiar case of unconscious knowledge, although we normally don't call it this, is that our bodies know how to digest food and must contain within them a representation of the complex biochemical operations required for this. Such an organic representation, which is analogous in many ways to the program of an electronic computer or the built-in instructions of any of the many automatic machines which exist in factories, is obviously *not* present in such physical systems as adding machines, telephone exchanges, or anti-missile computers. These, however, have represented in them various forms of knowledge not necessarily present in humans. But, unaided, one cannot make explicit these digestion principles any more than a computer can describe its program. If a biologically uneducated person is asked how digestion takes place, he can say almost nothing about it. Or again, the human eye perceives physical objects according to quite definite principles, different in part from those of many other animals. Yet again, unaided by inquiry, a person cannot directly make these principles explicit. Therefore, there is nothing unique about finding an organism or complex mechanism with implicit knowledge which is not subject to direct awareness and not capable of being made explicit directly.

In the case of language, we are from one point of view better off than in these other cases. While we do not possess direct, explicit knowledge of the underlying system of grammar as such, we do have some knowledge of sentences, either explicit, or easily made explicit with a little effort. Therefore, inquiry into the nature of grammars reasonably begins with sentences. We determine what some of the properties of these are. Only then can questions be raised about the kinds of finite systems which can describe the appropriate infinite set of sentences. Fortunately, many years of inquiry by a vast number of scholars and our basic intuitive knowledge provide us with a good deal of information about sentences.

IV. The Properties of Sentences

Human sentences, as abstract objects, are made up of certain quite distinct properties. Consider the following examples:

(10) Harry owns that house
(11) That house belongs to Harry
(12) Harry saw that house.

First of all, each of these sentences involves properties concerning knowledge of pronunciation. That is, one knows what sequence of movements must be made by the speech apparatus in order to produce utterances which will be understood as performances of the sentences. An account of this knowledge can be called a *phonetic representation*. The phonetic representation of a sentence is a sequence of *phonetic segments*, each of which is a complex of instructions for the different parts of the speech apparatus. A single phonetic segment determines the ideal behavior of the speech apparatus for a fixed period of time, roughly that needed for the production of a single "sound." Obviously (10), (11), and (12) have different, though partially similar, phonetic representations associated with them.

Secondly, each of the sentences involves properties concerning the knowledge of meaning. For instance, (10) and (11) have essentially the same meaning, which is quite different from the meaning of (12). The representation of the meaning of a sentence is called a *semantic representation*. A primary fact is that sentences consist of pairings or associations of information about meaning with information about pronunciation. We know that (10) and (11) have identical meanings paired with partially different pronunciations. But in the case of (13) and (14), below, we know that identical pronunciations are paired with different meanings:

(13) What annoyed Harry was being investigated by the committee
(14) What annoyed Harry was being investigated by the committee.

This utterance can mean either "Harry was annoyed that the committee was investigating him" or "The committee was investigating the thing that annoyed Harry."

Comparing the properties which semantic representations account for with the properties which phonetic representations account for, one observes an important contrast. Phonetic representations are relatively well understood with respect to their formal structure, the substantive constraints on them, and especially their relations to the world of observable behavior and objects. That is, phonetic representations are a system of instructions governing the movements of a physical system—the speech apparatus—and as such they are relatively easily understood. Semantic representations, on the other hand, are largely mysterious. Their relation to the observable world of objects and events is most unclear. Certain facts can, however, be ascertained. Since we know the meanings of an infinite number of expressions, which could not have been learned by rote, there must be some finite way of representing these meanings. Furthermore, meanings are analyzable into components. For example, among the words below, (15) through (17) share a semantic property which is not possessed by (18) and (19); similarly, (18) and (19) share a property not possessed by (15) through (17):

(15) boy
(16) rooster
(17) uncle
(18) woman
(19) daughter

What seems to emerge is a system of semantic primitives which represent components of meaning and which combine in various ways to form the semantic representations of sentences and their parts. Although knowledge about facts like those observed in (15) through (19) makes the study of semantic questions possible, inquiry into such matters is admittedly in its very beginning, and knowledge of these matters is very limited at present.

Finally, each sentence involves certain syntactic properties which are distinct from the meaning and the pronunciation of the sentence. That is, sentences are strings of words; these are made up of various elements; these elements are of different types, and there are various relations among them. A speaker of English knows that the expression in (20) is ambiguous:

(20) O'Hanrahan enjoys entertaining ladies.

That is, (20) has one analysis in which the relation between "entertain" and "ladies" is the same as it is in (21), and another in which it is the same as in (22), and yet a third in which it is the same as in (23):

(21) I am entertaining ladies
(22) The extremely entertaining ladies were unmarried
(23) Ladies who entertain should never be profane.

Similarly, we know that in (24) and (25) there exists an identical relation between "someone" and "who owns a Mercedes Benz." There is no such relation between these forms in (26):

(24) Someone drove away who owns a Mercedes Benz
(25) Someone who owns a Mercedes Benz drove away
(26) Someone drove away the boy who owns a Mercedes Benz.

We recognize that in structures like (27), the adjective "nice" "modifies" either "boys" alone or both "boys" and "girls," while in (28) it "modifies" only "boy":

(27) Carol met some nice boys and girls
(28) Carol met a nice boy and a girl.

We also recognize that the ambiguity of modification in (27) is related to two different possible pronunciations of the sentence: one in which there is a pause after "nice," and one in which there is a pause after "boys."

Also, our syntactic knowledge is manifested in the recognition that some strings are well formed while others are not, and to varying degrees. As speakers of English we know that (29) through (31) are natural or well-formed English sentences:

(29) Harry understands Cromwell

(30) Harry understands himself
(31) Cromwell was understood by Harry.

But neither (32) nor (33) is completely well formed:

(32) *Harry was understood by himself
(33) *himself was understood by Harry.

Notice that the deviation in (32) and (33) must be syntactic, since semantically they are perfectly all right and not even ambiguous. Furthermore, although both (32) and (33) violate some principles of English sentence formation, (33) is less grammatically correct or less well formed than (32).

In summary, we conclude that what we refer to as a sentence is actually a complex association of at least three kinds of properties: phonetic, semantic, and syntactic.

It is easy to see why sentences should have semantic and phonetic properties. Semantic properties represent the "message" or the "ideas" transmitted. They are, as it were, the very reason why languages exist. Similarly, it is understandable why phonetic properties exist, since they are concerned with correctly characterizing the modification of the physical medium needed to transmit a "message" or "idea." But the function of syntactic properties is much less clear. Unlike the semantic and phonetic properties, the syntactic properties seem to have no connection with the non-linguistic world of events and objects. This raises the general question of the relationship among the three kinds of properties.

V. The Overall Grammar

Suppose, for the moment, that one assumes *incorrectly* that the set of sentences in a language is not only finite but small enough to be learned directly. The description of such a language could consist simply of a large list of associations between semantic and phonetic representations. In other words, it could consist of a kind of sentence dictionary or *sentence lexicon.* Such a language would not have a grammar in the sense of our earlier discussion, and there would be no need for syntactic properties, since the lexicon would directly connect all semantic and phonetic information.

It has been observed, however, that human languages are not like this because they include an infinite number of semantic-phonetic associations which, by definition, cannot be listed in a lexicon. Real languages must, therefore, contain some apparatus other than a finite list of semantic-phonetic associations. That is, they must contain grammatical systems capable of generating an infinite number of structures—an apparatus analogous to the instructions of the simple illustrative "grammar" discussed in relation to the "language" consisting of *a*'s and *b*'s. This grammar is the chief basis for the existence of syntactic structure. Or, to put it more clearly, sentences have syntactic structure in addition to phonological and semantic characteristics, because they are not finite sets which are directly learnable, but infinite sets learnable only indirectly through internalization of some finite grammar which generates them.

Syntactic structure is basically a by-product or derivational process of a productive grammar which generates sentences rather than lists them. The existence of syntactic structure is closely linked to the fact that linguistic behavior typically involves operations with expressions which are *as wholes* novel. This is made possible only by the existence of productive grammars which associate syntactic organization with the sentences which they specify.

Once again we must distinguish between the two kinds of novelty— the novelty of utterances as wholes as opposed to that of utterances which are formed from parts which are not novel. This distinction should be clarified and related to the notion of lexicon. Although it is impossible for the description of a language to consist exclusively of an exhaustive list of phonetic-semantic associations, it is possible and, in fact, it is true that languages do contain such collections of associations. These collections link semantic and phonetic information, not for whole sentences but for certain parts of sentences. Every language has a finite lexicon containing a large number of associations of information about meaning and pronunciation and, to a lesser degree, about some syntactic properties. The dictionaries of our ordinary experience, the large books found on our shelves, can be regarded as rather gross attempts to state such associations. A lexicon will simply list all those arbitrary and unpredictable associations of facts of meaning with facts of pronunciation.

One obvious sense in which ordinary linguistic behavior does not involve novelty (or involves it only to a minor extent) is that this behavior is based on a previously known vocabulary of lexical items, each with inherent semantic and phonetic properties. This raises the question of the relation between semantic and syntactic properties.

A speaker of a language must learn a finite lexicon of semantic-phonetic associations directly. However, this speaker knows not this finite number of associations but rather an infinite number. The overall grammar must therefore provide some finite way for the possessor of a lexicon to *project* this finite knowledge of pronunciation to the infinite knowledge of the pronunciation of all sentences.

A natural framework to account for this linguistic projection, which is really the defining character of human language, would be the following. Assume that a grammar has three components, a *Syntax*, a *Se-*

mantics, and a *Phonology.* The Syntax contains a finite set of rules of some sort plus a finite lexicon. It generates an infinite set of *Syntactic Structures,* each of which contains individual lexical items (with their inherent semantic and phonological properties) as parts. The Syntax thus embodies the "creative power" of the grammar, that property which permits a finite system to generate an endless set.

However, the Syntax alone does not in principle account for our full knowledge of sentences. With respect to meaning, for example, the Syntax says nothing about the meaning of anything beyond the individual lexical items. It does not account for the semantic properties of whole sentences or of any of their parts "larger" than lexical items (such parts are technically called *constituents*). Observe, in particular, that there may be different syntactic structures containing identical lexical items which nonetheless have overall quite different meanings.

(34)   Harry loves Lucille
(35)   Lucille loves Harry.

The function of the semantic part of the grammar now becomes partially clear. It must operate on each of the syntactic structures specified by the Syntax and, on the basis of the *inherent semantic properties* of their lexical items, plus the *syntactic organization of these,* assign a semantic interpretation to the sentence as a whole as well as to each of its constituents. The function of the phonological part is now also clear. It must analogously operate on each of the syntactic structures specified by the Syntax and, on the basis of the *inherent phonological properties* of their lexical items plus the *syntactic organization of these,* assign a phonetic interpretation to the sentence as a whole and to each of its constituents.

It might seem that the Phonology is really unnecessary, since the pronunciation of each sentence might be fully determined by the sequence of pronunciations of each of its successive lexical items. But in fact the pronunciation of sentences in real languages is never determined exclusively in this elementary way. Many lexical items are pronounced one way in one context, another in another (compare *pirate/piracy; oblige/obligation*). Many aspects of pronunciation (for example, English stress and intonation) are not directly associable with any particular lexical items. There is thus a rich function for the Phonology to fulfill.

It has been emphasized repeatedly that the grammar of a human language is not just a device which *directly* associates meanings and pronunciations. But from this brief description of the form of grammar, it is clear that grammar is, in the sense of this discussion, a device which *indirectly* associates semantic and phonetic representations—indirectly because the process is mediated through the infinite number of syntactic structures. Each structure generated by the Syntax is semantically interpreted by the Semantics and phonetically interpreted by the Phonology. In this way the overall grammar does associate phonetic and semantic representations, but it does this *productively* through the mediation of the Syntax and not simply in a list. For the moment, a grammar can be represented schematically in the following manner:

(36)

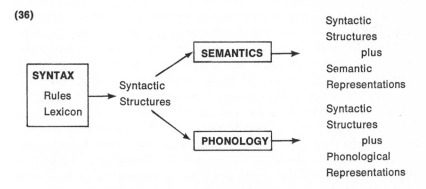

We shall presently see that even this apparently complex scheme of grammar is oversimplified in at least one crucial respect.

It can be seen from this discussion that the roles of the three components in a grammar are not equal. The Syntax is definitely primary; the Semantics and Phonology are both subsidiary. The Syntax is a system with no real *input*; it "creates" or generates an infinite number of structures. The other two components are *input-output* devices; they operate on the structures specified by the Syntax and assign further structure to them. In contrast to the creative character of the Syntax, the Semantics and Phonology are only interpretive. The Syntax is fundamental in that both of the other components operate on information provided by the Syntax. It is therefore no accident that the present book has dealt with syntactic questions, since an understanding of these is basic to any inquiry into the interpretive parts of language.

Suppose we say that that aspect of syntactic structure operated on by the Semantics for the purpose of semantic interpretation will be called *Deep Structure*. And let that aspect of syntactic structure operated on by the Phonology for the purpose of phonetic interpretation be called *Surface Structure*. Notice that thus far nothing substantive has been said since it is logically possible that the terminology is empty. That is, it is possible that the structures relevant for both types of interpretation are *identical*, a tacit assumption embodied in the diagram. This is, in effect, the assumption of almost all traditional linguistic discussion. But perhaps the fundamental revelation of the present approach to grammar, which is now referred to as *transformational*, is that this assumption is false, in fact drastically so. The structures relevant for semantic interpretation turn out to be very different indeed from those which are relevant for phonetic interpretation. Only the latter, or Surface Structures, are really similar to what we normally think of as the syntactic structures of sentences. The distinction between Deep and Surface Structures has been dealt with at length in the body of this book.

The fact that syntactic structure is bifurcated into two distinct aspects, Deep and Surface, requires modification of the diagram. One must now think of the Syntax as having two parts. One, the Base, consists of rules and a lexicon, which together generate the infinite set of Deep Structures. These are the inputs to the Semantic Component of the grammar. There is then a second or *Transformational* part of the Syntax, whose function is to associate Surface Structures with Deep Structures. That is, the Transformational subcomponent also takes Deep Structures as input. It is the output of this subcomponent, the Surface Structures, which are the input to the Phonology. The pairing of phonetic representations and semantic representations is thus even more indirect than indicated by the diagram. In reality, this pairing is mediated not through a single syntactic structure but through the association of two quite distinct forms of syntactic organization.

This outline discussion of the form of an overall grammar has been quite general. In this book, you have been introduced to the kinds of syntactic facts which must be dealt with in English: the kinds of Deep Structures which must be assumed, the kinds of rules which generate those structures, and some of the transformations which are involved in associating the proper Surface Structures with the Deep Structures.

VI. Linguistic Universals

We have spoken several times of the process of "learning a language," insisting that this involves the internalization of some finite system of rules, rather than simply the memorization of a fixed list of linguistic expressions. But even this unusual way of speaking, more accurate as it is, involves an underlying assumption which must be questioned. The usage "learning a language" implies that the whole system must be learned from scratch. That is, it implies that the overall linguistic system which the growing child represents internally is determined *entirely by his experience*. There is, however, not the slightest reason to believe this. Quite the contrary—it is definitely not the case.

A substantial portion of the structure of any particular language is not learned, but determined by the innate linguistic organization of the human organism. This innate organization specifies the overall structure of a grammar, the kinds of rules it can contain, the kinds of elements and the possible interrelations among these. It also determines to an unknown extent part of the actual content of particular grammars, that is, the particular rules and elements these contain.

The assumption of a rich, universal (innate) linguistic structure, which is the basis for every language and the real foundation which permits first language-learning to take place, is required on many grounds. First, it accounts for the many fundamental similarities manifested by all languages, similarities which are disguised by many factors, such as our general ignorance of anything but the most superficial facts of grammar. In particular, failure to recognize the Deep Structure–Surface Structure distinction, briefly described earlier, has obscured for many the rich system of similarities underlying the superficial syntactic differences which different languages reveal. Second, the assumption of an extensive, genetically determined linguistic organization accounts for the remarkable feat of first language-learning. This takes place so uniformly, rapidly, perfectly and independently of direct instruction, intelligence, etc., as to preclude the possibility that the total output system is a full function of the arbitrary, capricious, and limited experience of particular children. It is easy to overlook the extraordinary character of the task accomplished here because of a tendency to greatly underestimate the scope, complexity, and abstractness of the system actually constructed, i.e., a human language. A better appreciation of what is involved, and of the absurdity of assuming that the result can be fully a function of experience, is obtained by reviewing briefly even what we have concluded above. A child is necessarily restricted to a relatively small, certainly finite, and arbitrarily limited linguistic experience. Thus he hears only a finite number of utterances; many of these are ill-formed; there is much noise, irrelevance, etc. Yet he rapidly constructs a linguistic system which provides him with knowledge of an infinite system of linguistic expressions, no fraction of which he has ever experienced directly. Furthermore, these linguistic expressions are not simply strings of noises, but extraordinarily complicated combinations of semantic, syntactic, and phonological properties. Phrased in this way, it becomes clearer that language learning must be guided by a rich system of unlearned, inborn constraints. Otherwise, the task would be impossible.

Of course, languages do differ in many, often substantial, ways. But this does not preclude the existence of a far-reaching system of innate linguistic principles any more than the very real differences between molecules, tables, planets, and galaxies preclude the existence of a rich set of physical laws governing the behavior of all of them. What is perhaps most interesting about languages is that they reveal in complex and little understood ways the interaction between innate biological structure and experience in the formation of complex systems of knowledge.

The question of linguistic universals, or biologically determined linguistic structure, links the study of grammar to the wider study of human and animal psychology and biology, of which it is really a special part. It shows that in studying the structure of any particular language, one is not only detailing some accidental linguistic facts in space and time, but also necessarily dealing with a defining characteristic of human nature. It is the question of linguistic universals which makes the study of grammar today something beyond the parochial, often narrow, or even pedantic pursuit which it has not infrequently been in the past. Another key difference between grammar in the sense of this book and grammar as we may have encountered it in past schooling is that the principles of English syntax presented in this volume have been developed and been carefully considered within the context of the study of linguistic universals.

VII. Language Differences and Prescriptivism

We have used the term *English grammar* to refer to an overall system which fully describes our knowledge of the phonetic, semantic, and syntactic properties of all English sentences. This term seems to assume that *English* is a monolithic whole, a uniform language spoken by millions. But it is well known that there are vast differences in the languages of those we refer to as "speakers of English." In fact, it is almost certain that no two people really have completely identical languages. The most obvious difference in individual languages is lexicon: It is inconceivable that two people would know exactly identical sets of lexical items. Differences in phonology are also common and familiar to all of us. Nor are distinctions in syntax lacking.

These differences are not purely individual. Speakers of English, and other languages as well, fall into groups defined by associations of similarities and differences. These groups are called *dialects*. Dialects exist as a function of all forms of linguistic isolation and separation—in space, time, social class, occupation, age, etc. But the existence of dialects does not preclude the sensible use of the term *English grammar*, because it is obvious that both dialects and individual variations of our language do share a large number of underlying similarities. This is especially true of English syntax, and it may be even more true of semantics, although at present we have hardly any means to investigate the latter. By studying the deeper underlying principles of syntax, we are in a better position to appreciate how minor the differences among variants of the same language really are. Studies of phonetic differences have already revealed that dialectic variations in phonology may in fact be the function of an overlay of superficial rules on an extensive body of common phonological principles.

This aspect of the study of grammar brings us to another important difference between grammar as it has been presented in this book and the grammar we are familiar with from our previous schooling. School instruction in grammar is usually dominated by two considerations which are foreign to the subject matter and aims of this book: One is the teaching of writing and composition, a subject we will return to shortly; the other is the attempt to teach a more or less standardized dialect of English to students who often speak another dialect. A substantial portion of what is called "grammar" in schools is concerned with the minor features which distinguish different dialects. Long hours are spent rehearsing the difference between expressions such as those in (37) and (38):

(37) a. It is me
     b. It is I
(38) a. I am not going
     b. I ain't going.

But much less attention is given to the vast body of sentence formation principles common to *all* dialects of English—principles which for all speakers of English distinguish between the sequences in (39) and the sequence in (40):

(39) a. *I up to in come will should off so
     b. *I saw the boy you like him
     c. *I book John give
(40) a. I should come in
     b. I saw the boy that you like
     c. I gave John a book.

In short, much of school grammar is concerned with teaching the forms of the prestigious "standard" language to speakers of the less "standard" (often labeled "substandard") dialects of English. But the so-called "standard" language is itself a dialect or variant of English, specifically the one which is linked to literacy and to the literary tradition. This is really a kind of social engineering in which certain speakers are asked to alter certain details of their language to fit those of the more prestigious speakers. This kind of instruction is perhaps a socially defensible goal, defined more precisely and achieved more efficiently in a number of other countries. One difficulty in the United States is that the standard which is taught is not very standard and may vary considerably from place to place.

But whatever value we attach to this linguistic "engineering," it has no real linguistic interest or importance, and most of the "linguistic" justifications for it are either imaginary or completely silly. It is often claimed, for example, that various non-standard forms of speech not only involve linguistic "decay" but also prevent effective communication. This particular argument is as pompous and indefensible as it is empirically without basis.

Another aspect of school grammar, which we refer to here as *prescriptive* grammar, is its insistence that old, even now archaic, forms must continue in use and that many new formations must be excluded. A good example of this is the endless struggle to prevent the use of "like" in those places where older forms of English would have used "as." Prescriptive grammar, virtually by definition, involves resistance to the never-ending process of linguistic change. The baseless assumption behind this resistance is that we are headed for a "breakdown in communication" unless linguistic change is opposed by the guardians of the language. And this assumption, groundless though it may be, dominates much popular discussion of grammar and usage both within the schools and without, and even the most obvious evidence to the contrary does not seem to shake this false view. Does anyone wish to maintain seriously that modern French is a less adequate vehicle for communication than the Latin from which, in a certain sense, it developed, by just those processes of change which prescriptive grammar seeks to resist? Similarly, many hundreds of languages are maintained despite ongoing linguistic change without any tradition of grammatical prescriptivism, without any literary tradition, without any writing system. Prescriptive grammar tends to assume implicitly that human language is a fragile cultural invention, only with difficulty maintained in good working order. It fails to recognize that langauge is an innate attribute of human nature.

Prescriptive grammar is thus not very much concerned with the nature of language as such, nor with the nature of English in particular. It is interested instead in "correct English," that is, in enforcing the use of one particular dialect (that of the particular prescriptive grammarian, or at least that which he thinks is his). A final aspect of prescriptive approaches is a tendency to oppose colloquial styles of speech in favor of more formal ones (*is not* is better than *isn't*, etc.). This is linked to many things perhaps but probably most closely to a concern with the usages of the writing system which is more closely related to formal styles of speaking. There is a groundless tendency here to assume that writing has some sort of primacy over speech and to view colloquial styles as a "decay" from formal speaking, which is already taken to be a deviation from the "true language" given by writing.

Prescriptive grammar is closely linked to the curious assumption that it is necessary to teach "grammar" in schools—that is, to the assumption that the child comes to school with no knowledge of grammar. This assumption is obviously based on a very different conception of grammar from that discussed above. A five-year-old child already has a substantial grasp of most of the principles of sentence formation and interpretation. The truth of the assumption made by prescriptive grammar depends on interpreting the phrase "knowing grammar" to include the ability to discuss one's implicit linguistic knowledge, hence the teaching of concepts like the parts of speech; this interpretation of "knowing grammar" also involves knowledge of the writing system and its adequate use, and knowledge of the details of the prestigious or standard dialect.

It is important, therefore, that we do not confuse the concerns of this book with those of prescriptive grammar. When it has been said that an expression like (41) is a "well-formed English sentence" but an expression like (42) is not, it is not meant that the expression is well formed in some ideal, "standard" language:

(41) Harry wants to go
(42) *Harry wants going.

The expression in (41) is a well-formed sentence in the particular dialect being described, which is actually that of the authors. However, examples have generally been chosen which will almost certainly be valid for just about any dialect. The interest here is in the vast body of structural and syntactic principles which are common to *all* varieties of English rather than in the minor details which differentiate them. These details are what have occasioned so much argument and emotion within the framework of prescriptive grammar.

VIII. Writing

We mentioned above that prescriptive grammar tends to view writing as the primary aspect of language, and speech, or the vocal aspect of language, as a kind of unstable deviation from writing. But this view is completely erroneous. Writing systems are without exception parasitic on language; they are attempts (often rather bad attempts) to represent certain aspects of linguistic structure, usually phonological aspects. Furthermore, writing systems are relatively new inventions, dating back only a few thousand years, compared to the much more enormous span of time which must be assumed for language. Most of the languages on earth still have no writing systems associated with them, and they exist perfectly well without writing.

It is important not to misinterpret what was just said. We have not said that *speech* is primary; we do assert, however, that *language* is primary. Speech, after all, is behavior or performance. As we have seen, language is the system of knowledge which underlies this behavior. There are, however, many ways in which speech is more naturally related to language than any form of writing activity. The vocal-auditory medium is built right into the human organism, and all normal humans can use the medium of speech for performing sentences. But millions of humans cannot use any writing system. Although speech is the "natural" medium for performing language, and writing is a derived or secondary technique, this fact tends to be obscured for us by the great value of writing and by the role which it plays in more complex forms of highly developed social life.

It is therefore neither by mistake nor by accident that this book has considered language as if, in effect, writing systems did not exist. This approach recognizes that language, together with its "natural" performance medium of articulate speech, is a natural consequence of the human organism. Writing, on the other hand, is a special technique for performing the elements of language, and as such it is a clever invention rather like the telephone or algebra.

IX. The Present State of Grammatical Studies

One of the chief results of research within the framework of transformational grammar has been the realization that the depth, scope, complexity, and abstractness of linguistic structure have been almost always seriously underestimated. The informality and the lack of precision of most descriptions of grammar, particularly those underlying our school grammars, have produced a tendency to think of languages as much simpler and more obvious systems than they are in reality. The usual approach in these descriptions is to pick out arbitrary example sentences and then to say various things about them or analyze them in various ways. Such descriptions never really face the problem of determining the precise system of rules that tell one who knows the language all (and only) the facts about each example sentence. That is, they do not deal with the problem of providing a finite grammar which generates the infinite number of sentences in a language. But it is obviously a far simpler task to pick example sentences, even a very large number, and to say things about those particular sentences than it is to discover the exact mechanisms which generate these and all other sentences. In short, traditional linguistic discussion, and school grammars in particular, do not concern themselves with the problem of constructing an explicit system of grammatical rules.

The approach of this book has been quite different. The attempt has been made to provide a precise and explicit account of the system of rules underlying our syntactic knowledge. But this is a very complicated task. Consequently the class of constructions dealt with is much smaller than one might have expected from the older grammars. This is not a matter of deliberate omission, but rather a result of the limitations of our explicit knowledge of the complex, abstract system of principles which forms the grammar of a human language. Within those areas covered, however, this book has provided a degree of precision and explicitness in its discussion of various sentences—a degree of precision and explicitness which traditional grammars are precluded from obtaining by their vague rules and their reliance on the reader's built-in knowledge of the language and his presumed ability to extend the comments about particular examples to an infinite number of unlisted sentences.

The ultimate goal must be to combine breadth of coverage with depth and precision of analysis. But the attainment of this goal will require the intensive research of many grammarians for a long period of time. We must recognize that language in general, and English in particular, still remain largely beyond our serious understanding despite the many years of study by generations of scholars.

This book has been an introduction to the kinds of results that can be obtained by the attempt to construct a precise, explicit grammar of a language. These results are all the more impressive when we consider the fact that they represent what has been achieved by only the very beginning of precise studies of the form and content of the grammars of human languages.

FOR DISCUSSION AND REVIEW

1   How can you resolve the apparent paradox that human beings, who are finite organisms, "know" an infinite number of sentences?

2   How does Postal define *grammar*? Compare his definitions with those offered by W. Nelson Francis in "Revolution in Grammar" (p. 111).

3   Explain the distinction that Postal makes between *competence* and *performance*. Take into account his statement that "grammar is a description of part of what people *know*, not of what they *do*."

4   What properties do sentences have?

5   What are the principal components of a grammar, according to Postal? Describe each component and its function. What component is primary? Why?

6   Postal calls the distinction between deep and surface structures "perhaps the fundamental revelation" of transformational grammar. Look at the articles by Chomsky (p. 172), Miller (p. 132), and Lewis (p. 62). Using evidence from

them as well as what Postal says, can you support this claim? Explain.

7   What are "linguistic universals"? What arguments for their existence does Postal give? In this same regard, Postal says "language learning must be guided by a rich system of unlearned, inborn constraints." Discuss this statement.

8   How does Postal describe variations in phonology from one dialect to another?

9   In view of Postal's remarks concerning the teaching of usage in our schools, what position do you think he would take in the debate about bi-dialectalism? See the articles by William Labov (p. 393), William Raspberry (p. 412), William Stewart (p. 401), and James Sledd (p. 418).

10   What deficiencies of "prescriptive grammar" does Postal cite?

11   According to Postal, what is the relationship between writing, speech, and langauge?

6
Language and the Mind

Noam Chomsky

Transformational generative grammar is inextricably linked with the name Noam Chomsky, the M.I.T. linguist whose book *Syntactic Structures,* published in 1957, first brought this theory extensive attention. Chomsky himself, however, points to the connection between his ideas and those of rationalist, as opposed to empiricist, philosophy. Wilhelm von Humboldt, for example, in the early nineteenth century saw the necessity for describing speech production and interpretation through "a generative system of rules" in the human mind. In the following article, Chomsky discusses reasons for believing that the human mind contains "innate ideas and principles" that enable all normal children to acquire language. Far from being free to organize his linguistic experience in all possible ways, the child is predisposed to structure the data only in accordance with these innate principles, principles common to all human languages. Evident in Chomsky's article is the coming together of ideas from philosophy and psychology as well as linguistics.

H OW DOES the mind work? To answer this question we must look at some of the work performed by the mind. One of its main functions is the acquisition of knowledge. The two major factors in acquisition of knowledge, perception and learning, have been the subject of study and speculation for centuries. It would not, I think, be misleading to characterize the major positions that have developed as outgrowths of classical rationalism and empiricism. The rationalist theories are marked by the importance they assign to *intrinsic* structures in mental operations—to central processes and organizing principles in perception, and to innate ideas and principles in learning. The empiricist approach, in contrast, has stressed the role of experience and control by environmental factors.

The classical empiricist view is that sensory images are transmitted to the brain as impressions. They remain as ideas that will be associated in various ways, depending on the fortuitous character of experience. In this view a language is merely a collection of words, phrases, and sentences, a habit system, acquired accidentally and extrinsically. In the formulation of Willard Quine, knowledge of a language (and, in fact, knowledge in general) can be represented as "a fabric of sentences variously associated to one another and to nonverbal stimuli by the mechanism of conditioned response." Acquisition of knowledge is only a matter of the gradual construction of this fabric. When sensory experience is interpreted, the already established network may be activated in some fashion. In its essentials, this view has been predominant in modern behavioral science, and it has been accepted with little question by many philosophers as well.

The classical rationalist view is quite different. In this view the mind contains a system of "common notions" that enable it to interpret the scattered and incoherent data of sense in terms of objects and their relations, cause and effect, whole and part, symmetry, gestalt properties, functions, and so on. Sensation, providing only fleeting and meaningless images, is degenerate and particular. Knowledge, much of it beyond immediate awareness, is rich in structure, involves universals, and is highly organized. The innate general principles that underlie and organize this knowledge, according to Leibniz, "enter into our thoughts, of which they form the soul and the connection . . . although we do not at all think of them."

This "active" rationalist view of the acquisition of knowledge persisted through the romantic period in its essentials. With respect to language, it achieves its most illuminating expression in the profound investigations of Wilhelm von Humboldt. His theory of speech perception supposes a generative system of rules that underlies speech production as well as its interpretation. The system is generative in that it makes infinite use of finite means. He regards a language as a structure of forms and concepts based on a system of rules that determine their interrelations, arrangement, and organization. But these finite materials can be combined to make a never-ending product.

In the rationalist and romantic tradition of linguistic theory, the normal use of language is regarded as characteristically innovative. We construct sentences that are entirely new to us. There is no substantive notion of "analogy" or "generalization" that accounts for this creative aspect of language use. It is equally erroneous to describe language as a "habit structure" or as a network of associated responses. The innovative element in normal use of language quickly exceeds the bounds of such marginal principles as analogy or generalization (under any substantive interpretation of these notions). It is important to emphasize this fact because the insight has been lost under the impact of the behaviorist assumptions that have dominated speculation and research in the twentieth century.

In Humboldt's view, acquisition of language is largely a matter of maturation of an innate language capacity. The maturation is guided by internal factors, by an innate "form of language" that is sharpened, differentiated, and given its specific realization through experience. Language is thus a kind of latent structure in the human mind, developed and fixed by exposure to specific linguistic experience. Humboldt believes that all languages will be found to be very similar in their grammatical form, similar not on the surface but in their deeper inner structures. The innate organizing principles severely limit the class of possible languages, and these principles determine the properties of the language that is learned in the normal way.

The active and passive views of perception and learning have elaborated with varying degrees of clarity since the seventeenth century. These views can be confronted with empirical evidence in a variety of ways. Some recent work in psychology and neurophysiology is highly suggestive in this regard. There is evidence for the existence of central processes in perception, specifically for control over the functioning of sensory neurons by the brain-stem reticular system. Behavioral counterparts of this central control have been under investigation for several years. Furthermore, there is evidence for innate organization of the perceptual system of a highly specific sort at every level of biological organization. Studies of the visual system of the frog, the discovery of specialized cells responding to angle and motion in the lower cortical centers of cats and rabbits, and the somewhat comparable investigations of the auditory system of frogs—all are relevant to the classical questions of intrinsic structure mentioned earlier. These studies suggest that there are highly organized, innately determined perceptual systems that are adapted closely to the animal's "life space" and that provide the basis for what we might call "acquisition of knowledge." Also relevant are certain behavioral studies of human infants, for example those showing the preference for faces over other complex stimuli.

These and other studies make it reasonable to inquire into the possibility that complex intellectual structures are determined narrowly by innate mental organization. What is perceived may be determined by mental processes of considerable depth. As far as language learning is concerned, it seems to me that a rather convincing argument can be made for the view that certain principles intrinsic to the mind provide invariant structures that are a precondition for linguistic experience. In the course of this article I would like to sketch some of the ways such conclusions might be clarified and firmly established.

There are several ways linguistic evidence can be used to reveal properties of human perception and learning. In this section we consider one research strategy that might take us nearer to this goal.

Let us say that in interpreting a certain physical stimulus a person constructs a "percept." This percept represents some of his conclusions (in general, unconscious) about the stimulus. To the extent that we can characterize such percepts, we can go on to investigate the mechanisms that relate stimulus and percept. Imagine a model of perception that takes stimuli as inputs and arrives at percepts as "outputs." The model might contain a system of beliefs, strategies for interpreting stimuli, and other factors, such as the organization of memory. We would then have a perceptual model that might be represented graphically.

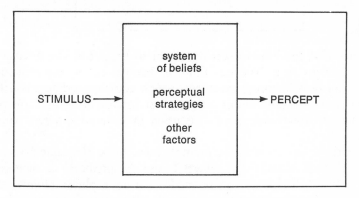

Consider next the system of beliefs that is a component of the perceptual model. How was this acquired? To study this problem, we must investigate a second model, which takes certain data as input and gives as "output" (again, internally represented) the system of beliefs operating in the perceptual model. This second model, a model of learning, would have its own intrinsic structure, as did the first. This structure might consist of conditions on the nature of the system of beliefs that can be acquired, of innate inductive strategies, and again, of other factors such as the organization of memory.

Under further conditions, which are interesting but not relevant here, we can take these perceptual and learning models as theories of the acquisition of knowledge, rather than of belief. How then would the models apply to language? The input stimulus to the perceptual model is a speech signal, and the percept is a representation of the

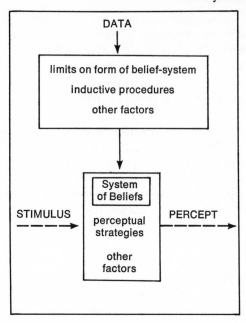

utterance that the hearer takes the signal to be and of the interpretation he assigns to it. We can think of the percept as the structural
description of a linguistic expression which contains certain phonetic,
semantic, and syntactic information. Most interesting is the syntactic
information, which best can be discussed by examining a few typical
cases.

The three sentences in the example seem to be the same syntactic
structure. Each contains the subject *I*, and the predicate of each consists of a verb (*told, expected, persuaded*), a noun phrase (*John*), and
an embedded predicate phrase (*to leave*). This similarity is only superficial, however—a similarity in what we may call the "surface structure"
of these sentences, which differ in important ways when we consider
them with somewhat greater care.

The differences can be seen when the sentences are paraphrased or
subjected to certain grammatical operations, such as the conversion
from active to passive forms. For example, in normal conversation the
sentence "I told John to leave" can be roughly paraphrased as "What
I told John was to leave." But the other two sentences cannot be paraphrased as "What I persuaded John was to leave" or "What I expected
John was to leave." Sentence 2 can be paraphrased as: "It was expected
by me that John would leave." But the other two sentences cannot undergo a corresponding formal operation, yielding: "It was persuaded by
me that John would leave" or "It was told by me that John should
leave."

(1)	I told John to leave
(2)	I expected John to leave
(3)	I persuaded John to leave

FIRST PARAPHRASE:

(1a)	What I told John was to leave (ACCEPTABLE)
(2a)	What I expected John was to leave (UNACCEPTABLE)
(3a)	What I persuaded John was to leave (UNACCEPTABLE)

SECOND PARAPHRASE:

(1b)	It was told by me that John would leave (UNACCEPTABLE)
(2b)	It was expected by me that John would leave (ACCEPTABLE)
(3b)	It was persuaded by me that John would leave (UNACCEPTABLE)

| (4) | I expected the doctor to examine John |
| (5) | I persuaded the doctor to examine John |

PASSIVE REPLACEMENT AS PARAPHRASE:

| (4a) | I expected John to be examined by the doctor (MEANING RETAINED) |
| (5a) | I persuaded John to be examined by the doctor (MEANING CHANGED) |

Sentences 2 and 3 differ more subtly. In Sentence 3 *John* is the direct object of *persuade,* but in Sentence 2 *John* is not the direct object of *expect.* We can show this by using these verbs in slightly more complex sentences: "I persuaded the doctor to examine John" and "I expected the doctor to examine John." If we replace the embedded proposition *the doctor to examine John* with its passive form *John to be examined by the doctor,* the change to the passive does not, in itself, change the meaning. We can accept as paraphrases "I expected the doctor to examine John" and "I expected John to be examined by the doctor." But we cannot accept as paraphrases "I persuaded the doctor to examine John" and "I persuaded John to be examined by the doctor."

The parts of these sentences differ in their grammatical functions. In "I persuaded John to leave" *John* is both the object of *persuade* and the subject of *leave.* These facts must be represented in the percept since they are known, intuitively, to the hearer of the speech signal. No special training or instruction is necessary to enable the native speaker to understand these examples, to know which are "wrong" and which "right," although they may all be quite new to him. They are interpreted by the native speaker instantaneously and uniformly, in accordance with structural principles that are known tacitly, intuitively, and unconsciously.

These examples illustrate two significant points. First, the surface structure of a sentence, its organization into various phrases, may not reveal or immediately reflect its deep syntactic structure. The deep structure is not represented directly in the form of the speech signal; it is abstract. Second, the rules that determine deep and surface structure and their interrelation in particular cases must themselves be highly abstract. They are surely remote from consciousness, and in all likelihood they cannot be brought to consciousness.

A study of such examples, examples characteristic of all human languages that have been carefully studied, constitutes the first stage of the linguistic investigation outlined above, namely the study of the percept. The percept contains phonetic and semantic information related through the medium of syntactic structure. There are two aspects to this syntactic structure. It consists of a surface directly related to the phonetic form, and a deep structure that underlies the semantic interpretation. The deep structure is represented in the mind and rarely is indicated directly in the physical signal.

A language, then, involves a set of semantic-phonetic percepts, of sound-meaning correlations, the correlations being determined by the kind of intervening syntactic structure just illustrated. The English language correlates sound and meaning in one way, Japanese in another, and so on. But the general properties of percepts, their forms and mechanisms, are remarkably similar for all languages that have been carefully studied.

Returning to our models of perception and learning, we can now take up the problem of formulating the system of beliefs that is a central component in perceptual processes. In the case of language, the "system of beliefs" would now be called the "generative grammar," the system of rules that specifies the sound-meaning correlation and generates the class of structural descriptions (percepts) that constitute the language in question. The generative grammar, then, represents the speaker-hearer's knowledge of his language. We can use the term *grammar of a language* ambiguously, as referring not only to the speaker's internalized, subconscious knowledge but to the professional linguist's representation of this internalized and intuitive system of rules as well.

How is this generative grammar acquired? Or, using our learning model, what is the internal structure of the device that could develop a generative grammar?

We can think of every normal human's internalized grammar as, in effect, a theory of his language. This theory provides a sound-meaning correlation for an infinite number of sentences. It provides an infinite set of structural descriptions; each contains a surface structure that determines phonetic form and a deep structure that determines semantic content.

In formal terms, then, we can describe the child's acquisition of language as a kind of theory construction. The child discovers the theory of his language with only small amounts of data from that language. Not only does his "theory of the language" have an enormous predictive scope, but it also enables the child to reject a great deal of the very data on which the theory has been constructed. Normal speech consists, in large part, of fragments, false starts, blends, and other distortions of the underlying idealized forms. Nevertheless, as is evident from a study of the mature use of language, what the child learns is the underlying ideal theory. This is a remarkable fact. We must also bear in mind that the child constructs this ideal theory without explicit instruction, that he acquires this knowledge at a time when he is not capable of complex intellectual achievements in many other domains, and that this achievement is relatively independent of intelligence or the particular course of experience. These are facts that a theory of learning must face.

A scientist who approaches phenomena of this sort without prejudice or dogma would conclude that the acquired knowledge must be determined in a rather specific way by intrinsic properties of mental organization. He would then set himself the task of discovering the innate ideas and principles that make such acquisition of knowledge possible.

It is unimaginable that a highly specific, abstract, and tightly organized language comes by accident into the mind of every four-year-old child. If there were not an innate restriction on the form of grammar, then the child could employ innumerable theories to account for his linguistic experience, and no one system, or even small class of systems, would be found exclusively acceptable or even preferable. The child could not possibly acquire knowledge of a language. This restriction on the form of grammar is a precondition for linguistic experience, and it is surely the critical factor in determining the course and result of language learning. The child cannot know at birth which language he is going to learn. But he must "know" that its grammar must be of a predetermined form that excludes many imaginable languages.

The child's task is to select the appropriate hypothesis from this restricted class. Having selected it, he can confirm his choice with the evidence further available to him. But neither the evidence nor any process of induction (in any well-defined sense) could in themselves have led to this choice. Once the hypothesis is sufficiently well confirmed, the child knows the language defined by this hypothesis; consequently, his knowledge extends vastly beyond his linguistic experience, and he can reject much of this experience as imperfect, as resulting from the interaction of many factors, only one of which is the ideal grammar that determines a sound-meaning connection for an infinite class of linguistic expressions. Along such lines as these one might outline a theory to explain the acquisition of language.

As has been pointed out, both the form and meaning of a sentence

are determined by syntactic structures that are not represented directly
in the signal and that are related to the signal only at a distance,
through a long sequence of interpretive rules. This property of abstractness in grammatical structure is of primary importance, and it is
on this property that our inferences about mental processes are based.
Let us examine this abstractness a little more closely.

Not many years ago, the process of sentence interpretation might
have been described approximately along the following lines. A speech
signal is received and segmented into successive units (overlapping at
the borders). These units are analyzed in terms of their invariant
phonetic properties and assigned to "phonemes." The sequence of
phonemes, so constructed, is then segmented into minimal grammatically functioning units (morphemes and words). These are again categorized. Successive operations of segmentation and classification will
lead to what I have called "surface structure"—an analysis of a sentence
into phrases, which can be represented as a proper bracketing of the
sentence, with the bracketed units assigned to various categories. Each
segment—phonetic, syntactic or semantic—would be identified in terms
of certain invariant properties. This would be an exhaustive analysis of
the structure of the sentence.

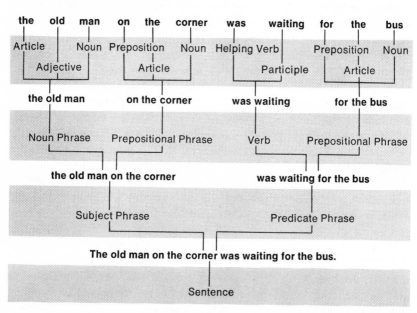

With such a conception of language structure, it made good sense
to look forward hopefully to certain engineering applications of linguistics—for example, to voice-operated typewriters capable of segment-
ing an expression into its successive phonetic units and identifying these,

so that speech could be converted to some form of phonetic writing in a mechanical way; to mechanical analysis of sentence structure by fairly straight-forward and well-understood computational techniques; and perhaps even beyond to such projects as machine translation. But these hopes have by now been largely abandoned with the realization that this conception of grammatical structure is inadequate at every level, semantic, phonetic, and syntactic. Most important, at the level of syntactic organization, the surface structure indicates semantically significant relations only in extremely simple cases. In general, the deeper aspects of syntactic organization are representable by labeled bracketing, but of a very different sort from that seen in surface structure.

There is evidence of various sorts, both from phonetics and from experimental psychology, that labeled bracketing is an adequate representation of surface structure. It would go beyond the bounds of this paper to survey the phonetic evidence. A good deal of it is presented in a forthcoming book, *Sound Pattern of English*, by myself and Morris Halle. Similarly, very interesting experimental work by Jerry Fodor and his colleagues, based on earlier observations by D. E. Broadbent and Peter Ladefoged, has shown that the disruption of a speech signal (for example, by a superimposed click) tends to be perceived at the boundaries of phrases rather than at the point where the disruption actually occurred, and that in many cases the bracketing of surface structure can be read directly from the data on perceptual displacement. I think the evidence is rather good that labeled bracketing serves to represent the surface structure that is related to the perceived form of physical signals.

Deep structures are related to surface structures by a sequence of certain formal operations, operations now generally called "grammatical transformations." At the levels of sound, meaning, and syntax, the significant structural features of sentences are highly abstract. For this reason they cannot be recovered by elementary data-processing techniques. This fact lies behind the search for central processes in speech perception and the search for intrinsic, innate structure as the basis for language learning.

How can we represent deep structure? To answer this question we must consider the grammatical transformations that link surface structure to the underlying deep structure that is not always apparent.

Consider, for example, the operations of passivization and interrogation. In the sentences (1) John was examined by the doctor, and (2) did the doctor examine John, both have a deep structure similar to the paraphrase of Sentence 1, (3) the doctor examined John. The same network of grammatical relations determines the semantic interpretation in each case. Thus two of the grammatical transformations of English must be the operations of passivization and interrogation that form such surface structures as Sentences 1 and 2 from a deeper structure which in its essentials also underlies Sentence 3. Since the transformations ultimately produce surface structures, they must produce labeled bracketings [see illustration p. 180]. But notice that these operations can apply in sequence: we can form the passive question "was John examined by the doctor" by passivization followed by interrogation. Since the result of passivization is a labeled bracketing, it follows that the interrogative transformation operates on a labeled bracketing and forms a new labeled bracketing. Thus a transformation such as interrogation maps a labeled bracketing into a labeled bracketing.

By similar argument, we can show that all grammatical transformations are structure-dependent mappings of this sort and that the deep structures which underlie all sentences must themselves be labeled bracketings. Of course, the labeled bracketing that constitutes deep structure will in general be quite different from that representing the surface structure of a sentence. Our argument is somewhat oversimplified, but it is roughly correct. When made precise and fully accurate it strongly supports the view that deep structures, like surface structures, are formally to be taken as labeled bracketings, and that grammatical transformations are mappings of such structures onto other similar structures.

Recent studies have sought to explore the ways in which grammatical structure of the sort just described enters into mental operations. Much of this work has been based on a proposal formulated by George Miller as a first approximation, namely, that the amount of memory used to store a sentence should reflect the number of transformations used in deriving it. For example, H. B. Savin and E. Perchonock investigated this assumption in the following way: they presented to subjects a sentence followed by a sequence of unrelated words. They then determined the number of these unrelated words recalled when the subject attempted to repeat the sentence and the sequence of words. The more words recalled, the less memory used to store the sentence. The fewer words recalled, the more memory used to store the sentence. The results showed a remarkable correlation of amount of memory and number of transformations in certain simple cases. In fact, in their experimental material, shorter sentences with more transformations took up more "space in memory" than longer sentences that involved fewer transformations.

Savin has extended this work and has shown that the effects of deep structure and surface structure can be differentiated by a similar technique. He considered paired sentences with approximately the same deep structure but with one of the pair being more complex in surface structure. He showed that, under the experimental conditions just described, the paired sentences were indistinguishable. But if the sequence of unrelated words precedes, rather than follows, the sentence being tested, then the more complex (in surface structure) of the pair is more difficult to repeat correctly than the simpler member. Savin's very plausible inference is that sentences are coded in memory in terms of deep structure. When the unrelated words precede the test sentence, these words use up a certain amount of short-term memory, and the sentence that is more complex in surface structure cannot be analyzed with the amount of memory remaining. But if the test sentence precedes the unrelated words, it is, once understood, stored in terms of deep structure, which is about the same in both cases. Therefore the same amount of memory remains, in the paired cases, for recall of the following words. This is a beautiful example of the way creative experimental studies can interweave with theoretical work in the study of language and of mental processes.

In speaking of mental processes we have returned to our original problem. We can now see why it is reasonable to maintain that the linguistic evidence supports an "active" theory of acquisition of knowledge. The study of sentences and of speech perception, it seems to me, leads to a perceptual theory of a classical rationalist sort. Representative of this school, among others, were the seventeenth-century Cambridge Platonists, who developed the idea that our perception is guided by notions that originate from the mind and that provide the framework for the interpretation of sensory stimuli. It is not sufficient to suggest that this framework is a store of "neural models" or "schemata" which are in some manner applied to perception (as is postulated in some current theories of perception). We must go well beyond this assumption and return to the view of Wilhelm von Humboldt, who attributed to the mind a system of rules that generates such models and schemata under the stimulation of the senses. The system of rules itself determines the content of the percept that is formed.

We can offer more than this vague and metaphoric account. A generative grammar and an associated theory of speech perception provide a concrete example of the rules that operate and of the mental objects that they construct and manipulate. Physiology cannot yet explain the physical mechanisms that affect these abstract functions. But neither physiology nor psychology provides evidence that calls this account into question or that suggests an alternative. As mentioned earlier, the most exciting current work in the physiology of perception shows that even the peripheral systems analyze stimuli into the complex properties of objects, and that central processes may significantly affect the information transmitted by the receptor organs.

The study of language, it seems to me, offers strong empirical evidence that empiricist theories of learning are quite inadequate. Serious efforts have been made in recent years to develop principles of induction, generalization, and data analysis that would account for knowledge of a language. These efforts have been a total failure. The methods and principles fail not for any superficial reason such as lack of time or data. They fail because they are intrinsically incapable of giving rise to the system of rules that underlies the normal use of language. What evidence is now available supports the view that all human languages share deep-seated properties of organization and structure. These properties—these linguistic universals—can be plausibly assumed to be an innate mental endowment rather than the result of learning. If this is true, then the study of language sheds light on certain long-standing issues in the theory of knowledge. Once again, I see little reason to doubt that what is true of language is true of other forms of human knowledge as well.

There is one further question that might be raised at this point. How does the human mind come to have the innate properties that underlie acquisition of knowledge? Here linguistic evidence obviously provides no information at all. The process by which the human mind has achieved its present state of complexity and its particular form of innate organization are a complete mystery, as much of a mystery as the analogous questions that can be asked about the processes leading to the physical and mental organization of any other complex organism. It is perfectly safe to attribute this to evolution, so long as we bear in mind that there is no substance to this assertion—it amounts to nothing more than the belief that there is surely some naturalistic explanation for these phenomena.

There are, however, important aspects of the problem of language and mind that can be studied sensibly within the limitations of present understanding and technique. I think that, for the moment, the most productive investigations are those dealing with the nature of particular grammars and with the universal conditions met by all human languages. I have tried to suggest how one can move, in successive steps of increasing abstractness, from the study of percepts to the study of grammar and perceptual mechanisms, and from the study of grammar to the study of universal grammar and the mechanisms of learning.

In this area of convergence of linguistics, psychology, and philosophy, we can look forward to much exciting work in coming years.

FOR DISCUSSION AND REVIEW

1 Distinguish between rationalist and empiricist theories concerning perception and learning.
2 Compare and contrast the empiricist and the rationalist view of the nature of knowledge, including language. In his article on the acquisition of language by children, which position does Lewis (p. 62) support?
3 Summarize von Humboldt's view of language acquisition.

4   What does Chomsky mean by *percept*? On what basis can he assert that "the general properties of percepts . . . are remarkably similar for all languages that have been carefully studied"? If percepts are similar, what does vary from language to language?

5   According to Chomsky, how does a child acquire language? How does Chomsky support this view?

6   Why does Chomsky describe "abstractness in grammatical structure" as "of primary importance"?

7   Define *deep* and *surface structures*. How are deep and surface structures related? How does this relationship affect comprehension of a sentence? (You may find it helpful to refer to Lewis's discussion of deep and surface structure, p. 68.)

8   What are *linguistic universals* and why are they important? Consider not only Chomsky's discussion but also those by Miller (p. 132) and Postal (p. 149).

7

Stratificational Grammar:
A New Theory of Language

John White

Stratificational grammar, as developed primarily by Sydney Lamb of Yale, is a recent theory of language that is attracting increasing attention; its proponents feel that within this decade it will supersede transformational generative grammar. The theory provides a hypothesis concerning the nature of the linguistic system in the human brain and deals with the several levels (or strata) of language, from distinctive features, which make up phonemes, to structures larger than sentences, such as complete texts.

IN THE broadest sense, grammar is the study of how a language works. Traditional grammar provides our most familiar model of a language, but this century has seen a number of attempts by linguists to give descriptions of languages which are more accurate and objective than those provided by traditional grammar. Structural linguistics and transformational grammar are the best known. This article is concerned with still another attempt to describe how a language works.

Stratificational grammar is a theory of language being developed by Sydney Lamb of the Linguistics Department at Yale University. Lamb's earliest thoughts about a stratificational model of language go back to the mid-1950's, but he dates the modern form of this theory from 1965. Dissemination of it has so far been limited mostly to professional journals, a book by Lamb entitled *Outline of Stratificational Grammar* (Georgetown University Press, 1966) and graduate courses taught by him. At present, transformational theory seems to be the most widely-held view of language, but Lamb predicts that by the early 1970's stratificational theory will have superseded it.

Aiding the development of this theory are H. A. Gleason of University of Toronto and Peter A. Reich of Yale. Reich works as a chief assistant to Lamb on the Linguistic Automation Project, which was started by Lamb in 1966 to test and evaluate his theory. From a small office in downtown New Haven, tests are programmed by Project personnel to be run at the nearby Yale Computer Center. In England, M. A. K. Halliday at University of London is developing a related view of language called systemic grammar, and it is of sufficient importance to stratificational theory to be credited here.

According to Lamb, *a language is the system which its speakers use to speak to each other and understand each other. Language is not to be understood in terms of words but rather in terms of mental systems.* Speech and writing are not language; they are only *manifestations* of the system which is language, just as a lighted bulb is a manifestation of electricity. Every speaker of a language has a representation of that system in his brain, but his representation is only part of the total system. One speaker's representation approximates another's in varying degrees, depending upon cultural background, education, etc. The representation in the brain of an illiterate ghetto-dweller is noticeably different from that of a college professor. No single person, however, has within his brain the complete system because it includes both the representations just mentioned as well as those of all other speakers of that language. A language is always more diverse and complex than the representation in any speaker's brain.

Language, then, is a finite system (among many in the brain) which can be used for encoding (speaking or writing) and decoding (understanding) any of an infinite set of texts in that language. Through the definition of "text" we may attain historical perspective on stratificational grammar. According to Lamb, a text consists of both a message and an expression. The message of a text pertains to its content; the expression of a text pertains to sound.

In connection with this definition, Lamb distinguishes two major traditions in the history of linguistic theory: the Bloomfieldian tradition and the Hjelmslevian tradition. Leonard Bloomfield, of course, was the well-known American linguist who taught at Yale in the 1930's. Louis Hjelmslev was a lesser-known but equally great Danish linguist who taught at University of Copenhagen in the 1930–50's. The Bloomfield-ian linguists, through structural linguistics, emphasized the study of the expressions of a language, while the Hjelmslevian linguists, through the system called glossematics, emphasized the study of the system which speakers use to produce the expressions. The two traditions may be out-lined as follows:

BLOOMFIELDIAN TRADITION	HJELMSLEVIAN TRADITION
(emphasizes expressions)	(emphasizes system)
Boas	de Saussure
Sapir	↓
Bloomfield (1930-45)	Hjelmslev (1935-55)
Neo-Bloomfieldians (1940-60)	↓
Hockett	Firth
Pike	↓
Bloch	Halliday
Trager	(Systemic grammar, 1960-?)
et al.	Lamb
Chomsky/Harris	(Stratificational
(Transformational	grammar, 1965-?)
grammar, 1955-70's)	

Lamb, then, is attempting to formulate a theory of language which accounts for the system which relates meaning and expression, content and sound. He terms his theory "stratificational" because "one of its chief features is its treatment of linguistic structure as comprising sev-eral layers or strata. A language, by its nature, relates sounds (or writ-ing) to meanings; the relationship turns out to be a very complex one, which can be analyzed in terms of a series of code-like systems, each of which has a structure analogous to that which earlier linguistic theories ascribed to language as a whole. . ." (*Outline*, p. 1). In making his analysis, it has appeared necessary to describe linguistic structures as consisting of levels or strata. Evidence to date suggests that "all natural languages have at least four [strata], and that at least some languages, including English, have six strata" (*Outline*, p. 1).

The six-strata structure of English may be regarded as made of three major components—phonology, semology and grammar. Pho-nology is concerned with speech; semology is concerned with meaning; and grammar relates the two. Each major component includes two of the six levels in the structure. From lowest (the expression side of lan-guage) to highest (the meaning side), the levels are named as follows: hypophonemic, phonemic, morphemic, lexemic, sememic, hyperseme-mic. The basic units of each level from lowest to highest are named hypophoneme, phoneme, morpheme, lexeme, sememe and hypersememe. The system of strata may be diagrammed as shown [below].

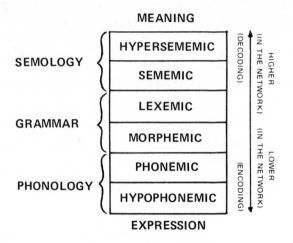

Speech sounds are produced by the articulatory mechanisms as signalled by the hypophonemic stratum. Hypophonemes, sometimes called distinctive features, are the components of phonemes. All the sounds of English can be produced by about fifteen hypophonemes (such as plosion, spirancy, nasality, labiality and voicing). For example, the Labial (Lb) hypophoneme closes or rounds the lips. In that position, nine phonemes can be produced, depending upon what other hypophonemes are used. If the oral passage is Closed (Cl), the phoneme /p/ is produced in the normal condition (no voicing). If the Voiced (Vd) component is present but all other features remain the same, the phoneme /b/ is produced. Therefore the phoneme /b/ differs from the phoneme /p/ by the addition of one hypophoneme:

/p/ = Lb Cl
/b/ = Lb Cl Vd

The concepts of phoneme and morpheme have been adequately discussed elsewhere, so here it will be sufficient to note only that the phonemic level deals with all possible combinations of sound in a language, while the morphemic level deals primarily with the structure of words in that language. The next higher stratum in the stratificational model, the lexemic, specifies the structure of clauses, while sentence structure and word meaning are dealt with at a still higher level, the sememic. Highest of all, the hypersememic stratum is concerned with the structure of narrative and units beyond the sentence from paragraphs to entire works.

This diagram is a graphic model of the system believed to be represented in the brain. The linguistic system itself is not directly observable. Only the manifestations of language, such as speech or writing, are observable. Lamb cautions that it is still too early to attempt any correlation between such models and actual neurological structures in the brain. New evidence may demand considerable alteration of the theory's mechanical processes. However, it is hoped that eventually the theory will be confirmed by physiological evidence showing that we really *do* communicate like that.

A language has both *structure* and *process*, corresponding to neurological network and neural impulse. Structure provides the means whereby process may occur. In a language, the primary processes are encoding and decoding. Impulses move through the network, but the network itself does not normally change in the ordinary use of language. In stratificational grammar, this is shown in the diagram as moving downward to expression (encoding) and moving upward to meaning (decoding). Each level of the structure is discrete and self-contained. The structure does not change one form into another. Rather it allows impulses to move from one level to another, with linguistic forms being produced only at the lower end. In the production of a sentence (encoding), meaning always precedes expression, while the reverse is true for decoding. Therefore all the decisions necessary to produce any linguistic form are made *before* the expression is actualized. It is the decision-event, standing outside the linguistic structure at the higher end, which sends impulses through the network. Their emergence outside the lower end of the structure is expression, either as speech or writing.

In attempting to give a precise description of linguistic activity, stratificational grammar has moved from traditional description in ordinary words to description based largely on graphs depicting networks. In addition to graphic diagram, stratificational grammar uses algebraic notation as a mode of description. Thus one type of linguistic activity may be described in ordinary words like this: "An impulse moving downward along line *a* goes simultaneously down line *b* and line *c*." The same relationship may also be described algebraically like this:

$$a \ / \ b \cdot c$$

and it may be diagrammed like this:

The example of hypophonemes given above could be indicated like this:

$$p \; / \; Cl \; Lb \qquad \text{and}$$

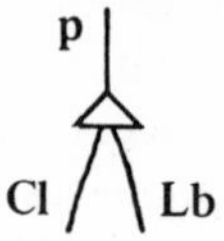

These can be translated as "An impulse moving downward along line p goes simultaneously down line Cl and line Lb." The triangular node in the center of the graphic diagram indicates a simultaneous "and" relationship. That is, both impulses are needed to make further transmission of impulse. If only one or the other is needed, this "either-or" relationship is indicated by a different node which looks like a bracket lying on its side.

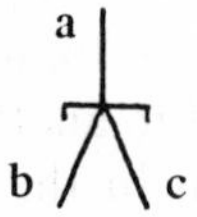

This graphic diagram shows "an impulse moving downward along line a goes down either line b or line c."

If impulses have a fixed, rather than simultaneous, order of transmission or arrival, it is shown through the lines' connection to a node, with priority being given to the left line. In this diagram an impulse

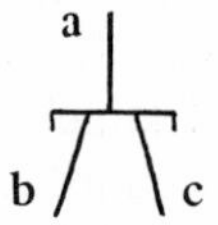

moving downward along line a will move first downward along line b, or (if a complete connection cannot be made further below in the network) it will return to the node and then move downward along line c.

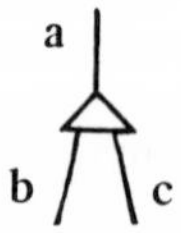

Likewise this diagram indicates that for an impulse to move upward along line a, there must arrive at the node, first, an impulse upward along line b and, second, an impulse upward along line c.

In brief, a triangular node indicates an "and" relationship while a bracket indicates an "either-or" relationship. The order of impulse arrival and transmission is indicated by the joining or separation of lines at a node, with priority in an ordered relationship given to the left-hand line on a non-joined multiple connection to a node.

Figure 1

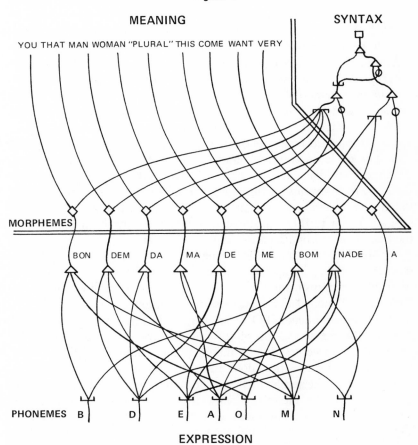

For the sake of example, Figure 1 shows the network grammar of a highly simplified artificial language having only two partially developed strata of seven phonemes and nine morphemes. The diagram indicates that the phoneme /B/[1] can move upward to either the morpheme /BON/ or the morpheme /BOM/. If we follow the line upward to

---

[1] Capital letters are used to indicate the difference between these phonemes of an artificial language and those of natural languages.

/BON/, we see the morpheme consists of three phonemes—/B/, /O/ and /N/—which have a definite ordering of first /B/, second /O/ and last /N/. Any other ordering to the arrival of impulses at the /BON/ morpheme node will result in no further transmission of impulse.

Suppose a speaker of this language received the message "Bon ma de bom." The ordered arrival of impulses through the phonemic section results in further transmission, indicating that each word is at least well-formed in that language, even if it is nonsensical.

Next the impulses are sent through the diamond node up the right-hand line to the syntax section, where their grammatical correctness is determined. Ungrammatical forms are not permitted to pass through the syntax section by virtue of the nodes and ordering of line connections.

The morpheme /BON/ sends an impulse up the right line from the diamond connection until it arrives at the bracket. Here, because the bracket indicates an "either-or" situation, the impulse is allowed to pass upward to the next node, the triangle indicating an "ordered and" situation. The circle on the right-hand line indicates a special situation in stratificational diagrams—an optional item—which is not absolutely necessary for transmission through an "ordered and" node. In this case, the line wtih a circle is connected to /DE/—which is a part of the message—and so a further transmission is made because both lines below the triangle have impulses arriving in the right order.

Passing upward from the triangle, the impulse goes through a bracket and then goes up the left-hand line because it would be blocked from further transmission if it took the right-hand line, since the "ordered and" node lacks the necessary prior impulse.

Thus the morpheme /BON/ has triggered a series of impulses which eventually arrive at the top of the syntax section, thereby proving its grammatical correctness in the message. The impulse will then return to the diamond connection along the path it chose and pass upward to meaning along the left-hand line. The same process will occur for all other items in the message. Each will have its syntactic correctness tested in the syntax section and, if not halted in transmission, eventually return to the diamond and then pass upward to meaning. By this process the message "Bon ma de bom" will be decoded and the hearer will understand it to mean "You women come."

This diagram (a simple one compared to stratificational descriptions of natural languages) illustrates one of stratificational grammar's advantages over other linguistic models: the capability to predict new words and phrases. /BO/ and /NA/ are possible morphemes existing in the structure of this artificial language which simply have not been used. Likewise *fribble* is a possibility that exists in the sound combinations of English but phonetic ŋñtx is not, and this can be demonstrated in stratificational terms such as those above. In transformational terms, however, this can be done only in part while the formation of new idioms such as "uptight" and "brinkmanship" cannot be shown at all. Stratificational grammar handles the formation of new idioms quite easily.

Besides its predictive capability, stratificational theory offers a hypothesis of what happens in the brain. (Transformational theory does not, since its emphasis is on the competence of a speaker, not the system he actually uses for linguistic performance.) In stratificational theory, the decisions are all made before any linguistic forms are produced with those forms being actualized only at the lower end of the network. Lamb maintains this is a simpler and more economical description than transformational theory's rewrite rules, which suggest that one linguistic form is changed into another, and then another and another.

Last of all, stratificational theory offers a unified picture of language from the distinctive features of expression to the formal structure of texts beyond the sentence. Theoretically, even the *Encyclopedia Britannica* could have a stratificational description of it made.

In summary, then, stratificational grammar is a new theory of language which may turn out to be the most precise, economical and complete of all existing models. It will become increasingly sophisticated as work on it proceeds at project headquarters and among other linguists. By the early 1970's stratificational theory may well replace transformational theory as a description of language.

FOR DISCUSSION AND REVIEW

1   Stratificational theory is complicated, and you should not expect to understand it after reading one short article. Nevertheless, try to discuss some of the conspicuous differences between it and both structural and transformational grammar.

2   What are the *strata* of language? Describe the strata of English. Are those of other languages always similar? Explain.

3   What advantages does White feel stratificational grammar offers over other theories?

8
Tagmemics

In the following article written specifically for this book, Peter H. Fries discusses the development and the future of tagmemics, and presents some of its fundamental concepts: language as purposive behavior; the interrelationship of form and meaning; description of each form-meaning composite in terms of its contrast, variation, and distribution; the necessity to describe language from different viewpoints (particle, wave, and field views); and the existence of hierarchy in language.

Peter H. Fries

Transformational generative grammar and stratificational grammar are not the only approaches to language analysis that are currently receiving much attention from linguists. Tagmemics is also providing new insights into the structure of languages. Developed primarily by Kenneth L. Pike and his students, tagmemics has been utilized mainly by people working on little-known languages and with preliterate cultures. Its principal application during the last twenty years has been in describing some three hundred of the world's languages. The extent of its use makes acquaintance with this approach desirable for anyone interested in language study.

Tagmemics is a slot and filler grammar; that is, because tagmemicists believe that neither form nor function alone adequately describes fundamental units, this grammar describes the basic units of language in terms of both their function (the slots in which they fit) and their form (the kinds of fillers they are). The importance of both form and function can be seen in the definition of a tagmeme, which Fries calls "the correlation of a grammatical function with the set of units which may play that function." The tagmeme is a unit at the grammatical level, one of three independent but interrelated levels of the tagmemic model of grammar—the phonological level, the lexical level, and the grammatical level.

TAGMEMIC theory has been developed primarily by Kenneth L. Pike and a number of colleagues in the Summer Institute of Linguistics over the past twenty years. Pike became interested in language and the description of language because of his interest in practical problems such as literacy and translation into the unwritten languages of the world. As of this writing, Pike and his colleagues have published articles and books describing about 300 different languages. In many cases the tagmemic descriptions are the only descriptions of these languages.

Pike's interest in practical problems remains his primary interest and it colors his view of linguistics. Specifically, linguistics is only a tool to be used for the more important end of understanding what people do and why they do it. As Pike put it recently: "I'm interested in truth about man, about how language is related to man, about how language is related to behavior. I wouldn't ever grant that I'm interested only in language."[1] The breadth of focus of tagmemicists in attempting to devise a theory which is adequate to describe both language and other types of human behavior is perhaps the most important distinguishing characteristic of tagmemic theory.

From the point of view of the tagmemicist, then, language is a kind of behavior; it is something people do. But since it is a kind of behavior, it occurs only within a more general behavioral context and this behavioral context is relevant to the understanding of language. We find ourselves in certain social situations and in these situations we use the language that is appropriate. Indeed, sequences of sentences can be found which make sense only if we realize that the social situation (a part of the behavioral context) has changed in some way. For example:

> "Double function occurs in three general situations. Could I have some cream and sugar, please? These three situations are. . . ."

At first glance it would seem that the speaker suddenly forgot what he was talking about. If it is explained that he was in a restaurant and that the waitress suddenly appeared, left a cup of coffee, and was about to leave, the sequence seems more understandable. Examples such as this one show that language must be considered in relation to the behavioral context in which it occurs.

Language as Purposive Behavior

The behavior of people is not random behavior. People do what they do in order to achieve some goal. The use of language is no excep-

[1] Discussion following Pike's "Crucial Questions in the Development of Tagmemics —the Sixties and Seventies," *Monograph Series on Language and Linguistics*, No. 24, 1971, pp. 79–98; quote from p. 162.

tion. Language is usually used to communicate a fairly specific message (*The redcoats are coming*). Most linguistic theories treat just this aspect of language. Language may also be used to communicate the speaker's attitude toward the message (*John got some more overtime, Poor John has to work overtime*) and the speaker's attitude toward the listener (*Get dem crates over here, Please move those boxes over here*). It may, in addition, be used as a tool to establish social contact (*Hello, this is the Internal Revenue Service office calling*), or to fill awkward silences once social contact has been made (most conversations about the weather fill this category).

The fact that language is purposive behavior leads us to note a general characteristic of language: that we must deal with purpose and that we must distinguish between the purpose and the means used to achieve this purpose (form). We can then say that the communication of meaning is the purpose, and this can be distinguished from the sequence of sounds used to communicate the meaning (that is, to achieve the purpose). The sounds (and the grammatical patterns) used to communicate meanings may be called *form*. So, in the description of language, linguists must distinguish between the *form* of language and the *meaning* communicated by the form.

But this distinction may be overdrawn. If linguists start to describe *only* the form of a language, they find suddenly that they are describing differences in form (differences in sounds, for example) which never correlate with differences in meaning in the language. Similarly, if they attempt to describe meaning independent of the form which expresses it, they may find themselves discussing metaphysical questions which have no answer (or whose answer is essentially irrelevant to the linguist).

Tagmemic theory holds that form cannot be discussed independent of meaning, nor can meaning be discussed independent of form. Clearly tagmemicists can focus on one aspect or the other, but as they discuss meaning they must also keep their eye on its formal expression, and as they discuss form they must also keep their eye on the meanings it may express. In other words, tagmemicists always deal with form-meaning composites. Each form-meaning composite may be regarded as a *unit* of language.

The Description of Units: Contrast, Variation, and Distribution

In order to describe a unit completely, we must describe it from three points of view: 1) what it contrasts with (what other similar units it is different from), 2) what its range of variation is (how many different physical objects may be called variants of the same unit and the range of difference), and 3) what the range of distribution of the unit is (i.e., where it may occur and where it may not occur).

Let me illustrate the description of a unit by describing a unit from the sound system of a language. A basic unit of the sound system of language is the phoneme. The English phoneme /k/ in *kill, coal, school, skill*, etc., for example, is distinct from all other sounds in the English language. During the pronunciation of /k/ the air stream is stopped. This keeps /k/ distinct from sounds such as vowels and fricatives (the first sounds in *sink, then*, and *fee* are fricatives) since the air stream is not stopped during the pronunciation of these sounds. During the pronunciation of /k/ the back of the tongue touches the roof of the mouth. This distinguishes /k/ from all sounds made at other points in the mouth, e.g., /p/, /b/, /m/, /t/, and /d/ (which involve either the lower lip touching the upper lip, or the tongue tip touching the ridge just behind the upper teeth). Once we have shown what sounds /k/ differs from and we have described the features which distinguish /k/ from these other sounds, our next task is to show the range of variants which may realize /k/. If you compare the position of the tongue as you say the words *kill* and *skill* with the position of the tongue as you say the words *cool* and *school*, you will find that the two positions are different. The tongue is farther back in the mouth for the production of the /k/'s in *school* and *cool* than it is for the production of the /k/'s in *kill* and *skill*. The difference between these /k/'s may be symbolized by writing a diacritic (.) underneath the ones made with the tongue farther back (*cool* and *school*) (ḳ), and no diacritic under the ones made with the tongue farther forward (*skill* and *kill*) (k).

Our last task in the description of /k/ is to give its distribution. There are two aspects of the distribution of a unit which must be described: 1) we must describe its distribution in higher units (such as syllables), and 2) we must describe its distribution with relation to other units of the same type (phonemes, in this case). The description of the distribution of /k/ in larger units would include statements such as: "Within a syllable, /k/ may occur either before the vowel (*kill*) or after the vowel (*Jack*)." (Compare this with /h/ which may only occur before the vowel of its syllable.) The description of the distribution of /k/ with relation to other units of the same type includes statements such as: "When /k/ precedes the vowel of its syllable, it itself may be preceded only by /s/ (*school* /skul/) and it may be followed only by /y/, /r/, /w/, /l/ (*skew* /skyu/, *scream* /skrim/, *squeal* /skwil/, and *clean* /klin/)." A systematic description of the distribution of /k/ and a comparison of its distribution with that of the other phonemes (sounds) of English would show that no other English phoneme has exactly the same distribution.

Particle, Wave, and Field

The description of units in language takes as its fundamental assumption the idea that the stream of speech consists of recurring bits and pieces, each self-contained and fully interpretable by itself. In this view of language, language is something like a brick wall. The wall itself is an entity, yet it is composed of a set of fully discrete and independent bricks. We can tell, for instance, where one brick stops and the next begins. This view of language we can call the *particle view*. It is useful to explain certain phenomena, but a number of aspects of language cannot be explained by such a view. For example, the stream of speech is not composed of a succession of disconnected sounds. The tongue must move from one position to another; as a result one sound flows into another with no sharp break between. Thus in the word *yes*, we can tell that it begins with a "y" sound and that soon after there is an "e" sound, but it is impossible to tell where the "y" stops and the vowel begins. Similarly, in the word *betty*, we know that there are two syllables, but it is impossible to point out a clear break between the two. The "t" sound in *betty* belongs *both* to the first syllable *and* to the second syllable of the word. In effect, what we are dealing with here is the overlapping of sound units because they occur in close sequence.

This phenomenon is not limited to the realm of sounds, however. Even in grammar we find units overlapping in analogous ways. Take for example the clause *John persuaded Mary to eat her rice pudding*. This is a complex clause in that it contains two verbs. *John* is obviously the subject of *persuade*, and *rice pudding* is obviously the object of *eat*. The role *Mary* plays within the clause is more difficult to describe. On the one hand, *Mary* is the object of *persuade* since it is moved when we make the clause passive (*Mary was persuaded to eat her rice pudding*) and it may be moved with other types of transformations (e.g., *The one whom John persuaded to eat her rice pudding was Mary*). But, on the other hand, *Mary* is the subject of *eat*. In a sense, then, *John persuaded Mary to eat her rice pudding* is really two clauses which happen to overlap, and in overlapping share a word between them.

The view of language which we have just illustrated may be called a *wave view* of language. In this view, the units of language are likened to waves on a lake. One can count the waves as they hit the beach, but it is impossible to tell where one wave stops and the next one begins. This view of language is useful when explaining the effect one unit has on the form of other units which occur in its environment.

The third view of language tagmemicists find necessary in describing languages may be called a *field view*. This view focuses on the role a unit plays within a system of contrasts. From this point of view units do not exist in and of themselves. Instead they play a role within a system.

We have already talked about the fact that units must be described from the standpoint of what they contrast with in order to be well defined. What we are now saying is an addition to that. Each unit takes a place within a well defined system of oppositions and thus one could say that the system defines the unit. Let us return to our description of the sound /k/.

Our description of how /k/ contrasts with all the other sounds of English did not present the sound system of English in the most effective way. In fact, it would have been difficult to present the sound system clearly since the focus at that time was on /k/ as a unit. If we were to focus away from the description of the individual sound and on the description of the sound system of English, we would show the various parameters by which sounds may vary in English; for example, the consonants of English may be voiced or voiceless, stops, fricatives, nasals, laterals, or semivowels; and they may have any one of five points of articulation: labial, dental, alveolar, alveopalatal, velar, or glottal. By shifting our focus from the individual sounds (e.g., /k/) to the various parameters of the system (e.g., voicing or point of articulation), we have now gained the ability to describe the system without losing sight of the individual parts of the system. The system is described by showing the various parameters and the general way they may intersect, while the units (in this case the individual sounds) are described as the points at which the various parameters intersect.

This situation may be easily shown with an n-dimensional chart. Tagmemicists call such charts *matrices*. Each dimension represents an independent parameter, and each cell on the chart represents a unit (or potential unit, since no language system is completely symmetrical). The consonant system of English may be represented by such a matrix as follows:

A Matrix Showing the Consonant System of English

	Labial		Dental	Alveolar	Alveo-palatal	Velar	Glottal
Stop	vl	p		t	č	k	
	vd	b		d	j	g	
Fricative	vl	f	θ	s	š		h
	vd	v	ð	z	ž		
Nasal	vd	m		n		ŋ	
Lateral	vd			l			
Semivowel	vd			r	y	w	

It should be apparent from the preceding discussion that the field view of language just presented and the particle view presented first are intimately related. Linguists are only interested in particles (units) which play a role in some system. But systems cannot exist apart from the particles (units) which form the system.

Hierarchy

So far we have talked about the units of a language as if they were all of approximately the same type. In fact, this is not true. We cannot regard the structure of a language merely as a series of sounds or words strung together like beads on a string. Instead we must talk about different sized units. In the sound system of a language, for example, one can find individual sounds such as /p/, /t/, /k/, /i/, and /u/, but one can also find syllables which are patterns of sequences of sounds. The word *betty* contains two syllables, for example, while *related* contains three and *cooperate* contains four. Sequences of syllables, however, are also patterned. Each of the examples above contained one syllable which was clearly louder and more prominent than the rest. These words, then, are examples of one stress group. (To show that a stress group is not always identical to a word, we need only cite an example of a single stress group which contains more than one word, e.g., *the word.*) A larger unit of the sound system may be the breath group (that portion of speech we say between breaths). We can call the units of the sound system of a language the *phonological hierarchy*, since it consists of sets of units of the sound system on different levels.

But the phonological hierarchy is not the only hierarchy. There is a *lexical hierarchy*, which consists of words and sequences of words, and a *grammatical hierarchy*, which consists of grammatical patterns of different sizes, e.g., word, phrase, clause, sentence, paragraph, and discourse. Each of these three hierarchies is independent (we do not have to know what a word means or know whether it is a noun in order to say what sounds it contains), but, on the other hand, the three hierarchies are interrelated in many complex ways. In addition, each of these hierarchies is open-ended. There is no largest unit. This is a direct consequence of the requirement that the distribution of each unit be described. If we say that we have not completely described /k/ until we describe where it occurs within the syllable, we have linked the description of /k/ to the description of a larger unit, in this case the syllable. But the same may be said about syllables. No syllable has been completely described until we describe its distribution within stress groups. Thus the description of any unit implies the existence of some larger unit which may include the first unit.

Perhaps a better understanding of the notion of hierarchy may be given if we examine some of the evidence for its existence. The best evidence comes from the grammatical hierarchy. One type of evidence is supplied by certain ambiguous constructions; for example, the phrase "an electric knife sharpener." The ambiguity arises because the phrase may be grouped in more than one way. That is, we do not know whether an electric knife sharpener is a sharpener of electric knives, or an electric sharpener of any old kind of knife. The implication of what has just been said is that the example given above is not just *one* construction, but *two* constructions. The two constructions differ from each other in that one has one grouping and the second has a different grouping. The differences in grouping may be shown by means of a diagram called a *tree*. The example then may be divided into two constructions: 1a) which may be paraphrased as "a sharpener of electric knives," and 1b) which may be paraphrased as "an electric sharpener of knives."

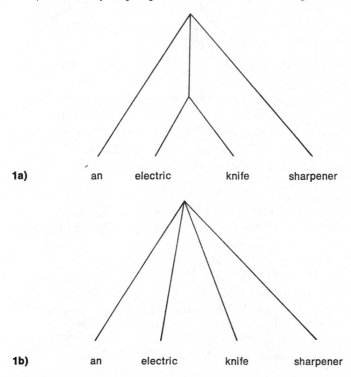

1a)   an   electric   knife   sharpener

1b)   an   electric   knife   sharpener

In such a diagram, each place where two or more lines intersect represents a group. Similarly, an end-point of a line (above a word) represents a group. Thus a comparison of the two diagrams shows that 1a) contains one more group than 1b).

The discussion of these constructions should make it obvious that in order to account for the type of ambiguity shown here, we *must* talk about a hierarchy of grouping within sentences and phrases. A further point needs to be made here and that is that even in unambiguous examples we must describe the groupings. The clause *The very old man will be walking out the door* contains, for example, the subgroups *the very old man, will be walking, out the door, the door, door, out*, etc. Again, the groupings involved in this example may be shown by means of the following tree diagram:

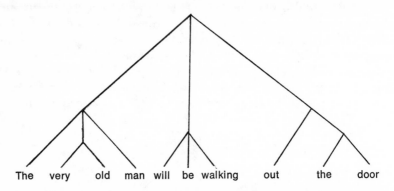

The   very   old   man will be walking   out   the   door

The notion of hierarchy is not merely one of different sizes of groupings within a construction, however. In fact, a primary reason for the use of hierarchy (in tagmemic theory) lies in the attempt to compare and relate the various constructions possible in English. That is to say, tagmemicists are interested in describing all the possible constructions of English within a framework which would make explicit the similarities and differences each construction has with every other construction. Tagmemicists are therefore interested in specific examples only in so far as they relate to the system of the language being described (in this case English). One help in comparing sentences would be to develop a vocabulary to describe the various parts of a sentence. From this point of view, we can say that groups such as *door* and *man* are nouns, *the very old man* and *the door* are noun phrases, *very old* is an adjective phrase, *will be walking* is a verb phrase, *out the door* is a prepositional phrase, and the whole construction *the very old man will be walking out the door* is an intransitive clause.

Such labeling enables us to compare clauses such as

1) *He will be walking out the door*
2) *Mary will be walking out the door*
3) *The girl will be walking out the door*

with the original clause given. 1) differs from the original example in that it begins with a pronoun instead of a noun phrase; 2) differs in that it begins with a personal name instead of a noun phrase; while 3) differs from the original in the degree of expansion within the noun phrase. Both *the girl* and *the very old man* are noun phrases, but *the very old man* contains an adjective phrase (*very old*) which *the girl* does not contain.

While labeling the groups which form the various parts of a construction helps us to compare constructions, this is not enough. We need to describe more than just the groupings a construction is divided into because it is possible to find constructions which are identical in groupings, yet are still ambiguous, e.g., *John was hit by the barrel*. This clause may be interpreted as telling either where John was hit, or what hit John. It should be emphasized that the groupings and the labels given to each group are the same for the two interpretations.

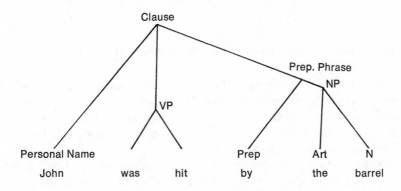

The example is ambiguous because the phrase *by the barrel* may function in two ways. In the first interpretation, it modifies the action of the clause by specifying the location of the action. In the second interpretation, *by the barrel* specifies the performer of the action. In other words, in order to describe a construction we must describe the groupings into which it is divided, we must label these groupings, and we must also describe the functions each one of these groupings plays within that particular construction. Thus a more complete grammatical description of the first example could be given in the form of the following tree. The labels at the end-points of the lines indicate labels of groups, while the labels along the lines describe the functions these groups play.

Notice that the overt mention of functional relations gives us a powerful tool for the comparison of constructions. We were implicitly using function before when we compared the clauses:

   o) *The very old man will be walking out the door*
   1) *He will be walking out the door*
   2) *Mary will be walking out the door*
   3) *The girl will be walking out the door*

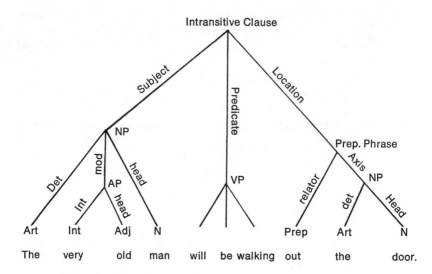

Notice that we only changed the construction which filled the role of subject (that is, we were holding the function constant). In other words, we can say that the four clauses given here are all examples of the same basic clause type. The functions of the various subgroups of the clauses remained the same.

Since we are really interested in the structure of the English language, not these specific examples, we must be interested in the potential clauses of this type. We must ask "What is the range of constructions available to the speaker of English?" A partial answer to this question would be to say the clause type exemplified above has three functions: subject, predicate, and location modifier. The subject could be a noun phrase (examples o and 3), it could be a pronoun (example 1), or it could be a personal name (example 2). The predicate may be filled by a verb phrase, and the location modifier may be filled by a prepositional phrase (*out the door*), a location pronoun (*there*), a location noun (*home*), or an independent relative clause (*wherever he usually walks*). This description has listed each grammatical function and the set of constructions which can play that function.

The correlation of a grammatical function with the set of units which may play that function is called a *tagmeme*.[2] Tagmemicists believe that it is essential to overtly describe both the grammatical functions and the set of units which may fill the functions. In other words,

---

[2] In much of the literature by tagmemicists and about tagmemics, one finds the term *slot* used instead of *grammatical function*. I have avoided using *slot* because for many people it has the connotation of being closely related to physical order. *Grammatical function* has no such connotations.

in our description of the potential intransitive clauses of English we have described three clause level tagmemes.

The description above still does not exhaust the range of clauses of this type, however. For one thing, it is not necessary to have a location modifier. *The very old man will be walking* is a grammatical sentence even without the phrase *out the door*. Similarly, we could have a time modifier added to the original example (*The very old man will be walking out the door next week*) or a manner modifier (*The very old man will be walking out the door in a hurry next week*). Notice that the time, location, and manner modifier tagmemes differ from the subject and the predicate tagmemes in that the subject and predicate tagmemes must occur in order to have a grammatical clause. If we omit them, an ungrammatical sequence results: **will be walking out the door* (no subject), **the very old man out the door* (no predicate). As a result, in the description of the potential clauses of English we must indicate whether a given function is obligatory (it must occur in order to have a grammatical clause) or optional (it may or may not occur, both situations result in a grammatical clause). We can summarize the information given above with the following formula:

Intransitive Clause = + Subject: Noun Phrase   + Predicate: Verb Phrase
                              Pronoun
                              Personal Name

± Location: Prep. Phrase$_{Loc.}$ ± Manner: Prep. Phrase$_{Ma.}$
            Location Noun
            Location Pronoun
            Indep. Rel. Clause

± Time: Prep. Phrase$_{Ti}$
        Time Noun
        Time Pronoun
        Time indep.
        rel.   clause

This formula describes a pattern which all English intransitive clauses fit. This pattern is a unit of the grammatical system of English. It is typical of the units of grammatical systems in that it is a pattern, not a specific sequence of particular words. Tagmemicists call such units *syntagmemes*. Like any other unit of language, syntagmemes must be described from the standpoints of contrast, variation, and distribution. The formula describes the variants which are considered examples of intransitive clauses in English by showing the various units which may fill each tagmeme and by showing which tagmemes may be omitted. The distribution of each syntagmeme is described implicitly by a complete grammar because the set of units which fill each tagmeme is specified overtly. The contrastive features of the syntagmeme may be described by placing the syntagmeme within a field of similar but contrasting syntagmemes. The intransitive clause described above may be placed within the system of contrasting English clauses:

A Matrix Illustrating Clause Level Contrasts
(only the obligatory constituents of the
clause syntagmemes have been included).

	declarative	*yes-no question*	*imperative*
intransitive	John came. +S+P	Did John come +Q+S+P	Come! +P
single transitive	John saw Bill. +S+P+O	Did John see Bill +Q+S+P+O	See Bill! +P+O
double transitive	John gave Bill a book. +S+P+IO+O	Did John give Bill a book +Q+S+P+IO+O	Give Bill a book! +P+IO+O
equative	John will be the center +S+P+Comp	Will John be the center +Q+S+P+Comp	Be the center! +P+Comp

The chart given above is no more than illustrative of the type of contrasts which occur on the clause level. It should be extended to include all the different clause syntagmemes of English. But once that has been done, we have a definition of the notion clause in English, and we can contrast this notion with other similar notions, such as phrase, sentence, and word. These concepts can be called *levels*, since they each are systems of contrasting syntagmemes. The set of levels of grammatical syntagmemes which a language contains is the grammatical hierarchy of that language.

Conclusion

The basic characteristics of tagmemics, then, may be summarized under the following five points: 1) Tagmemicists consider language to be part of human behavior and they attempt to describe language within a general behavioral framework. 2) Tagmemicists attempt to describe the language potential (what are the possible constructions of the language being described?). 3) Tagmemicists are interested in units and they insist that each unit has a formal manifestation and a meaning. To be well defined, each unit must be described from the standpoints of contrast, variation, and distribution. 4) Tagmemicists describe language in terms of three independent hierarchies—phonological, grammatical, and lexical—and they believe that each of these hierarchies is open-ended (that is, that there is no largest unit). Thus, a level within the grammatical hierarchy such as the sentence takes its place as merely one of the levels of that hierarchy and has no exceptional primary status assigned to it. 5) Within the grammatical hierarchy the grammatical units (syntagmemes) are described with respect to their makeup in terms of tagmemes. Each tagmeme is a correlation between a grammatical function and a set of units which may fill that function. Both the function and the set must be overtly described.

Prospect

As has been shown in the preceding sections, tagmemic grammars attempt to describe the potential constructions of the language being described. But so far the discussion has dealt only with the form these constructions might take: we have not discussed the meanings they might have. Much of the current work in tagmemics deals with the semantic interpretation of syntactic constructions. A number of factors enter into the semantic interpretation of a construction. The most obvious factor is the meaning of the words which make up the construction. In addition to meanings of words, however, the words interact in such a way as to signal relationships between the participants in the action. Thus, the meaning of a clause such as *The man will build a chair* includes, in addition to the meanings of the individual words, relationships such as performer of the action (*the man* in the example above) and result of the action (*a chair* in the example above). The semantic relations we have mentioned here are different from but related to the grammatical functions (such as subject and object) that we discussed in the last section. The grammatical subject, for example, may express any one of the following relations:

a) Performer of the action .... *John hit Mary with a bat.*
b) Instrument .... *The bat hit Mary.*
c) Undergoer of the action .... *Mary was hit with a bat by John.*

Not only may one grammatical function correlate with more than one semantic relationship, one semantic relationship may correlate with more than one grammatical function. The semantic relationship, performer of the action, may correlate with the following grammatical functions:

a) Subject of a clause .... *The emperor controlled trade.*
b) Determiner in a Noun Phrase .... *The emperor's control of trade.*
c) Modifier in a Noun Phrase .... *Imperial control of trade.*

As can be seen from these examples, the relation between grammatical units and their semantic interpretations is quite complex. In fact, it is only recently that these relations have been dealt with carefully at all by linguists. As a result, it is difficult to report much concrete progress in showing how the grammatical constructions of a language are linked to their semantic interpretations. Much of the current research (and hence the most interesting arguments) in linguistic theory can be described as attempts either to define semantic structure or to explain the relation betwen semantics and grammar. The next ten years will be a time of great advances in this realm of endeavour. Since tagemicists have worked fairly extensively on the description of several hundred languages, they will be able to contribute to the general trend toward semantics. Because of the current advances in semantics, linguistics will become more useful to other disciplines—for example, literary criticism and language teaching—since the more we can say about meaning and its expression in language, the better a tool linguistics will be to scholars interested in such areas.

Bibliography

Brend, Ruth M. "Tagmemic Theory: An Annotated Bibliography." *Journal of English Linguistics.* Vol. 4 (1970), 7–45.
————. "Tagmemic Theory: An Annotated Bibliography," Appendix I. *Journal of English Linguistics.* Vol. 6 (forthcoming).
Longacre, R. E. *Grammar Discovery Procedures.* The Hague: Mouton and Co., 1964.
Pike, K. L. "A Guide to Publications Related to Tagmemic Theory." *Current Trends in Linguistics.* Vol. 3 (1966), 365–94.
————. *Language in Relation to a Unified Theory of the Structure of Human Behavior.* The Hague: Mouton and Co., 1967.
Wares, Alan. *Bibliography of the Summer Institute of Linguistics, 1935–1968.* Santa Ana, Calif.: Summer Institute of Linguistics, 1968.

FOR DISCUSSION AND REVIEW

1   What does Fries consider the most important distinguishing characteristic of tagmemics?

2   What does Fries mean by the terms *form* and *meaning*? How does the tagmemicist feel they are related?

3   The tagmemicist argues that we must look at language from several points of view. Explain what Fries means by a *particle view* of language, a *wave view*, and a *field view*.

4   Explain *phonological hierarchy*, *lexical hierarchy*, and *grammatical hierarchy*. What importance does tagmemic theory attach to the notion of hierarchy?

5   Fries uses the English phoneme /k/ to illustrate the principles of contrast, variation, and distribution. Develop a similar description of another unit (e.g., the English phoneme /p/ or the English morpheme {un-}).

6   Fries discusses the ambiguous construction *an electric knife sharpener.* How would you analyze the following: *the old lady's hat; modern language teaching; they tore up the street?*

9
The Problem
of Describing
Syntactic
Complexity

"Our flourishing linguistic tree"—
a metaphor used by Sven Jacobson
in this article to describe the current situation in language study—
does by now have many different
branches. Some of them are no
longer really flourishing, while other,
newer branches are growing vigorously. There are many articles dealing with one or even two of these
branches, but Jacobson's discussion
is unusual: he compares the way in
which all four of the systems of
grammatical analysis included in
this section—structural, transformational generative, stratificational,
and tagmemic—would describe the
same two-sentence sequence.

Sven Jacobson

O NE OF THE most complex of human activities is linguistic performance. All over the world scholars and scientists who have set themselves the task of describing language in its many different aspects are
grappling with a number of intricate questions. One such problem is
the relationship between function and form,[1] which is one of the major
topics of syntax.

From my own schooldays I remember how in parsing exercises we
were asked to analyse a sentence simultaneously from two different
viewpoints: the part of speech (= the form class) was to be written
under each word and the part of the sentence (= the function class)
over each word or word-group. We were told always to keep the two
types of analysis strictly apart and not to mix them. Such mixing is,
however, not uncommon in some grammatical literature; one example
is the well-known formula S V O (subject-verb-object).

Anyone who undertakes to analyse language in a really scientific way
will soon find that the simple parsing technique that we were taught

---

[1] By "form" I mean not only the occurrence of bound morphemes, such as plural
endings, but also the presence of structure words, such as articles, and the order
in which the various elements occur in the sentence.

at school is not sufficient. For example, some words and word-groups can have several functions simultaneously, and elements that belong together functionally are often discontinuous in the sentence, so that one requires some special system of indicating their relationship. Also, in a discourse the various sentences can be described as links in a chain which are dependent on each other, so that full understanding of each separate sentence is usually achieved only by reference to what precedes or follows. A great deal of time and effort has been spent by linguists on the problem of how to achieve a grammatical description that accounts for these and other syntactic complexities, while at the same time satisfying the highest requirements as to brevity, accuracy and clarity. Some schools of linguists have tried to reach this goal by evolving systems in which ordinary explanations in words are supplemented with graphic or algebraic notation or even both these devices in combination. It has been objected that as a result their descriptions have often become totally inaccessible to the untutored public and thus hardly satisfy the demand for clarity. To this one might answer that clarity does not necessarily mean "simple and easy for the beginner." Moreover, one may wonder, as Sydney Lamb does,[2] how far, for instance, physics and chemistry or even a fine art like music would have advanced if scientists and composers had been dissuaded from using notational devices that require special study before they are understood.

In this article I propose to concentrate on one single example and demonstrate how it might be described syntactically by different linguistic schools. The example has been specially chosen because of its intricate syntactic relationships and runs as follows:

People moved to the cities. Especially was this the case in England.[3]

No doubt the attention of most readers will be focused on the adverb *especially*, which here fulfills a threefold function (cf. Jacobson 1964, p. 49):

(*a*) it is conjunctive, i.e. it links the two sentences together (the nature of the linking is described below under (*c*));

(*b*) it modifies the sentence it introduces; in fact its sentence modification is so strong that it is followed by the same kind of inverted word-order that we find in interrogative sentences;

(*c*) it directs our attention to the prepositional phrase *in England*, with which it may be said to form a split structure; this structure, in its turn, can be said to be a discontinuous modifier of the verb-phrase

[2] Lamb 1966, p. 8.
[3] The two sentences of this example may be assumed to form part of an account of the social upheaval caused in Europe by the Industrial Revolution. For two similar (but longer) examples excerpted from British books, see Jacobson 1964, pp. 47 and 49.

of the first sentence; if we put the three discontinuous constituents together, we get one long verb-phrase: *moved to the cities especially in England.*

Undoubtedly it is of great interest to see how different grammatical systems might tackle the problem of describing these three functions of *especially* within the general framework of a syntactic description of the two-sentence example in which it occurs. For this purpose I shall choose the following four types of grammatical approach:

(*a*) Immediate-constituent (IC) analysis.
(*b*) Tagmemics.
(*c*) Transformational grammar.
(*d*) Stratificational grammar.

Immediate-Constituent Analysis

Leonard Bloomfield, in his epoch-making book *Language* (1933), introduced the notion of levels of structure and said that at each level there are as a rule two immediate constituents. During the 1940's immediate-constituent analysis was further developed, especially by Rulon Wells, C. C. Fries, and W. Nelson Francis.[4]

The binary cuts made at each level of structure have frequently been rendered graphically. One of the major problems encountered here has, however, been the denotation of discontinuous constituents. W. Nelson Francis' solution is to use "Chinese boxes," some of which are so shaped as to depict the nature of such constituents. Fig. 1 shows Francis' diagram of a sentence with IC's A and B, where A is split into two parts by B, as in, for instance, *do you swim* (see Francis 1958, p. 295).

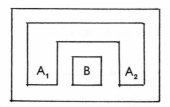

Fig. 1. Discontinuous constituents.

In immediate-constituent analysis each pair of IC's is taken to form a structure, the type of which may be indicated by means of various symbols or other devices. In the system used by Francis (1958, pp. 294–96) an arrow denotes modification, a P predication (i.e. subject-predi-

---

[4] See Wells 1947, Fries 1952, and Francis 1958.

cate relationship), and a C complementation. Prepositions are attached in a small box directly to their objects. On the basis of Francis' system the example chosen for this article may be rendered as in Fig. 2. In order to complete the description, I have added a dotted line to show the special referential, i.e. attention-directing, relationship between *especially* and *in England* (cf. Jacobson 1964, p. 42). Similarly, a broken line denotes the conjunctive function of *especially* by linking this adverb to the constituent *moved to the cities*. Another broken line indicates that the demonstrative pronoun *this* points back to the whole previous sentence.

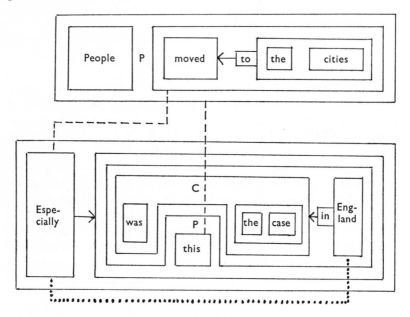

Fig. 2. Immediate-constituent analysis of the two sentences.

Tagmemics

The linguistic approach that is termed tagmemics was originated by Kenneth L. Pike, who in 1954 began the publication of his three-volume work *Language in relation to a unified theory of the structure of human behavior.* As his basic term Pike first used the word grameme but later changed it to tagmeme. Recently he has published a comprehensive list of contributors to tagmemic theory (see Pike 1966). The best popularizers of this theory are probably Benjamin Elson and Velma Pickett. In their book *An Introduction to Morphology and Syntax,* p. 57, they define a tagmeme as "a grammatical unit which is the correlation of a grammatical function or slot with a class of mutually substitutable items occurring in that slot." H. A. Gleason, Jr., in *Linguistics and English Grammar*, p. 140, characterizes tagmemic analysis as "a slot-and-filler technique combined with certain characteristic views of the general nature of language systems." Tagmemicists do not use diagrams but have instead evolved a rather complex algebraic notational system. Thus the slot and the filler of a tagmeme are symbolized by letters and separated by a colon, and tagmemes which are obligatory in a construction are preceded by + and those which are optional by ±. Tagmemes and the constructions into which they enter may be identified and described at several different levels.

With the use of tagmemic technique the previous two-sentence example may be analysed as follows.

(*a*) *Discourse level.*[5] At this level each of the two sentences [plus the function it fills] constitutes one tagmeme denoted in the following way:

+Base:Ind Sent±Sequence:Seq Sent.

The first sentence (*People moved to the cities*) forms a base consisting of an independent sentence, to which the second sentence (*Especially was this the case in England*) is added as an optional sequence consisting of a sequence sentence.

(*b*) *Sentence level.* For the sake of brevity I shall concentrate on the second sentence, which may be analysed as follows:

±C:padv+Base:eCl.

The first tagmeme consists of a connector slot (C) filled by a particularizing adverb (padv). After thus accounting for *especially*, I have denoted the rest of the sentence as a base slot filled by an equational clause (eCl), i.e. one containing a copula followed by a nounal complement. At the sentence level a symbol denoting the type of intonation may be added. A functional feature that seems impossible to account for, at this or any other level, is the connective nature of *this*.

(*c*) *Clause level.* Here I again analyse the second sentence, though this time I regard *especially* not as a connector but as a manner tagmeme, whose slot (Ma) is filled by a manner adverb (madv):

±MA:madv+eP:cn+S:dpr+L:l.
|_____±_____|

The second tagmeme consists of an equational predicate slot (eP) filled by a copula followed by a noun (cn), the third of a subject slot (S) filled by a demonstrative pronoun (dpr), and the fourth by a location slot (L) filled by a locative phrase (l). The line marked ± and tying the ± of the first tagmeme to the + of the fourth tagmeme

[5] Discourse is here used in the sense "connected speech or writing." Cf. Harris 1952, p. 18.

means that both these tagmemes are optional, with the reservation that the first tagmeme does not occur without the fourth. This line thus serves the purpose of indicating that a special relationship exists between *especially* and *in England*. Alternatively, we may drop the first tagmeme and regard *especially . . . in England* as a discontinuous allotagma of the L:1 tagmeme (for further analysis, see (*d*)). The inverted word-order of the clause is not indicated in the tagmemic analysis; it is simply regarded as an inverted allotagma of the eP:cn tagmeme. This word-order is here not emic, i.e. it is not distinctive in the way it is when it turns a declarative clause into an interrogative one.

(*d*) *Phrase level.* At this level I shall only analyse the discontinuous allotagma *especially . . . in England*, mentioned above:

±Ad:padv+R:prep+A:np.

The slot of the first tagmeme is an attention-director (Ad) filled by a particularizing adverb (padv), that of the second a relater (R) filled by a preposition (prep), and that of the third an axis (A) filled by a proper noun (np).

Transformational Grammar

The more accurate term for what is usually called "transformational grammar" is "transformational generative grammar." This grammatical approach came into prominence in 1957 when Noam Chomsky published his little book *Syntactic Structures*. Since then an enormous amount of work has been done not only in the form of applying transformational rules to more and more aspects of linguistics, such as semantics,[6] phonology,[7] and stylistics,[8] but also in the form of popularizing the basic rules for use in schools.[9] Whereas immediate-constituent analysis and tagmemics mainly describe the *state* of linguistic forms and relations as they appear in the surface structure, i.e. the actual spoken or written language, transformational grammar principally describes the *transition* from deep structure to surface structure. The deep structure of a sentence is considered as being composed of the underlying abstract forms and relations which constitute its semantic basis. This dynamic technique has a strong explanatory power. For example, it accounts in a very clear way for ambiguities like *the shooting of the soldiers*, and explains the difference between such ostensibly similar constructions as *John is easy to please* and *John is eager to please*.

Unfortunately, as far as the theme of this article is concerned, the point of departure in transformational grammar has been the sentence, and very little research has so far been devoted to analysing relations

[6] See, for instance, Katz and Fodor 1963 and Abraham and Kiefer 1966.
[7] See, for instance, Halle 1963.
[8] See, for instance, Ohmann 1964.
[9] See, for instance, Roberts 1964 and Thomas 1966.

at the discourse level. The following description of how the two inter-related sentences included in the example may be generated can there-fore only be tentative.

For the purpose of a treatment of inter-sentence relations it seems suitable to recognize three types of sentences: independent sentences, embedded sentences (= subordinate clauses) and sequence sentences. Any discourse contains at least one independent sentence, which may be followed by an infinite number of sequence sentences. To the ordi-nary formula for sentence generation ($S \rightarrow NP + VP$) should therefore be added an optional symbol Seq.

We now turn to the generation of the two sentences. This may be performed as follows:

1. THE FIRST SENTENCE (S_1)

Phrase-structure rules

$S_1 \rightarrow NP+VP+Seq$
$NP \rightarrow Det+N+Pl$
$Det \rightarrow \begin{Bmatrix} \varnothing \\ the \end{Bmatrix}$
$Pl \rightarrow \begin{Bmatrix} \varnothing \\ -es \end{Bmatrix}$
$VP \rightarrow Aux+MV$
$Aux \rightarrow Past$
$MV \rightarrow V_i+Dir$
$Dir \rightarrow Prep+NP$
$Seq \rightarrow S_2$

Abbreviations

NP = noun phrase
VP = verb phrase
Det = determiner
Pl = plural
$\varnothing$ = zero
Aux = auxiliary
MV = main verb
V_i = intransitive verb
Dir = adverbial of direction
Seq = sequence sentence

Lexicon (in simplified form):

N: people, city
V_i: move
Prep: to

By successively applying the phrase-structure rules and then inserting words from the lexicon, we get the terminal string

People+*Past*+move+to+the+city+-es.

After applying first an obligatory transformation that shifts *Past* to the position after *move* and then morphophonemic (or, in the case of the written language, morphographemic) rules, we finally get as a result the surface structure *People moved to the cities*.

2. THE SECOND SENTENCE (S_2)

This sentence is based on the previous sentence and may be said to have the following semantic content: "That people moved to the cities was the case in a special degree (and manner) in England." We must therefore use rules that generate a deep structure containing this information.

Phrase-structure rules	*Abbreviations (except those given above)*
$S_2 \rightarrow NP+VP$	Sg = singular
$NP \rightarrow Det+N+Sg(S)$[10]	Art = article
$Det \rightarrow \begin{Bmatrix} Art \\ Dem \end{Bmatrix}$	Dem = demonstrative
	Loc = locative
	$Pred$ = predicative
$Art \rightarrow \begin{Bmatrix} a(n) \\ the \\ \emptyset \end{Bmatrix}$	Dg/Ma = adverbial whose meaning is a mixture of degree and manner
$Dem \rightarrow this$	
$Sg \rightarrow \emptyset$	$Morph$ = special morpheme(s)
$VP \rightarrow Aux+MV+Loc$	-ly = adverb morpheme
$Aux \rightarrow Past$	$Emph$ = emphasis morpheme
$MV \rightarrow Be+Pred+Dg/Ma$	PRO_{Ni} = a deletable indefinite noun that may be translated by
$Pred \rightarrow NP$	"thing" or "circumstance."
$Dg/Ma \rightarrow Prep+NP+Morph$	See Thomas 1966, p. 87.
$Morph \rightarrow -ly+Emph$	Ni stands for "noun inanimate."
$Loc \rightarrow Prep+NP$	

Lexicon

N: PRO_{Ni}, case, degree/manner, England

Prep: in

In the derivation of the terminal string the optional symbol S listed in the rewriting of NP will be used twice, first to re-introduce S_1 and then to embed S_3, which will be a relative clause whose generation I will not deal with here. Suffice it to say that it gives this terminal string:

wh+degree/manner+*Past*+be+especial.

The terminal string of the whole of S_2, with S_1 and S_3 embedded, will be as follows:

This+PRO_{Ni}+People+*Past*+move+to+the+city+-es+*Past*+be+the+case+in+a+degree/manner+wh+degree/manner+*Past*+be+especial+-ly+Emph+in+England

This may be read in plain English as "This circumstance that people moved to the cities was the case in a degree (and manner) which was special in England."

Various transformations will now be applied to the terminal string. Among these may be. mentioned the deletion of PRO_{Ni} and the repeated S_1, so that all that remains of the first NP is the word *this*.

---

[10] Note that optional elements are placed within brackets and are not preceded by a plus sign.

Moreover, the degree/manner adverbial is followed by the adverb morpheme *-ly*, which transforms it into *especially*, and also an emphasis morpheme, which shifts it to the front and inverts the order of *this* and *Past+be*.

Figs. 3–5 show phrase-markers that graphically render the deep structure of the example. Similar tree diagrams can be drawn for the surface structure. Fig. 6 shows that of the second sentence. Here, because of the changed word-order, the derivational paths from Dg/Ma and Aux+be to S_2 no longer pass VP, as they do in the deep structure (see Fig. 4). This may seem a perfunctory way of accounting for discontinuities, but transformationalists argue that it is at the deep structure diagrams that one must look to see where the various elements really belong.

As appears from the rules and tree diagrams, transformational gram-

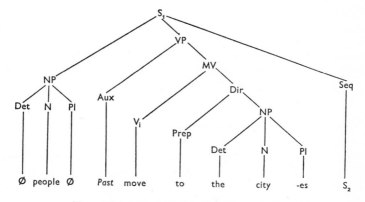

Fig 3. The deep structure of the first sentence.

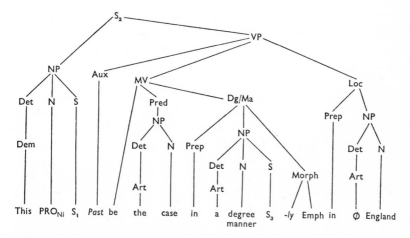

Fig. 4. The deep structure of the second sentence.

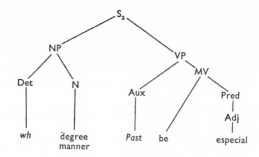

Fig. 5. The deep structure from which the adjectival
modifier *especial* is derived.

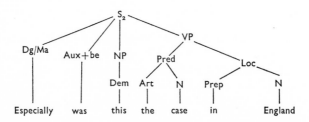

Fig. 6. The surface structure of the second sentence.

mar does not express syntactic functions by explicit symbols; they are
considered as inherent in the graphic subconfigurations of the deep
structure.[11] Figs. 3–5, which give the deep structure of the example,
fail, however, to indicate (*a*) that *especially* assumes a connective function when it is moved to the beginning of S_2 and (*b*) that there is a
special functional relationship between the elements *especially* and *in
England*. A possible solution might be to draw a special tree diagram
comprising these two elements (see Fig. 7) and attach it to the MV
node of the phrase-marker that shows the deep structure of S_1 (Fig. 3).
This phrase-marker would then represent the deep structure of the surface string *moved to the cities especially in England*. I have called this
addition to S_1 a function-phrase (FP) and suggest the introduction of
a rule that automatically deletes such a phrase in the transformational
process, as the elements of its terminal string also occur elsewhere. It
should be noted that in this function-phrase the node dominating what
later becomes *especially* is not called Dg/Ma but Att (= attention-
directer), which is specified as Part (= particularizer). A special morphophonemic rule should be introduced that gives the element that is

---

[11] See Chomsky 1965, pp. 68–74.

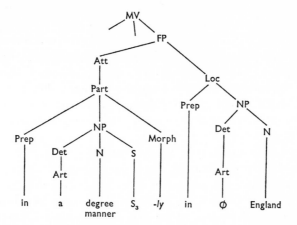

Fig. 7. Deep structure diagram showing the relationship between *especially* and *in England*.

configuratively combined with an attention-directer emphatic stress and intonation. If, as in the present case, this element occurs in a deletable function-phrase, then there should be a transformational rule to ensure that the emphatic stress and intonation are transferred to the same element in the undeleted counterpart.

The procedures of transformational grammar at first seem complicated, but they have the advantage of being algorithmic, i.e., they account for the generation of the surface structure in a mechanical way, so that a machine would be able to perform the operations necessary. And a machine does not mind performing a great number of operations whose products are simply deleted after they have served their purpose. To some extent such a process resembles the working of the human brain which, in a similar manner, performs a great number of tedious operations of which we, happily, are unaware, as our conscious minds simply concentrate on the result.

Stratificational Grammar

Stratificational grammar is one of the latest branches on our flourishing linguistic tree. Its main proponent is Sydney Lamb, who first published its basic tenets in an article entitled "MT (= machine translation) research at the University of California, Berkeley" in 1961. This article was followed by his *Outline of Stratificational Grammar*, which was published in a multilithed edition in 1962 and in a revised printed edition in 1966. Although H. A. Gleason, Jr., devotes the whole of his book *Linguistics and English Grammar* to other types of grammatical

approach, he says that his "own preference and conviction run to stratificational grammar" (p. vi).[12]

Stratificational grammar uses a graphic notation which resembles the
charts drawn by engineers to represent interconnections at, for instance,
an automatic telephone exchange. The main emphasis of this grammar
is on the relationships between linguistic elements. These relationships
can be analysed within several different strata, and it is not necessary
for the linguist to complete his analysis within one stratum before going
on to the next.

The graphic notation may be accompanied by an algebraic notation,
but this is considered subsidiary and is only used to describe the linguistic graphs. A graph is made up of lines branching off at nodes which
have the property of showing direction. The nodes are always turned
in the branching direction, which may be upwards, i.e. towards meaning, or downwards, i.e. towards expression. If two or more branching
lines touch each other when they converge at a node, they are unor-
dered; if, on the other hand, there is some space between them, they
operate from left to right.

The two concepts of meaning and expression correspond to the concepts of deep structure and surface structure in transformational grammar. Thus impulses are to be thought of as moving downwards in the
production process and upwards in the decoding process. Fig. 8 is an
attempt to give a graphic analysis of the example at the level of the
lexemic, i.e. syntactic, stratum. The graph is somewhat simplified;
though, for example, intonation and juncture play a lexemic as well as a
phonemic role, the lines and nodes pertaining to these concepts have
been omitted. Quite consistent is, however, the exclusion of such deriva-
tions as *especially* < *especial* + *ly* and *moved* < *move* + past, as these
belong to the morphemic stratum.

A look at the graph shows the following noteworthy features:

(*a*) If we read the terminal lexemes, i.e. the words, from left to right
and add the marks of punctuation that correspond to intonation and
juncture, we get the unchanged version of the example: *People moved
to the cities. Especially was this the case in England.*

(*b*) At the Pred node of S_1 three ordered lines branch off. The third
leads to *especially* and further to *in England*, which shows that there is
a relationship between these elements, so that we can read *People
moved to the cities especially in England.*

(*c*) The meaning of the lexeme *this* is explained by a line leading
from the Subj node of S_2 to the node S_1, i.e. the subject *this* refers back
to the whole previous sentence.

(*d*) The emphasis lexeme has first shifted *especially* to the front,

---

[12] For further works on stratificational grammar, see the bibliography in Lamb 1966
and footnote 64 in Hockett 1966.

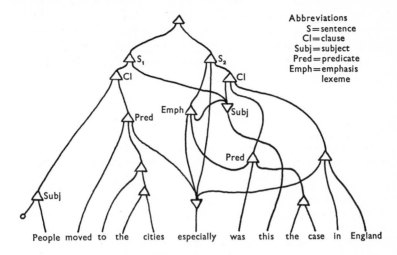

Fig. 8. The two sentences analysed at the level
of the lexemic stratum.

then reversed the order of *the case* and *was,* and lastly placed *this* between these two elements.

Like transformational grammar, stratificational grammar has proved a valuable tool for mechanical linguistic operations, especially machine translation. Typically, Sydney Lamb's first article on stratificational grammar (see above) was concerned with machine translation and his latest bears the title "Stratificational linguistics as a basis for machine translation" (see Lamb 1968?).

Conclusion

It is difficult to judge which of the four linguistic systems dealt with in this article offers the best description of the type of syntactic complexity that the particular example presents, for all of them have both advantages and disadvantages. Naturally these systems have been invented to cater for a very wide range of linguistic problems, and we should not be too surprised if they do not give ready-made answers to all questions concerning some specific points of grammar. As this article shows, I have consequently had to suggest several additions and amendments to the presentations I have found in the handbooks. Nor should we be surprised if, along with more or less satisfactory answers to the particular questions asked, we are also supplied with a great deal of additional information. After all, the aim of the article was to obtain these answers within the general framework of a syntactic description.

Personally I tend to favour the graphic presentation offered by stratificational grammar, as it seems to satisfy to a somewhat greater extent than the others the requirements mentioned earlier, namely, those of brevity, accuracy, and clarity. It is too early to judge, however, whether stratificational methods will also prove superior as regards the description of other types of syntactic complexity than those dealt with in this article.

References

Abraham, Samuel, and Kiefer, Ferenc, 1966. A *Theory of Structural Semantics*. The Hague: Mouton.

Bloomfield, Leonard, 1933. *Language*. New York: Henry Holt.

Chomsky, Noam, 1957. *Syntactic Structures*. The Hague: Mouton.

―――― 1965. *Aspects of the Theory of Syntax*. Cambridge, Mass.: M.I.T. Press.

Elson, Benjamin, and Pickett, Velma, 1965. *An Introduction to Morphology and Syntax*. Santa Ana, Calif.: Summer Institute of Linguistics.

Francis, W. Nelson, 1958. *The Structure of American English*. New York: The Ronald Press.

Fries, Charles C., 1952. *The Structure of English*. New York: Harcourt, Brace.

Gleason, H. A., Jr., 1965. *Linguistics and English Grammar*. New York: Holt, Rinehart and Winston.

Halle, Morris, 1962. "Phonology in Generative Grammar." *Word*, 18, pp. 54–72.

Harris, Zellig S., 1952. "Discourse Analysis." *Language*, 28, pp. 18–23.

Hockett, Charles F., 1966. "Language, Mathematics, and Linguistics." In Thomas A. Sebeok (ed.), *Current Trends in Linguistics* (The Hague: Mouton), pp. 155–304.

Jacobson, Sven, 1964. *Adverbial Positions in English*. Stockholm: AB Studentbok.

Katz, Jerrold J., and Fodor, Jerry, 1963. "The Structure of a Semantic Theory." *Language*, 39, pp. 170–210.

Lamb, Sydney, 1961. "MT Research at the University of California, Berkeley." In H. P. Edmundson (ed.), *Proceedings of the National Symposium on Machine Translation*. Englewood Cliffs, N.J.: Prentice-Hall.

―――― 1966. *Outline of Stratificational Grammar*. Washington, D.C.: Georgetown University Press.

―――― 1968? "Stratificational linguistics as a basis for machine translation." In Bulcsu Laszlo (ed.), *Approaches to Language Data Processing*. The Hague: Mouton.

Ohmann, Richard, 1964. "Generative Grammars and the Concept of Literary Style." *Word*, 20, pp. 423–29.

Pike, Kenneth L., 1954–60. *Language in relation to a unified theory of human behavior*, Vols. I–III. Glendale, Calif.: Summer Institute of Linguistics.

―――― 1966. "A Guide to Publications Related to Tagmemic Theory." In Thomas A. Sebeok, *Current Trends in Linguistics* (The Hague: Mouton), pp. 365–94.

Roberts, Paul, 1964. *English Syntax*. New York: Harcourt, Brace & World.

Thomas, Owen, 1966. *Transformational Grammar and the Teacher of English*. New York: Holt, Rinehart and Winston.

Wells, Rulon S., 1947. "Immediate Constituents." *Language*, 23, pp. 81–117.

FOR DISCUSSION AND REVIEW

1 What inadequacies of the traditional parsing technique does Jacobson identify? Do these limitations apply to the word *Especially*

in the two sentences analyzed? Explain.

2 Jacobson shows how four different grammatical systems would describe the syntax of *People moved to the cities. Especially was this the case in England.* He pays particular attention to the three functions of *Especially* and to how these systems would describe them. Compare and contrast the four descriptions; try to evaluate the particular strengths of each approach.

3 Jacobson notes that the syntactic descriptions of some linguists use notational systems that are often "totally inaccessible to the untutored public. . . ." To what extent is this statement true for the four systems discussed in this article and in this section of the book? Does Jacobson consider it proper or valuable to use the criterion "simple and easy for the beginner" in evaluating grammatical systems? Do you agree? Discuss.

PROJECTS FOR "THE SYSTEMS OF GRAMMAR"

1 Write a short paper describing your experiences with grammar: In what grades was it taught? How much time was devoted to it? What were the attitudes of teachers and students toward it? What kind of grammar was presented? Compare your conclusions with those of others in your class. Do you think your previous study of grammar enhanced your understanding of English or of other languages? If so, try to explain how; be specific.

2 Several of the articles in this book (Chomsky, Miller, Postal, Lewis) assert that children have an innate ability to acquire language and, in effect, "build" their own grammars on the basis of whatever linguistic data surround them. Observe several children of kindergarten age. How far has their grammar-building process progressed? Consider such things as vocabulary, sounds, the ability to adjust language to situation (functional variation), and both production and comprehension of a variety of syntactic structures. Write a paper summarizing your observations.

3 The articles in this section deal with developments in American linguistics since World War II. The study of English grammar, however, has a much longer history. Write a paper on one of the following topics: summarize the development of English grammar from its beginnings in the eighteenth century; describe the eighteenth-century attitude toward "ain't" and the double negative; compare eighteenth-century prescriptive statements with statements in modern handbooks. You may want to begin by reading Chapter 4, "English Grammar," in H. A. Gleason, Jr., *Linguistics and English Grammar* (New York: Holt, Rinehart & Winston, 1965), pp. 67–87.

4 In "Revolution in Grammar" (p. 111), W. Nelson Francis lists four main ways in which grammatical meaning is signaled in English. Examine the following:

These foser glipses have volbicly merfed the wheeple their preebs.[1]
Although you do not know the meaning of any of the underlined
words (How big is a wheeple? How does one merf? Are glipses good
to eat?), you do know a great deal about them. On the basis of the
devices Francis lists, what can you say about the form, function, and
meaning of the words?

5   In "Bilingualism and Information Processing" (p. 84), Kolers refers
to calques, instances of "the interference of one linguistic system with
another." He cites several examples, including "Throw mama from
the train a kiss," which shows interference from German. Collect other
examples of calques. If possible, include examples of interference
from several languages. Next, using any system of grammar with which
you feel comfortable, try to explain the precise nature of the ungram-
maticality.

6   Read the following paragraph:

The hunter crept through the leaves. The leaves had fallen. The leaves were
dry. The hunter was tired. The hunter had a gun. The gun was new. The
hunter saw a deer. The deer had antlers. A tree partly hid the antlers. The
deer was beautiful. The hunter shot at the deer. The hunter missed. The shot
frightened the deer. The deer bounded away.

Without changing important words or the meaning, rewrite the paragraph so as to avoid the many short, choppy sentences. Compare your
rewritten version with those prepared by other members of the class.
Are they alike? If they are not, describe the differences. How do you
account for the fact that passages that appear different can have the
same meaning?

7   Some non-linguists wrongly accuse the "new grammars" of being permissive. They are not; but they are descriptive rather than prescriptive
—that is, they are attempts to describe language as accurately as
possible. Do you think most Americans are ready to accept the descriptive approach to language? Collect evidence to support your conclusion. Good sources will be letters to the editor columns, vocabulary
sections in certain popular magazines, "how to" paperback books,
and some regular newspaper features dealing with language. Write
a paper summarizing your findings.

8   As a native speaker of English, you have an internalized knowledge
of the language—call it a "native-speaker intuition" if you will. For
example, you can recognize a grammatical English sentence, you can
interpret a sentence, you can perceive ambiguity, and you can determine when strings are synonymous. Examine the following groups of
sentences; what can you tell about each group?

---

[1] This example comes from Kenneth G. Wilson, "English Grammars and the Grammar of
English," which appears in the front matter of Funk & Wagnalls *Standard College Dictionary: Text Edition* (New York: Harcourt, Brace & World, 1963).

A 1 *The path ran around the fountain.*
    2 *The soldiers were told to stop marching on the parade ground.*
    3 *The chicken is too hot to eat.*

B 1 *That student continually sleeps in class.*
    2 *Student in class continually that sleeps.*
    3 *In class that student continually sleeps.*

C 1 *The Pittsburgh Pirates beat the Baltimore Orioles in the World Series.*
    2 *The ones that the Pittsburgh Pirates beat in the World Series were the Baltimore Orioles.*
    3 *The Baltimore Orioles were beaten by the Pittsburgh Pirates in the World Series.*

D 1 *Sam asked the students to build a display.*
    2 *Sam promised the students to build a display.*
    3 *Sam told the students to build a display.*

Do your statements about these groups of sentences support the claims made by Miller (p. 132), Postal (p. 149), and Chomsky (p. 172)? Consider especially the validity of such concepts as competence, performance, and deep and surface structures. Write a short paper describing your conclusions.

SELECTED BIBLIOGRAPHY

Cattell, N. R. *The New English Grammar: A Descriptive Introduction.* Cambridge, Mass.: The M.I.T. Press, 1969. (Outstanding introduction to transformational grammar.)

Chomsky, Noam. *Syntactic Structures.* The Hague: Mouton & Company, 1957. (Essential but difficult study.)

Cook, Walter A., S.J. *Introduction to Tagmemic Analysis.* New York: Holt, Rinehart & Winston, 1969. (Not for beginners; assumes background in linguistics and familiarity with phonetics and phonemics; extensive bibliography.)

Dykema, Karl. "Where Our Grammar Came From." *College English,* 22 (1961), 455–65. (Brief survey of the development of grammar.)

Elson, Benjamin and Velma Pickett. *An Introduction to Morphology and Syntax.* Santa Ana, Calif.: Summer Institute of Linguistics, 1965. (A presentation of Kenneth Pike's tagmemic method, with many illustrations from Indian languages of North and South America.)

Emig, Janet A., James T. Fleming, and Helen M. Popp, eds. *Language and Learning.* New York: Harcourt, Brace & World, 1966. (Excellent collection of articles on different aspects of language.)

Faust, George P. "Something of Morphemics." *College Composition and Communication,* 5 (1954), 65–69. (Introductory discussion of the smallest meaningful units of language.)

————. "Terms in Phonemics." *College Composition and Communication,* 5 (1954), 30–34. (Introductory discussion of the concept of the phoneme, important in structural linguistics.)

Francis, W. Nelson. *The Structure of American English.* New York: Ronald Press, 1958. (Influential structural linguistics text.)

Gleason, H. A., Jr. *Linguistics and English Grammar.* New York: Holt, Rinehart & Winston, 1965. (Excellent study; extensive general and topical bibliographies.)

Hall, Robert A., Jr. *Linguistics and Your Language.* Garden City, N.Y.: Doubleday and Co., 1960. (A readable, popular introduction to linguistics, excluding developments during the last decade.)

Herndon, Jeanne H. *A Survey of Modern Grammars.* New York: Holt, Rinehart & Winston, 1970. (An introductory book dealing with structural and transformational generative grammar, directed toward in-service and preservice teachers.)

Jacobs, Roderick A. and Peter S. Rosenbaum, eds. *Readings in English Transformational Grammar.* Waltham, Mass.: Ginn and Company, 1970. (Anthology of theoretical and descriptive articles; excellent bibliography.)

Joos, Martin, ed. *Readings in Linguistics.* Chicago: University of Chicago Press, 1966. (Traces the development of linguistics in the U.S. since 1925.)

Lamb, Sydney M. *Outline of Stratificational Grammar.* Washington, D.C.: Georgetown University Press, 1966. (Standard work by the pioneer in this field; bibliography.)

Lamberts, J. J. "Basic Concepts for Teaching from Structural Linguistics." *English Journal,* 49 (1960), 172–76. (Good introduction to basic ideas.)

Lester, Mark, ed. *Readings in Applied Transformational Grammar.* New York: Holt, Rinehart & Winston, 1970. (Intended for a nontechnical audience and including articles about psycholinguistic questions and the applications of transformational grammar.)

Levin, Samuel R. "Comparing Traditional and Structural Grammar." *College English,* 21 (1960), 260–65. (Short discussion pointing to weaknesses of traditional grammar.)

Live, Anna H. "Language: Universals and Divergences." *English Journal,* 56 (1967), 1177–84. (Interesting discussion of linguistic universals and language change.)

Lyons, John. *Noam Chomsky.* New York: The Viking Press, 1970. (Clear and complete account of Chomsky's central ideas.)

Reibel, David A. and Sanford A. Schane, eds. *Modern Studies in English: Readings in Transformational Grammar.* Englewood Cliffs, N.J.: Prentice-Hall, 1969. (Anthology of articles on the transformational analysis of English.)

Roberts, Paul. "Foreword." *A Linguistics Reader.* Ed. Graham Wilson. New York: Harper & Row, 1967. (Entertaining and informative introduction to the study of language.)

Thomas, Owen. "Generative Grammar: Toward Unification and Simplification." *English Journal,* 51 (1962), 94–99. (Introductory article describing some advantages of generative grammar.)

————. "Grammatici Certant." *English Journal,* 52 (1963), 322–26. (Brief but helpful comparison of traditional, historical, structural, and generative grammars.)

Wilkinson, Andrew. *The Foundations of Language.* New York and London: Oxford University Press, 1971. (Fascinating discussion of basic linguistic concepts and language acquisition in children.)

Wilson, Kenneth G. "English Grammars and the Grammar of English." *Funk and Wagnalls Standard College Dictionary: Text Edition.* New York: Harcourt, Brace & World, 1963. (Introductory comparison of traditional, structural, and transformational grammar.)

PART THREE

Words, Meanings, and the Dictionary

The great critical controversy that developed after the publication of *Webster's Third New International Dictionary* in 1961 (see the article by Albert H. Marckwardt on pp. 229–241) never really resolved any questions of lexicography. The arguments for and against this dictionary, however, did reveal something of significance which a good many Americans never really suspected. We are a people very much interested in words, meanings, and dictionaries, and we have many firm opinions about them; but we are either unaware or strangely reluctant to admit, even to ourselves, the intrigue these subjects have for us.

It is the purpose of this group of essays to be enlightening, but beyond that to affirm our fascination with a living language and how it remains alive. The essays on the dictionary inform the reader of the two basic dictionary-making traditions, prescriptive and descriptive, the effects of these traditions on the attitudes of Black Americans toward the language, and some recent developments in lexicography. The subjects of word formation and slang are then described and brought together in an essay on college slang. Finally, the section ends with discussions of euphemistic usage, the possible effects of dialect research on definitions, and the principles of semantic extension and radiation as revealed in recent usage of the word *existentialism*.

1

Dictionaries and the English Language

Albert H. Marckwardt sets the controversy over *Webster's Third New International Dictionary* against the history of descriptive and prescriptive dictionary making. He reveals the complex nature of attitudes toward dictionaries in general and the considerable misinformation concerning them that exists even in the minds of the critics. The descriptive and prescriptive traditions are not controversial in principle, but one might usefully ask to what extent they can be put into practice in any dictionary.

Albert H. Marckwardt

Now THAT much of the tumult and the shouting have subsided, and the controversy over *Webster's Third New International Dictionary* has attained the dignity of a casebook, it should be possible to consider both the dictionary and the varied reactions to it with a degree of detachment. Bergen Evans was quite correct in characterizing the storm of abuse provoked by the appearance of the new edition as a curious phenomenon. But how can it be explained? And more important still, what is there to be learned from it?

We must recognize, first of all, that a complete revision of our largest commercially produced dictionary of the English language has become a regularly recurring event in American life. Upon occasion the time table has varied a bit, but the following listing reveals an astonishing degree of regularity over the past century.

An American Dictionary of the English Language (Royal Quarto Edition, Unabridged)	1864	Webster's New International Dictionary	1909
Webster's International Dictionary	1890	Webster's New International Dictionary (Second edition)	1934
		Webster's Third New International Dictionary	1961

Of the five Webster editions listed above, probably none has called forth such extremes of critical comment upon its appearance as the recent Webster Third. It was characterized as "a very great calamity." Its general tone was described as "a dismaying assortment of the questionable, the perverse, the unworthy, the downright outrageous." At the same time, other reviewers spoke of the work as "an intellectual achievement of the very highest order," and "a reference work which worthily carries on a tradition of great reference works."

These extremes of praise and blame are reminiscent of the reception of the 1828 edition of *An American Dictionary of the English Language*, compiled by Webster himself and the real parent of the long line of dictionaries which bear his name. At that time a reviewer in *The Southern Literary Messenger* denounced the treatment of pronunciation as horrible and the orthography as abominable. The English *Quarterly Review* judged it "a decided failure, conducted on perverse and erroneous principles," and in much the same vein as some of the critics of the Webster Third, complained that "we do not recollect ever to have witnessed in the same compass a greater number of crudities and errors, or more pains taken to so little purpose." But Webster's 1828 work has its admirers as well, particularly among the Germans, who praised the profound learning that it reflected.

The disparate comments on Webster's early work are of interest today only as a historical phenomenon, but those which have been applied to the Webster Third still give rise to considerable confusion. It is scarcely possible for both the critics and the admirers to be right in all that they say, and one may reasonably ask what a more dispassionate evaluation might be.

Two Traditions

In approaching such an appraisal, we must understand first of all that the American lexicographer in his concern with current English faces something of a dilemma. He is the inheritor of two traditions clearly in conflict, both of which have their roots in England.

The earlier tradition is that of Samuel Johnson, the compiler of the 1755 *Dictionary of the English Language*, who lent the first touch of sheer genius to English lexicography. In the preface of this great work, he pointed out that "every language has its improprieties and absurdities, which it is the duty of the lexicographer to correct or proscribe." According to him, the function of a dictionary was one, "by which the pronunciation of our language may be fixed and its attainment facilitated; by which its purity may be preserved, its use ascertained, and its duration lengthened." That Johnson was expressing the spirit of his age is shown by comments such as that of Lord Chesterfield, who wrote, "We must have a resource to the old Roman expedient in times of confusion and choose a Dictator. Upon this principle I give my vote for Mr. Johnson to fill that great and arduous post."

This concept of the lexicographer as a linguistic legislator or arbiter, if not absolute dictator, is still strong in the United States. It is frequently reflected, and indeed encouraged, by the slogans which dictionary publishers—not the editors, let me hasten to say—choose to advertise their wares. The very phrase, "Supreme Authority," which the G. and C. Merriam Company used to employ, supported this view of the dictionary; whether intentionally or not is open to conjecture.

The slightly later and opposed tradition is that of the lexicographer as the objective recorder of the language. For the English-speaking nations this concept was first realized on a substantial scale in what is now known as *The Oxford English Dictionary* but originally entitled *A New English Dictionary on Historical Principles*. Here the purpose is stated as follows:

> The aim of this dictionary is to present in alphabetical series the words which have formed the English vocabulary from the time of the earliest records down to the present day, with all the relevant facts concerning their form, sense-history, pronunciation, and etymology. It embraces not only the standard language of literature and conversation, whether current at the moment or obsolete, or archaic, but also the main technical vocabulary, and a large measure of dialectal usage and slang.

Note that this statement contains not one word about fixing the language, about proscription or prescription of any kind. Operating on this basis, the lexicographer contents himself with setting down the record, leaving its interpretation to the reader. Needless to say, the prestige of the *Oxford English Dictionary* is enormous; it is generally conceded to be superior to the corresponding major dictionaries for the other western European languages. The principles on which it is based were formulated as early as 1859.

The conflict of principle which has been pointed out need not necessarily be troublesome. If the language involved is confined as to number of speakers and is the vehicle of a static and stabilized society, there is virtually no problem. An accurate description of the language as it is actually used, kept simple by the relative absence of variants, accurately designating social and regional status, will in itself serve prescriptive purposes. But this is not the case with English, which is spoken natively by some two hundred and seventy millions, spread over five continents of the globe. Under such circumstances, uniformity becomes a remote possibility. In the United States, at least, the language is that of a highly mobile society, both geographically and up and down the social scale. As a consequence the lines between class and regional dialects and the standard language inevitably tend to become blurred. Under such circumstances, the linguistic reporter and the legislator are more likely to seem to be working at cross purposes.

Nevertheless, it is clearly evident that as the various editions of Webster march down the century, the statements of principle which are to be found in them move steadily away from the Johnsonian or prescriptive concept toward the descriptive position of the Oxford editors. Even as early as 1864, Chauncey A. Goodrich, the chief editor of the first major revision after Webster's death, asserted that, "The chief value of a dictionary consists in its Definitions; in giving a clear, full, and accurate exhibition, of all the various shades of meaning which belong, *by established usage,* to the words of a language."

Nor was the reportorial concept limited to the Webster series of dictionaries in this country. One of the principal competitors during the early years of the present century, Dr. Isaac K. Funk, wrote in the preface of the 1913 *Standard Dictionary of the English Language,* "The chief function of a dictionary is to record usage." It is true that this forthright statement of the descriptive function was followed by a somewhat unsuccessful attempt to reconcile it with the authoritarian concept, but nevertheless the principle had been stated.

1934 Edition

The immediate predecessor of the new Webster Third was the 1934 edition. The following excerpt from its front matter (p. xvi) refers specifically to pronunciation, but it is a fair representation of the attitude of its editors toward all language matters:

> The function of a pronouncing dictionary is to record as far as possible the pronunciations prevailing in the best present usage, rather than to attempt to dictate what that usage should be. In so far as a dictionary may be known and acknowledged as a faithful recorder and interpreter of such usage, so far and no farther may it be appealed to as an authority.
>
> In the case of diverse usages of extensive prevalence, the dictionary must recognize each of them.

A somewhat broader treatment of the editorial function is to be found in the Introduction (p. xi) to the 1934 Webster:

> Both Samuel Johnson and Noah Webster conceived it to be a duty of the dictionary editor to maintain the purity of the standard language. However, with the growth in literacy of the past century, and the increase in fiction and drama, in radio and motion pictures, of the use of dialect, slang, and colloquial speech, it has become necessary for a general dictionary to record and interpret the vocabularies of geographical and occupational dialects, and of the livelier levels of the speech of the educated.

It would be difficult to imagine a more cogent or forthright exposition of the descriptive function of the dictionary than these two statements of editorial policy. The first of them apparently satisfied the editors of the Webster Third, for they repeat it in their Introduction (p. 6a) with only one minor expansion: "best present usage" of the earlier edition now reads, "General cultivated conversational usage, both formal and informal." This offers additional support for the conclusion that with respect to the conflict between opposing lexicographical concepts, the descriptive had been wholly accepted, the prescriptive completely rejected in 1934. Whatever differences there may be between the 1934 and 1961 editions, they are not matters of policy or principle. They are instead differences in the way in which a principle common to both dictionaries has been realized.

Lexicographical policy is not ordinarily a matter of absorbing interest, but it has been necessary to deal with it at some length because the Webster Third has been criticized on occasion for repudiating, even sabotaging the principles of the second edition. Such charges serve only to reveal a total lack of awareness on the part of the critic as to what these principles were, how they have developed in this country, and how they reflect a steadily changing concept of the function of the dictionary. Actually, the furor over the Webster Third is a sad commentary on how inadequately the dictionary has been presented in the English classrooms of the nation and how insufficiently English teachers are informed about one of the principal tools of their profession.

Practical Editorial Decisions

The extremes of public reaction to the new Webster must also be considered in terms of editorial decisions on a practical rather than a theoretical level. Such an understanding may best be attained by considering certain of the practical questions which confronted the editors, what the decisions on them were, and what the reasons for them may have been.

At the very outset of their preparations, the editors apparently felt an obligation to increase considerably the amount of evidence upon which the new dictionary was to be based. Dictionary evidence normally exists in the form of citation slips, the products of an extensive reading program. The citations are filed under their appropriate headwords, and in the editing process they constitute the raw material for the definitions and in fact for most of the word treatment.

At the time of the compilation of the second edition, the files in the Springfield offices held some 1,615,000 citation slips. In the years intervening between the two editions, as the result of what must have been a tremendous effort, this figure was nearly quadrupled. Just under

4,500,000 citations were added, resulting in a total of 6,000,000, a number approximately equalling the collection for the *Oxford English Dictionary*, but far more heavily concentrated on the language of the present day. In addition, the *Dictionary of American English* and the *Dictionary of Americanisms* had both been completed in the years 1944 and 1951 respectively, constituting a further increase in the size of the corpus available to the editors of the Webster Third. As a result, they found themselves with approximately 50,000 new words (words not entered in the Webster Second) and 50,000 new meanings for words already entered.

At this point physical and financial factors enter into consideration. For a number of reasons, undoubtedly based upon a century of business experience, the publishers are firmly committed to a single-volume dictionary. They had made the Webster Second as large, that is to say thick, as any one volume could possibly get and still assure a back that might withstand the rigors of long and constant use, particularly in schools and libraries. Thus it was manifestly impossible to increase the number of pages by the ten or fifteen percent necessary to accommodate the new entries. If these were to be included, something had to come out. The kind of material that was removed forms the basis of some of the criticisms of the present edition.

The first excision consisted of the materials which, in earlier editions, had been placed below the horizontal line running across the page. These included archaisms, dialect forms, variant spellings, and proper names. To quote the editors, "Many obsolete and comparatively useless or obscure words have been omitted. These include, in general, words that had become obsolete before 1755 unless found in well-known major works of a few major writers." Incidentally, the significance of the date 1755 can scarcely escape one's attention. In the first place it was the publication year of Dr. Johnson's dictionary. Moreover, as a deadline for obsolescence, it marks an advance of two centuries and a half over the corresponding date of 1500 for the Webster Second. Thus, in word selection as well as in other matters, the emphasis is clearly placed upon the current state of the language.

Getting rid of the obsolete and the obscure did not in itself solve the space problem. Still other things had to go, and these taken together constitute the parts essential to a peripheral function of the dictionary long cherished by Americans—the encyclopedic function. In the process of elimination, the editors removed among other things:

1. The gazetteer section.
2. The biographical section.
3. Titles of written works and works of art.
4. Names of characters in fiction, folklore, and mythology.

5. Names of battles, wars, organizations, cities, and states.
6. Mottoes and other familiar sayings.

There have been further excisions as well. Color plates and illustrations are reduced in a proportion somewhere between one-fourth and one-third. Even the number of pages has gone down from 3210 to 2720.

Elimination of Material

This elimination of encyclopedic material has caused anguish. "Think, if you can," complains Wilson Follett, "of an unabridged dictionary from which you cannot learn who Mark Twain was, or what were the names of the apostles, or that the Virgin was Mary, the mother of Jesus of Nazareth, or what and where the District of Columbia is." Actually, this is not at all difficult. The great Oxford comes immediately to mind, as does Henry Cecil Wyld's *Universal Dictionary of the English Language*, or any of the great academy dictionaries of such languages as French or Spanish.

Nevertheless, Follett's reaction will be shared by many Americans. In the past, dictionaries published in this country have cheerfully served an encyclopedic as well as a lexicographic function, and ironically enough it was Noah Webster himself who was primarily responsible. His first dictionary, published in 1806, included tables of the moneys of most of the commercial nations in the world, tables of weights and measures, ancient and modern, the divisions of time among the Jews, Greeks, and Romans, and an official list of the post-offices in the United States, to mention only a few of the extra features. Although the editors of the current volume have broken with their progenitor in cutting out these impedimenta, they have not at all departed from the essential principles of lexicography in so doing.

Undoubtedly they felt that the considerable increase in the number of illustrative citations would readily compensate for the loss of the peripheral material. Such citations do constitute the core of the reportorial dictionary. For instance, there were no citations for the adjective *oratorical* in the second edition; the Third has three. The second edition gave three identified citations for *chase*, verb. In the Third, there are four identified and seven unidentified citations.

According to the Preface of the current edition, "More than 14,000 different authors are quoted for their use of words or for the structural pattern of their words. . ." Many of these are contemporary. The reader is also informed that the verbal illustrations (citations apparently unidentified as to author) are "mostly from the twentieth century."

This innovation has met with something less than universal approval, a reaction not so much attributable to the editorial policy itself as to some of the advertising antics of the business office. The original brochure, announcing this edition as "one of the most remarkable literary achievements of all time," included among the list of authors cited such names as Billy Rose, Fulton Lewis, Jr., Art Linkletter, Dinah Shore, Ted Williams, and Ethel Merman. In addition there were Harry Truman, Dwight D. Eisenhower, John F. Kennedy, and Richard Nixon, whose names were undoubtedly signed to reams of material which they did not compose. To the sympathetic this signalled a conscious attempt to include a wide range of current authors. To the critical it betokened a lack of discrimination and responsibility. Actually, the citations from such sources are few in number and small in proportion.

A point which must be taken into account here is that which was made at the very outset of this essay, namely that the life of a Webster edition is roughly calculated at twenty-five years. Thus, the overriding concern of the dictionary is quite appropriately the language in its current state. It is on these grounds that the editors may logically justify the preponderance of citations from current authors, irrespective of lasting literary merit. It may be assumed that in the 1986 edition many of them will be discarded, to be replaced by others from the 1970's and early 1980's. In this respect the Webster practice will differ sharply from that of the *Oxford English Dictionary*, for which no new edition was contemplated, although certainly only a small proportion of the authors cited in that work are literary giants of lasting reputation.

Status Labels

Another departure in the Webster Third from the practice of earlier editions, which has given rise to considerable criticism, is the treatment of what are called *status labels*. Here again some of the disapproval has its source in misunderstanding. Basically, the editors have developed a terminology which is at once semantically neutral and more precise than that which has been employed in the past. The label *illiterate* has been discontinued. It has become a term of censure rather than a dispassionate indication of the inability to read and write. The current replacements, *substandard* and *nonstandard*, are matter-of-fact rather than pejorative and permit a gradation of acceptability, the latter indicating a wider range of occurrence than the former, although it is applied to a smaller number of words and expressions. American dialect ascriptions represent a great advance in precision over those of the second edition in that they reflect an adaptation of the terminology for the various dialect areas developed by Professor Hans Kurath, editor of the Linguistic Atlas and the most eminent linguistic geographer in the country. It was unfortunate, however, that the editors chose not to indicate those words current in all regions of the United States but not in England or other parts of the English-speaking world.

Another innovation in the Webster Third is the elimination of the label *colloquial*. There are two conceivable reasons for this: In the first place the term is ambivalent, signifying informality on the one hand and the spoken rather than the written medium on the other. It is customary now among students of the language to be somewhat more precise, recognizing not only colloquial but *casual* and *intimate* as further gradations of the spoken variety of the language, any of which not only may be but are regularly employed by speakers of unquestioned cultivation.

An even greater objection to the label *colloquial* is the persistence with which an unfavorable connotation has adhered to it. Dictionary users never interpreted the term in the way in which dictionary editors intended. It was not meant as a condemnation either in the Webster Second or in the various abridged dictionaries based upon it. The editors took great pains to say so, both in the prefatory material and in the definition of the word itself, but this went unheeded. So for the present edition the staff was faced with the alternative of finding an acceptable substitute less liable to misinterpretation, or of eliminating the label altogether. It chose the latter, partly perhaps because of the unsatisfactory experience of other dictionaries which had experimented with a substitute.

In general the changes in the choice and ascription of labels reflect an endeavor to achieve greater precision and objectivity. The attempt at precision undoubtedly finds some adherents, although there will be disagreements over the application of the labels in specific instances. The attempt at objectivity has, understandably enough, resulted in the disappearance of the censorious tone which for many seemed to be part of the proper function of the labels *colloquial* and *illiterate*. To such persons, the lack of censure has been understood as a lowering of standards.

Pronunciation

In dealing with pronunciation, the editors of the Webster Third had to contend with two factors which had not faced their predecessors. One was a new electronic development, namely voice amplification. The other was a new concept in the analysis of language, that of the phoneme or meaningful unit of sound.

Voice amplification affected the kind of pronunciation which the dictionary undertook to record. In pre-loud-speaker days, the second edition of Webster recorded what it called "formal platform speech," the speech of cultivated users of English, speaking formally with a view to being completely understood by their hearers. That there were other types of pronunciation wholly appropriate to less formal situations was readily conceded by the editors, but they evidently felt that their editorial responsibility could be discharged with the greatest amount of effectiveness and least confusion by indicating just the one.

The microphone has changed all this. Certain devices of articulation necessary for clarity when the speaker was forced to depend on lung power to make himself audible to the last row of a large auditorium are no longer necessary. Nor are they often employed today.

This change led the Webster editors into a complete revision of the manner in which evidence on pronunciation was collected. Where Webster Second had attempted a sampling, by means of written questionnaires, of the pronunciation of persons who did a considerable amount of public speaking, the Webster Third staff turned its attention directly to the language itself rather than to opinion about it. They listened to radio, television, and recordings; to speech in all parts of the country and in all types of situations. Again, as with the citations for word occurrences, forms, and meanings, the body of evidence was tremendously increased in range and scope, but certainly less skewed toward a single type of pronunciation.

In any English dictionary, and particularly one designed for use in the United States, a decision upon the particular system, or respelling, to indicate pronunciation always poses a problem. For a number of reasons, the American public has been unwilling to accept the International Phonetic Alphabet; nor is this a particularly economical device when a number of variants must be shown. The Webster Second continued with few changes the system of its predecessors, which was cumbersome in that a single sound was indicated by more than one transcription, and confusing in that a single character sometimes covered far more latitude than the user was likely to realize.

The editors of the current edition have attempted to take advantage of the phonemic concept, basic to present-day linguistic science. The general result has been the disappearance of a rash of diacritics which made the earlier dictionaries difficult to read and to interpret. Some useful characters have been taken over from the phonetic alphabet, notably the elongated n to indicate the usual sound of ng, and most important, the inverted e or schwa for the neutral vowel used in weakly stressed syllables. The latter, it must be confessed, is an innovation in which Webster followed some of its competitors. At all events, the public will no longer be misled into believing that the final vowel of *caucus* is somehow different from that of *fracas*.

Unfortunately the necessity of economizing on space has led to the excision of the authoritative treatments of the individual sounds of English which lent scholarly distinction to the second edition though perhaps read by only a few. Also, certain innovations of the Webster Third will cause annoyance until the public becomes accustomed to them. One of these may well be the indication of stress by a mark preceding rather than following the syllable. The removal of the pronunciation key from the bottom of the page is another. The use of a modified *d* character to indicate what the editors call, "the usual American pronunciation of *latter*," will seem to the critical like countenancing the slipshod, and it is possible that a *t* with a diacritic might have served quite as well without outraging quite so many sensibilities.

With pronunciation as with countless other features of the dictionary, the editors have attempted to present the facts of the language as they saw them. It is an honest presentation, maintaining the principles and the concept of the dictionary characteristic of previous editions, but carrying them out with greater consistency and basing them upon far more evidence. There have been errors of judgment, more often perhaps with respect to manner of presentation than in the interpretation of the facts which are reported, but this is inevitable in an undertaking of such magnitude.

My comments so far should have suggested, to a degree at least, the reasons for some of the changes which are to be found in the Webster Third. They have not yet given an answer to the question which was initially posed: why the extremes of praise and blame. The encomiums are easy to account for. They represent the approval of those who accept the descriptive principle and find in the current product a generally conscientious and more thorough implementation of it than is otherwise available.

Controversy

The chorus of protest is somewhat more complex in origin. It is in part the expression of a desire for linguistic authoritarianism, an attitude sincerely held by many, which can be explained only in terms of a number of complex and interrelated factors in American cultural history. Added to this is the mistaken notion that the Webster Third represents a change in lexicographical principle, an error which is fostered by the more complete coverage and greater accuracy of the edition. The excision of certain kinds of nonessential material represented a sudden departure from a time-honored practice. Moreover, there is, as always, a tendency toward careless reading and inept comparison; upon occasion a judgment objected to in the third edition was already present in the second. This reflects a not uncommon situation. Even those who are willing to concede that language standards must ultimately rest upon usage are not infrequently distressed when they encounter a detailed and factual inventory of that usage. At such a point the normal reaction is to question the accuracy of the inventory and the soundness of the method upon which it is based.

An excellent illustration of this is to be found in the treatment of the very word that has given rise to so many headlines and caused so much acid comment—*ain't*. The statement which gave rise to the excitement, namely that *ain't* is used orally in most parts of the United States by many cultivated speakers, is merely a condensation of what has already been noted in Bagby Atwood's *A Survey of Verb Forms in the Eastern United States*, a study based upon the materials of the Linguistic Atlas of the United States and Canada. "Cultivated, our foot," comments the editor of the Chicago *Daily News*; yet the cultivated informants for the various regional atlases were selected on the basis of as rigorous a set of standards in terms of family background, education, and occupation as could be established.

The presumed role of structural linguistics in the Webster Third reflects a most unfortunate confusion, and ironically it is the editor of the dictionary who is in part responsible for it. In an article in *Word Study* prior to the publication of the dictionary, Dr. Gove unintentionally left careless and uninformed readers with the mistaken impression that Leonard Bloomfield in 1926 first stated the postulate that correctness rests upon usage. Despite the fact that Dr. Gove then went on to mention any number of areas in lexicography where linguistics had had no appreciable influence, the first part of his article appears to have left many readers with the mental image of a fifth column of structuralists burrowing their way through the Merriam-Webster files in Springfield.

This notion is wrong on two counts. First, the importance of usage in the establishment of a linguistic standard had been maintained by a host of scholars from the turn of the century on. They included Thomas Lounsbury, George P. Krapp, Louise Pound, Charles C. Fries, and Sterling A. Leonard, to mention only a few of the more distinguished. The structuralists accept this as a matter of course, but they did not invent the idea. Second, except for the treatment of pronunciation, structural concepts do not appear with any great frequency in the dictionary. Words are traditionally classified as nouns, adjectives, verbs, and so on. There was no attempt to substitute a scheme consistently based either upon form or function. This is a dictionary of words rather than of morphemes. I find it difficult to detect even a hint of structuralism in the handling of the definitions. Yet Dwight Macdonald speaks of the "direct application" of structural linguistics "to making dictionaries," and the idea has been echoed by others.

It is the English-teaching profession which should be seriously disturbed by the dictionary controversy. If the Webster war has proved little or nothing about dictionaries, it has demonstrated our ineptitude, if not absolute failure, in teaching our students what a dictionary is for, how it is made, and the proper way to use it. Much of the misunderstanding of principle, of the confusion of principle and practice, of the failure to read and interpret accurately can, with considerable justice, be laid at our door. After all, the embattled critics were once our students; had our teaching of the dictionary been soundly based, this comedy of errors should have been at least somewhat less comic.

To return to the dictionary itself, however, one can only say that by a more literal acceptance of its declared function, and by running counter more obviously to what people want or think they want in a dictionary and to what they think they have been getting, the Webster Third represents a calculated risk. Depending on one's point of view, it is either a courageous or a foolhardy venture into the latter half of the twentieth century. For the staff, who in the face of the public clamor must wonder if it has been at all worthwhile, there is only the dubious comfort in Macaulay's words, "The best lexicographer may well be content if his productions are received by the world in cold esteem."

FOR DISCUSSION AND REVIEW

1   What were some of the objections made by reviewers and critics to *Webster's Third New International Dictionary*?

2   Define the words *prescriptive* and *descriptive*. How were these terms related to the controversy over *Webster's Third*?

3   Where does Marckwardt place much of the responsibility for the controversy over *Webster's Third*?

4   In what ways did the editors of *Webster's Third* reflect recent advances in linguistic science in the writing of their dictionary?

5   The word *ain't* and what *Webster's Third* said about it became a rallying point for critics of the dictionary. How does your desk dictionary describe the usage of this controversial word?

6   The editors of *Webster's Third* faced problems of pronunciation that the editors of the 1934 edition did not. What were these problems?

2

The English Language Is My Enemy!

In this short article, author, playwright, and actor Ossie Davis discusses a special kind of dictionary, Roget's *Thesaurus*, and what he sees as the prejudicial character of the English language. You may find it useful to consider whether the prejudice is latent in the language itself or in the people who make such word books.

Ossie Davis

A SUPERFICIAL examination of Roget's Thesaurus of the English Language reveals the following facts: the word WHITENESS has 134 synonyms; 44 of which are favorable and pleasing to contemplate, i.e. purity, cleanness, immaculateness, bright, shining, ivory, fair, blonde, stainless, clean, clear, chaste, unblemished, unsullied, innocent, honorable, upright, just, straight-forward, fair, genuine, trustworthy (a white man's colloquialism). Only ten synonyms for WHITENESS appear to me to have negative implications—and these only in the mildest sense: gloss over, whitewash, gray, wan, pale, ashen, etc.

The word BLACKNESS has 120 synonyms, 60 of which are distinctly unfavorable, and none of them even mildly positive. Among the offending 60 were such words as: blot, blotch, smut, smudge, sully, begrime, soot, becloud, obscure, dingy, murky, low-toned, threatening, frowning, foreboding, forbidden, sinister, baneful, dismal, thundery, evil, wicked, malignant, deadly, unclean, dirty, unwashed, foul, etc. . . . not to mention 20 synonyms directly related to race, such as: Negro, Negress, nigger, darky, blackamoor, etc.

When you consider the fact that *thinking* itself is sub-vocal speech —in other words, one must use *words* in order to think at all—you will appreciate the enormous heritage of racial prejudgement that lies in wait for any child born into the English Language. Any teacher good or bad, white or black, Jew or Gentile, who uses the English Language as a medium of communication is forced, willy-nilly, to teach the Negro child 60 ways to despise himself, and the white child 60 ways to aid and abet him in the crime.

Who speaks to me in my Mother Tongue damns me indeed! . . . the English Language—in which I cannot conceive my self as a black man without, at the same time, debasing myself . . . my enemy, with which to survive at all I must continually be at war.

FOR DISCUSSION AND REVIEW

1 If, as Davis observes, most of the definitions of *Blackness* are unfavorable, how does this contribute to prejudice against blacks?

2 Davis says that *"thinking* itself is sub-vocal speech." Is this a valid statement in your opinion? Can infants think? Explain.

3 Could women make a statement about sexual prejudice in dictionaries similar to the one Davis makes on racial prejudice? Does the fact that dictionaries are edited primarily by men have an influence on the way dictionaries define words? Explain.

3

How "White" Is Your Dictionary?

In this article from *ETC.: A Review of General Semantics*, William Walter Duncan deals less emotionally with the questions raised in the preceding article by Davis. Duncan offers some reasons why Davis may feel the way he does about the English language and in doing so returns to some principles of dictionary-making discussed in the article by Marckwardt (p. 229).

William Walter Duncan

DURING A recent discussion on semantics in one of my classes, I asked some twenty students to tell me what they think of when the word *white* is mentioned. I got such responses as: "purity," "the color," "snow," "something clean," but not one negative connotation for the word.

I then asked about the word *black* and got: "something very dark," "dirty," "black lies," "death," but not one positive connotation. When I pointed this out to the class, one "white" student immediately exclaimed, "But there are no positive connotations for *black*."

At this point one of the "black" students—all of whom had previously remained silent—responded angrily, and understandably so, pointing out that in his mind there are many negative connotations for *white* and many positive ones for *black*.

After a few moments of tension among some of the students, I turned the discussion into an examination of the word *black*, using the unabridged edition of *The Random House Dictionary of the English Language*. All of the definitions of the word in this dictionary are either negative or neutral in nature. Not until the phrases, specifically item no. 22, *in the black*, does one find a positive connotation for the word, the sole entry in more than fifty lines of fine print that can be said to be of a positive nature. Even when *black clothing* is mentioned, one finds: "esp. as a sign of mourning: *He wore black at the funeral.*"

In contrast with *black*, *white* has a preponderance of positive meanings, but none with negative connotations—not one word about *white* associated with death, as in *white as a ghost*, or with evil, as in *a white mask of deception*.

Now a dictionary is merely a report of the ways words are used. (The precedent set by Samuel Johnson for the expression of personal biases in the definition of some words has long since been rejected by lexicographers.) And the Random House dictionary, in its treatment of the words *white* and *black*, is not essentially different from other dictionaries. For example, here is the way *Funk & Wagnalls Standard College Dictionary* (Harcourt, Brace & World, 1963) treats the word:

> **black** adj. 1. Having no brightness or color; Reflecting no light; opposed to *white*. 2. Destitute of light; in total darkness. 3. Gloomy; dismal; forbidding: a *black* future. 4. Having a very dark skin, as a Negro. 5. Soiled; stained. 6. Indicating disgrace or censure: a *black* mark. 7. Angry; threatening: *black* looks. 8. Evil; wicked; malignant: a *black* heart. . .

While all of the dictionaries which I have examined treat the word *black* in a similar manner, the statement that lexicographers merely report the way a word is used, a defense which one editor of a well-known dictionary recently made to me, needs to be examined carefully.

A dictionary is supposedly merely a record of what a language *was* at some point in the past. Even at the moment of publication, a dictionary is dated. No one, therefore, can reasonably expect the dictionaries now in use to have statements about the way the word *black* is currently being used by many people, as in the slogan *black is beautiful*, and only time will tell if *black* is going to become the standard term for Negro.

But even if the above arguments are accepted, American dictionaries have not made complete reports of the word *black*. Why, for instance, in listing the phrase *black clothing* were not references made to the formal attire which men sometimes wear to look their best, or to the black robes worn by judges or by academicians? Why weren't references made to the *black opal* or *pearl* or to other contexts in which the word carries a positive connotation?

While a dictionary cannot perhaps explain why a *black lie* is a repugnant case of mendacity and a *white* one an excusable falsehood, a dictionary can suggest that a reader compare one phrase with the other. This might lead many to realize the logical inconsistency of the two phrases and possibly the evil we perpetuate when we use them.

While a dictionary cannot be expected to explain why we call some people "white" and others "black" when in reality there are no black or white people—we are all colored—a dictionary can say "a member of the so-called black race," as *Standard College* does, and "a member of the so-called white race," as *Standard College* does not.

While a correction and an improvement of the treatment of the words *black* and *white* in our dictionaries may not eliminate prejudice associated with skin color, it could be a contribution to this cause.

FOR DISCUSSION AND REVIEW

1 In the essay preceding this one, Ossie Davis claims that the English language is inherently prejudicial. Where does Duncan place the responsibility for prejudice in the language?

2 Duncan quotes one dictionary editor as saying that "lexicographers merely report the way a word is used." Can a dictionary ever be truly descriptive in this way? Why or why not?

3 If you were the editor of a dictionary today, what groups of people in American life might particularly interest you? How might this affect the dictionary?

4

Profile of a Best Seller

B. L. Trippett became interested in lexicography after doing a study of the reviews of *Webster's Third New International Dictionary*. In this essay, he relates *The American Heritage Dictionary* to the debate over *Webster's Third* and reviews the many innovative features that made *The American Heritage* a best seller.

B. L. Trippett

W<small>HEN</small> A dictionary remains on the best seller lists for some six months, it is some sort of milestone in the knowledge explosion.

The volume is called *The American Heritage Dictionary of the English Language* (AHD) and was produced by the American Heritage Publishing Company, Inc., and Houghton Mifflin Company.

Four quotations from a Houghton Mifflin Company advertisement are representative of the general reception the dictionary received in the news media.

". . . the handsomest dictionary in English." *Christian Science Monitor.*

". . . a remarkably good money's worth." *Wall Street Journal.*

". . . the most with-it ball of the year." *Saturday Review.*

". . . a kind of fire, a glow of genius." *New York Times Book Review.*

In perhaps the most balanced of the reviews, W. V. Quine in the *New York Review of Books,* called the American Heritage Dictionary "imposingly under-priced."

To verify these excerpts, I went back to the original articles. *Technical Communications* needed to be protected from the accusation that it was "puffing" the AHD, to use a vogue word current in Dr. Samuel Johnson's time. It is a matter of merchandising judgment, of course, but the quotations are actually understatements of the enthusiasm demonstrated.

The general climate of the dictionary-reading market was described succinctly by B. Hunter Smeaton, of the University of Calgary, Canada, writing in the *Library Journal.*

"The extraordinary output of new (and in large part, good) dictionaries of the English language in the present decade," Smeaton wrote, "may well have been triggered by the appearance in 1961 of Webster's

Third New International Dictionary, whose departures from precedent became such a cause célèbre. It is certain that there have been no makers of dictionaries since who have not capitalized on both the virtues of Webster's Third and its shortcomings."

Webster's Third Edition was a work of major scholarship that W. V. Quine said "sparked an unwonted if not unwanted public involvement by sparking a confusion between descriptive and prescriptive lexicography." The Webster Unabridged has stood for a century of proof of correctness. But, lo, the Third Edition shifted its allegiance from what should be to what is. The result spawned a series of what Brooks Atkinson of the *New York Times* called "savage reviews." Bergen Evans in the *Atlantic* said it was "a storm of abuse." Never, he said, had a scholarly work of this stature been attacked with such unbridled fury and contempt.

James Sledd and Wilma R. Ebbitt were inspired to write a sprightly text called *Dictionaries and That Dictionary,* published by Scott, Foresman, which was a casebook on "the aims of lexicographers and the targets of reviewers."

Even works of fiction got in the act. In Rex Stout's novel *Gambit* (Viking Press), the hero, Nero Wolfe, tore Webster's Third to bits page by page and burned it in the fireplace. Wolfe considered the dictionary subversive because it threatened the integrity of the English language. Wolfe asked a friend if he knew the difference between *infer* and *imply,* but could get no answer from his friend or from the dictionary.

Further, Webster's Third dropped the gazetteer section; biographical section; titles of written works and works of art; names of characters in fiction, folklore, and mythology; and of battles, wars, organizations, cities, states, and natural objects. In short, the encyclopedic material.

Dr. Philip B. Gove, editor-in-chief of Merriam-Webster, outlined the crux of the problem when he said, "Lexicography is not yet a science. It may never be. It is an intricate and subtle and sometimes overpowering art, requiring subjective analysis, arbitrary decisions, and intuitive reasoning. It often uses analogy, precedent, and probability, and it constantly has to distinguish between the typical and the atypical on the basis of knowledge and experience. It has no reason to scorn sprachgefühl, or to apologize for depending on it. But it should have no traffic with guesswork, prejudice, or bias or with artificial notions of correctness and superiority. It must be descriptive and not prescriptive."

According to Professor Sumner Ives of Syracuse University, who wrote a review of Webster's Third Edition, there are only three possible sources for what is given in a dictionary:

1. Other dictionaries, including the great, many-volumed *Oxford English Dictionary,* which all contemporary lexicographers use.

2. The common but unsystematic observations of educated men, including specialists in various fields.

3. A tremendous file of citations gathered over a long period of time, filed for reference, and constantly supplemented by continued observation of the language in use.

American Heritage went a step farther, as we shall see, by including computer analysis of the language.

It has also been said that all dictionaries are a development or re-writing of Dr. Samuel Johnson's great English dictionary, published in 1755.

Dr. Johnson outlined his procedures in a memorandum used to solicit financing. His aim was to provide more than a word list with etymologies and explanations for different terms. Instead, the Johnson dictionary was to offer comprehensive definitions of the different shades of meaning in the use of a word and to establish, by example, a flexible standard of propriety and good usage. Dr. Johnson made the decision to determine and illustrate meanings by selected quotations in order to offer a "kind of intellectual history." These standards were elastic and were to remain so in practice.

About a half century later, Noah Webster made seven specific criticisms of the Johnson Dictionary:

1. A multitude of words did not belong to the English language.
2. Selection of authorities was injudicious.
3. Dr. Johnson used "more of the lowest of all vulgar words."
4. Senses were not discriminated.
5. Dr. Johnson failed to define words nearly synonymous.
6. Illustrations were chosen from authors who did not write English with purity.
7. Etymologies were inaccurate.

The American Heritage people began their work with an extra century-and-a-half of experience, plus the inestimable advantage of following the celebrated Webster Third Edition and that merchandising bonanza, the Random House Dictionary.

Methods of compiling dictionaries are now fairly well established and need only to be followed. Previous dictionaries are available to be copied, expanded, or refined. Even so, scholars are assembled in large numbers; elaborate filing systems are devised; specialists in the graphic arts are recruited; and, as stated, American Heritage introduced computer analysis.

What are the innovative features of the American Heritage Dictionary that have made it a best seller?

Appearance. Pages are larger and more readable than those of other comparable dictionaries. Page formats are two columns of 17 picas each, and an outside column of 9 picas for illustrations, with the result that illustrations have no "runarounds."

Anthony Burgess, a British novelist writing in the *New York Times Book Review* said, ". . . the literal margins of the American Heritage are very heartening. Left-hand margin on the left-hand page, right-hand on the right, they have illustrations where illustrations are needed and sheer blankness where they are not."

Type size is 7.2 points with body type of "Times New Roman" and entry type of "Univers."

Abbreviations and symbols have been eliminated. Editor-in-Chief William Morris said this is an attempt to eliminate "dictionary short-hand"—the frustrating signs, symbols, and abbreviations that are commonplace in other dictionaries. Except for a few obvious abbreviations (*n.* for noun, *v.* for verb, and the like), the AHD followed a policy of spelling out all definitions.

A pronunciation key is located at the bottom of each two-page spread. Simplicity and clarity have been sought in the system of representing pronunciations, Morris observed, so that words can be pronounced from familiar symbols by the reader untrained in phonetics.

Publishers' Weekly, a trade publication considered the bible of the book publishing industry, reported that the AHD required a paper that had an opacity of 92 percent, was lightweight (30 pound), and had a high finish. Opacity and weight were the most important considerations, since the dictionary's unusual illustration program, which includes many halftones and as many as six cuts per page, precluded any but the lightest show-through. A canvass of some nine mills located one that agreed to develop a special paper to meet the publisher's specifications.

Information on Usage. Authoritative advice on the proper use of some 800 controversial words is provided in comprehensive usage notes, located right at the relevant entry. These notes reflect the opinions of 104 prominent writers, editors, scholars, and public figures, including Isaac Asimov, Gerald Carson, Roy Copperud, Mario Pei, Red Smith, Vermont Royster, Margaret Mead, and Margaret Nicholson. Theodore M. Bernstein and Gilbert Highet, who are listed on the consultant board of the Random House Unabridged Dictionary, are also on the Usage Panel, so the AHD is apparently getting the best of more than one world.

Polled by mail on lists of questionable words, the panelists reached a rough consensus that is tabulated in the dictionary text as approval or disapproval. *Time* magazine called the polling process "a Gallup through contemporary English and its linguistic hurdles."

Usage has been reenthroned, said Professor Smeaton—happily, not the prescriptive brand of yore but a more relativistic kind which recognizes the primacy of the spoken word and the fact that languages have to keep changing, but does not imply (as Webster's Third seems to) that "anything goes."

William Morris told *Time* that he feels that such standards are essential if readers are to have any indication of the social levels of words. But he rejects suggestions that the new dictionary is an American Fowler. Despite their prescriptive brilliance, Morris says, the Fowler brothers (*Dictionary of Modern English Usage*, 1926) could not possibly reflect a true cross section of the literate community of their time. As Morris sees it, "This is what we believe our Usage Panel has accomplished."

W. V. Quine found the usage notes an "unusual and commendable enrichment." It was an effective way of combining the benefits of description and prescription and even being descriptive about the prescriptions. Common uses are recorded and where evaluation is called for, the numerical vote of the panel is shown.

The panel fought to a draw on the grammatical number of *data*. The usage note states that *data* is now used both as a plural and as a singular collective. *These data are inconclusive. This data is inconclusive.* The plural construction is the more appropriate in formal usage. The singular is acceptable to 50 percent of the Usage Panel.

The word *finalize* has been making hackles rise for a decade, but according to Professor Ives, the word is coined according to established principles of word formation. The word is attested by many current uses, and even Dr. Gove himself approved it. Objections to it must be based on some consideration other than the normal processes of the language, Professor Ives said, such as personal whim or dislike of anything new.

Nevertheless, the AHD usage note states that *finalize* is closely associated with the language of bureaucracy, in the minds of many careful writers and speakers, and is consequently avoided by them. Isaac Asimov denounced *finalize* as "nothing more than bureaucratic illiteracy —the last resort of the communicatively untalented." The example *finalize plans for a class reunion* is termed unacceptable by 90 percent of the Usage Panel.

It would appear the Panel could have done better on the *-ize* shibboleth. In 1936 *The American Language* by H. L. Mencken listed *colonize, demoralize, hospitalize, minimize, modernize, scrutinize, synchronize,* and *winterize*. Serious students can add one more. As Dr. Gove said in a letter to the *New York Times*, the word *finalize* was recorded without stigma in the Second Edition, having appeared steadily in the Nineteen Twenties and Nineteen Thirties, and then regained popularity upon its use by President Eisenhower.

Morris Bishop, former president of the Modern Language Association, commented with perception on the Usage Panel, whose contributions William Morris said had the greatest significance to the dictionary. On specific questions the Usage Panel disagreed more than they agreed, revealing a fact often conveniently ignored—that among those best qualified to know, there is a considerable diversity of usage.

The panelists tended toward conservatism, Professor Bishop observed, but avoided overniceness and prissiness. They know the history of words and have tested the value of idioms. They have grown tired of overused vogue words.

None of them likes Business English, Professor Bishop said, and they betray a particular spite against the language of Madison Avenue. Yet they are anti-pedantic and have no absolute standard of rightness. They have given the reader the enlightened judgments of a cultivated elite on many interesting and troublesome expressions, but they do not presume to dictate.

From the start of editorial work on AHD, there was never any question in the minds of its editors and publishers of the propriety of inclusion of the entire range of vocabulary, including a handful of words omitted from most older American dictionaries. This position is one that would be taken by any reputable scholar, since to a linguist words are simply lexical items and if any are to be recorded, all should be.

Editor-in-Chief Morris told Tom Tiede of the NEA, "I suppose we have published more of what can be called 'the language of confrontation' than any other dictionary in history."

Morris means, of course, street talk. He means *nitty-gritty, up tight, black power, pot, bust,* and *make out.*

He also means four-letter words.

"We probably hold the record on four-letter ones," says Morris. "I don't know of any dictionary that carries more. We handle them like any other words. We do label them as 'vulgar' or 'vulgar slang' when necessary, but we indicate how to pronounce them and we give all of the various meanings, none of which, I should add, are written to excite the Freudian instincts of anyone."

Morris' feeling is that four-letter words are an active part of the language, and must be defined.

Morris is not the first lexicographer to think this way, Mr. Tiede observed, but is the first to think extensively this way. Four-letter words have been published in standard dictionaries since the 18th Century. The early works of Nathaniel Bailey (1721) and Reverend John Ash (1775) had explicit explanations of the same words used today.

In the 19th Century, such words fell into hard times. Says Morris: "Nobody dared dignify indecent words (then called *cants*) while Queen Victoria was on the throne."

The Victorian mores did not die easily. Dr. Allen Walker Read's article entitled "An Obscenity Symbol," which discussed the most vulgar word in the English language, appeared in the December 1934 issue of *American Speech* and never once mentioned the word. In 1961 Webster's still could not work up nerve to print the word.

In his column "Thinking Things Over," Vermont Royster, editor of the *Wall Street Journal*, said "Colloquialisms, vulgarisms, neologisms, even Madison Avenue malapropisms, all are now included as befits a dictionary of the living language."

Word Histories. Tracing the etymology of words, including those labeled "vulgar" or "vulgar slang," is a neat exercise in detective work.

Authorities say that many of Dr. Johnson's etymologies were pure fantasies. He cannot be blamed for this since the science of historical linguistics did not come into existence until the 19th Century. Modern dictionaries have access to a vast body of linguistic scholarship and they generally employ scholars to interpret the newest findings, which are often extremely complex.

The AHD is particularly strong in etymology. Its first linguistic consultant was Professor Calvert Watkins, then chairman of the Department of Linguistics at Harvard, a man recognized as one of the most brilliant historical linguists of today. He and the AHD's staff etymologist developed a system by which every word in English is traced to its ultimate known origins, in the reconstructed prehistoric language called Indo-European.

The Indo-European language, spoken in the early Bronze Age, is the ancestor not only of English but also of all the Germanic, Celtic, Italic, and Slavic languages, as well as of Greek, Persian, and Sanskrit. A massive task of research was undertaken by Professor Watkins and some 20 other members of his department in collaboration with 10 specialized editors at AHD, and the results are embodied in a 50-page appendix of Indo-European roots, to which the etymologies in the dictionary cross-refer.

Definitions. The selection, analysis, and writing of definitions is the central and by far the most laborious part of a dictionary. Casting a definition requires:

1. Precision, grace, clarity, and economy of language in wording entries.

2. Keen discrimination of senses.

3. A typographical system to guide the reader through the definition logically and on to further references.

In an article entitled "Guide to the Dictionary," Norman Hoss, the managing editor, explained how the AHD established the order of definitions.

When an entry has multiple numbered definitions, they are ordered by a method of synchronic semantic analysis intended to serve the convenience of the general user. The numerical order does not indicate the historical sequence of the senses. The first definition, then, is not necessarily the earliest sense of the word, though it may be. The first definition is the central meaning about which the other senses may be most logically organized. The organization seeks to clarify that the entry is a single "word" and not a number of separate words that happen to be spelled the same.

Two entries illustrate this principle:

hardware

1. Metal goods and utensils such as locks, tools, and cutlery. 2. *Technology*. a. A computer and the associated physical equipment directly involved in the performance of communications or data-processing functions. b. Broadly, machines and other physical equipment directly involved in performing an industrial, technological, or military function. 3. *Informal*. Weapons; especially, military weapons. 4. *Informal & Regional*. A pistol or pistols; a six-gun.

software

1. Written or printed data, such as programs, routines, and symbolic languages, essential to the operation of computers. 2. Documents containing information on the operation and maintenance of computers, such as manuals, circuit diagrams, and flow charts. [Coined after HARDWARE ("the machines").]

In selecting words for definition, the AHD used a significant innovation.

Academic linguists have for some years been using the computer to analyze large bodies of language with far greater speed and accuracy than is otherwise possible. A major study of this kind is the *Standard Corpus of Present-Day Edited American English*, performed at Brown University.

The Corpus contains 1,014,232 words broken down into a wide range of subject matter and prose style, from the sports page to the scientific journal, and from popular romantic fiction to abstruse philosophical discussion. (A full description of the Corpus can be found in the book by Henry Kučera and W. Nelson Francis, *Computational Analysis of Present-Day American English*, Brown University Press, Providence, 1967.)

Professor Kučera was one of the AHD's linguistic advisors, and he made two complete printouts of the Corpus available for use by the dictionary's editors. These printouts enabled a definer to trace a word, whether a very frequent one with many meanings, like *state*, or a rarer one like *pinkish*, and examine every context in which the word occurred in the Corpus. This method created striking benefits in selecting the basic word-list and in casting definitions that fit the facts of language.

The AHD negotiated through its 155,000 entries with remarkable skill and excellent taste, and maintains what *Time* called "a canny middle course" between prescriptive and descriptive.

It's apparently what the public wants.

FOR DISCUSSION AND REVIEW

1 What differences between *Webster's Third* and *The American Heritage Dictionary* does Trippett discuss?

2 What is the function of *The American Heritage* Usage Panel? What does Trippett consider interesting about their findings?

3 If a dictionary declares itself to be descriptive, can it avoid including four-letter taboo words? How have *Webster's Third* and *The American*

Heritage dictionaries solved this problem? Do you think that *The American Heritage Dictionary* is acceptable to buyers in all parts of the country?

4 What innovations in etymology did *The American Heritage Dictionary* incorporate into its dictionary?

5 How was the order of senses established in the definitions of words in this dictionary?

5

Computers in Language Analysis and in Lexicography

Henry Kučera

The increasing use of computers in lexicography, translation, and the compilation of word-indexes and concordances is one of the most exciting advances in language study today. Computers can be used to scan texts, make word counts, and set type. Henry Kučera discusses how computers were used in the creation of *The American Heritage Dictionary of the English Language.* His article is taken from the Preface to that dictionary.

AT THE time the editors of this Dictionary began their work the first contributions of computational linguistics to lexicography were becoming available. They have had at their disposal an analysis of a body of language data that would have cost many years of human labor to complete without the computer.

A lexicographer, contemplating the compilation of a new dictionary, is faced with a number of basic initial problems such as how many and which entries to include, which meanings to consider in defining a word, how to organize the definitions, and how to illustrate the usage of words. His decision will, of course, be based partly on such non-linguistic considerations as the size of the dictionary, the audience that he has in mind for the book, and the amount of money the publisher wishes to invest. But one thing the lexicographer must consider most carefully is the current state of the language he is planning to describe. For this reason, he collects citations illustrating the current usage of words, and studies the lexical, grammatical, and semantic properties of the language in normal discourse.

At the same time, the lexicographer may find it useful to have some knowledge of the basic lexical properties of large bodies of language data, knowledge that cannot be obtained from editorially chosen individual citations. Given a reasonably representative selection of contemporary texts, he may wish to know, for example, how many different words there are in such a textual corpus, what words they are, and with what frequency each occurs. In many instances the lexicographer may also be interested in the textual context that could provide useful information about particular shades of meaning in word usage. Such lexicographic interests naturally overlap, to a considerable extent, those of a linguist engaged in theoretical research on language structures or those of a practical specialist working to develop a machine that will automatically translate from one language to another.

Since any useful analysis of language usage has to be based on a large body of textual material, even elementary information could be obtained, before the advent of computers, only with enormous labor. Let us imagine that one wished to determine some very basic lexical properties of a textual corpus containing a million running words. If this were to be done by hand (or, more accurately, by the human brain), the task would require an inordinate amount of time; each of the one million words would have to be inspected individually, and each new word recorded after first checking to make sure it had not already been noted. If the analysis were also to preserve information about the frequency of occurrence of individual words, or perhaps references to the pages or lines of the text where their occurrences were to be found, the assignment would become more formidable still. Dedicated linguists and lexicographers—and their graduate students—have done limited analyses in the past by this painful method. But not only are projects of this kind extremely time-consuming, the monotony of the task is also apt to lead to errors. The modern computer, which is incapable of boredom and which does not make mistakes (provided that it is correctly programmed and free from technical defect), is ideally suited to this assignment.

A computer, in spite of its name and in spite of the definitions of it in some dictionaries, is much more than a machine for performing calculations. Aside from their mathematical operations, computers can process, organize, compare, and manipulate data of a nonnumerical nature, including textual information. It is precisely this capacity of computers to deal with letters, words, sentences, or even whole texts that has made these machines of considerable importance in the study of language. Linguists and lexicographers alike have found in the computer a new and useful tool that has not only made the analysis of languages less laborious and less time-consuming but has also opened new insights into important problems of language usage.

As it happened, the editors of this Dictionary began their work shortly after the completion of a computer analysis especially useful to an American lexicographer. A collection of texts, known as the *Standard Corpus of Present-Day Edited American English,* had been chosen, punched on cards, and analyzed at Brown University. The Corpus contains a total of 1,014,232 running words and is divided into 500 samples, each approximately 2,000 words long. These 500 samples are distributed among 15 types, or genre categories, representing a wide range of subject matter and prose style (poetry and drama are not included), from the sports page of the newspaper to the scientific journal, and from popular romantic fiction to abstruse philosophical discussion. All of the selections constituting the Corpus were chosen by a random sampling procedure from texts first printed in the United States in a single calendar year. (A full description of the Corpus and its basic properties can be found in the book by Henry Kučera and W. Nelson Francis, *Computational Analysis of Present-Day American English,* Brown University Press, Providence, 1967.)

Once the Corpus had become available in a form suitable for computer processing (that is, on punched cards and/or magnetic tape), the analysis of its basic properties and the retrieval of lexicographically useful information could be performed relatively easily and quickly.

Among other things, the analysis showed that in the more than one million running words of the Corpus, there were exactly 50,406 *different* words. The ten most frequent words turned out to be *the* (69,971 occurrences), *of* (36,411), *and* (28,852), *to* (26,149), *a* (23,237), *in* (21,341), *that* (10,595), *is* (10,099), *was* (9,816), and *he* (9,543 occurrences). (There were only 2,859 occurrences of *she,* which is perhaps something for ladies to contemplate.)

This list does not contain many surprises in itself. What was also discovered, however, and what may well turn out to be of considerable interest to linguists and literary specialists, is that the relative frequencies of even these common words vary significantly in different types of writing. Separate word-frequency studies made for each genre of the Corpus show that *the* still retains its first rank in all 15 categories. But already at the next rank, the genre classification affects the relative frequency of usage: *of* is the second most frequent word in ten genres, *and* in four, and *to* in one. What is more interesting still is that *of* is regularly the second most frequent word in what we have called *informative prose* (newspaper selections, popular articles, learned and scientific writings, for example), while *and* or *to* occurs in second place in almost all the genres of *imaginative prose* (fiction of various kinds and humor).

Significantly, *of*, the second most frequent word (mostly by a large margin) in informative prose, usually ranks only fourth or even lower in imaginative prose. This simple analysis and other, more detailed results clearly indicate that the frequency of particular words is a partial but interesting determinant of writing style, affecting even the most common words of a language.

New equipment and more ambitious linguistic and computing procedures will undoubtedly make it possible in the future to develop more revealing approaches to questions of style. One such approach, which is being currently pursued at Brown University, attempts to characterize the stylistic properties of a text not only in terms of word frequencies but also by the relative frequency of occurrence of various grammatical structures utilized in sentence formation.

Computer-produced word-indexes and concordances are also being widely used by linguists, lexicographers, and literary scholars. A word-index is simply a list of all the different words that occur in a given textual corpus; each index entry is followed by a precise indication of the location (for example, volume, page, and line) where the occurrence of the word can be found. The context in which a particular word has been used can then be looked up in the original text. But a computer can make even this task far easier by constructing a concordance that not only gives the reference to each occurrence but also prints the context itself (for example, each line or sentence in which the word occurred), so that manual searching through the original text becomes unnecessary.

Given a reasonably large computer, it is relatively easy to produce word-indexes and simple concordances even for large bodies of text. Such a computer-produced concordance has recently been made at the University of Texas for the complete works of James Joyce, and at the University of Toronto one is being made for the whole of Middle Welsh literature. It is possible as well to have more complex information-retrieval procedures, for example, a concordance program that prints only those lines (or sentences) fulfilling several specific conditions; such conditions could include the requirement that two or three or even more particular words must occur within a certain span of each other in the text before the textual segment is to be retrieved. The sophistication and the complexity of such concordances is limited chiefly by the availability of programming skill and of a sufficiently large computer.

To give a simple illustration of the potential lexicographic usefulness of multiple-condition concordances, let us assume that we are interested in retrieving from a textual corpus all occurrences of the construction *run up*. We may wish to study the exact usage of the different senses, such as *run up the hill* and *run up the flag*, which suggest different structures as well as different meanings. We have to bear in mind, of course, that *run* can be represented in such constructions also by its other inflected forms (*runs, running, ran*); moreover, the various forms of *run* may be separated from *up* by a number of other words, as in *He ran the blue flag up*. What we thus need is a concordance program that allows us to specify, roughly, the following conditions: "Retrieve all sentences in which any one of the forms *run, runs, running*, or *ran* is followed by *up* within the same sentence." This approach assumes, of course, that we have a reliable automatic procedure for dividing our text into sentences (the *Standard Corpus of Present-Day Edited American English* has been mechanically segmented into sentences on the basis of the occurrence of initial capital letters, periods, etc.). Alternatively, we could specify that *run* (or any of its forms) and *up* can be separated from each other by ten words or less; we could then be reasonably certain to catch all occurrences of the construction but might also get some accidental combinations of *run* and *up* which do not belong together and which we would have to eliminate through an inspection of the printout.

All concordance programs described so far require the specification of the particular words or expressions whose occurrences are to be retrieved. But linguists and lexicographers frequently need to study the occurrences of certain *grammatical classes* of words (such as adjectives, nouns, or auxiliary verbs). A computer, of course, cannot understand such a command as "retrieve all nouns," because this instruction is not explicit enough; the machine knows no grammar. Instead, either the formal properties of the relevant grammatical category must be specified, or a semiautomatic grammatical analysis must be resorted to. The word-index is first grammatically annotated by the appropriate designations (nouns, adjectives, etc.). Some parts of this annotating can be done automatically—the computer can be instructed, for example, to mark all entries ending in *-ify* as verbs. In some cases the automatic grammatical annotation may be erroneous and must be corrected manually; in other cases, only a skilled human analyst can determine the proper grammatical classification in the first place.

Some of the newer computer-related equipment is of considerable help in this kind of semiautomatic grammatical analysis. Among the most useful tools is the cathode-ray-tube console, a computer-connected instrument resembling a television set, which can display on its screen textual information from the computer's memory in easily readable form, and which allows the linguist to transmit his corrections and additions directly back to the computer, without having to punch cards or to use other slow procedures of information input.

Once a word-index is grammatically annotated, it is possible to retrieve all occurrences of a desired grammatical class of words. Similarly, a grammatical version of a multiple-condition concordance (that is, the printout of lines in which several grammatical conditions are satisfied) can be prepared. A portion of the million-word *Standard Corpus of Present-Day Edited American English* has been grammatically annotated and is now being used in the analysis of "grammatical style." In this project, the individual sentences of the text are broken down to reveal the grammatical rules that are represented in these sentences, and the relative frequency of the various grammatical rules of different complexity is then utilized in the characterization of the overall grammatical complexity of a textual passage.

Computers are also playing a significant role in advanced theoretical linguistic research. Methods of the mathematical theory of communication, various word-frequency-distribution models, and other mathematical techniques have been used in the comparative study of language structures. Attempts have been made to determine, with the aid of computers, certain aspects of the similarity of languages and to investigate the correlation between such quantitative results and the degree of known genetic linguistic relationship.

The validity of individual grammatical rules, of partial grammars, and even of semantic theories has been tested by simulating sentence production by computers. And, naturally, much theoretical research and practical work has been done in the various machine-translation projects, including the compilation of computer-based bilingual dictionaries (Russian-English, German-English, and others), which, although still very limited in size, contain useful lexical and grammatical information.

Not all, and not even most, aspects of linguistic research or of lexicographic work are suitable for computer-oriented approaches. Some of the most important linguistic problems, such as the determination of the underlying "deep" structure of sentences or the study of the semantics of discourse, are and will undoubtedly remain largely dependent on human imagination and effort. In lexicography, too, it is primarily the knowledge and the skill of the editorial staff that determine the value and usefulness of a dictionary. It would thus be a serious mistake for linguists and lexicographers to rush to computers in the hope of being provided with a quick solution to all problems. It is imperative that computers be used in language analysis in an informed and judicious manner that takes the limitations of the machine fully into account. But—as I have tried to illustrate in this essay—it would be equally foolhardy for linguists and especially for lexicographers to disregard the potential of computers as research tools. Not only can computers save labor and increase accuracy, but they can also help to bring important new insights into crucial problems of language use.

FOR DISCUSSION AND REVIEW

1 Discuss some of the uses of computers in language analysis and lexicography.

2 What is a *concordance*? How might it be useful to a student of literature? To a lexicographer?

3 The way the language is spoken is an important aspect of lexicography. Does Kučera discuss how computers might aid lexicographers in this area? Can you think of additional ways that computers could be used in language study?

4 Many problems are encountered when a computer is used in language study. *Traddutore, tradittore* is an old Italian adage which means "the translator is a traitor" and indicates how subtle and difficult the translator's task is. Imagine the problems that arise when a computer is used for translation. For example, a computer translated "out of sight, out of mind" into Japanese and back into English as "invisible, insane." What happened in the process?

6

Word-Making:

Some Sources of New Words

Word formation is not a haphazard procedure but one which is for the most part patterned. In this excerpt from his book *The English Language: An Introduction*, Professor W. Nelson Francis discusses the major ways, in addition to borrowing from other languages, that words are created or acquired and become a part of the vocabulary of English.

W. Nelson Francis

THOUGH BORROWING has been the most prolific source of additions to the vocabulary of English, we acquire or create new words in several other ways. Those which will be discussed here, in descending order of importance, are *derivation, compounding, functional shift, back formation* and *clipping, proper names, imitation, blending,* and *original coinage.*

1. *Derivation.* The derivational process consists of using an existing word—or in some cases a bound morpheme or morphemic structure— as a stem to which affixes are attached. Thus our imaginary word *pandle* might become the stem for such derivatives as *pandler, pandlette, depandle,* and *repandlize.* Affixes like these are called *productive;* all native speakers know their meanings and feel free to add them to various kinds of stems in accordance with analogy or the rules of English derivation. By this process any new word, whatever its source, may almost immediately become the nucleus of a cluster of derivatives. Thus *plane,* formed by clipping from *airplane,* has produced *emplane* and *deplane,* presumably by analogy with *entrain* and *detrain,* themselves formed by analogy with *embark* and *debark,* which were borrowed from French. When *telegraph* was formed by compounding of two Greek elements, it soon gave rise to *telegrapher, telegraphy, telegraphic,* and *telegraphist,* all of which were self-explaining derivatives.

So obvious is the process of forming derivatives with productive affixes that all of us probably do it much more frequently than we realize. The words we thus "create" in most cases have been frequently used before and are listed in the dictionary, but we may not know that. This process allows us to expand our vocabulary without specifically memorizing new words. But this reliance on analogical derivation may sometimes trap us into creating new words that are unnecessary because other derivatives already exist and have become standard. The student who wrote about Hamlet's *unableness to overcome his mental undecidedness* undoubtedly was familiar with *inability* and *indecision,* but under the pressure of an examination he forgot them and created his own derivatives instead.

2. *Compounding.* In a sense, compounding is a special form of derivation in which, instead of adding affixes (bound forms) to a stem, two or more words (or in some cases bound bases) are put together to make a new lexical unit. Compounding has been a source of new words in English since earliest times, and is particularly common in present-day English. Perusal of any daily paper will turn up countless examples of compounds that are new within the last few years or months: *launching pad, blast-off, jet-port, freeway, ski-tow, free loader, feather-bedding, sit-in.* Our writing system does not indicate whether items like *weather satellite* are compounds or constructions. Many of them begin as constructions but then assume the characteristic stress patterns of compounds: some people still pronounce *ice cream* with the stress pattern of a construction (as in *iced tea*), but most treat it as a compound

(as in *iceboat*). Some of the older compounds have gone through sound (and spelling) changes that have completely obscured their compound origin. Typical of these is *lord*, which began in early Old English as *hlāf-weard*, a compound of the ancestors of our *loaf* and *ward*, and passed through the stages of OE *hlāford* and ME *loverd* to its present monosyllabic form. Other examples are *woman*, originally a compound of the ancestors of *wife* and *man*, and *hussy*, from *house* and *wife*, hence etymologically a doublet of *housewife*.

The semantic relationships between the parts of compounds are very varied. If compounds are thought of as the product of a transformation process, this variety can be revealed by reconstructing the phrase from which the compound might have been created.[1] This may range from a simple modification, in which the transformation involves only a change in stress pattern (*hot dog, blackboard, bluebird*), to complete predication, where the transformation involves complicated reordering and deletion (as in *salesman* from *man who makes sales* or *movie camera* from *camera that takes movies*). Compounds may themselves enter into compounds to produce elaborate structures like *aircraft carrier* and *real estate salesman*. These must be considered compounds, since they have the characteristic stress-pattern with the strongest stress on the first element (*áircràft càrrier, réal estàte sàlesman*), in contrast to the stress pattern of modification constructions (as in *àircràft desígner* or *rèal estàte invéstment*).

One special group of compounds, most of them of quite recent origin, includes those words—mostly technical and scientific terms—which are made up of morphemes borrowed from Greek. Many of the elements so used were free forms—words—in Greek, but must be considered bound bases in English. The practice of compounding them began in Greek: *philosophia* is compounded from *philos* "fond of" and *sophia* "wisdom." Words of this sort were borrowed into Latin in ancient times, and ultimately reached English by way of French. Renaissance scholars, who knew Greek and recognized the combining elements, began to make new combinations which did not exist in the original Greek. With the growth of scientific knowledge from the seventeenth century on, new technical and scientific terms were commonly invented this way.

Words created can be roughly divided into two groups. The first includes those which have wide circulation in the general vocabulary—

---

[1] Full discussions of the types and meanings of compounds from differing grammatical points of view may be found in Otto Jespersen, *A Modern English Grammar on Historical Principles*, Part VI (Copenhagen: Ejnar Munksgaard, 1942), chapter IX, and Robert B. Lees, *The Grammar of English Nominalizations* (Bloomington, Indiana: Indiana University Research Center in Anthropology, Folklore, and Linguistics, 1960), chapter IV.

like *telephone, photograph,* and *thermometer.* These are constructed out of a relatively small number of morphemes, whose meanings are well known:

tele	"far, distant"	*meter*	"measure"
phone	"sound"	*dyna*	"power"
photo	"light"	*hydro*	"water, moisture"
graph	"write, mark"	*bio*	"life"
thermo	"heat"	*morph*	"shape, form"

Inventors and manufacturers of new products often create names for their inventions from elements of this sort. Sometimes the Greek elements are combined with Latin ones, as in *automobile* (Greek *autos* "self," Latin *mobilis* "movable") and *television,* or even with native English elements, as in *dynaflow.* Recent creations in this group are *astronaut* and *cosmonaut,* from Greek *aster* "star," *kosmos* "universe," and *nautes* "sailor." Actually *cosmonaut* was first used in Russian, whence it was borrowed, but since both of its bases were already in use in English (as in *cosmology* and *aeronaut*), it might just as well have originated in English.

The second group of Greek-based compounds comprises the large number of technical and scientific terms whose use is almost wholly restricted to specialists. As in the case of *cosmonaut,* most of these words are readily interchangeable among the languages in which scientific publication is extensive. Since it is often difficult if not impossible to determine the language in which they were first used, the Merriam-Webster editors have recently made use of the term *International Scientific Vocabulary* (abbreviated ISV) to describe them. A few examples of wide enough circulation to be included in an abridged dictionary, are the following:

hypsography: "recording (*graphy*) of elevation (*hypso*)"
telethermoscope: "instrument that perceives (*scope*) heat (*thermo*) at a distance (*tele*)"
electroencephalograph: "instrument that records (*graph*) electric current (*electro*) within (*en*) the head (*cephalo*)"
schizogenesis: "reproduction (*genesis*) by division (*schizo*)"

In all cases, since at least two of the combining elements are bases, these words must be considered compounds. They may also give rise to derivatives formed by the addition of affixes in regular patterns, such as *electroencephalography* and *schizogenetic.* It is in this way, rather than by direct borrowing, that Greek has made its great contribution to the English vocabulary.

3. *Functional Shift.* Since the late Middle English period, when most of the inflections surviving from Old English finally disappeared, it has been easy to shift a word from one part of speech to another without

altering its form, at least in the unmarked base form. A verb like *walk* can be turned into a noun simply by using it in a syntactic position reserved for nouns, as in *he took a walk*, where the determiner *a* marks *walk* as a noun, direct object of *took*. This process, called *functional shift*, is an important concomitant of the historical change of English from a synthetic to an analytic language, and has greatly enlarged the vocabulary in a very economical way. Since the words so created belong to a different part of speech and hence have a different grammatical distribution from that of the original, they must be considered new words, homonymous in the base form with the words from which they were derived, rather than merely extensions of meaning. From another point of view, they may be thought of as derivatives with zero affixes. In some cases they may take a different stress pattern in their new use: the noun *implement,* with weak stress and the weak central vowel /ə/ in the last syllable, when shifted to a verb took secondary stress on the last syllable, whose vowel was changed to /e/. Since there is overt change in pronunciation, this is true derivation rather than functional shift. But the two processes are obviously closely related.

   Older instances of functional shift commonly produced nouns from verbs: in addition to *walk*, already cited, we might mention *run, steal, laugh, touch, buy, break,* and many others. In present-day English the shift from noun to verb is much in favor. In the past, short words like *brush* and *perch* were sometimes shifted from noun to verb, but today, longer nouns like *implement, position, process, contact* are often used as verbs. Even compound nouns get shifted to verbs; the secretary who said "I didn't back-file the letter, I waste-basketed it" was speaking twentieth-century English, however inelegant.

   4. *Back Formation* and *Clipping* are two modes of word creation which can be classed together as different types of *reduction.* In each case, a shorter word is made from a longer one, so that the effect is the opposite of derivation and compounding. *Back formation* makes use of analogy to produce a sort of reverse derivation. The existence of *creation, create,* and *donation* readily suggests that if there is not a verb *donate* there should be. This seems so natural to us that it is hard to believe that less than a century ago *donate* was considered an American barbarism by many puristically inclined British speakers of English.[2] Other words that have come into English by back formation are *edit* (from *editor*), *burgle* (from *burglar*), *enthuse* (from *enthusiasm*), *televise* (from *television,* by analogy with pairs like *supervise: supervision*), *automate* (from *automation*), *laze* (from *lazy*), and many more. Once pairs of words like these have become established, only the historical

---

[2] See H. L. Mencken, *The American Language,* Fourth Edition (New York: Alfred A. Knopf, 1936), pp. 121, 165.

record proving prior use of the longer forms serves to distinguish them from normal derivational pairs.

Clippings, on the other hand, are shortenings without regard to derivational analogy. They are frequent in informal language, especially spoken, as in the campus and classroom use of *exam, lab, math,* and *dorm.* They are possible because often a single syllable, usually the one bearing the main stress, is sufficient to identify a word, especially in a rather closely restricted context, so that the remaining syllables are redundant and can be dropped. Most of them preserve a colloquial flavor and are limited to the special vocabularies of occupational groups. Others, however—often over the objections of purists—attain wide circulation and may ultimately replace the longer forms on most or all levels of usage. Some that have done so are *van* (from *caravan*), *bus* (from *omnibus*), *cello* (from *violoncello*), *mob* (from Latin *mobile vulgus* "unstable crowd"), *piano* (from *pianoforte*), and *fan* (in sense "ardent devotee," from *fanatic*). Others which are in acceptable, though perhaps characteristically informal, use alongside the longer unclipped words are *phone* (for *telephone*), *taxi* and *cab* (from *taxicab*), and *plane* (for *airplane* or older *aeroplane*). A rather special form of clipping is that which reduces long compounds or idiomatic fixed phrases to one of their elements—often the modifying element rather than the head—as in *express* from *express train*, *car* from *motor car*, and *outboard* from *outboard motor* (*boat*). This process often accounts for what otherwise seem strange transfers of meaning.

An extreme form of clipping is that which reduces words to their abbreviations and longer phrases to their initials. Abbreviation is, of course, a standard device of the writing system to save space by reducing the length of common or often repeated words. Usually it is confined to writing, and to rather informal writing at that. But some common abbreviations have been adopted in speech and ways have been found to pronounce them. The common abbreviations for the two halves of the day—A.M. and P.M.—which stand for the Latin phrases *ante meridiem* ("before noon") and *post meridiem* ("after noon") are frequently used in speech, where they are pronounced /é:+èm/ and /pí:èm/. These must indeed be considered words, though their spelling is that of abbreviations. The same is true of B.C. and A.D. in dates, O.K. (which has become an international word), U.S., G.I., L.P., TNT, TV, and DDT. In all these cases the pronunciation is simply the syllabic names of the letters, usually with the strongest stress on the last: /yù:+és/, /dì:+dì:+tí:/, and so on.

If the initial letters of a phrase, used as an abbreviation, happen to make a combination that is pronounceable, what results is an *acronym* —a word whose spelling represents the initial letters of a phrase. Though very popular in recent times, acronyms are by no means an

innovation of the twentieth century. The early Christians made a
famous one when they took the initials of the Greek phrase Ἰησοῦς
Χριστὸς θεοῦ υἱὸς σωτήρ ("Jesus Christ, son of God, Savior") to make the
Greek word ἰχθύς ("fish") and adopted the fish as a symbol of Christ.
Acronyms have become more frequent in English since World War II.
Everyone talks about NATO, UNESCO, and NASA, often without
being able to supply the longer title whose initials created the acronym.
In fact, acronyms have become so popular that some longer titles have
been created by a kind of back formation from the desired initials. It
was certainly more than a happy accident that led the Navy in World
War II to call its feminine branch "Women Assigned to Volunteer
Emergency Service," or WAVES. More recently an organization devoted to finding foster parents for orphan children from foreign lands
has called itself "World Adoption International Fund" so its initials
would spell WAIF.

5. *Proper Names.* The giving of individual names to persons, places,
geographic features, deities, and sometimes to animals is a universal
human practice, apparently as old as language itself. A proper name,
since it is closely restricted to a single specific referent, does not have
the general and varied distribution and reference that characterize
ordinary nouns. But there is frequent interchange across the line separating proper names from other words. Many proper names, such as
Taylor, Smith, Clark, and *Wright* are derived from common nouns
describing occupations; others like *Brown, Strong,* and *Wild* derive
from adjectives that may once have described the person so named.
Place-names also frequently show their derivation from common nouns,
as in *Northfield, Portsmouth,* and *Fairmount.*

There has also been interchange in the other direction, by which the
proper name of a person or place becomes generalized in meaning,
usually to refer to a product or activity connected with the referent of
the proper name. One famous example is the name *Caesar,* originally
a nickname coined from the Latin verb *caedo* "to cut" to describe
Julius Caesar, who was cut from his mother's womb by the operation
still called *Caesarian section.* The name was assumed by Julius's nephew
Octavius, the first Roman emperor, and then by the subsequent em-
perors, so that it became virtually a synonym for *imperator* "emperor."
In its later history it was borrowed into Germanic, ultimately becoming
German *Kaiser* (there was also a Middle English word *kayser,* now
obsolete), and into Slavonic, whence came *tsar.* Another interesting set
of words derived from names are the adjectives *mercurial, saturnine,*
and *jovial,* referring to temperaments supposed to be characteristic of
people under the dominance of the planets Mercury, Saturn, and
Jupiter. The corresponding *venereal* (from *Venus*) has been restricted
in meaning almost entirely to medical use, but *venery* is still a rather

high-flown word for love-making. Those supposed to derive instability from the changeable moon used to be called *lunatic* (from Latin *luna,* the moon). The punishment visited upon Tantalus, forever doomed to be within sight of food and water that receded when he reached for it, has given us the verb *tantalize,* formed by adding the productive suffix *-ize* (itself ultimately derived from Greek) to his name. Also ultimately Greek in origin are *hector* ("a bully, to bully") from the Trojan hero in the *Iliad* and *mentor* ("teacher"—now often used in the sports pages for "athletic coach") from the adviser of Telemachus in the *Odyssey.*

During the history of English since the beginning of the Middle English period, various words have been derived from proper names. Some earlier ones are *dunce* (from the scholastic philosopher Duns Scotus—used in ridicule of scholastic philosophy in the later sixteenth century), *pander* (from the character Pandarus in Chaucer's *Troilus and Criseyde,* c. 1385), *mawmet* (from Mahomet; at first it meant "idol," later "puppet, doll"). The Bible, widely read from Reformation times on and frequently discussed for its symbolic as well as its literal or historical meaning, has contributed many words of this sort, such as *jeremiad* ("a denunciatory tirade"), *babel, lazar* (from Lazarus; common for *leper* in Middle English), *maudlin* (from Mary Magdalen and her noted tears), and *simony* ("taking or giving money for church offices," from Simon Magus). On the border between proper and common nouns are names of Biblical and other personages taken in figurative meanings, though usually capitalized in writing, indicating that the transfer to common noun is not complete: *the old Adam, raising Cain, a doubting Thomas, a Daniel come to judgment.*

Some proper names that have assumed general meanings have undergone pronunciation changes that obscure their origins. The adjective *tawdry* ("cheap and flashy") comes from a clipping of *Saint Audrey,* and presumably was first used to describe a kind of cheap lace sold at St. Audrey's Fair. *Bedlam,* which to us means "uproar, total confusion," was a proper name as late as the eighteenth century, when it was used as a short name for *St. Mary of Bethlehem,* a London insane asylum. The word *mawkin,* used dialectally in England for "scarecrow," comes from *Malkyn,* a girl's name, ultimately a nickname from *Mary.* The parallel nickname *Moll* gave rise to an American slang word for a criminal's girl. The history of *doll* is similar but more complicated; it passed from a clipped form of *Dorothy* to describe a miniature (usually female) figure, then to describe a small and pretty girl.

The names of historical characters—often those of unsavory reputation—have given us some rather common words. One of the most interesting of these is *guy,* from *Guy Fawkes,* used in England to describe the effigies of that notable traitor which are customarily carried in procession and burned on November 5, the anniversary of the discovery of his "Gunpowder Plot." The term came to mean "a figure of fun, a butt of scorn," and as a verb "to poke fun at, tease." In America it has become a universal colloquial term for any male not held in high respect. In phrases like *a nice guy* (when not used ironically) it has lost all of its original pejorative flavor.

Names of products derived from the names of their places of origin are rather plentiful in English. Textiles like *calico* (from *Calicut*, or *Calcutta*), *denim* (*serge de Nîmes*), *cashmere* (*Kashmir*), and *worsted* (from the name of a town in Norfolk, England) are well known. So are products like *china* (clipped from *chinaware* from *China ware*), *gin* (clipped from *Geneva*), *cognac*, and *cayenne*. Specialized and technical vocabularies are especially fond of words adapted from proper names. Skiing has its *telemark* and *christiania* (usually clipped to *christy*); librarians speak of *Dewey decimal classification* and *Cutter numbers*; horticulturalists of *fuchsia, dahlia,* and *wistaria*; physicists of *roentgen rays, curies,* and *angstrom units*; electricians of *ohms, watts,* and *amperes*; doctors of *rickettsia* and *Bright's disease*.

6. *Imitation*. A relatively small number of words in English apparently owe their origin to attempts to imitate natural sounds. *Bow-wow, meow, baa, moo,* and other words for animal cries are supposed to remind us of the noises made by dogs, cats, sheep, and cows. They are not accurate imitations, since they are pronounced with sounds characteristic of the sound-system of English, which these animals, not being native speakers of English, do not use. Other languages have other, often quite different imitative words. Both *cock-a-doodle-doo* and *kikiriki* are supposedly imitative of a rooster's crow; unless we assume that English and Greek roosters make quite different sounds, we must attribute the difference between these words to the differing sound-systems of the two languages.

Related to imitation is the phenomenon sometimes called *sound symbolism*: the habit of associating a certain type or class of meanings with a certain sound or cluster of sounds. There seems to be in English an association between the initial consonant cluster *sn-* and the nose (*snarl, sneer, sneeze, sniff, snivel, snore, snort, snout,* and *snuffle*). When slang words referring to or involving the nose are coined they may begin with this cluster, as in *snook* and *snoop*. English speakers associate the sound-combination spelled *-ash* (/æš/) with a sudden loud sound or rapid, turbulent, or destructive motion, as in *crash, dash, flash, smash,* and *splash*; and a final *-er* on verbs suggests rapidly repeated, often rhythmic motion, as in *flicker, flutter, hover, quiver, shimmer, waver*. This last example is perhaps a morpheme in its own right, though to call it one would give us a large number of bound bases that occur nowhere else. But it is well on the way to the morphemic status which certainly must be accorded to the *-le* or *-dle* of *handle*, *treadle*, and *spindle*.

Imitation was once considered so important as to be made the basis for a theory of the origin of language—the so-called "bow-wow theory." This theory is commonly discounted nowadays.

7. *Blending* is a combination of clipping and compounding, which makes new words by putting together fragments of existing words in new combinations. It differs from derivation in that the elements thus combined are not morphemes at the time the blends are made, though they may become so afterward as a result of the blending process, especially if several blends are made with the same element and the phenomenon of *false etymology* is present.

The poem "Jabberwocky" in Lewis Carroll's *Through the Looking Glass* contains many ingenious blends, though only a few of them (called *portmanteau words* by Humpty Dumpty in the book) have passed into the general vocabulary. Thus *slithy* (from *lithe* and *slimy*) and *mimsy* (from *miserable* and *flimsy*) are not used outside the poem, but *chortle* (*chuckle* and *snort*) and *galumphing* (*galloping* and *triumphing*) are not uncommon words, though they are usually restricted to colloquial or facetious use.

The history of *-burger* illustrates the way in which blending can give rise to a new morpheme. The name *Hamburger steak* (varying with *Hamburg steak*) was given to a kind of ground beef in America in the 1880's. It was soon shortened by phrase-clipping to *hamburger*, losing its proper-name quality in the process. The *-er* here is simply the normal German suffix for making an adjective from a proper noun (as in *Brandenburger Tor* "Brandenburg Gate"). But to those who did not know German, the word looked (and sounded) like a compound of *ham* and *burger*. So the *-burger* part was clipped and combined with various other words or parts of words to make *cheeseburger, deerburger, buffaloburger*, and many more. These have the form of compounds made up of one free base and a bound base *-burger*. Meanwhile by further clipping, *hamburger*, already short for *hamburger steak sandwich*, was cut down to *burger*, which now became a free form—a word. Thus what began as the last two syllables of a German proper adjective has become first a bound morpheme and then a full word in English.

Other morphemes which owe their origin to blending are *-rama*, *-orium*, *-teria*, and *-omat*. The first of these began with words of Greek origin like *panorama* and *cyclorama*.[3] The combining elements in Greek were *pan* "all," *kyklos* "circle, wheel," and *horama* "view," a noun derived from the verb *horan* "see." But the *-rama* part of these words

---

[3] See John Lotz, "The Suffix '-rama,'" *American Speech*, 39:156–58, 1954.

was blended with *cine* (from *cinema*) to make *cinerama*, describing a type of wide-screen motion picture. Subsequently *-rama* was blended with various other elements to make new words like *colorama* and *vistarama*, as well as many trade and commercial names. It certainly must now be considered a separate morpheme, conveying a vague notion of grandeur and sweep (or so its users hope) to the words in which it is used. Similarly *-orium*, split off from *emporium* (a rather fancy Latin loan-word for "shop"), *-teria*, split off from the Spanish loan-word *cafeteria*, and *-omat*, split off from the trade name *Automat*, itself a clipping from *automatic*, have become separate morphemes, as in *lubritorium*, *valeteria*, and *laundromat*. The process of blending has thus produced not only new words but new morphemes capable of entering with some freedom into new compounds and derivatives. Many of the words thus coined never get any farther than their first application by an enterprising advertiser or proprietor, and those that do usually have a brief life. But a few seem to fill a real need and remain as part of the general vocabulary of English.

8. *Coinage.* Very few words are simply made up out of unrelated, meaningless elements. The other resources for making new words and the abundant vocabularies of other languages available for borrowing supply so many easy ways of producing new words that outright coinage seldom suggests itself. The outright coinage—unlike the compound, clipping, derivative, and blend—is also hard to remember because it has no familiar elements to aid the memory. So wholly new coinages are both harder to make and less likely to be remembered and used. It is no wonder that they are relatively rare. Some words, however, are indubitable coinages, and others for which etymologists have found no source may be tentatively assumed to be. Words like *quiz, pun, slang,* and *fun* have no cognates in other Germanic languages, cannot be traced to other languages as loan-words, and, since they are monosyllabic, are not compounds or derivatives, though they might be blends to which we have lost the key. One can imagine that *slang*—an eighteenth-century creation—combined elements from *slovenly* and *language,* but this is pure guesswork. These, together with more recent words, most of them facetious or slangy, like *hooch* and *pooch, snob* and *gob* ("sailor"), most probably originated as free coinages, sometimes involving sound symbolism.

More elaborate coinages, having more than one syllable, are likely to combine original elements with various other processes of word formation, especially derivation. Thus the stems of *segashuate, sockdologer,* and *spifflicated* seem to be coinages, but the suffixes are recognizable morphemes. In fact, it would be exceedingly unlikely for a native speaker to coin a word of more than one syllable without making use of one or more of the word-forming devices we have been discussing.

As even this brief chapter must have made obvious, the vocabulary of English is large, complex, highly diversified in origin, and constantly changing. No dictionary, however large, can contain it all. Or, if such a dictionary should be prepared, it would be out of date by the time it was printed, since new meanings, new borrowings, and new creations are being added every day. Nor can any single individual know it all. Speakers of English share a large vocabulary in common, it is true, but every individual speaker has his own unique inventory of the less commonly used words and meanings, reflecting his unique experience with language.

Many people—perhaps most people—go through life with a vocabulary adequate only to their daily needs, picking up new words when some new facet of life makes it necessary, but never indulging in curiosity and speculation about words. Others are wordlovers—collectors and connoisseurs. They like to measure one word against another, trace their etymologies and shifts of meaning, use them in new and exciting or amusing combinations. They play word-games like *Scrabble* and *Anagrams*, they do cross-word puzzles, they make puns and rhymes and nonsense jingles. Some make poems, which are the highest form of word-game. But even those who aspire no further than to the writing of good clear expository prose must become at least amateur connoisseurs of words. Only this way—not by formal exercises or courses in vocabulary-building—will they learn to make the best possible use of the vast and remarkable lexicon of English.

FOR DISCUSSION AND REVIEW

1   Francis makes references to *morphemes*. What is a morpheme and what importance does it have for the study of word formation?

2   Francis tells of a student who used the words *unableness* for *inability* and *undecidedness* for *indecision* while under the pressure of an examination situation. Can you recall ever forming new words by the derivative method? Explain.

3   When settlers first came to this country they frequently used the compounding technique to give names to specimens of the flora and fauna which were unfamiliar to them. They called unfamiliar ducks names such as *wood ducks, canvas back ducks, fan crested ducks,* and *dumpling ducks.* Naming in this particular field is no longer necessary, but science still makes great use of the compounding process. Can you give any examples of such compounds?

4   Identify the processes of word formation in the following words: *gas, contrail, happenstance, fan, elbow, peddle, ack ack, midwife, xerography, loran, positron, enthuse, piano, telecast, gin, quisling, tawdry, bang.*

7

Preface to the Dictionary of American Slang

When a fellow student asks you if you have any *bread*, he is most likely interested in money and not something to eat. As the following article by Stuart Berg Flexner indicates, food plays a major role in the imagery of our slang expressions. Mr. Flexner also discusses the origins of slang, its subgroups, and its place in American usage.

Stuart Berg Flexner

AMERICAN SLANG, as used in the title of this dictionary, is the body of words and expressions frequently used by or intelligible to a rather large portion of the general American public, but not accepted as good, formal usage by the majority. No word can be called slang simply because of its etymological history; its source, its spelling, and its meaning in a larger sense do *not* make it slang. Slang is best defined by a dictionary that points out who uses slang and what "flavor" it conveys.

I have called all slang used in the United States "American," regardless of its country of origin or use in other countries.

In this preface I shall discuss the human element in the formation of slang (what American slang is, and how and why slang is created and used). . . .

The English language has several levels of vocabulary:

Standard usage comprises those words and expressions used, understood, and accepted by a majority of our citizens under any circumstances or degree of formality. Such words are well defined and their most accepted spellings and pronunciations are given in our standard dictionaries. In standard speech one might say: *Sir, you speak English well.*

Colloquialisms are familiar words and idioms used in informal speech and writing, but not considered explicit or formal enough for polite conversation or business correspondence. Unlike slang, however, colloquialisms are used and understood by nearly everyone in the United States. The use of slang conveys the suggestion that the speaker and the listener enjoy a special "fraternity," but the use of colloquialisms emphasizes only the informality and familiarity of a general social situation. Almost all idiomatic expressions, for example, could be labeled colloquial. Colloquially, one might say: *Friend, you talk plain and hit the nail right on the head.*

Dialects are the words, idioms, pronunciations, and speech habits peculiar to specific geographical locations. A dialecticism is a regionalism or localism. In popular use "dialect" has come to mean the words, foreign accents, or speech patterns associated with any ethnic group. In Southern dialect one might say: *Cousin, y'all talk mighty fine.* In ethnic-immigrant "dialects" one might say: *Paisano, you speak good the English,* or *Landsman, your English is plenty all right already.*

Cant, jargon, and *argot* are the words and expressions peculiar to special segments of the population. *Cant* is the conversational, familiar idiom used and generally understood only by members of a specific occupation, trade, profession, sect, class, age group, interest group, or other sub-group of our culture. *Jargon* is the technical or even secret vocabulary of such a sub-group; jargon is "shop talk." *Argot* is both the cant and the jargon of any professional criminal group. In such usages one might say, respectively: CQ-CQ-CQ . . . *the tone of your transmission is good; You are free of anxieties related to interpersonal communication;* or *Duchess, let's have a bowl of chalk.*

Slang[1] is generally defined above. In slang one might say: *Buster, your line is the cat's pajamas,* or *Doll, you come on with the straight jazz, real cool like.*

Each of these levels of language, save standard usage, is more common in speech than in writing, and slang as a whole is no exception. Thus, very few slang words and expressions (hence very few of the entries in this dictionary) appear in standard dictionaries.

American slang tries for a quick, easy, personal mode of speech. It comes mostly from cant, jargon, and argot words and expressions whose popularity has increased until a large number of the general public uses or understands them. Much of this slang retains a basic characteristic of its origin: it is *fully* intelligible only to initiates.

Slang may be represented pictorially as the more popular portion of the cant, jargon, and argot from many sub-groups (only a few of the sub-groups are shown on page 274). The shaded areas represent only general overlapping between groups.

Eventually, some slang passes into standard speech; other slang flourishes for a time with varying popularity and then is forgotten; finally, some slang is never fully accepted nor completely forgotten. *O.K., jazz* (music), and *A-bomb* were recently considered slang, but they are now standard usages. *Bluebelly, Lucifer,* and *the bee's knees*

---

[1] For the evolution of the word "slang," see F. Klaeber, "Concerning the Etymology of Slang," *American Speech,* April, 1926.

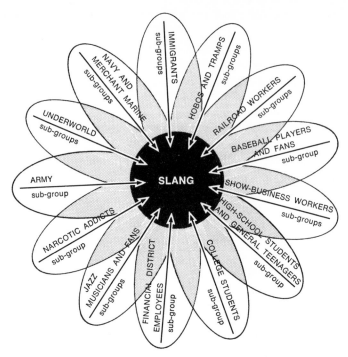

have faded from popular use. *Bones* (dice) and *beat it* seem destined to remain slang forever: Chaucer used the first and Shakespeare used the second.

It is impossible for any living vocabulary to be static. Most new slang words and usages evolve quite naturally: they result from specific situations. New objects, ideas, or happenings, for example, require new words to describe them. Each generation also seems to need some new words to describe the same old things.

Railroaders (who were probably the first American sub-group to have a nationwide cant and jargon) thought *jerk water town* was ideally descriptive of a community that others called a *one-horse town*. The changes from *one-horse town* and *don't spare the horses* to a *wide place in the road* and *step on it* were natural and necessary when the automobile replaced the horse. The automobile also produced such new words and new meanings (some of them highly specialized) as *gas buggy, jalopy, bent eight, Chevvie, convertible,* and *lube.* Like most major innovations, the automobile affected our social history and introduced or encouraged *dusters, hitch hikers, road hogs, joint hopping, necking, chicken* (the game), *car coats,* and *suburbia.*

The automobile is only one obvious example. Language always responds to new concepts and developments with new words.

Consider the following:

wars: *redcoats, minutemen, bluebelly, over there, doughboy, gold brick, jeep.*

mass immigrations: *Bohunk, greenhorn, shillalagh, voodoo, pizzeria.*

science and technology: *'gin, side-wheeler, wash-and-wear, fringe area, fallout.*

turbulent eras: *Redskin, maverick, speak, Chicago pineapple, free love, fink, breadline.*

evolution in the styles of eating: *applesauce, clambake, luncheonette, hot dog, coffee and.*

dress: *Mother Hubbard, bustle, shimmy, sailor, Long Johns, zoot suit, Ivy League.*

housing: *lean-to, bundling board, chuckhouse, W.C., railroad flat, split-level, sectional.*

music: *cakewalk, bandwagon, fish music, long hair, rock.*

personality: *Yankee, alligator, flapper, sheik, hepcat, B.M.O.C., beetle, beat.*

new modes of transportation: *stage, pinto, jitney, kayducer, hot shot, jet jockey.*

new modes of entertainment: *barnstormer, two-a-day, clown alley, talkies, d.j., Spectacular.*

changing attitudes toward sex: *painted woman, fast, broad, wolf, jail-bait, sixty-nine.*

human motivations: *boy crazy, gold-digger, money-mad, Momism, Oedipus complex, do-gooder, sick.*

personal relationships: *bunky, kids, old lady, steady, ex, gruesome two-some, John.*

work and workers: *clod buster, scab, pencil pusher, white collar, grave-yard shift, company man.*

politics: *Tory, do-nothing, mug-wump, third party, brain trust, fellow traveler, Veep.*

and even hair styles: *bun, rat, peroxide blonde, Italian cut, pony tail, D.A.*

Those social groups that first confront a new object, cope with a new situation, or work with a new concept devise and use new words long before the population at large does. The larger, more imaginative, and useful a group's vocabulary, the more likely it is to contribute slang. To generate slang, a group must either be very large and in constant contact with the dominant culture or be small, closely knit, and re-moved enough from the dominant culture to evolve an extensive, highly personal, and vivid vocabulary. Teen-agers are an example of a large sub-group contributing many words. Criminals, carnival workers, and hoboes are examples of the smaller groups. The smaller groups, because their vocabulary is personal and vivid, contribute to our general slang out of proportion to their size.

Whether the United States has more slang words than any other country (in proportion to number of people, area, or the number of words in the standard vocabulary) I do not know.[2] Certainly the French and the Spanish enjoy extremely large slang vocabularies. Americans, however, do use their general slang more than any other people.

American slang reflects the kind of people who create and use it. Its diversity and popularity are in part due to the imagination, self-confidence, and optimism of our people. Its vitality is in further part due to our guarantee of free speech and to our lack of a national acad-

---

[2] The vocabulary of the average American, most of which he knows but never uses, is usually estimated at 10,000-20,000 words. Of this quantity I estimate conservatively that 2,000 words are slang. Slang, which thus forms about 10 per cent of the words known by the average American, belongs to the part of his vocabulary most frequently *used*.

The English language is now estimated to have at least 600,000 words; this is over four times the 140,000 recorded words of the Elizabethan period. Thus over 450,000 *new words or meanings* have been added since Shakespeare's day, without counting the replacement words or those that have been forgotten between then and now. There are now approximately 10,000 slang words in American English, and about 35,000 cant, jargon, and argot words.

Despite this quantity, 25 per cent of all communication is composed of just nine words. According to McKnight's study, another 25 per cent of all speech is composed of an additional 34 words (or: 43 words comprise 50 per cent of all speech). Scholars do differ, however, on just which nine words are the most popular. Three major studies are: G. H. McKnight, *English Words and Their Background*, Appleton-Century-Crofts, Inc., 1923 (for spoken words only); Godfrey Dewey, "Relative Frequency of English Speech Sounds," *Harvard Studies in Education*, vol. IV, 1923 (for written words only); and Norman R. French, Charles W. Carter, and Walter Koenig, Jr., "Words and Sounds of Telephone Conversations," *Bell System Technical Journal*, April, 1930 (telephone speech only). Their lists of the most common nine words are:

McKnight's (speech)	Dewey's (written)	Bell Telephone (conversations)
	a	a
and	and	
be		
have	.	
	in	
		I
	is	is
it	it	it
		on
of	of	
	that	that
the	the	the
to	to	to
will		
you		you

emy of language or of any "official" attempt to purify our speech. Americans are restless and frequently move from region to region and from job to job. This hopeful wanderlust, from the time of the pioneers through our westward expansion to modern mobility, has helped spread regional and group terms until they have become general slang. Such restlessness has created constantly new situations which provoke new words. Except for a few Eastern industrial areas and some rural regions in the South and West, America just doesn't look or sound "lived in." We often act and speak as if we were simply visiting and observing. What should be an ordinary experience seems new, unique, or colorful to us, worthy of words and forceful speech. People do not "settle down" in their jobs, towns, or vocabularies.

Nor do we "settle down" intellectually, spiritually, or emotionally. We have few religious, regional, family, class, psychological, or philosophical roots. We don't believe in roots, we believe in teamwork. Our strong loyalties, then, are directed to those social groups—or sub-groups as they are often called—with which we are momentarily identified. This ever-changing "membership" helps to promote and spread slang.

But even within each sub-group only a few new words are generally accepted. Most cant and jargon are local and temporary. What persist are the exceptionally apt and useful cant and jargon terms. These become part of the permanent, personal vocabulary of the group members, giving prestige to the users by proving their acceptance and status in the group. Group members then spread some of this more honored cant and jargon in the dominant culture. If the word is also useful to non-group members, it is on its way to becoming slang. Once new words are introduced into the dominant culture, via television, radio, movies, or newspapers, the rapid movement of individuals and rapid communication between individuals and groups spread the new word very quickly.

For example, consider the son of an Italian immigrant living in New York City. He speaks Italian at home. Among neighborhood youths of similar background he uses many Italian expressions because he finds them always on the tip of his tongue and because they give him a sense of solidarity with his group. He may join a street gang, and after school and during vacations work in a factory. After leaving high school, he joins the navy; then he works for a year seeing the country as a carnival worker. He returns to New York, becomes a longshoreman, marries a girl with a German background, and becomes a boxing fan. He uses Italian and German borrowings, some teen-age street-gang terms, a few factory terms, slang with a navy origin, and carnival, dockworker's, and boxing words. He spreads words from each group to all other groups he belongs to. His Italian parents will learn and use a few street-gang, factory, navy, carnival, dockworker's, and boxing terms; his German in-laws will learn some Italian words from his parents; his navy friends will begin to use some of his Italian expressions; his carnival friends a few navy words; his co-workers on the docks some carnival terms, in addition to all the rest; and his social friends, with whom he may usually talk boxing and dock work, will be interested in and learn some of his Italian and carnival terms. His speech may be considered very "slangy" and picturesque because he has belonged to unusual, colorful sub-groups.

On the other hand, a man born into a Midwestern, middle-class, Protestant family whose ancestors came to the United States in the eighteenth century might carry with him popular high-school terms. At high school he had an interest in hot rods and rock-and-roll. He may have served two years in the army, then gone to an Ivy League college where he became an adept bridge player and an enthusiast of cool music. He may then have become a sales executive and developed a liking for golf. This second man, no more usual or unusual than the first, will know cant and jargon terms of teen-age high-school use, hot-rods, rock-and-roll, Ivy League schools, cool jazz, army life, and some golf player's and bridge player's terms. He knows further a few slang expressions from his parents (members of the Jazz Age of the 1920's), from listening to television programs, seeing both American and British movies, reading popular literature, and from frequent meetings with people having completely different backgrounds. When he uses cool terms on the golf course, college expressions at home, business words at the bridge table, when he refers to whiskey or drunkenness by a few words he learned from his parents, curses his next-door neighbor in a few choice army terms—then he too is popularizing slang.

It is, then, clear that three cultural conditions especially contribute to the creation of a large slang vocabulary: (1) hospitality to or acceptance of new objects, situations, and concepts; (2) existence of a large number of diversified sub-groups; (3) democratic mingling between these sub-groups and the dominant culture. Primitive peoples have little if any slang because their life is restricted by ritual; they develop few new concepts; and there are no sub-groups that mingle with the dominant culture. (Primitive sub-groups, such as medicine men or magic men, have their own vocabularies; but such groups do not mix with the dominant culture and their jargon can never become slang because it is secret or sacred.)

But what, after all, are the advantages that slang possesses which make it useful? Though our choice of any specific word may usually be made from habit, we sometimes consciously select a slang word because we believe that it communicates more quickly and easily, and more personally, than does a standard word. Sometimes we resort to slang because there is no one standard word to use. In the 1940's WAC, *cold war*, and *cool* (music) could not be expressed quickly by any standard synonyms. Such words often become standard quickly, as have the first two. We also use slang because it often is more forceful, vivid, and expressive than are standard usages. Slang usually avoids the sentimentality and formality that older words often assume. Taking a girl to a *dance* may seem sentimental, may convey a degree of formal, emotional interest in the girl, and has overtones of fancy balls, fox trots, best suits, and corsages. At times it is more fun to go to a *hop*. To be *busted* or without a *hog* in one's *jeans* is not only more vivid and forceful than being penniless or without funds, it is also a more optimistic state. A *mouthpiece* (or *legal beagle*), *pencil pusher, sawbones, boneyard, bottle washer* or a course in *biochem* is more vivid and forceful than a lawyer, clerk, doctor, cemetery, laboratory assistant, or a course in biochemistry—and is much more real and less formidable than a legal counsel, junior executive, surgeon, necropolis (or memorial park), laboratory technician, or a course in biological chemistry.

Although standard English is exceedingly hospitable to polysyllabicity and even sesquipedalianism, slang is not. Slang is sometimes used not only because it is concise but just because its brevity makes it forceful. As this dictionary demonstrates, slang seems to prefer short words, especially monosyllables, and, best of all, words beginning with an explosive or an aspirate.[3]

We often use slang *fad* words as a bad habit because they are close to the tip of our tongue. Most of us apply several favorite but vague words to any of several somewhat similar situations; this saves us the time and effort of thinking and speaking precisely. At other times we purposely choose a word because it is vague, because it does not commit us too strongly to what we are saying. For example, if a friend has been praising a woman, we can reply "she's *the bee's knees*" or "she's a real *chick*," which can mean that we consider her very modern, intelligent, pert, and understanding—or can mean that we think she is one of many nondescript, somewhat confused, followers of popular fads. We can also tell our friend that a book we both have recently read is *the cat's pajamas* or *the greatest*. These expressions imply that we liked the book

---

[3] Many such formations are among our most frequently used slang words. As listed in this dictionary, *bug* has 30 noun meanings, *shot* 14 noun and 4 adjective meanings, *can* 11 noun and 6 verb, *bust* 9 verb and 6 noun, *hook* 8 noun and 5 verb, *fish* 14 noun, and *sack* 8 noun, 1 adjective, and 1 verb meaning. Monosyllabic words also had by far the most citations found in our source reading of popular literature. Of the 40 words for which we found the most quotations, 29 were monosyllabic. Before condensing, *fink* had citations from 70 different sources, *hot* 67, *bug* 62, *blow* and *dog* 60 each, *joint* 59, *stiff* 56, *punk* 53, *bum* and *egg* 50 each, *guy* 43, *make* 41, *bull* and *mug* 37 each, *bird* 34, *fish* and *hit* 30 each, *ham* 25, *yak* 23, *sharp* 14, and *cinch* 10. (Many of these words, of course, have several slang meanings; many of the words also appeared scores of times in the same book or article.)

for exactly the same reasons that our friend did, without having to state what these reasons were and thus taking the chance of ruining our rapport.

In our language we are constantly recreating our image in our own minds and in the minds of others. Part of this image, as mentioned above, is created by using sub-group cant and jargon in the dominant society; part of it is created by our choice of both standard and slang words. A sub-group vocabulary shows that we have a group to which we "belong" and in which we are "somebody"—outsiders had better respect us. Slang is used to show others (and to remind ourselves of) our biographical, mental, and psychological background; to show our social, economic, geographical, national, racial, religious, educational, occupational, and group interests, memberships, and patriotisms. One of the easiest and quickest ways to do this is by using counter-words. These are automatic, often one-word responses of like or dislike, of acceptance or rejection. They are used to counter the remarks, or even the presence, of others. Many of our fad words and many student and quasi-intellectual slang words are counter-words. For liking: *beat, the cat's pajamas, drooly, gas, George, the greatest, keen, nice, reet, smooth, super, way out,* etc. For rejection of an outsider (implying incompetence to belong to our group): *boob, creep, dope, drip, droop, goof, jerk, kookie, sap, simp, square, weird,* etc. Such automatic counters are overused, almost meaningless, and are a substitute for thought. But they achieve one of the main purposes of speech: quickly and automatically they express our own sub-group and personal criteria. Counter-words are often fad words creating a common bond of self-defense. All the rejecting counters listed above could refer to a moron, an extreme introvert, a birdwatcher, or a genius. The counters merely say that the person is rejected—he does not belong to the group. In uttering the counter we don't care what the person is; we are pledging our own group loyalty, affirming our identity, and expressing our satisfaction at being accepted.

In like manner, at various periods in history, our slang has abounded in words reflecting the fear, distrust, and dislike of people unlike ourselves. This intolerance is shown by the many derogatory slang words for different immigrant, religious, and racial groups: *Chink, greaser, Heinie, hunkie, mick, mockie, nigger, spik.* Many counters and derogatory words try to identify our own group status, to dare others to question our group's, and therefore our own, superiority.

Sometimes slang is used to escape the dull familiarity of standard words, to suggest an escape from the established routine of everyday life. When slang is used, our life seems a little fresher and a little more personal. Also, as at all levels of speech, slang is sometimes used for the pure joy of making sounds, or even for a need to attract attention by making noise. The sheer newness and informality of certain slang words produces a pleasure.

But more important than this expression of a more or less hidden esthetic motive on the part of the speaker is slang's reflection of the personality, the outward, clearly visible characteristics of the speaker. By and large, the man who uses slang is a forceful, pleasing, acceptable personality. Morality and intellect (too frequently not considered virtues in the modern American man) are overlooked in slang, and this has led to a type of reverse morality: many words, once standing for morally good things, are now critical. No one, for example, though these words were once considered complimentary, wants to be called a *prude* or *Puritan*. Even in standard usage they are mildly derisive.

Moreover, few of the many slang synonyms for drunk are derogatory or critical. To call a person a standard drunk may imply a superior but unsophisticated attitude toward drinking. Thus we use slang and say someone is *boozed up, gassed, high, potted, stinking, has a glow on,* etc., in a verbal attempt to convey our understanding and awareness. These slang words show that we too are human and know the effects of excessive drinking.

In the same spirit we refer to people sexually as *big ass man, fast, John, sex pot, shack job, wolf,* etc., all of which accept unsanctioned sexual intercourse as a matter of fact. These words are often used in a complimentary way and in admiration or envy. They always show acceptance of the person as a "regular guy." They are never used to express a moral judgment. Slang has few complimentary or even purely descriptive words for "virgin," "good girl," or "gentleman." Slang has *bag, bat, ex, gold digger, jerk, money mad, n.g., old lady, square,* etc.; but how many words are there for a good wife and mother, an attractive and chaste woman, an honest, hard-working man who is kind to his family, or even a respected elderly person? Slang—and it is frequently true for all language levels—always tends toward degradation rather than elevation. As slang shows, we would rather share or accept vices than be excluded from a social group. For this reason, for self-defense, and to create an aura (but not the fact) of modernity and individuality, much of our slang purposely expresses amorality, cynicism, and "toughness."

Reverse morality also affects slang in other ways. Many use slang just because it is not standard or polite. Many use slang to show their rebellion against *boobs, fuddy-duddies, marks,* and *squares.* Intellectuals and politicians often use slang to create the "common touch" and others use slang to express either their anti-intellectualism or avant-garde leanings. Thus, for teen-agers, entertainers, college students, beatniks, jazz fans, intellectuals, and other large groups, slang is often used in preference to standard words and expressions. Slang is the "official" modern language of certain vociferous groups in our population.

In my work on this dictionary, I was constantly aware that most American slang is created and used by males. Many types of slang words—including the taboo and strongly derogatory ones, those referring to sex, women, work, money, whiskey,[4] politics, transportation, sports, and the like—refer primarily to male endeavor and interest. The majority of entries in this dictionary could be labeled "primarily masculine use." Men belong to more sub-groups than do women; men create and use occupational cant and jargon; in business, men have acquaintances who belong to many different sub-groups. Women, on the other hand, still tend to be restricted to family and neighborhood friends. Women have very little of their own slang.[5] The new words applied to women's clothing, hair styles, homes, kitchen utensils and gadgets are usually created by men. Except when she accompanies her boy friend or husband to *his* recreation (baseball, hunting, etc.) a woman seldom mingles with other groups. When women do mingle outside of their own neighborhood and family circles, they do not often talk of the outside world of business, politics, or other fields of general interest where new feminine names for objects, concepts, and viewpoints could evolve.

Men also tend to avoid words that sound feminine or weak. Thus there are sexual differences in even the standard vocabularies of men and women. A woman may ask her husband to set the table for dinner, asking him to put out the *silver, crystal,* and *china*—while the man will set the table with *knives, forks, spoons, glasses,* and *dishes.* His wife might think the *table linen attractive,* the husband might think the *tablecloth* and *napkins* pretty. A man will buy a *pocketbook* as a gift for his wife, who will receive a *bag.* The couple will live under the same roof, the wife in her *home,* the man in his *house.* Once outside of their domesticity the man will begin to use slang quicker than the woman. She'll get into the *car* while he'll get into the *jalopy* or *Chevvie.* And so they go: she will learn much of her general slang from him; for any word she associates with the home, her personal belongings, or any female concept, he will continue to use a less descriptive, less personal one.

Males also use slang to shock. The rapid tempo of life, combined with the sometimes low boiling point of males, can evoke emotions—

---

[4] It would appear that the word having the most slang synonyms is *drunk.*

[5] Women who do work usually replace men at men's jobs, are less involved in business life than men, and have a shorter business career (often but an interim between school and marriage). The major female sub-groups contributing to American slang are: airline stewardesses, beauty-parlor operators, chorus girls, nurses, prostitutes, and waitresses.

admiration, joy, contempt, anger—stronger than our old standard vocabulary can convey. In the stress of the moment a man is not just in a standard "untenable position," he is *up the creek*. Under strong anger a man does not feel that another is a mere "incompetent"—he is a *jerk* or a *fuck-off*.

Men also seem to relish hyperbole in slang. Under many situations, men do not see or care to express fine shades of meaning: a girl is either a *knockout* or a *dog*, liquor either *good stuff* or *panther piss*, a person either has *guts* or is *chicken*, a book is either *great* or nothing but *crap*. Men also like slang and colloquial wording because they express action or even violence: we *draw pay, pull a boner, make a score, grab some sleep, feed our face, kill time*—in every instance we tend to use the transitive verb, making ourselves the active doer.

The relation between a sub-group's psychology and its cant and jargon is interesting, and the relation between an individual's vocabulary and psychological personality is even more so. Slang can be one of the most revealing things about a person, because our own personal slang vocabulary contains many words used by choice, words which we use to create our own image, words which we find personally appealing and evocative—as opposed to our frequent use of standard words merely from early teaching and habit. Whether a man calls his wife *baby, doll, honey, the little woman, the Mrs.,* or *my old lady* certainly reveals much about him. What words one uses to refer to a mother (*Mom, old lady*), friend (*buddy, bunkie, old man*), the bathroom (*can, John, little boy's room*), parts of the body and sex acts (*boobies, gigi, hard, laid, score*), being tired (*all in, beat*), being drunk (*clobbered, high, lit up like a Christmas tree, paralyzed*), and the like, reveal much about a person and his motivations.[6]

The basic metaphors, at any rate, for all levels of language depend on the five senses. Thus *rough, smooth, touch; prune, sour puss, sweet; fishy, p.u., rotten egg; blow, loud; blue, red, square.* In slang, many metaphors refer to touch (including the sense of heat and cold) and to taste.

Food is probably our most popular slang image. Food from the farm, kitchen, or table, and its shape, color, and taste suggest many slang metaphors. This is because food can appeal to taste, smell, sight, and touch, four of our five senses; because food is a major, universal image to all people, all sub-groups; because men work to provide it and women devote much time to buying and preparing it; because food is before our eyes three times every day.

[6] For just the last example, *clobbered* may indicate that a drinker is punishing himself, *high* that he is escaping, *lit up like a Christmas tree* that he is seeking attention and a more dominant personality, and *paralyzed* that he seeks punishment, escape or death.

Many standard food words mean money in nonstandard use: *cabbage, kale, lettuce*. Many apply to parts of the body: *cabbage head, cauliflower ear, meat hooks, nuts, plates of meat*. Many food words refer to people: *apple, cold fish, Frog, fruitcake, honey, sweetie pie*. Others refer to general situations and attitudes: to *brew* a plot, to receive a *chewing out*, to find oneself *in a pickle* or something *not kosher*, to be unable to *swallow* another's story, to ask *what's cooking?* Many drunk words also have food images: *boiled, fried, pickled*; and so do many words for nonsense: *applesauce, banana oil, spinach*. Many standard food words also have sexual meanings in slang. The many food words for money, parts of the body, people, and sex reveal that food means much more to us than mere nourishment. When a *good egg brings home the bacon* to his *honey*, or when a *string bean* of a *sugar daddy* takes his *piece* of *barbecue* out to get *fried* with his hard-earned *kale*, food images have gone a long way from the farm, kitchen, and table.

Sex has contributed comparatively few words to modern slang,[7] but these are among our most frequently used. The use of sex words to refer to sex in polite society and as metaphors in other fields is increasing. Sex metaphors are common for the same conscious reasons that food metaphors are. Sex appeals to, and can be used to apply to, most of the five senses. It is common to all persons in all sub-groups, and so we are aware of it continually.

Slang words for sexual attraction and for a variety of sexual acts, positions, and relationships are more common than standard words. Standard non-taboo words referring to sex are so scarce or remote and scientific that slang is often used in referring to the most romantic, the most obscene, and the most humorous sexual situations. Slang is so universally used in sexual communication that when "a man meets a maid" it is best for all concerned that they know slang.[8] Slang words for sex carry little emotional connotation; they express naked desire or mechanical acts, devices, and positions. They are often blunt, cynical and "tough."

The subconscious relating of sex and food is also apparent from reading this dictionary. Many words with primary, standard meanings of food have sexual slang meanings. The body, parts of the body, and descriptions of each, often call food terms into use: *banana, bread, cheese cake, cherry, jelly roll, meat*, etc. Beloved, or simply sexually attractive, people are also often called by food names: *cookie, cup of tea*,

---

[7] Many so-called bedroom words are not technically slang at all, but are sometimes associated with slang only because standard speech has rejected them as taboo. However, many of these taboo words do have further metaphorical meanings in slang: *fucked, jerk, screw you*, etc.

[8] On the other hand, Madame de Staël is reported to have complimented one of her favorite lovers with "speech is not his language."

honey, peach, quail, tomato, etc. This primary relation between sex and food depends on the fact that they are man's two major sensuous experiences. They are shared by all personalities and all sub-groups and they appeal to the same senses—thus there is bound to be some overlapping in words and imagery. However, there are too many standard food words having sexual meanings in slang for these conscious reasons to suffice. Sex and food seem to be related in our subconscious.

Also of special interest is the number of slang expressions relating sex and cheating. Used metaphorically, many sex words have secondary meanings of being cheated, deceived, swindled, or taken advantage of, and several words whose primary meaning is cheating or deceiving have further specific sexual meanings: *cheating, fucked, make, royal screwing, score, turn a trick,* etc. As expressed in slang, sex is a trick somehow, a deception, a way to cheat and deceive us. To curse someone we can say *fuck you* or *screw you,* which expresses a wish to deprive him of his good luck, his success, perhaps even his potency as a man.[9] Sex is also associated with confusion, exhausting tasks, and disaster: *ball buster, screwed up, snafu,* etc. It seems clear, therefore, that, in slang, success and sexual energy are related or, to put it more accurately, that thwarted sexual energy will somehow result in personal disaster.

Language is a social symbol. The rise of the middle class coincided with the period of great dictionary makers, theoretical grammarians, and the "correct usage" dogma. The new middle class gave authority to the dictionaries and grammarians in return for "correct usage" rules that helped solidify their social position. Today, newspaper ads still implore us to take mail-order courses in order to "learn to speak like a college graduate," and some misguided English instructors still give a good speaking ability as the primary reason for higher education.

The gap between "correct usage" and modern practice widens each day. Are there valid theoretical rules for speaking good English, or should "observed usage" be the main consideration? Standard words do not necessarily make for precise, forceful, or useful speech. On the other

[9] See F. P. Wood, "The Vocabulary of Failure," *Better English,* Nov., 1938, p. 34. The vocabulary of failure is itself very revealing. Failure in one's personality, school, job, business, or an attempted love affair are all expressed by the same vocabulary. One gets the *brush off,* the *gate,* a *kiss off,* or *walking papers* in both business and personal relationships. As the previous discussion of counterwords demonstrates, slang allows no distinction or degree among individual failures. Incompetence does not apply to just one job or facet of life—either one belongs or is considered unworthy. This unworthiness applies to the entire personality, there are no alternate avenues for success or happiness. One is not merely of limited intelligence, not merely an introvert, not merely ugly, unknowing, or lacking in aggression—but one is a failure in all these things, a complete *drip, jerk,* or *square.* The basic failure is that of personality, the person is not a mere failure— he is an outcast, an untouchable; he is taboo.

hand, "observed usage" can never promise logic and clarity. Today, we have come to depend on "observed usage," just as eighteenth- and nineteenth-century social climbers depended on "correct usage," for social acceptance.

Because it is not standard, formal, or acceptable under all conditions, slang is usually considered vulgar, impolite, or boorish. As this dictionary shows, however, the vast majority of slang words and expressions are neither taboo, vulgar, derogatory, nor offensive in meaning, sound, or image. There is no reason to avoid any useful, explicit word merely because it is labeled "slang." Our present language has not decayed from some past and perfect "King's English," Latin, Greek, or pre-Tower of Babel tongue. All languages and all words have been, are, and can only be but conventions mutually agreed upon for the sake of communicating. Slang came to America on the Mayflower. In general, it is not vulgar, new, or even peculiarly American: an obvious illustration of this is the polite, old French word *tête*, which was originally slang from a Latin word *testa*—cooking pot.

Cant and jargon in no way refer only to the peculiar words of undesirable or underworld groups. Slang does not necessarily come from the underworld, dope addicts, degenerates, hoboes, and the like. Any cultural sub-group develops its own personal cant and jargon which can later become general slang. All of us belong to several of these specific sub-groups using our own cant and jargon. Teen-agers, steel workers, soldiers, Southerners, narcotic addicts, churchgoers, truck drivers, advertising men, jazz musicians, pickpockets, retail salesmen in every field, golf players, immigrants from every country, college professors, baseball fans—all belong to typical sub-groups from which slang originates. Some of these sub-groups are colorful; most are composed of prosaic, average people.

Many people erroneously believe that a fundamental of slang is that it is intentionally picturesque, strained in metaphor, or jocular. Picturesque metaphor (and metonymy, hyperbole, and irony) does or should occur frequently in all levels of speech. Picturesque metaphor is a frequent characteristic of slang, but it does not define slang or exist as an inherent part of it. The picturesque or metaphorical aspect of slang is often due to its direct honesty or to its newness. Many standard usages are just as picturesque, but we have forgotten their original metaphor through habitual use. Thus slang's *jerk* and *windbag* are no more picturesque than the standard *incompetent* and *fool*. *Incompetent* is from the Latin *competens* plus the negating prefix *in-* and = "unable or unwilling to compete"; *fool* is Old French, from the Latin *follis* which actually = "bellows or wind bag"; slang's *windbag* and the standard *fool* actually have the same metaphor.

As for picturesque sounds, I find very few in slang. Onomatopoeia, reduplications, harsh sounds and pleasing sounds, even rhyming terms, exist on all levels of speech. Readers of this dictionary will find no more picturesque or unusual sounds here than in a similar length dictionary of standard words. Many slang words are homonyms for standard words.

As has been frequently pointed out, many slang words have the same meaning. There seems to be an unnecessary abundance of counter-words, synonyms for "drunk," hundreds of fad words with almost the same meaning, etc. This is because slang introduces word after word year after year from many, many sub-groups. But slang is a scatter-gun process; many new words come at the general public; most are ignored; a few stick in the popular mind.

Remember that "slang" actually does not exist as an entity except in the minds of those of us who study the language. People express themselves and are seldom aware that they are using the artificial divisions of "slang" or "standard." First and forever, language is language, an attempt at communication and self-expression. The fact that some words or expressions are labeled "slang" while others are labeled "jargon" or said to be "from the Anglo-Saxon" is of little value except to scholars. Thus this dictionary is a legitimate addition to standard dictionaries, defining many words just as meaningful as and often more succinct, useful, and popular than many words in standard dictionaries.

FOR DISCUSSION AND REVIEW

1 What distinctions does Flexner make in discussing the terms *argot, slang, colloquial, cant, jargon,* and *dialect*?

2 How is slang created?

3 According to Flexner, what are the three cultural conditions that contribute to the creation of a large slang vocabulary?

4 Why is food imagery so prevalent in slang usage?

5 Flexner's essay was first published in 1960; at that time he claimed that "women have very little of their own slang" because they "still tend to be restricted to family and neighborhood friends." Is this still a fair assessment? Is there an increasing tendency on the part of women to use slang for its shock value? Explain.

6 The tremendous growth of the drug sub-culture has yielded a vast number of slang terms. Discuss some of these terms.

8

Collegiate Slang:

The following article by Richard K. Seymour, Professor of German at the University of Hawaii, brings together the subjects of the two preceding essays. In his discussion of collegiate slang, one of the subgroups referred to by Mr. Flexner (p. 274), Professor Seymour also illustrates some of the principles of word formation examined by Professor Francis (p. 260).

Aspects of Word Formation and Semantic Change

Richard K. Seymour

WATCH IT, you might rattle the troops." (Don't upset your parents.)

"Put on your quickstarts." (Put your tennis shoes on.)

"You are out of your tree." (You're nuts.)

"The girls like to go grub." (The girls like to wear old clothes.)

"I went into that on guts." (I didn't study for it.)

"He kicked her tires." (He checked her out before deciding to date her.)

"He shakes my tree." (I find him physically stimulating.)

"He has a good set of pits." (He is in dire need of a deodorant.)

These sentences contain few, if any, unknown words. However, the special meaning of certain words and the particular arrangement produce the unexpected meaning.

This paper presents examples of certain kinds of word formation, together with brief comments on semantic change, in the language of the college student. The corpus derives from the speech of students at a single Southern university, Duke University, a private institution with a rather homogeneous coeducational undergraduate population (numbering about 5,000), lacking close ties with metropolitan or cosmopolitan influences. The lexical items discussed were recently [in 1967] in vogue at least at Duke University, perhaps elsewhere.

The phrase "collegiate slang" is perhaps a misnomer.[1] It is correctly

---

[1] An excellent discussion of the meaning of the designation "college (or collegiate) slang" is given by Henry Kratz, "What Is College Slang?" *American Speech*, XXXIX (1964), 188–195. Cf. also Lawrence Poston, III, "Some Problems in the Study of Campus Slang," *ibid.*, XXXIX (1964), 114–123. This article contains several items of bibliography, supplementing the very useful list given by Alan

applied in those instances in which the student uses, among his peers at least, words and phrases peculiar to a particular situation, area, or group. For example, lexical items referring to academics, campus buildings, other students, professors, etc., may be classified as collegiate slang. On the other hand, the student uses countless words, not because he is a student somewhere, but because of his age, his generational identification. This kind of word or phrase does not belong to the specific college or university situation, but derives from the student's total background.

It will be noticed in the following that the examples often reveal or reflect an attitude toward society that is mostly negative. Thanks to Walt Disney, the student can express his attitude toward that which is tedious, time consuming, juvenile, foolish, or of little significance, by using the phrase *Mickey Mouse* as a noun qualifier or adjectival: "That is a Mickey Mouse course."; "What a Mickey Mouse think to do!"; and "That's so Mickey Mouse."

The semantic spread of the items discussed ranges from the sophisticated to the "gross," with a large measure of cynicism and ridicule. None of the items was found in the usual dictionaries of slang, such as Wentworth and Flexner, Farmer and Henley, etc.[2] The words and phrases are either too recently coined or perhaps too regional to appear in published dictionaries. To this extent the material is original.

I. Derivation

1) A popular breakfast food, especially in the South, is *grits*, a shortening of *hominy grits*. By extension the people who eat grits are called *grits*, the plural of a new noun: *grit* 'a Southerner.' The word frequently is used in a negative sense, especially by non-Southerners to characterize the Southerner and the latter's alleged negative attributes.[3]

Dundes and Manuel R. Schonhorn in "Kansas University Slang: A New Generation," *ibid.*, XXXVIII (1963), 163–177.

It may be mentioned in passing that what I would term the "peer language" of a student is an excellent source for synchronic linguistic anthropology.

[2] Wentworth, Harold, and Stuart Berg Flexner, *Dictionary of American Slang*, New York, 1960; Berrey, Lester V., and Melvin Van den Bark, *American Thesaurus of Slang*, 2nd ed., New York, 1953; Sagarin, Edward, *The Anatomy of Dirty Words*, New York, 1962; Weingarten, Joseph A., *An American Dictionary of Slang*, New York, 1954; Klein, Ernest, *A Comprehensive Etymological Dictionary of The English Language*, 2 vols., Amsterdam, 1967; and Farmer, J. S., and W. E. Henley, *Slang and Its Analogues Past and Present*, 7 vols. in 3, London, 1890–1904.

[3] The morpheme *grit* occurs as a noun qualifier in: *grit pants*. These are pants or trousers with tiny checks or stripes, worn primarily by Southern boys (so it is claimed).

Derivation, rhyme association, and semantic association are all involved in the formation *griticism* 'a typically Southern action.' Through the eyes of a non-Southerner, this is an action that is ostensibly provincial, stupid, pointless, or "slow-motion."

The suffix is *-ism*, as in *fanaticism*, derived from *fanatic*. Analogical formations include *witticism* for which there was no base adjective *wittic*. There likewise exists no adjective *gritic*, but since the use of the word *griticism* implies criticism, we undoubtedly are dealing here with analogy and rhyme and semantic association with *criticism*.

This word was chosen as the initial example because it so effectively points up the difficulties encountered in categorizing slang terms as a derivative, a compound, etc. Very often several devices of word formation are simultaneously at work.

2) Deverbative and denominative substantives with the suffix *-er* are numerous. Examples referring to people are: *greaser* 'one who has exceptionally long and/or unusually greasy hair'; *ricer*: 'a person who is on a rice diet at Duke Hospital in order to lose large quantities of weight' as in: "He likes to date ricers because there is so much of them."; *mini-juker*: 'a person who acts very childish' as in: "watching her dance, you could tell she was a real *mini-juker*"; *slimer*: 'one who changes his opinion hypocritically'; *booker*: 'one who studies too much'; *bridger*: 'one who is constantly playing bridge'; *grade-grubber*: 'one who tries to ingratiate himself with a professor in hopes of receiving a higher grade than his academic performance would objectively merit'; and *luncher*: 'one who has little social awareness': "That nurd is a real luncher"—one who is "out to lunch."

In some formations without an agential theme the meaning is transferred from an action to the object involved in the action: *griller*: 'a grilled hot dog'; *hip-huggers*: 'a pair of trousers or a blouse that fits low on the hips'; *popper*: 'can of beer with a pop top' as in: "Open me two poppers."; *water walkers*: 'sandals'; and *rimmer*: this is a general term for the grossest thing in the world. The grossest thing, however, is not known; but the *rimmer* is what it is called whatever it is. "I couldn't stand watching the movie; it approached a *rimmer*."

The denominative verb *skimmer* may be unique in that it represents a type not given in Marchand's[4] book on English word formation. "Bill, skimmer me, I'm thirsty." This is a request for Bill to buy the speaker some skimmed milk, which points to the origin of the formation.

Finally, to "pull" an *all nighter* means 'to stay up all night studying.'

3) The /-iy/ or /-siy/ suffix (*-ie, -ey, -y, -sie, -sey, -sy*), according to

---

[4] Marchand, Hans, *The Categories and Types of Present-Day English Word-Formation: A Synchronic-Diachronic Approach*, Wiesbaden, 1960 (reprinted as number 13 in the *Alabama Linguistic and Philological Series*).

Wentworth and Flexner, is found in derivatives indicating size, affection, or familiarity. Among the adjectives with this suffix are: *foxy* 'attractive, graceful'; *scuzzy* 'dirty'; *groady* 'dirty and grubby'; *wimpy* 'spineless'; *skoady* 'objectionable'; and *grungy* 'unclean.' Of these, *scuzzy, groady, skoady,* and *grungy* should probably be listed also under "Blends" (III, below). *Scuzzy,* for example, seems to imply *fuzzy* and *scummy*: "Your teeth are scuzzy."

Nouns are: *Eppie, youngy, woodsy,* and *chilly. Eppie* is a somewhat derogatory term for a female graduate student living in Epworth House, one of the dormitories. A *youngy* is a fashionable young lady in her teens. A bottle or can of beer that has been chilled is a *chilly.* A *woodsy* is an excursion to the woods, limited to one boy and one girl.

Four similar derivatives, occurring in the plural, are: *boonies, switchies, grubbies,* and *sipsies. Boonies,* probably derived from *boondocks,* means 'any secluded area where one is unlikely to be disturbed while making love.' Just as *nylons* is used for *nylon stockings, grubbies* is used for *grubby clothes. Switchies* means 'the exchanging of dates for any period of time, usually occurring between double-dating couples and not confined to any specific activity.' *Sipsies* means 'the first two sips of someone else's drink.' In effect it says: "Dibbies on your drink" or "Dibs on the first two sips."

4) The suffix *-ery* occurred in one derivative: *deanery.* The word refers collectively to the myriad deans on the campus and is used by students and faculty alike.

5) *Zit* is a common term for pimple. With the suffix *-o* we have *zitto.* It is a noun meaning 'someone whose face is covered with pimples (*zits*).'

6) "He thought his beard made him look *massable,*" i.e., 'masculine.' The word might be a playful pronunciation of *masterful;* perhaps more likely, it might be a pseudo-Negro formation: the base form *massa(h)* 'master' with the suffix *-(a)ble.*

7) Exasperation spawned a derivative with the suffix *-ness.* A conversation with a student went as follows: Student: "They said I could sign up now." (This referred to registration.) Response: "Who is *they?*" Student: "Allen Building [the administration building]. The epitome of *theyness.*"

8) The verb *to grouse* means 'to have physical intimacy': "You can almost always find a couple grousing in the parlor." This verb coupled with the infrequently occurring suffix *-atorium* has yielded the formation: *grouse-atorium* which is a room in which several couples are *grousing.*[5]

---

[5] It is claimed that the brothers of Sigma Chi invented the term.

9) The verb *to bulken*, usually followed by *up*, means 'to get bigger from lifting weight.' Most verbs with the suffix *-en* currently are formed from adjectives, although according to Jespersen the formations were historically extensions of existing verbs. In the case of *bulken*, however, derivation from the adjective is very unlikely, as it means 'packed or handled in bulk, as in bulk cargo.' Thus, the derivative source must ultimately be taken to be either the verb or the noun *bulk*, although as Marchand mentions, desubstantive formations, likewise of historical significance, have no bearing on the present-day situation.

II. Clippings

Clipping is the reduction of a word to one of its (assumed) parts. The back clippings, such as *lab* for *laboratory*, are: *libe* for *library*, *porn* for *pornography*, *lech* for *lecher*, *bod* for *body*, and *nook* /nuwk, nɨwk/ for *newcomer*. *Bod* can mean either person or body: "I can't believe there are so many *bods* going to class this morning; what a beautiful *bod*." A *nook* is the low person in a stratified situation.

The five fore-clippings, such as *plane* for *airplane*, are: *za* (/za/) for *pizza*, *viz* (/vayz/) for *Levis*, *bot* for *robot*, *ball* for *to blackball*, and *cept* for *concept*. "All cept and no fact makes dull lectures."

A room in which vending machines are located is the *robot room*, usually termed the *bot room* (obvious allusion?). A clipping compound, like *Eurasia* from *Europe* and *Asia*, is *minibot* 'a smaller room with vending machines,' from *miniature* and *robot room*.

III. Blending

Among the many blends, such as *gritch* ('grouchy female'; from *grouchy* and *witch* or *bitch*), *scrummy* (from *scrumptious* and *yummy*), *fantabulous* ('remarkable, wonderful'; from *fantastic* and *fabulous*), etc., two deserve special mention:

  twud: 'an ordinary Joe,' combined from *twit* and *stud*. A *twit* is someone who thinks studying is important and doesn't necessarily date every weekend; the opposite (in many ways) of a *twit* is *stud*. Thus the combination would apparently mean the 'Jack Armstrong' of the campus.

  spasmastic: 'awkward, uncoördinated,' as in: "Mother is spasmastic when she drinks." This might be termed in part a "reduplicated blend," meaning the blend is a combination of parts of two, perhaps three, words which in themselves derive ultimately from a single root.

IV. Acronyms

Acronyms occurred in abundance in the corpus. Three examples of the *radar*-type are *PO* /pow/ 'post office,' *GAPO* /geypow/ 'giant armpit aroma,' as in: "Boy, George, you have GAPO.", and *UNCCH* /ənč/ 'University of North Carolina at Chapel Hill,' almost entirely limited to the phrase: "Crunch Uncch!" Of the *UN*-type of acronym the following warrant mention: *KK* 'campus cops,' with obvious reference to the Ku Klux Klan; *PK* 'preacher's kid'; Duke is historically a Methodist institution and there are many PK's enrolled; *AKA* 'alcohol kills all'; *OTR* to be explained later, and *EB* 'electric blanket': This occurs in the sentence: "Turn your EB up to mother." The expression means 'to set the control on one's electric blanket to the highest temperature, thus a return to the womb.'

D, Z, and U may be called abbreviations. D stands for decibel; Z refers to sleep; and U stands for university: "Give me some D's!", i.e., 'make more noise'; "the Z's are calling me to the rack" and "to catch some Z's." A very telling example of resignation in the face of pseudo-pre-destination is the phrase *Saigon U.* "After flunking out comes Saigon U," that is: 'being sent to Vietnam.'

V. Conversion

Conversion is the transfer of a word from one class to another, such as *to service* from the noun *service*. The majority of the formations in the corpus are desubstantival verbs. Examples: *to machine* 'to copy an assignment, using a copying machine, a Xerox machine.' The clipping compound *minibot* (see above) also is used as a verb: *to minibot* 'to go to the minibot.' *To book it* means 'to study,' *to eyeball* means 'to cheat.' A cigarette is commonly known as a *fag* and the phrase *fag me* means 'Give me a cigarette'.[6]

Two rather unexpected conversions occurred. One was that of a verb to an adverb: *maul*: "That football game was the maul greatest (game)." The other is the conversion of a French phrase into an English noun. French *pas de tout* ('not at all') in slang usage means: 'the economic class below the bourgeoisie.' "Students are members of the pas de tout," thus an equivalent of "the have-nots."

Conversion of a clipping of a French noun to an English verb is present in *to theque it* 'to go to the library,' a shortening of the French word *bibliothèque* 'library.'

---

[6] Restaurant names such as Foys Grill, The Zoom Zoom Restaurant, The Ranchhouse, The Rathskeller, and Ballentines Cafeteria have produced (some via clipping): *to foy, to zoom, to ranch, to rate,* and *to tines.*

VI. Rhyme Formations

Everyone is familiar with the phrase *zoot suit*. Many such formations occur in collegiate slang, for example: *fruit boots* 'white-buck
shoes' alluding to the notion that such shoes are worn by a *fruit*, a term
for 'homosexual.' The Duke campus is divided into two parts called the
East Campus and the West Campus. The women students live on
East Campus and are known as *east beasts*, the men students live on
West Campus and are often known as *west pests*.

The West Campus, the main campus, is centered around the chapel.
The large square in front of the chapel is known as *God's quad*.

VII. Alliteration

Alliteration is undoubtedly at least a force in the following combinations: *queer quad* 'the dormitory quad where members of several
rather "unpopular" fraternities live,' *Watts witch* 'a nurse that works
at Watts Hospital,' and *Menopause Manor*: a derogatory term applied
to Epworth House, a dormitory for women graduate students (thus the
aged among the female students).

A formation based on an alliterative ablaut association is: *group
grope* 'a party at which many couples are intimate.'

In the above discussion I have alluded to several examples of semantic change. I would like to give some further examples at this point.
The process of conversion frequently involves extension. For example,
the verb *to tube* is a conversion of the noun *tube*, which in turn is a
clipping of *picture tube*, as contained in the television set. Thus a part
of the whole becomes a name for the whole, then converted to a verb:
Let's tube it for *Let's watch television*.

The word *board* shows an interesting semantic development. Originally it meant the table at which a council sat; then the word came to
be applied to the people who made up the council, thus an official body
of persons directing or supervising some activity, such as a *board of
directors*. The pre-collegiate existence for students at many universities
inevitably implied the taking of certain tests, devised and published
under the title CEEB examinations. The designation of the authority
that devised and administered the tests became the name of the tests
themselves.

The examinations for entrance into a medical school or law school
are called *med boards* and *law boards*, respectively. Nowadays, however,
boards may also be tests to qualify to stay out of something: *war boards*,
the Selective Service Qualifying Test.

The word *bar* in the plural is used to mean examination, test, specifically in another phrase for the Selective Service Qualifying Test that involves a pun with intended insult: *the Hershey bars,* so named after General Hershey, former Director of the Selective Service System.

The reverse process is in evidence with the word *wallet.* In this case we have an example of extension or transfer from the object to the person: nowadays the students use the word to mean 'father': "The wallet will pay for my trip to Europe."

In racing terminology a *pit stop* is a common phrase. This phrase has been borrowed by students, male and female, to refer to the necessity for stopping during a trip at a gas station to go to the men's or ladies' room.

A very frequent type of semantic transfer is that of facetious descriptions of courses to the names of the big courses. There are countless examples, some of which are:

     trees: Forestry
     genes: Introduction to Genetics
     monkeys: course in Zoology dealing with human evolution
     leaves: Botany courses
     tanks and jeeps: course in Military History
     ducks and geese: Comparative Psychology
     dirt farming: History of American Democracy
     rocks: Geology
     pre-God: Religion courses
     God: courses in the Divinity School
     play-a-day: English Drama

There are many phrases of two or more words which involve a variety of kinds of semantic extension or transfer. For example, a *queen* is a common term for a male homosexual and a *closet* is a small storage room. A *closet queen* is used to describe a 'homosexual who conceals his problem.' The word *muscle* assumes a rather opposite meaning, namely 'fat,' in the phrase *Milwaukee muscle* 'beer-belly.' A *sandwich date* is a threesome, two boys and one girl.

In days of yore there were many words in the taboo and related concepts category which were undoubtedly known to girls (and possibly even used by them among themselves), but which were avoided in mixed company. Nowadays there appears to have been some sort of disintegration or collapse in the distinction between words that are used in mixed company. So many items dealing with sex and body functions are in the gray zone: used with very little restraint by both sexes in mixed groups of their peers. Several of the so-called four letter words have gone the way of *hell* and *damn:* they are merely exclamations of disgust or anger, having become dissociated from their referents.

One example is the acronym OTR /ow tiy aə(r/ as well as the three words to which these letters refer: *on the rag.* This was a phrase originally used among females to refer to the menstrual period, which for many women brings a certain edginess and irritability. The phrase was then extended to mean simply: 'in a foul mood,' and currently is readily applied to males! "Jack has really been on the rag this week. He has been otr since she dumped on him." Neither the acronym nor the complete phrase is connected with the original concept.

The following illustrates well the possible scope of semantic extension. Male athletes very commonly wear a protective garment known as an athletic supporter. The everyday term for this item is jockstrap. By extension the first part of that term is now applied to athletes or actually any other male with an athletic build. The word is used by both men and women. During the homecoming weekend, campus tradition requires that many living groups put on a skit during a program on the night before the "big game." One of the women's living groups, Jarvis House, did so participate in the fall of 1967. Probably in imitation of the Radio City Rockettes and in reference to athletes, "jocks," these girls called themselves the Jarvis Jockettes.

FOR DISCUSSION AND REVIEW

1 What is collegiate slang? How is it differentiated from other slang groups? Is it a valid category? Why or why not?

2 According to Seymour, what are some of the processes by which collegiate slang is created?

3 Are the examples of collegiate slang that Seymour cites dated? Can you give more recent examples of collegiate slang which illustrate the principles of word formation discussed by both Seymour and Francis (pp. 288 and 260)?

4 Seymour provides examples of semantic transfer in the facetious titles that students give courses. Can you find examples of such semantic transfer on your campus? What might be the proper titles for the courses with the following student titles: foods and nuts, kiddie lit, weeds and seeds, the un-math, cuts and guts, mug the bug?

9

The Agonies
of Acronymania

Acronyms are words made from initials or abbreviations and most serve their purposes quite well. Consider, however, the problems and humorous situations that result from the proliferation of acronyms during the last decade as discussed in this article published in Time in 1970.

Time Magazine

TODAY'S ACRONYMS, designed to be time- and labor-saving devices, are often harder to use than the words they are meant to replace. Consider the monsters that the Navy alone has spawned: EPDOPAC (Enlisted Personnel Distribution Office-Pacific Fleet) and PAMIPAC (Personnel Accounting Machine Installation-Pacific Fleet). Worse, they have now grown so prolific that MAD may stand for anything from Mutual Assured Destruction to the New York Stock Exchange symbol for the Madison Fund—with 13 other alternatives in between.

The very word acronym is a neologism, which a Bell Laboratories researcher created in 1943 from the Greek *akros* (tip) and *onyma* (name). By 1960, when the Gale Research Company of Detroit published the first edition of what is now called *Acronyms and Initialisms Dictionary* (lumping wordlike acronyms with unpronounceable abbreviations) 12,000 of both were already on the loose. This summer's third edition will list more than 80,000. Nor is English the only language to be acronymized. The Library of Congress publishes a glossary of 23,600 Russian acronyms and abbreviations, ranging from the familiar MIG plane (designed in part by Mikhail Iosifovich Gurevich) to AGITPROP (for Agitation and Propaganda Department).

Planned to save words in print and speech, acronyms have created new ones instead (radar, sonar, loran) and even corrupted spelling, producing "snick" out of SNCC and "rotsy" from ROTC. Today inappropriate acronyms are a constant hazard. When the Nixon Administration set up its new Office of Management and Budget (OMB), for example, it seemed clear that the awkward initials were invented to avoid the more logical name, Bureau of Management and Budget (BOMB). Military men seldom avoid such errors. The Army is especially prone to fatuous acronyms like BAMBI, which stands for Ballistic Missile Boost

Intercept. Some civilian agencies are equally dense: ACHE (Alabama Commission on Higher Education), or something the Albuquerque payroll office of the Bureau of Indian Affairs calls Wage and Manpower Process Utilizing Machines, which tactlessly yields WAMPUM. From conservationists: FOE (Friends of the Earth) and ACNE (Alaskans Concerned for Neglected Environments).

The worst hazard is the acronym's tendency to create doubles. As soon as an acronym becomes common, it breeds a litter of identical children. When a man says that he works for AID, is he part of the Agency for International Development or Americans of Italian Descent? Perhaps he is a doctor concerned with Artificial Insemination by Donor, or a lexicographer employed by the *Acronyms and Initialisms Dictionary*, which now lists 18 different AIDs.

Even the Strategic Air Command must compete with other SACs, from sprayed acoustical ceiling to the Society of the Catholic Apostolate—not to mention SACC (either Supplemental Air Carrier Conference or Supporting Arms Coordination Center) and SAK (a Finnish trade union confederation called Suomen Ammattiliittojen Keskuslitto).

Ironically, people have a natural reluctance to clutter their memories with clusters of letters. Even those in the midst of the highest acronymic concentrations occasionally lose one. During the Apollo 12 mission, according to *The Washington Monthly*, controllers discovered that a minor malfunction was due to something called the Digital Uplink Assembly. "We think we've figured it out—your DUA was off," they radioed to the vicinity of the moon. Replied Apollo: "What is a DUA?"

FOR DISCUSSION AND REVIEW

1 What is an *acronym*? A *neologism*? Give some examples of both.

2 Ecologists worried about the dangers of off-shore oil spills have recently coined the word GOO (Get Oil Out). Imagine that you have been given the responsibility for the formation of an appropriate acronymn for a group concerned with each of the following issues: a) oil pipelines through the state of Alaska; b) noise pollution in New York City; c) the immediate release of all prisoners of war; d) airport congestion; e) full citizenship for Chicanos; f) the detection of potential airplane hijackers.

3 What is your opinion of acronyms? Do you agree with *Time* that they "are often harder to use than the words they are meant to replace"? Are there any alternatives to the use of acronyms? Explain.

10

Speaking
of Space

David McNeill

Part of the thrill of space flights is the exposure to the otherworldliness of a seemingly new language. Professor David McNeill, Associate Professor of Psychology at the University of Michigan, examines "space speak" and reveals that, while some aspects of this language are unique, much of it is based on a single grammatical device which transforms underlying phrases into nominal compounds.

W̲E READ of "space speak" on every hand. Newspapers and magazines discuss it in their science columns, and popular fancy seems to have been captured by it. The belief is that the space effort has given us, in addition to the possibility of going to the moon, a new linguistic phenomenon. However, it is not easy to escape the confines of English, and in "space speak" there is nothing novel, nor even very much that is unique. The name itself is a misnomer. "Space speak" is not much spoken; and, linguistically, the most important thing that NASA engineers do is not peculiar to the space effort. On the other hand, there is a jargon of engineering that is fully used by space technologists. My task in this article is the analysis of such jargon.

The major part of space jargon is an overabundance of a linguistic form that is available to all speakers of English. There is, however, a much smaller part that is unique; these are the words, seemingly occult, that give rise to the impression of linguistic novelty. Some familiar examples are *pad, abort, umbilical*. Others, less well known, are *eyeballs in* and *eyeballs out* (describing conditions of extreme acceleration and deceleration respectively) and *milk stool* (describing an arrangement of three rocket engines on the lunar spacecraft). As these examples show, such terms in the jargon of space engineering are of two types. Most are metaphors (for example, *umbilical, milk stool*), where the conventional meaning of the word and its meaning in space jargon have something in common. A much smaller number are metonyms (for example, *eyeballs in*), where the conventional term refers to something that typically accompanies the referent of the space term. Metaphors depend on similarity of referent; metonyms depend on contiguity. Both types of term are the ingredients of most professional jargons. Psychologists, for example, talk of *thresholds*; anthropologists, of cultural *diffusion*; sailors, of *Jacob's ladders*.

Metaphors and metonyms are usually apt, but, by the same token, they are difficult to come by. The process of finding a good metaphor or metonym is not given automatically by the rules of English syntax. It demands a kind of creativity that is unregimented. Thus, whereas metaphors and metonyms are ordinarily "good," in the sense of capturing an intended meaning succinctly and vividly, they are also rare. If a technical jargon must provide large numbers of terms, reliance on metaphors and metonyms simply will not be sufficiently productive.

What is needed is a systematic procedure. One solution is to coin new words, as the medical sciences have done. Their procedure is systematic and useful if one knows a little Greek or Latin and the rules for combining roots in these languages. Had engineering experienced its great growth at a time when schooling in Greek and Latin was still part of the college curriculum, perhaps space jargon would have followed the same path. (NASA's penchant for naming programs and vehicles after the Greek and Roman gods is, of course, a different matter altogether.) Words also can be created *de novo* within English, and there are some examples of this in space jargon (for instance, *rockoon*, a rocket launched from a balloon). Neologism, however, is no more systematic than the formation of metaphors, though it may demand less in the way of creative powers, and so it is not likely to have a larger yield of technical terms.

In official NASA dictionaries of space terms,[1] metaphors and metonyms account for about one-eighth of the entries. In absolute terms, this is less than 100 words. Most of the remaining entries are combinations of words, put together into a particular grammatical construction, the so-called nominal compound. The solution for increasing the technical vocabulary, then, has been to resort to English syntax.

The advantages of this solution are considerable. The method is endlessly productive, since there are no limits on the constructions that may be generated by a grammatical device. It requires no exotic knowledge, since it draws only on the English lexicon and employs only rules that are general in English. Moreover, nominal compounds, however long, are always nouns and this means that they have all the maneuverability of single words. Some examples will make clear the type of construction a nominal compound is: *launch vehicle; escape propulsion system; battery discharger test set; separation and destruct system ordi-*

---

[1] "Short Glossary of Space Terms," NASA (*Nat. Aeron., Space Admin.*) *Publ.* SP-1 (1962); "Apollo Terminology," NASA (*Nat. Aeron. Space Admin.*) *Publ.* SP-6001 (1963).

nance equipment.[2] These terms reveal several features worth noting about engineers' nominal compounds. Most obvious is the flexibility in length. Two words are the minimum, but there is, in theory, no upper limit. The longest nominal compound I have seen occurred in the *Congressional Record* and contained 13 words—*liquid oxygen liquid hydrogen rocket powered single stage to orbit reversible boost system.* The statement that each compound is grammatically a noun can be verified by placing the compounds in the sentence frame, "The ——— is here." Actually, the grammatical class of the compound is the class of the final word, which is always a noun. Perhaps less obvious than the grammatical class of nominal compounds is the constraint on the order in which words can appear. *Vehicle launch* is not the same thing as *launch vehicle;* nor is *discharger set battery test* the same as *battery discharger test set.* I return below to the constraint on word order, but first I must support two points already made.

One is the statement that nominal compounds are part of general English grammar, a relationship that can be simply exemplified with some familiar compounds from ordinary English. We buy from *vending machines,* park in *driveways,* and worry about *girl friends;* and we even read in Dr. Seuss of "three seater zatzit nose patting extensions."[3] It is not accidental that the obvious examples of nominal compounds in general English are short; the main difference between engineering jargon and general English is that long compounds are more frequent in engineering jargon. Otherwise, the two classes of compounds are the same—that is, order of words makes a difference, and the compounds are grammatically nouns.

The second point is basic to the theme of this article and so warrants elaborate treatment. It is, actually, two related points: (i) in spite of the fact that nominal compounds are general in English, they are used by engineers in response to a special pressure for technical terminology; (ii) because of this, nominal compounds are not peculiar to the space effort but appear equally often in the jargon of other engineering fields.

There is no way to measure pressure on a field to form a technical vocabulary. But it seems safe to assume that engineers are under greater pressure to do this than social scientists, who in turn experience greater pressure than literary critics or historians. Therefore, we should expect that writings by these three groups will show corresponding differences in the frequency with which nominal compounds are used, and such

---

[2] *Destruct* is another neologism, which in many cases replaces the verb *destroy;* the reason for the neologism, I was told, is to avoid the warlike overtones of *destroy.*

[3] T. S. Geisel (Dr. Seuss), *On Beyond Zebra!* (Random House, New York, 1955); I am indebted to Nobuko McNeill for bringing this example to my attention.

is the case. Samples were taken from 18 technical reports published by NASA, from six papers by psychologists, which appeared in the *Psychological Review* and the *Psychological Bulletin* (both professional journals), and from six articles from *The American Scholar*. The samples ranged in size from 3000 to 6000 words of text. Nineteen percent of all words in the NASA reports were in nominal compounds. The corresponding average for the psychologists was 8 percent, and for *The American Scholar*, 3 percent. The number of metaphors and metonyms, on the other hand, did not differ among the three samples, which perhaps indicates that this source is used to its fullest even in *The American Scholar*. Thus, most of the nominal compounds used by the engineers were probably used in response to the need for technical terms.

The average for NASA—19 percent—is duplicated almost exactly in the technical writing of other engineering fields. Twenty percent of the words in a sample of reports issued by the Operations Research Center of M.I.T. were in nominal compounds; most of the writers were electrical engineers. Similarly, 17 percent of the words in the departmental announcements of the M.I.T. departments of mechanical engineering and physics were in nominal compounds. In short, the nominal compound is used by diverse fields, apparently to meet the common need for technical terms in greater numbers than metaphors, metonyms, or neologisms can supply.

Linguistic Analysis

The basic fact about nominal compounds is that they all derive from underlying phrases, through the application of one or more grammatical rules. It is in this sense that the nominal compound is a grammatical device. *Launch vehicle*, for example, comes from the phrase *vehicle for launching*. The grammatical transformation has the effect of reversing word order and deleting the preposition and the bound morpheme *-ing*. Phrases with different structure are similarly transformed, but by different rules. *Simulation of flight*, which is a sequence of noun-preposition-noun (in contrast to noun-preposition-verb in the foregoing example) becomes the compound *flight simulation*. The rule is slightly different, but it has the same effect of reversing order and deleting the preposition. The various rules thus have similar effects; their differences consist in the type of underlying structure on which they operate.

The rules for transforming underlying phrases into compounds have been formulated in detail by the linguist R. B. Lees.[4] I need not restate these rules here, nor take into account their complete forms. For present

[4] R. B. Lees, *Intern. J. Amer. Linguistics* **26**, No. 3 (July 1960).

purposes it is sufficient to note that such rules exist and that they pair compounds with underlying phrases.[5]

An underlying phrase can be regarded as the origin of the corresponding compound, and the process of forming nominal compounds in space jargon can be conceived of as taking place in two steps: production of the underlying phrase and transformation of the phrase into a compound by the appropriate rule. There are many rules, and so virtually any phrase can become a nominal compound. Also, as we shall see shortly, underlying phrases can be of any length, and so, therefore, can their compounds. In these two points lie the major advantages of the nominal compound as a means of increasing technical vocabulary. Given a knowledge of the rules, all that is required is a capacity to produce phrases in English.

The process is illustrated in Table 1. On the left are phrases; each row contains everything contained in the immediately preceding row plus one additional phrase or word. On the right are the corresponding compounds. We can see here how compounds grow in length, and we can also see something of the variety of phrase structures that can be transformed into nominal compounds.

Also, we can now see the basis of the constraint on the order of words in a compound. It is simply the order of words in the underlying phrase. Note that one can roughly reconstruct each phrase from the corresponding compound by reading the words of the compound in reverse order.

Table 1. Nominal compounds and corresponding phrases.

Phrase	Nominal compound
the system	the system
the system that controls	the control system
the system that controls attitude	the attitude control system
the system that controls attitude of the ship	the ship attitude control system
the system that controls attitude of the ship by ejecting	the ejection ship attitude control system
the system that controls attitude of the ship by ejecting gas	the gas ejection ship attitude control system
the system that controls attitude of the ship by ejecting gas through nozzles	the nozzle gas ejection ship attitude control system

[5] Actually, transformations do not operate on phrases, but operate on the abstract structure out of which phrases are built. The distinction is critical in most discussions of syntax. In the present case, however, the reader will not be seriously misled by thinking of phrases rather than structures. It should be borne in mind, nonetheless, that the term *underlying phrase* is really a loose figure of speech. For a complete discussion of the relation between phrases and underlying syntactic structures, see N. Chomsky, *Aspects of the Theory of Syntax* (M.I.T. Press, Cambridge, Mass., 1965).

One way to demonstrate that compounds correspond to phrases is to show that they can be bracketed in the same way. Bracketing is grammatical parsing done with brackets; it is a notation showing where the constituents of the compound or phrase are. (In the present case, contrary to usual practice, the brackets have been drawn above and below the string of words.) For the compound of Table 1 we get,

The nozzle gas ejection ship attitude control system,

which corresponds exactly to

The system that controls attitude of the ship by ejecting gas through nozzles.

Most of the constituents marked off in this fashion overlap. (One pair of constituents does not, which is the reason why row 5 of Table 1 seems incomplete; in fact, it is not complete, since one constituent is only half represented.) However, not all compounds or phrases have overlapping constituents. For phrases of a different structure, the relative positions of the brackets are different. For example, the pseudo-space phrase

a program that orbits astronauts, makes modules, and embarrasses Russians

becomes the compound

a Russian embarrassing module making astronaut orbiting program

As the bracketing shows, no constituents overlap. The cases of overlapping and nonoverlapping constituents, plus combinations of the two, appear to encompass all the situations in which long phrases can be transformed into single nominal compounds. Other phrase structures, such as the "self-embedding construction," in which a sentence is constructed like an onion (for example, "The race that the car that the people whom the man called sold won was held last summer"), cannot be transformed into nominal compounds. With allowable phrase structures, however, long compounds can be generated from long phrases through successive application of Lees's rules. Each rule produces only a two-word compound, but by applying the rules in a left-to-right direction throughout the phrase, one produces a right-to-left growth of the compound. The result is an orderly and predictable dependence of compounds on underlying phrases, a relation that is sufficient basis for use of the nominal compound as a source of technical terminology.

Psycholinguistic Implications

In the actual use of nominal compounds as technical terms, more is involved than the application of Lees's rules of transformation. One might suppose that the rules for forming compounds would work in two directions, from underlying phrase to compound and back again. In theory, of course, they do; it is always possible to retransform a compound into a phrase. But transformations in the two directions are not equally determined. Whereas transformation of a phrase is unique, retransformation of a compound is often ambiguous. *Mission suitability*, for example, could derive from either "suitability *for* the mission" or "suitability *of* the mission," which are quite different things. To NASA engineers, the term has the former meaning. Similarly, *time critical equipment* could mean "equipment for which there is a critical time [during which it is usable]" or "equipment for which there is a critical time [for performing a function]." Again, the former is the correct meaning.

Although such ambiguities exist, NASA engineers seem unaware of them. I interviewed four engineers at the Marshall Space Flight Center in Huntsville, Alabama; all were actively engaged in the design or testing of apparatus used in the Apollo program. They were alert and cooperative informants, but none was aware of ambiguities of the sort just mentioned. In view of the fact that nominal compounds are *constructed*, this is rather remarkable. One explanation is that these engineers had "recoded" certain of the nominal compounds into single units, quite as if they were simple nouns. Possibly, such recoding is due to a suspension of the process of transformation, and tends to occur in the case of nominal compounds that are used frequently. Presumably the status of these recoded compounds is similar to that of the nominal compounds of ordinary English. *Driveway* means "way *for* driving," but "way *of* driving" is equally possible. The fact seems to be that we do not disassemble *driveway* in order to understand it, and so we are, like the engineers, unaware of the ambiguity.

If we make the assumption that frequently occurring nominal compounds in engineering jargon are understood as unified nouns, we can see that it is for the encoder of terms, not the decoder, that this grammatical device is advantageous. Moreover, since an established nominal compound that is understood as a unit probably is produced as a unit as well, the advantages are not primarily for every encoder, but for the encoder who is producing a new term. The result is that the nominal compound is a device that mainly benefits the "culture," guaranteeing that new technical terms will be available when needed.

That frequently occurring nominal compounds can be recoded does not mean that the rules for forming nominal compounds are linguistic fictions. On the contrary, they conform to actual psychological processes. When asked to "unravel" nominal compounds, the engineers interviewed at Huntsville produced phrases in which the words of the compound appeared in reverse order. And, conversely, when the engineers were asked to create nominal compounds to go with definitions (which were unfamiliar to them but taken from a NASA dictionary), they selected two or more words in the definition, reversed their order, and placed them into a compound. Usually, in this latter experiment, the term the engineers created was not the term defined in the dictionary. But that does not alter the conclusion that, psychologically as well as linguistically, nominal compounds are transformed phrases.

Many people suspect that engineers use the nominal compound because of a careless lack of concern for the requirements of style. This seems to be a general opinion among nontechnical readers of engineering prose. It is an opinion, however, which overlooks the fact that nominal compounds are transformations, and so require the user to go at least one step beyond formulating an underlying phrase. Consider the following data. The proportion of all words in nominal compounds has already been given as 19 percent for several NASA technical reports. For some of the writers of these reports, samples of spoken language also were available (from written and oral testimony before a congressional committee). If the nominal compound is overused through carelessness, it should occur more often when an individual is speaking extempore than when he is writing. However, this is not the case; the nominal compound is a literary phenomenon.

Compared to the figure of 19 percent for written materials, only 7 percent of spoken words are in nominal compounds. The pressure of spontaneous speech thus has an effect quite opposite from the effect the hypothesis of carelessness would predict. Evidently, use of the nominal compound in technical writing reflects literary care, not lack of it. The nominal compounds that are used in speech are short and among the most common. In all probability, they are recoded compounds. If that is the case, the 12 percent comprised of compounds used in written language but not in speech would for the most part be newly created terms. There is psychological evidence[6] that speech containing many transformations is more difficult to understand than speech containing few transformations. Probably there is a similar difference in difficulty when speech is produced, so the nominal compound is used less frequently in spoken than in written language. It simply takes too much time and causes too much confusion to transform phrases as frequently when one is speaking as one does when writing.

Influence of Space Jargon

There are at least two ways in which space jargon may influence the general language. One is through what may be called *specific* influence. In this case, a particular term passes into nontechnical language. There

[6] G. A. Miller, *Amer. Psychologist* 17, 748 (1962).

are numerous familiar examples: *countdown, astronaut, space probe,* and so on. Metaphors, metonyms, neologisms, and nominal compounds —all might be introduced into the general language as specific terms. The basis of specific influence is some knowledge, on the part of the speaker or writer, of the hardware or concept that the technical term names. Thus, specific influence is limited by the extent of the infusion of technical knowledge, but, by the same token, terms carried into the language through specific influence do not importantly change meaning in their passage from jargon to general language.

However, some of these terms appear to undergo a further development once they have been taken into the general language. For example, one hears people speak of starting something from a "launching pad of . . . ," by which they mean a "basis of. . . ." This is a metaphorical use of the space term *pad.* Some of the adopted terms that change in this way are already metaphors in space jargon, being adaptations of ordinary English words. *Pad* is an example. These new metaphors, then, actually are attachments of new meanings to old words, a process known to linguists as polysemy. Specific influence, therefore, can have two rather different effects. One derives from the simple introduction of technical terms; the consequences of this should be narrow for the general language. The other derives from the attachment of new meanings to old words, and it has more devastating possibilities. Polysemy is held to be a major force for change in language, and, through it, terms such as *pad* could conceivably lose their present meaning: our descendants may talk about the pad of our democracy being free speech.

Not all words that pass as "space speak" come from space technology. Indeed, some of the most popular specimens are spurious, having been invented by newsmen. Among the most notable of these are *A-OK, blast off,* and *spin off.* Nonetheless, many such words are examples of polysemy, and so are potential sources of change of meaning.

In contrast to specific influence, there is a second, more *generic* influence. In this case, elaborate use of the grammatical device of the nominal compound itself is adopted. Generic influence in no way depends on technical knowledge; it consists simply of extensive use of a construction already available in the general language. One way in which generic influence is mediated was suggested by some of the engineers whom I interviewed at Huntsville. On occasion, they said, engineers will deliberately overuse the nominal compound in order to impress their auditors. Apparently the nominal compound has about it an aura of technical sophistication. Such exploitation of the nominal compound could work also in the opposite direction, in that non-technologists who desire to resemble technologists can use the nominal compound as a kind of poor man's engineering jargon. This would be an example of generic influence.

These considerations suggest computation of a measure, called here the "pretension index," for analyzing samples of prose for evidence of generic influence. The name pretension index is used to indicate that, by overusing the nominal compound, one can pretend to possess a degree of technical knowledgeability that, in fact, one does not have. There are two senses in which the nominal compound could be "overused," and the pretension index might measure either one of them. Overuse could be taken to mean simply increased frequency of use of these compounds. However, such an increase could occur simply because the content of a passage required it, and this would have nothing to do with generic influence. Because of this possibility, the pretension index measures overuse in the second sense—an increased use of the number of long compounds relative to the number of short compounds. The idea is that unnecessary use of the nominal compound would favor both increased frequency and increased length, but that where technical content requires unusually frequent use of some nominal compounds in a given passage, it would not ordinarily require, at the same time, an increase in their length. Greater length can come only from (i) a need to make technical terms more specific or from (ii) use of the nominal compound without regard to technical terminology.

The pretension index is computed from the number of compounds of length 2, 3, 4, 5, . . . words that occur in a sample of prose. There is a simple relation between length and frequency, known as Zipf's law, that holds for a great variety of textual material. Zipf's law states that the logarithm of frequency and the logarithm of length are negatively related to each other by a straight line. In brief, the law states that the frequency of words (or compounds) is proportional to their shortness. The shorter the word or compound, the more frequent its occurrence. The slope of the line relating frequency and length, the "Zipf slope," depends on the relative number of long and short words or compounds. The pretension index is based on the "Zipf slope," but not directly, for it is necessary also to make some reference to a standard. An appropriate standard is the "Zipf slope" for the entries in a dictionary of space terminology. Such dictionaries contain only technical terms, and thus provide an estimate of the relative numbers of long and short compounds in the true technical vocabulary. The pretension index for a sample of speech, then, is computed by dividing the "Zipf slope" of the standard by the measured "Zipf slope" of the sample. The higher the index, the more "pretentious" the sample of speech.

Equipped with an index, we can now see whether there is any evidence for generic influence of space jargon. Pretension indices have been computed for samples of writing by NASA engineers (the same material that was used in the study cited above); for samples of spoken material by NASA personnel (oral testimony before a congressional committee); for samples of spoken material by some members of Congress; and for samples of writing from a popular magazine on space technology. In these computations NASA represents the engineering profession; the Congressmen and the space magazine represent laymen who deal a good bit with space technology. The results are given in Table 2.

Table 2. Pretension indices for several samples of speech.

Sample	Pretension index
NASA, written	1.00
NASA, spoken	0.79
Magazine on space technology, written	1.46
Congress, spoken	0.94

The proper comparisons here are within modes of communication—written-to-written and spoken-to-spoken. Clearly, the space magazine uses relatively too many long compounds for all of them to be true technical terms. Since the pretension index is based on logarithms, small numerical differences reflect large differences in length of the compounds; expressed as percentages, these data are much more impressive. In the space magazine there are 220 percent more five-word compounds than there are in the NASA written reports, and 300 percent more six-word compounds. There is no reason to suppose that only the long compounds in the space magazine are nontechnical; no doubt many of the short compounds also result from generic influence.

The slopes for the two oral samples are both lower than those for the written samples—an effect that derives, in all probability, from the need to avoid complicated transformations in spontaneous speech. Nonetheless, Congressmen have an index nearly as high when speaking as NASA engineers have when writing, and possibly this too reflects generic influence.

Generic influence, of course, need not be limited to the nonengineer who attempts to appear knowledgeable about space technology. The nominal compound can be a source of borrowed dignity for any professional jargon. On the other hand, it would be a mistake to assume that every extensive use of the nominal compound by nonengineers is a case of generic influence. Other professional people may turn to it for the same reasons that engineers do, for technical terms. I know of no way to distinguish generic influence throughout the language from independent discovery of the nominal compound as a form of professional jargon. However, those who dread the influence of engineering jargon may be heartened to learn that newspapers, outside their science columns, show little indication of adopting the nominal compound.

Acronyms

As already indicated, Zipf's law asserts that the shorter compounds are the more frequent. The relation is often interpreted as showing causality: words (or compounds) become shorter because they are more frequently used. Indeed, Zipf concluded from his law that language users follow a principle of least effort. Whether or not Zipf's theory is correct, his law—which is a purely mathematical statement—implies that particular compounds should become shorter as their frequency of use increases. It is clear that such a shortening does take place in the case of individual words, as the erosion of *television* to *video* to *TV* illustrates. However, it is equally clear that compounds cannot be shortened in this way, for the reason that they have grammatical structure. When a word is shortened, the abbreviation appears to be made almost arbitrarily; it must remain pronounceable, but there are no other requirements. In England, for example, *television* has changed to *telly*. Comparable freedom does not exist with compounds. One cannot shorten *escape propulsion system* to *escape system, escape propulsion,* or *propulsion system* without changing the original meaning. The abbreviations correspond to new underlying phrases that are not identical with the original phrase. The solution to this problem, of course, is the acronym. Thus, *escape propulsion system* becomes *EPS*, while *propulsion system, escape system,* and *escape propulsion* becomes *PS, ES,* and *EP,* respectively. The original structural distinctions among the compounds are all represented among the acronyms. I suspect that most cases of "acronyming" can be explained as efforts to conform to Zipf's law without changing meaning at the same time. However, not all acronyms result from increased frequency of use of compounds. In some cases the sequence apparently is reversed: the acronym is devised first, then a compound is found to fit it. In these cases the acronym often spells a word whose meaning is somehow relevant to the meaning of the compound. This is a literary game, not the outcome of the natural linguistic development implied by Zipf's law. One such playful acronym is *EGADS*, which names the system used to destroy a malfunctioning missile after it has been launched, and "goes" with the compound *electronic ground automatic destruct sequencer.*

It is not possible, obviously, to disassemble an acronym into a kernel phrase. But, since frequently used compounds tend to be recoded and thus are not disassembled anyway, nothing is lost by reducing these compounds to acronyms. The ultimate outcome of compounding followed by "acronyming" is the creation of new vocabulary. In effect, acronyms are new words. However, they are words manufactured according to definite principles and so can be coined in abundance.

A Concluding Remark

Professional jargon is a topic that stands at the intersection of several academic fields. Sociology, anthropology, linguistics, and psychology, at least, can find something of interest in it. The emphasis here has been on the psycholinguistic aspects, not because they are the most notable in the study of jargon, but, on the contrary, because they have been the most neglected. However, it is not likely that psychologists or linguists will be entirely satisfied with the results. The psychologist will find the data scanty; the linguist will find the statement of rules informal. Both will be correct, for this psycholinguistic study of jargon should be regarded as preliminary. The purpose here has been merely to indicate some interesting lines of inquiry.

But until further work has been done, we can conclude that the following statement is probably true: space speak is an engineering technology concept expression manuscript sentence grammar device.[7]

FOR DISCUSSION AND REVIEW

1 What is a *nominal compound*? Why are they found so frequently in technical speech and writing?

2 Why have there not been more names coined from Greek and Latin root words in the field of space technology?

3 McNeill says, "Perhaps less obvious than the grammatical class of nominal compounds is the constraint placed on the order in which words can appear." Is there a difference between *launch vehicle* and *vehicle launch*? Explain.

4 McNeill makes the point that nominal compounds are derived from "underlying phrases" and are the products of "transformations." What does he mean by the use of these terms?

5 What is "Zipf's law"? What is a "pretension index"?

6 Now that you have read the McNeill article and have learned how nominal compounds are constructed, try making nominal compounds from the following: a) a device that detects metal for the purpose of preventing hijackings; b) an assembly which is made of wood, operated by hand, and used to remove the tops from aluminum cans which once held soda.

[7] Preparation of this article was supported in part by a grant (No. NsG-253-62) from the National Aeronautics and Space Administration to the American Academy of Arts and Sciences, Committee on Space, and in part by a grant (No. 5-TI-GM-1011-02) from the National Institutes of Health to Harvard University, Center for Cognitive Studies. Final preparation of the article was supported in part by a grant (No. 1PO1 HD01368-01) from the National Institute of Child Health and Human Development to the Project on Language Development. University of Michigan, and in part by a contract (No. OE-5-14-036) between the U.S. Office of Education and the Center for Research on Language and Language Behavior, University of Michigan.

11
American Euphemisms for Dying, Death, and Burial
An Anthology

Louise Pound

When we use the expressions *pre-owned* for *used*, *exterminator* for *rat-catcher*, and *vertical surface sanitation engineer* for *window cleaner*, we are using *euphemisms*. We camouflage reality to a certain degree by their use, and perhaps nowhere do we feel they are more necessary than when we talk about death. You may be surprised to learn that Homer used the expression "bit the dust" and that Shakespeare used "gave up the ghost." In the following article, Louise Pound has compiled and categorized an extensive collection of such euphemisms.

THE SUPERSTITION that to name a thing is to gain power over it seems to receive little credence when death and its trappings are concerned. It appears, in fact, that one of mankind's gravest problems is to avoid a straightforward mention of dying or burial. Every ingenuity is practiced to find words which will shroud the idea of death. The number and variety of such euphemisms is amazing, and, although a list of the expressions may not be of much value, a curious interest attaches to them. They represent an essential human trait which to the devout may seem an inherent reverence before the name of a mystery, to the cynical, a cowardly evasion of reality.

The following expressions were collected from time to time in a purely incidental fashion. They came largely from oral sources, sermons and conversations, with occasional expressions from newspapers and books. For the sake of imposing limitations, only American expressions have been listed, although, of course, many of these are traditional from Britain or are held in common with the mother country. All of the material, including the older literary expressions, came from the current usage of the nineteenth and twentieth centuries. No earlier sources were used. It is doubtless true that of late certain taboos have been dropped and, as regards death as well as life, downright words are often preferred to periphrases. Yet scores and scores of euphemistic terms are still in use.

Because certain expressions seem related, they are grouped together in the following six sections. Many smaller classes might have been possible or even advisable, but for convenience these larger general divisions have been made, with only a few subdivisions. It would be absurd to claim that the lists given here are exhaustive. They never could be complete; but they may at least give an idea of the number and variety of ways in which English-speaking people have been able to suggest without actually naming dying, death, and burial.

I. Sentimental and Poetic Expressions

By far the greater number of current euphemisms are sentimental or poetic. Some of them have a high literary ancestry; others are the inventions of modern funeral orators or newspaper biographers. In all there is an attempt to evoke gentle emotions and to find in death and burial a melancholy romance or noble dignity. Shakespeare supplied several of the figures, Homer at least one, and the Scriptures half a dozen others. Even the American Indian influence may be detected in a small group of expressions.

In this section are listed the various personifications of death, metaphors of light and darkness, sleep and rest, and the familiar figures of departure, setting out, or return, in which death becomes a journey. There is genuine poetry in many of the expressions, but more often the effect is that of a pointless substitute for straightforward speech. A jarring element obtrudes itself as the metaphor shifts from the 'flickering lamp' to the 'run-down clock,' from the 'fiddle and the bow' to the 'knife and fork,' and legend chronicles as the ultimate failure the trope of the rattled clergyman who said, pointing to the corpse, 'This is only the shell—the nut is gone.'

GENERAL LITERARY AND FIGURATIVE EXPRESSIONS

Released from the burden of the weary world.
Laid down his burden.
Laid down the burden of life's weary load.
The lamp of life flickered out.
The dews of death were upon him.
The cord is broken.
The golden cord is severed.
The thread is snapped.
Taken to Paradise.
Translated into another world.
Joined the great majority.

Is out of his misery.
Breathed his last.
Called home.
Called to his reward/final reward.
Fallen by the wayside.
Met his end.
Gathered to his fathers.
His soul has flown.
He has left us.
He has left a vacant chair.
He gave up earthly life.
The angel of death claimed him in his youth.

His clock has run down.

Slipped into the great democracy of the dead.

Passed from earth's uncertainties into the infinite varieties.

Clasped in the cold embrace of death.

Climbed the golden stair.

Answered the call of the unknown.

Is with the angels.

Has paid the last tribute/debt of nature.

Is now playing the harp.

Has laid down the knife and fork.

Laid away.

Laid/placed under the daisies.

Laid under the sod.

Laid in the cold, cold ground.

Borne forth amid the daisies.

Consigned to the earth.

Put under a little mound of earth.

Enshrined in his mausoleum.

His light is put out.

Has clothed himself in light.

Withdrawn in silence from the living.

Granted/given/handed his quietus.

Suffered the last great change.

Life's last demand has been met.

The immortal occupant has deserted its tenancy/tenement.

He lay down in darkness and his light is in ashes.

Called to God.

Called to Jesus.

Called beyond.

Launched into eternity.

God in his providence saw fit to remove him.

Hung up the fiddle and the bow. (From the songs by Stephen C. Foster, 'Old Uncle Ned' and 'Massa's in the Cold Cold Ground.')

Bit the dust. (Homer.)

Gave up the ghost. (Shakespeare.)

Shuffled off this mortal coil. (Shakespeare.)

There cracked a noble heart. (Shakespeare.)

For him the sunset gates unbarred. (From Whittier's 'Snowbound.')

Personifications of Death

The Grim Reaper.

The Pale Horseman.

The Spoiler.

The Destroying Angel.

The Grim Monster.

The Twin Brother of Sleep.

The Arch Foe.

METAPHORS OF SLEEP AND REST

Gone to enduring sleep.

Asleep in Jesus.

Safe in the arms of Jesus.

Asleep in the valley.

Fallen asleep in God.

Sunk into his last sleep.

Sleeps the long sleep.

Sleeps with his fathers.

Is sleeping the final sleep.

Gone to the mansions of rest.

Gone to his last sleep.

Gone to a well-earned rest.

Called to heavenly rest.

Laid to rest.

Fallen quietly into the sleep which knows no earthly waking.

Rests in peace till we meet again.

Gone to rest from his long labors.

Sleeps the sleep that knows no waking. (From Scott's 'The Lady of the Lake.')

Called to the eternal sleep.

METAPHORS OF DEPARTURE, SETTING OUT, RETURN

Passed on/away/out/over.

Passed to a better home.

Passed/crossed over the river.

Passed to his reward.

Passed from the shadows below to the sunlight above.

Passed into the unknown night.

Passed within the pearly gates.

Crossed/gone over the range.
Crossed the bar/barrier/frontier/ border.
Crossed over.
Crossed/passed/went over the Great Divide.
Slipped into outer darkness.
Gone from us.
Gone forward.
Gone onward.
Gone home.
Gone aloft.
Gone through the Black Door.
Gone to Heaven.
Gone to his heavenly home.
Gone to the marble city where you and I are going.
Gone beyond the horizon.
Gone to meet the beyond.
Gone to the Great Beyond.
Gone to stand before the Great White Throne.
Gone to the land of Heart's Desire.
Gone to the land of Cockaigne.
Gone to Glory.
Gone to his Heavenly Father.
Gone to meet his Saviour.
Gone to Abraham's bosom.
Gone to his fathers.
Gone out of the darkness into the light.

Gone up yonder.
Gone to meet his Maker.
Gone to his reward.
Gone to his account.
Gone to his long home.
Gone to the Great Adventure.
Gone to prepare a place for us.
Gone the way of all flesh.
Gone out of the darkness into the light.
Gone to the Happy Hunting Grounds. (Indian.)
Gone to see the face of Wakondah. (Indian.)
Gone West. (Indian. Also used in France during World War I.)
Gone to the bourne whence no traveler returns. (Shakespeare.)
Went out with the ebb.
Went to Jordan's banks.
Slipped into outer darkness.
Was guided into the shade.
Descended into the valley of the shadow.
Hit the long trail.
Exited.
Reached his journey's end.
Returned to his native soil.
Departed this life.
Entered the marble orchard.
The bell rang and he went.

II. Flippant and Slang Expressions

As a reaction, no doubt, against the tradition of sentiment, slang and flippancy in the mention of death enjoy a certain favor. No single class is answerable for the popularity of these expressions. College students and pioneer farmers, gangsters and playwrights have all had a part in their creation, and they are kept alive by speakers of every sort. There is a little humor, much vulgarity, and a general spirit of defiance and insolence in the terms. While some of them are actually descriptive, others, particularly contemporary slang from the world of the outlaw, have an esoteric quality. To the more obscure of these expressions definitions have been attached. The terms at the end of the list, from *Take for a ride* on, are from contemporary criminal slang.

Winked out.
Shuffled off.
Ran down.
Kicked the bucket.

Kissed the dust.
Petered out.
Coiled up his cables.
Turned up his toes.

Cocked up his toes.
Turned up his toes to the daisies.
Is done for/erased/finished/flattened out.
Is a deader.
Is a goner.
Now installed in Furnace No. 10.
Went bung.
Salted down.
Placed on the shelf.
Placed in cold storage.
Put to bed with a shovel.
Is pushing up the daisies.
Gone to grass.
Grounded for good.
Paid St. Peter a visit.
Went pfft. (From flattening automobile tires.)
Stepped off the deep end.
Stepped into his last bus.
Is counting the daisy roots.
Is pushing the clouds around/about.
His hash is settled.
Is potted/gone to pot. (Reference to urn burial.)
Got his everlasting.
Made a stiff.
Gone home in a box.
Gone under.
Gone cold.
Popped off.
Hopped the twig.
Dropped off.
Bound for glory.
His goose is cooked.
Got the ax.
Snuffed it.
Snuffed out.
Now picking at the coverlet.

Made a die of it.
Knocked off/up/over.
Knocked the daylights out of.
Went up the handle.
Croaked.
Went home feet first.
Became filling for a casket.
Is counting the worms.
They put the skids under him and kicked him into the Great Beyond.
Planted. (Pioneers' slang.)
Is holding up the Bermuda (grass).
He has a little garden on his stomach.
Is lying on the cooling board.
Gone to kingdom come.
Finishee. (Pidgin English.)
Mak finishee. (Pidgin.)
Makee die. (Pidgin.)
Catchee killum. (Pidgin.)
Take for a ride.
Bump off.
Put on the spot.
Give lead poison.
Liquidate.
Give the works.
Put on ice.
Give the heat.
Give the rap.
Let the daylight into.
Drill.
Fog (shoot).
Send by the gun/rod/pistol route.
Put the cross on (mark for death).
Rub out. (A *rubber* is a professional killer.)
Wipe out.
Give a pineapple (bomb).
Take the back gate parole. (Die in prison.)

III. Terms from Work and Recreation

Another group is composed of metaphors from a variety of human activities. The expressions in the first part of the section derive from the occupations, professions, and trades. As might be expected, several of the figures originate in the business of war; a few of the others are nautical, and a miscellaneous group represents a range of pursuits from banking to butchering. Among the figures in the second division are those taken from sports and recreations. Here are terms from the theater, moving pictures, the prize ring, racing, hunting, football, and cards. They show much of the levity of the expressions in the foregoing section, and, like many of these, gain effectiveness from the incongruity between implication and actual expression. Most of the terms listed here are self-explanatory.

METAPHORS FROM OCCUPATIONS, PROFESSIONS, AND TRADES

Stopped a shrapnel.
Stopped a bullet.
Answered the last roll call.
Answered the last muster.
Heard the final call.
Received the final call.
Fired his last shot.
Gave up the ship.
Went to Davy Jones's locker.
Spilled the drink.
Fed the fishes (died by drowning).
Dropped off the hooks. (From butchering.)
Died in harness (at work).
It was '30' for him, flashed across the unending wires. ('30' is the newsman's and telegrapher's sign that he has come to the end of the string, or the day's work.)
Checked out.

Passed in his checks.
Cashed his checks.
Handed in his checks.
Went to the pay off.
Died with his boots on. (From range riding.)
Laid down the shovel and the hoe. (From Stephen C. Foster's song, 'Old Uncle Ned.')
Closed up his accounts with the world.
Answered the final/last summons. (Perhaps legal.)
The tailor (undertaker) measured the man for a new overcoat (casket).
Pulled in at the last terminal. (Railroading.)
Went to the last roundup.

METAPHORS FROM SPORTS AND RECREATIONS

Played his last card.
Went to the races.
Ran the good race.
His race is run.
Pegged out. (Cribbage.)
Struck out. (Baseball.)
Kicked off. (Football.)
Took the jump.
The curtain for him. (Theater.)
Took the curtain call.
Has taken his last cue from life's

stage.
His number was up.
Jumped his last hurdle.
Is knocked out.
He took the last/the long, long count. (Prize fighting.)
Threw in the sponge.
Passed from the picture.
Made a fadeout.
Handed in his chips. (Poker.)
Threw sixes. (Dice.)

IV. Terms for Hanging, Lynching, and Electrocution

A number of expressions, largely from the criminal world, have been evolved to cover the horrors of hanging, lynching, and electrocution. They are grim in their playfulness and often only too pictorial. Among the older expressions are those which designate hanging and lynching. They come for the most part from the sixties and seventies and suggest the lawlessness of the West in the early days. Of more recent origin are the euphemisms for electrocution. They are more terse and forbidding than the word itself, yet somehow suggestive of nonchalance in the face of punishment. The terms from *Burn* on are used for electrocution.

Kicked the clouds/air/wind.
Go up.
Go up a tree.
Put on the hempen collar/cravat/ necktie/necklace/anodyne necklace/choker/halter.
Put in a state of suspense.
Hoist.
Salivate.
Stretch.
Swing.
Run up.
Tuck up.
Turn off.
Top.
Scrag.
String up.
Exalt.
Crack the neck.
Cause to die of a hempen fever.
Justly jerk.
Jerk to Jesus.
Legally lasso.
Give the rope.

Die in a horse's nightcap.
Give the California collar.
Neck.
Hold a necktie party (lynch).
Give a lynching bee.
Yield to Judge Lynch.
Hold a dance of death.
Burn.
Cook.
Fry.
Fry in the chair.
Be jumped.
Ride Old Smoky.
Take the smoky seat/rocker.
Burn in the chair/flame chair/juice chair/hot seat.
Take the hot squat.
Heat the hot spot.
Take the hot/warm sit-down.
Take the electric cure.
Take the juice/shock.
Step into the chair.
Get a permanent wave.
Sit down and burn up.

V. Miscellaneous Euphemisms

Even more necessary than circumlocutions for the abstract idea of death, are those to suggest the material adjuncts of the funeral and burial. The corpse, the coffin, and the cemetery are given new names, sometimes jocose, often serious. Even the name of the dead person is avoided by means of a series of pious epithets. Eulogists and scoffers alike shun a forthright mention of the concrete evidences of death. The elaborateness of the figures suggests the strength of the taboo.

The Dead

The defunct.
The departed.
The deceased.
The late lamented.
The body.
The remains.
Food for worms.
Late specimen of humanity.

The Cemetery

The broken pitcher. (Clergyman: 'Useless now this broken pitcher.')
Cold meat. (The hearse is the 'cold meat cart.')
The marble orchard.
The bone orchard.
The Marble City.
The boneyard.

Memorial park.
Permanent rest camp.
City/village of the dead.
Skeleton park.

Hell's half acre.
Last home.
Underground jungle.

The Coffin

The Grave

Wooden overcoat.
Wooden kimona.
Crate.
Planting crate.
Six-foot bungalow.
Wooden suit.
Casket.
Box.
Bone box.
Man box.
Bone house.
Cold meat box.
Eternity box.

Long home.
Cold mud.
Deep six.
Earth bath.
Dust bin.
Great divide.
A neat oblong hole in the ground.
Narrow home.

The Funeral

Buryin'.
Dead march.
Planting.
Cold meat party.

VI. Predictions of Death

It is quite as difficult to prophesy death as to announce it, and to smooth the difficulty various periphrases have been invented. Although many of the predictions are jocular, they derive from the same instinct that prompts the creation of the serious euphemisms. Man evades the mention of death either as an accomplished fact or an inevitable outcome. His scruples may goad him to painful exertion but they are always obeyed, and nothing can be more circuitous than the sayings that result.

You'll wake up some morning and find some one patting you in the face with a spade.
Your number is up.
You are on your last legs/pegs.
You are slated for a fancy epitaph.
You have one foot in the grave and another on a banana peel.
You have no more chance than a rabbit.
One more clean shirt is all you'll need.
We'll be looking at each other and one of us won't know it.
Your expectancy of life is zero.
Soon you'll be lying down with a spade patting you in the face.

You'll be put to bed with a shovel.
Earth that nourished thee shall claim thy growth. (Bryant.)
You'll be sent home in a box.
Step softly, kind friend, for you, too, will meet your end. (On a tombstone.)
You are under sailing orders.
You'll soon hold a lily in your hand.
They'll be playing slow music and you won't hear it.
You are booked.
There'll be eight going out and seven coming back. (From 'Frankie and Johnnie.')
Tomorrow you'll be crowbait.

FOR DISCUSSION AND REVIEW

1 What is the reasoning behind the following euphemistic expressions for death: "He laid down the knife and fork"; "His clock has run down"; "He has slipped into the democracy of the dead"? What is wrong with the expression "This is only the shell—the nut is gone"?

2 Can you think of any euphemisms for death in professions or sports that Pound has not listed?

3 Is euphemistic usage an example of the Whorfian hypothesis as discussed by Woolfson on pp. 3–11 of this book? Explain. Does the statement "Death has not lost its sting, only the words for it have" alter your opinion?

12
Cobweb
and Spider Web

Ideally, the work of the dialect researcher and the lexicographer should show much interaction. Dr. Underwood, who teaches at the University of Arkansas, shows how results of research on *Linguistic Atlas* material can influence the lexicographer's estimates of semantic change and innovation.

Gary N. Underwood

THE DEFINITIONS for *cobweb* and *spider web* in *Webster's Third* indicate that, while the two terms are often used synonymously, *cobweb* has acquired extended meanings. Consequently, for some people there exists a semantic distinction between *spider web* and *cobweb*. In *Webster's Third* the entry for *spider web* includes this definition:

> A silk web constructed by a spider especially to entrap prey of threads composed of a viscid fluid that is secreted by glands in the abdomen, is discharged through minute orifices in the spinnerets, and hardens on exposure to the air in a form often characteristic of its family or genus . . . (p. 2194).

The entry for *cobweb* contains the following:

> 1a: the network spread by a spider to catch its prey b: a single thread spun by a spider; also: tangles of such thread with adherent dirt and dust that have accumulated . . . c: a thread or web spun by an insect larva . . . (p. 434).

Of course, there are figurative meanings for each, but they are irrelevant to the purpose of this article. The important point is that the dictionary records that *cobweb* can be distinguished from *spider web* in that it may denote (1) a single thread instead of a web, (2) a dust-covered spider web, or (3) a thread or web produced by an insect instead of a spider. The semantic confusion recorded in *Webster's Third* makes pertinent the publication of relevant data that cast light on further semantic changes with regard to *cobweb* and *spider web*.

The evidence upon which the present study is based is provided by the files of the Linguistic Atlas of the Upper Midwest.[1] Since the purpose of the linguistic atlas survey is to determine the regional distribution of pronunciation, meaning, grammar, vocabulary, and syntax in the states of Minnesota, Iowa, North Dakota, South Dakota, and Nebraska, the fieldworkers not only determined whether or not the informant uses *spider web*, *cobweb*, or another variant, but also recorded the referent for each variant. In response to this particular item on the work sheet the informants responded with a total of twelve variants: *boo chaser, cobweb, dangler, dust web, heat web, Indian smoke, mare's tail, mosquito web, spider nest, spider net, spider* (occasionally *spider's*) *web,* and *web.* Of immediate interest, however, are only the two most widespread terms, *cobweb* and *spider web.*

Of 206 informants responding to this item, 42 (20%) have only one of the two terms in their active vocabularies. Twenty-three informants (11%) use *spider web* and 19 (9%) say *cobweb.* Of the remaining 164 informants (80%) who have both *cobweb* and *spider web* in their vocabularies, 29 regard them as synonyms. However, 135 (66% of all informants and 82% of those using both terms) make a semantic distinction between *cobweb* and *spider web.*

While all informants attribute spider webs to spiders, the same is not true for cobwebs. (As one would expect, not a single informant indicated an awareness of the fact that *cob-* is etymologically derived from Old English *ātorcoppe* "spider.") In fact, 31 informants say that spiders do not make cobwebs. Curiously, although one of the three meanings recorded in *Webster's Third* for *cobweb* is "a thread or web spun by an insect larva," only a single informant says rather vaguely that a cobweb is made by "a kind of fly." For the remaining 30 *cobweb* has a meaning which is not recorded in *Webster's Third*. For these people a cobweb is not a filament spun by either a spider or an insect; rather it is composed of an accumulation of dust or lint, or a combination of both. For

---

[1] For details about the Linguistic Atlas of the Upper Midwest see Harold B. Allen, "The Primary Dialect Areas of the Upper Midwest," in *Readings in Applied English Linguistics*, 2nd ed., ed. Harold B. Allen (New York, 1964), pp. 231–241. The files of the atlas are used for this study through the courtesy of Mr. Allen, to whom I am also grateful for his helpful criticism of this paper.

all 31 informants a cobweb is found indoors only, but a spider web may be found either indoors or outside.

The remaining 104 informants who distinguish between *spider web* and *cobweb* say that both are created by spiders; for them the distinction is either the location or appearance of the web. Almost half of them (49) distinguish on the basis of appearance, but they offer a wide variety of criteria, as Table A indicates.

Table A

No. of infs.	Distinction
23	A spider web is a patterned web; a cobweb is a strand
8	A cobweb is a spider web with dust on it
7	A spider web is a patterned web; a cobweb is either a web or a strand
4	A cobweb is smaller in design
1	A cobweb is heavier and thicker
1	A cobweb is looser in design
1	A spider web is a strand; a cobweb is a patterned web
1	A spider web is neatly patterned; a cobweb is "a messy mass"
1	A cobweb is a collection of tangled old spider webs
1	A cobweb is "many webs in one place"
1	A spider web if the spider is on it; a cobweb if the spider is gone

It seems significant that none of the three most frequent of these distinctions, roughly equivalent to the distinctions reported by *Webster's Third*, have widespread distributions. The fact that each of these meanings is not shared by a great number of informants is paralleled in importance by the fact that so many differences in meaning exist. Since the rival forms are in complementary fluctuation, the natural, but unpredictable, process of semantic innovation is at work destroying the synonymity.

The semantic confusion is further compounded by still another distinction between the two terms. That is, for a large number of informants the location of the spider's web or strand will determine whether or not they call it a *cobweb* or a *spider web*. Table B indicates the confusion with regard to this distinction.

Table B

No. of infs.	Distinction
68	A spider web is found outdoors; a cobweb is found indoors
17	A spider web is found either indoors or outdoors; a cobweb is found only indoors
2	A spider web is found outdoors; a cobweb is found either indoors or outdoors
1	A spider web is found indoors; a cobweb is found outdoors

First, it will be noted that none of these distinctions are recorded in *Webster's Third*, yet 88 informants (85% of those who distinguish between filaments spun by spiders) separate spider webs and cobwebs on this basis. Even more confusion will be noted by the fact that the numbers for Table A and Table B total to considerably more than 104; some informants distinguish on the basis of both the location and the appearance of the filament. If we consider all 135 informants for whom a cobweb is different from a spider web, a total of 77% distinguish the two on the basis of location or appearance, not on the criteria recorded in *Webster's Third*. For still another informant the distinction is based upon a combination of locational and pejorative factors. According to a college graduate in Faribault, Minnesota, webs found in the house are spider webs, but those in a barn are cobwebs. In his mind, "Cobweb is too bad a word to use for a web in the house."

From this evidence we can draw the following conclusions. (1) While *spider web* denotes only a filament spun by a spider, *cobweb* has acquired semantic extensions so that it often denotes something other than a strand or web spun by either a spider or an insect. (2) Among those for whom both spider webs and cobwebs are created by spiders, many classify the referents on the basis of the location of the referent. Although some disagreement exists, the indoor variety is commonly referred to as a cobweb, and the outdoor variety as a spider web. The evidence for other regions may indicate otherwise, but in the Upper Midwest the most frequently noted distinctions cannot be correlated with either geography and/or education of the informant. In view of the evidence, at least two of the semantic innovations, the extended meaning of cobweb and the locational differentiation, are significant enough to warrant further investigation by the lexicographer.

FOR DISCUSSION AND REVIEW

1 In general, what are Underwood's conclusions about popular distinctions between *cobweb* and *spider web*?

2 What use could a lexicographer make of the information that Underwood has provided in this article?

3 How do you and your friends differentiate *cobweb* and *spider web*? Do you agree or disagree with Underwood's findings?

4 How do you differentiate the following pairs: *pants* and *slacks; rest home* and *convalescent home; demonstration* and *protest; hippie* and *freak*?

13

Existential:

When certain words capture the fancy of a sizeable portion of society, they often go through a process of semantic change that results in their becoming virtually meaningless. Professor Benjamin DeMott of Amherst College illustrates this process with *existentialism*, a word he considers unlikely to have gone through such a change.

Sixties' Cinderella Word

Benjamin DeMott

POP QUESTION: Can *existential* make it big?

Prospects were poor until recently. A foreign entry, heavy, hard to pronounce, fast in the forties, faded in the fifties, the word looked a foot too long. Worse, it came from philosophy instead of from showbiz or sports. And as for the timing of its sixties' bid—crazy. Camp, charisma, nitty-gritty, dialogue, relevance, thrust—jargonville was jammed to the rails with winners: how could a "newcomer" break through? Despite the handicaps, though, *existential* is breaking through. Improving its place steadily, unfazed by cheapening, inflation, or technical correction, it's closing once again on high fashion. Given a boost from nonlinear media, its future could be immense.

As might be guessed, adaptability plays a key part in this success story. Useful in a variety of fields, *existential* has won strong support across a whole spectrum of nontechnical writing—magazines, newspapers, and books. (In the space of a week this season it was used in public prints to distinguish revolutionaries from gamblers, rioters from students, party candidates from write-ins, and the ovum from sperm.) But other elements besides adaptability figure in the tale—in particular, an Image Factor. Embarrassing to mention that, of course; it implies (falsely) that *existential* is just another contemporary blur-word, no core of meaning at its heart. (The standard pop core is as follows: Existential, adj.—*Not-knowing-what-will-happen-next*. Cf. Norman Mailer at the New York Theater for Ideas: "It was existential [the Columbia strike], because these kids went out and did something that they had never done before, and they did not know how it was going to turn out." Or cf. Steve Cohn, in the Amherst College literary magazine: ". . . the trick is not to know what's going to happen next, that's existential, that's being."

But embarrassing or not, image-talk is necessary. You can't understand *existential* today without leaving the narrow denotative band and seeing the term in its largest dimensions, as an item closer to trade names than to ordinary parts of speech. Like Marlboro, Mustang, or Ma Griffe, the word sings, has mystery in its nimbus, casts a shadow, evokes the gut response. Charged atmospheres gather at its mention —the unexpected, the reckless, the unconstrained, the spontaneous, the indomitable, the solitary, the purified, the intense, the elemental. . . . The "meaning" of *existential* lies, in short, in the content of the Existential Image—beautifully controlled intimations of safe audacity swinging round the don't-know-what-happens-next core. And, as indicated, the goodwill roused by these intimations already ranks as a major popcultural capital reserve.

Writers who draw on the capital aren't hung up about how and where to spend it. Neither are they oblivious to its potential as a prestige-builder—a means of instant sanctification both of oneself and the cause one favors. For Nat Hentoff the cause one favors is the Concerned Parents movement, pro-community control of schools—therefore he describes the cause as that of "existential education" in his column in *The Village Voice*. For Charles Marowitz (another *Voice* column) the cause one favors is that of the Living Theater, the La Mama Company and Tom O'Horgan—therefore he cries up *Hair* as "existential thunder." For Mary Ellmann the cause one likes is female superiority; hence in her *Thinking About Women* (1968) she identifies sperm as humdrum and herdlike ("jostling masses, swarming out on signal like a crowd of commuters"), and finds the ovum to be adventurous-glamorous-existential ("the ovum travels singly . . . in [a] kind of existential loneliness . . . a daring and independence").

Connotations of daring and independence are by no means the term's only plus values. *Portentousness*—a sense that something grave and grand, though incomprehensible, is nigh—also enfolds the word. One is aware of it, a misty penumbra, in a *Commentary* essay by Diana Trilling, wherein instead of the flatness of "special" or "peculiar," we savor the excitement of *existential*: "In the meanwhile one's friendly neighborhood suffered in its own existential fashion and went unnoticed. . . ." One feels it, too, in an article by Robert Somma in the *New York Free Press Critique*, wherein *existential* stands in deliciously for "usual" ("negation, despair, abulia [are] not the existential conditions of super spades or super stars"). And the Reverend William Jones, of Brooklyn's Bethany Baptist Church, achieves portentousness by dropping *existential* in to replace *real*:

> "[State Trustee] Johnson was just a puppet. He was not a free man. The existential question is: Is Firman free?"
>
> [*New York Post*, December 4, 1968]

There is, as should be acknowledged, a squarish pop usage, one that takes the term as synonymous with phrases like "existing, that which is," or "pertaining to real life." In *Cinema Now* (1968) the film maker Stan Brakhage reflects on the Beat Generation as a "form of life which is destructive of the self," and recalls that he used to say, when asked to comment on it, "We've got beyond the stage of existentialism, we've got to the stage of desistentialism."[1] And the word does have a few snipers, characters who concede its prestige grudgingly or ironically, if at all. The dustjacket of a first novel published this month—*Yes*, by Bibi Wein—is sniffish about the book's hero on the ground that he "accepts love incidentally," and "romanticizes the existential freedom he thinks he wants." And a recent Sunday *Times* magaziner about the 20th Century-Fox production of *Che!* quotes an extra praising the star of the film for seeing Che Guevara as a businesslike "casino gambler" rather than as a wildboy "existential" type.

On the whole, however, disrespect is rare. When Michel Crozier, the sociologist, invokes "the existential anguish of the hippies" as an opposing force to the business-government faith in the "science of decision-making . . . the omnipotence of reason," he isn't knocking hippies. When Michael Rossman, the New Left leader, writes in the *American Scholar* that the student activist movement is beyond politics, and works in "unstructured temporary groups in which the dominant themes are existential involvement and effective (potent) freedom," he's not lamenting the Democratic decline. When Margot Hentoff declares in *The Village Voice* that her voting-booth decision to write her own name in on the presidential ballot was an "existential act," she isn't confessing she's a silly woman. When David Cohen, of Country Joe and the Fish, tells *The New Yorker*'s "Talk" reporter that he had a breakdown—"the beginning of the existential dilemma—I just fell apart"—as a student at Los Angeles State College, he doesn't see himself as a cloddish, insensitive chap. And when Miss Renata Adler writes, in *The Times*, that Steve McQueen has "existential" features, she hardly means the man looks bad. The plain case is, to repeat, that *existential* has come through, bears no negative scars, has a uniformly positive valence: at the end of the sixties it means good, like pop knows it should.

For the student of popular culture, the questions arising from this evolution are these: How and why has the word arrived at its present

[1] Surprisingly, something of the same flavor—*existential* as pertaining to that which is, concrete life—turns up in Mr. Nat Hentoff's recent remark, in *Evergreen Review*, about the congressional education of Allard Lowenstein:

> As for transforming the Democratic Party into the agent of our salvation, that too is not in the immediate future as Allard Lowenstein, for one, is going to find out existentially in encounters with his party leadership in the House.

state? What were the chief stages of its progress? And neither question is quickly answerable offhand. It seems likely that when the American *existential* record is thoroughly investigated, significant contributions to it will prove to have been made in two books by one author—*Advertisements for Myself* (1959) and *The Presidential Papers* (1963) by Norman Mailer. For while *existential* did have an early run in the forties, it dropped from pop sight thereafter—until Mr. Mailer set it on a comeback trail. *Advertisements* was the first publication in book form of the author's ruminations on the Hip and the Square—chat that freshened the association of *existential* and romantic. And *The Presidential Papers* was no less notable, partly because it laid down the first pop definition of the word ("an act . . . is existential precisely because its end is unknown"), and developed the themes of existential glamour adumbrated in *Advertisements*, and partly because it was dense with suggestive new coinages—"existential legislation," "existential orgasm," "existential politics," "existential vibrations," "existential fatigue," "existential heroine" (Jacqueline Kennedy), to cite just a few.—But these notes on the *existential* past are at best scratchy impressions: the subject demands at the minimum a solid AmStuds doctoral thesis or two.

Nor are AmStuds' doctors the only likely researchers. For students of the history of philosophy this evolution also presents interesting problems, namely, How could a term be so efficiently, swiftly, ruthlessly stripped of intellectual content? What distinctively American gifts figured in the transformation?—Irrepressible American humor clearly had something to do with the redefinition. (Jean-Paul Sartre himself acknowledged this, indirectly, upon learning in 1947 that the American producers of *No Exit* had brightened the piece, and were playing it strictly for laughs. M. Sartre's churlish comment at the time was that "Les Américains ne comprendront jamais rien à l'existentialisme.")

And American production genius was also involved. Changing the meaning of *existential* sharply reduced the amount of time needed to produce a philosopher, even a "first philosopher of hip," and eliminated the need for mental labor. In former days talking philosophy of any kind required extensive training—profitless, time-consuming—in the analysis of concepts, and some consciousness of intellectual tradition as well. Talking existential philosophy was especially burdensome, furthermore, because on its strong side (the phenomenological side, developing from Husserl through Merleau-Ponty) this school conceived the philosophical task to be that of laboriously, responsibly uncreating previous philosophies, descriptions, perceptions, standardized structurings of experience, in order to begin the infinitely difficult task of knowing a thing.[2]

---

[2] ". . . we bypass [the world of perception] in critical thought—almost to the point of forgetting the contributions of perception to our idea of truth. For critical

For the American market a substitute was vital—some means of enabling people to sound philosophical without suffering the pain of thought. And the drive to meet this need helped to create the automated, or Hentoff, philosophical style—that device by which a man can think existential by signing his name, pulling the lever, uttering the word.

And finally, some degree of influence on the redefinition may have been exerted by American theories of experience and self-realization, and by the national idealization of isolated, autonomous, closed-system selves. European existentialists tend to be, if a frank word may be spoken, a shade chicken in their concept of freedom, stressing that, while I can realize my being in conflict with others, I must understand that others are themselves engaged in realizing their being in conflict with me; the resulting tension *between* freedoms defines the general human struggle and is the root of our need for balance. Americans are less inhibited, as the theme of creative violence in Norman Mailer attests.[3] We know better than to be distracted by complications stemming from too much brooding on the truth that, although human beings can be treated as objects, none is less than a subject to himself. We also know better than to be gulled into the idea that thinking is a kind of experience; we know, as did our lesser forefathers from the beginning, that reflection is at bottom an evasion of or even escape from experience—and Experience is All. And this knowledge has in turn nourished the determined American effort to simplify existentialist key-terms.

As goes without saying, though, these matters of genesis, influence, etc. are at bottom purely academic. What counts isn't the nature of the forces that are shooting this word into the center of popular consciousness, but rather the simple fact that the word will arrive there, will have a life in pop usage. There are, admittedly, many unknowns in the equation. (How will the word make itself at home in social discourse? My

---

thought encounters only bare propositions which it discusses, accepts or rejects. Critical thought has broken with the naïve evidence of things, and when it affirms, it is because it no longer finds any means of denial. However necessary this activity of verification may be, specifying criteria and demanding from our experience its credentials of validity, it is not unaware of our contact with the perceived world which is simply there before us, beneath the level of the verified true or false."
—Merleau-Ponty, *The Primacy of Perception*.

[3] Writing from a European, hence narrowly critical, point of view in a coterie journal called *Minnesota Review*, Samuel Hux recently remarked that "Mailer tends to force 'conflict with' to an insane logic, to change it to 'destruction of.' No longer does he realize himself in the *tension* of inevitable conflict, but in the apocalypse of chosen violence . . . This is not existentialism, but popular surrealism."

unusual weekday-night third martini, for instance, formerly known as an extra drink—will I come to call it my existential belt?)

And there will also be, in time, some sadness. Older types, witnessing the slow descent of the term into phone-book listings—Existential Bagel, Existential Body and Fender, Existential Casket—will keen to each other, asking how a word could have been so corrupted. How could such rot be taught? Learning without studying . . . Thinking without thought . . . Philosophizing without wisdom . . . But this elitist rant, this maundering about yesteryear, won't for an instant turn the trend. For way out on the what-comes-next precipice, free, giddy, gutsy, orgasmic, alone, there's no nostalgia, Pops, no looking back over the shoulder—so man like uh y'know what cat in that crib *could* give a good existential goddam?

FOR DISCUSSION AND REVIEW

1 Why does DeMott say it was unlikely for *existentialism* to go through the meaning changes that it did?

2 How do *Webster's Third New International Dictionary* and the more recent desk dictionaries define *existentialism*? Do you feel these definitions are adequate? Explain.

3 The author uses the expression "AmStuds' doctors," an interesting example of word formation. What does he mean and how did he form the expression?

4 DeMott says of *existentialism*, "Like Marlboro, Mustang, and Ma Griffe, the word sings, has mystery in its nimbus, casts a shadow, evokes the gut response." Discuss the responses the word evokes in you.

5 According to DeMott, what does the use of the word *existentialism* tell us about Americans' attitudes toward philosophy?

PROJECTS FOR "WORDS, MEANINGS, AND THE DICTIONARY"

1 *There are many different kinds of dictionaries published today. Dictionaries of foreign languages, artists, slang, psychology, and music are only a few. Consult the reference section of your library and describe the different dictionaries it contains.*

2 *A worthwhile and enjoyable project for the class as a whole is a dictionary debate. Each of three or four groups is given the responsibility to become very familiar with one of the various recently published desk dictionaries. In turn, members of each group are responsible for particular aspects of their dictionary. After the necessary research is completed, the groups meet and debate the merits of their dictionaries. Care should be taken to avoid comparisons between abridged and unabridged dictionaries.*

3 Write a paper on how the Random House, American Heritage, and Webster's New World *dictionaries have responded to criticisms directed at* Webster's Third New International Dictionary. *Reviews of these dictionaries would be the most helpful place to begin your study and the* Book Review Digest *will provide you with references. For reviews of* Webster's Third, *see:* Dictionaries and That Dictionary, *ed. James Sledd and Wilma R. Ebbitt (Glenview, Illinois: Scott, Foresman and Company, 1962).*

4 *Either as a class project or individually, compile a lexicon of slang (or of short-order cooking terms, skiing, fraternity life, etc.) used on your campus. If the project is to be done by the whole class, care should be taken in defining words to include the variety of usages offered by all members of the class. A related project could center on the principles of wordmaking revealed in these dictionaries. (Some of the difficulty of writing definitions may be seen in exercise 5.)*

5 *If you were compiling a dictionary and had before you only the following quotations, what definition would you write for the word* lasto? *Do not try to find a one-word synonym; write a ten to twenty-word definition:*

   a. *A lasto is sometimes difficult to clean.*

   b. *Mary put too much food into her lasto and it overflowed.*

   c. *A knife will do many of the jobs that a lasto will do but cannot do them as efficiently.*

   d. *The blades on a lasto must be bent for it to work well.*

   e. *Some lastos have only three speeds while others have as many as ten.*

6 *William Walter Duncan in his essay "How White Is Your Dictionary?" (p. 243) has investigated the unabridged Random House Dictionary of the English Language and the Funk and Wagnalls Standard College Dictionary, but he says that what he has found holds true for other dictionaries as well. Examine two other dictionaries, see how they define* black *and* white, *and write a paper describing the results of your research. Is Duncan correct?*

7 *Louise Pound has compiled a list of euphemisms concerning death (p. 312). Discuss in class more recently used terms for dying, death, and burial. Make a list of euphemistic terms used in other "taboo" subjects.*

8 *DeMott's article (p. 324) examines what happened to the word* existentialism. Funky, banquet, freak, artificial, *and* paranoid *are also words that are going or have gone through similar processes. Write a paper on one of these words or on a word of your own choosing which illustrates the processes of semantic radiation and extension.*

SELECTED BIBLIOGRAPHY

Adler, Mortimer. "How To Read A Dictionary." *Saturday Review of Literature,* 24, No. 34, 13 December 1941, 3–4, 18–20. (A brief but interesting perusal of the dictionary with some historical references.)

Anon. "The Euphemism: Telling It Like It Isn't." *Time,* 94, 19 September 1969, 26–27. (A *Time* essay devoted to recent euphemistic usage, which makes passing reference to the connection between the Whorfian hypothesis and euphemisms.)

Barnhart, C. L. "Problems in Editing Commercial Dictionaries." *Problems in Lexicography.* Ed. Fred W. Householder and Sol Saporta. Bloomington: Publication Twenty-one of the Indiana Research Center in Anthropology, Folklore, and Linguistics, 1962. (Analyzes technical problems facing dictionary editors and discusses ways they have been solved.)

Bolinger, Dwight. "Structure in Language: The Higher Levels." *Aspects of Language.* New York: Harcourt, Brace & World, 1958. (Excellent introductory section on morphemes and their role in word formation.)

————. "The Life and Death of Words." *The American Scholar,* 22, No. 3 (Summer 1953), 323–35. (Discusses attempts to see words as being affected by the families in which they exist and argues against "straight-line" etymologizing.)

Bradley, Henry. "Word-Making in English." *The Making of English.* New York: Collier-Macmillan Ltd. and St. Martin's Press, Inc., 1904. (Analyzes the word formation processes of composition, derivation, back-formation, shortening, and root-creation.)

Chapman, Robert L. "A Working Lexicographer Appraises Webster's III." *American Speech,* 42, No. 3 (October 1967), 202–10. (Concise criticisms of *Webster's Third* by a lexicographer who used it for three years.)

Current Slang. Published by the English Department at the University of South Dakota, Vermillion, South Dakota. (Attempts to keep up-to-date on the latest slang usage in America.)

Dundes, Alan, and Manuel R. Schonhorn. "Kansas University Slang: A New Generation." *American Speech,* 38 (October 1963), 163–77. (A comparative study which raises questions about the definition of college slang.)

ETC.: *A Review of General Semantics.* Published by the International Society for General Semantics, San Francisco, California. (A popularly written journal of semantics founded by S. I. Hayakawa.)

Gove, Philip B., ed. *The Role of the Dictionary.* New York: The Bobbs-Merrill Company, Inc., 1967. (A short but readable collection of essays including two useful ones on repetition in defining and usage in the dictionary.)

Gray, Jack., ed. *Words, Words, and Words About Dictionaries.* San Francisco: Chandler Publishing Company, 1963. (A book of readings with considerable sample material.)

Greenough, James B., and George L. Kittredge. *Words and Their Ways in English Speech.* New York: Crowell-Collier and Macmillan, Inc., 1901. (Paperbound by Beacon Press, 1962.) (An older book but still valuable especially on meaning changes and slang.)

Hockett, Charles F. "Analogical Creation." *A Course in Modern Linguistics.* New York: The Macmillan Company, 1958. (A description of a specific type of word formation used particularly by children.)

Laird, Charlton. "Words and Their Waywardnesses in Present-Day Speech." *Col-*

lege Composition and Communication, 22, No. 3 (October 1971), 221–28. (Discusses the tendency toward phrase making and specialization in present-day English.)

Lloyd, Donald J., and Harry R. Warfel. "The Dictionary." *American English in Its Cultural Setting.* New York: Alfred A. Knopf, Inc., 1956. (The best short history of the American dictionary.)

Lodwig, Richard R., and Eugene F. Barrett. *The Dictionary and the Language.* New York: Hayden Book Companies, 1967. (Good section on the making of a modern dictionary.)

Mathews, Mitford M. "The Freshman and His Dictionary." *College Composition and Communication,* 6 (December 1955), 187–90. (Discusses the ways in which the dictionary is a useful tool.)

Mencken, H. L. *The American Language: The Fourth Edition and the Two Supplements.* Abridged and ed. Raven I. McDavid, Jr. New York: Alfred A. Knopf, Inc., 1963. (A classic study on the subject with an interesting section on euphemisms.)

Potter, Simeon. "Slang and Dialect." *Our Language.* Rev. ed. Baltimore: Penguin Books Ltd., 1950. (Good examples of English slang and dialect and a good chapter on meanings.)

Pyles, Thomas. "Words and Meaning." *The Origin and Development of the English Language.* New York: Harcourt, Brace & World, 1964. (An examination of how and why meanings change.)

Scott, Kenneth W. "The Slang of the Victorian Underworld." *Word Study,* 28, No. 5 (May 1953), 7–8. (A catalog and an analysis helpful to the student of literature and as a model of such studies.)

Sledd, James, and Wilma R. Ebbitt. *Dictionaries and That Dictionary.* Glenview, Ill.: Scott, Foresman and Company, 1962. (A casebook on the controversy concerning the publication of *Webster's Third International Dictionary.*)

Whitehall, Harold. "The Development of the English Dictionary." *Webster's New World Dictionary of the English Language.* New York: The World Publishing Company, 1958. (A basic historical survey.)

Wilson, Kenneth G., R. H. Hendrickson, and Peter Alan Taylor. *Harbrace Guide to Dictionaries.* New York: Harcourt, Brace & World, Inc., 1963. (Thorough, but does not treat recently published dictionaries.)

PART FOUR

Americans
Speaking

Dialect study, especially with its recent historical, sociological, and educational applications, is a fascinating and integral part of linguistics. The word *dialect*, however, is generally misunderstood, largely as a result of the negative connotations it has acquired.

Most Americans mistakenly view dialect as an ignorant corruption of the language; little do they realize that they and their close associates speak a variety of English which can be called a dialect. In a strict sense, each person has his own unique dialect, his *idiolect*. Since the majority of the native speakers in any given region or social class share many features of pronunciation, vocabulary, and grammatical usage, dialectologists can make general statements about geographical and social dialect distributions.

This section first introduces the student to the concept of dialect, to the dialectologist, and to his field methods. The subsequent readings illustrate specifically the studies and applications of research that has been undertaken with respect to regional, functional, and social varieties of American English. Scholars have explored and sought to explain not only the regional, social, and educational aspects of dialect, but also the linguistic problems encountered by the speaker of "nonstandard" English.

1
Speech Communities

Age, geography, education, occupation, and social position are among the factors shaping dialect variations within a language. Professor Roberts, in this excerpt from his book *Understanding English*, discusses the effects of speech communities upon the language patterns of persons who come into contact with them. Recall your own experiences with childhood and adolescent speech communities while reading this selection.

Paul Roberts

Directions of Change in Language

IMAGINE a village of a thousand people all speaking the same language and never hearing any language other than their own. As the decades pass and generation succeeds generation, it will not be very apparent to the speakers of the language that any considerable language change is going on. Oldsters may occasionally be conscious of and annoyed by the speech forms of youngsters. They will notice new words, new expressions, "bad" pronunciations, but will ordinarily put these down to the irresponsibility of youth, and decide piously that the language of the younger generation will revert to decency when the generation grows up.

It doesn't revert, though. The new expressions and the new pronunciations persist, and presently there is another younger generation with its own new expressions and its own pronunciations. And thus the language changes. If members of the village could speak to one another across five hundred years, they would probably find themselves unable to communicate.

Now suppose that the village divides itself and half the people move away. They move across the river or over a mountain and form a new village. Suppose the separation is so complete that the people of New Village have no contact with the people of Old Village. The language of both villages will change, drifting away from the language of their common ancestors. But the drift will not be in the same direction. In both villages there will be new expressions and new pronunciations, but not the same ones. In the course of time the language of Old Village and New Village will be mutually unintelligible with the language they both started with. They will also be mutually unintelligible with one another.

An interesting thing—and one for which there is no perfectly clear explanation—is that the rate of change will not ordinarily be the same for both villages. The language of Old Village changes faster than the language of New Village. One might expect that the opposite would be true—that the emigrants, placed in new surroundings and new conditions, would undergo more rapid language changes. But history reports otherwise. American English, for example, despite the violence and agony and confusion to which the demands of a new continent have subjected it, is probably essentially closer to the language of Shakespeare than London English is.

Suppose one thing more. Suppose Old Village is divided sharply into an upper class and a lower class. The sons and daughters of the upper class go to preparatory school and then to the university; the children of the lower class go to work. The upper-class people learn to read and write and develop a flowering literature; the lower-class people remain illiterate. Dialects develop, and the speech of the two classes steadily diverges. One might suppose that most of the change would go on among the illiterate, that the upper-class people, conscious of their heritage, would tend to preserve the forms and pronunciations of their ancestors. Not so. The opposite is true. In speech, the educated tend to be radical and the uneducated conservative. In England one finds Elizabethan forms and sounds not among Oxford and Cambridge graduates but among the people of backward villages.

A village is a fairly simple kind of speech community—a group of people steadily in communication with one another, steadily hearing one another's speech. But the village is by no means the basic unit. Within the simplest village there are many smaller units—groupings based on age, class, occupation. All these groups play intricately on one another and against one another, and a language that seems at first a coherent whole will turn out on inspection to be composed of many differing parts. Some forces tend to make these parts diverge; other forces hold them together. Thus the language continues in tension.

The Speech Communities of the Child

The child's first speech community is ordinarily his family. The child learns whatever kind of language the family speaks—or, more precisely, whatever kind of language it speaks to him. The child's language learning, now and later, is governed by two obvious motives: the desire to communicate and the desire to be admired. He imitates what he hears. More or less successful imitations usually bring action and reward and tend to be repeated. Unsuccessful ones usually don't bring action and reward and tend to be discarded.

But since language is a complicated business it is sometimes the unsuccessful imitations that bring the reward. The child, making a stab at the word *mother*, comes out with *muzzer*. The family decides that this is just too cute for anything and beams and repeats *muzzer*, and the child, feeling that he's scored a bull's eye, goes on saying *muzzer* long after he has mastered *other* and *brother*. Baby talk is not so much invented by the child as sponsored by the parent.

Eventually the child moves out of the family and into another speech community—other children of his neighborhood. He goes to kindergarten and immediately encounters speech habits that conflict with those he has learned. If he goes to school and talks about his *muzzer*, it will be borne in on him by his colleagues that the word is not well chosen. Even *mother* may not pass muster, and he may discover that he gets better results and is altogether happier if he refers to his female parent as his ma or even his old lady.

Children coming together in a kindergarten class bring with them language that is different because it is learned in different homes. It is all to some degree unsuccessfully learned, consisting of not quite perfect imitations of the original. In school all this speech coalesces, differences tend to be ironed out, and the result differs from the original parental speech and differs in pretty much the same way.

The pressures on the child to conform to the speech of his age group, his speech community, are enormous. He may admire his teacher and love his mother; he may even—and even consciously—wish to speak as they do. But he *has* to speak like the rest of the class. If he does not, life becomes intolerable.

The speech changes that go on when the child goes to school are often most distressing to parents. Your little Bertram, at home, has never heard anything but the most elegant English. You send him to school, and what happens? He comes home saying things like "I done real good in school today, Mom." But Bertram really has no choice in the matter. If Clarence and Elbert and the rest of the fellows customarily say "I done real good," then Bertram might as well go around with three noses as say things like "I did very nicely."

Individuals differ of course, and not all children react to the speech community in the same way. Some tend to imitate and others tend to force imitation. But all to some degree have their speech modified by forces over which neither they nor their parents nor their teachers have any real control.

Individuals differ too in their sensitivity to language. For some, language is always a rather embarrassing problem. They steadily make boners, saying the right thing in the wrong place or the wrong way.

They have a hard time fitting in. Others tend to change their language slowly, sticking stoutly to their way of saying things, even though their way differs from that of the majority. Still others adopt new language habits almost automatically, responding quickly to whatever speech environment they encounter.

Indeed some children of five or six have been observed to speak two or more different dialects without much awareness that they are doing so. Most commonly, they will speak in one way at home and in another on the playground. At home they say, "I did very nicely" and "I haven't any"; these become, at school, "I done real good" and "I ain't got none."

The Class as a Speech Community

Throughout the school years, or at least through the American secondary school, the individual's most important speech community is his age group, his class. Here is where the real power lies. The rule is conformity above all things, and the group uses its power ruthlessly on those who do not conform. Language is one of the chief means by which the school group seeks to establish its entity, and in the high school this is done more or less consciously. The obvious feature is high school slang, picked up from the radio, from other schools, sometimes invented, changing with bewildering speed. Nothing is more satisfactory than to speak today's slang; nothing more futile than to use yesterday's.

There can be few tasks more frustrating than that of the secondary school teacher charged with the responsibility of brushing off and polishing up the speech habits of the younger generation. Efforts to make *real* into *really*, *ain't* into *am not*, *I seen him* into *I saw him*, *he don't* into *he doesn't* meet at best with polite indifference, at worst with mischievous counterattack.

The writer can remember from his own high school days when the class, a crashingly witty bunch, took to pronouncing the word *sure* as *sewer*. "Have you prepared your lesson, Arnold?" Miss Driscoll would ask. "Sewer, Miss Driscoll," Arnold would reply. "I think," said Miss Driscoll, who was pretty quick on her feet too, "that you must mean 'sewerly,' since the construction calls for the adverb not the adjective." We were delighted with the suggestion and went about saying "sewerly" until the very blackboards were nauseated. Miss Driscoll must have wished often that she had left it lay.

Confronting the Adult World

When the high school class graduates, the speech community disintegrates as the students fit themselves into new ones. For the first time in the experience of most of the students the speech ways of adult communities begin to exercise real force. For some people the adjustment is a relatively simple one. A boy going to work in a garage may have a good deal of new lingo to pick up, and he may find that the speech that seemed so racy and won such approval in the corridors of Springfield High leaves his more adult associates merely bored. But a normal person will adapt himself without trouble.

For others in other situations settling into new speech communities may be more difficult. The person going into college, into the business world, into scrubbed society may find that he has to think about and work on his speech habits in order not to make a fool of himself too often.

College is a particularly complicated problem. Not only does the freshman confront upperclassmen not particularly disposed to find the speech of Springfield High particularly cute, but the adult world, as represented chiefly by the faculty, becomes increasingly more immediate. The problems of success, of earning a living, of marriage, of attaining a satisfactory adult life loom larger, and they all bring language problems with them. Adaptation is necessary, and the student adapts.

The student adapts, but the adult world adapts too. The thousands of boys and girls coming out of the high schools each spring are affected by the speech of the adult communities into which they move, but they also affect that speech. The new pronunciation habits, developing grammatical features, different vocabulary do by no means all give way before the disapproval of elders. Some of them stay. Elders, sometimes to their dismay, find themselves changing their speech habits under the bombardment of those of their juniors. And then of course the juniors eventually become the elders, and there is no one left to disapprove.

The Space Dimension

Speech communities are formed by many features besides that of age. Most obvious is geography. Our country was originally settled by people coming from different parts of England. They spoke different dialects to begin with and as a result regional speech differences existed from the start in the different parts of the country. As speakers of other languages came to America and learned English, they left their mark on the speech of the sections in which they settled. With the westward movement, new pioneers streamed out through the mountain passes and down river valleys, taking the different dialects west and modifying them by new mixtures in new environments.

Today we are all more or less conscious of certain dialect differences in our country. We speak of the "southern accent," "the Brooklyn accent," the "New England accent." Until a few years ago it was often said that American English was divided into three dialects: Southern American (south of the Mason-Dixon line); Eastern American (east of the Connecticut River); and Western American. This description suggests certain gross differences all right, but recent research shows that it is a gross oversimplification.

The starting point of American dialects is the original group of colonies. We had a New England settlement, centering in Massachusetts; a Middle Atlantic settlement, centering in Pennsylvania; a southern settlement, centering in Virginia and the Carolinas. These colonies were different in speech to begin with, since the settlers came from different parts of England. Their differences were increased as the colonies lived for a century and a half or so with only thin communication with either Mother England or each other. By the time of the Revolution the dialects were well established. Within each group there were of course subgroups. Richmond speech differed markedly from that of Savannah. But Savannah and Richmond were more like each other than they were like Philadelphia or Boston.

The Western movement began shortly after the Revolution, and dialects followed geography. The New Englanders moved mostly into upper New York State and the Great Lakes region. The Middle Atlantic colonists went down the Shenandoah Valley and eventually into the heart of the Midwest. The southerners opened up Kentucky and Tennessee, later the lower Mississippi Valley, later still Texas and much of the Southwest. Thus new speech communities were formed, related to the old ones of the seaboard, but each developing new characteristics as lines of settlement crossed.

New complications were added before and after the Revolution by the great waves of immigration of people from countries other than England: Swedes in Delaware, Dutch in New York, Germans and Scots-Irish in Pennsylvania, Irish in New England, Poles and Greeks and Italians and Portuguese. The bringing in of Negro slaves had an important effect on the speech of the South and later on the whole country. The Spanish in California and the Southwest added their mark. In this century movement of peoples goes on: the trek of southern Negroes to northern and western cities, the migration of people from Arkansas, Oklahoma, and Texas to California. All these have shaped and are shaping American speech.

We speak of America as the melting pot, but the speech communities of this continent are very far from having melted into one. Linguists today can trace very clearly the movements of the early settlers in the still living speech of their descendants. They can follow an eighteenth century speech community West, showing how it crossed this pass and followed that river, threw out an offshoot here, left a pocket there, merged with another group, halted, split, moved on once more.

If all other historical evidence were destroyed, the history of the country could still be reconstructed from the speech of modern America.

Social Differences

The third great shaper of speech communities is the social class. This has been, and is, more important in England than in America. In England, class differences have often been more prominent than those of age or place. If you were the blacksmith's boy, you might know the son of the local baronet, but you didn't speak his language. You spoke the language of your social group, and he that of his, and over the centuries these social dialects remained widely separated.

England in the twentieth century has been much democratized, but the language differences are far from having disappeared. One can still tell much about a person's family, his school background, his general position in life by the way he speaks. Social lines are hard to cross, and language is perhaps the greatest barrier. You may make a million pounds and own several cars and a place in the country, but your vowels and consonants and nouns and verbs and sentence patterns will still proclaim to the world that you're not a part of the upper crust.

In America, of course, social distinctions have never been so sharp as they are in England. We find it somewhat easier to rise in the world, to move into social environments unknown to our parents. This is possible, partly, because speech differences are slighter; conversely, speech differences are slighter because this is possible. But speech differences do exist. If you've spent all your life driving a cab in Philly and, having inherited a fortune, move to San Francisco's Nob Hill, you will find that your language is different, perhaps embarrassingly so, from that of your new acquaintances.

Language differences on the social plane in America are likely to correlate with education or occupation rather than with birth—simply because education and occupation in America do not depend so much on birth as they do in other countries. A child without family connection can get himself educated at Harvard, Yale, Princeton. In doing so, he acquires the speech habits of the Ivy League and gives up those of his parents.

Exceptions abound. But in general there is a clear difference between the speech habits of the college graduate and those of the high school graduate. The cab driver does not talk like the Standard Oil executive, the college professor like the carnival pitch man, or an Illinois merchant like a sailor shipping out of New Orleans. New York's Madison Avenue and Third Avenue are only a few blocks apart, but they are widely separated in language. And both are different from Broadway.

It should be added that the whole trend of modern life is to reduce rather than to accentuate these differences. In a country where college education becomes increasingly everybody's chance, where executives and refrigerator salesmen and farmers play golf together, where a college professor may drive a cab in the summertime to keep his family alive, it becomes harder and harder to guess a person's education, income, and social status by the way he talks. But it would be absurd to say that language gives no clue at all.

Good and Bad

Speech communities, then, are formed by many features: age, geography, education, occupation, social position. Young people speak differently from old people, Kansans differently from Virginians, Yale graduates differently from Dannemora graduates. Now let us pose a delicate question: aren't some of these speech communities better than others? That is, isn't better language heard in some than in others?

Well, yes, of course. One speech community is always better than all the rest. This is the group in which one happens to find oneself. The writer would answer unhesitatingly that the noblest, loveliest, purest English is that heard in the Men's Faculty Club of San Jose State College, San Jose, California. He would admit, of course, that the speech of some of the younger members leaves something to be desired; that certain recent immigrants from Harvard, Michigan, and other foreign parts need to work on the laughable oddities lingering in their speech; and that members of certain departments tend to introduce a lot of queer terms that can only be described as jargon. But in general the English of the Faculty Club is ennobling and sweet.

As a practical matter, good English is whatever English is spoken by the group in which one moves contentedly and at ease. To the bum on Main Street in Los Angeles, good English is the language of other L.A. bums. Should he wander onto the campus of UCLA, he would find the talk there unpleasant, confusing, and comical. He might agree, if pressed, that the college man speaks "correctly" and he doesn't. But in his heart he knows better. He wouldn't talk like them college jerks if you paid him.

If you admire the language of other speech communities more than you do your own, the reasonable hypothesis is that you are dissatisfied with the community itself. It is not precisely other speech that attracts you but the people who use the speech. Conversely, if some language strikes you as unpleasant or foolish or rough, it is presumably because the speakers themselves seem so.

To many people, the sentence "Where is he at?" sounds bad. It is bad, they would say, in and of itself. The sounds are bad. But this is very hard to prove. If "Where is he at?" is bad because it has bad sound combinations, then presumably "Where is the cat?" or "Where is my hat?" are just as bad, yet no one thinks them so. Well, then, "Where is he at?" is bad because it uses too many words. One gets the same meaning from "Where is he?" so why add the *at*? True. Then "He going with us?" is a better sentence than "Is he going with us?" You don't really need the *is*, so why put it in?

Certainly there are some features of language to which we can apply the terms *good* and *bad*, *better* and *worse*. Clarity is usually better than obscurity; precision is better than vagueness. But these are not often what we have in mind when we speak of good and bad English. If we like the speech of upper-class Englishmen, the presumption is that we admire upper-class Englishmen—their characters, culture, habits of mind. Their sounds and words simply come to connote the people themselves and become admirable therefore. If we knew the same sounds and words from people who were distasteful to us, we would find the speech ugly.

This is not to say that correctness and incorrectness do not exist in speech. They obviously do, but they are relative to the speech community—or communities—in which one operates. As a practical matter, correct speech is that which sounds normal or natural to one's comrades. Incorrect speech is that which evokes in them discomfort or hostility or disdain. . . .

FOR DISCUSSION AND REVIEW

1 Identify the factors which, according to Roberts, shape speech communities.

2 Does education have an influence on dialect? If so, what exactly is the nature of this influence?

3 Roberts feels that there is a marked difference between the speech communities of one generation and the next. Observe and describe speech differences between students and faculty in your school. Compare your findings with those of your teacher. Does a similar situation exist between you and your parents?

4 Do men and women speak different dialects? Try to describe the language of the opposite sex. Compare your results with those of other members of the class. What generalizations can you make about the language of women and the language of men? You may find

it helpful to review Flexner's discussion (p. 282).

5 Roberts talks of the "enormous pressures" on a person to conform to the speech of his age group and his speech community. Discuss the pressures that you felt while growing up.

6 Embarrassing situations can arise, according to Roberts, when a person moves to a new area and discovers that his language is different from that of his new acquaintances. Silas Lapham, the rustic hero of William Dean Howells' *The Rise of Silas Lapham*, moves his family from rural Vermont to Boston's exclusive Beacon Street. Read chapter 14 of Howells' novel, and discuss the embarrassing situations that the Laphams encounter at the dinner party as a result of speech differences.

2

The

Reasons

for Dialect

Differences

After reading the preceding selection by Paul Roberts, you should not be surprised that speech behavior is patterned. The following excerpt from *Discovering American Dialects* by Roger W. Shuy considers the contributing influences of settlement, population shift, and physical geography on the patterned behavior of American dialects. Have any of these factors discussed by Professor Shuy had a marked effect on your area of the country?

Roger W. Shuy

The Patterns of Settlement History

RECENTLY I was driving through the rural Midwest with some friends from California, who noticed things which I had always taken for granted. One Californian, for example, was struck by what he called "little red lollipops" in the front yards of the farmhouses. Later, when he saw another one and called my attention to it, I saw only a red reflector on a stick, used by Indianans as a guide to their driveways at night. My guests were also impressed with poppies growing along the roadside and the quaint country grocery stores with cases of empty soft drink bottles stacked near the front steps. If one grows up in an area in which people usually say "quarter to four," a different but equally common expression, "quarter till four," may seem as strange as the little red lollipops seemed to my friend.

Whether we realize it or not, our language is influenced by the people who settled and established our area. The influence of the early settlers may remain strong for many years; for example, German pronunciations and vocabulary are still found in Grundy County, Illinois; the linguistic effects of the Irish are present on Beaver Island in Lake Michigan; the Dutch influences, in Holland and Grand Rapids, Michigan; and Briticisms, in many American communities which were settled directly from England (such as Albion, Illinois, and New Harmony, Indiana). The first large migration of English people to our country came chiefly from the southeastern counties of England, but there were also some families from Yorkshire, Lancashire, and even the counties farther north. Each of these counties in England has its own local dialects, and the settlers brought these dialects to the New World with them. Later, Ulster Scots, Palatinate Germans, Dutchmen, and others brought features of their own languages or dialects to America, and remnants of these may be clearly seen over one hundred years later.

Sometimes we find a relatively small dialect area surrounded by another, larger one; the former is called a dialect "island." A good example roughly includes parts of northwestern Illinois and southeastern Wisconsin. This lead mining region was settled in the 1850's primarily by people from the Ohio River area, especially Kentucky. Traveling to the region on the Ohio and Mississippi Rivers, these Midland people and some immigrant Cornishmen formed the nucleus of the Lead Region population. To this day, Midland speech predominates here, even though people in all the surrounding areas of both states use Northern speech. Note, too, that this "island" has no regard for political boundaries; it spreads over parts of Illinois, Wisconsin, and Iowa.

Local settlement history, a study often neglected, is vital to the dialectologist as he begins his research. Sometimes he can even supply "missing links" to settlement histories by observing and analyzing speech; for example, a Midwestern area with dialect features usually found in New England is quite likely to have been settled by New Englanders.

The current dialect, although useful, is not a foolproof guide to settlement history, for later layers of settlement may tend to cancel out earlier speech characteristics.

The first American settlers, of course, came from England. At the time of the earliest settlements in Massachusetts, Virginia, Maryland, and Rhode Island, dialect differences in England were even greater than they are today—and today they are still more striking than ours. Speakers of these various dialects crossed the Atlantic Ocean and settled, dialect and all, on the eastern coast of America. The various colonies of the New World found communication very difficult, and the mixed dialects of English settlers who inhabited each colony gradually became distinctive in themselves. The infrequent visits from "outsiders," the lack of safe and efficient transportation methods, and the tendency of each colony to act as a social unit did much to make their dialects distinctive. To this day the eastern coast of our country has smaller and more clearly defined dialect areas than does almost any region to the west.

Patterns of Population Shift

Ask almost anyone what the dialects of America are, and you probably will be told that they are Southern, Eastern, and General American (meaning Midwestern and Western). Even though some textbooks en-

courage this notion, Americans simply are not divided that neatly. Nor
are regional dialects organized along state lines, as we have already seen.
There is simply no such thing as a single New York, Ohio, or Florida
dialect; the dialects of these and other states are formed along the lines
of population shift. Nor do national borders necessarily mark dialect
(or, for that matter, language) differences. The U.S.-Canadian border
has been crossed many times by immigrants from both nations. One interesting example of this movement occurred during the Civil War
when groups of New Englanders, hoping to avoid conscription, felt the
urge to move to New Brunswick. Such immigrants were referred to as
Skedaddlers, and to this day one of their settlements is known locally as
Skedaddlers Ridge.

Since the American population shift generally has been from east
to west, dialect boundaries are more apt to run horizontally than ver-
tically. People from, say, western New York who moved to Michigan,
Wisconsin, northern Illinois, and northern Ohio took their western
New York dialect with them.

Population shift is affected by the opening of new travel routes, by
the invention of new means of transportation, by the development of
industry, and by other aspects of American history. And speech patterns
are thus moved and changed. For instance, the steamboat ushered in a
whole new concept of American migration, allowing New Englanders
and the more recent immigrants to move west across the Great Lakes.

The effects of population shift caused by industrialization can be
seen in cities like Akron, Ohio. This area was settled later than most
urban areas of Ohio because it is located on a high spot (Summit
County) just south of the general migration route through Cleveland
and just north of the route through Columbus. When the rubber industry began to develop, Akron drew thousands of laborers from the handiest source of labor: southern Ohio, West Virginia, and Kentucky. The
tremendous in-pouring of Midlanders has had such a noticeable effect
on the speech of Akronites that, despite its Northern location, Akron
might well be considered part of the Midland speech area. The migration of Midlanders, especially West Virginians, in the past twenty years
is also clearly evident in the Cleveland area, where it is estimated that
Cuyahoga County has received 150,000 migrants from other states since
World War II. Professor Raven I. McDavid, Jr., of the University of
Chicago has observed that Kentucky and West Virginia, like western
New England in our country's earlier days, have the two qualities necessary for emigration: a high fertility in the population and a low fertility
in the soil.

Along with mention of the shift of population, we must also note
the development of urban prestige. Cities like New York, Philadelphia,

New Orleans, and San Francisco have acquired a certain prestige and have become culturally influential. Of course, no one city dominates American culture or American speech; a combination of factors causes Americans to use regional forms rather than a "national" pattern of speech.

One such factor is found in the very size of our country. It is simply too large for one city to develop a network of influence over every other city. If such an influence had ever existed, today we would most likely be imitating the speech of New York City, Boston, Philadelphia, Washington, D.C., or some other city significant in our nation's history.

Democracy also affects the thinking of Americans. If we should be told suddenly that we should pattern our speech, dress, buying habits, religion, and political views after those of Cedar Rapids, Iowa, most of us would react violently. Why Cedar Rapids? The spirit of American regionalism may be seen in people from almost any area of the country. The most traditional example might be a Texan, whose loyalty is notorious. But it can also be seen in the regional loyalty of the natives of Washington State, the Great Lakes area, and New England. This feeling is encouraged by local businessmen whose constant plea is "Buy local products," and by the pressures of family life which cause people to take local jobs rather than to move to some other part of the country.

As a result of this loyalty, various urban areas become focal points in the culture, including the dialect, of a given area. Pronunciations, words, and even grammatical choices of a city are often copied, consciously or subconsciously, by people around it. The influence of Chicago speech patterns can be clearly seen as far west as Wheaton, Illinois (twenty-five miles from Chicago), for example, where such characteristic Chicago words as *prairie* (for vacant lot) and *clout* (political influence) are known. The spread of the Minneapolis influence into Wisconsin was recently noted by Frederic G. Cassidy, who observed that the Minneapolis term *rubber-binder* (for rubber band) was gaining across the state line. On the other hand, the exact influence of an urban area is difficult to judge. The mere presence of a word or pronunciation in the city and its surrounding area does not guarantee that the primary influence came from the city. The flat farm land west of Chicago was actually settled before that city began its phenomenal growth, and it is difficult to sort out the influences of both areas. William Labov has recently observed that lower income New York City residents often ridicule their own speech. The pronunciations *dis* and *dese* (for *this* and *these*) are thought of as characteristic of lower social levels and are not highly valued.

More recent immigration patterns also have had their influence on American English. There can be little doubt about the impact of foreign languages in the past century. The influence of German settlers on the vocabulary and syntax of certain parts of Pennsylvania has long been recognized; likewise, one can easily find Polish terms in Detroit, Hungarian in Cleveland, and Spanish in Los Angeles. New people bring new customs and, quite frequently, new ways of expressing them. Other aspects of American history have also contributed to the dialect mixtures of the present day. Many of our earlier settlements in the Rocky Mountains, for example, dissolved along with the mines which attracted the settlers in the first place. Similarly, those early eastern Coloradans who tried the wrong farming techniques soon moved to other parts, taking their dialect heritage with them and leaving the dust bowl behind.

Patterns of Physical Geography

Today we are seldom hindered in our travels by physical barriers such as rivers, deserts, or mountains. Bridge building, improved water travel, earthmoving techniques, and air transportation have removed most of the barriers which hampered communications and population shift in the last century. Consequently, dialect differences which are found on opposite sides of a river, a mountain range, or a desert were probably established many years ago. In more recently settled areas we find the influences of physical geography less important; however, there are some recent examples of cultural and linguistic isolation. Until about forty years ago river transportation was almost the only way for residents of Calhoun County, Illinois, to travel outside the county to Alton, Illinois, for a distance of about one hundred miles. Likewise Leslie County, Kentucky, had only one paved road as recently as ten years ago. This type of isolation can be seen today in parts of eastern Kentucky and southern Virginia, and more examples might be found in many other states.

In the East, rivers, mostly because they were early physical barriers, are rather clear markers of dialect areas. The Connecticut River still separates *pahk the cah* from *park the car*. As far west as Illinois, the prairie south of the Rock River and north of the Illinois River provided easy access for the settlement of Yankees who came to Illinois across the Great Lakes and Midlanders who came north by way of the Mississippi and Illinois Rivers. Today this prairie area contains a mixture of Northern and Midland dialects. West of the Mississippi, however, geographical barriers are seldom important, since settlement often developed along with the railroad or even followed it, instead of being determined by water routes and boundaries.

FOR DISCUSSION AND REVIEW

1 What are the three reasons for dialect differences that Shuy discusses? Provide an example of each. Compare Shuy's explanations for dialect differences with those presented by Professor Roberts (pp. 335–343).
2 The names of cities, towns, rivers, and mountains often provide clues to settlement and migration patterns. Using a map of your area, list some important local place names and discuss their significance.
3 Discuss the ways in which settlement patterns, population shifts, and physical geography have influenced the dialect of your region.

3

Standard English

Charles C. Fries

The concept of "standard English" has caused much misunderstanding and debate. For many Americans, "standard" implies that one variety of English is more correct or more functional than other varieties of English. In this passage from *American English Grammar*, the late Professor Fries defines "standard English" as those particular language habits that are "used in the conduct of the important affairs of our people." Do you agree?

IN ORDER to grasp the significance of . . . social differences in language practice for the obligation of the schools one must understand clearly what is meant by "standard" English, and that can perhaps best be accomplished by tracing the course by which a particular kind of English became "standard." As one examines the material written in England during the twelfth and thirteenth centuries—a period from one hundred to two hundred years after the Norman Conquest—he finds a situation in which three things are of especial note:

1. Most of the legal documents, the instruments which controlled the carrying on of the political and the business affairs of the English

people, were not written in the English language but in French or in Latin. This fact was also true of much of the literature and books of learning familiar to the upper classes.

2. Although some books, especially historical records and religious and moral stories and tracts, were written in English, there was no single type of the English language common to all English writings. The greatest number used what is called the Southern dialect. This particular kind of English had been centered in Winchester, which was the chief city of King Alfred and his successors until the time of the Norman Conquest.

3. There was, therefore, no "standard" English in twelfth and thirteenth century England, for no single type of the English language furnished the medium by which the major affairs of English people were carried on. Instead, English people used for these purposes French, Latin, and at least four distinct varieties of English. The particular kind of English spoken in southern England came nearest to fulfilling the function of a "standard" English because more writings and more significant writings were produced in this type of English than in any other.

In the fourteenth and early fifteenth centuries, however, this situation changed. London had become the political and in some respects the social head of English life in a much more unified England. Many of the major affairs of the realm had to be handled in London. More and more the English language, the English of London, was used in the legal documents of politics and business. Solely because of the fact that more of the important affairs of English life were conducted in this London English rather than in Winchester English, London English became "standard" English. Naturally, then, the growing use of this particular type of English for the important affairs of English life gathered such momentum that even writers to whom other types of English were more natural felt constrained to learn and to use the fashionable London English. Gower, for example, a Kentishman, did not write his native kind of English but practically the same forms, constructions, and spellings as Chaucer, a Londoner born. Naturally, too, this London English gained a social prestige because of the fact that its use connoted or suggested relations with the center of affairs in English life, whereas the inability to use London English suggested that one did not have such social contacts. "Standard" English, therefore, is, historically, a local dialect, which was used to carry on the major affairs of English life and which gained thereby a social prestige.[1]

---

[1] "Standard" French, "Standard" Italian, "Standard" Dutch, etc., have similar histories.

Many changes occurred in this dialect of English and these changes especially affected the usage of the younger rather than of the older generations in the centers of fashionable social life. Thus the continued use of the older forms rather than the newer changes always suggested a lack of direct contacts with those who were active in the conduct of important matters. In this connotation lay the power of "standard" English to compel the ambitious to conform to its practices.

In America, however, we have had no one recognized center for our political, business, social, and intellectual affairs. More than that, the great distances between various parts of the United States made very difficult frequent actual social contacts in the earlier days. Our coast cities, Boston and New York, maintained direct relations with London long after the earlier settlers had moved west, but the middle western settlements had practically no relations with Boston and New York. This fact can probably explain the differences between our middle-western speech and that of nineteenth century Boston and New York. Because of the fact that New England so long dominated our intellectual life there has been a good deal of feeling in many parts of the United States that the language usages of New England connoted a connection with a higher culture than did the language of the Middle West. Hence the rather widespread attempt to imitate certain New England speech characteristics. On the whole, however, if we ignore the special differences that separate the speech of New England, the South, and the Middle West, we do have in the United States a set of language habits, broadly conceived, in which the major matters of the political, social, economic, educational, religious life of this country are carried on. To these language habits is attached a certain social prestige, for the use of them suggests that one has constant relations with those who are responsible for the important affairs of our communities. It is this set of language habits, derived originally from an older London English, but differentiated from it somewhat by its independent development in this country, which is the "standard" English of the United States. Enough has been said to enforce the point that it is "standard" not because it is any more correct or more beautiful or more capable than other varieties of English; it is "standard" solely because it is the particular type of English which is used in the conduct of the important affairs of our people. It is also the type of English used by the *socially acceptable* of most of our communities and insofar as that is true it has become a social or class dialect in the United States.

FOR DISCUSSION AND REVIEW

1 According to Fries, how did the concept of "standard English" develop?

2 In "Speech Communities" (pp. 335–343), Paul Roberts stated that "good English is whatever En-

glish is spoken by the group in which one moves contentedly and at ease." What do you think Fries' reaction to this statement would be?

3 Fries believes that in the United States standard English is a social

or class dialect. How does he justify this conclusion? Do you agree with him?

4 What exactly, according to Fries, is the "power" of standard English?

4

Sense and Nonsense About American Dialects

Raven I. McDavid

Professor Raven I. McDavid is among a growing number of linguists who are exploring the various implications of American dialects. In the following speech delivered at the meeting of the Modern Language Association in Chicago in December, 1965, McDavid takes a penetrating look at the phenomena of dialect. As the title of his address indicates, McDavid's purpose is twofold. He wants to correct some commonly held misconceptions concerning American dialects and to present some valid generalizations about them.

IN MY BOYHOOD—more years ago than I care to remember—we used to define an expert as "a damned fool a thousand miles from home." Since I am considerably less than a thousand miles from where I grew up, and stand but a few minutes from my residence in Hyde Park, it behooves me to avoid any claim to expertness about the problems faced in practical situations where the dialect of the school child is sharply divergent from what is expected of him in the classroom. For many of these situations, neither I nor any other working dialectologist knows what the local patterns actually are; for some, there has been no attempt, or at best a partial and belated one, to find out the patterns. Nevertheless, the implications of dialectology for the more rational teaching of English in the schools—and not only in the schools attended by those we currently euphemize as the culturally disadvantaged—are so tremendous that I am flattered to have John Fisher ask for my observations. The problems are not limited to Americans of any race or creed or color, nor indeed to Americans; they are being faced in England today, as immigrants from Pakistan and the West Indies compete in the Midlands for the same kinds of jobs that have drawn Negro Americans to Harlem and the South Side, and Appalachian whites to the airplane factories of Dayton. In fact, such problems are faced everywhere in the world as industrialization and urbanization take place, on every occasion when people, mostly but not exclusively the young, leave the farm and the village in search of the better pay and more glamorous life of the cities. In all parts of the world, educators and politicians are suddenly realizing that language differences can create major obstacles to the educational, economic, and social advancement of those whose true integration into the framework of society is necessary if that society is to be healthy; they are realizing that social dialects—that is, social differences in the way language is used in a given community—both reflect and perpetuate differences in the social order. In turn, the practicing linguist is being called on with increasing frequency to devise programs for the needs of specific groups—most often for the Negroes dwelling in the festering slums of our northern and western cities; and generous government and private subsidies have drawn into the act many teachers and administrators—most of them, I trust, well meaning —who not only have made no studies of dialect differences, but have ignored the studies and archives that are available, even those dealing with their own cities.

Perhaps a data-oriented dialectologist may here be pardoned an excursion into the metaphors of siegecraft, recalled from the time when under the tutelage of Allan Gilbert I learned something of the arts of war and gunnery, if not all their Byronic applications. In confronting our massive ignorance of social dialects, the professional students of the past generation have been a forlorn hope—burrowing into a problem here, clawing their way to a precarious foothold of understanding there, seizing an outwork yonder. Like many forlorn hopes, they have been inadequately supported, sometimes ignored, even decried—not only by their literary colleagues, with the usual patronizing attitude toward anything smacking of affiliation with the social sciences, but also by their fellow linguists who are interested in international programs for teaching English as a second language, in machine translation, in formulaic syntax, or in missionating to convert the National Council of Teachers of English. It is small wonder that some students of dialects have withdrawn from the assault to participate in these better-heeled campaigns; it is a tribute to the simple-minded stubbornness of the survivors that they have not only persisted but advanced. Today their work, their aims,

are embarrassingly respectable, as legions spring from the earth in response to the golden trumpet sounding on the banks of the Pedernales.
It is inevitable, perhaps even fitting, that the practical work in social
dialects should be directed by others than the pioneers in research. But
it is alarming that many of those now most vocally concerned with social dialect problems not only know nothing about the systematic work
that has been done, about the massive evidence (even if all too little)
that is available, but even have a complete misconception about the
nature and significance of dialects. At the risk of drawing the fire of the
House Un-American Activities Committee, I would agree with my
sometime neighbor James H. Sledd that our missionaries should at
least know what they are talking about before they set out to missionate.

I have a particular advantage when I talk on this subject: I am one
of those who speak English without any perceptible accent. I learned
to talk in an upper-middle-class neighborhood of Greenville, South Carolina, among corporation lawyers, bankers, textile magnates, and college
presidents, among families with a long tradition of education and general culture. Many of my playmates, like myself, represented the sixth
generation of their families in the same county. It never occurred to
any of us to tamper with our language; our only intimate acquaintance
with non-standard grammatical forms in writing came from stories in
literary dialect or from the quaint and curious exercises that infested
our textbooks—though we knew that less privileged forms of speech
than ours were found in our community, and were not above imitating
them for rhetorical effect. Not a single English teacher of an excellent
faculty—our superintendent had his doctorate, not from Peabody or
from Teachers College, Columbia, but from the University of Berlin in
1910—made a gesture of tampering. Nor have I ever heard anything in
the exotic dialects of the Northeast or the Middle West that would
make me feel less content with a way of speaking that any educated
person might want to emulate. And yet, a few years ago, my younger
sister, who has remained in the South Carolina upland, told me over
the telephone: "Brucker, you've been North so long that you talk just
like a Yankee." Even though I doubt if I would fool many real Yankees, I know that something has rubbed off from my travels and teaching to make me talk a little different from the boys I grew up with.
Still, whenever I go back and start talking with them again, I find myself slipping into the old ways; it is natural for us to shift our way of
talking, according to the people we are talking with. In fact, it is the
people we talk with habitually who give us our way of talking. Here, in
essence, is the way dialects originate. And until everybody lives in a
sterile, homogenized, dehumanized environment, as just a number on
the books of an all-powerful state, we can expect differences in environment to be reflected in those differences in speech that we call dialects.

An appreciation of this fact would avoid a lot of nonsense expressed in categorical statements in educational literature. Two amusing if distressing examples are found in *Language Programs for the Disadvantaged: Report of the NCTE Task Force*, a booklet released at the 1965 convention of the NCTE. These statements, the more distressing because so much of the report is magnificently phrased, probably arose from the inevitable wastefulness of haste (the Task Force was in the field only last summer) and from the imbalance of the Task Force itself: there was only one linguist and not a single sociologist or anthropologist or historian in a group heavily loaded with supervisors and (to coin a term, which is probably already embalmed in educationese) curriculologists:

> Most disadvantaged children come from homes in which a nonstandard English dialect is spoken. It may be pidgin, Cajun, Midland, or any one of a large number of regional or cultural dialects. Many preschool teachers are concerned about the dialect of their children and take measures to encourage standard pronunciation and usage. (p. 70)
> . . . the general feeling is that some work in standard English is necessary for greater social and job mobility by disadvantaged students with a strong regional or racial dialect. (p. 89)

Among the bits of nonsense to be found in these two statements we may notice:

1. A belief that there is some mystical "standard," devoid of all regional association. Yet the variety that we can find in cultivated American English, as used by identifiable informants with impeccable educational and social credentials, has been repeatedly shown in works based on the American Linguistic Atlas, most recently and in greatest detail in Kurath's and my *Pronunciation of English in the Atlantic States* (Ann Arbor: University of Michigan Press, 1961).

2. A belief that there are "racial" dialects, independent of social and cultural experiences.

3. A snobbishness toward "strong" dialect differences from one's own way of speaking. Would Bobby Kennedy, politically disadvantaged after the Atlantic City convention, have run a better race in New York had he learned to talk Bronx instead of his strong Bostonian?

4. A glib juggling of terms, without understanding, as in the parallelism of "pidgin, Cajun, Midland." *Pidgin* denotes a minimal contact language used for communication between groups whose native languages are mutually unintelligible and generally have markedly different linguistic structures; typical examples are the Neo-Melanesian of New Guinea and the Taki-taki of Surinam. However scholars may debate the existence of an American Negro pidgin in colonial days, speakers of

pidgin constitute a problem in no Continental American classroom, though it would be encountered in Hawaii and the smaller Pacific islands. *Cajun* properly describes the colonial varieties of French spoken in southwestern Louisiana and in the parts of the Maritime Provinces of Canada from which the Louisiana Acadians were transported; even if by extension we use the term to describe the varieties of English developing in the French-speaking areas of Louisiana and the Maritimes, the problems of teaching English in these areas are really those of teaching English as a second language. *Midland* is a geographical designation for those dialects stemming from the settlement of Pennsylvania and embracing a broad spectrum of cultural levels. At one extreme, we may concede, are the impoverished submarginal farmers and displaced coal miners of Appalachia; at the other are some of the proudest dynasties of America—the Biddles of Philadelphia, the Mellons of Pittsburgh, the Tafts of Cincinnati, and their counterparts in Louisville and in St. Louis, in Memphis and in Dallas—people it were stupid as well as impractical to stigmatize in language like that of the Task Force Report. So long as such glib generalities are used about social dialects, we must conclude that our educators, however well intentioned, are talking nonsense.

And regrettably, such nonsense is no new phenomenon in American culture; it has long been with us. Much of it, fortunately, runs off us like raindrops off a mallard's back. But enough lingers in the schoolroom to do positive harm. My friend Bob Thomas, the anthropologist—a Cherokee Indian and proud of it, though with his blond hair and blue eyes he looks far less like the traditional Cherokee than I do—tells of his traumata when he moved to Detroit from Oklahoma at the age of fourteen. Although Cherokee was his first language, he had picked up a native command of Oklahoma English. Since he had always lived in a good neighborhood, and his family had used standard English at home, he had no problems in grammar; through wide reading and a variety of experiences he had acquired a large and rich vocabulary. But his vowels were Oklahoma vowels; and some benevolent despot in Detroit soon pushed him into a class in "corrective speech." The first day the class met, he looked around the classroom and noticed everybody else doing the same. As eyes met eyes, it became apparent that the class in "corrective speech" contained no cleft palates, no stammerers, no lispers, no foreign accents, not even any speakers of substandard English —for again, the school was in a good neighborhood. The only thing wrong with the boys and girls in the class was that they had not learned English in Michigan, but in Oklahoma, Arkansas, Missouri, Kentucky, Tennessee, West Virginia, Mississippi, and Alabama. "We all realized immediately," Bob told me years afterward, "that they were planning to brainwash us out of our natural way of speaking; and it became a point of honor among us to sabotage the program." To this day, Bob flaunts his Oklahoma accent belligerently; if the teachers had let him alone, he might have adapted his pronunciation to that of the Detroit boys he played with, but once he felt that the school considered his home language inferior, nothing could make him change. The first principle of any language program is that, whatever the target, it must respect the language that the students bring with them to the classroom.

Another kind of nonsense was demonstrated by the head of the speech department at the University of Michigan during my first Linguistic Institute. Impelled by the kind of *force majeur* that only a four-star general can exert, I had compromised with my scientific interest in linguistics to the extent of enrolling in a course in "stage and radio diction," only to find myself bewildered, frustrated, and enraged from the outset. Typical of the petty irritations was the panjandrous insistence on the pronunciation /'pradjus/, though all my friends who raised fruits and vegetables for market, many of them gentlemen with impeccable academic credentials, said /'prodjus/. But far more distressing were the pronunciations advocated in the name of elegance. We were advised to reject the Middle Western and Southern /æ/, not only in *calf* and *dance* and *command*, but even in *hat* and *ham* and *sand*, for an imitation of the Boston /a/ in environments where Bostonians would never use it, so that we would say /hat/ and /ham/ and /sand/, pronunciations legitimate in no American dialect except that of the Gullah Negroes of the South Carolina and Georgia coast. A few departmental underlings even went all out for an equally phony British [a], again in the wrong places, yielding [hat] and [ham] and [sand], and all of them plumped for replacing the Midwestern [a] of *cot* and *lot* with an exaggerated [ɔ]. Of course, Midwesterners ordering [hɔt ham 'sandwɪčɪz] are as suspect as counterfeit Confederate $3 bills. It is possible that some compulsive aspirants to social elegance docilely lapped up this pap; but those of us who were seriously concerned with English structure and usage laughed the program out of court and left the course, never to return. A second principle can be deduced from this experience: to imitate a dialect sharply different from one's own is a tricky and difficult assignment. A partial imitation is worse than none, since the change seems an affectation to one's neighbors, and the imperfect acquisition seems ridiculous to those whose speech is being imitated. Any attempts at teaching a standard dialect to those who speak a nonstandard one should be directed toward an attainable goal, toward one of the varieties of cultivated speech which the student might hear, day after day, in his own community.

At this point, perhaps, some of you may be muttering, "But what do these experiences have to do with dialects? I always thought that a dialect was something strange and old-fashioned." Many will share your opinion, especially in such countries as France and Italy, where an academy accepts one variety of the language as standard and casts the rest into outer darkness. In such countries the word *dialect* implies a variety of the language spoken by the rustic, the uneducated, the culturally isolated. To say that someone "speaks a dialect"—as one Italian professor patronizingly described one of the best soldiers working with me on our Italian military dictionary—is to exclude him forever from the company of educated men. For a dialect, to such intellectuals, is a form of the language they had rather be found dead than speaking.

True, there are other attitudes. Germans and Austrians make a distinction between the standard language—literary High German—and the dialects, local and predominantly rural forms of speech. But educated Germans do not always avoid dialect speech forms; in some areas, such as the Austrian Tyrol, an educated person will take particular pains to use some local forms in his speech, so as to identify himself with his home. The attitude may be a bit sentimental, but it does help to maintain one's individual dignity in a homogenizing world.

A more extreme attitude was prevalent in the Romantic Era. If the Augustans of the seventeenth and eighteenth centuries looked upon dialects as corruptions of an originally perfect language, the Romantics often alleged, in Wordsworth's terms, that people in humble and rustic life used "a purer and more emphatic language" than that to be met with in the cities. In this viewpoint, the dialects represent the pure, natural, unchanging language, unencumbered by the baggage of civilization. This attitude has long prevailed in Britain; even today the English Dialect Survey is heavily slanted toward archaic forms and relics and ignores modern innovations.

Nor are Americans wholly free from this attitude that a dialect is something archaic and strange. Time and again, a fieldworker for our Linguistic Atlas is told, "We don't speak no dialect around hyur; if you want *rale* dialect you gotta go down into Hellhole Swamp"—or up into Table Rock Cove, or at least across the nearest big river. To many of us, as my student Roger Shuy put it, a dialect is something spoken by little old people in queer out-of-the-way places.

When we become a little more sophisticated—as we must become on a cosmopolitan campus—we realize that cities as well as rural areas may differ in the ways in which their inhabitants talk. Thus we next conclude that a dialect is simply the way everybody talks but us and the people we grew up with; then, by force of circumstance, we realize that we speak a dialect ourselves. But at this point we still feel that a dialect is something regional or local. When we notice that people of our own community speak varieties of English markedly different from our own, we dismiss them as ignorant, or simply as making mistakes. After all, we live in a democratic society and are not supposed to have class markers in our speech. It is a very sophisticated stage that lets us recognize social dialects as well as regional ones—dialects just as natural, arising out of normal, everyday contacts.

By this time we have elaborated our definition of a dialect. It is simply a habitual variety of a language, regional or social. It is set off from all other such habitual varieties by a unique combination of language features: words and meanings, grammatical forms, phrase structures, pronunciations, patterns of stress and intonation. No dialect is simply good or bad in itself; its prestige comes from the prestige of those who use it. But every dialect is in itself a legitimate form of the language, a valid instrument of human communication, and something worthy of serious study.

But even as we define what a dialect is, we must say what it is not. It is different from slang, which is determined by vogue and largely distinguished by transient novelties in the vocabulary. Yet it is possible that slang may show regional or social differences, or that some regional and social varieties of a language may be particularly receptive to slang.

A dialect is also different from an argot, a variety of the language used by people who share a common interest, whether in work or in play. Everyone knows many groups of this kind, with their own peculiar ways of speaking and writing: Baptist preachers, biophysicists, stamp collectors, model railroad fans, Chicago critics, narcotic addicts, jazz musicians, safecrackers. But in the normal course of events a person adopts the language of such subcultures, for whatever part of his life it may function in, because he has adopted a particular way of life; he uses a dialect because he grows up in a situation where it is spoken. Again, some argots may show regional or social variations; the term *mugging*, to choose one example, is largely found on the Atlantic Seaboard; the sport has different designations in the Great Lakes region and on the Pacific Coast.

Nor are dialect differences confined to the older, pre-industrial segments of the vocabulary. Here European and American attitudes differ sharply. The late Eugen Dieth chided the editors of the *Linguistic Atlas of New England* for including such vocabulary items as window shades, the razor strop, and the automobile, such pronunciation items as *library* and *postoffice* and *hotel*, on the ground that these are not genuine dialect items. Yet if they have regional and social variants, as all of these have in North American English, they warrant inclusion. In my lifetime I have seen the *traffic circle* of the Middle Atlantic States become the *rotary* of Eastern New England; the *service plaza* of the Pennsylvania *Turnpike* become the *oasis* of the Illinois *Tollway*; the *poor boy* of New Orleans—a generous sandwich once confined to the Creole Gomorrah and its gastronautic satellites—appearing as a *grinder* in upstate New York, a *hoagy* in Philadelphia, a *hero* in New York City, a *submarine* in Boston. Nor will dialect terms be used only by the older and less sophisticated: a Middle Western academician transplanted to MIT quickly learns to order *tonic* for his children, not *soda pop*, and to send his clothes to a *cleanser*. And though some would consider dialect a matter of speech and not of writing, one can find regional and local commercial terms on billboards and television as well as in the advertising sections of local newspapers.

Finally, dialect terms are not restricted to sloppy, irresponsible usage —a matter of personality type rather than of specific vocabulary items. And though regional and local terms and usages are likely to appear most frequently in Joos's casual and intimate styles, the example of William Faulkner is sufficient evidence that they may be transmuted into the idiom of the greatest literature.

All of these comments are the fruit of centuries of observation, at first casual and anecdotal, later more serious and systematic. The grim test of the pronunciation *shibboleth*, applied by Jephthah's men to the Ephraimites seeking to ford the Jordan, the comic representations of Spartan and Theban speech by Aristophanes, the aspiration of the Roman cockney Arrius-Harrius, immortalized by Horace, the Northern English forms in the Reeves Tale—these typify early interest. With the Romantic search for the true language in the dialects came the growth of comparative linguistics, and the search for comparative dialect evidence in translations of the Lord's Prayer and the proverb of the prodigal son. The search for comparable evidence led, in the 1870's, to the monumental collections for Georg Wenker's *Deutscher Sprachatlas*, later edited by Ferdinand Wrede and Walther Mitzka—44,251 responses, by German village schoolmasters, to an official request for local dialect translations of forty-four sentences of Standard German. Designed to elicit fine phonetic data, the collections proved notably refractory for that purpose, but the sheer mass of evidence corrected the unevenness of individual transcriptions. More important, the discovery that questions designed for one purpose may yield a different but interesting kind of evidence—as *Pferd* proved useless for the /p: pf/ consonant alternation in dialects where the horse is *Roß* or *Gaul*—was reflected in greater sophistication in the design and use of later questionnaires. Less happy was the effect on German dialectology, with later investigations, such as Mitzka's *Wortatlas*, sticking to correspondence techniques, a short questionnaire, an immense number of communities, and an expensive cartographic presentation of the data. But the *Sprachatlas* and *Wortatlas*, and the Dutch investigations modeled upon them, provided us with the evidence on which to determine their own defects.

A valuable innovation was made at the turn of the century in the *Atlas linguistique de la France*, directed by Jules Gilliéron. Correspondence questionnaires gave way to field interviews on the spot, in a smaller number of selected communities (some six hundred in this instance) with a longer questionnaire; a trained investigator interviewed a native of the community in a conversational situation and recorded his responses in a finely graded phonetic alphabet. As with the German atlas, however, the communities chosen were villages; larger places were first investigated in the Atlas of Italy and Southern Switzerland, under the direction of the Swiss scholars Karl Jaberg and Jakob Jud, who also introduced the practice of interviewing more than one informant in the larger communities. With certain refinements, then, the basic principles of traditional dialect study were established by World War I. Some subsequent investigations have followed Wenker, others Gilliéron; some, like the current Czech investigations, have combined both methods, relying primarily on field interviews but using correspondence surveys in the early stages, so that the selection of communities can be made most effectively. Only the British Isles have lagged, perhaps because Joseph Wright's *English Dialect Dictionary*, with its claim to have recorded ALL the dialect words of English, has erected a Chinese Wall worthy of Mr. Eliot's scorn. Not till the 1950's did any kind of field work get under way in either England or Scotland; in both countries it was handicapped by a shortage of funds and fieldworkers, and in England by an antiquarian bias that over-emphasized relics, shunned innovations, and neglected opportunities to provide data comparable to that obtained in the American surveys. Yet both Harold Orton in England and Angus McIntosh in Scotland have enriched our knowledge of English.

Perhaps because American linguists have kept in touch with European developments, the *Linguistic Atlas of New England*, launched in 1930, drew on the lessons of the French and Italian atlases. Although the transition from casual collecting to systematic study was not welcomed by all students, nevertheless—even with the Hoover Depression, World War II, the Korean intervention, and the tensions of the Cold War—a respectable amount of progress has been made toward a first survey of American English. *The Linguistic Atlas of New England* was published in 1939–43; scholars are now probing for the changes that a generation has brought. For four other regional surveys, field work has been completed and editing is under way: (1) the Middle and South Atlantic States, New York to central Georgia, with outposts in Ontario and northeastern Florida; (2) the North-Central States: Wisconsin, Michigan, southwestern Ontario, and the Ohio Valley; (3) the Upper Midwest: Minnesota, Iowa, Nebraska, and the Dakotas; (4) the Pacific Southwest: California and Nevada. Elsewhere, field work has been completed in Colorado, Oklahoma, Washington, and eastern Montana; respectable portions have been done in several other states, Newfoundland, Nova Scotia, and British Columbia; with a slightly different method the late E. Bagby Atwood produced his memorable *Regional Vocabulary of Texas*. In all of these surveys the principles of European dialect investigations have been adapted to the peculiarities of the American scene. Settlement history has been studied more carefully before field work, since English-speaking settlement in North America is recent, and its patterns are still changing. At least three levels of usage are investigated—partly because cultivated American speech has regional varieties, just like uneducated speech, and the cultivated speech of the future may be foreshadowed in the speech of the intermediate group; partly because until very recently general education has been a more important linguistic and cultural force in the United States than in most of the countries of Europe. Urban speech as well as rural has been investigated in each survey, and intensive local investigations have been encouraged. The questionnaires have included both relics and innovations. All of these modifications were suggested by Hans Kurath, first Director of the Atlas project, who is currently drawing on his experience in developing a new theory for the interpretation of dialect differences.

Just as warfare is still decided ultimately by infantrymen who can take and hold territory, so dialect study still depends on competent investigators who can elicit and record natural responses in the field. The tape recorder preserves free conversation for later transcription and analysis, and permits the investigator to listen repeatedly to a response about whose phonetic quality he is in doubt; but the investigator must still ask the right questions to elicit pertinent data. He must remember, for instance, that *chicken coop* is both a vocabulary and a pronunciation item—that the pronunciation in the American North and North Midland is /kup/, in the South and South Midland /kvp/, that *coop* in the North designates the permanent shelter for the whole flock, in the South a crate under which a mother hen can scratch without an opportunity to lead the little ones off and lose them in the brush. The full record for such an item may require three or four questions, which only a human interviewer can provide.

But if the fieldworker remains essential, the objects of his investigation may change. Recent studies have turned increasingly to urban areas, urbanizing areas, and minority groups. To a long list of impressive early investigations one can now add such contributions as Lee Pederson's study of Chicago pronunciation and Gerald Udell's analysis of the changes in Akron speech resulting from the growth of the rubber industry and the consequent heavy migration from West Virginia. Among special groups investigated in detail are the Spanish-American bilinguals in San Antonio by Mrs. Janet Sawyer, the American Norwegians by Einar Haugen, the New York City Greeks by James Macris, the New England Portuguese by Leo Pap, the Chicago Slovaks by Mrs. Goldie Meyerstein, the Gullah Negroes by Lorenzo Turner, and the

Memphis Negroes by Miss Juanita Williamson. In all of these studies the emphasis has been on the correlation between linguistic and social forces.

Another significant development has been the investigation of the way language attitudes are revealed by the choice among linguistic variants under different conditions. The most impressive work of this kind has been done by William Labov of Columbia University, in his study of the speech of the Lower East Side of New York. Limiting himself to a small number of items—the vowels of *bad* and *law*, the initial consonants of *think* and *then*, the /-r/ in *barn* and *beard*—phonological details that can be counted on to appear frequently and in a large number of contexts during a short interview, Labov gathers specimens of linguistic behavior under a wide range of conditions. At one end of the spectrum is the reading of such putatively minimal pairs as *bed* and *bad*; at the other is the description of children's games or the recounting an incident when the informant thought he was going to be killed. The difference between pronunciations in the relaxed situation and those when the informant is on what he considers his best linguistic behavior is an index of his social insecurity. Almost as revealing is the work of Rufus Baehr with high-school students in the Negro slums of the Chicago West Side. It is no surprise that in formal situations the students with greater drive to break out of their ghetto reveal striking shifts of their speech in the direction of the Chicago middle-class norm. This kind of discovery should give heart to all who believe that a directed program of second-dialect teaching can make at least a small dent in our problem of providing a wider range of economic and educational opportunities for the aspiring young Negro.

Out of all these investigations two patterns emerge: (1) a better understanding of the origin and nature of dialect differences; (2) a set of implications for those who are interested in providing every American child with a command of the standard language adequate for him to go as far as his ability and ambition impel him.

No dialect differences can, as yet, be attributed to physiology or to climate. Perhaps anatomists will discover that some minor speech-differences arise from differences in the vocal organs; but so far there is no evidence for any correlation between anatomy and dialect, and the burden of proof is on those who propose such a correlation. As for climate: it is unlikely that nasality could have arisen (as often asserted) both from the dusty climate of Australia and the dampness of the Tennessee Valley. And though it is a favorite sport among Northerners to attribute the so-called "Southern drawl" to laziness induced by a hot climate, many Southerners speak with a more rapid tempo than most Middle Westerners, and the Bengali, in one of the most enervating tropical climates, speak still more rapidly. For an explanation of dialect differences we are driven back, inevitably, to social and cultural forces.

The most obvious force is the speech of the original settlers. We should expect that a part of the United States settled by Ulster Scots would show differences in vocabulary, pronunciation, even in grammar from those parts settled by East Anglians. We should expect to find Algonkian loans most common in those regions where settlers met Algonkian Indians, French loans most frequent in Louisiana and in the counties adjacent to French Canada, Spanish loans most widespread in the Southwest, German loans clustering in cities and in the Great Valley of Pennsylvania, and indubitable Africanisms most striking in the Gullah country.

Speech forms are also spread along routes of migration and communication. The Rhine has carried High German forms northward; the Rhone has taken Parisian forms to the Mediterranean; in the United States, the same kind of dissemination has been found in the valleys of the Mississippi, the Ohio, and the Shenandoah.

If speech forms may spread along an avenue of communication, they may be restricted by a physical barrier. As Kurath has observed, there is no sharper linguistic boundary in the English-speaking world than the Virginia Blue Ridge between the Potomac and the James. The tidal rivers of the Carolinas, the swamps of the Georgia coastal plain, have contributed to making the Old South the most varied region, dialectally, in the English settlements of the New World.

The economic pattern of an area may be reflected in distinctive dialect features. *Fatwood*, for resin-rich kindling, is confined to the turpentine belt of the Southern tidewater; *lightwood*, with a similar referent, to the Southern coastal plain and lower Piedmont. *Case weather*, for a kind of cool dampness in which it is safe to cut tobacco, occurs over a wide area, but only where tobacco is a money crop. *To run afoul of*, a maritime phrase in the metaphorical sense of "to meet," seems to be restricted to the New England coast.

Political boundaries, when long established, may become dialect boundaries; in the Rhineland, pronunciation differences coincide strikingly with the boundaries of the petty states of pre-Napoleonic Germany. In the New World, on the other hand, political boundaries have seldom delimited culture areas. Yet *county site*, for the more usual *county seat*, is common in Georgia but unknown in South Carolina, and Ontario Canadians speak of the *reeve* as chief officer of a township, the *warden* as chief officer of a county, and a *serviette* instead of a table napkin—terms unfamiliar in the United States.

Each city of consequence may have its distinctive speech forms. The grass strip between the sidewalk and the curb, undesignated in South Carolina, is a *tree belt* locally in Springfield, Massachusetts (and hence unlabeled in *Webster's Third New International Dictionary*), a *tree lawn* in Cleveland, a *devil strip* in Akron, and a *boulevard* in Minneapolis and St. Paul. And only Chicagoans naturally refer to political influence as *clout*, or to a reliable dispenser of such influence as a *Chinaman*.

Nor are differences in the educational system without their effect. Where separate and unequal education is provided to particular social groups, we can be sure that a high-school diploma or even a college degree will be no indication by itself of proficiency in the standard language. That this problem is not confined to any single racial or cultural group has been shown by institutions such as West Virginia State College, which have undergone the process of reverse integration. This particular school, which once drew an elite Negro student body, is now eighty percent white, with the white students mostly from the disadvantaged mountain areas along the Kanawha. Since the teachers in the mountain schools are not only predominantly local in origin, but often have had little education beyond what the local schools offer, and then, since most of them habitually use many non-standard forms, it has been difficult for the college to maintain its academic standards in the face of increasing white enrollment, however desirable integration may be.

Most important, perhaps, is the traditional class structure of a community. In a Midwestern small town, it is still possible for one brother to stay home and run a filling station, and another to go off and become a judge—and nobody mind. But in parts of the South there is a social hierarchy of families and occupations, so that it is more respectable for a woman of good family to teach in an impoverished small college than to do professional work for the government at twice the salary. Here, too, an aristocratic ideal of language survives, and the most cultivated still look upon *ain't* as something less reprehensible than incest—but use it only in intimate conversation with those whom they consider their social equals. Here too we find the cultural self-assurance that leads an intelligent lawyer to ask the linguistically naive question: "Why is it that the educated Northerner talks so much like the uneducated Southerner?"

If social differences among the WASP population are reflected in linguistic differences, we should not be surprised if similar differences among later immigrants are reflected in the extent of linguistic borrowing from particular foreign-language groups, or even from the same foreign-language group at different times. Our longest continuous tradition of borrowing, with probably the largest and most varied kinds of words, is that from various kinds of German. Even the bitterness of two world wars cannot prevent us from seeing that of all foreign-language groups the Germans have been most widely distributed, geographically and socially, throughout the United States—as prosperous farmers, vaudeville comedians, skilled craftsmen, merchants, intellectuals. In contrast, the hundreds of thousands of Italian- and Slavic-speaking immigrants of the last two generations have left few marks on the American vocabulary; most of them were of peasant stock, often illiterate, and settled in centers of heavy industry as basic labor.

Even more striking is the change in the incidence of Texas borrowings from Mexican Spanish. In her study of the bilingual situation in San Antonio, Mrs. Sawyer has shown that although early Spanish loans were numerous, quickly assimilated, and widely spread—*canyon, burro, ranch, lariat, broncho, silo* are characteristic examples—there have been few such loans in the last seventy years. The explanation is the drastic change in the relationships between Anglos and Latins. When English-speaking settlers first moved into Texas, they found the hacienda culture already established, and eagerly took over culture and vocabulary from the Latins who constituted the local elite. Anglo and Latin, side by side, died in the Alamo 4 March 1836 and conquered at San Jacinto seven weeks later. But since 1890 the Texan has encountered Mexican Spanish most often in the speech of unskilled laborers, including imported braceros and illegally entered wetbacks; derogatory labels for Latins have increased in Texas English, and loans from Spanish have declined. We borrow few words from those we consider our inferiors.

We can now make a few clear statements about the facts of American dialects, and their significance:

1. Even though much work remains to be done, we can describe in some detail most of the principal regional varieties of American English and many of the important sub-varieties; we can indicate, further, some of the kinds of social differences that are to be found in various dialect areas, and many of the kinds that are to be found in some of the most important cities.

2. We can be sure that in many situations there are tensions between external norms and the expectations of one's associates. These tensions, most probably, are strongest in the lower middle class—a group anxious to forget humbler backgrounds but not sure of their command of the prestige patterns. Since the teaching profession, on all levels, is heavily drawn from the lower middle class, we can expect—as Marjorie Daunt found years ago—that anxiety is the characteristic attitude of the English teacher toward variations in usage. There is a strong urge to make changes, for the sake of making changes and demonstrating one's authority, without stopping to sort out the significance of differences in usage. This attitude is reflected in the two most widely known programs for teaching better English to the disadvantaged: a socially insignificant problem, such as the distinction between *Wales* and *whales,* is given the same value as the use of the marker for the third singular in the present indicative. Future programs should use the resources of the

dialect archives, at least as a start, even though more detailed and more recent information may be necessary before one can develop teaching materials. The inevitable prescription in a pedagogical situation can be no better than the underlying description.

3. There is evidence that ambitious students in slum areas intuitively shift their speech patterns in the direction of the prestigious local pattern, in situations where they feel such a shift will be to their advantage. Some actually achieve, on their own, a high degree of functional bidialectalism, switching codes as the situation demands. In any teaching program it would seem intelligent to make use of this human facility.

4. The surest social markers in American English are grammatical forms, and any teaching program should aim, first of all, at developing a habitual productive command of the grammar of standard English— with due allowance for the possibility that the use of this grammar may be confined to formal situations in which the speaker comes in contact with the dominant culture.

5. Relatively few pronunciation features are clear social markers, though in many Northern cities there is a tendency to identify all Southern and South Midland pronunciations as those of uneducated rural Negroes. How much one should attempt to substitute local pronunciations for those which are standard in regions from which migrants come would probably depend on the extent to which variations in standard English are recognized and accepted in the community: Washington, for instance, may be more tolerant than New York City. In any event, programs to alter pronunciation patterns should concentrate on those pronunciations that are most widely recognized as substandard.

6. Few people can really identify the race of a speaker by pronunciation and voice quality. In experiments in Chicago, middle-class Middle Westerners consistently identified the voice of an educated urban white Southerner as that of an uneducated rural Negro, and many identified as Negro the voice of an educated white Chicagoan. Similar experiments in New York have yielded similar results. And many white Southerners can testify to personal difficulties arising from this confusion in the minds of Northerners. In Ithaca, New York, I could not get to see any apartment advertised as vacant until I paid a personal visit; over the telephone I was always told that the apartments had just been rented; James Marchand, a Middle Tennessean now on the Cornell faculty, must carefully identify himself as "Professor Marchand," if he wants a garageman to come and pick up his car. And the telephone voice of my Mississippi-born chairman, Gwin Kolb, is racially misidentified with alarming regularity.

7. There can be no single standard in programs for the disadvantaged; the target dialect must vary according to the local situation. In Mississippi, the same program can be used for Negroes and whites,

because they share most of the same grammatical deviations from the local standard, and share phonological patterns with that standard; in Cleveland, grammatical features in writing are sufficient to distinguish Negro college applicants from white better than ninety percent of the time, and deviations from local standard pronunciation are far more striking and numerous among Negroes than among locally-born disadvantaged whites.

8. To the suggestion that Southern Negroes should not be taught local standard pronunciation, but some external standard—the hypothetical variety some call "network English"—there is a simple answer in the form of a question: "Do you want integration in the South?" The Southern patterns of race relations have suffered too long from too many separate standards for Negro and white; it would be ironical if those speaking most loudly in behalf of the aspirations of the Southern Negro should create new obstacles to those aspirations. The language problems of the uneducated Southern Negro are the language problems, even to fine detail, of the uneducated Southern white in the same community; the South may well solve the language problems in its schools before Detroit does. Once the races are brought into the same classroom, a community will need only one intelligent program based on a solid body of dialect evidence.

9. While we are planning language programs for our disadvantaged, we must educate the dominant culture in the causes and significance of dialect differences; it is particularly urgent that we educate teachers on all levels, from kindergarten through graduate school. The disadvantaged will have enough to do in learning new patterns of language behavior; the dominant culture must meet them part way, with greater understanding, with a realization that dialect differences do not reflect intellectual or moral differences, but only differences in experience. Granted that this reeducation of the dominant culture is bound to be difficult, we should not be so cynical as to reject it, on the ground that it cannot take place. In an age when we are turning the heat off under the melting pot and accepting the cultural contributions of Americans with ancestral languages other than English, in an age when we are learning the art of peaceful coexistence with a variety of economic and political and cultural systems, it should not be difficult to extend this acceptance to fellow Americans of different cultural backgrounds and linguistic habits, and especially to recognize that cultured American English may be found in many regional and local varieties. It is a poor cultural tolerance that would accept all cultivated speech except that in other parts of our own country.

With my deep-ingrained horror of patent-medicine salesmen, I would not leave you with the impression that we already have all the answers, or even all the evidence we need to arrive at those answers.

We need many more kinds of investigation, and we should like to think that John Fisher, with his unlimited license to stalk money-bearing animals, might help us conduct some of them. We are still to do even the preliminary surveys in such parts of the country as Tennessee and Arkansas; we need many more studies of the actual patterns of social dialects in most American cities. We really have no serious evidence on regional and social differences in such prosodic features as stress and pitch and juncture. The recognition of paralanguage—the non-linguistic modulation of the stream of speech—is so recent that we have no idea as to the kinds of regional and social differences that may be found in tempo and rhythm, in range of pitch and stress, in drawl and clipping, in rasp and nasality and mellifluousness. We have not even begun to study regional and social variations in gesture and other kinds of body movement. But we do have a framework which we can fill in detail, continually building our teaching programs on solid research into the ways in which Americans communicate in various localities, and into the attitudes of specific speakers toward those whose usage differs from their own. In comparison with the immensity of our social problems, our linguistic knowledge is as a little candle in the forest darkness at midnight; let us not hide that candle under a basket, but put it in a lantern and use it to find our way.

Bibliographical Note

The significance of dialect differences has been often discussed, notably in Leonard Bloomfield, *Language* (New York, 1933), Ch. xix. The most detailed summary of dialect investigations to the mid-century is Sever Pop, *La Dialectologie*, 2 vols. (Louvain, 1950). Kurath's *Areal Linguistics: Problems, Methods, Results* (Bloomington, Ind., 1967), will be shorter but more up to date.

The most widely known summary of American dialects is to be found in Ch. ix of W. Nelson Francis, *The Structure of American English* (New York, 1958); the most accessible bibliographical summary is in the footnotes of Ch. vii of the one-volume 1963 edition of H. L. Mencken, *The American Language*. Annual summaries of research will be found in the reports of the Committee on Regional Speech and Dialectology, in *Publications of the American Dialect Society*; recent research is reported in the quarterly bibliographies in *American Speech*, less extensively in the supplement to *PMLA*. The method of the American atlases is discussed in detail in Kurath's *Handbook of the Linguistic Geography of New England* (Providence, R.I., 1939). For summaries of particular dialect features along the Atlantic seaboard, see Kurath, *A Word Geography of the Eastern United States* (Ann Arbor, Mich., 1949); Atwood, *A Survey of Verb Forms in the Eastern United States* (Ann Arbor, Mich., 1952); Kurath and McDavid, *The Pronunciation of English in the Atlantic States* (Ann Arbor, Mich., 1961). Atwood's *The Regional Vocabulary of Texas* was published by the University of Texas Press, Austin, in 1962. For particular regions see articles by A. H. Marckwardt for the Great Lakes, Harold B. Allen for the Upper Midwest, Marjorie M. Kimmerle and Clyde Hankey for Colorado, David W. Reed and David DeCamp for California. A *Dictionary of American Regional English*, directed by Frederic G. Cassidy, is currently under way at the University of Wisconsin.

The first direct attention to American social dialects is McDavid, "Dialect Geography and Social Science Problems," *Social Forces*, XXV, 168–172; basic for the problems of Negro speech is Raven I. and Virginia McDavid, "The Relationship of the Speech of American Negroes to the Speech of Whites," *American Speech*, XXVI, 3–17. A 1964 conference on social dialects, held at Bloomington, Indiana, is reported in *Social Dialects and Language Learning*, a publication of the NCTE, edited by A. L. Davis and Roger Shuy (Champaign, Ill., 1965); in 1965 the NCTE also published *Language Programs for the Disadvantaged: A Report of the NCTE Task Force*, and reprinted two of McDavid's articles as a monograph, *American Social Dialects*. A teachers' manual on the subject has been requested by the U.S. Office of Education; it is hoped that work can begin in the summer of 1966.

The most familiar American analysis of stress, pitch, and juncture was first sketched in G. L. Trager and H. L. Smith, Jr., *Outline of English Structure, Studies in Linguistics:* Occ. Paper 3 (Norman, Okla., 1951); a more detailed exposition is found in A. A. Hill, *Introduction to Linguistic Structures* (New York, 1958). A different analysis is that of Kenneth L. Pike, *The Intonation of American English* (Ann Arbor, Mich., 1945). The importance of paralanguage, previously discussed by Trager and Smith, is shown in Robert E. Pittenger, Charles F. Hockett, and John J. Danehy, *The First Five Minutes* (Ithaca, N.Y., 1960); the most detailed treatment of gesture is in Ray Birdwhistell, *Introduction to Kinesics* (Washington, 1952), later reprinted by the University of Louisville. A good popular treatment of communication in culture is Edward T. Hall, *The Silent Language* (New York, 1959), now available in paperback. Martin Joos's theories of style are summed up in *The Five Clocks* (Bloomington, Ind., 1962).

FOR DISCUSSION AND REVIEW

1   Briefly summarize McDavid's definition of *dialect*.

2   Recount the "bits of nonsense" about dialects that McDavid points out. Have you ever encountered any of these misconceptions about dialects? Discuss them.

3   How would McDavid react to Fries' definition of standard English (pp. 349–352)?

4   McDavid sees a connection between dialects and some of the pressing social issues confronting the United States. What exactly is this connection? Do you believe that a knowledge of dialects has social value?

5   Professor McDavid says that "the surest social markers in American English are grammatical forms." Collect examples of grammatical forms used in your community. What social classes are represented?

5

Regional Variations of American English

Dialectologists usually divide American English into three major regional patterns: Northern, Midland, and Southern. Professor Nist of Auburn University indicates that each of these speech areas fosters its own regional subdivisions. In this passage from A *Structural History of English*, the distinguishing features of the ten leading regionalisms are discussed. Can you identify yours?

John Nist

G EORGE P. KRAPP declared in 1919 that "Relatively few Americans spend all their lives in one locality, and even if they do, they cannot possibly escape coming into contact with Americans from other localities. . . . We can distinguish with some certainty Eastern and Western and Southern speech, but beyond this the author has little confidence in those confident experts who think they can tell infallibly, by the test of speech, a native of Hartford from a native of Providence, or a native of Philadelphia from a native of Atlanta, or even, if one insists on infallibility, a native of Chicago from a native of Boston." Despite some minor regional vocabulary differences, a leveling of speech habits has been a primary factor in the similarity of American regionalisms. The reasons for that leveling, according to Mencken, are "The railroad, the automobile, the mail-order catalogue, the movie and, above all, radio and television. . . ." As a present-day indication of regional leveling in American English, the omitted *r* in the pronunciation of Eastern New England, New York City, and the South is beginning to reassert itself.

Regionalisms do, nevertheless, exist. They now constitute three major speech areas in the United States: Northern, Midland, and Southern. These speech areas foster their own regional subdivisions, which at times have little to do with geographical location. Thus the pronunciation habits of the Southwest area of Arizona, Nevada, and California are generally of Northern derivation, whereas the speech patterns of the Northwest (Montana, Idaho, Oregon, and Washington) are basically of Midland origin. West Texas speech shows the dominance of Appalachian; East Texas speech is an outgrowth of Southern.

Since Appalachian is a regional version of Midland, the differences between the pronunciations of East and West Texas are marked.

American English, then, is characterized by three major speech areas
that have generated ten leading regionalisms:

Northern

1) *Eastern New England.* This Atlantic seaboard regionalism, with
Boston as its center, lengthens the vowel /a/ to compensate for the loss
of r in a word like *barn* /bahn/; tends to use the broad British /a/ in
words like *ask, dance, path, aunt,* and *rather;* interjects a final r in words
like *idea* and *Cuba;* distinguishes the low-central vowel of *cot* /kat/
from the low-back vowel of *caught* /kɔt/; prefers /æ/ as the stressed
vowel of *barren;* lowers the stressed vowel of *hurry* to /ə/; often interjects the glide /y/ after /d/ in a word like *due* /dyuw/; centers the low-
back vowel of *log* to /a/; either lengthens or *schwa*-glides the vowel of
horse and *hoarse* to compensate for the loss of r: /hɔhs/ or /hoəs/;
pronounces *greasy* with an /s/.

2) *North Central.* This regionalism extends from Western New
England across the Champlain and Great Lakes basins to the central
Dakotas; Hartford, Syracuse, Cleveland, Detroit, Chicago, and Minneapolis are centers. North Central American English pronounces its
medial and final r's; prefers the flat /æ/ in words like *ask;* does not
interject a final r in words like *idea;* also distinguishes *cot* from *caught;*
usually prefers /e/ as the stressed vowel of *barren;* heightens the stressed
vowel of *hurry* to /ɨ/; does not interject the glide /y/ into the pronunciation of *due* /duw/; employs the low-back vowel /ɔ/ in the word *log;*
uses r in both *horse* and *hoarse* so that they sound alike: /hɔrs/; pronounces *greasy* with an /s/.

3) *Southwest.* This regionalism covers Arizona, Nevada, and California; Phoenix, San Francisco, and Los Angeles are centers. Southwest
American English is almost identical with North Central. A higher
incidence of Mexican Spanish vocabulary constitutes the primary difference.

Midland

1) *New York City.* This regionalism covers a small area (southern
New York, southwestern Connecticut, and northeastern New Jersey),
but it is big in importance because of the population and prestige of its
center. Agreeing with Eastern New England in many of its pronunciation patterns, New York City American English is different in several

major respects, for it often articulates medial and final *r's*; does not interject a final *r* after a terminal vowel; makes a clearer phonemic distinction between the /a/ of *cot* and the /ɔ/ of *caught*; and refuses to employ the glide /ə/ in any actualization of *hoarse*. Known for its heavy nasal quality and Yiddish influence, this regionalism is often hard and metallic in intonation; it also permits such variants as /c/ for /j/, /t/ for /θ/, /d/ for /ð/. Brooklyn versions of /ɔy/ and /ɨr/ are notorious.

2) *Middle Atlantic.* Extending from New Jersey to Maryland and from Delaware to the mountains of Pennsylvania, with Philadelphia as center, this regionalism does not permit the complex /ah/ to replace the *r* in *barn*; allows /z/ as a phonemic variant of /s/ in the pronunciation of *greasy*; often rounds and elevates the /ɔ/ of *horse* to /o/; permits both /lag/ and /log/ for *log*; and resembles New York City in the use of either /e/ or /æ/ as the stressed vowel of *various*.

3) *Western Pennsylvania.* This small regionalism covers western Pennsylvania, the eastern tip of Ohio, and the northern portion of West Virginia. With Pittsburgh as center, Western Pennsylvania American English is noted for its "Pennsylvania Dutch" vocabulary and idioms. Much like Middle Atlantic, Western Pennsylvania differs in that it backs the /a/ in *orange* to /ɔ/; it makes absolutely no distinction between *cot* and *caught*; it does not permit /æ/ as the stressed vowel of *various*; it consistently pronounces *log* as /lɔg/.

4) *Central Midland.* This vast regionalism covers the heartland of the United States from Ohio to Utah and from west Texas to Wyoming, with such centers as Cincinnati, Indianapolis, St. Louis, Kansas City, Denver, Albuquerque, and Salt Lake City. Because it dominates such a large area of the country and is the immediate progenitor of Northwest American English, Central Midland is perhaps the best candidate for the office of Standard American, the outstanding characteristics of which are the articulation of medial and terminal *r*; the distinction between the vocalic phonemes of *cot* and *caught*; the preference for /e/ over /æ/ as the stressed vowel of *barren*; the universal use of the flat /æ/ in words like *ask* and *path*; the tolerance of /s/ and /z/ as phonemic variants in the pronunciation of *greasy*; the preference for /ɨ/ over /ə/ as the stressed vowel of *hurry*; the rejection of interjectional /y/ in words like *due* /duw/; the interchangeability of /ɔ/ and /o/ as the stressed vowel of *hoarse*; and the exclusive use of /ɔ/ as the stressed vowel of *log*.

5) *Northwest.* With Seattle as center, this regionalism covers Washington, Oregon, Idaho, and Montana, and small portions of northern California, Nevada, Utah, of northwestern Wyoming, and of western North Dakota and South Dakota. In most respects, Northwest Ameri-

can English is identical with Central Midland. It differs slightly by permitting a higher-tongued and tenser pronunciation of the stressed vowel in *various* and by allowing /lag/ as a variant of /lɔg/.

6) *Appalachian.* Commonly referred to as "hillbilly" American English, this regionalism covers the eastern area of the United States known as Appalachia (most of West Virginia, Kentucky, Tennessee, and portions of eastern Virginia, North Carolina, South Carolina, and northern Georgia, Alabama, and Mississippi). Noted for the archaic features of its grammar and the substandard usage of its "folk speech," Appalachian partakes of certain Midland characteristics that distinguish it from Southern—especially in retaining *r* in words like *barn*; in refusing to add the breaking glide /ə/ to diphthongs; in maintaining /æ/ as a simple vowel without tension and in adding the breaking glide /ɫ/; in backing Southern /a/ to /ɔ/ in words like *orange*; in permitting /e/ as a phonemic variant of /æ/ in the pronunciation of *barren*; and in the preference for /duw/ over /dyuw/. Appalachian is like Southern in its distinction between *cot* and *caught*; in its use of flat /æ/ in words like *ask* and *path*; in its complete use of /z/ in the pronunciation of *greasy*; in its universal preference for /ə/ as the stressed vowel of *hurry* and for /ɔ/ as the stressed vowel of *log*.

Southern

A complex of various subregionalisms, this vast speech variety extends from Virginia through most of the old Confederacy to western Texas. With centers in Richmond, Charleston, Atlanta, Miami, Montgomery, New Orleans, and Houston, Southern American English is famous for its loss of final *r*; for its conversion of *r* to either the breaking glide /ə/ or the offset glide /h/ when the *r* is followed by another consonant or by a juncture; for its transmutation of simple vowels to diphthongs, as in *dog* /dɔəg/ and *class* /klæɫs/; for reducing complex narrow vowels to complex wide vowels, as in *time* /tahm/ and *oil* /ɔhl/, so that words like *Mike* and *Mark* sound identical: /mahk/; and for a generally slower rate of speech that gives the intonation a "honey-and-molasses" effect.

The characteristics for each of these regionalisms are merely representative and not exhaustive. Both Hawaiian and Alaskan American English, furthermore, need detailed study. But the ten major regionalisms listed above are *speech varieties*; they are not confined within arbitrary borders. From the migration of munitions workers during World War II, for example, Appalachian gained an entrance into, and thus an influence upon, North Central American English. Appalachian, as a matter of fact, spills way beyond its traditional confines—into Texas as far east as the Brazos River, into southern Missouri, Illinois, Indiana,

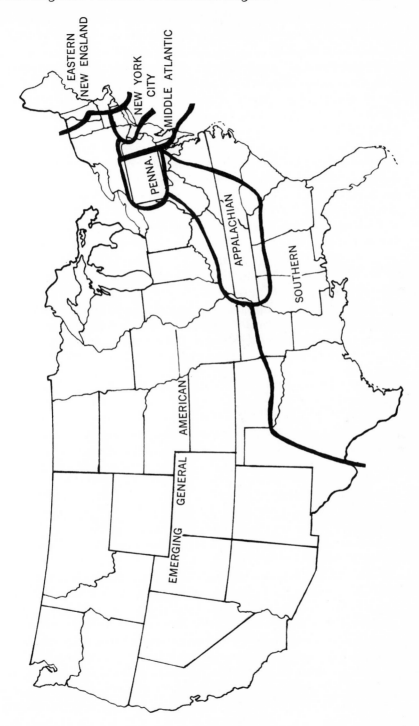

and Pennsylvania. Some of the most interesting phonemic features of American English have to do with Southern pronunciations. The nasalizations of the South tend to raise the preceding vowel; hence it is that *pin* is articulated as /piyn/, *pen* as /pin/, and *pan* as /pen/. Southern American English shows several signs that a major sound shift is taking place within its area of dominance: 1) back vowels tend to be fronted whenever possible; 2) checked "short" vowels generally develop a high-central glide before voiceless consonants and a mid-central glide before voiced consonants: /ɨ/ and /ə/ respectively; 3) the /ɨ/ glide tends to form before post-apical consonants, as in /θeɨŋk/ for *thank*, /bæɨs/ for *bass*, and /puɨš/ for *push*; 4) tense vowels, therefore, tend to break into two segments (or syllables) at points of pitch change—hence the Southern *drawl*, as in /rihəst/ for *wrist*.

Far more important than the phonemic features of Southern speech habits, however, is the gradual wearing away of pronunciation differences among the four regionalisms that cover most of the land mass of the continental United States: North Central, Southwest, Central Midland, and Northwest. Because of the vast increase in population mobility and the immense impact of the mass media, at present these four regionalisms constitute an Emerging General American, which in time may become the accepted American Standard. The resultant seven major speech varieties of present-day American English are distributed as shown in the preceding map.

FOR DISCUSSION AND REVIEW

1   What speech pattern, according to Nist, may in time become the accepted American Standard? What evidence does Nist supply to support this conclusion?

2   Of what major speech area and regional subdivision are you a native? Compare the features of your speech with those listed by Nist as characteristic of your subdivision. How closely do they compare?

3   Select several members of your class to pronounce the following words: *car, wash, cot, caught, almond, horse, hurry, dog, class,* and *idea.* Can you identify the area and regional subdivision from which each one comes?

4   Read a portion of James Russell Lowell's *Biglow Papers* and/or Joel Chandler Harris' *Uncle Remus,* noting carefully the author's literary representation of dialect. Can you identify the regional subdivisions presented?

6

Dialect Distribution and Settlement Patterns in the Great Lakes Region

As Professor Shuy has indicated (pp. 344–349) settlement patterns serve as one explanation for the patterned distribution of American dialects. On the basis of data provided by the collections of the *Linguistic Atlas of the United States and Canada,* Alva Davis studies dialect distribution in the eastern United States and in the secondary settlement areas of the Great Lakes Region. He discovers many interesting correlations between the linguistic features and the settlement patterns of these regions.

Alva L. Davis

THE STUDY of dialect distribution in the eastern United States and in the secondary settlement areas of the Great Lakes Region has now reached a point where it is possible to show some interesting correlations between the linguistic features and the settlement patterns of these regions. It is simple, perhaps even obvious, to say that when large, homogeneous groups of people migrate to new territories, they take with them the speech patterns of their old communities and that these speech patterns will be gradually modified as various cultural influences are brought to bear on them. However, the validity of any correlation depends upon a solid foundation of extensive and painstaking research, rather than on generalities, and for this particular problem, such research materials are provided by the collections of the *Linguistic Atlas of the United States and Canada.*[1]

---

[1] This paper is limited to a discussion of Michigan, Ohio, Indiana, and Illinois. For an account of the Wisconsin data, see Frederic G. Cassidy, "Some New England Words in Wisconsin," *Language,* XVII (1941), 324–339. The name "Great Lakes Region" has been applied to this area.

Other articles based on *Atlas* field work in the region are Albert H. Marckwardt, "Folk Speech in Indiana and Adjacent States," *Indiana Historical Bulletin,* XVII (1940), 120–140; "Middle English o in the American English of the Great Lakes Area," *Papers of the Michigan Academy of Sciences, Arts, and Letters,* XXVI (1941), 56–71; "Middle English WA in the Speech of the Great Lakes Region," *American Speech,* XVII (1942), 226–254.

The *Linguistic Atlas,* which proposes to be a comprehensive survey of American English, was begun in 1931 under the directorship of Professor Hans Kurath, then at Brown University. In that year the first of the regional atlases, *The Linguistic Atlas of New England,* got under way. Upon completion of the records for New England, field work was extended to the Middle Atlantic and South Atlantic states and these records were finally completed during the spring of 1949. *The Linguistic Atlas of New England*[2] has been published, and the Middle Atlantic and South Atlantic materials are on file at the University of Michigan, where they are to be edited and prepared for publication.

The technique employed by the *Linguistic Atlas* is modeled upon the personal interview methods developed by European linguists. After a careful analysis of the geography and history of the region to be surveyed, the director of the project plots the communities for investigation. These communities are spaced so as to furnish a balanced sampling of speech forms in the area, the number of the communities varying with the complexity of the region. A trained phonetician then visits each community and interviews native speakers, asking several hundred standardized questions designed to bring out regional and social differences in dialect. Each interview requires about eight hours and is conducted in such a way that the informant uses his normal pronunciation, grammar, and vocabulary. According to the plan of the *Linguistic Atlas,* two speakers are chosen from each community, one a representative of the oldest generation with relatively little education, and another of the middle age group (ordinarily from fifty to sixty years old) with considerably more formal education and wider social contacts. Occasionally college educated informants are interviewed to represent the cultured speech of the area. In the eastern states—from Maine to Florida—over 1,600 field interviews have been completed. The geographical spacing of the communities permits the plotting of the informants' responses on maps so that regional dissemination of speech forms can be related to topographical, historical, and cultural influences. By using informants from different age groups and from varying social backgrounds much useful data can be obtained about innovation, obsolescence, and prestige values of speech forms.

Since 1937 *The Linguistic Atlas of the North Central States,* under the supervision of Professor Albert H. Marckwardt of the University of Michigan, has been making steady progress.[3] Work in this region was

---

[2] Hans Kurath, ed. (6 vols., Providence, 1939–43).

[3] This atlas includes the five states named above (footnote 1) plus Kentucky. The research in this area has been made possible by grants from the Rackham Foundation of the University of Michigan, from the University of Illinois, University of Wisconsin, Western Reserve University, Ohio State University, and the Ohio State Archaeological and Historical Society.

begun with an exploratory survey of Ohio, Indiana, Illinois, Wisconsin, and Michigan, limited to ten field records in each state. This initial survey was completed in 1940 and the project was then expanded to cover from fifty to seventy records per state. The additional field work has already been done in Wisconsin and Michigan and is currently being carried on in Illinois and Ohio.

The historical background for dialect distribution in the Great Lakes Region is well known. The settlement patterns for Ohio, Indiana, Illinois, and Michigan are easily traced, partly because the region is new, comparatively speaking, and partly because a wealth of information on the subject is available.[4] Three main streams of migration entered the area. The southernmost and earliest of these used the Ohio River system and peopled the lands within easy reach of the river and its tributaries. This group of settlers was for the most part from the Middle Atlantic states and the hill regions of the old slave states. In the north the important avenue of approach was the Great Lakes. Although some New Englanders, following Moses Cleaveland's party of 1796, had settled in the Connecticut Western Reserve, the opening of the Erie Canal in 1825 started the great land rush into that area, made up principally of Yankees from New York state. This migration, which reached its peak in the 1840's and 1850's, completed the settlement of the Ohio counties bordering Lake Erie and filled up most of Michigan and northern Illinois. The third general migration was the overland movement, especially along the National Road. The Conestoga wagon carried Pennsylvanians into Ohio and westward, and Buckeyes and Hoosiers themselves joined in this search for cheap land.

Within the Great Lakes Region are two important small areas distinctive in the composition of their population: in southeastern Ohio, the Marietta colony, founded in 1788 by the Ohio Company, from Massachusetts, and in northwestern Illinois, the Lead Region settled in the 1820's by miners from all parts of the country.[5]

Even though much field work is still to be done in the Great Lakes Region, the present data is adequate for a preliminary comparison to the Eastern findings. The handiest material for such a comparison is

---

[4] Information concerning settlement is available in such works as Frederic L. Paxson, *History of the American Frontier 1763–1893* (Boston, 1924); Lois K. Mathews, *The Expansion of New England* (Boston, 1909); Beverley W. Bond, Jr., *The Foundations of Ohio* (*History of the State of Ohio*, edited by Carl Wittke, I, Columbus, 1942); Solon J. Buck, *Illinois in 1818* (Springfield, 1917). Tables I and VII, *U.S. Census, 1870: Population*, are of great value for determining the geographical extent of these settlements.

[5] The Lead Region also includes southwestern Wisconsin. See Cassidy, *loc. cit.*, 326. Foreign population settlements, such as that at Holland, Michigan, may be of importance but our present data shows little permanent influence on American English in this area.

the folk vocabulary, the everyday words of life around the house and farm.

On the basis of the vocabulary variants of the Eastern *Atlas* records, Professor Kurath has discovered three main dialect areas,[6] differing considerably from the traditional three-fold Eastern, Southern, and General American classification.[7] The Eastern records show a Northern area including New England, New York, the northern half of New Jersey and approximately the northern quarter of Pennsylvania; a Midland area including the rest of Pennsylvania and New Jersey, parts of Delaware and Maryland, and the mountainous South, beginning at the Blue Ridge; and a Southern area consisting of the coastal South from Delaware to Florida.

None of these areas is completely uniform, but divided into several subareas. The North is composed of Eastern New England (roughly from the Connecticut River) Western New England and Upstate New York, the Hudson Valley, and metropolitan New York. The Midland may be divided conveniently into two large subareas: North Midland for most of Pennsylvania and northern West Virginia, and South Midland for the speech of the mountain area to the south. The South (identified most easily by loss of post-vocalic *r*) contains many subareas, many of them centering around such cities as Richmond, Charleston, and Savannah.

The general patterns which folk terms make in the Great Lakes Region are shown on the accompanying map.[8] The "Yankee" settlement is consistent in using Northern words, and the area to the south of it is almost without exception Midland. Between the two major areas, some smaller transition areas of mixed usage occur.[9] The Lead Region of northwestern Illinois reflects its different settlement history by the retention of many Midland forms, and the Marietta region retains many Yankeeisms.[10]

The following words, arranged according to their Eastern distribu-

---

[6] A *Word Geography of the Eastern United States* (Ann Arbor, 1949). This work gives a detailed explanation of the Eastern areas, with helpful maps.

[7] George Philip Krapp, *The English Language in America* (2 vols., New York, 1925), I, 35–42.

[8] The atlas records have been augmented by a correspondence questionnaire given to 233 informants in these four states. See Alva L. Davis, A Word Atlas of the Great Lakes Region (unpublished doctoral dissertation, University of Michigan, 1948). It should be noted that most of the information thus far obtained is from the older age group.

[9] Raven I. McDavid, Jr. and Alva L. Davis, "Northwestern Ohio: a Transition Area," *Language*, XXVI (1950), 264–273, is a preliminary study of one of these areas.

[10] Among the Yankee terms in the Marietta area are *pail, swill, dutch cheese, boss!,* and *angleworm.* In the Lead Region are found *roasting ears, sook!,* and *fishworm.*

small areas indicate
mixed usage

Dialect Areas in the Great Lakes Region

tions, may be used to demonstrate the folk vocabulary differences in the Great Lakes Region:

NORTHERN WORDS

A. GENERAL NORTH:
  pail; swill, 'food for hogs'; *comforter,* 'tied quilt'; *johnnycake; whiffletree; boss!,* 'call to cows'; *angleworm; (devil's) darning needle,* 'dragonfly'; *sick to his stomach*

B. HUDSON VALLEY:
  stoop, 'small porch'; *sugar bush,* 'sugar maple grove'; *coal scuttle*

C. THE NORTH EXCEPT THE HUDSON VALLEY:
  spider, 'cast-iron frying pan'; *dutch cheese,* 'cottage cheese'; *fills,* 'shafts of a buggy'; *nan(nie)!* and *co-day!,* 'calls to sheep'; *curtains,* 'roller shades'; *scaffold,* 'improvised platform for hay'; *rowen,* 'second crop of hay'

D. WESTERN NEW ENGLAND AND UPSTATE NEW YORK:
  fried-cakes, 'baking powder doughnuts'; *loppered milk,* 'thick, sour milk'; *hard maple,* 'sugar maple tree'

This group of words, as a whole, is limited to northern Ohio, Michigan and northern Illinois, with rare instances in the Midland area. Those words restricted to subareas of the East—as in B, C, D—do not make any definite geographical patterns within the Great Lakes Northern area, though further research may show that some new subareas are to be set up.[11] Most conspicuous is the fact that many of these words are becoming old-fashioned, being supplanted by words of wider regional and national usage, or being forgotten with changes in customs. *Johnnycake* is a childhood memory for many speakers, *dutch cheese* and *fried-cakes* are now *cottage cheese* and *doughnuts* most commonly, the *whiffletree* (sometimes *whippletree*) and the *fills* (or *thills*) are of little use in a tractor and automobile age, the old *spider* is likely to be an aluminum frying pan, and the more fashionable term *window shades* is taking the place of *curtains.* Rarest on this list are *scaffold, rowen,* and *loppered milk* (sometimes *lobbered milk*): the general terms are *loft* or *mow*—the improvised platform is now a permanent structure in the modern barn—*second cutting,* and *sour milk.*

MIDLAND WORDS

A. GENERAL MIDLAND:
  quarter till (eleven); blinds, 'roller shades'; *skillet; dip,* 'sweet sauce for pudding'; *sook!,* 'call to cows'; *sheepy!; fish(ing) worm; snake feeder,* 'dragonfly'; *poison vine,* 'poison ivy'; *belling,* 'noisy celebration after a wedding'

[11] *Sewing needle,* 'dragonfly,' for example, is current in the Upper Peninsula of Michigan and in the Duluth area of Minnesota.

B. NORTH MIDLAND:
    spouting, 'guttering at edges of roof'; *smearcase*, 'cottage cheese'; *hay doodles*, 'small piles of hay in the field'; *sugar camp*, 'sugar maple grove'; *baby buggy*

C. SOUTH MIDLAND:
    fire board, 'mantlepiece'; *clabbered milk*, 'thick, sour milk'; *trestle*, 'implement to hold planks for sawing'

D. SOUTH MIDLAND AND SOUTH:
    evening, 'afternoon'; *light-bread*, 'white bread'; *clabbered cheese*, 'cottage cheese'; *hay shocks*, 'small piles of hay in the field'; *nicker*, 'noise made by horse at feeding time'

E. MIDLAND AND SOUTH:
    dog irons, 'andirons'; *bucket*; *slop*, 'food for hogs'; *comfort*, 'tied quilt'; *pully bone*, 'wishbone'; *corn pone*, 'corn bread'; *cherry seed*; *butter beans*, 'lima beans'; *roasting ears*, 'corn-on-the-cob'; *singletree*; *polecat*; *granny woman*, 'midwife'; *Christmas gift!*, 'familiar greeting at Christmas time'
    NOTE—No terms limited to the South are common in this region.

The General Midland words are in common use in the Ohio Valley, though *poison vine* is obsolescent, and *blinds* may be. *Belling* is now common only in Ohio and scatteringly in northern Indiana and southern Michigan; it has been replaced in most of the area by *shivaree*, the most common term in the Middle West.[12]

The North Midland contains many expressions which are common only in Ohio; some of them have spread into Indiana (especially the northern part of the state), and occasionally they are found in Illinois. *Spouting* is restricted to Ohio, *hay doodle* is old-fashioned in Ohio and Indiana and very rare in Illinois, *sugar camp* is most common in Ohio and Indiana, and *smearcase* is common in Ohio, Indiana, and most of Illinois (*clabbered cheese* is fairly common in southern Illinois and Indiana). These North Midland words as a group form an irregular wedge-like pattern: generally current in Ohio, occasional in Indiana, and rare in Illinois. The Upper Ohio Valley may be the home of *baby buggy*, which is now the most usual of the words for the perambulator in all of the Great Lakes Region. It is, of course, a trade term, and therefore little affected by settlement patterns. The *Dictionary of American English* gives 1852 as the first date for *baby wagon*, the earliest of the terms.

The South Midland has few terms of its own; in vocabulary it seems to be a transition zone between the North Midland and the South. Words typical of the region are those listed, along with *sugar orchard*; *ridy horse*, 'seesaw'; *pack*, 'carry'; and *favor*, 'resemble.' None of these

[12] See McDavid and Davis, " 'Shivaree': an Example of Cultural Diffusion," *American Speech*, XXIV (1949), 249–255.

words is especially common in this region, but they are most frequent in the southern portion.

Words common to large parts of the South and the South Midland are well represented in the Great Lakes Midland and for this reason these terms have been included with the Midland group. They seem to be slightly less common in Ohio than in Indiana and Illinois, further differentiating these subareas. *Light-bread*, for example, is only fairly common in Ohio, but is the prevailing term of southern Indiana and southern Illinois. *Nicker* has probably spread from the Virginia Piedmont; it is common in the entire Great Lakes Midland, even spreading into southern Michigan.

The words shared by the Midland and the South are also well distributed in the Great Lakes Midland, but many are becoming old-fashioned. *Dog irons* become the modern 'andirons,' *corn pone*, like Northern *johnnycake*, has yielded to store-bought bread, the general term *skunk* occurs alongside *polecat*, and few communities have a *granny woman* to deliver the babies. *Christmas gift!*, usually a children's greeting, is rather rare in the region, but information is not sufficient to tell whether it was ever more widely used here.

The evidence of regional differentiation shows, in this comparison, surprisingly little disturbance of the "expected" dialect patterns, in spite of the steady leveling influences of national advertising, ease in transportation with its resultant mobility of population, intermarriage, and changes in modes of living. These influences have tended to blur some regional differences, but the vocabulary of everyday usage is so extremely conservative that there is far from complete uniformity. As yet there is no indication that trade and culture centers have developed distinctive dialect areas as has happened in the case of Boston and some Southern cities.[13] The dialect information makes, instead, a faithful reconstruction of the settlement patterns. The significance of this historical comparison, even in its present incompleteness, is that speech habits are brought into the realm of historical fact—the usage of the word *spider*, for example, becomes as real as the use of the Cape Cod lighter or the hip-roofed barn.

FOR DISCUSSION AND REVIEW

1 What use did Davis make of the Linguistic Atlas materials available?
2 Discuss the possible influences of physical geography on the settlement pattern and dialect distribution in the Great Lakes Region. You may find it helpful to return to the Shuy article (p. 344) and to con-

---

[13] *Tonic*, 'soda-pop,' is one of the terms current in the Boston trade area. The prestige of Boston pronunciation is well known.

sult the maps on pages 375 and 381.

3 In his conclusion, Davis notes that he found "surprisingly little disturbance of the 'expected' dialect patterns, in spite of the steady leveling influences." Discuss the influences that national advertising, radio, television, and improved methods of transportation have had upon dialect.

7

Cultural Levels and Functional Varieties of English

John S. Kenyon

Professor Kenyon, seeing the need to distinguish levels and varieties of American English, presents a classification of language which recognizes two distinct categories: *cultural levels* and *functional varieties*. In this excerpt from "Cultural Levels and Functional Varieties of English," he discusses, first, levels which have cultural or social associations, and, second, formal and familiar varieties of language usage. Reflect on your own experiences with language while reading this article. How helpful do you find Kenyon's classification?

T HE WORD *level,* when used to indicate different styles of language, is a metaphor, suggesting higher or lower position and, like the terms *higher* and *lower,* figuratively implies 'better' or 'worse,' 'more desirable' or 'less desirable,' and similar comparative degrees of excellence or inferiority in language.

The application of the term *level* to those different styles of language that are not properly distinguished as better or worse, desirable or undesirable, creates a false impression. I confess myself guilty of this error along with some other writers. What are frequently grouped together in one class as different levels of language are often in reality false combinations of two distinct and incommensurable categories, namely, *cultural levels* and *functional varieties.*

Among *cultural levels* may be included, on the lower levels, illiterate speech, narrowly local dialect, ungrammatical speech and writing, excessive and unskillful slang, slovenly and careless vocabulary and construction, exceptional pronunciation, and, on the higher level, language used generally by the cultivated, clear, grammatical writing, and pronunciations used by the cultivated over wide areas. The different cultural levels may be summarized in the two general classes *substandard* and *standard*.

Among *functional varieties* not depending on cultural levels may be mentioned colloquial language, itself existing in different degrees of familiarity or formality, as, for example, familiar conversation, private correspondence, formal conversation, familiar public address; formal platform or pulpit speech, public reading, public worship; legal, scientific, and other expository writing; prose and poetic belles-lettres. The different functional varieties may roughly be grouped together in the two classes *familiar* and *formal* writing or speaking.

The term *level*, then, does not properly belong at all to functional varieties of speech—colloquial, familiar, formal, scientific, literary language. They are equally "good" for their respective functions, and as classifications do not depend on the cultural status of the users.

The two groupings *cultural levels* and *functional varieties* are not mutually exclusive categories. They are based on entirely separate principles of classification: *culture* and *function*. Although we are here principally concerned with the functional varieties of standard English (the highest cultural level), yet substandard English likewise has its functional varieties for its different occasions and purposes. Thus the functional variety colloquial English may occur on a substandard cultural level, but the term *colloquial* does not itself designate a cultural level. So the functional variety formal writing or speaking may occur on a lower or on a higher cultural level according to the social status of writer or speaker, and sometimes of reader or audience. It follows, for instance, that the colloquial language of cultivated people is on a higher cultural level than the formal speech of the semiliterate or than some inept literary writing. . . .

The term *colloquial* cannot properly designate a substandard cultural level of English. It designates a functional variety—that used chiefly in conversation—and in itself says nothing as to its cultural level, though this discussion, and the dictionary definitions, are chiefly concerned with cultivated colloquial, a functional variety of standard English. When writers of . . . standing slip into expressions that imply lower cultural status of colloquial English, it is not surprising that some teachers fall into the error. One teacher expressed the conviction that colloquialisms should not be represented as standard American speech. But the context of the statement indicated that its author was using *colloquialism* in the sense of 'localism.' I could hardly believe how frequent this gross error is, until I heard it from a well-known American broadcaster.

The best dictionaries, at least in their definitions, give no warrant for the various misuses of *colloquial, colloquially, colloquialism, colloquiality*. I urge the reader to study carefully the definitions in the *Oxford English Dictionary*, with its many apt examples from standard writers, and in *Webster's New International Dictionary, Second Edition*, with its quotations from George Lyman Kittredge. Kittredge's views on the standing of colloquial English are well known. It is said that somebody once asked him about the meaning of the label "Colloq." in dictionaries. He is reported to have replied, "I myself speak 'colloke' and often write it." I cannot verify the story, but it sounds authentic.

It seems to me inevitable that the frequent groupings of so-called "levels" such as "Literary, Colloquial, Illiterate," and the like, will lead the reader to suppose that just as Illiterate is culturally below Colloquial, so Colloquial is culturally below Literary. While I can scarcely hope that my humble remonstrance will reform all future writing on "levels of English," I believe that writers who confuse the meaning of the term *level* must accept some part of the responsibility for the popular misunderstanding of the true status of colloquial English; for I cannot avoid the belief that the popular idea of colloquial English as something to be looked down upon with disfavor is due in part to the failure of writers on the subject to distinguish between *cultural levels of English* and *functional varieties of standard English*.

FOR DISCUSSION AND REVIEW

1 What distinction does Kenyon draw between the words *level* and *variety*?

2 According to Kenyon, what are the problems connected with the misuse of the word *level*?

3 Why does Kenyon maintain that colloquial language is a functional variety and not a cultural level?

4 As Kenyon suggests, study the definitions of *colloquial, colloquially, colloquialism*, and *colloquiality* in the *Oxford English Dictionary* and *Webster's New International Dictionary, Second Edition*. Compare the definitions you find with the definitions in a recently published dictionary. What differences do you note?

5 Imagine that you just received a traffic ticket for speeding. How would you describe the incident to your roommate, to your parents, to the judge? Compare the functional varieties of English found in your descriptions.

6 Can you improve upon Kenyon's classifications? Explain the rationale of your improvements.

8

Another Look
at Kenyon's
Levels

In this article, Professor J. J. Lamberts of Arizona State University reassesses John Kenyon's classification of cultural levels and functional varieties of English (pp. 385–387). He feels that Kenyon's categories and terminology greatly oversimplify the complex issue of English usage. Review the major points made by Kenyon before reading Lamberts' rejoinder.

J. J. Lamberts

Among the enduring preoccupations of language scholars has been the search for a formula by which it will be possible to reduce to order the vast and chaotic realm of English usage. Call it what you will, what we are after is a set of reasonably tidy rules or generalizations.

There are two ways of producing these. We may impose a prearranged order upon the language from the outside, or we may attempt to derive a pattern of regularity from the language itself. The first approach is familiar as the one that captured the imaginations of many eighteenth century grammarians and which was implemented in their efforts to reduce the language to rule. The same attitude continues to dominate much of our classroom instruction, to say nothing of popular folklore with respect to good and bad English.

The alternative to this has been formulated in several ways. Its advocates maintain that usage cannot be legislated, nevertheless it possesses a certain degree of regularity which we can discern if we look earnestly and intelligently. This idea received what was doubtless its most heartening encouragement during the 1920's when a number of investigators converged almost simultaneously upon the concept of "levels of usage." Here at last was an interpretation which could convincingly set at naught the assumption that some words are inherently good and others inherently bad. Language differences were simply to be correlated with social differences and these could presumably be studied as purely objective data.

In the brief, the levels of usage doctrine asserted that linguistic acceptability and social acceptability go hand in hand, and vice versa, to be sure. People had spoken about social classes for hundreds of years; now here was the same thing in language. One wonders, as a matter of fact, why it took so long for anyone to stumble on so obvious a relation. We speak of social levels, and it follows clearly that there must be levels of usage. These levels were identified at once. "Standard" usage ranked at the top, "substandard" at the bottom and between these extremes a shadowy middle ground that went by several names. The most elaborate specification of this view presently appeared in C. C. Fries *American English Grammar* in which the three levels of usage were derived from three social levels. "Standard" English was equated with the language of people engaged in the professions; "common" English with that of persons employed in the service occupations; "vulgar" English with the language of those doing unskilled labor. With minor modifications here and there the levels concept now went into the textbooks, having achieved the status of dogma.

The levels theory, however, incorporated two basic difficulties. The first was its assumption that American society is stratified like the society of a typical West European country into fairly clear class divisions. England has its aristocracy, and this aristocracy has its characteristic speech, as Nancy Mitford indicated several years ago (1956) in a little book called *Noblesse Oblige*. It has also a middle class and these people speak middle-class English. Finally, it has a laboring class with a typical manner of speaking. By contrast America has neither a hereditary aristocracy nor a hereditary peasantry. In a few generations the descendant of an immigrant laborer can be President of the United States and can speak middle-class English. Finally, it has a laboring class with a typical class society, we do better to think of it as a status society. The absence of any clear class structure in this country explains why no one has been able to isolate a characteristic middle-class speech, and why the investigators have been frustrated in trying to fit in designations like "common" or "colloquial" or "informal" or some such thing.

The other difficulty is closely related to this one and it was pointed out by John S. Kenyon a dozen or more years ago.[1] It is simply that language differences are not so much distinctions in level as in function. When we apply terms like "formal" or "informal" or "colloquial" or "technical" or any one of scores of others, we are actually dealing with functional varieties. These are quite independent of levels of usage.

Identifying functional varieties for what they were explained a good deal that had been obscure, but there remained some contrasting types of usage which did not fit any such category and Kenyon called them cultural levels. In these, it was apparent, some reference had to be made to social standing. To avoid being caught in the trap that had

---

[1] "Levels of Speech and Colloquial English," *The English Journal*, 37 (January 1948), 25–31; "Cultural Levels and Functional Varieties of English," *College English*, 10 (October 1948), 31–36.

plagued his predecessors, Kenyon confined himself to two levels and these he identified as "standard" and "substandard." Some of the more recent textbooks have also followed this shift in dogma and speak of only two levels.

What gives the entire usage problem significance, of course, is the tendency of users of the language to react unfavorably toward certain expressions. More specifically, we say that in one way or another speakers of standard English disapprove of the language of speakers of substandard English. In other words, an unguarded use of the latter will certainly bar a person from certain coveted employments, and will further exclude him from other social privileges. For this reason the schools are committed to teach standard English. Every boy and girl is to have an equal opportunity to make good.

Having said this much, I should like now to examine more closely the entire notion of levels as a device for explaining the vagaries of English usage. The concept of functional varieties has accounted for many of the differences and it has done so quite accurately; but to assume that everything else can be explained in reference to two social levels, one superior and the other inferior, seems to me an oversimplification.

Suppose we look briefly at three quite typical reactions toward certain usage situations. The first is described in an article by J. M. Steadman, Jr.[2] which appeared in *American Speech*. Apart from Steadman's comments, it consisted of a list of expressions which students at Emory University had regarded as affected and for that reason objectionable. First on the list was *limb* in the sense of "leg." This was followed in order by *It is I* and *retire* (go to bed). Then came *elegant, expectorate, cease, prevaricate, cinema, deceased, ablutions, conflagration, domicile, one* (as indefinite pronoun), *whom, anybody's else, arise, commence, dine, erudite, mortician,* and *piazza*.

The second appeared in an article by Norman Lewis in *Harpers*.[3] There is no need to summarize the article; let me simply quote a comment on the word *whom*, offered by Kyle Crichton, who was at the time associate editor of *Colliers*. Said Crichton: "The most loathsome word (to me, at least) in the English language is 'whom.' You can always tell a half-educated buffoon by the care he takes in working the word in. When he starts it I know I am faced with a pompous illiterate who is not going to have me long as company."

And now a personal experience. Some time ago I was visiting a friend, a man who had never gone beyond the eighth grade in school and who was employed as a welder in a factory. The generator in my

---

[2] "Affected and Effeminate Words," *American Speech*, 136 (February 1938), 13–18.
[3] "How Correct Must Correct English Be?" *Harpers*, 198 (March 1949), 68–79.

Chevrolet was about to give out, so at my friend's suggestion I decided to call an auto wrecker to see what used parts he might have. I had already dialed the telephone number when my friend reached over, took the phone out of my hand with these words: "Here, Doc; let me talk to him. The way you talk costs you money."

In each of these three situations we have one person consciously disapproving of the language habits of another person, not because they are too crude—as we commonly expect—but because they are too precious. Crichton and the college students objected to *whom*, which for many people is the very touchstone of refinement. My none-too-literate friend apparently found the whole package of my speech abominable.

Here we have more than a mere disapproval. Our reaction to most substandard usages is essentially passive. We may not like them, but it would never occur to us to make remarks about them. It is only the exceptional usage, the one that troubles us tremendously, that calls forth any kind of comment. The fact then that in each of these three cases the respondents were so articulate suggests what we seem to have overlooked, namely, that hearers and readers become greatly involved in these expressions. Evidently these precious usages are capable of generating more powerful rejections than we had supposed.

Over against standard English, Kenyon proposed simply a substandard level, in other words, a type of language we reject as being too crude, or as reflecting a general poverty of cultivated influences. Let me propose another level, this time not too crude, but too affected or too refined, that is to say, "hyperstandard." It does not indicate a lack of culture so much as the wrong kind of culture. A person can fall flat on his face, but he can also bend over too far backward.

All of this means that we have three levels again: hyperstandard, standard, and substandard. To lump the two extremes into a single category, nonstandard, ignores some significant attitudes toward usage.

Are we possibly begging the question when we call these "levels"? The only connection in which the term "level" makes any sense is when it has been tied to social differences, specifically social levels. Substandard usage we like to associate with substandard social conditions, and yet one can push the association too far. When we endeavor to determine social status by means of language, we are obviously arguing in a circle.

The real difficulty with these categories is their utter disregard for logic, plus their curious way of overlapping each other. One man's standard is another's substandard. Conversely, one man's standard is another's hyperstandard. This produces a very real problem in our schools. We have all heard tales of illiterate or semi-illiterate parents who belabored their children for refusing to say *ain't* and *it don't* and *can't hardly*. To such parents *isn't* and *it doesn't* and *can hardly* sound affected and therefore offensive. We may compare our own reactions to phrases like *I feel badly* or *None of the parents is here* or *It was a question of whom was to be in charge*. To make it even more pointed, what would we do if a teacher indicated that our preference for *I feel bad* or *None of the parents are here* or *It was a question of who was to be in charge* betrayed us as persons of dull sensibilities and limited taste. In other words, the reason many people refuse to adopt standard usages instead of substandard usages may not be cussedness or stupidity, but the uncomfortable feeling that some hyperstandard forms are being foisted on them.

Possibly instead of "level" we should speak of "quality" or "type." The distinctions are, after all, qualitative rather than geometrical.

When the linguists of the 1920's set up their three-part division of usage distinctions, they were playing a worthy hunch. They realized evidently that the differences were more complex than a mere contrast between acceptability and inacceptability. But they appear to have felt, and reasonably so, that their own language was best, and should therefore be standard.

I am not sure that the recognition of this organization of usage structure is going to make our problems any easier. But it should make our handling of them more realistic. These many years we have been busy trying to construct a ceiling over crudity as we belabored substandard usages. Possibly it is time to begin building a floor under preciosity too. As a matter of fact, maybe we should measure the house once more and determine the exact location of the ceiling and the floor.

FOR DISCUSSION AND REVIEW

1 According to Lamberts, how was the "assumption that some words are inherently good and others inherently bad" refuted?

2 Why does Lamberts prefer to think of America as having a "status society" as opposed to a "class society"?

3 What are the two basic difficulties with the levels theory cited by Lamberts?

4 With what aspect of Kenyon's classification does Lamberts find fault? Why? What suggestion does he offer to improve Kenyon's system?

5 List several of the words that Lamberts cites as being "too precious." What exactly does Lamberts mean by the word *precious*? Discuss with other members of the class "precious" words that you find particularly irritating.

9

The Study of Nonstandard English

William Labov

Professor Labov is well known for his studies of New York City speech, especially Negro speech. In this selection, he argues for the need to study nonstandard dialect, explains some of its distinguishing characteristics, and discusses the relationship between nonstandard dialect and standard English. In other studies, Labov advocates functional bidialectalism for speakers of a nonstandard dialect. He urges Negroes to learn standard English because of its value for coping with social situations and operating in the business world.

Three Reasons for Studying Nonstandard Language

SINCE LANGUAGE learning does take place outside of the classroom, and the six-year-old child does have great capacity for learning new language forms as he is exposed to them, it may be asked why it should be necessary for the teacher to understand more about the child's own vernacular. First, we can observe that automatic adjustment does *not* take place in all cases. Even the successful middle class student does not always master the teacher's grammatical forms; and in the urban ghettos we find very little adjustment to school forms. Students continue to write I *have live* after ten or twelve years in school; we will describe below failures in reading the -*ed* suffix which show no advance with years in school. Second, knowledge of the underlying structure of the nonstandard vernacular will allow the most efficient teaching. If the teacher knows the general difference between standard negative attraction and nonstandard negative concord, he can teach a hundred different standard forms with the simple instruction: *The negative is attracted only to the first indefinite.* Thus by this one rule we can make many corrections:

He don't know nothing	⟶	He doesn't know anything
Nobody don't like him	⟶	Nobody likes him
Nobody hardly goes there	⟶	Hardly anybody goes there
Can't nobody do it	⟶	Nobody can do it

Third, the vernacular must be understood because ignorance of it leads to serious conflict between student and teacher. Teachers in ghetto schools who continually insist that *i* and *e* sound different in *pin* and *pen* will only antagonize a great number of their students. The knowledge that *i* and *e* actually sound the same before *m* and *n* for most of their students (and "should" sound the same if they are normal speakers) will help avoid this destructive conflict. Teachers who insist that a child meant to say *He is tired* when he said *He tired* will achieve only bewilderment in the long run. Knowledge that *He tired* is the vernacular equivalent of the contracted form *He's tired* will save teacher and student from this frustration.

Granted that the teacher wishes to learn about the student's language, what methods are available for him to do so? Today, a great many linguists study English through their own intuitions; they operate "out of their own heads" in the sense that they believe they can ask and answer all the relevant questions themselves. But even if a teacher comes from the same background as his students, he will find that his grammar has changed, that he no longer has firm intuitions about whether he can say *Nobody don't know nothing about it* instead of *Nobody knows nothing about it*. He can of course sit down with a student and ask him all kinds of direct questions about his language, and there are linguists who do this. But one cannot draw directly upon the intuitions of the two major groups we are interested in, children and nonstandard speakers. Both are in contact with a superordinate or dominant dialect, and both will provide answers which reflect their awareness of this dialect as much as of their own. One can of course engage in long and indirect conversations with students, hoping that all of the forms of interest will sooner or later occur, and there are linguists who have attempted to study nonstandard dialects in this way. But these conversations usually teach the subject more of the investigator's language than the other way around. In general, one can say that whenever a speaker of a nonstandard dialect is in a subordinate position to a speaker of a standard dialect, the rules of his grammar will shift in an unpredictable manner towards the standard. The longer the contact, the stronger and more lasting is the shift. Thus adolescent speakers of a vernacular make very unreliable informants when they are questioned in a formal framework. The investigator must show considerable sociolinguistic sophistication to cope with such a situation, and indeed the teacher will also need to know a great deal about the social forces which affect linguistic behavior if he is to interpret his students' language.

Nonstandard Dialects as "Self-Contained" Systems

The traditional view of nonstandard speech as a set of isolated deviations from standard English is often countered by the opposite view:

that nonstandard dialect should be studied as an isolated system in its own right, without any reference to standard English. It is argued that the system of grammatical forms of a dialect can only be understood through their internal relations. For example, nonstandard Negro English has one distinction which standard English does not have: there is an invariant form *be* in *He always be foolin' around* which marks habitual, general conditions, as opposed to the unmarked *is, am, are,* etc., which do not have any such special sense. It can be argued that the existence of this distinction changes the value of all other members of the grammatical system and that the entire paradigm of this dialect is therefore different from that of standard English. It is indeed important to find such relations within the meaningful set of grammatical distinctions, if they exist, because we can then *explain* rather than merely describe behavior. There are many co-occurrence rules which are purely descriptive—the particular dialect just happens to have X' *and* Y' where another has X and Y. We would like to know if a special nonstandard form X' *requires* an equally nonstandard Y' because of the way in which the nonstandard form cuts up the entire field of meaning. This would be a tremendous help in teaching, since we would be able to show what sets of standard rules have to be taught together to avoid confusing the student with a mixed, incoherent grammatical system.

The difficulty here is that linguistics has not made very much progress in the analysis of semantic systems. There is no method or procedure which leads to reliable or reproducible results—not even among those who agree on certain principles of grammatical theory. No one has yet written a complete grammar of a language—or even come close to accounting for all the morphological and syntactic rules of a language. And the situation is much more primitive in semantics; for example, the verbal system of standard English has been studied now for many centuries, yet there is no agreement at all on the meaning of the auxiliaries *have . . . ed* and *be . . . ing.* The meaning of *I have lived here,* as opposed to *I lived here,* has been explained as a) relevant to the present, b) past *in* the present, c) perfective, d) indefinite, e) causative, and so on. It is not only that there are many views; it is that in any given discussion no linguist has really found a method by which he can reasonably hope to persuade others that he is right. If this situation prevails where most of the investigators have complete access to the data, since they are native speakers of standard English, we must be more than cautious in claiming to understand the meaning of *I be here* as opposed to *I am here* in nonstandard Negro English, and even more cautious in claiming that the meaning of nonstandard *I'm here* therefore differs from standard *I'm here* because of the existence of the other form. Most teachers have learned to be cautious in accepting a grammarian's statement about the meaning of their own native forms, but they have no way of judging statements made about a dialect which they do not speak, and they are naturally prone to accept such statements on the authority of the writer.

There is, however, a great deal that we can do to show the internal relations in the nonstandard dialect as a system. There are a great many forms which seem different on the surface but can be explained as expressions of a single rule, or the absence of a single rule. We observe that in nonstandard Negro English it is common to say *a apple* rather than *an apple*. This is a grammatical fault from the point of view of standard speakers, and the school must teach *an apple* as the written, standard form. There is also a rather low-level, unimportant feature of pronunciation which is common to southern dialects: in *the apple*, the word *the* has the same pronunciation as in *the book* and does not rhyme with *be*. Finally, we can note that, in the South, educated white speakers keep the vocalic schwa which represents *r* in *four*, but nonstandard speakers tend to drop it (registered in dialect writing as *fo' o'clock*). When all these facts are put together, we can begin to explain the nonstandard *a apple* as part of a much broader pattern. There is a general rule of English which states that we do not pronounce two (phonetic) vowels in succession. Some kind of semi-consonantal glide or consonant comes in between: an *n* as in *an apple*, a "*y*" as in *the apple*, an *r* as in *four apples*. In each of these cases, this rule is not followed for nonstandard Negro English. A teacher may have more success in getting students to write *an apple* if he presents this general rule and connects up all of these things into a single rational pattern, even if some are not important in themselves. It will "make sense" to Negro speakers, since they do not drop *l* before a vowel, and many rules of their sound system show the effect of a following vowel.

There are many ways in which an understanding of the fundamental rules of the dialect will help to explain the surface facts. Some of the rules cited above are also important in explaining why nonstandard Negro speakers sometimes delete *is*, in *He is ready*, but almost always delete *are*, in *You are ready*; or why they say *they book* and *you book* but not *we book*. It does not always follow, though, that a grammatical explanation reveals the best method for teaching standard English.

Systematic analysis may also be helpful in connecting up the nonstandard form with the corresponding standard form and in this sense understanding the meaning of the nonstandard form. For example, nonstandard speakers say *Ain't nobody see it*. What is the nearest standard equivalent? We can connect this up with the standard negative "foregrounding" of *Scarcely did anybody see it* or, even more clearly, the literary expression *Nor did anybody see it*. This foregrounding fits in with the general colloquial southern pattern with indefinite subjects:

Didn't anybody see it, nonstandard *Didn't nobody see it*. In these cases, the auxiliary *didn't* is brought to the front of the sentence, like the *ain't* in the nonstandard sentence. But there is another possibility. We could connect up *Ain't nobody see it* with the sentence *It ain't nobody see it*, that is, "There isn't anybody who sees it"; the dummy *it* of nonstandard Negro English corresponds to standard *there*, and, like *there*, it can be dropped in casual speech. Such an explanation is the only one possible in the case of such nonstandard sentences as *Ain't nothin' went down*. This could not be derived from **Nothin' ain't went down*, a sentence type which never occurs. If someone uses one of these forms, it is important for the teacher to know what was intended, so that he can supply the standard equivalent. To do so, one must know a great deal about many underlying rules of the nonstandard dialect, and also a great deal about the rules of English in general.

Nonstandard English as a Close Relative of Standard English

Differences between standard and nonstandard English are not as sharp as our first impressions would lead us to think. Consider, for example, the socially stratified marker of "pronominal apposition"—the use of a dependent pronoun in such sentences as

My oldest sister she worked at the bank.

Though most of us recognize this as a nonstandard pattern, it is not always realized that the "nonstandard" aspect is merely a slight difference in intonation. A standard speaker frequently says the same thing, with a slight break after the subject: *My oldest sister—she works at the bank, and she finds it very profitable*. There are many ways in which a greater awareness of the standard colloquial forms would help teachers interpret the nonstandard forms. Not only do standard speakers use pronominal apposition with the break noted above, but in casual speech they can also bring object noun phrases to the front, "foregrounding" them. For example, one can say

My oldest sister—she worked at the Citizens Bank in Passaic last year.
The Citizens Bank, in Passaic—my oldest sister worked there last year.
Passaic—my oldest sister worked at the Citizens Bank there last year.

Note that if the foregrounded noun phrase represents a locative—the "place where"—then its position is held by *there*, just as the persons are represented by pronouns. If we are dealing with a time element, it can be foregrounded without replacement in any dialect: *Last year, my oldest sister worked at the Citizens Bank in Passaic.*

It is most important for the teacher to understand the relation between standard and nonstandard and to recognize that nonstandard

English is a system of rules, different from the standard but not necessarily inferior as a means of communication. All of the teacher's social instincts, past training, and even faith in his own education lead him to believe that other dialects of English are merely "mistakes" without any rhyme or rationale.

In this connection, it will be helpful to examine some of the most general grammatical differences between English dialects spoken in the United States. One could list a very large number of "mistakes," but when they are examined systematically the great majority appear to be examples of a small number of differences in the rules. The clearest analysis of these differences has been made by Edward Klima (1964). He considers first the dialect in which people say sentences like

Who could she see?
Who did he speak with?
He knew who he spoke with.
The leader who I saw left.
The leader who he spoke with left.

What is the difference between this dialect and standard English? The usual schoolbook answer is to say that these are well-known mistakes in the use of *who* for *whom*. But such a general statement does not add any clarity to the situation; nor does it help the student to learn standard English. The student often leaves the classroom with no more than an uneasy feeling that *who* is incorrect and *whom* is correct. This is the state of half-knowledge that leads to hypercorrect forms such as *Whom did you say is calling?* In the more extreme cases, *whom* is seen as the only acceptable, polite form of the pronoun. Thus a certain receptionist at a hospital switchboard regularly answers the telephone: "Whom?"

The nonstandard dialect we see here varies from standard English by one simple difference in the order of rules. The standard language marks the objective case—the difference between *who* and *whom*—in a sentence form which preserves the original subject-object relation:

Q—She could see WH-someone.

The WH-symbol marks the point to be questioned in this sentence. When cases are marked in this sentence, the pronoun before the verb receives the unmarked subjective case and the pronoun after the verb the marked objective case.

Q—she(subjective case)—could—see—WH-someone(objective case)

The combination of WH, indefinite pronoun, and objective case is to be realized later as *whom*. At a later point, a rule of *WH-attraction* is applied which brings the WH-word to the beginning of the sentence:

Q—Whom—she—could—see

and finally the Q-marker effects a reversal of the pronoun and auxiliary, yielding the final result:

Whom could she see?

Here the objective case of the pronoun refers to the underlying position of the questioned pronoun as object of the verb.

The nonstandard dialect also marks cases: *I, he, she, they* are subjective forms, and *me, him, her, them* are objective. But the case marking is done after, rather than before, the WH-attraction rule applies. We begin with the same meaningful structure, *Q-She could see* WH-*someone,* but the first rule to consider is W*H-attraction:*

Q—WH someone—she—could—see

Now the rule of case marking applies. Since both pronouns are before the verb, they are both unmarked:

Q—WH-someone(unmarked)—she(unmarked)—could see.

Finally, the question flip-flop applies, and we have

Who could she see?

The same mechanism applies to all of the nonstandard forms given above.

We can briefly consider another nonstandard grammatical rule, that which yields *It's me* rather than *It's I.* The difference here lies again in the rule of case marking. As noted above, this rule marks pronouns which occur after verbs; but the copula is not included. The nonstandard grammar which gives us *It's me* differs from standard English in only one simple detail—the case-marking rule includes the verb *to be* as well as other verbs. It is certainly not true that this nonstandard grammar neglects the case-marking rule; on the contrary, it applies the rule more generally than standard English here. But the order of the rules is the same as that for the nonstandard grammar just discussed: we get W*ho is he?* rather than W*hom is he?* Like the other verbs, the copula marks the pronoun only after WH-attraction has applied.

In all of the examples just given, we can observe a general tendency towards simplification in the nonstandard grammars. There is a strong tendency to simplify the surface subjects—that is, the words which come before the verb. This is most obvious in pronominal apposition. The foregrounded part identifies the person talked about, *my oldest sister;* this person is then "given," and the "new" predication is made with a pronoun subject: *she worked at the Citizens Bank.*

A parallel tendency is seen in the nonstandard grammars which confine the objective marker to positions after the verb. But this tendency to simplify subjects is not confined to standard colloquial English. Sentences such as the following are perfectly grammatical but are seldom if ever found in ordinary speech:

> For him to have broken his word so often was a shame.

Most often we find that the rule of "extraposition" has applied, moving the complex subject to the end of the sentence:

> It was a shame for him to have broken his word so often.

In general, we find that nonstandard English dialects are not radically different systems from standard English but are instead closely related to it. These dialects show slightly different versions of the same rules, extending and modifying the grammatical processes which are common to all dialects of English.

Any analysis of the nonstandard dialect which pretends to ignore other dialects and the general rules of English will fail (1) because the nonstandard dialect is *not* an isolated system but a part of the sociolinguistic structure of English, and (2) because of the writer's knowledge of standard English. But it would be unrealistic to think that we can write anything but a superficial account of the dialect if we confine our thinking to this one subsystem and ignore whatever progress has been made in the understanding of English grammar.

FOR DISCUSSION AND REVIEW

1   According to Labov, why is it important to study nonstandard language?

2   Labov states that "nonstandard English dialects are not radically different systems from standard English but are instead closely related to it." What evidence does Labov present to document this conclusion?

3   In what ways would an understanding of nonstandard dialect be of value to a teacher in an urban school system?

4   "Nonstandard English," according to Labov, "is a system of rules, different from the standard but not necessarily inferior as a means of communication." What are some of these rules? Illustrate them. How does an understanding of the fundamental rules of Black English help to explain the speech patterns of blacks?

10

Sociolinguistic Factors in the History of American Negro Dialects

William A. Stewart, a leading authority on American Negro dialects, examines nonstandard Negro dialects from an historical point-of-view. The logical, coherent, and grammatical nature of the Negro's nonstandard speech is soundly documented by Stewart. The pedagogical implications of the differences between standard English, as discussed by Charles C. Fries (pp. 349–352), and nonstandard Negro dialects are invaluable for the prospective teacher.

William A. Stewart

WITHIN THE last few years, the increased national commitment to bettering the lot of socially and economically underprivileged groups of Americans—the so-called "disadvantaged"—has caused educators to consider ways in which the schools may involve themselves in this task. Of the many possibilities, certainly one of the most obvious is to deal with the chronic language problems associated with many of the disadvantaged. Yet, although there is a general awareness that certain of the disadvantaged do have language problems, there is at the same time a lack of agreement as to what these problems entail, and therefore what to do about them. Some investigators (often educational psychologists) have maintained that the disadvantaged characteristically do not use verbal communication to the extent that members of the middle class do, and are thus impoverished in "communicative skills." To alleviate this situation, they have recommended programs aimed at encouraging the use of verbal communication of a variety of kinds by disadvantaged pupils. A few investigators have theorized that members of disadvantaged groups may even engage less in abstract thinking than do middle-class persons. For this there have been suggested programs designed to teach more perception and conceptualization on the part of the disadvantaged pupils.

On the other hand, linguists have tended to emphasize one other type of language problem which some disadvantaged groups often have, and for which evidence is quite accessible—being encountered every day in the nation's classrooms. This is the purely structural conflict between on the one hand the patterns of a non-standard dialect which an individual may have learned at home or in peer-group interaction, and on the other hand the equivalent patterns of standard English—the language of modern technology and of the middle class. This is one kind of problem which many of the nation's schools ought to be ready and willing to cope with. One indication of the readiness of the schools is the fact that traditional English teachers are rapidly abandoning the older "sloppy speech" and "lazy tongue" views of non-standard speech in favor of a realization that it usually represents the speaker's use of some language system which, though it may differ from standard English in form and sometimes even in function, is nevertheless logical, coherent, and (in its own way) grammatical. Another indication of the readiness of schools to cope with the problem of dialect differences is the growth of a cadre of specialists in the teaching of English to speakers of other languages. With them, there has come into being a set of new techniques for teaching English to persons coming from a different language background.

Just as they are ready, America's schools certainly ought to be willing to deal with dialect-based problems, since there are a number of ways in which, by themselves, they can render a non-standard speaker dysfunctional in exchanges with standard-English-speaking members of the middle class. One way is for minor pronunciation differences between a non-standard dialect and standard English—each one perhaps trivial by itself—to pile up in an utterance to such an extent that the non-standard version becomes unintelligible to a middle-class listener, even though in grammar and vocabulary it may be quite similar to its standard equivalent. Thus, a non-standard version of "I don't know where they live" might, in one dialect, become cryptic to the standard-speaking listener, merely because of its being pronounced something like *Ah 'own know wey 'ey lib.* Or, a standard English speaker may misunderstand a non-standard utterance, even though he thinks he has deciphered it correctly, because it contains non-standard grammatical constructions which are unknown to him. For example, a middle-class listener may take a non-standard sentence *Dey ain't like dat* to mean "they aren't like that," when it really means "They didn't like that." The standard-English speaker is simply unaware that *ain't* is this particular dialect's way of negating verbs in the past tense, as he is unaware that the usual equivalent in the same dialect of "They aren't like that" would be either *Dey not like dat* or *Dey don't be like dat* (the two variants indicating a difference in meaning which is not easily expressed in standard English). Of course, similar breakdowns in intelligibility may also occur in the other direction, when the non-standard speaker tries to understand standard English. Finally, even when he does succeed in making himself understood by his middle-class listeners, the non-standard speaker may still fall victim to the difference in social prestige between his dialect and standard English. In other words, although middle-class persons may understand what he is saying, they may still consider him uncouth for saying it the way he does.

Professionally able though the schools may now be to embark on programs which would deal effectively with this kind of problem, the likelihood of their actually doing so in the near future is certainly not increased by the unwillingness of many educators and even some applied linguists to approach the problem in any but the most general terms. For, unfortunately, the technical know-how necessary to teach standard English to speakers of non-standard dialects is simply not embodied in an awareness of the problem at the level of "Some children should probably be taught standard English as a second dialect"—no matter how true such statements may be. The necessary know-how will begin to be adequate when and only when applied linguists can give, and educators will take seriously, details of the type "The verb system of such-and-such a non-standard dialect operates in such-and-such a way, and the verb system of standard English operates in such-and-such a way, so that structural interference is most likely to occur at points *a*, *b*, and *c*. Therefore, the following lessons and drills in the standard English verb system is what children who speak this non-standard dialect will need."[1]

One reason why there is little remedial English now being taught based upon a systematic comparison of the differences between non-standard dialects and standard English is that information about one of the pedagogically most important features of non-standard dialects— their grammatical systems—is still largely lacking. This lack is due in great part to the fact that American dialect studies have traditionally emphasized differences in pronunciation and vocabulary, at the expense of information on systematic grammatical differences.

Now that linguists have begun to fill this information gap, however, they are finding their observations on language variation among the disadvantaged received with uneasiness and even hostility by many teachers, administrators, and community leaders. The reason for this is undoubtedly that the accurate description of dialect variation in American communities—particularly in urban centers—is turning out to show a disturbing correlation between language behavior on the one hand and socio-economic and ethnic stratification on the other.[2] The

---

1 See William A. Stewart, editor, *Non-Standard Speech and the Teaching of English* (Washington, D.C., Center for Applied Linguistics, 1964).

2 The American Dream notwithstanding, it is well known to social scientists that American society is stratified into a number of social classes and ethnic groups, and that each of these exhibits a "characteristic" configuration of customs, attitudes, roles, life-ways and, as it turns out, speech patterns. The literature on social

correlation is particularly controversial insofar as it involves the speech of large numbers of American Negroes, since at the present time Negro leadership (and this includes most Negro educators) is probably more achievement-oriented than any other. Because of this orientation, Negro elites tend not to welcome any evidence of uniform or stable behavioral differences between members of their own group (even lower-class ones) and those of the white-dominated middle class. Yet the fact is that Negroes account for most of the most pedagogically problematic non-standard dialect speakers in the larger cities, and also include within their group speakers of the most radically non-standard dialects of natively-spoken English in the entire country.[3] Furthermore, because *de facto* segregation in housing has caused non-standard-dialect-speaking Negroes to predominate in many schools and because these Negroes appear in many cases to have different kinds of problems with standard English than non-standard-dialect-speaking whites have (even in the same area), the sweeping, for political purposes, of Negro dialect descriptions under the white-oriented geographic dialect rug would probably be more detrimental to disadvantaged Negro children than it would be advantageous to Negro elites.[4]

On the other hand, linguists should realize that the fears and anxieties of Negro leaders about public discussion of ethnically correlated behavioral differences may have some foundation. It is possible, for example, that quite objective and innocently-made statements about dialect differences between whites and Negroes might be interpreted by white racists as evidence of Negro cultural backwardness or mental inferiority, or even seized upon by black racists as evidence of some sort of mythical Negro "soul." Linguists should not censor their data, but they should make sure that their statements about Negro-white

---

and ethnic stratification is extensive, but good introductions are Egon Ernest Bergel, *Social Stratification* (New York, McGraw-Hill Book Co., 1962), and Tamotsu Shibutani and Kian M. Kwan, *Ethnic Stratification* (New York, The Macmillan Co., 1965). For an exhaustively documented study of the correlation between language variation and social class, ethnicity, and age in an American metropolis, see William Labov, *The Social Stratification of English in New York City* (Washington, D.C., The Center for Applied Linguistics, 1966).

[3] These two facts may not be entirely unrelated. For a graphic indication of the relatively more non-standard grammatical norms of Negro children over white children in a single city, see Figure 18 (page 53) in Walter Loban, *Problems in Oral English: Kindergarten Through Grade Nine* (Champaign, Ill., National Council of Teachers of English, 1966).

[4] For a discussion of Negro dialect in one urban community, see William A. Stewart, "Urban Negro Speech: Sociolinguistic Factors Affecting English Teaching" in Roger W. Shuy, editor, *Social Dialects and Language Learning* (Champaign, Ill., National Council of Teachers of English, 1965). The non-standard dialect patterns cited earlier in the present article are also Negro dialect.

differences are not divorced from an awareness of the historical, social, and linguistic reasons why such differences may have come into existence and been maintained. Perhaps it would serve that end to point out here some of the sociolinguistic factors involved in the evolution of American Negro dialects, factors which explain why certain kinds of American Negro dialects are both different from the non-standard dialects of American whites, and more radically deviant from standard English.

Although the linguistic history of the Negro in the United States can be reconstructed from the numerous literary attestations of the English of New World Negroes over the last two and a half centuries, and by comparing these with the English of Negroes in the United States, the Caribbean, and West Africa today, this has never been done for the English teaching profession. In presenting a historical sketch of this type, I realize that both the facts presented and my interpretations of them may embarrass or even infuriate those who would like to whitewash American Negro dialects by claiming that they do not ex'st —that (in spite of all sorts of observable evidence to the contrary) they are nothing but Southern white dialects, derived directly from Great Britain. I will simply make no apologies to those who regard human behavior as legitimate only if observed in the white man, since I feel that this constitutes a negation of the cultural and ethnic plurality which is one of America's greatest heritages. On the other hand, I do regret that such a historical survey, although linguistically interesting, may at times conjure up out of the past memories of the Negro-as-slave to haunt the aspirations of the Negro-as-equal.

Of those Africans who fell victim to the Atlantic slave trade and were brought to the New World, many found it necessary to learn some kind of English. With very few exceptions, the form of English which they acquired was a pidginized one, and this kind of English became so well established as the principal medium of communication between Negro slaves in the British colonies that it was passed on as a creole language to succeeding generations of the New World Negroes, for whom it was their native tongue.[5] Some idea of what New World

---

[5] In referring to types of languages, linguists use the terms *pidgin* and *creole* in a technical sense which has none of the derogatory or racial connotations of popular uses of these terms. When a linguist says that a variety of language is pidginized, he merely means that it has a markedly simplified grammatical structure compared with the "normal" (i.e., unpidginized) source-language. This simplification may be one way in which speakers of different languages can make a new language easier to learn and use—particularly if they have neither the opportunity nor the motivation to learn to speak it the way its primary users do. In addition, some of the unique characteristics of a pidgin language may be due, not to simplification, but to influences on it from the native languages of its users. What is important to realize, however, is that pidginized languages do have grammatical

Negro English may have been like in its early stages can be obtained from a well-known example of the speech of a fourteen-year-old Negro lad given by Daniel DeFoe in *The Family Instructor* (London, 1715). It is significant that the Negro, Toby, speaks a pidginized kind of English to his boy master, even though he states that he was born in the New World. A sample of his speech is:[6]

> *Toby.* Me be born at Barbadoes.
> *Boy.* Who lives there, Toby?
> *Toby.* There lives white mans, white womans, negree mans, negree womans, just so as live here.
> *Boy.* What and not know God?
> *Toby.* Yes, the white mans say God prayers,—no much know God.
> *Boy.* And what do the black mans do?
> *Toby.* They much work, much work,—no say God prayers, not at all.
> *Boy.* What work do they do, Toby?
> *Toby.* Makee the sugar, makee the ginger,—much great work, weary work, all day, all night.

Even though the boy master's English is slightly non-standard (e.g. *black mans*), it is still quite different from the speech of the Negro.

An idea of how widespread a pidginized form of English had become among the Negro population of the New World by the end of the Seventeenth Century can be gathered from the fact that it had even become the language of the coastal plantations in the Dutch colony of Surinam (i.e., Dutch Guiana), in South America. In an early description of that colony, the chapter on the Negro ends with a sample

---

structure and regularity, even though their specific patterns may be different from those of the related unpidginized source-language of higher prestige. Thus, the fact that the sentence *Dem no get-am* in present-day West African Pidgin English is obviously different from its standard English equivalent "They don't have it" does not necessarily indicate that the Pidgin English speaker "talks without grammar." In producing such a sentence, he is unconsciously obeying the grammatical rules of West African Pidgin English, and these determine that *Dem no get-am* is the "right" construction, as opposed to such ungrammatical or "wrong" combinations as *No dem get-am, No get dem-am, Get-am dem no*, etc. If a pidgin finally becomes the native language of a speech community (and thereby becomes by definition a creole language), it may expand in grammatical complexity to the level of "normal" or unpidginized languages. Of course, the resulting creole language may still exhibit structural differences from the original source-language, because the creole has gone through a pidginized stage. For more details, see Robert A. Hall, Jr., *Pidgin and Creole Languages* (Ithaca, N.Y., Cornell U. Press, 1966).

[6] The same citation is given in a fuller form, along with a number of other attestations of early New World Negro speech, in George Philip Krapp, *The English Language in America* (New York, The Century Co., 1925), Vol. I, pp. 255–265. Other attestations are cited in Tremaine McDowell, "Notes on Negro Dialect in the American Novel to 1821," *American Speech*, V (1930), pp. 291–296.

conversation in the local Negro English dialect. The dialogue includes such sentences as *Me bella well* "I am very well," *You wantee siddown pinkininne?* "Do you want to sit down for a bit?", and *You wantee go walka longa me?* "Do you want to take a walk with me?"[7] In these sentences, the use of the enclitic vowel in *wantee* recalls the same in DeFoe's example *makee*. Also, the speaker, like Toby, uses *me* as a subject pronoun. In the first Surinam sentence, we see an early example of a construction without any equivalent of the standard English verb "to be." Toby also would probably have said *Me weary*, since the *be* in his first sentence was in all likelihood a past-tense marker (as it is in present-day West African Pidgin English)—the sentence therefore meaning "I was born in Barbadoes." In the last Surinam sentence, a reflex of English *along* is used with the meaning of standard English "with." It may or may not be accidental that in the Gullah dialect, spoken by the Negroes along the South Carolina coastal plain, the same phenomenon occurs, e.g., *Enty you wantuh walk long me?* "Do you want to take a walk with me?" Some Gullah speakers even still use *me* as a subject pronoun, e.g., *Me kyaan bruk-um* "I can't break it," and enclitic final vowels seem to have survived in such Gullah forms as *yerry, yeddy* "to hear."

Early examples of Negro dialect as spoken in the American colonies show it to be strikingly similar to that given by DeFoe for the West Indies and by Herlein for Surinam. In John Leacock's play, *The Fall of British Tyranny* (Philadelphia, 1776), part of the conversation between a certain "Kidnapper" and Cudjo, one of a group of Virginia Negroes, goes as follows:[8]

> *Kidnapper.* . . . what part did you come from?
> *Cudjo.* Disse brack man, disse one, disse one, disse one, come from Hamton, disse one, disse one, come from Nawfok, me come from Nawfok too.
> *Kidnapper.* Very well, what was your master's name?
> *Cudjo.* Me massa name Cunney Tomsee.
> *Kidnapper.* Colonel Thompson—eigh?
> *Cudjo.* Eas, massa, Cunney Tomsee.
> *Kidnapper.* Well then I'll make you a major—and what's your name?
> *Cudjo.* Me massa cawra me Cudjo.

[7] J. D. Herlein, *Beschryvinge van de volksplantinge Zuriname* (Leeuwarden, 1718), pp. 121–123. Herlein gives the Negro English dialogues in Dutch orthography. I have retranscribed these sentences in the kind of spelling which his English contemporaries would have used in order to show better the relationship between the Surinam dialect and the other examples. In the Dutch spelling, these sentences appear as *My belle wel, Jou wantje sie don pinkinine?*, and *Jo wantje gaeu wakke lange mie?*

[8] This citation also occurs in Krapp, and with others in Richard Walser, "Negro Dialect in Eighteenth-Century American Drama," *American Speech*, XXX (1955), pp. 269–276.

Again, the enclitic vowels (e.g., *disse*) and the subject pronoun *me* are prominent features of the Negro dialect. In the sentence *Me Massa name Cunney Tomsee* "My master's name is Colonel Thompson," both the verb "to be" and the standard English possessive suffix *-s* are absent. Incidentally, Cudjo's construction is strikingly similar to sentences like *My sister name Mary* which are used by many American Negroes today.

One possible explanation why this kind of pidginized English was so widespread in the New World, with widely separated varieties resembling each other in so many ways, is that it did not originate in the New World as isolated and accidentally similar instances of random pidginization, but rather originated as a *lingua franca* in the trade centers and slave factories on the West African coast.[9] It is likely that at least some Africans already knew this pidgin English when they came to the New World, and that the common colonial policy of mixing slaves of various tribal origins forced its rapid adoption as a plantation *lingua franca*.

In the course of the Eighteenth Century, some significant changes took place in the New World Negro population, and these had their effect on language behavior. For one thing, the number of Negroes born in the New World came to exceed the number of those brought over from Africa. In the process, pidgin English became the creole mother-tongue of the new generations, and in some areas it has remained so to the present day.[10]

In the British colonies, the creole English of the uneducated Negroes and the English dialects of both the educated and uneducated whites were close enough to each other (at least in vocabulary) to allow the speakers of each to communicate, although they were still different enough so that the whites could consider creole English to be "broken" or "corrupt" English and evidence, so many thought, of the mental limitations of the Negro. But in Surinam, where the European settlers spoke Dutch, creole English was regarded more objectively. In fact, no less than two language courses specifically designed to teach creole English to Dutch immigrants were published before the close of the Eighteenth Century.[11]

[9] See, for example, Basil Davidson, *Black Mother; The Years of the African Slave Trade* (Boston, Little, Brown and Co., 1961), particularly p. 218.

[10] In the West Indies, creole English is usually called *patois*, while in Surinam it is called *Taki-Taki*. In the United States, the only fairly "pure" creole English left today is Gullah, spoken along the coast of South Carolina.

[11] These were Pieter van Dijk, *Nieuwe en nooit bevoorens gexiende onderwijzinge in het Bastert Engeles, of Neeger Engels* (Amsterdam, undated, but probably 1780), and G. C. Weygandt, *Gemeenxame leerwijze om het Basterd of Neger-Engelsch op een gemakkelijke wijze te leeren verstaan en spreeken* (Paramaribo, 1798).

Another change which took place in the New World Negro population primarily during the course of the Eighteenth Century was the social cleavage of the New World-born generations into underprivileged field hands (a continuation of the older, almost universal lot of the Negro slave) and privileged domestic servants. The difference in privilege usually meant, not freedom instead of bondage, but rather freedom from degrading kinds of labor, access to the "big house" with its comforts and "civilization," and proximity to the prestigious "quality" whites, with the opportunity to imitate their behavior (including their speech) and to wear their clothes. In some cases, privilege included the chance to get an education and, in a very few, access to wealth and freedom. In both the British colonies and the United States, Negroes belonging to the privileged group were soon able to acquire a more standard variety of English than the creole of the field hands, and those who managed to get a decent education became speakers of fully standard and often elegant English. This seems to have become the usual situation by the early 1800's, and remained so through the Civil War. In Caroline Gilman's *Recollections of a Southern Matron* (New York, 1838), the difference between field-hand creole (in this case, Gullah) and domestic servant dialect is evident in a comparison of the gardener's "He tief one sheep—he run away las week, cause de overseer gwine for flog him" with Dina's " 'Scuse me, missis, I is gitting hard o'hearing, and yes is more politer dan no" (page 254). A more striking contrast between the speech of educated and uneducated Negroes occurs in a novel written in the 1850's by an American Negro who had traveled extensively through the slave states. In Chapter XVII, part of the exchange between Henry, an educated Negro traveler, and an old "aunty" goes as follows:[12]

> 'Who was that old man who ran behind your master's horse?'
> 'Dat Nathan, my husban'.'
> 'Do they treat him well, aunty?'
> 'No, chile, wus an' any dog, da beat 'im foh little an nothin'.'
> 'Is uncle Nathan religious?'
> 'Yes, chile, ole man an' I's been sahvin' God dis many day, fo yeh baun! Wen any on 'em in de house git sick, den da sen foh 'uncle Nathan' come pray foh dem; 'uncle Nathan' mighty good den!'

After the Civil War, with the abolition of slavery, the breakdown of the plantation system, and the steady increase in education for poor

---

[12] Martin R. Delany, *Blake; or the Huts of America,* published serially in *The Anglo-African Magazine* (1859). The quotation is from Vol. I, No. 6 (June 1859), page 163.

as well as affluent Negroes, the older field-hand creole English began to lose many of its creole characteristics, and take on more and more of the features of the local white dialects and of the written language. Yet, this process has not been just one way. For if it is true that the speech of American Negroes has been strongly influenced by the speech of whites with whom they came into contact, it is probably also true that the speech of many whites has been influenced in some ways by the speech of Negroes.[13]

Over the last two centuries, the proportion of American Negroes who speak a perfectly standard variety of English has risen from a small group of privileged house slaves and free Negroes to persons numbering in the hundreds of thousands, and perhaps even millions. Yet there is still a sizeable number of American Negroes—undoubtedly larger than the number of standard-speaking Negroes—whose speech may be radically non-standard. The non-standard features in the speech of such persons may be due in part to the influence of the non-standard dialects of whites with whom they or their ancestors have come in contact, but they also may be due to the survival of creolisms from the older Negro field-hand speech of the plantations. To insure their social mobility in modern American society, these non-standard speakers must undoubtedly be given a command of standard English; that point was made in the early part of this paper. In studying non-standard Negro dialects and teaching standard English in terms of them, however, both the applied linguist and the language teacher must come to appreciate the fact that even if certain non-standard Negro dialect patterns do not resemble the dialect usage of American whites, or even those of the speakers of remote British dialects, they may nevertheless be as old as African and European settlement in the New World, and therefore quite widespread and well-established. On various occasions, I have pointed out that many speakers of non-standard American Negro dialects make a grammatical and semantic distinction by means of *be*, illustrated by such constructions as *he busy* "He is busy (momentarily)" or *he workin'* "he is working (right now)" as opposed to *he be busy* "he is (habitually) busy" or *he be workin'* "he is working (steadily)," which the grammar of standard English is unable to make.[14] Even this distinction goes back well over a century. One observer in the 1830's noted a request by a slave for a permanent supply of soap as "(If) Missis only give we, we be so clean forever," while *be* is absent

[13] See Raven I. McDavid, Jr. and Virginia Glenn McDavid, "The Relationship of the Speech of American Negroes to the Speech of Whites," *American Speech*, XXVI (1951), pp. 3-17.

[14] See, for example, *The Florida FL Reporter*, Vol. 4, No. 2 (Winter 1965–1966), page 25.

in a subsequent report of someone's temporary illness with "She jist sick for a little while."[15]

Once educators who are concerned with the language problems of the disadvantaged come to realize that non-standard Negro dialects represent a historical tradition of this type, it is to be hoped that they will become less embarrassed by evidence that these dialects are very much alike throughout the country while different in many ways from the non-standard dialects of whites, less frustrated by failure to turn non-standard Negro dialect speakers into standard English speakers overnight, less impatient with the stubborn survival of Negro dialect features in the speech of even educated persons, and less zealous in proclaiming what is "right" and what is "wrong." If this happens, then applied linguists and educators will be able to communicate with each other, and both will be able to communicate with the non-standard-speaking Negro child. The problem will then be well on its way toward a solution.

FOR DISCUSSION AND REVIEW

1 What, according to Stewart, are some common misconceptions about nonstandard dialects? How do these compare with the "bits of nonsense" about dialects enumerated by Professor McDavid (pp. 352–370)? How has the work of the linguist helped to correct these misconceptions?

2 What distinctions does Stewart make in discussing *pidgin language, creole language,* and *dialect*?

3 Stewart concludes that "nonstandard Negro dialects represent a historical tradition." What evidence does he utilize to arrive at this conclusion?

4 According to Stewart, why should educators be less concerned with "proclaiming what is 'right' and what is 'wrong' " and more concerned with trying to understand the pronunciation, vocabulary, and grammatical forms of nonstandard speech?

15 Frances Anne Kemble, *Journal of a Residence on a Georgian Plantation in 1838–1839* (New York, 1862). The first quotation is from page 52, and the second is from page 118.

11
Should
Ghettoese
Be Accepted?

William Raspberry, a columnist for the *Washington Post*, discusses a question that educators are facing at present. On the basis of the evidence available, how does one approach the conflict between patterns of a nonstandard dialect which the child learns either at home or from his peers and the equivalent patterns of standard English? Raspberry advocates the desirability of making slum children bidialectal. In order to implement such a program, he feels that teachers sensitive to nonstandard language are needed in ghetto schools.

William Raspberry

BY THE time I get there, he will have gone."

"Time I git dere, he be done gone."

You and I were taught to recognize the first example as good English and the second as bad. According to a growing number of linguists, we were taught wrong.

The two sentences, these linguists tell us, don't represent proper and improper usage; they represent two distinct languages, equally consistent and, in that they communicate meaning, equally valid.

The first is standard American English; the second, the nonstandard English of the black slums. These linguists, who include some of the leading lights at Washington's Center for Applied Linguistics, are attempting to build on the validity of the second as a means of teaching the first.

English teachers don't find it necessary to make a Spanish-speaking child feel that his native language is bad in order to get him to learn English. But when confronting children who speak the native tongue of the black slums, too many of them do precisely that. One unfortunate result, the linguists tell us, is that slum children become ashamed of their language and, therefore, ashamed of themselves.

The child who points to the rose on his teacher's desk and says, "Dere go a flyvuh," will too frequently be told flatly that a rose is a *flower* and that it isn't going anywhere.

Such instruction is more likely to confuse than help. The child knows very well that his meaning would be unmistakable at home; his mother might have put it just the same way. Furthermore, if his efforts at free expression are criticized too often, he may simply shut up and say nothing at all.

And so the teacher dubs him "nonverbal," a typical label for the ghetto child.

Nonverbal, hell! Follow him out the schoolhouse door and listen while his playmate tries to get a word in edgewise.

The teacher has made a classical error. He has tried to teach his pupil a new language by condemning the pupil's old one. And the result is that the child shrinks from the teacher, making it very difficult if not impossible for him to teach the pupil anything at all.

Wouldn't it be better, the linguists ask, to accept the validity of the child's native language if that facilitates teaching him a new one?

The answer would be obvious if the child's native tongue were French or Spanish. The difference is that French and Spanish are respected languages *and they don't sound like standard English.* Thus, *voici and voilà* aren't wrong; they simply aren't English. Their exact equivalent in ghettoese, "here go" and "dere go" are just close enough to standard English that teachers are tempted to brand them as bad standard English rather than good nonstandard.

Nonstandard English, or ghettoese, it must be admitted, is a lot easier to recognize than to describe. (Try describing *standard* English!)

The linguists emphasize two things about ghettoese: First, it is the language spoken almost universally among low-income black Americans (and understood by almost all black Americans) and second, it is consistent in syntax.

Ghettoese is not slang: The latter is little more than a one-for-one substitution of nonstandard words for standard ones. Nor is it simply mispronunciation of standard English words.

"Sue is a boss chick" is slang. Boss is a synonym for "fine" and chick for "girl." But the sentence isn't ghettoese, although something very like it might be heard among ghetto residents.

On the other hand, the statement, "Dat Sue sho a boss chick," is ghettoese—but not solely because of the mispronunciation of "that" and "sure," for "Sue a boss chick" is also ghettoese, although each word may be given the standard pronunciation. It is ghettoese because of the missing "is," a feature common to ghetto speech patterns.

The linguists make another point: Ghettoese is not necessarily less *precise* than standard English. In some instances, it may be more precise than the standard.

Ask a slum child why his father missed last night's meeting, and the answer might be, "He sick." Ask him why his father misses so many meetings, and he might answer, "He be sick." The first describes a temporary illness; the second, a chronic or recurring one. No such distinction exists in standard English. The answer to both questions in standard English would be, "He is sick."

This example seems to be a favorite among the linguists who want standard English taught as a foreign language, which has led me on occasion to refer to them as the he-be-sick school.

This designation suggests, unfairly, that the linguists who have been addressing themselves to the language problems of slum children are of a single mind. Not so. There is something less than unanimity among them even on the notion of teaching standard English as a foreign language.

For some, it is a direct analogy to the teaching of English to a Spanish-speaking child. For others, it means using some of the techniques that are used in the teaching of foreign languages.

It is pointed out, for instance, that one reason middle-class children learn to read more easily than slum children is that the former have to make but a single translation: from print to sound. A slum child, on the other hand, has to make a second translation: from the standard English to his native nonstandard, just as a French-speaking youngster would have to make the additional translation to his native French.

The argument loses a little in light of the fact that translation increasingly is thought of as a rather poor way of teaching foreign languages. Total immersion is the current trend. If you want to learn Russian in a hurry, you might find yourself in a classroom where only Russian is spoken. No tedious translations. You learn to speak Russian because you have to speak Russian to get along in the class.

The method has a lot to recommend it. After all, isn't that how you learned English?

If the total immersion system is an effective way of teaching foreign languages and if our linguist friends want to teach English as a foreign language, then why not total immersion in standard English?

As a matter of fact, that is what almost always happens. Good teachers don't spend their time reminding their pupils that the "flyvuh" isn't going anywhere. They are careful to say, "Here is a flower." They believe that if they say something in standard English distinctly enough and often enough the child will learn to say it that way, too.

That is a very great deal different from translating from nonstandard into standard, which some of the linguists seem to be suggesting.

At least one of them, William A. Stewart, explicitly makes that suggestion. He tells of the time a young "problem reader" from the inner city happened across his ghettoese translation of *The Night Before Christmas*:

It's the night before Christmas, and here in our house
It ain't nothing moving, not even no mouse.
There go we-all stockings, hanging high up off the floor,
So Santa Claus can full them up, if he walk in through our door.

Says Stewart:
Lenora was one of the "problem readers" of the public schools; she read school texts haltingly, with many mistakes and with little ability to grasp the meaning of what she read. Yet, when she began to read the nonstandard version of the poem, her voice was steady, her word reading [was] accurate, and her sentence intonation was natural. . . .

This unexpected success in reading so surprised Lenora that she began to discuss the experience with her little brother. They decided that there was something different about the text, but were unable to tell exactly what it was.

To compare, I then had Lenora read the standard English version of the poem. . . . When she did, all the "problem reader" behavior returned.

Stewart's point goes far beyond pronunciation; its essence is grammar. His translation closely approximated the grammar of Lenora's native ghettoese, leaving her to make the single print-to-sound translation. Clement Moore's original required her to make the second standard-to-nonstandard translation and, thus, exposed her as being a problem reader.

It is for this reason that some linguists have proposed that early reading material for inner-city children be written in the slum dialect. They point to experiments, notably in Sweden, which indicate that children who are introduced to reading through their own nonstandard dialects and then are switched to standard surpass those who use standard materials from the beginning.

If this is so, they suggest, then we should be able to improve drastically the reading abilities of young slum dwellers simply by first teaching them to read in their native tongue.

The theory makes a good deal of sense, but it may be asking too much to expect the average classroom to implement it effectively. The more likely result is either to hopelessly confuse such children or to reinforce their nonstandard speech patterns.

But more is involved here than the teaching of reading. Involved, too, is the assessment of a child's intelligence, an assessment often based on his language proficiency in standard English.

Joan C. Baratz of the Education Study Center makes that point in the September 1969 issue of *Child Development*:

"If the criterion for language development is the use of a well-ordered systematic code," she says, "then the continued use of measures of language development that have standard English as the criterion of a developed form will only continue to produce the results that the Negro, lower-class child is delayed in language development because he has not acquired the rules that the middle-class child has been able to acquire. . . ."

What that means, I think, is that there are two distinct questions to be asked: To what degree has this child developed language skills? To what degree has this child developed facility *in standard English?*

Most of our written tests pretend to ask the first question, when in fact they ask the second. The answer to the first question is obviously a more valid measure of intelligence. But that is not the end of it.

What you, I, and the linguists want is to have slum children learn the language that will help them get along in the American society. That means standard English.

It may be academically interesting to be aware that, from a purely linguistic point of view, nonstandard is just as valid as standard. Interesting, but not particularly useful.

If employers, personnel officers, and the others whom we find it useful to impress with our intelligence were fluent in nonstandard English and understood its validity and if books and newspapers were written in nonstandard, then it would be unnecessary to teach standard (But in that case, nonstandard would, by definition, be standard!)

The reason we want slum children to learn standard is that nonstandard is a good deal less negotiable—just as trading stamps are less negotiable than cash.

But that doesn't mean that trading stamps are *bad*. It is here that the linguists make the heart of their case. The way we speak is such an integral part of who we are that to deprecate our speech is to deprecate us.

What the linguists want to do is to give slum children facility with standard English without forcing them to forget their native nonstandard—to give them cash without confiscating their trading stamps. The nonstandard, lest we forget, may be *the* negotiable language back home in the slum neighborhood or within the family or on the playground. After all, you can't pay cash for that lamp at the redemption center.

What we are talking about, then, is the desirability of making slum children bilingual, just as most educated blacks are bilingual. (Forget the black teacher, recently escaped from the slums, who pretends she doesn't understand when Johnny says, "I'mo take me a brick an' bus' you upsi' yo' head." Her kind, happily, is disappearing.) Giving slum children this kind of bilinguality has far less to do with understanding the inner workings of ghettoese than with being sensitive to the inner workings of people.

No teacher expects a pupil to learn arithmetic if he calls him a dunderhead every time the child delivers himself of a wrong answer. Nor should the teacher expect him to learn standard English (or anything else, for that matter) if, by his attitude, he conveys "you are a dunderhead" every time the child opens his mouth. (This, however, is simply psychology, not linguistics.)

In that light, linguists who emphasize the beauties of ghettoese may be showing their contempt for teachers. Their implication is that teachers are too stupid to distinguish between form and substance, that if a child says something really clever—but in ghettoese—the teacher will hear nothing but the ghettoese.

If that is the case, if substantial numbers of teachers believe nonstandard equals stupid, then forget linguistics. Forget everything, for any teacher so insensitive that he will shame a child into silence every time he opens his mouth is beyond the help even of the Center for Applied Linguistics.

FOR DISCUSSION AND REVIEW

1   Why does Raspberry believe that "ghettoese" should be accepted? Does he set limits to this acceptance?

2   According to Raspberry, why should slum children be given facility with standard English?

3   In "Sense and Nonsense about American Dialects" (p. 352), Raven I. McDavid advises that "the first principle of any language program is that, whatever the target, it must respect the language that the students bring with them to the classroom." If you were establishing a program to make slum children bidialectal, would you heed this advice? Why or why not?

12

Bi-Dialectalism:
The Linguistics
of White
Supremacy

James Sledd

In this article, Professor Sledd responds to the programs advocating functional bi-dialectalism that have been proposed by William Labov (p. 393), William Raspberry (p. 412), William Stewart (p. 401), and others. In essence, Sledd doubts the possibility of successfully teaching bi-dialectalism in the classroom. Furthermore, he feels that even if it were possible, enforced bi-dialectalism should not be tolerated because of its inherent white prejudices. Carefully consider the racist implications of bi-dialectalism as disclosed by Sledd.

BECAUSE PEOPLE who rarely talk together will talk differently, differences in speech tell what groups a man belongs to. He uses them to claim and proclaim his identity, and society uses them to keep him under control. The person who talks right, as we do, is one of us. The person who talks wrong is an outsider, strange and suspicious, and we must make him feel inferior if we can. That is one purpose of education. In a school system run like ours by white businessmen, instruction in the mother tongue includes formal initiation into the linguistic prejudices of the middle class.

Making children who talk wrong get right with the world has traditionally been the work of English teachers, and more recently of teachers of that strange conglomerate subject which we call speech. The English teacher in the role of linguistic censor was once a kind of folk heroine (or anti-heroine), the Miss Fidditch of the linguists' diatribes. Miss Fidditch believed in taking a strong stand. It never occurred to her that her main job was making the lower classes feel so low that they would try to climb higher. Instead, Miss Fidditch taught generations of schoolchildren, including future linguists, to avoid *ain't* and double negatives and *used to could* and *hadn't ought*, not because *ain't* would keep them from getting ahead in the world, but because *ain't* was wrong, no matter who used it, and deserved no encouragement from decent people who valued the English language. She did her job all the better for thinking that she was doing something else.

Miss Fidditch is not popular any longer among educators. Though the world at large is still inclined to agree with her, the vulgarizers of linguistics drove her out of the academic fashion years ago, when they replaced her misguided idealism with open-eyed hypocrisy. To the popular linguists, one kind of English is as good as another, and judgments to the contrary are only folklore; but since the object of life in the U.S.A. is for everybody to get ahead of everybody else, and since linguistic prejudice can keep a man from moving up to Schlitz, the linguists still teach that people who want to be decision-makers had better talk and write like the people who make decisions. The schools must therefore continue to cultivate the linguistic insecurity which is already a national characteristic but must teach the youngsters to manipulate that as they manipulate everything else; for neither Miss Fidditch's dream of a language intrinsically good, nor a humbler ideal of realizing the various potentialities of the existing language in its responsible use, can get in the way of the citizenry in its upward anguish through the pecking order. The linguists think that people who do knowingly what Miss Fidditch did in her innocence, will do it more efficiently, as if eating the apple made a skilled worker out of Eve.

As long as most people agreed that up is toward Schlitz and another TV set, and as long as they could pretend that every American eaglet can soar to those great heights, Fidditch McFidditch the dialectologist could enforce the speech-taboos of the great white middle class without complaint: either the child learned the taboos and observed them, or he was systematically penalized. But the damage done to the Wasps' nest by World War II made difficulties. People who talked all wrong, and especially black people, began to ask for their share of the loot in a world that had given them an argument by calling itself free, while a minority of the people who talked right began to bad-mouth respectability and joined the blacks in arguing that it was time for a real change. Some black people burned up the black parts of town, and some students made study impossible at the universities, and in general there was a Crisis. Optimists even talked of a revolution.

The predictable response of the frightened white businessman's society was to go right on doing what it had done before—which had caused the crisis—but to do it harder and to spend more money at it. Education was no exception. Government and the foundations began to spray money over the academic landscape like liquid fertilizer, and the professional societies began to bray and paw at the rich new grass. In that proud hour, any teacher who could dream up an expensive scheme for keeping things as they were while pretending to make a change was sure of becoming the director of a project or a center and of flying first-class to Washington twice a month. The white business-man strengthened his control of the educational system while giving the impression of vast humanitarian activity.

Black English provided the most lucrative new industry for white linguists, who found the mother lode when they discovered the inter-esting locutions which the less protected employ to the detriment of their chances for upward mobility. In the annals of free enterprise, the early sixties will be memorable for the invention of functional bi-dialectalism, a scheme best described by an elderly and unregenerate Southern dame as "turning black trash into white trash." Despite some signs of wear, this cloak for white supremacy has kept its shape for almost a decade now, and it is best described in the inimitable words of those who made it. Otherwise the description might be dismissed as a malicious caricature.

The basic assumption of bi-dialectalism is that the prejudices of middle-class whites cannot be changed but must be accepted and in-deed enforced on lesser breeds. Upward mobility, it is assumed, is the end of education, but white power will deny upward mobility to speak-ers of black English, who must therefore be made to talk white English in their contacts with the white world.

An adequate florilegium may be assembled from a volume entitled *Social Dialects and Language Learning* (NCTE, 1964), the proceed-ings of a conference of bi-dialectalists which was held in 1964. William A. Stewart of the Center for Applied Linguistics begins the chorus (p. 13) by observing among our educators "a commendable desire to emphasize the potential of the Negro to be identical to white Amer-icans"—a desire which is apparently not overwhelming, however, among the Black Muslims or among the young men who have enjoyed pot-shooting policemen for the past few summers. Editor Roger W. Shuy next speaks up (p. 53) for social climbing by our American Indians, who have been notably reluctant, throughout their unfortunate asso-ciation with their conquerors, to adopt our conquering ways. Our lin-guistic studies, Shuy remarks in the purest accents of fidditchery, "should reveal those elements, both in speech and writing, which prevent In-dians from attaining the social status which, with socially acceptable language, they might otherwise attain." A similar desire to be at peace with status-holders is suggested (p. 66) by Ruth I. Golden, who opines that "a human being wants most of all to be recognized as an indi-vidual, to be accepted, and to be approved." Since Southern speech brings "negative reactions when heard by employers in Detroit," where Dr. Golden labors in the schools, she devotes herself to stamping out /i/ for /e/ in *penny* and to restoring /l/ in *help* (pp. 63 f.).

An admirable scholar from New York, William Labov, then agrees (p. 88) that "recognition of an external standard of correctness is an inevitable accompaniment of upward social aspirations and upward social mobility," and advises that people who (like Jesus) prefer not to take excessive thought for the morrow can probably be made to. In Labov's own words, "since the homes of many lower class and working people do not provide the pressures toward upward social mobility that middle-class homes provide," and since adults in those lower reaches are sometimes resistant to middle-class values, we must "build into the community a tolerance for style shifting which is helpful in educational and occupational advancement," and we must build into the children, "starting from a level not much above the nursery school and going on through high school, a tolerance for practice in second role playing" (pp. 94–97, 104).

Presumably Labov sees nothing wrong in thus initiating children into the world of hypercorrection, insecurity, and "linguistic self-hatred" which marks, as he has said elsewhere, "the average New Yorker" (*The Social Stratification of English in New York City*, Center for Applied Linguistics, 1966, Chapter XIII); and Charles Ferguson, the eminent ex-director of the Center for Applied Linguistics, is equally confident of *his* right and duty to remake his fellow men in his directorial image. Talking about the Negroes in our Northern cities, Ferguson says that "we have to face a rather difficult decision as to whether we want to make these people bi-dialectical . . . [please to remark Ferguson's choice of verbs] or whether we want . . . to impose some kind of standard English on these people and to eradicate the kind of substandard English they speak" (p. 116). To cite another NCTE volume (*Language Programs for the Disadvantaged* [NCTE, 1965], p. 222), if the black children of the ghetto "do not learn a second kind of dialect, they will be forever prevented from access to economic opportunity and social acceptance." Middle-class white prejudice will rule eternally.

The bi-dialectalists, of course, would not be so popular with government and the foundations if they spoke openly of the supremacy of white prejudice; but they make it perfectly clear that what they are dealing with deserves no better name. No dialect, they keep repeating, is better than any other—yet poor and ignorant children must change theirs unless they want to stay poor and ignorant. When an NCTE "Task Force" set out to devise *Language Programs for the Disadvantaged* (NCTE, 1965), it laid down a perfect smoke screen of such hypocrisy, as one would expect from persons who felt called upon to inform the world that "without the experience of literature, the individual is denied the very dignity that makes him human" (p. v) but that not "all disadvantaged children are apathetic or dull" (pp. 24 f.).

"In this report" (p. 117), "teachers are asked to begin by accepting the dialect of their students for what it is, one form of oral communication. . . ." Teachers are warned particularly that they "need to accept the language which Negro children bring to school, to recognize that it is a perfectly appropriate vehicle for communicating ideas in the Negro home and subculture" (p. 215), that it is "essentially respectable and good" (p. 227). But though teachers must not attack "the dialect which children associate with their homes and their identity as Negroes" (p. 215), they must still use all the adult authority of the school to "teach standard informal English as a second dialect" (p. 137), because the youngster who cannot speak standard informal English "will not be able to get certain kinds of jobs" (p. 228).

The most common result of such teaching will be that white middle-class Midwestern speech will be imposed as mandatory for all those situations which middle-class white businessmen think it worth their while to regulate. In the words of Chicago's Professors Austin and McDavid (p. 245), "future educational programs should be developed in terms of substituting for the grammatical system of lower-class Southern speech [read: black Chicago speech] that of middle-class Chicago white speech—at least for those economic and social situations where grammatical norms are important." Labov goes so far as to ask (*Social Dialects and Language Learning*, p. 102) whether Northern schools should tolerate Southern speech at all—whether they should not also correct the "cultivated Southern speech" of privileged children who move North.

The description of compulsory bi-dialectalism may be completed by examining the methods which its proponents advocate for perpetuating the supremacy of white prejudice. Essentially, those methods are derived by analogy from structuralist methods of teaching foreign languages—methods whose superiority has been claimed but never demonstrated and whose intellectual foundations vanished with the demise of structuralist ideas. As an eminent grammarian privately observed after a recent conference, "The achievements of the operators will continue to lie in the field of getting and spending government money. . . . They seem to have an unerring instinct for finding ways of spending it unprofitably—on conferences at which they listen to each other, for example. Now they're out to teach standard English as a second dialect through techniques that have served very poorly in teaching second languages."

High on the list of those techniques is incessant drill on inessentials. In theory, the drills are the end-product of a long process of systematic comparison of the children's nonstandard dialects with the standard dialect which they are to be taught; but since the systematic comparisons have never been made, the bi-dialectalists fall back on a simple enumeration of a few dozen "features of pronunciation, grammar, and vocabulary which can be considered indices of social stratification" (Roger Shuy, "Detroit Speech," in A. L. Davis, ed., *On the Dialects of*

Children, p. 13). Professor Rudolph Troike of the University of Texas was thus simply platitudinizing piously when he told the TESOL convention in 1968 that "any instructional program . . . must begin with as full an *objective* knowledge as possible" of both or all the dialects involved. The escape hatch in Troike's statement is the phrase *as full as possible.* What is usually possible is an unsystematic list of shibboleths—the simplification of consonant clusters, the Southern pronunciations of *walk,* and *right, ax* for *ask,* the dropping of postvocalic /r/, *ain't* and *fixin' to, bofe* and *mouf* for *both* and *mouth,* and the like. These innocent usages, which are as familiar as the sun in the late Confederacy, are apparently the terror of Northern employers, who the bidialectalists assume are almost suicidally unconcerned with such details as character, intelligence, and training for the job. The fact is, of course, that Northern employers and labor leaders dislike black faces but use black English as an excuse.

Having established, however, that a child of darkness under her tutelage says *mouf,* the pretty white lady sets out to rescue his soul. First she plays tapes of Southern speech to convince her victims, who understand Southern speech far better than they understand hers, that Southern speech often makes "complete understanding of content . . . difficult," "not readily comprehensible"—as is demonstrated by the fact that the pretty white lady would never have detected her victim's four-letter word just by listening and without watching his lips (New York Board of Education, *Nonstandard Dialect,* pp. 1, 14, 17). The difficulty of detecting him is all the more reason for fearing the iniquitous *mouf*-sayer: it proves he is a cunning devil who probably says *dentissoffice* too and who perpetrates such subversive "malapropisms" as "The food in the lunch room is not fitting to eat" (*On the Dialects of Children,* p. 23). How else *would* he spell *fitten?* But for such a hardened rogue, a good many "motivational activities" are likely to be necessary before the pretty white lady can really start twisting the thumbscrew with her drills.

Yet the drills are available, and the pretty white lady will use them when she sees her time. She has drills of all kinds—repetition drills, substitution drills, replacement drills, conversion drills, cued answer drills, the reading in unison of 'long lists of words like *teeth / reef, toothbrush / waffle, bathtub / alphabet, weather / weaver.* To get rid of *dentissoffice,* she may have students debate such propositions as "Ghosts do exist" or "Formal school tests should be eliminated"; and before a really "culminating activity" like playing "Pack the Trunk" she may "divide the class into consonant-cluster committees to seek out words containing" clusters like *sks, sps,* or *kt* (*Nonstandard Dialect, passim*). At this point the class might be invited to suggest a context for a replacement drill—maybe something like "Teacher! teacher! Billy Joe say

that Tommy ————— Bessy!" This last suggestion, it must be confessed, has not yet been made in the literature, but it seems considerably more stimulating than choral recitation of Poe's "Bells" (*ibid.*,
p. 35).

Perhaps it need not be added that existing tests and evaluations of
such "instructional materials" are something of a farce. If bi-dialectalism
is really harder to acquire than bilingualism (Einar Haugen in *Social
Dialects and Language Learning*, p. 125), teachers and texts ought
surely to be superb, and judgments on them ought to be severe; but
New York City's curriculum developers can give "highest priority" to
making the children change *a* to *an* before nouns beginning with a
vowel (*Nonstandard Dialect*, p. 14), and Texas' Professor Troike can
argue the success of his methods by showing that after six months of
drills a little black girl could repeat *his hat* after her teacher, instead of
translating automatically to *he hat*. Unfortunately, tapes do not record
psychological damage, or compare the effectiveness of other ways of
teaching, or show what might better have been learned in the same
time instead of learning to repeat *his hat*.

So much for a description of mandatory bi-dialectalism, a bit en-
livened (since the subject is dreary) by irreverent comment, but not
distorted in any essential way. In the U.S.A., we are being told, everybody wants approval—not approval for doing anything worth approv-
ing, but approval for doing whatever happens to be approved. Because
approval goes to upward mobility, everybody should be upwardly mobile; and because upward mobility is impossible for underdogs who
have not learned middle-dog barking, we must teach it to them for
use in their excursions into the middle-dog world. There is no possibility either that the present middle class can be brought to tolerate
lower-class English or that upward mobility, as a national aspiration,
will be questioned. Those are the pillars on which the state is built, and
the compassionate teacher, knowing the ways of his society, will change
the color of his students' vowels although he cannot change the color
of their skins.

It is not at all certain that the bi-dialectalists, for all their absurdities, can be dislodged from their well-carpeted offices. They are supported by the National Council of Teachers of English, the Modern
Language Association of America, the Center for Applied Linguistics,
the federal government, the foundations, the governments of a number
of major cities, and by black people who have made it into the middle
class and so despise their origins and their less efficient fellows. In the
best of times our top dogs are pleased by docility, if not mobility,
among the beasts below; and in 1969 a new ice age is beginning. Newspaper headlines tell us that the Department of Health, Education, and
Welfare has been urged to relax its requirements for desegregation of

schools immediately but quietly, and President Nixon loses his Miami tan at the thought that militant students will "politicize" our universities—as if government grants to upwardly mobile faculty had not politicized them long ago. In Lyndon Johnson's Texas the citizens of Austin vote down an open housing law, their board of education then justifies segregated schooling by the established pattern of segregated housing, and the governor of the state praises the state university as the source of brain-power to assist the businesman in the lucrative exploitation of what the governor proudly calls the "insatiable appetite" of Texans. The only revolution we are likely to see is the continued subversion, by the dominant white businessman, of the political and religious principles on which the nation was founded.

Yet though the times are bad, they are not hopeless, at least not in the small, undramatic world of English education; and the bi-dialectalists are so gorgeously absurd that the breath of laughter may collapse their card-house if only enough people can be brought to see it as it is. It is not simply quixotic, then, to add to a laughing description of imposed bi-dialectalism a more serious statement of reasons why it cannot succeed and should not be tolerated even if it could—a statement which can lead, in conclusion, to the proposing of an alternative policy.

The argument that bi-dialectalism cannot be forced is easy to make out, even, in part, from the reluctant admissions of some of its proponents. Two principal reasons have already been suggested, the ignorance and unproved methods of the bi-dialectalists. The term *ignorance* is used literally, and in all fairness. Whatever one thinks of teaching standard English by methods like those for teaching foreign languages, contrastive analyses of our different dialects are a prerequisite—but a prerequisite which has not yet been supplied. Until very recently, the principal sources of information were the collections for the *Linguistic Atlas;* but they are unsystematic, partially out-of-date, and in some respects inaccurate and superficial. Where, for example, should one go for descriptions of intonation and its dialectal variants, for accurate accounts of the system or systems of verbal auxiliaries, for analyses of the speech of ghetto children instead of rustic ancients? Such minimal essentials are simply lacking. In fact, it might be said that for all the talk about revolutionary advances in linguistics, neither the structural nor the generative grammarians have yet produced a satisfactory basic description of even standard English.

The best descriptions of all our kinds of English would still not be enough to make coercive bi-dialectalism a success. The English teacher's forty-five minutes a day for five days in the week will never counteract the influence, and sometimes the hostility, of playmates and friends and family during much the larger part of the student's time. Formal education could produce real bi-dialectals only in a vast system of state nurseries and boarding schools to which the children of the poor and ignorant would be consigned at an early age; but such establishments would be prohibitively expensive, intolerable to the people, and still not absolutely certain of success, because the most essential of all conditions might not be met—namely, the desire of the children to talk like the white middle class.

When one thinks about it in these realistic terms, the whole argument about bi-dialectalism begins to look schizophrenic, as out-of-this-world as an argument whether Lee should surrender at Appomattox or fight back. There is no evidence that the bi-dialectalists, if they actually had good textbooks, better teachers, and as much money as the country is spending to devastate Vietnam, would really know what to do with those fictional resources. Instead of clear ideas, they offer clichés, like the familiar attacks on "traditional methods and approaches" or the protected pedagogue's arrogant assurance that illiterates can have no human dignity. They fly off quickly into high-sounding vaguenesses, talking (for example) about "differences in social dialect and associated versions of reality" (*Social Dialects and Language Learning*, p. 68), as if metaphysics rested on a preconsonantal /r/. At their most precise, they suggest the prudential avoidance of Southern pronunciations of *walk* and *cough* in Washington because Negroes there look down on new arrivals from Georgia and the Carolinas. They happily assume what they should prove—that intensive training in "standard informal English as a second dialect" has produced or can produce large numbers of psychologically undamaged bi-dialectals, whose new accomplishment has won them or will win them jobs that otherwise would have been impossible for them to get. When their guard is down, the bi-dialectalists actually confess that they *have* no concrete program, since "no one program at any level yet seems applicable to a significant number of other classes at the respective level" (*Language Programs for the Disadvantaged*, pp. 30 ff.).

Some awareness of their difficulties, and some uncertainty about priorities, seem indeed to be spreading among the bi-dialectalists (though it would be too much to hope that if their present bandwagon falls apart they will consider themselves discredited and resign their membership in the Society of Mandarin.) For one thing, they have become aware of the significance of reading, which William A. Stewart, as late as 1964, could reduce to the level of "socially desirable embellishments" (*Social Dialects and Language Learning*, p. 10). In his latest book, however, *Teaching Black Children To Read*, Editor Shuy announces "the simple truth that speaking standard English, however desirable it may be, is not as important as learning to read" (p. 118). His colleagues Walter A. Wolfram and Ralph W. Fasold are even closer to enlightenment. In the same new volume (p. 143), they hesitantly admit that "there is some question about the degree to which Standard English can be taught to the ghetto child in the classroom at all"; and Fasold meant what he said, for he had said it before at the Milwaukee convention of the NCTE. Though that august body was still congratulating itself on its concern with "a language component for the so-called culturally divergent," it had to bear with Fasold's embarrassing confession: "Because of the operation of social forces in the use of language," he said, "forces which are only poorly understood, it may not be possible to teach Standard English as a second language to Black English-speaking children unless they are interacting with Standard English speakers in a meaningful way outside the classroom" (*Convention Concerns—1968*, p. 10). The Center's linguistician came as close as standard English would allow to saying that it is segregation which makes black people talk different and that there would be no slum children if there were no slums.

No doubt the most important of Fasold's poorly understood social forces is one which everybody but white linguists has understood for a long time: black people may just not want to talk white English. Several years ago, Labov observed that some of his more rebellious New York subjects were deliberately turning away from social-climbing New York speech toward a black Southern model (*Social Dialects and Language Learning*, pp. 96 f.), and today comment on "the new feeling of racial pride among black Americans" (*Teaching Black Children to Read*, p. 142) is a platitude. Wolfram and Fasold go on to the quite unsurprising speculation that that pride may even extend to the Negro's speech. "If a realization develops that this dialect, an important part of black culture, is as distinctively Afro-American as anything in the culture, the result may well be a new respect for Black English within the community" (p. 143). More plainly, condescending middle-class white charity is not wanted any more, if it ever was, in language-teaching or anywhere else. We should learn from the example of the British: the social cataclysm of the Second World War, and the achievement of political power by labor, did more to give the "disadvantaged" English youngster an equal chance than charitable bi-dialectalism ever did. We are past the stage when white teachers, whether Africans or Caucasians, can think well of themselves for trying to turn black people into uneasy imitations of the whites.

The immorality of that effort is the chief reason why enforced bi-dialectalism should not be tolerated even if it were possible. Predators can and do use dialect differences to exploit and oppress, because ordinary people can be made to doubt their own value and to accept subservience if they can be made to despise the speech of their fathers. Obligatory bi-dialectalism for minorities is only another mode of exploitation, another way of making blacks behave as whites would like

them to. It is unnecessary for communication, since the ability to understand other dialects is easily attained, as the black child shows when
she translates her teacher's prissy white model *"his* hat" into *"he* hat."
Its psychological consequences are likely to be nervous affectation, self-
distrust, dislike for everyone not equally afflicted with the itch to get
ahead, and eventual frustration by the discovery that the reward for so
much suffering is intolerably small. At best the altered student will get
a somewhat better job and will move up a few places in the rat-race of
the underlings. At worst he will be cut off from other blacks, still not
accepted among whites, and economically no better off than he was
before.

White teachers should hope, then, that their black students will be
recalcitrant, so that bi-dialectalism as a unilateral condition for employ-
ment can be forgotten. It would make better sense, if pedagogues insist
on living in a fantasy world, to require whites to speak black English
in their dealings with blacks, since the whites have more advantages
than the blacks and consider themselves more intelligent; or perhaps we
should be hard-headedly consistent in our brutalities and try to eradicate the vices which really do enrage employers—like intellectual questioning, or the suspicion that ours is not the best of possible worlds.

Indeed, the educationists' faith in education would be touching if
it were not their way of keeping up their wages. Nothing the schools
can do about black English or white English either will do much for
racial peace and social justice as long as the black and white worlds
are separate and hostile. The measure of our educational absurdity is
the necessity of saying once again that regimented bi-dialectalism is no
substitute for sweeping social change—*necessity* being defined by the
alternative of dropping out and waiting quietly for destruction if the
white businessman continues to have his way.

The reply that the educational system should not be politicized is
impossible for bi-dialectalists, since bi-dialectalism is itself a political
instrument. They may purge themselves of inconsistency, and do what
little good is possible for English teachers as political reformers, if instead of teaching standard English as a second dialect they teach getting out of Vietnam, getting out of the missile race, and stopping the
deadly pollution of the one world we have, as horribly exemplified by
the current vandalism in Alaska.

One use for a small fraction of the resources that would thus be
saved would be to improve the teaching of the English language. Bi-
dialectalism would never have been invented if our society were not
divided into the dominant white majority and the exploited minorities.
Children should be taught that. They should be taught the relations
between group differences and speech differences, and the good and bad
uses of speech differences by groups and by individuals. The teaching

would require a more serious study of grammar, lexicography, dialectology, and linguistic history than our educational system now provides —require it at least of prospective English teachers.

In the immediate present, the time and money now wasted on bi-dialectalism should be spent on teaching the children of the minorities to read. Already some of the universal experts among the linguists have boarded this new bandwagon, and the next round of government grants may very well be for programs in reading and writing in black English. That might be a good thing, particularly if we could somehow get rid of the tired little clique of operators who have run the professional societies of English teachers for so long. Anyway, the direct attack on minority language, the attempt to compel bi-dialectalism, should be abandoned for an attempt to open the minds and enhance the lives of the poor and ignorant. At the same time, every attempt should be made to teach the majority to understand the life and language of the oppressed. Linguistic change is the effect and not the cause of social change. If the majority can rid itself of its prejudices, and if the minorities can get or be given an education, differences between dialects are unlikely to hurt anybody much.

(The phoniest objections to this proposal will be those that talk about social realism, about the necessity for doing something even—or should one say particularly?—if it's wrong. That kind of talk makes real change impossible, but makes money for bi-dialectalists.)

FOR DISCUSSION AND REVIEW

1 For what reasons is Sledd against enforced bi-dialectalism?

2 Are there distinct advantages in using standard English rather than vernacular or uneducated English? Explain.

3 Many linguists feel that nonstandard English is intrinsically a perfectly good form of expression. Do you agree? Cite evidence presented by Labov (p. 393), Raspberry (p. 412), Stewart (p. 401), and Sledd that supports your position.

4 In "Sense and Nonsense about American Dialects" (p. 352), Professor McDavid recounts the story of his friend Bob Thomas, a Cherokee Indian. Although Bob had picked up a native command of Oklahoma English, he found himself in a class in "corrective speech" soon after his family moved from Oklahoma to Detroit. Bob remembers that the students in this class "all realized immediately that [the teachers] were planning to brainwash us out of our natural way of speaking; and it became a point of honor among us to sabotage the program." Is this reaction typical of minority students? How, according to Raspberry and Stewart, can such a situation be avoided? What would be Sledd's reaction to this issue?

5 In 1962, Lamberts stated that "our reaction to most substandard usages is essentially passive. We may not like them, but it would never occur to us to make remarks about them." After reading the selections by Labov, Stewart, Raspberry, and

Sledd, do you feel that Lamberts' assessment of the situation is still correct? Explain.

6 What does Sledd propose as an alternative to forced bi-dialectalism? Do you agree with his proposals? Can you suggest others?

13

Social Aspects of Bilingualism in San Antonio, Texas

Janet B. Sawyer

For many Mexican-Americans living in the southwestern part of the United States, Spanish is the first language. In recent years, however, English has made inroads into Spanish-speaking communities so that now both languages exist side by side. As a result, Mexican-Americans experience the frustrations and social pressures of being caught between two cultures. In this article, Professor Sawyer presents her findings from an investigation of bilingualism in San Antonio, Texas. This study considers conditions common to other bilingual situations in the United States.

A RECENT dialect survey of English in San Antonio, Texas,[1] a community where over 40 percent of the people are Spanish-speaking immigrants from Mexico, yielded two important types of data: first, interviews with native speakers of English provided knowledge of the pronunciation features and vocabulary of a relatively unstudied part of Texas;[2] second, a study of the English spoken in the same community by Spanish-speaking informants revealed at least two degrees of second-language skill and unexpected evidence of the social stresses felt by

[1] Janet B. Sawyer, "A Dialect Study of San Antonio, Texas, a Bilingual Community" (University of Texas diss., 1957).

[2] See E. Bagby Atwood, *The Regional Vocabulary of Texas* (Austin: University of Texas Press, 1962) for a more recent analysis of the larger dialect area.

speakers from a low-status culture who found no advantage in being identified as members of the Spanish-speaking minority.

The study of the pronunciation and vocabulary of the English-speaking informants, whom we will call *Anglos* in this report, following the custom of the community, was helpful in establishing the predominant influences upon the regional dialect. The informants were selected from various age, education, and culture groups within the Anglo community, and the tabulated records[3] gave the following pronunciation features as characteristic of San Antonio:

1) "Vocalized /r/": *here* [hɪə].
2) Diphthongal /æy/: *pass* [pæys].
3) Monophthongal "long i": *five* [faˑv].
4) Diphthongal /ɔw/: *fought* /fɔwt/.
5) /ɪ/ in certain unstressed syllables: *Dallas, wanted*.
6) /iw/ or /yuw/ after /t/, /d/, /n/: *tune, due*.

A comparison of these features with the known features of the dialect areas studied in the East[4] proved that such features are typical of the Southern dialect area, a somewhat surprising fact since a study of the immigration to San Antonio during the critical years between 1865 and 1880[5] states that 47 percent of the Anglo immigrants were from the Midland and South Midland speech areas, and only 44 percent were from the Gulf states. The prestige of the Southern settlers must have been high, judging from the persistence of the Southern speech characteristics. Of the six features listed above, only (1) is receding sharply in the speech of the youngest Anglo informants; (4) may be receding slightly.

---

3 The items used for this study are those included in the worksheets made by Hans Kurath in 1939 (see note 4 below), as revised by E. Bagby Atwood for the Southwest regional study. The worksheets were supplemented by taped readings of Dagwood comic strips and other selections which provided additional information about pronunciation features in various styles of speech. For example, although in citation forms [ai] (in *five*) was often heard in the speech of certain Anglo speakers, in the reading of the comic strip, monothongal [aˑ] was more frequent for these same speakers.

4 Hans Kurath, M. L. Hanley, B. Bloch, G. S. Lowman, Jr., and M. L. Hansen, *Linguistic Atlas of New England* (3 vols. in 6 parts. Providence: Brown University, 1939–43); Hans Kurath, *A Word Geography of the Eastern United States* (Ann Arbor: University of Michigan Press, 1949); and E. Bagby Atwood, "Outline of the Principle Speech Areas of the Eastern United States" (mimeographed pamphlet, Austin, 1950).

A book which gives detailed information on the Linguistic Atlas materials was not available at the time that this dialect study of San Antonio, Texas, was made: Hans Kurath and Raven I. McDavid, Jr., *The Pronunciation of English in the Atlantic States* (Ann Arbor: University of Michigan Press, 1961).

5 Homer Lee Kerr, "Migration Into Texas 1865–1880" (University of Texas diss., 1953).

In matters of lexicon, the survey disclosed that San Antonio English is not so strikingly Southern, partially because many of the words known to be characteristic of the South, such as *lightwood, chittling,* and *co-wench,* are obsolescent in this urban community. Words which spread from the South into the South Midland area appear with the greatest frequency in San Antonio. Terms such as *pully bone* and *clabber* are known to all the Anglo informants. Thus, in the Anglo community of San Antonio, we find a frequency of 53 percent for words common to the South and South Midland.

The English vocabulary of San Antonio has its distinctive regional flavor because of a continual contact with the Spanish culture and language during the early settlement years. We found numerous Spanish words pertaining particularly to Southwestern ranching and cattle raising: *burro, lariat, hackamore, tank, norther, acequia, arroyo, chaps, corral,* and *mesa* are in very common usage; however, others such as *nopal, guajilla, tuna, pīnata, yobero* and *potro* were known only by the older members of the Anglo community, since the items they name are characteristic terms in a receding rural way of life.

The comparison of the English of seven Spanish-speaking informants, who will be referred to as *Latin* informants since the name *Latin-Americans* is the term preferred by this group, with the English of the seven Anglo informants made it possible to distinguish varying degrees of second-language skill. We were able to classify three informants as basically *unilingual* Spanish speakers, since they spoke Spanish exclusively at home and whenever possible away from home. (All of them were native second-generation residents of San Antonio with grade school educations.) Their English was characterized by constant interference from the phonological structure of Spanish, numerous errors in basic grammatical contrasts, and a limited, inaccurate use of English vocabulary. These informants were L2, a female midwife, 53 years old; L3, a male gardener, 46 years old; and L5, a female actress, 41 years old.

The remaining four Latin informants were classified as *bilinguals,* because their English was extremely competent. Very few errors occurred in their speech in either phonology or grammar, and they were able to respond to eight or more hours of interviewing in fluent English. These informants were L1, a retired female seamstress, 74 years old; L4, a female saleslady and housewife, 45 years old; L6, a male university graduate, 32 years old; and L7, a male university student, 21 years old.

In classifying these four informants as bilinguals, we do not mean that they had completely mastered English. Anyone speaking to either of the two women informants would immediately recognize the fact that English was not their native language. But they were competent within a limited vocabulary, and they had no difficulty making their ideas clear in English. Neither had had more than an elementary school education, but their jobs, which brought them into contact with English speakers, made it possible and even necessary for them to speak English well. The two male informants were much superior to them in the range and relative perfection of their English; L6, at least, was near the dividing line between bilingual Spanish and bilingual English, since he felt some embarrassment when speaking Spanish to anyone outside of San Antonio. Of course, neither L6 nor any of the other bilinguals felt completely at ease in English either.

The unilinguals experienced greater embarrassment and frustration when speaking English. However, L5, the unilingual actress, criticized the Spanish spoken in San Antonio, calling it "Tex.-Mex." Having been well-educated in cultured Spanish, thanks to the training of her Cuban husband and years in the Spanish theater, she disapproved of the way the Spanish speakers of the area interspersed English words among the Spanish words when speaking Spanish.

In order to ascertain the actual features of this Tex.-Mex., we also recorded the Spanish of the Latin informants and compared these records with those of Spanish students studying at the University of Texas from various parts of Mexico and the rest of the Spanish-speaking world. And no matter how diverse Tex.-Mex. may be in its vocabulary, the records proved that it is almost identical in its phonology to Mexican-Spanish, so this dialect of Spanish was used in the comparative study of the two languages.[6]

The phonology of standard Southern English as spoken by the Anglo informants of San Antonio was the dialect of English used in judging the skill of the Latin informants since it seems reasonable to assume that the model they were striving to attain in English was not Northern or New England speech, or even "General American," but simply that variety of American English found in the Anglo community into which they were striving to integrate. Therefore, in making the analysis of the bilinguals' achievement, we did not consider them to be skilled if they used [ɑʊ] in cow, even if these phones happened to be found in this word in many varieties of American English, since the Anglo informants of San Antonio used only [æʊ] or [aʊ] in such words.

The English phonology of the unilingual Latins and the bilingual Latins can be briefly summarized:

Several vowel contrasts caused particular difficulty for the unilinguals:

[6] Harold V. King, "Outline of Mexican Spanish Phonology," *Studies in Linguistics*, X (1952), 51–62.

1) /i/ and /ɪ/. The unilinguals commonly substituted Spanish /i/ (which lacks the high off-glide of English /i/) for English /ɪ/ in such words as *pig*.
2) /u/ and /ʊ/. The unilinguals commonly substituted Spanish /u/ (which lacks the lip-rounding off-glide of English /u/) for English /ʊ/ in such words as *pull*.
3) /æ/. This phoneme does not occur in Spanish, and the unilinguals commonly substituted either the close [e] or the open [ɛ] allophone of the Spanish /e/ in such words as *man*.
4) /ə/ also does not occur in Spanish. The unilingual Spanish speakers substitute either the [ɑ] of Spanish /ɑ/ or the [ɔ] allophone of Spanish /o/ in such words as *one*.

The bilingual informants very seldom had difficulty with the simple vowel contrasts. The most difficult vowel qualities for them were the [æʊ] (in *cow*), the monophthongal [a·] (in *five*), and the fronted [ʉ] (in *school*). L6, the university graduate, was the only Latin informant who had mastered these regional features.

A variety of errors occurred in the attempt of the Latins to produce the English consonant system. Those of highest incidence in the records of the San Antonio unilingual informants were the following:

1) Fricative allophones of Spanish stops such as [β] often occurred in place of the labiodental [v] of English, following the Spanish distributional pattern. There is no /v/ phoneme in Spanish.
2) Final voiced consonants are often devoiced following the Spanish pattern, which permits only a few consonants to be final of word and commonly devoices those that do occur. Example: [wepᶜ] for *web*; [pikᶜ] for *pig*.
3) The fricatives and affricates /š/, /č/, and /ǰ/ often replace each other in a form of free variation. *Sheep* [čiˑp], *chair* [šɛr], *jump* [čɔmp], and *fudge* [fɔš] are typical occurrences in unilingual Latin speech.

Such phenomena were typical of unilingual speech. But such interference by the Spanish consonant system was rare in bilingual English. Apparently, the bilinguals had mastered the essential contrasts between the voiced and voiceless consonants and had learned the new phonemes which occur only as allophones in Spanish. The most difficult pattern for the bilinguals to master seemed to be the contrast between /s/ and /z/, which are separate phenomes in English. In Spanish, however, the [z] is an allophone of /s/, occurring only when /s/ is followed by a voiced consonant in close transition. In the speech of L5, one of the unilinguals, an example of this Spanish distributional pattern occurred: In the phrase "twice better" *twice* was pronounced as [twɑɪz], but when *twice* occurred before a pause, it was pronounced as [twɑis]. Although the bilinguals never made a total transfer of the Spanish pattern, the most persistent feature of "accent" in their speech (as well as in the speech of the unilinguals) is the occurrence of the tense voiceless [s] or the only partially voiced [z̦] in final position where [z] should occur in English. The high frequency of /s/ in both languages as a plural suffix and as a verb inflexional suffix may be one of the causes of the persistence of the difficulty in mastering the phoneme /z/ in English. It is a feature of the speech of even L6, who has attained most of the features of Texas English.

An interesting and unexpected feature of the pronunciation of the San Antonian bilinguals can be directly linked to the social pressures of the bilingual community, rather than to the interference of Spanish language habits. It became obvious after even the most superficial study of the community that the Latin-American population, commonly called *Mexicans*, or more derogatory terms such as *Meskans, pilau, greasers*, or *wet backs*, were regarded as inferior. One of the Anglo informants of a prominent San Antonio family commented, "Many of my friends and relatives don't think Negroes and Mexicans are human beings—just animals. I didn't even know we had many Mexicans in San Antonio until I came back from college in Virginia." The Latin informants were well aware of the situation. The granddaughter of L1, herself a skilled bilingual, talked of her difficulty in getting a job upon her return from a good position in a psychiatrist's office in a western city. "Every ad for a good job here in San Antonio says 'Only *Anglos* need apply'!"

How this almost insurmountable pressure would affect the language achievement of the bilinguals was not immediately clear. It would seem logical that the ultimate degree of their effort would be the mastery of English as spoken in San Antonio. But the bilinguals interviewed for this survey (and others observed at various times before and after this survey) had gone even further. So determined were they to erase any influence of their low-prestige language upon their use of English that they treated Spanish words in two very special ways. First, Spanish words that they could not avoid in English received different pronunciations depending upon who was listening. Second, Spanish words that could be avoided were not used even though they were the typical regional terms in the English-speaking community.

Let us illustrate each of these facets of bilingual behavior in greater detail. Whenever a Spanish word could not be avoided in English, for example, when a bilingual speaker had to pronounce a Spanish personal name or a Spanish place-name, he pronounced it in two different ways. If the listener was also a bilingual speaker, he gave the word a Spanish pronunciation. If the listener was a member of the English-speaking prestige group, the bilingual gave the word an Anglicized pronunciation. The bilingual informants even pronounced their own names in two different ways in English: *Lorenzo:* [loɾɛnso] to other bilinguals;

[lowrɛnzow] to Anglos. Other examples follow: (In each case, the Spanish pronunciation has been given first.) *Dolores:* [dolɔ́řes] or (dəlɔ́rɛs]; *San Antonio:* [Sanantónio] or [sænæntówniə]; *burro:* [búřo] or [bɔ́row]; *plaza:* [plása] or [plǽzə]; *corral:* [kořál] or [kəráel]. The bilinguals gave the same double treatment for other indispensable borrowings from Spanish. It must be emphasized that this is not the way a speaker of Spanish from any Latin American country or from Spain would treat Spanish words when speaking English. It would be a matter of pride to pronounce them in the true Spanish way and even to correct English speakers who mispronounced them. This writer remembers the horror of a bilingual from one South American country when he heard a San Antonio bilingual mispronounce his own Spanish name. The South American took an instant dislike to the Texan solely on the basis of this strange linguistic behavior.

As we mentioned above, if a Spanish word could be avoided in English, the bilinguals would not use it at all. In this way they were like the unilinguals, who never used Spanish words in English. This was in direct contrast to the freedom with which all the Latin informants used *English* words in *Spanish*, the main distinguishing feature of San Antonio Spanish, according to various informants. (Examples: "Dame mi *pokebuk.*" [Give me my *pocket book.*], or "Es un *eswamp.*" [It's a *swamp.*].) Some of the Spanish words rejected in English by all the Latin informants were used normally by the Anglo informants: *morral, lariat, cinch, remuda, pilon, frijoles, chaps, hackamore, quirt.* Other words, which may have been borrowed from Latin or French rather than from Spanish, were also rejected by some of the Latin informants, because they were so similar to Spanish words: *gallery, melon, rancid.*

This rejection of the typical regional vocabulary of the English-speaking community illustrates the cultural isolation of even the bilingual speakers. In fact, if a Northern term happened to be more common in print, the Latin informants were likely to use that instead of the term preferred by all age levels in the Anglo group. Words such as *light bread, clabber,* and *corn shuck* were unknown to the Latin informants. They used the terms *corn husk* and *wish bone* rather than *corn shuck* and *pully bone*. The phrase *setting hen* was not known by even the most skilled bilingual Latin, L6, because such items are commonly learned in the home, and in the homes of the Latins only Spanish words for such things were used. Other terms typical of the regional English culture such as *Christmas Gift* or *snap beans* were unknown to the Latins, who used instead the general greeting, *Merry Christmas* and the commercial term *string beans.*

In evaluating our findings, we must remember that the number of bilinguals interviewed for this survey is out of all proportion to their number in the Spanish-speaking community, since it was our intent to study bilingualism. Actually only a small number of people attempt to break through their isolation into the larger, prestige culture. Generally, they are content to consider themselves part of the Mexican culture and to live out their lives in relative security. Those who are more ambitious are called *agringados*, from the term *gringo*, with no compliment intended. Even members of the younger generation in the public schools generally stick together and talk Spanish outside of class. This is a sort of voluntary segregation; yet they would be the first to protest any actual segregation for the purpose of teaching them English as it should be taught to speakers of a second language. As a result, they are taught English along with the native speakers who need to learn the special kind of English known as formal written style. Those students who wish to become competent bilinguals adopt the "book-words" and formal usage rules of this special style for ordinary English speech situations, and this precise, elegant style often sets off a bilingual from the English-speaking community quite as much as the "errors" of the unilinguals do.

The isolation of the Latin Americans results in a series of social isoglosses separating their speech from that of the Anglo community. Although these lines cannot be drawn on the map like the geographical isoglosses which separate one dialect from another, they are quite as real and as enduring. In the long run, the acquiring of the regional standard speech depends upon acculturation, which means the elimination of social barriers. Only when this is achieved (a necessity, from the point of view of democracy) can social isoglosses be eliminated.

FOR DISCUSSION AND REVIEW

1 Briefly, what were Sawyer's findings concerning Latin bilinguals in San Antonio? Latin unilinguals? Anglos?

2 What factors, according to Sawyer, contributed to the language behavior found among the Latin informants?

3 Discuss the linguistic and social problems confronting Mexican-Americans in San Antonio. Which of these problems are shared by Black Americans?

4 Cite several examples of Spanish words that have become a part of the English lexicon. English has borrowed words from other foreign languages, too. Look up the following words in your desk dictionary: *maize, police, cole slaw, brigade, muggy, patio, ski, folio, urban, janitor, cigarette, barbecue, fugue.* Discuss your findings.

14

Harpin' Boont in Boonville

Timothy Tyler

In the small village of Boonville nestled in California's Anderson Valley, one of the oldest invented languages in the United States survives. In 1968, *Time* sent correspondent Timothy Tyler to interview the people of Boonville. Tyler's report was published in February, 1969. Since that time, Boonville lingo has been collected and studied by Charles C. Adams in *Boontling: An American Lingo* (Austin: The University of Texas Press, 1971). While reading Tyler's article, consider reasons that might account for the longevity of Boontling. Do you think it can survive the "space age"?

THE ROAD had been hairpin turns through foggy mountains for the past 20 miles. All at once there was the sign: Boonville, pop. 1,003. Sure enough, there were some shacks along the road. No lights anywhere except the eerie blue glow of a television coming from one window. We stopped there, and after a minute one of the oldest men alive appeared. Stooped, toothless mouth indented, wearing glasses with handmade brass temples that could have been a hundred years old, he looked happy to have someone to talk to. We asked him about a place to stay. He looked surprised:

"You piked to boont in your moche geekin' on a motel?" he said. "Motel's strung, kimmie, but pike in the nook an' whittle a slib by the jeffer. Got enough zeese for a gormin' tidric. You from Belk?" We repeated our question, more slowly. He seemed to understand. "There's a nonch sluggin' nook ye can pike to," he said and gestured up the road. We thanked him and went back to our rented car, which wouldn't start. Finally, we walked the way he pointed, found the rickety New Boonville Hotel, roused a pale clerk, and were shown to a room where the floor had the solidarity of a trampoline and the only decoration was a 1948 calendar from a Chinese laundry in San Francisco.

Boonville is the Cannery Row of the '60s, a case study of isolated humanity intertwined with the land and the elements. It lies 100 miles north of San Francisco at the southern end of Mendocino County's Anderson Valley, a corridor 30 miles long that takes the Navarro River northwest to the Pacific. The southern half looks like Scotland: steep hills, lush fields dotted with sheep and shacks with wood smoke coming out of the chimneys. The valley is beautiful and silent. Two thousand people in maybe 150 square miles. Having few of the distractions of urban life, they see death clearly and have no urge to escape it. All they ask is a little sex, a little booze and a little humor in the meantime.

For more than half a century, their humor has come largely out of their exotic argot. It is their link now with a more exciting, more amusing past. We went back next morning to the house of the old man who spoke the language. His name is Phocian McGimsey, but everybody calls him Levi. He is 73. His grandfather came West to Boonville in 1852. He told us that the language is "Boontling," which is a corruption of Boonville Lingo. In English sprinkled with Boontling, Levi described what Boonville was like in those days: a rough frontier town first settled in the 1850s by subsistence farmers and sheep and cattle ranchers, most of them of Scotch-Irish descent.

One day in '92, sitting around the Anytime Saloon, Reg and Tom Burger and the Duff brothers started putting some of their old Scotch-Irish dialect words together with some on-the-spot code words into a language that the enemies—be they womenfolk, their rivals, their elders, their children—could not possibly understand. It caught on, rapidly losing its value as a code; soon "Boontlingers" and their friends were eagerly trying to shark (con) each other with new inventions.

It was more fun to call coffee *zeese* instead of coffee, because it recalled old Z. C., a cook who made coffee so strong you could float an egg on it. Or to call working *ottin'*, after an industrious logger named Otto. To call a big fire in the grate a *jeffer*, because old Jeff Vestal always had a big fire going. To say *charlie ball* for embarrass, because old Charlie Ball, a local Indian, was so shy he never said a word. To say *forbes*, short for four bits, and *tubes*, for two bits. To call a phone a *buckywalter* after Walter Levi, known back then for having a phone at home. To say *ball* for good, because the old standard of quality was the Ball-Band shoe, with the red ball on the box.

Other words came right out of old Scotch-Irish dialect—*wee* for small, *kimmie* for man, *tweed* for young man, *deek* for look at. Still other words were borrowed from the Pomo Indians, who moved off to a reservation after an early settler set up his general store in the middle of their camping ground. A few words are corruptions of French, like *gorm* (gourmand) for eat.

Gorming has its full terminology. Pie is *charlie brown* because the latter had to have pie at every meal. *Dom* is chicken, after the

Dominique, a particular breed. *Broadie* is a cow or a steak. *Gano* is the name of a very hard kind of apple they used to grow in the valley and, by extension, Boontling for all apples. Bacon is *bowrp* (a contraction of boar pig), eggs are *easters*, as in "If I don't shy to the sluggin' region [sleeping place] soon, I may as well set me a jeffer and gorm bowrp and easters."

For a child learning his nursery rhymes, *Old Mother Hubbard* would go like this: "The old dame piked for the chigrel nook/ For gorms for her ball belljeemer;/ The gorms had shied, the nook was strung,/ And the ball belljeemer had neemer."[1] Then there were the code names for *nonch* (not-nice) subjects. To go to bed with a girl was to *burlap* her, because one day in the 1890s someone walked into the general store, found no clerk, checked the storeroom and found him making love to a young lady on a pile of sacks. The word caught on, although it got competition from *ricky-chow*, an onomatopoeic description of the twanging bedsprings in the Boonville Hotel's honeymoon suite.

Some of the language was developed to cushion tragedy: everybody feared having their sheep frozen or starved by a sudden change in the weather. That was too big a disaster just to report baldly, so they would say "That frigid perel [cold rain, which resembles little pearls] made many white spots [dead lambs]. There'll be nemer croppies [no more sheep, which crop the grass] come boche season [*boche*, meaning deer, is derived from a Pomo word]."

Boontling was in full bloom between 1900 and 1940. "We would make fun of the visitors when the mail stage came through every three weeks," recalls Levi. "They all thought we was crazy. I spoke Boontling ever since I could talk. When they drafted me in '17, I had to learn to talk English all over again."

With bad times in the '30s, some of the Boonters lost their sense of humor, and the number of Boontlingers declined. In the '40s, when a logging boom began, the population of Boonville temporarily tripled to 3,000. This was the first real influx of new people from the outside world since the town was settled, and the strangers dealt the language another blow. Television also has brought change, as Boonters soak up pernicious English from the machines.

Now Boontling is spoken by only a minority of Boonters. They have a club that meets every other week in one of the members' houses to *harp* (speak). There are 20 members, though more like 200 harp and understand. Mack Miller, in his 60s, drives down from Ukiah, a

---

[1] *Piked* is went, *chigrel* is food, *book* is place, *belljeemer* is hound or dog, which comes from *beljeek*, the word for rabbit (a corruption of Belgian hare), plus a suffix that makes it a rabbit dog, *shied* is gone away, *strung* is dead or empty.

larger town on the coast, "because I'm tonguecuppy [sick] when there's nemer to harp Boont with." The local highway patrolman, a young fellow who lives up the valley in the state park, has picked up Boontling and started to lose his tenuous grasp of the mother tongue. "You're arking the japeway," he said to a stranger recently. "Sorry, I mean you're blocking the driveway." They predict that the cop will start attending meetings soon.

But *codgiehood*, their word for old age, is overtaking most of the Boontlingers. The oldtimers—Wee Ite and Buzzard, and Fuzz and Deekin', Wee Tumps and Highpockets, and Iron Mountain, Skeeter and Sandy—are dwindling. They are saying their last sayings in Boont: "A dom in the dukes is baller than dubs in the sham [bush]." A couple of dude ranches have sprung up in the valley, and just a year ago, for the first time ever, a bank dared open a branch in once-woolly Boonville. The end is near.

FOR DISCUSSION AND REVIEW

1 What are some of the ways in which words are formed in Boontling? Give some examples.

2 According to W. Nelson Francis in "Revolution in Grammar" (p. 111), American English uses five devices to signal structural meaning. To what extent are these devices used in Boontling? How does Boontling differ from American English?

3 What factors have accounted for the preservation of Boontling? Why does Tyler feel that its "end is near"?

4 How does Flexner define *argot* in "Preface to the *Dictionary of American Slang*" (p. 272)? Does Boontling conform to his definition? Explain.

15

As

I Listened

to Archie

Say "Hebe" . . .

The lexicon of American English abounds with terms of abuse and contempt for members of racial, religious, and nationality groups. These terms reveal many of the latent social prejudices existent in the United States. Archie Bunker, the blue-collar bigot hero of CBS's hit comedy "All in the Family," frequently uses such words as *Hebe*, *pinko*, *jungle bunny*, and *Polack*. After a somewhat shaky start, the show skyrocketed to the top of the Nielsen ratings. Critics have acclaimed it as an "honest show" that produces "honest laughter." Laura Z. Hobson, author of *Gentleman's Agreement* and *The Tenth Month*, does not agree. Her criticism of "All in the Family" appeared in *The New York Times*.

Laura Z. Hobson

I HAVE a most peculiar complaint about the bigotry in the hit TV comedy, "All in the Family." There's not enough of it.

Hebe, spade, spic, coon, Polack—these are the words that its central character Archie Bunker is forever using, plus endless variations, like jungle bunnies, black beauties, the chosen people, yenta, gook, chink, spook and so on. Quite a splashing display of bigotry, but I repeat, nowhere near enough of it.

Let me back up a little. Years ago, after *Gentleman's Agreement*, I decided I'd never again write about bigotry or prejudice, at least not about the racial or religious kinds. I've stuck to it. No lectures, no articles, no books about discrimination against Jews, against blacks, against whites, against Puerto Ricans. Perhaps I did not want to keep harping on one theme; perhaps I had nothing to say.

But after 24 years something happened. A television show that treated bigotry for laughs appeared on the screens of the nation and after a shaky start, when it was way down at the bottom of the Nielsen ratings, it went on to win the Emmy for the best new situation comedy of the year and soon after achieved the glory of the Number One rating of all sitcoms.

The Number One Nielsen, I'm told, means an audience of some 40 million families per week. Forty million families means about 100 million people. Old people, young people, black, white, Protestant, Catholic, Jewish, well-educated, ill-educated, secure, insecure—100 million people every week.

I didn't see the show at its beginnings except for a few minutes of one episode about Archie's horror that a black family had bought a house in his neighborhood. Those few minutes were all I could take so I didn't get to know the show until after it won the Emmy, and then it was rerun time and I had to make my private little study that way, with an additional pair of kinescopes obligingly shown me at CBS by the Press Relations Department. Thus, though I may have missed one or two of the original 13, I did get to see the majority, with the kinescopes assuring me I had caught two of "the best."

At the start, "All in the Family" drew a few harsh criticisms—of these, more later—but mostly the TV critics and columnists, like the telephoners, all cheered. Cleveland Amory, that historian of the proper and crusader against cruelty to animals, the four-legged kind, gave it perhaps the greatest and most widely read rave, a full page in *TV Guide*. "Not just the best-written, best-directed and best-acted show on television, it is the best show on television." Tom Mackin, in the *Newark Evening News*, called it "excruciatingly funny . . . the best situation comedy yet." Norman Dresser, in the *Toledo Blade*, said the show had "everything . . . honesty, true wit, a bite which is no mushy quasi-love bite, sharp and literate writing and fine acting."

And Jack Gould in this newspaper, and in many other papers that reprinted his column, wrote a follow-up piece some six weeks after the January debut of the show, presumably after plenty of time for watching it and for reflection about it, which ended, "Some of Archie's words may chill the spine, but to root out bigotry has defied man's best efforts for generations, and the weapon of laughter just might succeed. The possibility entitles 'All in the Family' to a chance."

Mr. Gould himself did not use any of those words that might chill the spine, did not come right out in hard print with spade and coon and Hebe and spic and Polack. For reasons of his own, he preferred to sum them up as "a string of epithets and slurring remarks that understandably provoke the affected parties."

Of the adverse critics, John Leonard in *Life* called the show "a wretched program" in which "bigotry becomes a form of dirty joke," and asked, "Why review a wretched program? . . . Well, why fix the septic tank?" Long before Jack Gould's piece, *The New York Times* ran two other pieces, both adverse, one by Fred Ferretti the morning

before the show premiered, and one by Stephanie Harrington 12 days
later, both of which reveal their authors' disapproval, even disgust.
Phrases like "vulgar and silly" and "painfully offensive lines" showed
what Miss Harrington felt, and Mr. Ferretti said the bigot-words "don't
make one laugh so much as they force self-conscious, semi-amused
gasps."

The *Boston Herald Traveler* said, "The same network that fired the
Smothers Brothers presents a show crackling with racist remarks . . .
crude and coarse . . . and often offensive." And out in the *Los Angeles
Sentinel,* in what must have been one of the last things he wrote before
his sudden death in March, Whitney Young Jr. of the Urban League
was even more vigorous. "Gratuitous insults" is what he called those
words and remarks, and the show itself "A new low in taste." "It is irresponsible," he wrote, "to air a show like this at a time when our nation
is polarized and torn by racism."

That came closest to what I felt, but beyond that I began to be
haunted by the notion that there was something else I had to get hold
of, for myself if for nothing else. Something the critics weren't saying,
something nobody seemed to be saying, not even the people I sought
out as experts in the field of race relations. As I kept on ploughing
through all the reviews, the feeling intensified. I was pulled up often
by the phrases "honest show" and "honest laughter" and "a lovable
bigot."

This last particularly impressed me. I found it many times in one
form or another, the first time in a longish interview by Don Freeman
in the *San Diego Union* and the *Cincinnati Enquirer.* In it, after con-
tending that reality was the core of his show, Norman Lear, its writer,
director and, with Bud Yorkin, its producer, had said, "My father was
what you might call a lovable bigot, as Archie is."

A lovable bigot. Your neighborhood bigot. This is an honest show.
This is the way it really is. These bouquets cropped up again and again
in the reviews and special stories. I must have read them all, for on my
desk are no less than 97 clippings from all over the country, the few
bad notices right in with the raves and the lets-wait-and-see straddlers,
all supplied me by no less a collector than that same Press Relations
Department at CBS.

A kind word here about the Press Relations Department at CBS,
for, alas, some unkind words about other CBS matters may crop up
later. The kind words arose with my first phone call to a vice president
there, about two months after Emmy night, and I began by explaining,
"I'm going to write a hostile piece about 'All in the Family,' and I
wonder if I could bother you with some questions?" This perhaps naive
way of putting it seemed to endear me to the vice president, for though
he later asked to remain anonymous, he couldn't have been more re-

sponsive to the questions I asked on the phone or in person, nor more forthcoming about running those kinescopes, at a cost, he said, of about $150 to CBS, nor about delegating various people in his department to collect and send me those 97 clippings and supply me with all sorts of pertinent facts, dates, titles, credits, everything I asked. Except the answer to one question.

On that particular question I got nowhere. It was tied into the special point I was trying to get hold of and day by day it mattered more to me. I asked it of the vice president during a good solid talk in his office and he said he would call Hollywood where the show originated and then call me back, but after he did call me back, I still got nowhere. As I began talking to and interviewing all sorts of people, and it began to get around town that I was writing something about the show, a man named Buddy Clarke, who introduced himself as Norman Lear's public relations man, called me and offered any help he could give. Again I said it would be a hostile piece, and again that was taken in stride, but when I tried my One Question on him, I again got nowhere. He said he would call the Coast and get back to me. A day later he did, and it was the same old story. Nowhere.

But it seems to me such a natural question, such an inevitable question, if you really let yourself think about this bigotry-for-laughs that's shown to 100 million people each week by a responsible network—so responsible that for a while last winter, an avuncular voice-over assured the listener during the credits that " 'All in the Family' . . . seeks to throw a humorous spotlight on our frailties, prejudices and concerns."

I kept asking that same question outside CBS as I phoned or went to see certain leaders in the field of fighting discrimination and prejudice. Mostly my question startled them—they had never thought to ask it themselves. At the Anti-Defamation League of B'Nai B'Rith, I talked for more than an hour to Benjamin R. Epstein, its national director, and Oscar Cohen, director of its National Program Division, and was surprised that their organization had taken "no official position" on the show, though several months had gone by since its premiere.

No official position had been taken by the National Conference of Christians and Jews either, another of the nation's best-known and longest-established human-relations organizations. There I talked to Dr. Sterling Brown, its president, following a full hour with Harry A. Robinson, a young vice president, and neither of them had considered the point my special question raised. By telephone I talked with Dore Schary, recently Mayor Lindsay's Commissioner of Cultural Affairs; he had not seen the show, had heard people say it was funny, and also reacted strongly to the one point I was trying to examine.

I don't know about the NAACP and any official position it may have taken, for despite some six or eight separate efforts over a period of two weeks to get past Roy Wilkins's secretary, to whom I explained what I was calling about, I was never able to get through to Mr. Wilkins himself, even for a telephone interview.

In all these major groups, by the way, the secretaries to whom I talked also surprised me—they all liked the show, thought it was funny. The young vice president, Mr. Robinson, also thought it was funny; he saw Archie Bunker, the blue-collar "hero," as an ill-educated boob who constantly revealed his lower classness by spouting stuff like "misconscrued ideas," "detergent to crime," "I'm mortifried" and "not German to the conversation." I asked Mr. Robinson if this might not be an elitist point of view; he himself was indeed superior to Archie Bunker and thus could discount him, but did he think most of the 100 million viewers were college graduates and executives as he was? He willingly conceded that this was a matter he had overlooked.

None of these people at the head of these organizations, of course, nor others at the Catholic Archdiocese, at the Italian-American Civil Rights League, at the PR office of the Commonwealth of Puerto Rico— none of them wondered that I was disturbed at seeing bigotry aired weekly to the nation as a laughable little matter, nor did they disagree that the rebuttal, supposedly built into each show, was pretty feeble. Indeed they agreed that the chiding of Archie by his "liberal" daughter Gloria and her college-student husband, also "liberal" and jobless and living off her family, were merely two more butts for Archie in other kinds of stereotypic prejudice, giving him endless chances to get off nifties about "radical liberal garbage" or "pinko atheistic meathead," as well as "pinko bleedin' heart lawyers" and endless variations of "you dumb Polack." Even his wife Edith, with her stream of dimwitticisms, supplies him with the cue to use his frequent injunction, "Will you stifle, dingbat?" and to hold forth in general on the dopey inferiority of all dingbats, i.e., women.

Somewhere in there among all the phone calls and personal interviews I began to go back to the night I first really tangled with "All in the Family," long before I thought of breaking my 24-year vow. It was the night of May 9, the night of the Emmy Awards, and it involved the word Hebe.

Johnny Carson was the glamorous master of ceremonies that night, with a glamorous audience of TV professionals, actors, writers, directors, producers, the works—and beyond them the national audience looking on. Just after the announcement that "All in the Family" had won the Emmy, and of course in the spirit of the show, Johnny Carson wisecracked, "Norman Lear—a nice guy for a Hebe." The audience roared with laughter.

I suppose Norman Lear laughed too. Would he have laughed, I suddenly wondered, if Johnny Carson had said, "Norman Lear, a nice guy for a kike"?

Unthinkable. Johnny Carson would never never—

I know he wouldn't. Besides, it was never never used in the show. Hebe, yes; chosen people, yes; yenta, yes; yid, yes. But kike? Never.

I began to listen for it as I began my little study of the re-runs. Never. And sheeny? Never.

Had Norman Lear never realized that what bigots really called Jews was kike or sheeny? That they didn't really go around talking about the chosen people or one of that tribe or yenta? That their own words, the words they actually used, were kike and sheeny? Then why did Norman Lear, in this honest portrayal of the bigot next door, never say either?

And that other word. Where was that one, among the spades and coons and jungle bunnies and black beauties? I was listening to the shows regularly by then, pad and pencil at the ready, jotting down the actual words Archie was so free with, and I never once heard it. But do the bigots of this world really talk about spades moving in next door, or not breaking bread with no jungle bunnies, or signing petitions to keep black beauties from ruining real estate values on the street?

You know the word they use. The one word, the hideous word.

Unthinkable too. Don't even print it. Nigger.

You know and I know and Mr. Lear knows and the anonymous vice president of the Press Relations Department at CBS knows that Archie Bunker in the flesh would be holding forth about niggers moving in next door, and not breaking bread with no niggers, and getting up a petition for keeping niggers from wrecking real estate values on the street.

Everybody knows it. Then why doesn't this honest show use the real words that real bigots always use?

Is there a little list of Forbidden Words floating around CBS? Is it a little list self-imposed by Mr. Lear himself? Or is it a little list imposed by the Program Practices Department, and the CBS executives in charge of that department?

That was my one big question. Instinctively I knew the answer, but tied into it was that other point: what was that list for? Were the honest producer and the responsible network trying to make bigotry more acceptable? Were they trying to clean it up, deodorize it, make millions of people more comfy about hearing it, indulging in it?

It strikes me that, unconsciously or not, that's just what they were doing. And of course it was the essential trick, to make this show laughable not only to the bigots among that 100 million out there, but also to the "bigotees," the very Hebes and coons and spades and spics and Polacks themselves.

Do you think that any of the nation's blacks would laugh if Archie Bunker constantly said nigger? Do you think many Jews would laugh if he said kike?

I gather that in the first show he did say yid, for nearly every one of the early reviews include that little word, but then something drastic must have happened, for yid was not once said in all the shows I saw myself.

Another missing word was Mafia, though I did catch one remark about a Dago artist painting a ceiling in Rome. Missing also was any name-calling of Catholics. None of that "hotline to the Vatican" and "Pope in the White House" that was so rampant among bigots in the 1960 election, not even any micks and Irish micks.

Strange, all these omissions. But then there are some 20 to 35 million first-and-second-generation Italian-Americans in this country, and some 13 million Irish-Americans and, often overlapping, over 48 million Catholics, and if you got *them* good and sore, as well as nine million Spanish-speaking people and six million Jews and 23 million blacks, where would your Nielsen ratings be?

Don't risk it. Don't tell it like it is. Clean it up, deterge it, bleach it, enzyme it, and you'll have a show about a lovable bigot that everybody except a few pinko atheistic bleedin' hearts will love.

Well, I differ. I don't think you can be a bigot and be lovable; I don't think you can be a black-baiter and lovable, nor an anti-Semite and lovable. And I don't think the millions who watch this show should be conned into thinking that you can be.

And there you have the basis for my peculiar complaint: there's nowhere near enough bigotry in "All in the Family," not by a long sight. How about showing the real thing for a while, before accepting any more praise for honest shows and honest laughter? What about laying it on the line about bigots and then seeing whether CBS switchboards light up with nothing but cheers?

But this is supposed to be a comedy! I know, but a network is supposed to care about the public interest. And one thing that's nearly as nasty as exposing those millions, and their children, week after week to bigotry, is to expose them constantly to hypocrisy.

Particularly since more children than ever will be watching in the new season that starts this week. As I finish this piece, in late August, CBS has just announced a last-minute switch in its schedules. Here in the East the show had been on at 9:30 Tuesday nights; in May, word went out that this would shift in the fall to 10:30 Monday nights, in an effort, some said, to cut away from the younger, more impressionable kids in its vast audience. But now all that has been ditched and the new time—oh, triumph—will be Saturday nights at 8, a time when even the kindergarten set can be in on the laughable business of bigotry.

To be among the first to teach impressionable children that they're not wanted in certain neighborhoods, that there's something that makes people laugh at them and look down on them and call them names, seems to me callous, even cruel. Indeed, to teach other children that it's quite all right to go around saying spade and Hebe and coon and spic—for of course kids always imitate what they see on TV—that seems to me pretty cruel too.

Is there a difference between laughter and cruel laughter? I went back to some unused notes I had made way back at the start when I first felt caught up in this show, and the notes suddenly seemed pertinent. When it comes to writing something like this piece, I'm sort of a nut about doing 10 times more research than I could ever possibly use, talking to 10 times more people, reading 10 times more material. One of the things I did was to re-read a book I hadn't looked at in all the years since college, Henri Bergson's *Laughter*, published 70 years ago.

Right off on page four, Bergson talks of "the absence of feeling which usually accompanies laughter," and speaks of "a momentary anesthesia of the heart." All through the book are lines that are so pertinent they make you flinch. "Comedy can only begin at the point where our neighbor's personality ceases to affect us. It begins, in fact, with a growing callousness. . . . In laughter we always find an unavowed intention to humiliate."

Of course "All in the Family" doesn't mean to do that, nor does CBS. Just now, in the avalanche of spot promotions that herald the new season, they seem to be stepping pretty warily. In one of these promos, Archie puts on his pained face as Edith explains that she sent $3 to OTB because she thought it was for "treating lung disease." In another he tells her that no, the Pentagon Papers weren't what's delivered on people's doorsteps in the morning, and in the third she's worrying about Queen Elizabeth and the Common Market, and why couldn't the poor thing afford a really good market.

Nowhere in any of these promos is there one whiff of bigotry. Not one word about Hebes and spics and spades and coons. Was this whiter-than-white advertising one more aspect of that Forbidden List nobody had ever yet acknowledged?

That tore it. I picked up the phone and at last made the one call I had been telling myself all along was futile—to California and Norman Lear. The anonymous vice president had long since told him I might call him, had briefed him on the one question I most certainly would ask him, had even given me the phone number I was to use.

Mr. Lear was tied up on another line, his secretary said, and illogically enough, while I waited, I thought about network censors and censorship in general. I am unalterably opposed to all forms of censorship, not only the interior hidden kinds within an organization or a government, but also to any external and public forms, such as pressure on sponsors and libraries and the press. Equally unalterably, I believe in a citizen's right to protest, in peaceful assembly, on lecture platforms, in books and plays and films, and in the newspapers.

Two or three times the secretary came back and apologized for the lengthening delay and finally she said that Mr. Lear couldn't manage it at all just now and would have to call me back later on.

It was some hours before the call came and when it did, it was not Norman Lear out there in Hollywood, but his PR man, Buddy Clarke, right here in town.

"Norman Lear," he began, "says if you would go out to California, he would be delighted to meet you, run some tapes for you, spend all the time you might want in a personal interview about 'All in the Family,' but he feels that this is too sensitive a subject to discuss on the phone."

And that was that. One last time, nowhere.

Or was it?

FOR DISCUSSION AND REVIEW

1 Why does Laura Hobson say that there is "nowhere near enough [bigotry]" in "All in the Family"?
2 Hobson feels that there is no such thing as a "lovable bigot." Do you agree?
3 Do you believe that by throwing "a humorous spotlight on our frailties, prejudices and concerns" "All in the Family" is fighting discrimination and prejudice? Defend your position.
4 Collect terms of abuse and contempt for a racial, religious, or nationality group in your area. Do you feel that these terms can be ranked in a hierarchy of offensiveness? Does your conclusion validate Laura Hobson's conclusion? Explain.
5 Four weeks after Laura Hobson's review appeared, Norman Lear, creator-producer of "All in the Family," responded in an article entitled "As I Read How Laura Saw Archie . . ." (The New York Times, October 10, 1971, Section D, pp. 17, 30). Read Lear's rebuttal. How effectively do you feel Lear responds to Hobson's criticisms?

PROJECTS FOR "AMERICANS SPEAKING"

1 Make a report on the purposes and methods of the Linguistic Atlas of the United States. Use the library card catalogue, Hans Kurath's Handbook of the Linguistic Geography of New England, the PMLA Bibliography, and the International Index to the Social Sciences and Humanities to locate materials for this project.
2 Many authors, in order to enhance the aura of realism, try to represent dialect in their writing. Consider the following passage from Mark Twain's The Adventures of Huckleberry Finn:

> "Why, Huck, doan' de French people talk de same way we does?"
> "No, Jim; you couldn't understand a word they said—not a single word."
> "Well, now, I be ding-busted! How do dat come?"

"I don't know; but it's so. I got some of their jabber out of a book. S'pose a man was to come to you and say *Polly-voo-franzy*—what would you think?"

"I wouldn' think nuff'n; I'd take en bust him over de head. Dat is, if he warn't white. I wouldn't 'low no nigger to call me dat."

"Shucks, it ain't calling you anything. It's only saying do you know how to talk French."

"Well, den, why couldn't he *say* it?"

"Why, he *is* a-saying it. That's a Frenchman's *way* of saying it."

"Well, it's a blame' ridicklous way, en I doan' want to hear no mo' 'bout it. Dey ain' no sense in it."

"Looky here, Jim; does a cat talk like we do?"

"No, a cat don't."

"Well, does a cow?"

"No, a cow don't, nuther."

"Does a cat talk like a cow, or a cow talk like a cat?"

"No, dey don't."

"It's natural and right for 'em to talk different from each other, ain't it?"

"Course."

"And ain't it natural and right for a cat and a cow to talk different from *us*?"

"Why, mos' sholy it is."

"Well, then, why ain't it natural and right for a *Frenchman* to talk different from *us*? You answer me that."

"Is a cat a man, Huck?"

"No."

"Well, den, dey ain't no sense in a cat talkin' like a man. Is a cow a man? —er is a cow a cat?"

"No, she ain't neither of them."

"Well, den, she ain' got no business to talk like either one er the yuther of 'em. Is a Frenchman a man?"

"Yes."

"*Well*, den! Dad blame it, why doan' he *talk* like a man? You answer me *dat!*"

I see it warn't no use wasting words—you can't learn a nigger to argue. So I quit.

What devices does Twain use to evoke the grammatical, lexical, and phonological peculiarities of this regional and social speech?

3 *Select the work of an author whose characters speak a social or regional dialect, e.g., William Dean Howells,* The Rise of Silas Lapham; *Bret Harte,* The Luck of Roaring Camp and Other Sketches; *Sarah Orne Jewett,* The Country of the Pointed Firs; *William Faulkner,* The Sound and the Fury; *Willa Cather,* My Antonia; *or John Steinbeck,* Grapes of Wrath. *Identify the dialect presented and discuss the devices the author uses to represent dialect. Read a passage aloud; how closely does it approximate actual speech?*

4 *According to Paul Roberts (p. 335), you are presently a member of a college speech community. As a class or individual project, collect vocabulary items which are either unique to your student community*

or used in an unusual way by the community. Compare your listing with lexicons of collegiate slang in back issues of Current Slang.

5   *Having read the arguments by William Labov (p. 393), William Rasp-berry (p. 412), and James Sledd (p. 418) about functional bi-dialectal-ism, discuss their ideas. Do you consider the sociologic and economic factors raised by the various authors important? What issues do not appear to be relevant? From an educational point of view, which argu-ment is the strongest? Defend your position in an essay.*

6   *As evidenced by Alva Davis' study (p. 377), word geography is a fas-cinating aspect of dialect study. Usually the vocabulary items of a dia-lect are collected by direct questions. For example, to the question "What do you call a paper container for groceries, etc.?", informants responded either bag, sack, toot, or poke. Discuss with members of your class terms elicited by the following questions:*

   a. *What do you call onions that are served raw early in the year?*

   b. *What do you call a round breakfast food made with flour and eaten with butter and syrup?*

   c. *What do you call a machine for playing records?*

   d. *What formal terms do you have for a maternal parent?*

   e. *What informal terms do you have for a paternal parent?*

   f. *What do you call a carbonated, non-alcoholic beverage?*

   g. *What do you call land that usually has some standing water with trees and bushes growing in it?*

   h. *What words do you use that mean "opposite"?*

   i. *What nicknames or pejorative terms do you have for groups of people living in nearby settlements?*

   j. *When a clock has the big hand on 9 and the little hand almost on 5, what time is it?*

7   *Compose a questionnaire of your own that is designed to ascertain vocabulary items of a dialect. You may wish to consult the extensive questionnaire compiled by Frederic Cassidy in A Method for Collecting Dialect, Publication of the American Dialect Society, No. 20 (November 1953), 19–96, while preparing your own. Distribute the questionnaire on campus and tabulate your results. Do any regional patterns emerge?*

8   *Dialect differences in pronunciation abound. Here are some words in which such differences exist. Compare your pronunciation of these items with those of others in the class: collar, car, apricot, paw, empty, dog, tomato, door, clientele, marry, washed, garage, mangy, Mary, oil, house, roof, can, very, sorry, greasy, either, fog, lot, caller, water. What pronunciation differences do you note among the members of your class? Are there any regional or social patterns of pronunciation evident? Compare your results with the regionalisms discussed by John Nist (p. 371).*

SELECTED BIBLIOGRAPHY

Allen, Harold B. "The Linguistic Atlases: Our New Resource." *English Journal*, 45 (April 1956), 188–94. (A discussion of *Linguistic Atlas* data and their applications.)

——. "The Primary Dialect Areas of the Upper Midwest." *Studies in Language and Linguistics in Honor of Charles C. Fries.* Ed. Albert H. Marckwardt. Ann Arbor: The English Language Institute, The University of Michigan, 1964. (A study of the lexical, phonological, and morphological features of the speech in the Upper Midwest region.)

——, and Gary N. Underwood, eds. *Readings in American Dialectology.* New York: Appleton-Century-Crofts, 1971. (An anthology of essays dealing with important aspects of American dialectology.)

Atwood, E. Bagby. " 'Grease' and 'Greasy': A Study of Geographical Variation." *University of Texas Studies in English*, 29 (1950), 249–60. (A classic study of geographical variation in pronunciation based on *Linguistic Atlas* materials.)

Brown, Claude. "The Language of Soul." *Esquire*, April 1968, p. 88. (An examination of one variety of Afro-American speech.)

Cassidy, Frederic G. *A Method for Collecting Dialect. Publication of the American Dialect Society*, No. 20 (November 1953), 5–96. (Entire issue devoted to a discussion of field methods and the presentation of a comprehensive dialect questionnaire.)

Cordasco, Frank M. "Knocking Down the Language Walls." *Commonweal*, October 6, 1967, pp. 6–8. (A discussion of legislation to establish bilingual American education programs.)

Drake, James A. "The Effect of Urbanization upon Regional Vocabulary." *American Speech*, 36 (February 1961), 17–33. (A study of regional dialect items and urbanization in Cleveland, Ohio.)

Fasold, Ralph W. "Distinctive Linguistic Characteristics of Black English." *Linguistics and Language Study: 20th Roundtable Meeting.* Ed. James E. Alatis. Washington, D.C.: Georgetown University Press, 1970. (An examination of the distinctive differences between the nonstandard speech of poor blacks and the speech of whites.)

Francis, W. Nelson. *The English Language: An Introduction.* New York: W. W. Norton & Company, 1965. (See pp. 223–260 for a consideration of regional, social, educational, and functional variations in English.)

Hinton, Norman D. "The Language of Jazz Musicians." *Publication of the American Dialect Society*, No. 30 (November 1958), 38–48. (A glossary of words used by jazz musicians in their everyday speech.)

Hoffman, Melvin J. "Bi-dialectalism Is Not the Linguistics of White Supremacy: Sense Versus Sensibilities." *The English Record*, 21 (April 1971), 95–102. (An argument refuting Sledd's position.)

Houston, Susan. "A Sociolinguistic Consideration of the Black English of Children in Northern Florida." *Language*, 45 (September 1969), 599–607. (A linguistic and sociolinguistic examination of Black English as spoken in one of Florida's northern counties.)

Ives, Sumner. "Dialect Differentiation in the Stories of Joel Chandler Harris." *American Literature*, 17 (March 1955), 88–96. (A study of the social implications of Harris's dialects.)

——. "A Theory of Literary Dialect." *Tulane Studies in English*, 2 (1950), 137–82. (An essential reference for all students doing work in literary dialects.)

Labov, William. *The Nonstandard Vernacular of the Negro Community: Some Practical Suggestions.* Washington, D.C.: Education Resources Information Center, 1967. (Some advice to teachers concerning bi-dialectalism for the speaker of a nonstandard dialect.)

———. *The Social Stratification of English in New York City.* Washington, D.C.: Center for Applied Linguistics, 1966. (A landmark sociolinguistic study of New York City speech.)

———. "Stages in the Acquisition of Standard English." *Social Dialects and Language Learning.* Ed. Roger W. Shuy. Champaign, Illinois: NCTE, 1964. (An investigation of the acquisition of standard English by children in New York.)

Marckwardt, Albert H. *American English.* New York: Oxford University Press, 1958. (An introduction to American dialects from an historical point of view.)

———. "Principal and Subsidiary Areas in the North-Central States." *Publication of the American Dialect Society,* No. 27 (April 1957), 3–15. (A regional study of dialect variation which includes seven maps.)

Maurer, David W. *The Argot of the Racetrack.* Publication of the American Dialect Society, No. 16 (November 1951), 3–70. (Entire issue devoted to a discussion of racetrack terms with a lexicon.)

———, and Victor H. Vogel. "The Argot of Narcotics Addicts." *Narcotics and Narcotic Addiction.* 3rd edition. Springfield, Illinois: Charles C. Thomas, 1967. (A discussion of argot formation followed by a glossary of terms.)

McDowell, Tremaine. "The Use of Negro Dialect by Harriet Beecher Stowe." *American Speech,* 6 (June 1931), 322–26. (A study in literary dialect.)

Mencken, H. L. *The American Language: The Fourth Edition and the Two Supplements.* Abridged and ed. Raven I. McDavid, Jr. New York: Alfred A. Knopf, 1963. (A classic study of American English.)

Miller, Mary R. "Bilingualism in Northern New England." *Publication of the American Dialect Society,* No. 52 (November 1969), 1–23. (A detailed study of French-English bilingualism.)

Ortego, Philip D. "Schools for Mexican-Americans: Between Two Cultures." *Saturday Review,* April 17, 1971, pp. 62, 63, 64, 80, 81. (A discussion of bilingual education for Mexican-American children.)

Pederson, Lee A. "Negro Speech in *The Adventures of Huckleberry Finn.*" *Mark Twain Journal,* 13 (1966), 1–4. (An examination of the literary representation of Negro dialect in Twain's classic novel.)

———. "Terms of Abuse for Some Chicago Social Groups." *Publication of the American Dialect Society,* No. 42 (November 1964), 26–48. (A detailed study of terms of abuse and contempt for members of racial, religious, and nationality groups in Chicago.)

Pyles, Thomas. *Words and Ways of American English.* New York: Random House, 1952. (An introduction to American English from colonial times to present.)

Rawles, Myrtle Read. " 'Boontling'—Esoteric Speech of Boonville, California." *Western Folklore,* 25 (1966), 93–103. (A discussion of the lingo used by the people of Boonville.)

Reed, Carroll E. *Dialects of American English.* New York: The World Publishing Company, 1967. (An introduction to dialect study with a unit devoted to sectional atlas studies.)

———. "The Pronunciation of English in the Pacific Northwest." *Language,* 37 (October–December 1961), 559–64. (A description of the pronunciation of vowels and consonants by people in the Pacific Northwest.)

Shuy, Roger W. "Detroit Speech: Careless, Awkward, and Inconsistent, or Systematic, Graceful, and Regular?" *Elementary English,* 45 (May 1968), 565–69. (A discussion of nonstandard speech in Detroit, Michigan.)

Stockton, Eric. "Poe's Use of Negro Dialect in 'The Gold-Bug.' " *Studies in Language and Linguistics in Honor of Charles C. Fries.* Ed. Albert H. Marckwardt. Ann Arbor: The English Language Institute, The University of Michigan, 1964. (An analysis of Jupiter's speech as an example of literary dialect used by pre-Civil War writers.)

Underwood, Gary N. "Vocabulary Change in the Upper Midwest." *Publication of the American Dialect Society,* No. 49 (April 1968), 8–28. (An investigation of language change which utilizes four generations of informants.)

Williamson, Juanita V., and Virginia M. Burke, eds. *A Various Language: Perspectives on American Dialects.* New York: Holt, Rinehart and Winston, Inc., 1971. (An anthology of essential articles dealing with American dialects.)

Wood, Gordon R. "Word Distribution in the Interior South." *Publication of the American Dialect Society,* No. 35 (April 1961), 1–16. (A regional dialect study for the southern United States.)

Yelsma, Paul L. "Words Used by the Fire Fighters of the Denver Fire Department." *Publication of the American Dialect Society,* No. 52 (November 1969), 24–36. (A discussion of occupational idioms with a lexicon.)

PART FIVE

Space
and the
Language
of the Body

When people think of language, they tend to consider it primarily in terms of the words that they say or write. To look at language in this way, however, is to ignore the very significant role played by nonverbal communication. For example, it has been estimated that in a conversation between two people, only 35% of the message is conveyed by the words. The remaining 65% is communicated nonverbally, by how they speak, move, gesture, and handle spatial relationships. Thus both *kinesics,* the study of movement (related to Greek *kinēsis,* movement) and *proxemics,* the study of the ways in which space is handled (related to Latin *proximus,* nearest) are important aspects of nonverbal communication. Awareness of their importance is not really new—writers and artists have long utilized very effectively their observations of nonverbal communication. But for most of us, the idea that "language is more than words" *is* new; we have not sufficiently realized the important role that is played in all kinds of interpersonal relationships by kinesics and proxemics. We need to study them systematically, especially because of their many practical applications in medicine, diplomacy, education, race relations, business negotiations—any situation in which people interact and need to understand one another.

The first articles in this section provide a general introduction to nonverbal communication, followed by more detailed studies of specific kinds of kinesic and proxemic situations. The photographs, drawings, and charts illustrate points made in the articles. Finally, the three concluding selections point out the ways in which different people, in different fields, over a span of almost seventy-five years, have looked for practical applications of the developing knowledge of nonverbal communication. An interesting trend noticeable in these three selections is a movement away from prescription and toward description and understanding.

1

The Sounds of Silence

Until recently, most Americans were largely unaware of the existence, let alone the importance, of nonverbal communication. Yet it is omnipresent in interpersonal situations and affects powerfully our judgments about other people and theirs about us. One of the men who has pioneered in the study of nonverbal communication is anthropologist Edward Hall. In this article, Edward and Mildred Hall discuss the crucial effects that "your posture, gestures, facial expression, costume, the way you walk, even your treatment of time and space and material things" may have, and emphasize the importance of respecting the power and diversity of "the sounds of silence."

Edward T. Hall and Mildred Reed Hall

Bob LEAVES his apartment at 8:15 a.m. and stops at the corner drugstore for breakfast. Before he can speak, the counterman says, "The usual?" Bob nods yes. While he savors his Danish, a fat man pushes onto the adjoining stool and overflows into his space. Bob scowls and the man pulls himself in as much as he can. Bob has sent two messages without speaking a syllable.

Henry has an appointment to meet Arthur at 11 o'clock; he arrives at 11:30. Their conversation is friendly, but Arthur retains a lingering hostility. Henry has unconsciously communicated that he doesn't think the appointment is very important or that Arthur is a person who needs to be treated with respect.

George is talking to Charley's wife at a party. Their conversation is entirely trivial, yet Charley glares at them suspiciously. Their physical proximity and the movements of their eyes reveal that they are powerfully attracted to each other.

José Ybarra and Sir Edmund Jones are at the same party and it is important for them to establish a cordial relationship for business reasons. Each is trying to be warm and friendly, yet they will part with mutual distrust and their business transaction will probably fall through. José, in Latin fashion, moved closer and closer to Sir Edmund as they spoke, and this movement was miscommunicated as pushiness to Sir Edmund, who kept backing away from this intimacy, and this was miscommunicated to José as coldness. The silent languages of Latin and English cultures are more difficult to learn than their spoken languages.

In each of these cases, we see the subtle power of nonverbal communication. The only language used throughout most of the history of humanity (in evolutionary terms, vocal communication is relatively recent), it is the first form of communication you learn. You use this preverbal language, consciously and unconsciously, every day to tell other people how you feel about yourself and them. This language includes your posture, gestures, facial expressions, costume, the way you walk, even your treatment of time and space and material things. All people communicate on several different levels at the same time but are usually aware of only the verbal dialog and don't realize that they respond to nonverbal messages. But when a person says one thing and really believes something else, the discrepancy between the two can usually be sensed. Nonverbal-communication systems are much less subject to the conscious deception that often occurs in verbal systems. When we find ourselves thinking, "I don't know what it is about him, but he doesn't seem sincere," it's usually this lack of congruity between a person's words and his behavior that makes us anxious and uncomfortable.

Few of us realize how much we all depend on body movement in our conversation or are aware of the hidden rules that govern listening behavior. But we know instantly whether or not the person we're talking to is "tuned in" and we're very sensitive to any breach in listening etiquette. In white middle-class American culture, when someone wants to show he is listening to someone else, he looks either at the other person's face or, specifically, at his eyes, shifting his gaze from one eye to the other.

If you observe a person conversing, you'll notice that he indicates he's listening by nodding his head. He also makes little "Hmm" noises. If he agrees with what's being said, he may give a vigorous nod. To show pleasure or affirmation, he smiles; if he has some reservations, he looks skeptical by raising an eyebrow or pulling down the corners of his mouth. If a participant wants to terminate the conversation, he may start shifting his body position, stretching his legs, crossing or uncrossing them, bobbing his foot or diverting his gaze from the speaker. The more he fidgets, the more the speaker becomes aware that he has lost his audience. As a last measure, the listener may look at his watch to indicate the imminent end of the conversation.

Talking and listening are so intricately intertwined that a person cannot do one without the other. Even when one is alone and talking to oneself, there is part of the brain that speaks while another part listens. In all conversations, the listener is positively or negatively reinforcing the speaker all the time. He may even guide the conversation without knowing it, by laughing or frowning or dismissing the argument with a wave of his hand.

The language of the eyes—another age-old way of exchanging feelings—is both subtle and complex. Not only do men and women use their eyes differently but there are class, generation, regional, ethnic and national cultural differences. Americans often complain about the way foreigners stare at people or hold a glance too long. Most Americans look away from someone who is using his eyes in an unfamiliar way because it makes them self-conscious. If a man looks at another man's wife in a certain way, he's asking for trouble, as indicated earlier. But he might not be ill mannered or seeking to challenge the husband. He might be a European in this country who hasn't learned our visual mores. Many American women visiting France or Italy are acutely embarrassed because, for the first time in their lives, men really look at them—their eyes, hair, nose, lips, breasts, hips, legs, thighs, knees, ankles, feet, clothes, hairdo, even their walk. These same women, once they have become used to being looked at, often return to the United States and are overcome with the feeling that "No one ever really looks at me anymore."

Analyzing the mass of data on the eyes, it is possible to sort out at least three ways in which the eyes are used to communicate: dominance vs. submission, involvement vs. detachment and positive vs. negative attitude. In addition, there are three levels of consciousness and control, which can be categorized as follows: (1) conscious use of the eyes to communicate, such as the flirting blink and the intimate nose-wrinkling squint; (2) the very extensive category of unconscious but learned behavior governing where the eyes are directed and when (this unwritten set of rules dictates how and under what circumstances the sexes, as well as people of all status categories, look at each other); and (3) the response of the eye itself, which is completely outside both awareness and control—changes in the cast (the sparkle) of the eye and the pupillary reflex.

The eye is unlike any other organ of the body, for it is an extension of the brain. The unconscious pupillary reflex and the cast of the eye have been known by people of Middle Eastern origin for years—although most are unaware of their knowledge. Depending on the context, Arabs and others look either directly at the eyes or deeply *into* the eyes of their interlocutor. We became aware of this in the Middle East several years ago while looking at jewelry. The merchant suddenly started to push a particular bracelet at a customer and said, "You buy this one."

What interested us was that the bracelet was not the one that had been consciously selected by the purchaser. But the merchant, watching the pupils of the eyes, knew what the purchaser really wanted to buy. Whether he specifically knew *how* he knew is debatable.

A psychologist at the University of Chicago, Eckhard Hess, was the first to conduct systematic studies of the pupillary reflex. His wife remarked one evening, while watching him reading in bed, that he must be very interested in the text because his pupils were dilated. Following up on this, Hess slipped some pictures of nudes into a stack of photographs that he gave to his male assistant. Not looking at the photographs but watching his assistant's pupils, Hess was able to tell precisely when the assistant came to the nudes. In further experiments, Hess retouched the eyes in a photograph of a woman. In one print, he made the pupils small, in another, large; nothing else was changed. Subjects who were given the photographs found the woman with the dilated pupils much more attractive. Any man who has had the experience of seeing a woman look at him as her pupils widen with reflex speed knows that she's flashing him a message.

The eye-sparkle phenomenon frequently turns up in our interviews of couples in love. It's apparently one of the first reliable clues in the other person that love is genuine. To date, there is no scientific data to explain eye sparkle; no investigation of the pupil, the cornea or even the white sclera of the eye shows how the sparkle originates. Yet we all know it when we see it.

One common situation for most people involves the use of the eyes in the street and in public. Although eye behavior follows a definite set of rules, the rules vary according to the place, the needs and feelings of the people, and their ethnic background. For urban whites, once they're within definite recognition distance (16–32 feet for people with average eyesight), there is mutual avoidance of eye contact—unless they want something specific: a pickup, a handout or information of some kind. In the West and in small towns generally, however, people are much more likely to look at and greet one another, even if they're strangers.

It's permissible to look at people if they're beyond recognition distance; but once inside this sacred zone, you can only steal a glance at strangers. You *must* greet friends, however; to fail to do so is insulting. Yet, to stare too fixedly even at them is considered rude and hostile. Of course, all of these rules are variable.

A great many blacks, for example, greet each other in public even if they don't know each other. To blacks, most eye behavior of whites has the effect of giving the impression that they aren't there, but this is due to white avoidance of eye contact with *anyone* in the street.

Another very basic difference between people of different ethnic backgrounds is their sense of territoriality and how they handle space.

This is the silent communication, or miscommunication, that caused friction between Mr. Ybarra and Sir Edmund Jones in our earlier example. We know from research that everyone has around himself an invisible bubble of space that contracts and expands depending on several factors: his emotional state, the activity he's performing at the time and his cultural background. This bubble is a kind of mobile territory that he will defend against intrusion. If he is accustomed to close personal distance between himself and others, his bubble will be smaller than that of someone who's accustomed to greater personal distance. People of North European heritage—English, Scandinavian, Swiss and German—tend to avoid contact. Those whose heritage is Italian, French, Spanish, Russian, Latin American or Middle Eastern like close personal contact.

People are very sensitive to any intrusion into their spatial bubble. If someone stands too close to you, your first instinct is to back up. If that's not possible, you lean away and pull yourself in, tensing your muscles. If the intruder doesn't respond to these body signals, you may then try to protect yourself, using a briefcase, umbrella or raincoat. Women—especially when traveling alone—often plant their pocketbook in such a way that no one can get very close to them. As a last resort, you may move to another spot and position yourself behind a desk or a chair that provides screening. Everyone tries to adjust the space around himself in a way that's comfortable for him; most often, he does this unconsciously.

Emotions also have a direct effect on the size of a person's territory. When you're angry or under stress, your bubble expands and you require more space. New York psychiatrist Augustus Kinzel found a difference in what he calls Body-Buffer Zones between violent and nonviolent prison inmates. Dr. Kinzel conducted experiments in which each prisoner was placed in the center of a small room and then Dr. Kinzel slowly walked toward him. Nonviolent prisoners allowed him to come quite close, while prisoners with a history of violent behavior couldn't tolerate his proximity and reacted with some vehemence.

Apparently, people under stress experience other people as looming larger and closer than they actually are. Studies of schizophrenic patients have indicated that they sometimes have a distorted perception of space, and several psychiatrists have reported patients who experience their body boundaries as filling up an entire room. For these patients, anyone who comes into the room is actually inside their body, and such an intrusion may trigger a violent outburst.

Unfortunately, there is little detailed information about normal people who live in highly congested urban areas. We do know, of course, that the noise, pollution, dirt, crowding and confusion of our cities induce feelings of stress in most of us, and stress leads to a need for greater space. The man who's packed into a subway, jostled in the street, crowded into an elevator and forced to work all day in a bull pen or in a small office without auditory or visual privacy is going to be very stressed at the end of his day. He needs places that provide relief from constant overstimulation of his nervous system. Stress from over-crowding is cumulative and people can tolerate more crowding early in the day than later; note the increased bad temper during the evening rush hour as compared with the morning melee. Certainly one factor in people's desire to commute by car is the need for privacy and relief from crowding (except, often, from other cars); it may be the only time of the day when nobody can intrude.

In crowded public places, we tense our muscles and hold ourselves stiff, and thereby communicate to others our desire not to intrude on their space and, above all, not to touch them. We also avoid eye contact, and the total effect is that of someone who has "tuned out." Walking along the street, our bubble expands slightly as we move in a stream of strangers, taking care not to bump into them. In the office, at meetings, in restaurants, our bubble keeps changing as it adjusts to the activity at hand.

Most white middle-class Americans use four main distances in their business and social relations: intimate, personal, social and public. Each of these distances has a near and a far phase and is accompanied by changes in the volume of the voice. Intimate distance varies from direct physical contact with another person to a distance of six to eighteen inches and is used for our most private activities—caressing another person or making love. At this distance, you are overwhelmed by sensory inputs from the other person—heat from the body, tactile stimulation from the skin, the fragrance of perfume, even the sound of breathing —all of which literally envelop you. Even at the far phase, you're still within easy touching distance. In general, the use of intimate distance in public between adults is frowned on. It's also much too close for strangers, except under conditions of extreme crowding.

In the second zone—personal distance—the close phase is one and a half to two and a half feet; it's at this distance that wives usually stand from their husbands in public. If another woman moves into this zone, the wife will most likely be disturbed. The far phase—two and a half to four feet—is the distance used to "keep someone at arm's length" and is the most common spacing used by people in conversation.

The third zone—social distance—is employed during business transactions or exchanges with a clerk or repairman. People who work together tend to use close social distance—four to seven feet. This is also the distance for conversations at social gatherings. To stand at this distance from someone who is seated has a dominating effect (e.g., teacher to pupil, boss to secretary). The far phase of the third zone—seven to twelve feet—is where people stand when someone says, "Stand back so I can look at you." This distance lends a formal tone to business or social discourse. In an executive office, the desk serves to keep people at this distance.

The fourth zone—public distance—is used by teachers in classrooms or speakers at public gatherings. At its farthest phase—25 feet and beyond—it is used for important public figures. Violations of this distance can lead to serious complications. During his 1970 U.S. visit, the president of France, Georges Pompidou, was harassed by pickets in Chicago, who were permitted to get within touching distance. Since pickets in France are kept behind barricades a block or more away, the president was outraged by this insult to his person, and President Nixon was obliged to communicate his concern as well as offer his personal apologies.

It is interesting to note how American pitchmen and panhandlers exploit the unwritten, unspoken conventions of eye and distance. Both take advantage of the fact that once explicit eye contact is established, it is rude to look away, because to do so means to brusquely dismiss the other person and his needs. Once having caught the eye of his mark, the panhandler then locks on, not letting go until he moves through the public zone, the social zone, the personal zone and, finally, into the intimate sphere, where people are most vulnerable.

Touch also is an important part of the constant stream of communication that takes place between people. A light touch, a firm touch, a blow, a caress are all communications. In an effort to break down barriers among people, there's been a recent upsurge in group-encounter activities, in which strangers are encouraged to touch one another. In special situations such as these, the rules for not touching are broken with group approval and people gradually lose some of their inhibitions.

Although most people don't realize it, space is perceived and distances are set not by vision alone but with all the senses. Auditory space is perceived with the ears, thermal space with the skin, kinesthetic space with the muscles of the body and olfactory space with the nose. And, once again, it's one's culture that determines how his senses are programmed—which sensory information ranks highest and lowest. The important thing to remember is that culture is very persistent. In this country, we've noted the existence of culture patterns that determine distance between people in the third and fourth generations of some families, despite their prolonged contact with people of very different cultural heritages.

Whenever there is great cultural distance between two people, there are bound to be problems arising from differences in behavior and expectations. An example is the American couple who consulted a psychiatrist about their marital problems. The husband was from New England and had been brought up by reserved parents who taught him to control his emotions and to respect the need for privacy. His wife was from an Italian family and had been brought up in close contact with all the members of her large family, who were extremely warm, volatile and demonstrative.

When the husband came home after a hard day at the office, dragging his feet and longing for peace and quiet, his wife would rush to him and smother him. Clasping his hands, rubbing his brow, crooning over his weary head, she never left him alone. But when the wife was upset or anxious about her day, the husband's response was to withdraw completely and leave her alone. No comforting, no affectionate embrace, no attention—just solitude. The woman became convinced her husband didn't love her and, in desperation, she consulted a psychiatrist. Their problem wasn't basically psychological but cultural.

Why has man developed all these different ways of communicating messages without words? One reason is that people don't like to spell out certain kinds of messages. We prefer to find other ways of showing our feelings. This is especially true in relationships as sensitive as courtship. Men don't like to be rejected and most women don't want to turn a man down bluntly. Instead, we work out subtle ways of encouraging or discouraging each other that save face and avoid confrontations.

How a person handles space in dating others is an obvious and very sensitive indicator of how he or she feels about the other person. On a first date, if a woman sits or stands so close to a man that he is acutely conscious of her physical presence—inside the intimate-distance zone—the man usually construes it to mean that she is encouraging him. However, before the man starts moving in on the woman, he should be sure what message she's really sending; otherwise, he risks bruising his ego. What is close to someone of North European background may be neutral or distant to someone of Italian heritage. Also, women sometimes use space as a way of misleading a man and there are few things that put men off more than women who communicate contradictory messages—such as women who cuddle up and then act insulted when a man takes the next step.

How does a woman communicate interest in a man? In addition to such familiar gambits as smiling at him, she may glance shyly at him, blush and then look away. Or she may give him a real come-on look and move in very close when he approaches. She may touch his arm and ask for a light. As she leans forward to light her cigarette, she may brush him lightly, enveloping him in her perfume. She'll probably continue to smile at him and she may use what ethologists call preening gestures —touching the back of her hair, thrusting her breasts forward, tilting her hips as she stands or crossing her legs if she's seated, perhaps even exposing one thigh or putting a hand on her thigh and stroking it.

She may also stroke her wrists as she converses or show the palm of her hand as a way of gaining his attention. Her skin may be unusually flushed or quite pale, her eyes brighter, the pupils larger.

If a man sees a woman whom he wants to attract, he tries to present himself by his posture and stance as someone who is self-assured. He moves briskly and confidently. When he catches the eye of the woman, he may hold her glance a little longer than normal. If he gets an encouraging smile, he'll move in close and engage her in small talk. As they converse, his glance shifts over her face and body. He, too, may make preening gestures—straightening his tie, smoothing his hair or shooting his cuffs.

How do people learn body language? The same way they learn spoken language—by observing and imitating people around them as they're growing up. Little girls imitate their mothers or an older female. Little boys imitate their fathers or a respected uncle or a character on television. In this way, they learn the gender signals appropriate for their sex. Regional, class and ethnic patterns of body behavior are also learned in childhood and persist throughout life.

Such patterns of masculine and feminine body behavior vary widely from one culture to another. In America, for example, women stand with their thighs together. Many walk with their pelvis tipped slightly forward and their upper arms close to their body. When they sit, they cross their legs at the knee or, if they are well past middle age, they may cross their ankles. American men hold their arms away from their body, often swinging them as they walk. They stand with their legs apart (an extreme example is the cowboy, with legs apart and thumbs tucked into his belt). When they sit, they put their feet on the floor with legs apart and, in some parts of the country, they cross their legs by putting one ankle on the other knee.

Leg behavior indicates sex, status and personality. It also indicates whether or not one is at ease or is showing respect or disrespect for the other person. Young Latin-American males avoid crossing their legs. In their world of *machismo*, the preferred position for young males when with one another (if there is no older dominant male present to whom they must show respect) is to sit on the base of their spine with their leg muscles relaxed and their feet wide apart. Their respect position is like our military equivalent; spine straight, heels and ankles together— almost identical to that displayed by properly brought up young women in New England in the early part of this century.

American women who sit with their legs spread apart in the presence of males are *not* normally signaling a come-on—they are simply (and often unconsciously) sitting like men. Middle-class women in the presence of other women to whom they are very close may on occasion throw themselves down on a soft chair or sofa and let themselves go. This is a signal that nothing serious will be taken up. Males, on the other hand, lean back and prop their legs up on the nearest object.

The way we walk, similarly, indicates status, respect, mood and ethnic or cultural affiliation. The many variants of the female walk are too well known to go into here, except to say that a man would have to be blind not to be turned on by the way some women walk—a fact that made Mae West rich before scientists ever studied these matters. To white Americans, some French middle-class males walk in a way that is both humorous and suspect. There is a bounce and looseness to the French walk, as though the parts of the body were somehow unrelated. Jacques Tati, the French movie actor, walks this way; so does the great mime, Marcel Marceau.

Blacks and whites in America—with the exception of middle- and upper-middle-class professionals of both groups—move and walk very differently from each other. To the blacks, whites often seem incredibly stiff, almost mechanical in their movements. Black males, on the other hand, have a looseness and coordination that frequently makes whites a little uneasy; it's too different, too integrated, too alive, too male. Norman Mailer has said that squares walk from the shoulders, like bears, but blacks and hippies walk from the hips, like cats.

All over the world, people walk not only in their own characteristic way but have walks that communicate the nature of their involvement with whatever it is they're doing. The purposeful walk of North Europeans is an important component of proper behavior on the job. Any male who has been in the military knows how essential it is to walk properly (which makes for a continuing source of tension between blacks and whites in the Service). The quick shuffle of servants in the Far East in the old days was a show of respect. On the island of Truk, when we last visited, the inhabitants even had a name for the respectful walk that one used when in the presence of a chief or when walking past a chief's house. The term was *sufan*, which meant to be humble and respectful.

The notion that people communicate volumes by their gestures, facial expressions, posture and walk is not new; actors, dancers, writers and psychiatrists have long been aware of it. Only in recent years, however, have scientists begun to make systematic observations of body motions. Ray L. Birdwhistell of the University of Pennsylvania is one of the pioneers in body-motion research and coined the term kinesics to describe this field. He developed an elaborate notation system to record both facial and body movements, using an approach similar to that of the linguist, who studies the basic elements of speech. Birdwhistell and other kinesicists such as Albert Sheflen, Adam Kendon and William Condon take movies of people interacting. They run the film over and over again, often at reduced speed for frame-by-frame analysis, so that they can observe even the slightest body movements not perceptible at normal interaction speeds. These movements are then recorded in notebooks for later analysis.

To appreciate the importance of nonverbal-communication systems, consider the unskilled inner-city black looking for a job. His handling of time and space alone is sufficiently different from the white middle-class pattern to create great misunderstandings on both sides. The black is told to appear for a job interview at a certain time. He arrives late. The white interviewer concludes from his tardy arrival that the black is irresponsible and not really interested in the job. What the interviewer doesn't know is that the black time system (often referred to by blacks as C. P. T.—colored people's time) isn't the same as that of whites. In the words of a black student who had been told to make an appointment to see his professor: "Man, you *must* be putting me on. I never had an appointment in my life."

The black job applicant, having arrived late for his interview, may further antagonize the white interviewer by his posture and his eye behavior. Perhaps he slouches and avoids looking at the interviewer; to him, this is playing it cool. To the interviewer, however, he may well look shifty and sound uninterested. The interviewer has failed to notice the actual signs of interest and eagerness in the black's behavior, such as the subtle shift in the quality of the voice—a gentle and tentative excitement—an almost imperceptible change in the cast of the eyes and a relaxing of the jaw muscles.

Moreover, correct reading of black-white behavior is continually complicated by the fact that both groups are comprised of individuals—some of whom try to accommodate and some of whom make it a point of pride *not* to accommodate. At present, this means that many Americans, when thrown into contact with one another, are in the precarious position of not knowing which pattern applies. Once identified and analyzed, nonverbal-communication systems can be taught, like a foreign language. Without this training, we respond to nonverbal communications in terms of our own culture; we read everyone's behavior as if it were our own, and thus we often misunderstand it.

Several years ago in New York City, there was a program for sending children from predominantly black and Puerto Rican low-income neighborhoods to summer school in a white upper-class neighborhood on the East Side. One morning, a group of young black and Puerto Rican boys raced down the street, shouting and screaming and overturning garbage cans on their way to school. A doorman from an apartment building nearby chased them and cornered one of them inside a building. The boy drew a knife and attacked the doorman. This tragedy would not have occurred if the doorman had been familiar with the behavior of boys from low-income neighborhoods, where such antics are routine and socially acceptable and where pursuit would be expected to invite a violent response.

The language of behavior is extremely complex. Most of us are lucky to have under control one subcultural system—the one that reflects our sex, class, generation and geographic region within the United States. Because of its complexity, efforts to isolate bits of nonverbal communication and generalize from them are in vain; you don't become an instant expert on people's behavior by watching them at cocktail parties. Body language isn't something that's independent of the person, something that can be donned and doffed like a suit of clothes.

Our research and that of our colleagues has shown that, far from being a superficial form of communication that can be consciously manipulated, nonverbal-communication systems are interwoven into the fabric of the personality and, as sociologist Erving Goffman has demonstrated, into society itself. They are the warp and woof of daily interactions with others and they influence how one expresses oneself, how one experiences oneself as a man or a woman.

Nonverbal communications signal to members of your own group what kind of person you are, how you feel about others, how you'll fit into and work in a group, whether you're assured or anxious, the degree to which you feel comfortable with the standards of your own culture, as well as deeply significant feelings about the self, including the state of your own psyche. For most of us, it's difficult to accept the reality of another's behavioral system. And, of course, none of us will ever become fully knowledgeable of the importance of every nonverbal signal. But as long as each of us realizes the power of these signals, this society's diversity can be a source of great strength rather than a further—and subtly powerful—source of division.

FOR DISCUSSION AND REVIEW

1   Give some examples of nonverbal positive and negative reinforcement in talking and listening situations.

2   Describe the phenomenon the Halls call "pupillary reflex." Have you ever noticed any examples of it? Explain.

3   To what extent, according to the Halls, does ethnic background produce differences in nonverbal communication behavior? Give some examples of situations in which these differences may be of great importance.

4   What do the Halls mean by the "invisible bubble of space" surrounding each of us? What factors may affect its size at any given time?

5   What are the four distances used by most white middle-class Americans in social and business situations? Describe the varying sensory inputs at each distance (auditory, olfactory, tactile, visual, etc.). Are there significant cross-cultural differences? Explain.

6   According to the Halls, how and when do people learn body lan-

guage? Why have nonverbal communication systems developed?

7 What are "preening gestures"? Give some examples. Are they used only by humans? (Before answering, be sure you know what an *ethologist* is.)

8 How important is "leg behavior"? How much does it vary between men and women and among different cultures?

9 Discuss the implications of the Halls' statement: "Once identified and analyzed, nonverbal-communication systems can be taught, like a foreign language. Without this training, we respond to nonverbal communications in terms of our own culture; we read everyone's behavior as if it were our own, and thus we often misunderstand it."

Seeing
Language

Nonverbal communication is in large part visual; and the more you learn about kinesics and proxemics, the more clearly you will perceive and understand what you see around you. Gestures and spatial relationships can be highly informative and expressive. The photographs that follow illustrate some of the kinesic and proxemic principles discussed in the articles in this section. What emotions do you think are expressed by each face in the group of movie stills? Analyze the pictures to see if you can determine how these emotions are conveyed. Although important, the face is only a part of nonverbal communication, and the next group of photographs shows the whole human body and the interrelationships of individuals. Artists have long utilized a knowledge of body language in making their work more communicative and effective. An interesting example of conscious manipulation of this principle is seen in the two paintings by Holbein the Younger commissioned by Henry VIII.

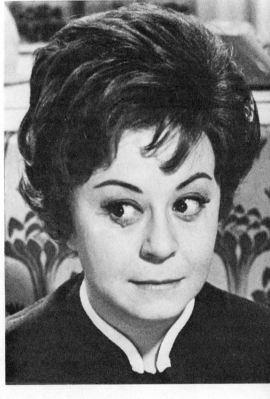

If you were HenryVIII,which princess would you marry?

Here are details from two famous portraits of eligible young princesses, Christina of Denmark on the left and Anne of Cleves on the right. Holbein the Younger painted both for Henry VIII, to help the English king choose his fourth wife without making a tedious trip across Europe to meet the princesses in person.

Holbein wanted his patron to know something about each girl's personality, as well as her appearance. And so, as John Canaday points out in the Metropolitan Museum Seminars in Art, the artist painted lively, intelligent Christina in a subdued costume that does little to distract attention from the girl herself. In contrast, he portrayed the sweet but rather dull Anne in an elaborate jeweled headdress and robe, far more interesting than her face. Christina looks forthrightly at us, while Anne's eyes evade us. Christina's hands are full of graceful movement, while Anne's are submissively folded.

What Holbein suggested about the contrasting personalities of the two princesses, through the details and composition of their portraits, turned out to be true. The more discerning Christina was not charmed by Henry's reputation as a husband, and turned down the thrice-married king. Placid, obedient Anne then accepted—but a bored Henry divorced her with indecent haste.

Every major work of art contains clues to what the artist is trying to reveal. Yet a surprising number of well-educated people are blind to these clues. It was to help such people that the Metropolitan Museum and John Canaday, now art critic of The New York Times, created the Seminars in Art.

Each seminar is a handsome portfolio, the core of which is a lecture on one aspect of painting. Each is illustrated with many black-and-white pictures and twelve large separate full-color reproductions of notable paintings. As you compare these masterpieces, Mr. Canaday's lectures clarify their basic differences and similarities, and so reveal what to look for in any painting you may see.

Soon, paintings will be more than just "good" or "bad" to you. You will be able to talk knowledgeably when you visit a gallery or museum. And parents will find themselves sharing their understanding with their children, providing a foundation for a lifelong interest in art.

You can study the first seminar by mailing the coupon to the Book-of-the-Month Club, which administers the program for the Museum. You will receive the first of the twelve portfolios, What Is a Painting?, for a two week trial examination. Subsequent portfolios, sent at the rate of ap-

proximately one a month, are devoted to realism, expressionism, abstraction, composition, painting techniques and the role of the artist as social critic and visionary.

If you choose not to continue, return the portfolio, canceling your subscription. There's no obligation. Otherwise, you pay only $5.50, plus postage and handling, for this and each portfolio you accept.

Courtesy of Metropolitan Museum of Art Seminars in the Home, c/o Book-of-the-Month Club, 280 Park Avenue, New York, N.Y. 10017.

2

Other Ways of Packaging Information

Randall P. Harrison

The information conveyed by both verbal and nonverbal communication is "packaged" or coded for transmission; the packages, however, vary with their content. In this article, Randall P. Harrison discusses these different ways of packaging and reviews several different communication models. Notice, throughout the article, the way in which the verbal elements are supplemented and reinforced by the visual. How effective is this technique?

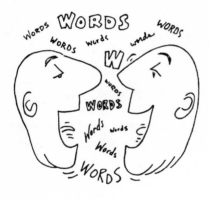

We *are* a verbal lot. Not only we communicators, in conclave, but we human beings—the communicating animals. The words flow trippingly off the tongue; they cascade endlessly upon the ear.

We are somewhat surprised when someone like Ray Birdwhistell[1] estimates that in a normal, two-person conversation the verbal band carries less than 35% of the social meaning of the situation; more than 65% is transmitted via nonverbal bands. This doesn't square very well with our common sense notions about the communication process.

We, after all, spend a good deal of time packaging—and unpackaging—verbal messages. It takes a lot of conscious thought. It's real work. We spend years in school learning how to read, how to spell, how to put together a grammatical sentence, how to make a speech.

We tend to be less aware of the other packages of information we produce—and use. We tend to learn these packaging procedures in what Ed Hall[2] calls an "informal" manner. They are often "out-of-awareness." They are learned by imitation or accident. They are not taught explicitly.

This lack of awareness has been one stumbling block for the communication theorist who would like to examine the communication process. He's often tripped up by a nonverbal element. But he doesn't have the tools for analysis. He doesn't even have a conceptual perspective—so he knows what to look for.

---

[1] Ray L. Birdwhistell, "Paralanguage: 25 Years After Sapir," unpublished (1959).
[2] Edward T. Hall, The Silent Language (Garden City, N.Y.: Doubleday, 1959).

Recently, several trends have forced nonverbal communication upon our attention. In the mass media, we've seen the advent of powerful new institutions with strong nonverbal components—first, film, and then its younger, big brother—television. Even the old print media have taken on a new look. Books, magazines, newspapers—all have been treated to a pictorial facelift. And now they're cosmetically color coordinated.

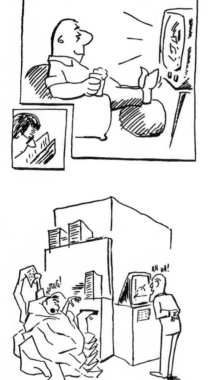

From an audience viewpoint—(emphasis on the *view*)—we find the average American spending 30 to 40 hours a week with television—and two to four hours a week with the print media.

But even in esoteric communication areas such as the man-computer interface, we're finding a nonverbal trend. Once the computer's output was totally digital—in the form of a "print-out." But now, we may soon see the day when 50% of the computer's output will be in the form of "visual display"—charts, drawings, graphs—presented on a cathode-ray tube or even on animated film.[3] (Parenthetically, the computer was originally called a "computer" because it could compute. Perhaps it would be more appropriate to call the present generation "informers.")

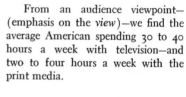

Advances in computer technology are important to the communication scholar, but there's another spot where nonverbal communication is apparently hitting the researcher where he lives . . .

[3] Ivan E. Sutherland, "Computer Inputs and Outputs," in Scientific American Editors, *Information* (San Francisco: W. H. Freeman, 1966), pp. 40–55.

This is work—such as Rosenthal's at Harvard[4]—which shows the extent to which the experimenter may be influencing the outcome of his experiments—often nonverbally. From some of Rosenthal's research we might conclude that sometimes the only naïve subject in the lab is the experimenter. What we've said so far bears on the first problem I see before us, namely . . .

HOW IMPORTANT ?

How important is nonverbal communication? How important are these other ways of packaging information? It seems the answer to this question should be reflected to some extent in the amount of time, energy, and resources we invest in studying nonverbal communication. By several criteria it would appear that nonverbal communication is quite important.

QUANTITY

We've touched, for instance, on quantity. Apparently, a great deal of nonverbal communication goes on about us. In fact, the domain of communication seems to be spreading into areas that once we didn't define as communication. And in these areas much of the communication is nonverbal. Too, we've seen trends—particularly in the mass media—which lead us to believe that the quantity of nonverbal communication may be increasing.

4 Robert Rosenthal, *Experimenter Effects in Behavioral Research* (New York: Appleton-Century-Crofts, 1966).

PRIMACY

We might next mention primacy. And here we mean both that nonverbal communication is first in development, setting the pattern for later communication developments in the individual—and primacy in the sense that "seeing is believing." Often, the nonverbal messages take precedence because of sheer stimulus strength. In a somewhat related vein, it's often assumed by a receiver that the nonverbal message is harder to "fake"—whether it's a photo or a facial expression.

SUBTLETY

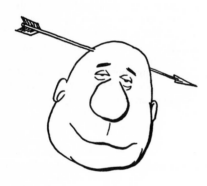

Finally, nonverbal communication acts with subtlety. We may be unaware that we are sending nonverbal messages. We may be unaware that we are receiving nonverbal messages. In complex nonverbal messages, we may not know to what we respond. This subtlety makes communication breakdowns hard to analyze. It makes the process of nonverbal communication hard to teach.

HOW STUDY?

RESEARCH

TEACH

This then leads to our second major problem area: How to study nonverbal communication? This comprises the twin problems of how to research and how to teach. Although we often assume these are identical problems, the goals of research and teaching may be quite different. Research moves toward fruitful and comprehensive theories which in turn lead to more research. Meanwhile, teaching is concerned with effective operation in some context. The role of research *in* teaching may be quite a separate issue. . . .

But we might assume that to study nonverbal communication we will need to go through some steps—which we might label: sensitize, analyze, organize, utilize. Within the research frame, *sensitize* means problem awareness, an articulation of relevant variables. *Analyze* means the operationalization of variables—the sorting, the labeling, the sifting of relevant from irrelevant. *Organize* introduces theorizing, the integration and structuring of conceptual systems. Finally, *utilize* refers to testing, to hypotheses and experiment. For the teacher, perhaps a parallel process occurs, ending with application.

In attacking the problem, the process is perhaps not so neatly linear. To the extent, for instance, that we have a well-articulated nomenclature, we will find it easier to sensitize ourselves. And to the degree we're sensitive we're better able to analyze. And so on. But let us start with "sensitize."

For both the researcher and the would-be practitioner, we have a growing battery of tools that help focus attention on nonverbal cues, that help us dissect the on-going nonverbal process. Included are videotapes—with instant re-play—motion pictures, still photos, recordings, and so on. We can produce these ourselves, and a growing list of already produced materials is becoming available. (As one sensitizing technique, we have taken a standard film—such as the Nixon-Kennedy debates—and played it without the sound. In a few moments, the viewer feels he's seen "everything." But as he watches, he becomes aware of more and more.)

For the researcher, sensitizing—as well as analyzing and organizing—frequently begins with a review of the literature. Fortunately, there's a growing—although far-flung—body of research, representing several frames of reference. . . .

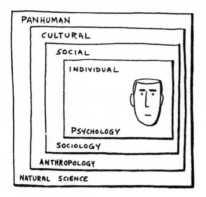

Certain panhuman characteristics emerge from the study of natural science—mapping the boundaries of what can be perceived, what can be performed, what biological needs undergird communication. Similarly, we find determinants—constraints—at the cultural, at the social, and at the individual level. To sample briefly from each level, we might start with . . .

. . . Charles Darwin,[5] who made an early attempt to link expression in man to expression in other animals. He tried to isolate human universals and make the link to earlier noncommunicative functions. This work continues today in animal studies of emotion, learning, cooperation, territoriality, and so on.

Anthropologist Edward Hall[6] points out cultural differences in the use of time and space and what he calls the "primary message systems." He most recently has articulated the area of "proxemics"—the language of space.

---

[5] Charles Darwin, *Expression of Emotions in Man and Animals* (New York: Philosophical Library, 1955).
[6] Hall, *op. cit.*, and Edward T. Hall, *The Hidden Dimension* (Garden City, N.Y.: Doubleday, 1966).

Ray Birdwhistell,[7] working in the anthropological and linguistic traditions, has focused on "kinesics"—the study of gestural communication. In his cross-cultural research, he notes that the eye and hand are important "situation definers" in our culture, but not in all.

At a sociological level, scholars like Erving Goffman[8] point to the "management of personal front" that goes on in any social "gathering"—the socialization of potential communication performance depending on status, age, role and group norms. The work of Hall, Birdwhistell, and Goffman has filtered into the psychological area, particularly in . . .

Psychiatric communication—in the interview situation between counselor and client—and also in communication between emotionally disturbed individuals. Men in the clinical tradition—like Jurgen Ruesch[9] and Joel Davitz[10]—have increasingly explored the nonverbal domain. Davitz, for instance, was frustrated at the nonspecific advice given fledgling psychiatrists: "be sensitive" or "grow a third ear. . . ." He tried experimentally to isolate some of the nonverbal cues being used by experienced clinicians.

[7] Ray L. Birdwhistell, "Background to Kinesics," ETC., Vol. 13 (1955), pp. 10–18.
[8] Erving Goffman, The Presentation of Self in Everyday Life (Garden City, N.Y.: Doubleday, 1959); and Behavior in Public Places (London: Collier-Macmillan, 1963).
[9] Jurgen Ruesch and Weldon Kees, Nonverbal Communication (Berkeley: University of California Press, 1956).
[10] Joel R. Davitz, The Communication of Emotional Meaning (New York: McGraw-Hill, 1964).

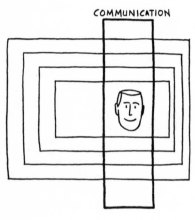

COMMUNICATION

In other areas of psychology, new evidence is pouring in from the study of emotions, person perception, the perceptual processes generally. Researchers include men like Charles Osgood,[11] Sylvin Tompkins,[12] Paul Ekman,[13] and Jeffrey Shapiro.[14]

Recently, an additional frame of analysis has emerged, namely . . .

. . . Communication theory and research itself. This frame partakes deeply in the levels of analysis already mentioned, and adds new perspectives —drawing from the spectrum of communication arts and tapping relevant disciplines ranging from the philosophy of language to electrical engineering.

This audience hardly needs a review of communication models, but let me touch briefly on what I see as the unique calculus underlying communication theory.

Perhaps the simplest communication model possible is what we might call the A-B model—where two systems join—sharing an interface—so that changes in the states of one system influence the states of the other system. This diagram, of course, could apply equally to a mechanical system, a hydraulic system, etc. The communication theorist, however, is primarily interested in those systems where the flow across the interface is information, not merely energy or matter.

[11] Charles E. Osgood, "Dimensionality of the Semantic Space for Communication via Facial Expressions," *Scandinavian Journal of Psychology*, Vol. 7 (1966).

[12] S. S. Tompkins and Robert McCarter, "What and Where Are the Primary Affects? Some Evidence for a Theory," *Perceptual and Motor Skills*, Vol. 18 (1964), pp. 119–158.

[13] Paul Ekman, "Body Position, Facial Expression and Verbal Behavior During Interviews." *Journal of Abnormal and Social Psychology*, Vol. 68 (1964).

[14] Jeffrey Shapiro, "Responsivity to Facial and Linguistic Cues," unpublished, privately distributed (1966).

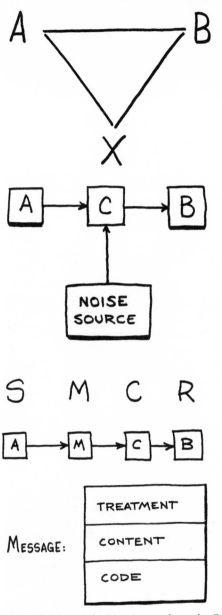

Newcomb's A-B-X model[15] is an early elaboration which adds an X component—some referent of orientation in the environment. This model, of course, was elaborated further in the Westley-MacLean model[16] to apply to more complex mass media phenomena.

The Shannon-Weaver model[17] might be termed an A-B-C model—the C standing for "channel." Shannon, of course, was particularly interested in channel capacity and the problems of communicating in the face of various noise levels.

Berlo's S-M-C-R model[18] might be called an A-B-C-M model—with the M standing for "message." With the emergence of the M component we seem to be squarely in a communication framework—no longer in electrical engineering, in physical systems, or even in traditional social psychology. For our present topic—other ways of packaging information—it is this message component which we will wish to explore in some detail.

Berlo originally suggested that a message could be analyzed in terms of its code, its content, and its treatment. What we have been calling "packaging" is first a coding problem —but with implications for the selection of content, treatment, and channel.

[15] T. M. Newcomb, "An Approach to the Study of Communicative Acts," *Psychological Review*, Vol. 60 (1953), pp. 393–404.

[16] Bruce H. Westley and Malcolm S. MacLean, "A Conceptual Model for Communication Research," *Journalism Quarterly* (1957), pp. 31–38.

[17] Claude E. Shannon and Warren Weaver, *The Mathematical Theory of Communication* (Urbana: Univ. of Illinois Press, 1963).

[18] David K. Berlo, *The Process of Communication* (New York: Holt, Rinehart and Winston, 1960).

MESSAGE

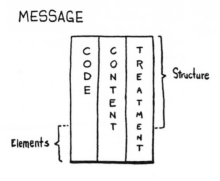

Berlo also noted that code, content, and treatment can all be analyzed in terms of, first, elements. And elements combine to form structure. The concept of "levels" becomes important here since elements at one level combine to form structures, which—at the next level of analysis—become elements which, in turn, combine into structures. Any given message can be analyzed at several levels and it can be considered a miniature system—with interrelated code, content, and treatment.

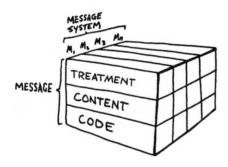

In many of the situations which interest us most, however, the receiver is being bombarded with simultaneous messages which to some extent are interrelated. These multiple messages—bounded by time, place, receiving communicator or producing communicator—can be analyzed as one level of message system.

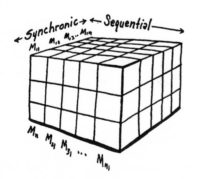

But in addition to this synchronic message system we are frequently interested in message chains—i.e., sequential message systems. We can go on to map more encompassing message systems—on up to national and international levels—as indeed George Gerbner[19] has done. But in terms of our present topic, we can begin by focusing on three small cells. . .

---

[19] George Gerbner, *Mass Communications and Popular Conceptions of Education: A Cross-Cultural Study* (Cooperative Research Project No. 876, Office of Education, U.S. Department of Health, Education and Welfare, 1964).

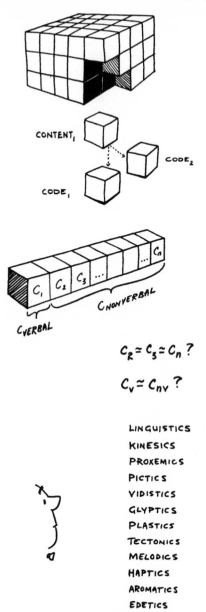

CONTENT₁

CODE₂

CODE₁

C_{VERBAL}

$C_{NONVERBAL}$

C_1 | C_2 | C_3 | ... | ... | C_n

$$C_2 \cong C_3 \cong C_n \; ?$$

$$C_v \cong C_{nv} \; ?$$

LINGUISTICS

KINESICS

PROXEMICS

PICTICS

VIDISTICS

GLYPTICS

PLASTICS

TECTONICS

MELODICS

HAPTICS

AROMATICS

EDETICS

Phrased as "other ways of packaging information" we have the underlying assumption that there is some block of content which could be encoded in either Code One or Code Two. Now to the extent that we are dealing with a system, we might not expect to shift from one code to another without eliminating—or adding —some information, and indeed without changing the treatment. We have much anecdotal speculation on this point—including Marshall McLuhan's dictum that "the medium is the message."[20] But at the moment we seem to lack adequate data on the problem—partly because of inadequate information measures—and partly because alternative code systems have not been thoroughly articulated.

In trying to solve the latter problem, two issues arise immediately. First, are there enough underlying similarities among the nonverbal codes so that they can be studied together? Second, does our knowledge of the verbal code system provide a useful model for the analysis of nonverbal code systems? If the answer to those two questions is "yes" we've made some giant strides forward; if not, we've a lot of basic conceptualizing to do.

So far, the linguistic analog has been best pursued by Birdwhistell in his kinesics. Hall has moved in a similar direction with his proxemics. We've done some work on "pictics" —an analysis of the pictorial code.[21] Sol Worth[22] is pursuing a parallel analysis of cinema, which he calls "vidistics." And Martin Krampen[23] has suggested a nomenclature for sev-

[20] Marshall McLuhan, *Understanding Media* (New York: McGraw-Hill, 1964).

[21] Randall Harrison, "Pictic Analysis: Toward a Vocabulary and Syntax for the Pictorial Code; with Research on Facial Communication," unpublished Ph.D. dissertation, Michigan State University (1964).

[22] Sol Worth, "Cognitive Aspects of Sequence in Visual Communication," unpublished, privately distributed (1965).

[23] Randall Harrison and Clyde D. J. Morris, "Communication Theory and Typographic Research," *Journal of Typographic Research*, Vol. 1 (1967), pp. 115–24.

eral other areas, such as glyptics, plastics, tectonics, haptics, aromatics, and edetics.

Looking down the road, it seems very likely that verbal and nonverbal codes will diverge in important ways. Similarly, key differences are likely to divide the various nonverbal codes. I'm hoping that we can profitably pursue a common path—although some theorists feel that already differences far outweigh similarities—that we are following deadened trails —and we need to remap our research strategy.

VERBAL	
DISCRETE	CONTINUOUS
ARBITRARY	NATURAL
INVARIABLE	VARIABLE
DENOTATIVE	CONNOTATIVE

In particular, we hear the arguments that verbal codes are "discrete" while nonverbal codes tend to be "continuous." In the sematic dimension, verbal codes are "arbitrary" while nonverbal codes are "natural." It's suggested that for the nonverbal codes, greater variability persists in both encoding and decoding. And similarly, the nonverbal codes tend to be strongly connotative whereas verbal codes are more abstractly denotative. Each proposition raises interesting research questions. Many of these questions, however, rest on appropriate information measures.

SENT?
MEANT?
RESPONSE?

Looking at the receiver at any given moment in the communication process, we might assume that he has certain uncertainties—needs for various types of information. At one level is technical uncertainty: what was sent? Next, semantic uncertainty: what was meant? Finally, pragmatic uncertainty: what is the appropriate response?

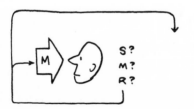

S?
M?
R?

This, in turn, leads to higher level, or longer-range uncertainties. If communicator B makes response X, what will communicator A send next? And how will this relate to previous messages? Does it modify their meanings, etc.?

This, in turn, feeds into a still higher level of analysis of the communication system. Here, we might suggest successive stages: I. Pre-initiation, when messages relate to availability for interaction; II. Initiation, when messages examine reward potentials and establish communication traffic patterns; III. Interaction, the main body of communication, where messages relate to goal achievement and interaction maintenance; IV. Termination, where the communication system suspends its current interaction. Each stage may have certain uncertainty-reducing priorities. At each stage, different code systems may be brought into play. And similar cues may shift their meaning from stage to stage.

For each communication system, then, we have a message space which reflects the information or uncertainty space of the communicators. This complex matrix changes from stage to stage. And it changes as we introduce more communicators or change the means of interposing our communicators.

Returning to our original topic—other ways of packaging information—it seems that many superficial tips might be given. But perhaps our central problem is that, on one hand, we are still struggling to conceptualize that key communication variable: information. And on the other hand, we have all too little knowledge of alternative ways of packaging—i.e., the code systems available to man. Meanwhile, the state of our art—like Venus de Milo—may be beautiful to look at, but it lacks the hands that are needed for an effective science.

FOR DISCUSSION AND REVIEW

1   According to Harrison, how important are nonverbal bands of communication?

2   Why does Harrison say that Americans have become more aware recently of nonverbal communication?

3   Harrison argues that nonverbal communication is important because of quantity, primacy, and subtlety. How significant do you consider each of these factors?

4   Harrison lists four steps in the study of nonverbal communication: sensitize, analyze, organize, utilize. What does he mean by these terms? Give examples of each, if possible.

5   What relationship exists between the first and second items in these pairs: panhuman/natural science; cultural/anthropology; social/sociology; and individual/psychology? What constraints operate in each area so far as nonverbal communication is concerned?

6   Harrison describes briefly four communication models. How do they differ?

7   Define *pictics, vidistics, glyptics, plastics, tectonics, haptics, aromatics,* and *edetics.* You may have trouble finding these words in some dictionaries. Does etymology help you to determine their meanings? Explain.

8   In what ways do verbal and nonverbal codes differ?

9   Look at Rosenthal's report of his research (footnote 4), and describe the extent to which an experimenter may influence the outcome of his experiments. What explanations are offered for these results?

3

Kinesics and Communication

Ray L. Birdwhistell

Much of the pioneering work in kinesics has been carried out by Ray L. Birdwhistell. In this article, he distinguishes three units of kinesics —pre-kinesics, micro-kinesics, and social kinesics—and explains the kinds of analysis appropriate to each. Birdwhistell has developed a detailed notational system for recording bodily movements. Utilizing what he calls *kinegraphs,* it divides the human body into eight principal sections and provides a means for recording, unambiguously, in a standard "orthography," significant body motions. Some examples of kinegraphs are included in this article.

KINESICS IS the study of the visual aspects of non-verbal, interpersonal communication. It is divided into three units: *Pre-kinesics* deals with physiological, pre-communicational aspects of body motion. *Micro-kinesics* is concerned with the derivation of kines (least particles of isolatable body-motion) into manageable morphological classes. And *social kinesics* is concerned with these morphological constructs as they relate to communication.

Pre-kinesics

Present research in kinesics assumes that visually perceptible body shifts, whose variations have been repetitively observed and are subject to systematization, are learned. This assumption does not preclude consideration of physiological influence. Generalizations about individual variations of velocity and intensity must await more definitive neuromuscular and endocrine research. But failure to keep pre-kinesics separate from micro-kinesics and social kinesics leads to reductionism. In the early stages of investigation, important data were overlooked by being dumped into the wastepaper baskets of "an itch," "weariness," "muscular relaxation," "tonus," and the like. But such stimuli to body movement are often, if not usually, dependent upon the context of the act and its social definition. To "scratch," to "shift," to "stretch," to "relax," and to "tense" are but a few of many apparently simple physiological reactions that are socially defined and controlled. To equivocate by calling them psychosomatic is to sacrifice experimental clarity for interdisciplinary fellowship.

In this discussion I shall use the closing and opening of the lids of one eye for illustration. This example contains much behavior that is non-significant (at the present) to kinesiological research. For instance, a high-speed camera records almost a thousand positions of the lid in closing and opening. A graph derived from such a film strip shows rests, reverses, and velocity shifts that are imperceptible to the unassisted eye. Any society "selects" but a portion of this range for interactional definition.

The least isolated particle we call a *kine*. Members of a group use only certain of the discriminated range of kines for social interaction.

Micro-kinesics

Micro-kinesics deals with the systematization of kines with meaning into manageable classes. In a series of tests, five young nurses reported they could discriminate eleven positions of lid closure (eleven kines with discriminational meaning). All agreed that only four "meant" anything (four kines with differential meaning). Retesting of the nurses revealed that the latter were not precise positions but ranges of positions, which the nurses reported as "open-eyed," "droopy-lidded," "squinting," and "eyes squeezed tight," all of which they distinguished from just "open" and "closed."

Consequent to this research, it was found that only one of the five nurses could reproduce more than five of the twenty-three positions that they recognized to have differential meaning. Using a male control group of college students of comparable age, it was established that all could reproduce at least ten, with an average of fifteen. One extremely versatile young man produced thirty-five kines and easily got the twenty-three with differential meaning. Significantly, far less sex difference was noted in the ability of our Japanese and German informants. (This may be related to the small number of informants in the non-American groupings.) From this experiment, alone, we feel we have isolated significant recognition and reproduction differences within the informant range and between sexes. Just as we have a larger reading and hearing vocabulary than we do a speaking one, so we may have a larger viewing than acting list. Parenthetically, only morphological research has given us any feeling of security in describing any particular motion as *idiokinesic*.

To return to our methodological procedure: As soon as it was discovered that the variation of one or the other of the kines in a given area in the composite changed the differential meaning of the composite, we described the abstracted combination as a kinemorph. For example, "droopy-lidded," combined with "bilaterally raised, median portion depressed brows," has an evident differential meaning from "droopy-lidded" combined with a "low unilateral brow lift."

The discovery that the variation of *either* brow or lids may vary the differential meaning of the kinemorph relieves us from the over-easy temptation of indulging in discussion concerning modifiers and subjects or predicators. Nevertheless, I have a hunch that cross-cultural research is going to lead to the development of kinesic syntax. Present research seems to indicate that in middle-majority American culture circum-eye movement takes priority in definition of situation over movement of the hands, the arms, the trunk, and even over the head. This becomes apparent when we compare such data with that derived from Southern European and Southeast Asian informants.

Let me illustrate several of these points with an excerpt from an experiment:

Left eye closed; right open
Left orbital margin squinted
Mouth held in "normal"
Tip of nose depressed (bunnynose)
(This projection held for no more than five seconds. Retest with shorter duration.)

Right eye closed; left open
Left orbital margin squinted
Mouth held in "normal"
Tip of nose depressed (bunnynose)
Informant's remark: "They look different, but they wouldn't mean anything different."
Tentative analysis: Shift from closing of right eye to left eye does not shift meaning. Leftness and rightness allokinic in this case. Use of unilateral squint unnoticed by informant.

Left eye closed; right open
Mouth held in "normal"
Tip of nose depressed
Neither orbital margin squinted
Informant's remark: "That's the same as the first."
Tentative analysis: Squint morphologically insignificant.

Left eye closed; right open
Left orbital margin squinted (or unsquinted)
Mouth drawn into pout
Tip of nose depressed
Informant's remark: "Well, that changes things."
Tentative analysis: Mouth position morphologically significant.

Here are two examples of recording situations. Both were taken in context, one on a bus, the second in a home. In only the second was there any direct information other than that supplied by the situation itself. Except insofar as there are regional cultural differences in the United States, these can be described as members of the common American culture. Mother and child spoke with a Tidewater, Virginia, accent. The hostess is a native of Cleveland, Ohio, resident in Washington since 1945; the guest is from a small Wisconsin town and is presently residing in Chicago. Both the hostess and the guest could probably be assigned an upper-middle-class position as measured by a Warner-type analysis. The bus route on which the bus event was recorded leads to a similar neighborhood. The way in which the mother and child were dressed was not consistent with the other riders, who disembarked, as did the observer, before the mother and child did. Both the hostess and her guest were in their late thirties. The child was about four, while his mother seemed to be about twenty-seven to thirty.

In Figures 1 and 2 stress and intonation are indicated above the pertinent text, using symbols provided in Trager and Smith's *Outline of English Structure*; voice-qualifiers, e.g., the drawl ($\frown$), are indicated by symbols developed by them. In a few places a phonemic transcription of the text is also provided. Kinesic symbols are given below the pertinent text, but are merely illustrated, not translated.

1. This situation was observed on a street at about 2:30 P.M., April 14. The little boy was seated next to the window. He seemed tired of looking out of the window, and, after surveying all of the car ads and the passengers, he leaned toward his mother and pulled at her sleeve, pouted and vigorously kicked his legs.

2. His mother had been sitting erectly in her seat, her packages on her lap, and her hands lightly clasped around the packages. She was apparently "lost in thought."

3. When the boy's initial appeal failed to gain the mother's attention, he began to jerk at her sleeve again, each jerk apparently stressing his vocalization.

4. The mother turned and looked at him, "shushed" him, and placed her right hand firmly across his thighs.

5. The boy protested audibly, clenched both fists, pulled them with stress against his chest. At the same time he drew his legs up against the restraint of his mother's hand. His mouth was drawn down and his upper face was pulled into a tight frown.

6. The mother withdrew her hand from his lap and resettled in her former position with her hands clasped around the packages.

7. The boy grasped her upper arm tightly, continued to frown. When no immediate response was forthcoming, he turned and thrust both knees into the lateral aspect of her left thigh.

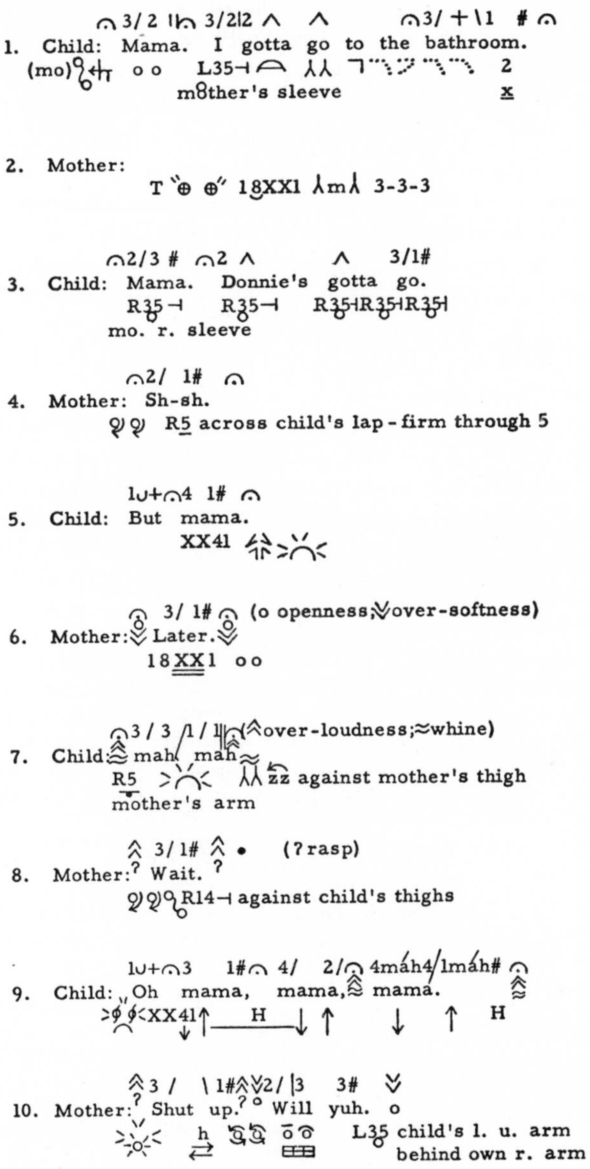

1. Child: Mama. I gotta go to the bathroom.
   (mo) ⌇ o o L35⊣ ⌒ ʎʎ ⊐ ˙˙ ˙˙ ˙˙ 2
        m8ther's sleeve   x

2. Mother:
        T ⊕ ⊕ 18XX1 ʎmʎ 3-3-3

3. Child: Mama. Donnie's gotta go.
        R35⊣   R35⊣   R35⊣R35⊣R35⊣
        mo. r. sleeve

4. Mother: Sh-sh.
        ℘ ℘ R5 across child's lap - firm through 5

5. Child: But mama.
        XX41 ⥮ >⌒<

6. Mother: Later.   (o openness; over-softness)
        18XX1 o o

7. Child: mah mah (over-loudness; whine)
        R5 >⌒< ʎʎ zz against mother's thigh
        mother's arm

8. Mother: Wait. • (?rasp)
        ℘℘℘R14⊣ against child's thighs

9. Child: Oh mama, mama, mama.
        >ɸ ɸ<XX41↑ H ↓ ↑   ↓ ↑ H

10. Mother: Shut up. Will yuh. o
        >⌖< h ⇄ ōō L35 child's l. u. arm
                        behind own r. arm

Figure 1

8. She looked at him, leaned toward him, and slapped him across the anterior portion of his upper legs.

9. He began to jerk his clenched fists up and down, vigorously nodding between each inferior-superior movement of his fists.

10. She turned, frowning, and with her mouth pursed, she spoke to him through her teeth. Suddenly she looked around, noted that the other passengers were watching, and forced a square smile. At the same time that she finished speaking, she reached her right hand in under her left arm and squeezed the boy's arm. He sat quietly.

Guest of honor forty-five minutes late. Three couples waiting, plus host and hostess. Host had arranged guest list for function.

1. As the hostess opened the door to admit her guest, she smiled a closed-toothed smile. As she began speaking she drew her hands, drawn into loose fists, up between her breasts. Opening her eyes very wide, she then closed them slowly and held them closed for several words. As she began to speak she dropped her head to one side and then moved it toward the guest in a slow sweep. She then pursed her lips momentarily before continuing to speak, indicating that he should enter.

2. He looked at her fixedly, shook his head, and spread his arms with his hands held open. He then began to shuffle his feet and raised one hand, turning it slightly outward. He nodded, raised his other hand, and turned it palm-side up as he continued his vocalization. Then he dropped both hands and held them, palms forward, to the side and away from his thighs. He continued his shuffling.

3. She smiled at him, lips pulled back from clenched teeth. Then, as she indicated where he should put his coat, she dropped her face momentarily into an expressionless pose. She smiled toothily again, clucked and slowly shut, opened, and shut her eyes again as she pointed to the guest with her lips. She then swept her head from one side to the other. As she said the word "all" she moved her head in a sweep up and down from one side to the other, shut her eyes slowly again, pursed her lips, and grasped the guest's lapel.

4. The guest hunched his shoulders, which pulled his lapel out of the hostess' grasp. He held his coat with both hands, frowned, and then blinked rapidly as he slipped the coat off. He continued to hold tightly to his coat.

Social Kinesics

In this discussion I avoid the word "gesture," for gesture is restricted to those actions whose descriptions contain vocalized rationalizations by the actor or viewer. Research has revealed, however, that gestures are no more "meaningful" than other acts. The subjective, vocalized meanings attached to them do not necessarily supply us with insight into the meaning of the action, of which the gesture is an independent but deceptively visible aspect. Consider the variety of messages relayed by an action of which the "thumbed-nose" is the *explicit* focus. The delusory availability of gestures has provided the same handicap to the development of kinesics that formal grammar has to the understanding of lin-

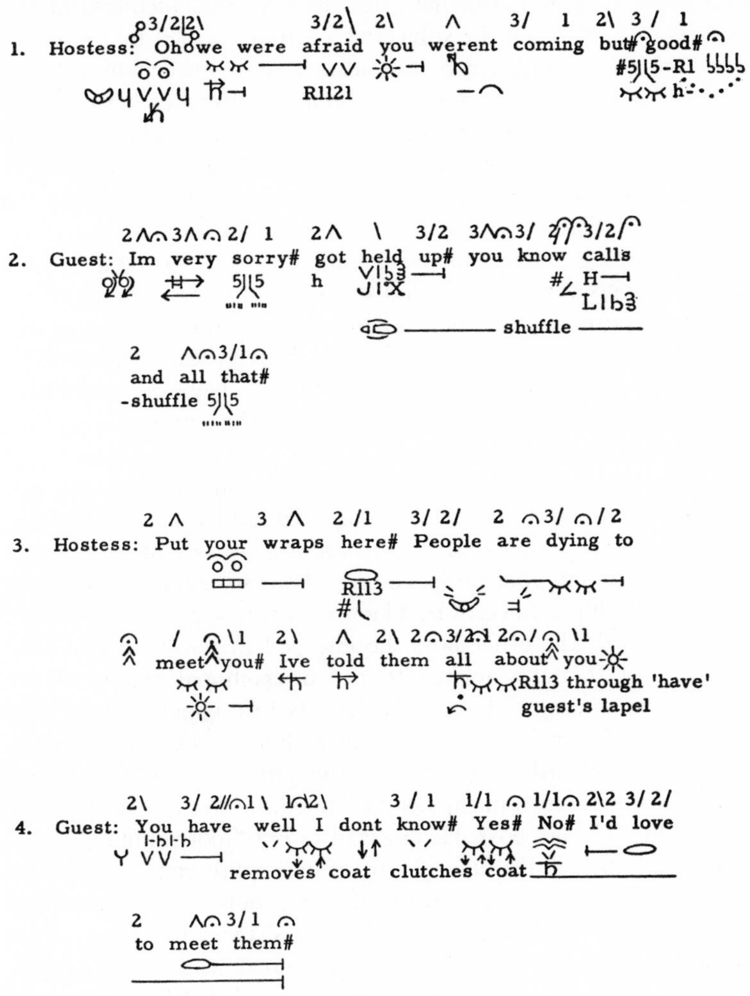

1. Hostess: Ohowe were afraid you werent coming but good#

2. Guest: Im very sorry# got held up# you know calls

   and all that#
   -shuffle

3. Hostess: Put your wraps here# People are dying to

   meet you# Ive told them all about you

   through 'have'
   guest's lapel

4. Guest: You have well I dont know# Yes# No# I'd love

   removes coat   clutches coat

   to meet them#

Figure 2

guistics. The most successful research in the field of kinesics has come
from the attempt to understand the relationship between visible and
audible communication. New developments in linguistics make possible
the organic relationship between such phonema; particularly intonation
patterns, phrase superfixes, and voice qualifiers. So intimate is this relationship that the trained linguist-kinsiologist has at times been able to
describe many of the movements of a speaker from hearing a recording
or listening to a telephone conversation. Further, we have found that
an auditor may "hear" intonational shifts that were not spoken but
moved by the informant, and vice versa. Yet these phenomena are not

inseparable. Smith and Trager have described as *meta-incongruent* the situation that occurs when the subjective meaning carried by the words in an utterance is contradicted by the intonation or voice-qualifiers used with it. A comparable situation occurs when the utterance has one contextual meaning and the accompanying action another. The utilization of such data has evident value for interviewers. Meta-incongruences are as important for those interested in "unconscious behavior" as is the recognition that there occur kinesic "slips" and "stuttering."

Of more interest perhaps to the non-linguist is the working process of in-group conversation. As part of a study of an adolescent clique, we paid particular attention to the "origin-response ratio." Three of the nine boys in this group were, by word count, heavy vocalizers. In fifteen recorded scenes (five scenes for each of the three), they were responsible for from seventy-two to ninety-three per cent *of the words* spoken. One of the three was regarded by the group as a leader. (Incidentally, he originated more conversations or new trends to conversation than any of the other boys.) But the other recognized leader had one of the lowest word count percentages of the group. He originated, by our count, at a median rate, but he spoke only about sixteen per cent of the words. His leadership seemed to be a kinesic one.

Compared with the other boys, he engaged in few unrelated acts, that is, acts not traceably related to the interactional chain. (These "unrelated acts" appear to be abortive efforts to originate action; they seem related to similar behavior in smaller children, except that older children more frequently realize when the group is not responsive.) Compared with the adults in the neighborhood, he was kinesically more "mature" than the other boys. He engaged in less "foot shuffling," "dramatic thought"—a substitution (?) of kinemorphic constructions for verbal descriptions was characteristic of this group—and he exhibited fewer hand-mouth kinemorphic constructions than his peers. Even though he vocalized relatively little, he was known as a good conversationalist. Kinesiological analysis of this boy revealed that he was a "good listener." His responses were seldom meta-incongruent, he steered the conversation with face and head kinemorphs, and he seldom engaged in leg and foot "jiggling," which generally conveys a contextual meaning of restlessness, malaise, or negation.

FOR DISCUSSION AND REVIEW

1 Birdwhistell uses the terms *pre-kinesics, micro-kinesics,* and *social kinesics.* Define each term.
2 What is a *kine*? Give several examples.
3 What differences between male and
female American subjects did Birdwhistell find in testing discrimination and reproduction of eyelid closure kines? Do these differences hold across cultures? Explain.
4 Language teachers distinguish be-

tween active vocabulary items, words which we actually speak or write, and passive vocabulary items, words that we recognize but do not use ourselves. Is there a similar distinction with regard to kines? Can you give any examples based on your own experience?

5 Look up the definition of *idiolect*. Now explain what Birdwhistell means by *idiokinesic*. After looking up the definition of *morpheme* and *allomorph*, explain *kinemorph* and *allokine*.

6 Study the transcription of the ex-change between hostess and guest on p. 499. Birdwhistell does not explain the kinesic notations that appear underneath the phonemic transcription. See how well you can understand them. How pictographic are they? (An explanation of the symbols appears on pp. 255–302 of Birdwhistell's book *Kinesics and Context*.)

7 How does Birdwhistell describe the term *meta-incongruent*? Can you give an example of such a situation?

4

Winking, Blinking and Nods

Julius Fast

It is a widely-held belief that our eyes are capable of communicating a vast range of emotions, and many examples from literature, the arts, and popular belief can be cited to support this observation. Our eyes, however, do not communicate by themselves; they operate in conjunction with other facial and body movements to convey a person's feelings. In this selection from *Body Language*, Julius Fast discusses just how telling our eyes are, how we can learn to read them, and how eye movements are culturally related.

The Stare that Dehumanizes

THE COWPUNCHER sat his horse loosely and his fingers hovered above his gun while his eyes, ice cold, sent chills down the rustler's back. A familiar situation? It happens in every western novel, just as in every love story the heroine's eyes *melt* while the hero's eyes *burn* into hers. In literature, even the best literature, eyes are *steely, knowing, mocking, piercing, glowing* and so on.

Are they really? Are they ever? Is there such a thing as a burning glance, or a cold glance or a hurt glance? In truth there isn't. Far from being windows of the soul, the eyes are physiological dead ends, simply organs of sight and no more, differently colored in different people to be sure, but never really capable of expressing emotion in themselves.

And yet again and again we read and hear and even tell of the eyes being wise, knowing, good, bad, indifferent. Why is there such confusion? Can so many people be wrong? If the eyes do not show emotion, then why the vast literature, the stories and legends about them?

Of all parts of the human body that are used to transmit information, the eyes are the most important and can transmit the most subtle nuances. Does this contradict the fact that the eyes do not show emotion? Not really. While the eyeball itself shows nothing, the emotional impact of the eyes occurs because of their use and the use of the face around them. The reason they have so confounded observers is because by length of glance, by opening of eyelids, by squinting and by a dozen little manipulations of the skin and eyes, almost any meaning can be sent out.

But the most important technique of eye management is the look, or the stare. With it we can often make or break another person. How? By giving him human or nonhuman status.

Simply, eye management in our society boils down to two facts. One, we do not stare at another human being. Two, staring is reserved for a non-person. We stare at art, at sculpture, at scenery. We go to the zoo and stare at the animals, the lions, the monkeys, the gorillas. We stare at them for as long as we please, as intimately as we please, but we do not stare at humans if we want to accord them human treatment.

We may use the same stare for the side-show freak, but we do not really consider him a human being. He is an object at which we have paid money to stare, and in the same way we may stare at an actor on a stage. The real man is masked too deeply behind his role for our stare to bother either him or us. However, the new theater that brings the actor down into the audience often gives us an uncomfortable feeling. By virtue of involving us, the audience, the actor suddenly loses his non-person status and staring at him becomes embarrassing to us.

As I said before, a Southern white may stare at a black in the same way, making him, by the stare, into an object rather than a person. If we wish pointedly to ignore someone, to treat him with an element of contempt, we can give him the same stare, the slightly unfocused look that does not really see him, the cutting stare of the socially elite.

Servants are often treated this way as are waiters, waitresses and children. However, this may be a mutually protective device. It allows the servants to function efficiently in their overlapping universe without too much interference from us, and it allows us to function comfortably without acknowledging the servant as a fellow human. The same is true of children and waiters. It would be an uncomfortable world if each time we were served by a waiter we had to introduce ourselves and indulge in social amenities.

A Time for Looking

With unfamiliar human beings, when we acknowledge their humanness, we must avoid staring at them, and yet we must also avoid ignoring them. To make them into people rather than objects, we use a deliberate and polite inattention. We look at them long enough to make it quite clear that we see them, and then we immediately look away. We are saying, in body language, "I know you are there," and a moment later we add, "But I would not dream of intruding on your privacy."

The important thing in such an exchange is that we do not catch the eye of the one whom we are recognizing as a person. We look at him without locking glances, and then we immediately look away. Recognition is not permitted.

There are different formulas for the exchange of glances depending on where the meeting takes place. If you pass someone in the street you may eye the oncoming person till you are about eight feet apart, then you must look away as you pass. Before the eight foot distance is reached, each will signal in which direction he will pass. This is done with a brief look in that direction. Each will veer slightly, and the passing is done smoothly.

For this passing encounter Dr. Erving Goffman in *Behavior in Public Places* says that the quick look and the lowering of the eyes is body language for, "I trust you. I am not afraid of you."

To strengthen this signal, you look directly at the other's face before looking away.

Sometimes the rules are hard to follow, particularly if one of the two people wears dark glasses. It becomes impossible to discover just what they are doing. Are they looking at you too long, too intently? Are they looking at you at all? The person wearing the glasses feels protected and assumes that he can stare without being noticed in his staring. However, this is a self-deception. To the other person, dark glasses seem to indicate that the wearer is always staring at him.

We often use this look-and-away technique when we meet famous people. We want to assure them that we are respecting their privacy, that we would not dream of staring at them. The same is true of the crippled or physically handicapped. We look briefly and then look away before the stare can be said to be a stare. It is the technique we use for any unusual situation where too long a stare would be embarrassing. When we see an interracial couple we use this technique. We might use it when we see a man with an unusual beard, with extra long hair, with outlandish clothes, or a girl with a minimal mini-skirt may attract this look-and-away.

Of course the opposite is also true. If we wish to put a person down we may do so by staring longer than is acceptably polite. Instead of dropping our gazes when we lock glances, we continue to stare. The person who disapproves of interracial marriage or dating will stare rudely at the interracial couple. If he dislikes long hair, short dresses or beards he may show it with a longer-than-acceptable stare.

The Awkward Eyes

The look-and-away stare is reminiscent of the problem we face in adolescence in terms of our hands. What do we do with them? Where do we hold them? Amateur actors are also made conscious of this. They are suddenly aware of their hands as awkward appendages that must somehow be used gracefully and naturally.

In the same way, in certain circumstances, we become aware of our glances as awkward appendages. Where shall we look? What shall we do with our eyes?

Two strangers seated across from each other in a railway dining car have the option of introducing themselves and facing a meal of inconsequential and perhaps boring talk, or ignoring each other and desperately trying to avoid each other's glance. Cornelia Otis Skinner, describing such a situation in an essay, wrote, "They re-read the menu, they fool with the cutlery, they inspect their own fingernails as if seeing them for the first time. Comes the inevitable moment when glances meet, but they meet only to shoot instantly away and out the window for an intent view of the passing scene."

This same awkward eye dictates our looking behavior in elevators and crowded buses and subway trains. When we get on an elevator or train with a crowd we look briefly and then look away at once without locking glances. We say, with our look, "I see you. I do not know you, but you are a human and I will not stare at you."

In the subway or bus where long rides in very close circumstances are a necessity, we may be hard put to find some way of not staring. We sneak glances, but look away before our eyes can lock. Or we look with an unfocused glance that misses the eyes and settles on the head, the mouth, the body—for any place but the eyes is an acceptable looking spot for the unfocused glance.

If our eyes do meet we can sometimes mitigate the message with a brief smile. The smile must not be too long or too obvious. It must say, "I am sorry we have looked, but we both know it was an accident."

Bedroom Eyes

The awkward eye is a common enough occurrence for all of us to have experienced it at one time or another. Almost all actions and interactions between humans depend on mutual glances. The late Spanish philosopher José Ortega y Gasset, in his book *Man and People*, spoke of "the look" as something that comes directly from within a man "with the straight-line accuracy of a bullet." He felt that the eye, with its lids and socket, its iris and pupil, was equivalent to a "whole theatre with its stage and actors."

The eye muscles, Ortega said, are marvelously subtle and because of this every glance is minutely differentiated from every other glance. There are so many different looks that it is nearly impossible to name them, but he cited, "the look that lasts but an instant and the insistent look; the look that slips over the surface of the thing looked at and the look that grips it like a hook; the direct look and the oblique look whose extreme form has its own name, 'looking out of the corner of one's eye.' "

He also listed the "sideways glance" which differs from any other oblique look although its axis is still on the bias.

Every look, Ortega said, tells us what goes on inside the person who gives it, and the intent to communicate with a look is more genuinely revealing when the sender of the look is unaware of just how he sends it.

Like other researchers into body language Ortega warned that a look in itself does not give the entire story, even though it has a meaning. A word in a sentence has a meaning too, but only in the context of the sentence can we learn the complete meaning of the word. So too with a look. Only in the context of an entire situation is a look entirely meaningful.

There are also looks that want to see but not be seen. These the Spanish philosopher called sideways glances. In any situation we may study someone and look as long as we wish, providing the other person is not aware that we are looking, providing our look is hidden. The moment his eyes move to lock with ours, our glance must slide away. The more skilled the person, the better he is at stealing these sideways glances.

In a charming description Ortega labels one look "the most effec-

tive, the most suggestive, the most delicious and enchanting." He called
it the most complicated because it is not only furtive, but it is also the
very opposite of furtive, because it makes it obvious that it is looking.
This is the look given with lidded eyes, the sleepy look or calculating
look or appraising look, the look a painter gives his canvas as he steps
back from it, what the French call *les yeux en coulisse*.

Describing this look, Ortega said the lids are almost three-quarters
closed and it appears to be hiding itself, but in fact the lids compress
the look and "shoot it out like an arrow."

"It is the look of eyes that are, as it were, asleep but which behind
the cloud of sweet drowsiness are utterly awake. Anyone who has such
a look possesses a treasure."

Ortega said that Paris throws itself at the feet of anyone with this
look. Louis XV's DuBarry was supposed to have had it, and so was
Lucien Guitry. In our own Hollywood, Robert Mitchum certainly had
it and it set him up for years as a masculine sex symbol. Mae West
copied it and the French actress Simone Signoret has it so perfectly
controlled that even in middle age she comes across as a very sexy and
attractive woman.

Other Cultures, Other Looks

The recognition of the eye as a means of communication, or of a
look as having special significance is nothing new. Looking is something
that has always had strong emotions attached to it and has been forbidden, under certain circumstances, in prehistory and legend. Lot's
wife was turned to a pillar of salt for looking back, and Orpheus lost
Eurydice by looking at her. Adam, when he tasted the fruit of knowledge, was afraid to look at God.

The significance of looking is universal, but usually we are not sure
of just how we look or how we are looked at. Honesty demands, in our
culture, that we look someone straight in the eye. Other cultures have
other rules, as a principal in a New York City high school recently
discovered.

A young girl at the high school, a fifteen-year-old Puerto Rican, had
been caught in the washroom with a group of girls suspected of smok-
ing. Most of the group were known troublemakers, and while this
young girl, Livia, had no record, the principal after a brief interview
was convinced of her guilt and decided to suspend her with the others.

"It wasn't what she said," he reported later. "It was simply her attitude. There was something sly and suspicious about her. She just
wouldn't meet my eye. She wouldn't look at me."

It was true. Livia at her interview with the principal stared down at the floor in what was a clear-cut guilty attitude and refused to meet his eyes.

"But she's a good girl," Livia's mother insisted. Not to the school, for she was too much of a "troublemaker" the principal felt, to come to the authorities with her protest. Instead, she turned to her neighbors and friends. As a result there was a demonstration of Puerto Rican parents at the school the next morning and the ugly stirrings of a threatened riot.

Fortunately, John Flores taught Spanish literature at the school, and John lived only a few doors from Livia and her family. Summoning his own courage, John asked for an interview with the principal.

"I know Livia and her parents," he told the principal. "And she's a good girl. I am sure there has been some mistake in this whole matter."

"If there was a mistake," the principal said uneasily, "I'll be glad to rectify it. There are thirty mothers outside yelling for my blood. But I questioned the child myself, and if ever I saw guilt written on a face— she wouldn't even meet my eyes!"

John drew a sigh of relief, and then very carefully, for he was too new in the school to want to tread on toes, he explained some basic facts of Puerto Rican culture to the principal.

"In Puerto Rico a nice girl, a good girl," he explained, "does not meet the eyes of an adult. Refusing to do so is a sign of respect and obedience. It would be as difficult for Livia to look you in the eye as it would be for her to misbehave, or for her mother to come to you with a complaint. In our culture, this is just not accepted behavior for a respectable family."

Fortunately the principal was a man who knew how to admit that he was wrong. He called Livia and her parents and the most vocal neighbors in and once again discussed the problem. In the light of John Flores' explanation it became obvious to him that Livia was not avoiding his eyes out of defiance, but out of a basic demureness. Her slyness, he now saw, was shyness. In fact, as the conference progressed and the parents relaxed, he realized that Livia was indeed a gentle and sweet girl.

The outcome of the entire incident was a deeper, more meaningful relationship between the school and the community—but that of course is another story. What is of particular interest in this story is the strange confusion of the principal. How did he so obviously misinterpret all the signals of Livia's behavior?

Livia was using body language to say, "I am a good girl. I respect you and the school. I respect you too much to answer your questions, too much to meet your eyes with shameless boldness, too much to defend myself. But surely my very attitude tells you all this."

How could such a clear-cut message be interpreted as, "I defy you.

I will not answer your questions. I will not look you in the eyes because I am a deceitful child. I will evade your questions slyly—"

The answer of course is a cultural one. Different cultures have different customs and, of course, different body language. They also have different looks and different meanings to the same looks.

In America, for instance, a man is not supposed to look at a woman for any length of time unless she gives him her permission with a body language signal, a smile, a backward glance, a direct meeting of his eye. In other countries different rules apply.

In America, if a woman looks at a man for too long a period of time, she commits herself to a verbal approach. Her signal says, "I am interested. You can approach me." In Latin countries, though freer body movements are permissible, such a look might be a direct invitation to a physical "pass." It becomes obvious then why a girl like Livia would not look the principal in the eye.

Again, in our country, two men are not allowed to stare at each other for more than a brief period of time unless they intend to fight or to become intimate. Any man who looks at another man for too long embarrasses and annoys him and the other man begins to wonder just what he wants.

This is another example of the rigidity of the rules of looking. If someone stares at us and we meet his eye and catch him staring, it is his duty to look away first. If he does not look away as we engage his eye, then we become uncomfortable and aware that something is wrong. Again we become embarrassed and annoyed.

A Long Look at Oneself

In an attempt to discover just how some of these rules for visual communication work, Dr. Gerhard Neilson of Copenhagen analyzed the "looks" of the subjects in his self-confrontation studies. To discover just how long, and when, the people being interviewed looked at the interviewer, he filmed interviews and replayed them a number of times in slow motion.

While he started with no clear-cut idea of how long one man would look at another during an interview, he was surprised to find how little looking there actually was. The man who looked at his interviewer the most, still looked away 27 percent of the time. The man who looked at his interviewer the least looked away 92 percent of the time. Half of the people interviewed looked away for half of the time they were being interviewed.

Dr. Neilson found that when people spoke a lot they looked at their partners very little; when they listened a lot they also looked a lot. He reports that he expected people to look at each other more when they listened more, but he was surprised to find them looking less when they spoke more.

He found that when people start to speak, they look away from their partners at first. There is a subtle timing, he explains, in speaking, listening, looking and looking away. Most people look away either immediately before or after the beginning of one out of every four speeches they make. A few look away at the beginning of half their speeches. As they finish speaking, half the people look at their partners.

As to why so many people refuse to meet the eyes of their partners during a conversation, Dr. Neilson believes this is a way of avoiding distraction.

How Long Is a Glance?

Another study, carried out by Dr. Ralph V. Exline at the University of Delaware, involved 40 men and 40 women, all freshmen and sophomores. In the study a man interviewed 20 men and 20 women and a woman interviewed the other 20 of each sex. Half the students were questioned by both interviewers about intimate subjects, their plans, desires, needs and fears. The other half were asked about recreational interests, reading, movies, sports.

Dr. Exline found that when the students were interviewed about personal subjects, they didn't look at the interviewer as often as they did when they were interviewed about recreational subjects. Women, however, in both types of interview, looked at the interviewers more frequently than men did.

What seems to come across from both these studies, and others of a similar nature, is that when someone looks away while he's speaking, it generally means he's still explaining himself and doesn't want to be interrupted.

A locking of his gaze with his partner's at this point would be a signal to interrupt when he paused. If he pauses and is not looking at his conversational partner, it means he hasn't yet finished. He is signaling, "This is what I want to say. What is your answer?"

If you look away from the person who is speaking to you while you are listening, it is a signal, "I am not completely satisfied with what you are saying. I have some qualifications."

If you look away while you are speaking it may mean, "I am not certain of what I am saying."

If while you are listening, you look at the speaker, you signal, "I agree with you," or "I am interested in what you are saying."

If while you are speaking, you look at the listener, you may be signaling, "I am certain of what I am saying."

There are also elements of concealment in looking away from your
partner. If you look away while he is speaking, you signal, "I don't want
you to know what I feel." This is particularly true if the partner is critical or insulting. It is something like an ostrich burying his head in the
sand. "If I cannot see you, you cannot hurt me." This is the reason
children will often refuse to look at you when you are scolding them.

However, there are more complexities here than meet the eye . . .
or the glance. Looking away during a conversation may be a means of
concealing something. Therefore when someone else looks away, we
may think he is concealing something. To practice deceit we may sometimes deliberately look at our partner instead of refusing to meet his
glance.

In addition to length and direction of glances, there is a good deal
of signaling involved in the act of closing the lid. In addition to the
half-lidded look Ortega described, Birdwhistell states that five young
nurses, in a series of tests, reported twenty-three different positions of
lid closure that they could distinguish.

But they all agreed that only four out of the twenty-three "meant
anything." Retesting allowed Dr. Birdwhistell to label these four positions, "open-eyed, droopy-lidded, squinting, eyes-closed-tight."

Working from the opposite end, trying to get the girls to reproduce
the lid positions, was not so successful. All could reproduce five of the
twenty-three positions, but only one could reproduce more than five.

Using a group of men in the same type of experiment, he found
that all could reproduce at least ten positions. Unexpectedly men were
more facile at winking. Some of the men could reproduce fifteen different positions, and one—fantastically eloquent in body language—
came up with thirty-five different eyelid positions.

Branching out into cultural comparisons Dr. Birdwhistell found that
among the Japanese both sexes were similar in the number of eyelid
positions they could reproduce. But even the Japanese could recognize,
in others, more positions than they could assume themselves.

When movement of the eyebrows is added to movement of the lids,
many more recognizable signals are produced. Some scientists have
found as many as forty different positions of the brows alone, though
most agree that less than half of them are significant. It is only when
the significant eyebrow movements are combined with the significant
lid movements and we add forehead creases that the permutations and
combinations are endless.

If each combination has a different implication, then there is no
end to the number of signals we can transmit with our eyes and the
skin around them.

FOR DISCUSSION AND REVIEW

1 What does the ability to stare at an object or person tell you about your attitude toward that person or object?

2 Why is it often considered impolite to wear dark glasses? Do dark glasses annoy you? Explain.

3 What does Fast mean by *awkward eyes?*

4 What are *les yeux en coulisse?* What do they tell us about the observer and the observed?

5 According to Dr. Neilson, why in a conversation do speakers not look at their partners more often than they do? Do you agree with his interpretation? Explain.

6 What does a meeting of the eyes in a conversation say to the person who is not talking?

7 The claim has been made that it is easier to lie verbally than kinesically. Do you think the Halls (pp. 459–471) and Fast would agree with this statement? Do you agree? Explain.

5
Communication
by Gesture
in the
Middle East

Leo Hamalian

In the preceding selection, Julius Fast related an anecdote that illustrated how eye movements are linked to culture and how a misunderstanding was avoided when this fact was realized. In this essay on gesture in the Arab world, Leo Hamalian offers a more complete picture of body language in a foreign culture. His analysis of the belly dance, the Arab handshake, the courting gestures of Arab males and females, and the influence of social position and education on such gestures is interesting as a study in itself. It is also significant for the contrast it provides in the study of our own body language.

I T WAS, I believe, an Englishman with an eye for epigram as well as for ethnology who remarked that Arabs fight with their mouths and talk with their hands. Even if the events of the next few years in the

Middle East should invalidate the first half of this observation, nevertheless the second half will remain true for sometime to come. Of course, Arabs also talk with their mouths, but they have attained such an eloquence of gesture that often words seem superfluous in a conversation. Watching two Arabs conduct a conversation, you begin to feel that you do not have to understand their tongue in order to understand their conversation.

During the first months of my stay in the Middle East (chiefly in Syria, but with frequent visits to Lebanon and Jordan), it seemed to me that these gestures were not subject to classification or generalization, and therefore perhaps without much significance to the semanticist. However, as I continued my observations over the following months, certain patterns began to emerge and now I believe that I can risk several broad statements that may prove useful or interesting to the semanticist who is concerned with the ways of communication in other parts of the world. These statements, incidentally, have been subject to the scrutiny of some of my colleagues at the Syrian University, and while they took issue with a particular point here and there, they agreed in general with the conclusions drawn below.

• Gestures in the Arab world are apparently confined to the hands—although an expert knows how to use all parts of the body to communicate.

• The gestures are usually sex-linked; that is, certain gestures are associated exclusively with men, others with women; also, women seem to depend upon gesture far less than men do.

• Gesture is associated with the level of education—educated Arabs use gesture far less than uneducated Arabs.

• Gestures appear to be associated with expressions of three main emotions: of friendly feelings, of hostile feelings and of erotic feelings.

Most gesture language seems to be confined to the hands, but in that most expressive form of gesture, the dance, the Arab uses the shoulders, the torso, and the legs "to speak"; these gestures often signify an invitation to sexual encounter, but sometimes they express rejection as well. For instance, slowly raising the leg apparently expresses the desire to copulate; the manipulation of the arms may suggest loveplay; and the movement of the hips in a certain manner indicates that the dancer has arrived at a climax. The use of the body to communicate in the so-called "belly dance" (a corruption of the *hareem* dance) is an elaborate art as practiced by the expert; and one of the most baffling yet fascinating experiences for a Westerner fresh to the Middle East is watching an audience respond to the gestures of the dancer. There is conducted, in effect, a dialogue, half in gesture, half in words: the calls of the audience will encourage the dancer to attain new peaks of frenzied movement, which in turn will drive the audience into a state of wild cries and clapping. In panting pantomime, the dancer beckons, tempts, accepts, and consummates, her arms, bosom, hips, and thighs blending in a series of fluid undulations that convey meaning to admiring males as words never could.

For Arab men, this experience is often the only outlet for sexual feelings permitted by the mores of the society, and thus a skilled "belly dancer" holds the same status with them as Marilyn Monroe once had among American men. The varied movements and positions of the "belly dancer" is a subject for a separate paper, preferably by a specialist in the field of dance, but I wanted to indicate briefly in this paper that silent communication is far from limited to the hands.

Certain gestures which correspond to the vocabulary of the men's room are almost never practiced by women. (This is a carry-over from spoken Arabic). Other gestures associated with masculinity are considered to be unsuited to the image of soft femininity. Often this seems to be a matter related to social class: the closer a woman is to the working class, the more likely she is to move into the domain of masculine gesture. For example, sometimes you will see a woman who conducts a stall in the *souq* ball her hand and thrust it with a twist in the direction of a potential purchaser who has haggled too long over price: the gesture plainly says in the Middle East as elsewhere in the Mediterranean area, "Your offer is too low—go screw yourself, friend."

The most common of gestures in the Middle East, lifting the chin upwards to indicate the negative, has been given several nuances by women. The defiant toss of the head usually means "Absolutely not!" A more temperate tilt of the eyebrows while widening the eyes (without any gesture of the head itself) can mean, "I think it is not likely, but you may try to persuade me otherwise." Men use the gesture also, but without the ability to bestow it with the range of meanings that women do. There are, I am sure, many other gestures connected with gender that an experienced anthropologist might bring to light, but I myself found that women of this part of the world are loathe to discuss intimate customs. The fact that there is no literature on the subject does not help such investigation.

Arabs are people of passion who need to express their feelings through gesture as well as words; but the more educated an Arab is, the less he uses gesture, possibly because he has been conditioned by education to inhibit the expression of extravagant feelings. Thus, one of my Syrian colleagues who read this paper discovered much in it that he had not known before. Also, Arabs who have learned Western ways regard communication by gesture as a form of vulgarity, an extension of "lower class" manners. In Damascus, the *souq Hamadiyeh* or the shops lining "The Street Called Straight" are the best places to see Arab conversation in action.

In the Arab world, people like to express their feelings of friendship or antagonism—traditionally among the most important relationships here—in a manner more dramatic than words allow. For example, if an Arab accepts you as a friend, he will place his two index fingers side by side as a sign that he considers you to be his equal in all respects. (From this meaning, the gesture has taken on a secondary significance: "The two things we are talking about are the same.") In Jordan, if a bedouin extends his little finger and invites you to lock pinkies, he is offering friendship; the same gesture involving the second finger means that you are henceforth his enemy. In Syria and Lebanon, these meanings seem to be reversed.

There is also a special way of shaking hands to denote the degree of friendship. Between close friends, the hand is held up and out, as though prepared to make a fast gun-draw, then brought down in an arc to meet the hand of the friend in what becomes an explosive contact of flesh. No one can mistake the warmth and vigor of feeling that two friends put into this gesture. When the same friends take leave of each other, each will place a hand over his heart to indicate that he is sincerely grieved by the parting. The same gesture is used when one refuses the proffer of food or drink. Again, it carries the implication of sincere sorrow.

If one can read signs of friendship clearly, then the signs of antagonism are no less distinct. Perhaps it is necessary for Arabs, who value friendship above anything else, to communicate this basic emotion in a simple, unmistakable language understood everywhere in the Arab world. For example, the index fingers pointing at each other in opposition is one way by which hostility is expressed. If the speaker has passed beyond this stage into open animosity, he will join his index finger and thumb in a circle, draw back his lips in a snarl, and thus silently convey his sentiments: "Watch out, you son of a dog; I'll break your neck if you continue to provoke me." Taxi drivers frequently flash this sign at one another, knowing that they could never make their anger heard above the din of an Arab city.

When one feels happiness or joy at the expense of another person or wishes to show that he is rejoicing in the misfortune of an enemy, he will grind coffee in pantomime or turn his hands into a mortar-and-pestle.

If an Arab feels neither friendly nor hostile, he makes another gesture: he places his thumbs behind the lapels of his jacket and lifts the jacket gently backwards and forwards. A sign of lack of interest, this gesture says: "It is no skin off my nose" or "This matter has nothing to do with me."

The bunched finger-tips, that familiar Mediterranean gesture, has received skillful variations in the hands of the Arabs. Vibrated back and forth, bunched finger-tips can mean, "What is the matter with you, stupid son of a donkey?" Held towards the speaker and drawn back towards his body gradually, it means, "Please—go more slowly" or "Relax, friend, Rome was not built in a century." Tilted out towards the listener, bunched fingers may mean, "What would you like?" or, in our familiar idiom, "What's yours, bud?"

In the domain of sex, which between two unmarried people requires a more covert approach in the Middle East than anywhere else in the world, gesture appears to be indispensable for the tryst. A man who encounters a young lady in public may run his hand over his hair as a way of saying, "Hello, you cool chick." If the response is the same from the young lady, it signifies a willingness to improve relationships. Having struck up an acquaintance, the young man may be emboldened to twist his moustache and close one eye slightly, his way of saying, "I would now like to sleep with you if you don't mind." The young lady who does not draw her veil up indignantly and flee from the premises insulted is apparently ready to hear or see more. Should the young man carry out a successful assignation, he may boast about his conquest to his friends with a scrub-brush motion of his fingers: it usually means, "I slept with her and I am willing to go shares with you." Or the young man may silently signal to his friends, by lifting his leg, stiff-kneed, that the lady is free with her favors. However, if none of his advances were successful, then he may mimic a man turning a light bulb on the wall at hip-level. This generally means, "Well, that's how the cookie crumbles —nothing doing there."

As S. I. Hayakawa says, there are occasions "when it is felt that language is not sufficiently affective by itself to produce the results wanted." On such occasions, the Arab has an unusually rich storehouse of nonverbal communication to draw upon. It gives Middle Eastern life a colorful and exciting quality and perhaps deserves more careful study in the future than it has received in the past. For instance, it is interesting to ask to what extent the success of a Nasser depends upon his mastery of nonverbal communication.

FOR DISCUSSION AND REVIEW

1 What general emotional categories are represented through gesture in the Arab world?

2 According to Hamalian, is gesture in the Middle East confined to a particular area of the body? Explain.

3 How does the term "gesture" fit

into the definition of kinesics that Birdwhistell (p. 493) gives?

4 What is the relationship between sex and social class in the use of gesture in the Middle East?

5 Does education in the Arab world eliminate gesture or does it change it? Explain.

6

Space Speaks

When we observe a man and a woman whispering to each other, we should realize that they are also communicating something to us. That is, we should recognize that there is a certain degree of intimacy between them because they are close together. We have not in the past considered this kind of information to be communication, nor, until recently, have we attempted to study how space speaks to us. In this chapter from his book *The Silent Language*, Edward T. Hall examines the subject of proxemics and its principles, the concept of territoriality, how Americans view space in a personal and equalitarian manner, and how cultures vary in their use of space.

Edward T. Hall

EVERY LIVING thing has a physical boundary that separates it from its external environment. Beginning with the bacteria and the simple cell and ending with man, every organism has a detectable limit which marks where it begins and ends. A short distance up the phylogenetic scale, however, another, non-physical boundary appears that exists outside the physical one. This new boundary is harder to delimit than the first but is just as real. We call this the "organism's territory." The act of laying claim to and defending a territory is termed territoriality. It is territoriality with which this chapter is most concerned. In man, it becomes highly elaborated, as well as being very greatly differentiated from culture to culture.

Anyone who has had experience with dogs, particularly in a rural setting such as on ranches and farms, is familiar with the way in which the dog handles space. In the first place, the dog knows the limits of his master's "yard" and will defend it against encroachment. There are also certain places where he sleeps: a spot next to the fireplace, a spot in the kitchen, or one in the dining room if he is allowed there. In short, a dog has fixed points to which he returns time after time depending upon the occasion. One can also observe that dogs create zones around them. Depending upon his relationship to the dog and the zone he is in, a trespasser can evoke different behavior when he crosses the invisible lines which are meaningful to the dog.

This is particularly noticeable in females with puppies. A mother who has a new litter in a little-used barn will claim the barn as her territory. When the door opens she may make a slight movement or stirring in one corner. Nothing else may happen as the intruder moves ten or fifteen feet into the barn. Then the dog may raise her head or get up, circle about, and lie down as another invisible boundary is crossed. One can tell about where the line is by withdrawing and watching when her head goes down. As additional lines are crossed, there will be other signals, a thumping of the tail, a low moan or a growl.

One can observe comparable behavior in other vertebrates—fish, birds, and mammals. Birds have well-developed territoriality, areas which they defend as their own and which they return to year after year. To those who have seen a robin come back to the same nest each year this will come as no surprise. Seals, dolphin, and whales are known to use the same breeding grounds. Individual seals have been known to come back to the same rock year after year.

Man has developed his territoriality to an almost unbelievable extent. Yet we treat space somewhat as we treat sex. It is there but we don't talk about it. And if we do, we certainly are not expected to get technical or serious about it. The man of the house is always somewhat apologetic about "his chair." How many people have had the experience of coming into a room, seeing a big comfortable chair and heading for it, only to pull themselves up short, or pause and turn to the man and say, "Oh, was I about to sit in your chair?" The reply, of course, is usually polite. Imagine the effect if the host were to give vent to his true feelings and say, "Hell, yes, you're sitting in my chair, and I don't like anybody sitting in my chair!" For some unknown reason, our culture has tended to play down or cause us to repress and dissociate the feelings we have about space. We relegate it to the informal and are likely to feel guilty whenever we find ourselves getting angry because someone has taken our place.

Territoriality is established so rapidly that even the second session in a series of lectures is sufficient to find a significant proportion of most audiences back in the same seats. What's more, if one has been sitting in a particular seat and someone else occupies it, one can notice a fleeting irritation. There is the remnant of an old urge to throw out the interloper. The interloper knows this too, because he will turn around or look up and say, "Have I got your seat?" at which point you lie and say, "Oh no, I was going to move anyway."

Once while talking on this subject to a group of Americans who were going overseas, one very nice, exceedingly mild-mannered woman raised her hand and said, "You mean it's natural for me to feel irritated when another woman takes over my kitchen?" Answer: "Not only is it natural, but most American women have very strong feelings about their kitchens. Even a mother can't come in and wash the dishes in her daughter's kitchen without annoying her. The kitchen is the place where 'who will dominate' is settled. All women know this, and some can even talk about it. Daughters who can't keep control of their kitchen will be forever under the thumb of any woman who can move into this area."

The questioner continued: "You know that makes me feel so relieved. I have three older sisters and a mother, and every time they come to town they march right into the kitchen and take over. I want to tell them to stay out of my kitchen, that they have their own kitchens and this is my kitchen, but I always thought I was having unkind thoughts about my mother and sisters, thoughts I wasn't supposed to have. This relieves me so much, because now I know I was right."

Father's shop is, of course, another sacred territory and best kept that way. The same applies to his study, if he has one.

As one travels abroad and examines the ways in which space is handled, startling variations are discovered—differences which we react to vigorously. Since none of us is taught to look at space as isolated from other associations, feelings cued by the handling of space are often attributed to something else. In growing up people learn literally thousands of spatial cues, all of which have their own meaning in their own context. These cues "release" responses already established in much the same way as Pavlov's bells started his dogs salivating. Just how accurate a spatial memory is has never been completely tested. There are indications, however, that it is exceedingly persistent.

Literally thousands of experiences teach us unconsciously that space communicates. Yet this fact would probably never have been brought to the level of consciousness if it had not been realized that space is organized differently in each culture. The associations and feelings that are released in a member of one culture almost invariably mean something else in the next. When we say that some foreigners are "pushy," all this means is that their handling of space releases this association in our minds.

What gets overlooked is that the response is there in toto and has been there all along. There is no point in well-meaning people feeling guilty because they get angry when a foreigner presents them with a spatial cue that releases anger or aggression. The main thing is to know what is happening and try to find out which cue was responsible. The next step is to discover, if possible, whether the person really intended to release this particular feeling or whether he intended to engender a different reaction.

Uncovering the specific cues in a foreign culture is a painstaking and laborious process. Usually it is easier for the newcomer to listen to the observations of old-timers and then test these observations against his own experience. At first he may hear, "You're going to have a hard time getting used to the way these people crowd you. Why, when you are trying to buy a theater ticket, instead of standing in line and waiting their turn they all try to reach in and get their money to the ticket seller at once. It's just terrible the way you have to push and shove just to keep your place. Why, the last time I got to the ticket window of the theater and poked my head up to the opening, there were five arms and hands reaching over my shoulder waving money." Or he may hear the following: "It's as much as your life is worth to ride the streetcars. They're worse than our subways. What's more, these people don't seem to mind it at all." Some of this stems from the fact that, as Americans we have a pattern which discourages touching, except in moments of intimacy. When we ride on a streetcar or crowded elevator we will "hold ourselves in," having been taught from early childhood to avoid bodily contact with strangers. Abroad, it's confusing when conflicting feelings are being released at the same time. Our senses are bombarded by a strange language, different smells, and gestures, as well as a host of signs and symbols.

However, the fact that those who have been in a foreign country for some time talk about these things provides the newcomer with advance warning. Getting over a spatial accent is just as important, sometimes more so, than eliminating a spoken one. Advice to the newcomer might be: Watch where people stand, and don't back up. You will feel funny doing it, but it's amazing how much difference it makes in people's attitudes toward you.

How Different Cultures Use Space

Several years ago a magazine published a map of the United States as the average New Yorker sees it. The details of New York were quite clear and the suburbs to the north were also accurately shown. Hollywood appeared in some detail while the space in between New York and Hollywood was almost a total blank. Places like Phoenix, Albuquerque, the Grand Canyon, and Taos, New Mexico, were all crowded into a hopeless jumble. It was easy to see that the average New Yorker knew little and cared less for what went on in the rest of the country. To the geographer the map was a distortion of the worst kind. Yet to the student of culture it was surprisingly accurate. It showed the informal images that many people have of the rest of the country.

As a graduate student I lived in New York, and my landlord was a first-generation American of European extraction who had lived in New York all his life. At the end of the academic year as I was leaving, the landlord came down to watch me load my car. When I said goodby, he remarked, "Well, one of these Sunday afternoons I put my family in the car and we drive out to New Mexico to see you."

The map and the landlord's comment illustrate how Americans treat space as highly personalized. We visualize the relationship between places we know by personal experience. Places which we haven't been to and with which we are not personally identified tend to remain confused.

Traditionally American space begins with "a place." It is one of the oldest sets, comparable to, but not quite the same as, the Spanish *lugar*. The reader will have no difficulty thinking up ways in which place is used: "He found a place in her heart," "He has a place in the mountains," "I am tired of this place," and so on. Those who have children know how difficult it is to get across to them the whole concept of place—like Washington, or Boston, or Philadelphia, and so on. An American child requires between six and seven years before he has begun to master the basic concepts of place. Our culture provides for a great variety of places, including different classes of places.

Contrasted with the Middle East, our system is characterized by fine gradations as one moves from one space category to the next. In the world of the Arab there are villages and cities. That is about all. Most non-nomadic Arabs think of themselves as villagers. The actual villages are of varying population, from a few families up to several thousands.

The smallest place category in the United States is not covered by a term like hamlet, village, or town. It is immediately recognizable as a territorial entity, nevertheless, because such places are always named. They are areas with no recognizable center where a number of families live—like Dogpatch of the funny papers.

Our Dogpatches present the basic American pattern in uncomplicated form. They have scattered residences with no concentration of buildings in one spot. Like time, place with us is diffused, so that you never quite know where its center is. Beyond this the naming of place categories begins with the "crossroads store" or "corner" and continues with the "small shopping center," the "county seat," the "small town," "large town," "metropolitan center," "city," and "metropolis." Like much of the rest of our culture, including the social ranking system, there are no clear gradations as one moves from one category to the next. The "points" are of varying sizes, and there are no linguistic cues indicating the size of the place we are talking about. The United States, New Mexico, Albuquerque, Pecos are all said the same way and used the same way in sentences. The child who is learning the language has no way of distinguishing one space category from another by listening to others talk.

The miracle is that children eventually are able to sort out and pin down the different space terms from the meager cues provided by others. Try telling a five-year-old the difference between where you live in the suburbs and the town where your wife goes to shop. It will be a frustrating task, since the child, at that age, only comprehends where *he* lives. His room, his house, his place at the table are the places that are learned early.

The reason most Americans have difficulty in school with geography or geometry stems from the fact that space as an informal cultural system is different from space as it is technically elaborated by classroom geography and mathematics. It must be said in fairness to ourselves that other cultures have similar problems. Only the very perceptive adult realizes that there is anything really difficult for the child to learn about space. In reality, he has to take what is literally a spatial blur and isolate the significant points that adults talk about. Sometimes adults are unnecessarily impatient with children because they don't catch on. People do not realize that the child has heard older people talking about different places and is trying to figure out, from what he hears, the difference between this place and that. In this regard it should be pointed out that the first clues which suggest to children that one thing is different from another come from shifts in tone of voice which direct attention in very subtle but important ways. Speaking a fully developed language as we do, it is hard to remember that there was a time when we could not speak at all and when the whole communicative process was carried on by means of variations in the voice tone. This early language is lost to consciousness and functions out of awareness, so that we tend to forget the very great role it plays in the learning process.

To continue our analysis of the way a child learns about space, let us turn to his conception of a road. At first a road is whatever he happens to be driving on. This doesn't mean that he can't tell when you take a wrong turn. He can, and often will even correct a mistake which is made. It only means that he has not yet broken the road down into its components and that he makes the distinction between this road and that road in just the same way that he learns to distinguish between the phoneme *d* and the phoneme *b* in initial position in the spoken language.

Using roads for cross-cultural contrast, the reader will recall that Paris, being an old city as well as a French city, has a street-naming system that puzzles most Americans. Street names shift as one progresses. Take Rue St.-Honoré, for example, which becomes Rue du Faubourg St.-Honoré, Avenue des Ternes, and Avenue du Roule. A child growing up in Paris, however, has no more difficulty learning his system than one of our children learning ours. We teach ours to watch the intersections and the directions and that when something happens—that is,

when there is a change of course at one of these points—you can expect
the name to change. In Paris the child learns that as he passes certain
landmarks—like buildings that are well known, or statues—the name of
the street changes.

It is interesting and informative to watch very young children as
they learn their culture. They quickly pick up the fact that we have
names for some things and not for others. First, they identify the whole
object or the set—a room, for instance; then they begin to fixate on
certain other discrete objects like books, ashtrays, letter openers, tables,
and pencils. By so doing they accomplish two things. First, they find
out how far down the scale they have to go in identifying things. Second, they learn what are the isolates and patterns for handling space
and object nomenclature. First children are often better subjects than
second children, because, having learned the hard way, the first one will
teach the second one without involving the parents.

The child will ask, "What's this?" pointing to a pencil. You reply,
"A pencil." The child is not satisfied and says, "No, this," pointing to
the shaft of the pencil and making clear that she meant the shaft. So
you say, "Oh, that's the shaft of the pencil." Then the child moves her
finger one quarter inch and says, "What's this?" and you say, "The
shaft." This process is repeated and you say, "That's still the shaft; and
this is the shaft, and this is the shaft. It's all the shaft of the pencil.
This is the shaft, this is the point, and this is the eraser, and this is the
little tin thing that holds the eraser on." Then she may point to the
eraser, and you discover that she is still trying to find out where the
dividing lines are. She manages to worm out the fact that the eraser
has a top and sides but no more. She also learns that there is no way to
tell the difference between one side and the next and that no labels are
pinned on parts of the point, even though distinctions are made between the lead and the rest of the pencil. She may glean from this that
materials make a difference some of the time and some of the time
they do not. Areas where things begin and end are apt to be important,
while the points in between are often ignored.

The significance of all this would undoubtedly have escaped me if
it hadn't been for an experience on the atoll of Truk. In a rather detailed series of studies in technology I had progressed to the point of
having to obtain the nomenclature of the canoe and the wooden food
bowl. At this point it was necessary for me to go through what children
go through—that is, point to various parts after I thought I had the
pattern and ask if I had the name right. As I soon discovered, their system of carving up microspace was radically different from our own. The
Trukese treat open spaces, without dividing lines (as we know them),
as completely distinct. Each area has a name. On the other hand, they
have not developed a nomenclature for the edges of objects as elab-

orately as Westerners have done. The reader has only to think of rims and cups and the number of different ways in which these can be referred to. There is the rim itself. It can be square or round or elliptical in cross section; straight, flared, or curved inward; plain or decorated, and wavy or straight. This doesn't mean that the Trukese don't elaborate rims. They do; it just means that we have ways of talking about what we do and not as many ways of talking about what happens to an open area as they do. The Trukese separate parts which we think of as being "built in" to the object.

A certain decoration or carving at either end of a canoe-shaped food bowl is thought of as being separate or distinct from the rim in which it has been carved. It has an essence of its own. Along the keel of the canoe the carving, called the *chunefatch*, has characteristics with which it endows the canoe. The canoe is one thing, the chunefatch something else. Open spaces without obvious markers on the side of the bowl have names. Such distinctions in the dividing up of space make the settling of land claims unbelievably complicated in these islands. Trees, for instance, are considered separate from the soil out of which they grow. One man may own the trees, another the soil below.

Benjamin Whorf, describing how Hopi concepts of space are reflected in the language, mentions the absence of terms for interior three-dimensional spaces, such as words for room, chamber, hall, passage, interior, cell, crypt, cellar, attic, loft and vault. This does not alter the fact that the Hopi have multi-room dwellings and even use the rooms for special purposes such as storage, grinding corn, and the like.

Whorf also notes the fact that it is impossible for the Hopi to add a possessive pronoun to the word for room and that in the Hopi scheme of things a room in the strict sense of the word is not a noun and does not act like a noun.

Since there is a wealth of data on how strongly the Hopi feel about holding onto things which are theirs, one has to rule out the possessive factor in Whorf's references to their inability to say "my room." It's just that their language is different. One might be led to assume by this that the Hopi would then lack a sense of territoriality. Again, nothing could be farther from the truth. They just use and conceive of space differently. We work from points and along lines. They apparently do not. While seemingly inconsequential, these differences caused innumerable headaches to the white supervisors who used to run the Hopi reservation in the first part of this century.

I will never forget driving over to one of the villages at the end of a mesa and discovering that someone was building a house in the middle of the road. It later developed that the culprit (in my eyes) was a man I had known for some time. I said, "Paul, why are you building your house in the middle of the road? There are lots of good places on either side of the road. This way people have to knock the bottoms out of their cars driving around on the rocks to get to the village." His reply was short and to the point: "I know, but it's my right." He did have a right to a certain area laid down long before there was a road. The fact that the road had been used for many years meant nothing to him. Use and disuse of space in our terms had nothing to do with his ideas of possession.

Space as a Factor in Culture Contact

Whenever an American moves overseas, he suffers from a condition known as "culture shock." Culture shock is simply a removal or distortion of many of the familiar cues one encounters at home and the substitution for them of other cues which are strange. A good deal of what occurs in the organization and use of space provides important leads as to the specific cues responsible for culture shock.

The Latin house is often built around a patio that is next to the sidewalk but hidden from outsiders behind a wall. It is not easy to describe the degree to which small architectural differences such as this affect outsiders. American Point Four technicians living in Latin America used to complain that they felt "left out" of things, that they were "shut off." Others kept wondering what was going on "behind those walls." In the United States, on the other hand, propinquity is the basis of a good many relationships. To us the neighbor is actually quite close. Being a neighbor endows one with certain rights and privileges, also responsibilities. You can borrow things, including food and drink, but you also have to take your neighbor to the hospital in an emergency. In this regard he has almost as much claim on you as a cousin. For these and other reasons the American tries to pick his neighborhood carefully, because he knows that he is going to be thrown into intimate contact with people. We do not understand why it is that when we live next to people abroad the sharing of adjacent space does not always conform to our own pattern. In France and England, for instance, the relations between neighbors are apt to be cooler than in the United States. Mere propinquity does not tie people together. In England neighbor children do not play as they do in our neighborhoods. When they do play, arrangements are sometimes made a month in advance as though they were coming from the other side of town!

Another example has to do with the arrangement of offices. In this case one notices great contrast between ourselves and the French. Part of our over-all pattern in the United States is to take a given amount of space and divide it up equally. When a new person is added in an office, almost everyone will move his desk so that the newcomer will have his share of the space. This may mean moving from positions that have been occupied for a long time and away from favorite views from the window. The point is that the office force will make its own adjustments voluntarily. In fact, it is a signal that they have acknowledged the presence of the new person when they start rearranging the furniture. Until this has happened, the boss can be sure that the new person has not been integrated into the group.

Given a large enough room, Americans will distribute themselves around the walls, leaving the center open for group activities such as conferences. That is, the center belongs to the group and is often marked off by a table or some object placed there both to use and save the space. Lacking a conference table, members will move their chairs away from their desks to form a "huddle" in the middle. The pattern of moving from one's place to huddle is symbolized in our language by such expressions as, "I had to take a new position on that point," or "The position of the office on this point is . . ."

The French, by contrast, do not make way for each other in the unspoken, taken-for-granted way that we do. They do not divide up the space with a new colleague. Instead they may grudgingly give him a small desk in a dark corner looking toward the wall. This action speaks eloquently to Americans who have found themselves working for the French. We feel that not to "make a place" accents status differences. If the rearrangement which says, "Now we admit you to the group, and you are going to stay," fails to take place, Americans are likely to feel perilously insecure. In French offices the key figure is the man in the middle, who has his fingers on everything so that all runs smoothly. There is a centralized control. The French educational system runs from the middle, so that all students all over France take the same class at the same time.

It has already been mentioned that ordering is an important element in American patterns. As a general rule, whenever services are involved we feel that people should queue up in order of arrival. This reflects the basic equalitarianism of our culture. In cultures where a class system or its remnants exist, such ordinality may not exist. That is, where society assigns rank for certain purposes, or wherever ranking is involved, the handling of space will reflect this.

To us it is regarded as a democratic virtue for people to be served without reference to the rank they hold in their occupational group. The rich and poor alike are accorded equal opportunity to buy and be waited upon in the order of arrival. In a line at the theater Mrs. Gotrocks is no better than anyone else. However, apart from the English, whose queueing patterns we share, many Europeans are likely to look upon standing in line as a violation of their individuality. I am reminded of a Pole who reacted this way. He characterized Americans as sheep, and the mere thought of such passiveness was likely to set him off crashing into a line at whatever point he pleased. Such people can't stand the idea of being held down by group conformity as if they were an automaton. Americans watching the Pole thought he was "pushy." He didn't bother to hide the fact that he thought we were much too subdued. He used to say, "What does it matter if there is a little confusion and some people get served before others?"

Formal Space Patterns

Depending upon the culture in question, the formal patterning of space can take on varying degrees of importance and complexity. In America, for example, no one direction takes precedence over another except in a technical or utilitarian sense. In other cultures one quickly discovers that some directions are sacred or preferred. Navajo doors must face east, the mosques of the Moslems must be oriented toward Mecca, the sacred rivers of India flow south. Americans pay attention to direction in a technical sense, but formally and informally they have no preference. Since our space is largely laid out by technical people, houses, towns, and main arteries are usually oriented according to one of the points of the compass. The same applies to roads and main highways when the topography allows, as it does in the flat expanses of Indiana and Kansas. This technical patterning allows us to locate places by co-ordinates (a point on the line). "He lives at 1321 K Street, N.W." tells us that he lives in the northwest part of town in the thirteenth block west of the line dividing the town into east-west halves and eleven blocks north of the line dividing the town into north-south halves, on the left side of the street, about one quarter of the way up the block.

In the country we will say, "Go out of town ten miles west on Highway 66 until you get to the first paved road turning north. Turn right on that road and go seven miles. It's the second farm on your left. You can't miss it."

Our concept of space makes use of the edges of things. If there aren't any edges, we make them by creating artificial lines (five miles west and two miles north). Space is treated in terms of a co-ordinate system. In contrast, the Japanese and many other people work within areas. They name "spaces" and distinguish between one space and the next or parts of a space. To us a space is empty—one gets into it by intersecting it with lines.

A technical pattern which may have grown out of an informal base is that of positional value or ranking. We have canonized the idea of the positional value in almost every aspect of our lives, so much so that even children four years old are fully aware of its implications and are apt to fight with each other as to who will be first.

In addition to positional value, the American pattern emphasizes equality and standardization of the segments which are used for measuring space or into which space is divided, be it a ruler or a suburban subdivision. We like our components to be standard and equal. American city blocks tend to have uniform dimensions whereas towns in many other parts of the world are laid out with unequal blocks. This suggests that it was no accident that mass production, made possible by the standardization of parts, had its origins in the Untied States. There are those who would argue that there are compelling technological reasons for both mass production and parts standardization. However, an examination of actual practice indicates that Europeans have produced automobiles in the past—and very good ones too—in which the cylinders were all of different sizes. The difference in dimensions was not great, of course, a matter of a very few thousands of an inch. This, however, was enough to cause the car to make noise and use too much oil if it was repaired by an American mechanic unfamiliar with the European patterns that lack the uniformity isolate.

Japan, too, has a passion for uniformity, though it is somewhat different from ours. All mats (*tatami*) on the floors of Japanese houses and all windows, doors, and panels are usually of identical dimensions in a given district. In newspaper advertisements of houses for sale or rent the dimensions are usually given in terms of the number of mats of a specific area. Despite this example of uniformity, the Japanese differ from us in a way which can have considerable economic results. In one case, for example, they manufactured a very large order of electronics parts according to rigid specifications which they were quite able to meet. When the product arrived in the United States, it was discovered that there were differences between various batches of these parts. The customer subsequently discovered that while the whole internal process of manufacture had been controlled, the Japanese had failed to standardize their gauges! It is no accident that in the United States there is a Bureau of Standards. Much of the success of this country's technical skill and productivity, which we are trying to pass on to other nations, rests on these and similar unstated patterns.

How Space Communicates

Spatial changes give a tone to a communication, accent it, and at times even override the spoken word. The flow and shift of distance between people as they interact with each other is part and parcel of the communication process. The normal conversational distance between strangers illustrates how important are the dynamics of space interaction. If a person gets too close, the reaction is instantaneous and automatic—the other person backs up. And if he gets too close again, back we go again. I have observed an American backing up the entire length of a long corridor while a foreigner whom he considers pushy tries to catch up with him. This scene has been enacted thousands and thousands of times—one person trying to increase the distance in order to be at ease, while the other tries to decrease it for the same reason, neither one being aware of what was going on. We have here an example of the tremendous depth to which culture can condition behavior.

One thing that does confuse us and gets in the way of understanding cultural differences is that there are times in our own culture when people are either distant or pushy in their use of space. We, therefore, simply associate the foreigner with the familiar; namely those people who have acted in such a way that our attention was drawn to their actions. The error is in jumping to the conclusion that the foreigner feels the same way the American does even though his overt acts are identical.

This was all suddenly brought into focus one time when I had the good fortune to be visited by a very distinguished and learned man who had been for many years a top-ranking diplomat representing a foreign country. After meeting him a number of times, I had become impressed with his extraordinary sensitivity to the small details of behavior that are so significant in the interaction process. Dr. X. was interested in some of the work several of us were doing at the time and asked permission to attend one of my lectures. He came to the front of the class at the end of the lecture to talk over a number of points made in the preceding hour. While talking he became quite involved in the implications of the lecture as well as what he was saying. We started out facing each other and as he talked I became dimly aware that he was standing a little too close and that I was beginning to back up. Fortunately I was able to suppress my first impulse and remain stationary because there was nothing to communicate aggression in his behavior except the conversational distance. His voice was eager, his manner intent, the set of his body communicated only interest and eagerness to talk. It also came to me in a flash that someone who had been so successful in the old school of diplomacy could not possibly let himself communicate something offensive to the other person except outside of his highly trained awareness.

By experimenting I was able to observe that as I moved away slightly, there was an associated shift in the pattern of interaction. He had more trouble expressing himself. If I shifted to where I felt comfortable (about twenty-one inches), he looked somewhat puzzled and hurt, almost as though he were saying: "Why is he acting that way? Here I am doing everything I can to talk to him in a friendly manner and he suddenly withdraws. Have I done anything wrong? Said something that I shouldn't?" Having ascertained that distance had a direct effect on his conversation, I stood my ground, letting him set the distance.

Not only is a vocal message qualified by the handling of distance, but the substance of a conversation can often demand special handling of space. There are certain things which are difficult to talk about unless one is within the proper conversational zone.

Not long ago I received a present of some seeds and chemicals along with the information that if I planted the seeds the chemicals would make them grow. Knowing little about hydroponics except that the plants should be suspended above the fluid in which chemicals are dissolved, I set out to find a suitable flowerpot. At every flower shop I was met with incredulity and forced to go through a routine involving a detailed explanation of just what it was I wanted and how hydroponics worked.

My ignorance of both hydroponics and florist shops made me feel somewhat ill at ease, so that I did not communicate in the manner that I use when I am speaking on a familiar subject in a familiar setting. The role that distance plays in a communication situation was brought home to me when I entered a shop in which the floor was filled with benches spaced at about twenty-inch intervals. On the other side of the benches was the female proprietor of the shop. As I entered, she craned her neck as though to reach over the benches, raised her voice slightly to bring it up to the proper level, and said, "What was it you wanted?" I tried once. "What I'm looking for is a *hydroponic* flowerpot." "What kind of flowerpot?" still with the neck craned. At this point I found myself climbing over benches in an effort to close up the space. It was simply impossible for me to talk about such a subject in a setting of this sort at a distance of fifteen feet. It wasn't until I got to within three feet that I was able to speak with some degree of comfort.

Another example is one that will be familiar to millions of civilians who served in the Army during World War II. The Army, in its need to get technical about matters that are usually handled informally, made a mistake in the regulations on distance required for reporting to a superior officer. Everyone knows that the relationship between officers and men has certain elements which require distance and impersonality. This applied to officers of different ranks when they were in command relationship to each other. Instructions for reporting to a superior officer were that the junior officer was to proceed up to a point three paces in front of the officer's desk, stop, salute, and state his rank, his name, and his business: "Lieutenant X, reporting as ordered, sir." Now, what cultural norms does this procedure violate, and what does it communicate? It violates the conventions for the use of space. The distance is too great, by at least two feet, and does not fit the situation. The normal speaking distance for business matters, where impersonality is involved at the beginning of the conversation, is five and a half to eight feet. The distance required by the army regulations borders on the edge of what we would call "far." It evokes an automatic response to shout. This detracts from the respect which is supposed to be shown to the superior officer. There are, of course, many subjects which it is almost impossible to talk about at this distance, and individual army officers recognize this by putting soldiers and junior officers at ease, asking them to sit down or permitting them to come closer. However, the first impression was that the Army was doing things the hard way.

For Americans the following shifts in the voice are associated with specific ranges of distances:

1. *Very close* (3 in. to 6 in.) Soft whisper; top secret

2. *Close* (8 in to 12 in.) Audible whisper; very confidential

3. *Near* (12 in. to 20 in.) Indoors, soft voice; outdoors, full voice; confidential

4. *Neutral* (20 in. to 36 in.) Soft voice, low volume; personal subject matter

5. *Neutral* (4½ ft. to 5 ft.) Full voice; information of non-personal matter

6. *Public Distance* (5½ ft. to 8 ft.) Full voice with slight overloudness; public information for others to hear

7. *Across the room* (8 ft. to 20 ft.) Loud voice; talking to a group

8. *Stretching the limits of distance* 20 ft. to 24 ft. indoors; up to 100 ft. outdoors; hailing distance, departures

In Latin America the interaction distance is much less than it is in the United States. Indeed, people cannot talk comfortably with one another unless they are very close to the distance that evokes either sexual or hostile feelings in the North American. The result is that when they move close, we withdraw and back away. As a consequence, they think we are distant or cold, withdrawn and unfriendly. We, on the other hand, are constantly accusing them of breathing down our necks, crowding us, and spraying our faces.

Americans who have spent some time in Latin America without learning these space considerations make other adaptations, like barricading themselves behind their desks, using chairs and typewriter tables to keep the Latin American at what is to us a comfortable distance. The result is that the Latin American may even climb over the obstacles until he has achieved a distance at which he can comfortably talk.

FOR DISCUSSION AND REVIEW

1 What are some of the ways in which territoriality communicates?

2 What is *culture shock* and what does the use of space have to do with it? How might a lack of awareness of the ways foreign cultures use space create embarrassing situations?

3 What is the connection between Hall's discussion of the territoriality of an individual and commuting by car as opposed to public transportation? How does the concept of

territoriality help to explain irritability caused by rush-hour traffic?

4 It has been theorized that the concept of American equality is related to the way we use space. What is the basis of this theory?

5 Review the articles by Woolfson (pp. 3–11) and Greenfield and Bruner (pp. 12–26). What are some of the possible implications of the Whorfian hypothesis on the study of space?

7

When Space Is Invaded

Julius Fast

Julius Fast, like anthropologist Edward Hall (p. 516), recognizes the complex significance of spatial relationships—how, for example, they impart status, rank, and dominance. In this chapter from *Body Language*, Fast discusses the situations that can occur when one's personal space or territory is invaded and the kinesic signals one uses to defend against intrusion. Within the structured status system of the business world, he explores the import of hierarchies, signals, and symbols, and points to an interesting relationship between rank and the vulnerability of one's territory.

Defending Body Zones

AT FIRST glance it might be hard to see the exact relationship between personal spaces, zones or territories and kinesics, body language. But unless we understand the basic principles of individual territories we cannot appreciate what happens when these territories are invaded. How we react to personal invasion of our territory is very much related to body language. We should know our own aggressive behavior and our reactions to others' aggressions if we are to become aware of what signals we are sending and receiving.

Perhaps the most touching account of the inviolability of body zones was a novel written almost half a century ago by H. DeVere Stacpool, called *The Blue Lagoon*. It is the story of a young child shipwrecked on a tropical island with an old sailor. The sailor raises the boy to self-sufficiency and then dies, and the child grows to manhood alone, meets a young Polynesian girl and falls in love with her. The novel deals with the boy's love affair with the Polynesian girl who has been declared taboo from infancy. She has grown up forbidden to allow herself to be touched by any man. The struggle between the two to break down her conditioning and allow him to touch her makes a fascinating and moving story.

It was the early recognition of just how defensive a human can become about his body zones and personal privacy that led Stacpool to explore this theme, but it has only been in the last decade that scientists have begun to understand the complex significance of personal space.

In an earlier chapter I told of a psychiatrist who, with the aid of a pack of cigarettes, taught me a lesson about the invasion of personal space. He in turn had learned much of what he knew from the reaction of patients in hospitals for the mentally ill. A mental hospital is a closed microcosm, and as such often reflects and exaggerates attitudes of the larger world outside. But a mental hospital is also a very special type of place. The inmates are more susceptible to suggestion and aggression than are normal men and women and often their actions distort the actions of normal people.

How aggressive a mental patient is to someone depends on the rank of the other person. It is a test of dominance. In any mental hospital one or two patients will attain superior rank by aggressive behavior, but they can always be cowed by one of the attendants. In turn, the attendant is beneath the nurse and she is subordinate to the doctor.

There is a very real hierarchy developed in these institutions and it is reflected in the outer world in organizations like the army, or in business where there is a definite order of dominance. In the army, dominance is achieved by a system of symbols, stripes for the noncommissioned officers and bars, leaves, birds and stars for the commissioned officers. But even without the symbols, the pecking order remains. I have seen privates in a shower room deferential to sergeants without knowing who they were or what their rank was. The sergeants, through their manner and bearing, were able to convey an obvious body language message of rank.

Advice for Status Seekers

In the business world, where neither stripes nor other obvious symbols are worn, the same ability to project a sense of superiority is the common attainment of the executive. How does he do it? What tricks does he use to subdue subordinates, and what tricks does he bring out for in-fighting in his own rank?

An attempt to study this was made by two researchers in a series of silent films. They had two actors play the parts of an executive and a visitor, and switch roles for different takes. The scene had one man at his desk while the other, playing the part of a visitor, knocks at the door, opens it and approaches the desk to discuss some business matter.

The audience watching the films was asked to rate the executive and the visitor in terms of status. A certain set of rules began to emerge from the ratings. The visitor showed the least amount of status when he stopped just inside the door to talk across the room to the seated man. He was considered to have more status when he walked halfway up to the desk, and he had most status when he walked directly up to the desk and stood right in front of the seated executive.

Another factor that governed status in the eyes of the observers was the time between knocking and entering, and for the seated executive, the time between hearing the knock and answering. The quicker the visitor entered the room, the more status he had. The longer the executive took to answer, the more status *he* had.

It should be obvious that what is involved here is a matter of territory. The visitor is allowed to enter the executive's territory, and by that arrangement the executive automatically achieves superior status.

How far into the territory the visitor penetrates, and how quickly he does it, in other words how he challenges the personal space of the executive, announces his own status.

The "big boss" will walk into his subordinate's office unannounced. The subordinate will wait outside the boss's office until he is permitted in. If the boss is on the phone, the subordinate may tiptoe off and come back later. If the subordinate is on the phone, the boss will usually assert his status by standing above the subordinate until he murmurs, "Let me call you back," and then gives the boss his full attention.

There is a continuous shifting or fighting for status within the business world, and therefore status symbols become a very necessary part of the shift or dance. The executive with the attaché case is the most obvious one, and we all know the joke of the man who carries only his lunch in his attaché case but insists on carrying the case simply because it is so important to the image he must project. I know of a black minister and educator in America who travels around the country a great deal. He told me that he would never go into any Southern city, into the downtown area or a hotel, without a business suit and an attaché case. These two symbols gave him a certain amount of authority that differentiated him from the "nigger" in the same city.

Big business sets up a host of built-in status symbols. A large drug firm in Philadelphia earned enough money through the sale of tranquilizers to put up a new building that would house their rapidly expanding staff. The building could have been designed with any number of offices and workrooms, but quite deliberately the company set up a built-in status symbol in the offices. The corner offices on the very highest floor were reserved for the very highest personnel. The corner offices on the floor below were reserved for the next rank of top personnel. Lesser, but still important executives had offices without corner windows. The rank below this had offices without windows at all. Below them were the men with partitioned cubicles for offices. These had frosted glass walls and no doors and the next rank down had clear glass cubicles. The last rank had desks out in an open room.

Rank was arrived at by an equation whose elements consisted of time on the job, importance of the job, salary and degree. The degree of M.D., for example, gave any man, no matter what his salary or time on the job, the right to have a closed office. Ph.D.'s might or might not have such an office, depending on other factors.

Within this system there was room for many other elements to demonstrate degree of status. Drapes, rugs, wooden desks as opposed to metal desks, furniture, couches, easy chairs, and of course, secretaries, all set up subhierarchies.

An important element in this set-up was the contrast between the frosted glass cubicles and the clear glass cubicles. By allowing the world to see in, the man in the clear glass cubicle was automatically reduced in importance or rank. His territory was that much more open to visual invasion. He was that much more vulnerable.

How to Be a Leader

Opening of territory and invasion of territory are important functions of rank in business. What about leadership? By what tricks or by what body language does a leader assert himself?

Back in the years just before World War II, Charlie Chaplin did a motion picture called The Great Dictator. As with all of Chaplin's movies, it was filled with bits of body language, but the most delightful sequence was one that took place in a barber shop.

Chaplin as Hitler and Jack Oakie as Mussolini are shown getting shaves in adjacent chairs. The scene centers around the attempts of each to put himself in a dominant position to the other in order to assert his superior leadership. Trapped within their chairs, lathered and draped, there is only one way to achieve dominance, and that is by controlling the height of the chairs. They can reach down and jack them up. The higher man wins, and the scene revolves around the attempt of each to jack his own chair to a higher position.

Dominance through height is a truism that works from the animal kingdom to man. Among wolves, recent studies have shown that the pack leader asserts his dominance by wrestling a yearling or subordinate wolf to the ground and standing over him. The subordinate expresses his subservience by crawling beneath the pack leader and exposing his throat and belly. It becomes a matter of who is higher.

The same positioning occurs with humans. We are all aware of the tradition of abasement before a king, before idols, before altars. Bowing and scraping in general are all variations of superiority or inferiority by height. They are all actions to point out the body language message, "You are higher than I am, therefore you are dominant."

A young man I know, well over six feet tall, was extremely successful in business because of his ability to show empathy for his associates. Observing him in action in some successful business transactions I became aware that whenever possible he stooped, sloped his body, or sat, in order to allow his associate to achieve dominance and feel superior.

In family seatings the dominant member, usually the father, will hold sway at the head of a rectangle table or an oval table. Often the choice of a round table will tell something of the family set-up. In the same way in discussion groups around a table, the leader will automatically assume the head of the table position.

That this is no new concept is obvious in the story of King Arthur and his round table. The table was round so that there could be no question of dominance and every knight could share equally in the honor of being seated at the table. However, this whole idea was weakened by the fact that Arthur himself, wherever he sat, became the dominant figure and status decreased as the distance from the King increased.

The boss of a large drug company I have worked in has an office that contains, in addition to his desk and desk chair, a couch, an easy chair and a coffee table with one or two chairs around it. This man announces the formality or informality of a situation by where he sits during that situation. If a visitor comes whom he wants to treat in an informal manner, he will come around from his desk and guide the visitor to the couch, to the easy chair or to the coffee table. In this way, by his positioning, he indicates just what type of interview he will have. If it's to be an extremely formal one he will remain seated behind his desk.

The Space We Hold Inviolate

The need for personal space and the resistance to the invasion of personal space is so strong a thing that even in a crowd each member will demand a given amount of space. This very fact led a journalist named Herbert Jacobs to attempt to apply it to crowd size. Since estimation of crowd size tends to vary according to whether the observer is for the crowd or against it, the sizes of political rallies, peace rallies and demonstrations are inflated by the marchers and deflated by the authorities.

Jacobs, by studying aerial photographs of crowds where he could actually count heads, concluded that people in dense crowds need six to eight square feet each, while people in loose crowds require an average of ten square feet. Crowd size, Jacobs finally concluded, could be gauged by the formula, *length* times *width* divided by a *correction factor* that took density of the crowd into account. This gave the actual number of people in any gathering.

On the subject of crowds, it is important to realize that the personal territory of the people in a crowd is destroyed by the very act of crowding. The reaction to this destruction can, in some cases, change the temper of the crowd. Men react very strongly when their personal space or territory is invaded. As a crowd gets larger and tighter and more compact, it may also get uglier. A loose crowd may be easier to handle.

This need for personal space was known to Freud, who always arranged his sessions so that the patient would lie on the couch while he sat in a chair out of the patient's sight. In this way there was no intrusion upon the patient's personal space.

The police are also well aware of this fact, and they take advantage of it in their interrogation of prisoners. A textbook on criminal interrogation and confessions suggests that the questioner sit close to the suspect and that there be no table or other obstacle between them. Any kind of obstacle, the book warns, gives the man being questioned a certain degree of relief and confidence.

The book also suggests that the questioner, though he may start with his chair two or three feet away, should move in closer as the questioning proceeds, so that "ultimately one of the subject's knees is just about in between the interrogator's two knees."

This physical invasion of the man's territory by the police officer, the crowding in as he is questioned, has been found in practice to be extremely useful in breaking down a prisoner's resistance. When a man's territorial defenses are weakened or intruded upon, his self-assurance tends to grow weaker.

In a working situation the boss who is aware of this can strengthen his own position of leadership by intruding spatially on the man under him. The higher-up who leans over the subordinate's desk throws the subordinate off balance. The department head who crowds next to the worker while inspecting his work makes the worker uneasy and insecure. In fact, the parent who scolds the child by leaning over him is compounding the relationship between them, proving and reinforcing his own dominance.

Can we use this intrusion of personal space to arouse defensive measures in others, or can we, by avoiding it, also avoid the sometimes dangerous consequences of an intrusion? We know that tailgating a car is dangerous from a purely physical point of view. If the car ahead stops short we can smack into it, but no one talks about what the act of tailgating can do to the nerves of the driver ahead.

A man driving a car often loses an essential part of his own humanity and is, by virtue of the machine around him, once removed from a human being. The body language communication that works so well for him outside the car often will not work at all when he is driving. We have all been annoyed by drivers who cut in front of us, and we all know the completely irrational rage that can sometimes fill the driver who has thus had his space invaded. The police will cite statistics to show that dozens of accidents are caused by this cutting in, by the dangerous reaction of the man who has been cut off. In a social situation few men would dream of acting or reacting in this fashion. Stripped of the machine we adopt a civilized attitude and allow people to cut in front of us, indeed we step aside quite often to permit people to board a bus or elevator ahead of us.

A car, however, seems to act much like a dangerous weapon in the hands of many drivers. It can become a weapon that destroys many of our controls and inhibitions. The reason for this is obscure, but some psychologists have theorized that at least a part of it is due to the extension of our personal territories when we are in a car. Our own zones of privacy expand and the zone of privacy of the car becomes much greater and our reaction to any intrusion on that zone is greater still.

Of Space and Personality

There have been many studies attempted to find out just how the reaction to invasion of personal space is related to personality. One, a master's thesis by John L. Williams, determined that introverts tended to keep people at a greater conversational distance than extroverts. The man who is withdrawn needs greater defenses to insure the sanctity of his withdrawn state. Another study, for a doctoral thesis, by William E. Leipold arrived at the same conclusion by a clever experiment. Students were first given personality tests to see if they were introverted or extroverted, and then were sent to an office to be interviewed about their grades.

Three types of instructions to the students were given by the experimenter. These were called *stress, praise* or *neutral* instructions. The stress instructions were geared to upset the man. "We feel that your course grade is quite poor and that you haven't tried your best. Please take a seat in the next room till the interviewer can speak to you."

The student then entered a room with a desk and two chairs, one in front of it and one behind it.

The praise interview started with the student being told that his grades were good and that he was doing well. In the neutral interview the instructions were simply, "We are interested in your feelings about the course."

Results of the study showed that the students who were praised sat closest to the interviewer's chair. The students under stress sat farthest away, and the ones receiving neutral instructions sat midway. Introverted and anxious students sat farther away than extroverted students under the same conditions.

With this much charted, the next step was to determine the reactions of men and women when their territory was invaded. Dr. Robert Sommer, professor of psychology and chairman of the Psychology Department at the University of California, describes a set of experiments conducted in a hospital environment where, dressed in a doctor's white coat to gain authority, he systematically invaded the patients' privacy, sitting next to them on benches and entering their wards and day rooms. These intrusions, he reported, invariably bothered the patients and drove them from their special chairs or areas. The patients reacted to Dr. Sommer's physical intrusion by becoming uneasy and restless and finally by removing themselves bodily from the area.

From his own observations and the observations of others Dr. Sommer has discovered a whole area of body language that the individual uses when his private territory is invaded. Aside from the actual physical retreat of picking up and going somewhere else, there will be a series of preliminary signals, rocking, leg swinging or tapping. These are the first signs of tension, and they say, "You are too near. Your presence makes me uneasy."

The next series of body language signals are closed eyes, withdrawal of the chin into the chest and hunching of the shoulders. These all say, "Go away. I do not want you here. You are intruding."

Dr. Sommer tells of another researcher into the field of spatial invasion, Nancy Russo, who used a library as her theater of operations. A library is a perfect place to observe reactions. It is a subdued atmosphere geared to privacy. In most cases a newcomer to a library will isolate himself from the other researchers by taking a seat some distance from anyone else.

Miss Russo would take an adjacent chair and then move closer to her victim, or sit across from him. While she found no single universal reaction to people sitting close, she found that most spoke with body language to transmit their feelings. She described "defensive gestures, shifts in posture, attempts to move away unobtrusively." Eventually, she concluded, if all of a man's body language signals are ignored, he will take off and move to another location.

Only one out of eighty students whose area was intruded on by Miss Russo asked her verbally to move away. The rest used body language to communicate their disapproval of the closeness.

Dr. Augustus F. Kinzel, who now works at the New York Psychiatric Institute, evolved a theory while working at the U.S. Medical Center for Federal Prisoners which may point the way toward detecting, predicting and even treating violent behavior in men.

In his early animal studies Dr. Kinzel noted that animals will often react with violence to any intrusion of their personal territory. While working at the prison in a population selected for violent action against society, he noticed that certain men preferred isolation cells despite the deprivations of such living. He found that these same men were sometimes troubled by senseless outbursts of violence. Could it be that these men required more space to maintain their self-control?

Dr. Kinzel found that many men who were guilty of assault with violence complained that their victims had "messed around with them," though a careful check disclosed that they had assaulted men who had done nothing but come close to them. The fits of violence were similarly provoked in and out of prison, so the prison atmosphere could not explain it. What could?

To find out, Dr. Kinzel conducted an experiment in the prison with fifteen volunteer prisoners. Eight had violent histories and seven didn't. The men were asked to stand in the center of an empty room while the "experimenter" approached them slowly. Each was to say, "Stop!" when the experimenter came too close.

When the experiment was repeated again and again, each man was found to have a definite body zone, territory or bubble, a personal space Dr. Kinzel labeled a "body buffer zone."

"The violent group," Dr. Kinzel said, "kept the experimenter at twice the distance the non-violent ones did." Their body buffer zones were four times larger in volume than the zones of the non-violent group. When someone got too close to one of these men, he resisted as though the intruder were "looming up" or "rushing in."

In this experiment the same feeling had been induced in the violent men as when they had assaulted other prisoners for "messing around." These men, Dr. Kinzel decided, went into an unreal panic when someone intruded upon their larger-than-normal body zones. This panic and its resulting violence occurred at a distance that other people would consider normal.

Much of what Dr. Kinzel calls "the quickly spiraling character of violence between 'overcrowded' ghetto groups and the police" may be due to a poor understanding by the police of the sanctity of body zones. Dr. Kinzel's study seems to indicate that we are only beginning to understand the origins of violent outbreaks in human beings, and how to detect and manage them, outbreaks which seldom occur in the animal kingdom where a tacit understanding of territorial needs exists until man interferes.

Sex and Non-Persons

There is, in the whole business of invasion, a strong sexual link. A girl moving into a man's territory encounters a different set of signals than if she were moving into a woman's territory. There is more acceptance and the possibility of a flirtation makes the man less likely to resent the intrusion. The same situation reversed, however, generally puts a woman on her guard.

The signal that invariably is sent by intruders is, "You are a non-person, and therefore I can move in on you. You do not matter."

This signal, in the context of a business situation between boss and employee, can be demoralizing to the employee and useful to the boss. It can in fact reaffirm the boss's leadership.

In a crowded subway there is a slightly different interpretation of the signals. There it is important that the two people regard each other as non-persons. Otherwise the fact that they are forced into such intimate terms may be awkward. The person who intrudes on another verbally in a crowded subway is guilty of a gaucherie. It may in fact be a little left of gauche. Here a rigid withdrawal is necessary in order to endure an uncomfortable situation. We have never seen any movies in which a boy and a girl meet on a crowded subway. It just isn't done, even in Hollywood.

The crowding in subway trains is only bearable, Sommer believes, because the riders tend to think of each other as non-persons. If they are forced to acknowledge each other's presence because of an abrupt stop, for instance, they may resent the situation in which they find themselves.

The reverse is also true. In an uncrowded situation a person will resent being treated as a non-person. Our library researcher noticed one man who lifted his head and stared at her coldly, signaling with body language, "I am an individual, by what right do you intrude?"

He was using body language to resist her intrusion and she all at once became the person aggressed against, instead of the aggressor. So strongly did she feel this man's disapproval that she was unable to follow through her experiment for the rest of that day.

Her inability to continue was because the man whose privacy she was invading suddenly cut through her own defenses and for the first time in the experiment she perceived him as a human instead of an object. This ability to realize humanity in another individual is an extremely important key to how we act and react in body language as well as in all relationships. Dr. Sommer points out that an object, a non-person, cannot invade someone else's personal space, any more than a tree or a chair can. Nor is there any problem with invading the personal space of a non-person.

As an example Sommer cites the hospital nurses who discuss the patient's condition at his bedside, or the black maid in the white household who serves dinner while the guests debate the race question. Even the janitor who empties the waste basket in an office may not bother to knock when he enters, nor does the occupant of the office mind this intrusion. The janitor is not a real person to him. He's a non-person just as the man in the office is a non-person to the janitor.

Ceremonies and Seating

How we recognize and react to invasions includes a number of what Sommer calls "recognition ceremonies." In normal circumstances when you invade another's territory in either a library or a cafeteria, you send out a set of deferential signals. Verbally you apologize and ask, "Is this seat taken?" In body language you lower your eyes when you sit down.

When you take a seat on a crowded bus the proper ceremony is to keep your eyes straight ahead and avoid looking at the person sitting next to you. For other situations there are other ceremonies.

Defending personal space, according to Dr. Sommers, involves using the proper body language signals or gestures and postures as well as a choice of a location. How do you sit at an empty table when you wish to discourage other people from joining you? What body language do you use? A study by Sommers among university students showed that sitting down at an empty table when you wanted privacy usually involved use of two procedures. Either you look for privacy by positioning yourself as far as possible from other distracting people, or you attempt to get privacy by keeping the entire table to yourself alone.

If you look for privacy by retreating from others, you approach the problem from an avoidance viewpoint. You take a retreat position, usually at the corner of the table. In body language you say, "Share my table if you wish, but leave me alone. I am putting myself here at a corner so that the next person can sit as far from me as possible."

The other approach would be to try to keep the entire table to yourself. This is an offensive attitude and the aggressive person who chooses it would seat himself in the center of either side. He is saying, "Leave me alone. You cannot sit down without annoying me, so find another table!"

Among other findings of Dr. Sommer's study were the following: students who are in retreat, who wish to be as far away from others as they can get, will face away from the door. Students who wish to hog the entire table, who are in defense, will face the door. Most students, retreaters and defenders, preferred the back of the room, and most preferred small tables or tables against the wall.

In body language, students who sat squarely in the center of the table were asserting their dominance, their ability to handle the situation and also their desire to have the table to themselves.

The student who sat at the corner of the table signaled his wish to be left alone. "I don't mind if you share the table, but if you do, I have placed myself far away. You should do likewise. In that way we can both have our privacy."

The same is true of park benches. If you want privacy and you take a seat on an empty park bench you will most likely sit on the far end of either side indicating, "If you must sit here too, there is room enough to leave me alone."

If you don't want to share the bench you will position yourself in the center and communicate, "I want this bench as my own. Sit and you are intruding."

If you are willing to share your bench and your privacy then you will sit to one side, but not at the far end.

These approaches to the struggle for privacy reflect our inner personality. They indicate that the extroverted man will tend to go after his privacy by holding off the world. The introverted one will look for his by sharing his place with others, but keeping them at a distance. In both cases the body language involved includes a different set of signals, not a signal of body movement, but rather a signal of placement. "I put myself here and by doing so I say, 'Keep off' or 'Sit here but do not intrude.' "

This is similar to the signal transmitted by arranging the body in various postures relating to the environment: behind the desk in an office, to signal, "Keep off, I am to be respected"; at the top of a judge's bench, the highest point in a courtroom, to signal, "I am far above you and therefore my judgment is best"; or close to someone else, violating their zone, to say, "You have no rights of your own. I move in on you at will and therefore I am superior."

FOR DISCUSSION AND REVIEW

1 How does Fast relate personal spaces, zones, and territories to body language?

2 What is the relationship between rank and the vulnerability of one's territory? Cite several examples which support your answer.

3 How, acording to Fast, does a person convey dominance?

4 The next time you go to a movie or watch television, carefully note the utilization of space by the characters involved. How do people react when their territory is invaded? What defenses are employed against invasion? How does the invader act?

5 Fast states that "dominance through height is a truism." Do you agree?

Why or why not? Discuss the many facets of this issue with other members of the class.

6 According to Fast, "when a man's territorial defenses are weakened or intruded upon, his self-assurance tends to grow weaker." As a modest experiment, try invading the territory of a friend or roommate; for example, look over his shoulder while he is typing. What happens? Does your experience tend to confirm Fast's generalization? Explain.

7 What is a "non-person"?

8 What is the relationship between space and personality? In what ways can this information be valuable to a parent? A teacher? A psychiatrist? A prison warden?

Teacher's Desk

Psychology Today

Much of what happens in a class-room can be affected by the spatial arrangement of the seats. Certain seating arrangements, for example, are more comfortable than others and are, therefore, more conducive to certain types of classroom activities. Open discussions seem to be promoted when the students and teachers can all face one another. In order to ascertain the significance of seating arrangements with respect to degree of comfort, psychologist Fred C. Feitler and two associates asked students at Syracuse University to rate seven classroom seating charts. The implications of their results are pertinent to student and teacher alike.

WHICH OF these classroom seating arrangements would you find the most and the least comfortable if you were a student? If you were a teacher?

Psychologist Fred C. Feitler of the Southern Tier Regional Educational Center in Horseheads, New York, and two fellow researchers asked these questions of 276 graduates and undergraduates at Syracuse University's School of Education. Some of the results:

Either as student or as teacher, most subjects said they would feel most comfortable in setting four. Many of them also picked settings three and seven as most comfortable.

In the least-comfortable category, most picked settings six and one, both as student and as teacher. And, despite the general popularity of settings seven and four, many thought that these settings would be uncomfortable for students.

Theorizing that the choices relate to a person's need to be controlled by or to control others, the researchers say they expected setting six to be a least-comfortable choice since it creates ambivalence for both teachers and students. "The setting is one of high teacher control, although the teacher is not in a traditional teaching position," they say. And the arrangement does nothing for those students who want to con-

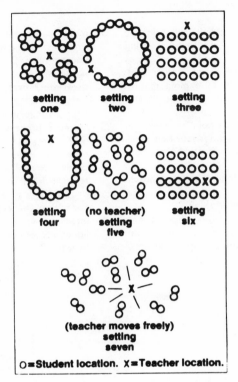

setting
one

setting
two

setting
three

setting
four

(no teacher)
setting
five

setting
six

(teacher moves freely)
setting
seven

O=Student location. X=Teacher location.

trol other persons, since "it does not facilitate either student-student or student-teacher interaction."

There were a couple of surprises. Though they expected setting five to be selected overwhelmingly as the least comfortable, it "was not selected for any category with any consistency worth noting." They speculate that "the notion of a learning situation without a teacher is not even considered as feasible," despite a trend toward independent study and individual instruction.

A bigger surprise was the selection of setting one as a least-comfortable choice. It was surprising, they say, because "the concept of students working in small groups with the teacher helping as needed would appear as one which is desirable and often used," particularly in science laboratory work. One possible explanation is "the belief that students working without the direct assistance of the teacher are not efficient."

Feitler and his colleagues say that more studies of this sort are needed because "the traditional classroom setting—the teacher in front of a class in neat rows—is undergoing significant, if not revolutionary, changes." They reason that comfortable seating arrangements "facilitate the learning process."

FOR DISCUSSION AND REVIEW

1   In terms of proxemics, why do you
    think the students found "setting
    four" to be so "comfortable"? Does
    Fast's discussion of space (pp.
    531–543) help to explain the re-
    sults of Feitler's experiment? Dis-
    cuss.

2   From a teacher's point of view, why
    do you think settings four and seven
    might be uncomfortable for stu-
    dents?

3   Why do you think that the research-
    ers expected "setting five" to be
    the least comfortable?

4   Is it really surprising that "setting
    one" was selected as one of the
    least comfortable arrangements?
    Why?

5   Make arrangements to give this
    same test to another class. Tabulate
    your results. Do your conclusions
    agree with those of Feitler and his
    associates? Explain.

6   Do you feel that "comfortable seat-
    ing arrangements 'facilitate the
    learning process' "? Why or why
    not? Arrange the seats in your
    classroom differently on three suc-
    cessive days. Do you notice a dif-
    ference from one arrangement to
    another? Try to explain any differ-
    ences that you experience. Did the
    three seating arrangements selected
    have any effect on the "learning
    process"?

9
from
The American Speaker for Boys and Girls

Benjamin Walter

For centuries man has been aware of the importance of gestures to daily communication. Only within the last two decades, however, have scholars begun to scientifically describe, analyze, and systematize the whole range of human gestures. The following three selections illustrate, from an historical point of view, attempts that have been made to utilize gesture effectively. The first selection is from *The American Speaker for Boys and Girls,* an early twentieth-century elocution book, in which the author carefully depicts the "proper" gestures for a particular oratorical situation. Then, in a selection from the *Secrets of Charm* (1954), Powers and Miller discuss the impressions that can be conveyed with delicate manipulations of the eyes. Finally, Nierenberg and Calero (1971) analyze and discuss the importance of gesture in the business world. While reading these three selections, note the movement from a highly prescriptive presentation of gesture to a more informed presentation based upon descriptive analysis.

GESTURE.—Oratory without proper gesture loses half its charm. The ancient Greeks and Romans attached great importance to gesture. Their rhetoricians taught their pupils graceful gestures as well as how to manage their voices. He who gestures spontaneously conforms to his subject, and who in other respects is truly eloquent, can, in the most effectual manner, make himself a master of other men's minds. Such an orator has power "to stir a fever in the blood of age, and make an infant's sinews strong as steel." Gesture should be used only when it will aid in expressing more forcibly, and to be appropriate and impressive, must always be natural; excess in gestures is to be avoided as well as awkward ones. The following rules have been given by one who has given much thought to this subject, and will be found of great value to the student, taken in connection with the illustrations contained in this article.

"1. The gesture employed most frequently is the movement used in handing a book or other article to a friend, and the delivery of an oration is simply the presentation of ideas to an audience.

"POSITION OF THE HAND.—The hand open, the first finger straight, the other slightly curved, and generally the palms of the hands open toward the audience, so that they may be seen by the audience.

"2. The *Argumentative* gesture may, and should be, used most frequently in debate and argumentative declamation.

"POSITION OF THE HANDS.—First finger straight, the others closed or nearly so.

"This gesture is very useful in earnest debate, as it was often remarked of Clay that the argument seemed to drop from the ends of his fingers. These gestures are of great value in any discourse.

"3. The *Fist*, sometimes called the 'sledge-hammer' gesture, should be used in the expression of the most earnest, powerful, *moving* sentiments, where strong arguments are to be brought out with telling effect. This gesture was a favorite one with Daniel Webster; and in those memorable debates with Hayne in the United States Senate, he is said to have riveted his arguments with the force of a giant when at every appropriate place he brought down his 'sledge-hammer' gesture."

Denial

Bashfulness

Regret

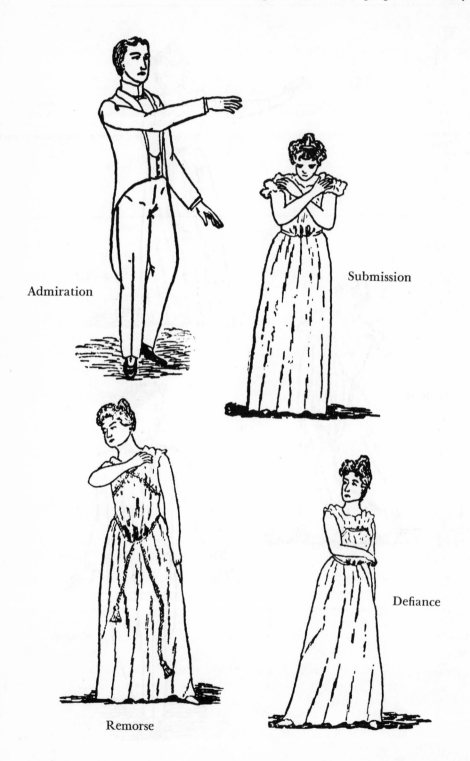

Admiration

Submission

Remorse

Defiance

10

from Secrets of Charm

John Robert Powers
and Mary Sue Miller

EYES HAVE a language all their own. They can smile, glower or record boredom. And although your lips may speak thoughts of which a diplomat would be proud, it would be better never to have spoken at all if your eyes register denial.

It's possible that through unconscious habit your eyes play you false. To make sure, study the antics of your eyes before a mirror. Open and close your eyes slowly. You will discover very soon that it is the movement of the upper lid that gives the eye its range and expression. The lower lid never moves unless you brown-study some object or thought. When it does, it gives your face the expression of a Doubting Thomas. Try it, and you will see how uncomplimentary the expression is to your face or to anyone else's words.

Next, squint. Does this feel natural? If so, chances are that you are going about with a squint that gives people the idea that you are as stubborn as a Missouri mule—or too vain to wear glasses.

How do you look when you are lost in contemplation? Let your lid come halfway down over the pupil and there you have it. Be guilty of this expression when holding a conversation, and you will be considered rudely inattentive.

You probably know at least one person who looks bored or indifferent most of the time. Both his or her eyelids and mouth droop. This is mainly an affectation of young people who believe that such an expression makes them appear sophisticated. But boredom is not, never was or never will be chic! Stamped on the face, it announces just one message: "You tire me, irk me, and I hope you leave soon." No expression is better calculated to kill any spontaneous feeling others might have for the wearer.

Your eyes tell quite another story and say the most appealing things about you when they are wide-open, alight with interest and look the other person right in the eye.

11

from How to Read
a Person Like a Book

*Gerard I. Nierenberg
and Henry H. Calero*

MANY professional salesmen and buyers with whom we have discussed nonverbal communication have stated that they could tell at once when something was wrong by the way a customer or vendor walked into the office and sat down. It is not until we have discussed the details in depth that they begin to see how much they already know about interpreting gestures.

In many typical sales transactions both parties adopt the "I am going to win and you are going to lose" attitude. This causes an elevation of emotional reactions. Let us outline such a situation.

The buyer sits back, away from the desk, folds his arms, crosses his legs, and suspiciously says, "What do you want to talk about?" The seller might respond by getting up on the edge of his chair, feet in a sprinter's position, body leaning forward in a take-charge attitude, waving his hands and using his index finger to drive home his point. The seller's initial gestural advances can cause the buyer to become suspicious, especially if he is one of those who bitterly resent a hard sell. The "Tell you what I'm going to do" approach causes the buyer to withdraw and become defensive.

Instead of changing to an alternate plan, or motivating the buyer to get involved, the seller now becomes insecure because his ideas are not accepted. At this point the seller's gestures tend to be defensive. He may push himself away from the desk, twist his body in a silhouette, cross his legs and arms, then ask such ineffective questions as "What's the matter with you? Don't you understand?" or "Why are you being so unreasonable?" This line of questioning only serves to drive the two further apart.

When this stage is reached there are very few instances where either a buyer or a seller is expert enough to restructure or wind down the emotions in order to solve their problem or reach an agreement. A "Let's call it off or postpone it" attitude prevails. Often the atmosphere becomes so negatively charged that each side starts accusing the other of causing the breakdown. In day-to-day situations this is the point where we rationalize that "It was the other guy's fault we didn't settle. How can we do business with people like that?"

Those executives attending our video-taped practice seminars, however, have a second chance. We can replay what took place and objectively review why and how the negotiation failed. Being able to see and hear their mistakes gives each participant a greater insight into a degenerating process that they can avoid in future life situations.

Some businessmen, both buyers and sellers, believe that once they have been exposed to this form of training-by-viewing, they have an overwhelming advantage over their opposers. But this is not completely true. All they have is a better understanding of the attitudes and emotions that are being communicated by their opposers. They still must develop their ability to read congruency of gestures, to evaluate by testing, and, most important, to understand how they themselves are responding to gestures. The phrase "putting it all together" probably best explains what we hope may happen.

To young, inexperienced salesmen many purchasing agents are ogres like the one in [the illustration below].

And some purchasing agents assume this characteristic pose because they like to have others squirm, talk too much, or simply perform while they themselves act as spectators rather than participants. A hard man to sell? Yes indeed! But if the salesman can get him involved by asking questions that deal with his needs, the glacial attitude may melt. If not, the buyer's next gesture may be to put down his glasses ("That's it!

Get out"), cross his arms ("Your time is running out"), or begin to shuffle papers ("I've got more important things to do").

Experienced salesmen know how important it is to "close the gap" between buyer and seller, so they usually manage to have available photographs, reports, or other visual presentations. With these they try to move around the desk, either to the same side as the buyer or at a right angle to him. If the buyer reacts to the salesman moving closer by crossing his arms or making some other defensive gesture, this communicates his displeasure. The salesman should take care to return to his original position on the opposite side of the desk. Some people are extremely sensitive about their position of dominance behind a desk and will fight to maintain their image.

[The illustration below] presents gesture-clusters that might be seen in a typical buyer/seller relationship.

The buyer is leaning far back in his chair, away from the seller, and is steepling. His coat is buttoned and his legs are crossed while he swings one foot as if impatient with what is being said. A slight scowl indicates he is not ready to buy or accept what the seller is offering. The seller is leaning forward in an action-oriented position. His gesture with the upturned palms of his hands, his simple smile, and unbuttoned coat indicate he is being open and desires the buyer to feel comfortable. He has reached the critical stage of his sales presentation. If he says the wrong thing now, the buyer may signal this by crossing his arms over his chest or recrossing his legs so that the elevated foot points away from the seller and toward the nearest exit.

FOR DISCUSSION AND REVIEW

1 Do the postures and gestures depicted in *The American Speaker* selection strike you as posed? Is there, then, a distinction to be made between the proper gestures of the rhetorician and the gestures of everyday life? Explain any distinction you see.

2 Observe someone giving a speech or a lecture. How does he use his hands? Can you recognize any of the hand gestures described in the selection from *The American Speaker*? Were the gestures used effectively? Explain.

3 Do you agree with Powers and Miller that a person can say one thing and have his eyes "register denial"? Provide an example to illustrate your answer.

4 As Powers and Miller suggest, "study the antics of your eyes before a mirror." What messages can you convey with your eyes?

5 After reading the article by Nierenberg and Calero, why would you say that kinesics (or, more popularly, body language) has become the concern of businessmen, professionals, and laymen?

6 What are "gesture clusters"? Do you find it valuable to think in terms of clusters of gestures instead of single, isolated gestures?

7 Discuss any movements or developments in man's knowledge about and use of body language as reflected in these three excerpts.

PROJECTS FOR "SPACE AND THE LANGUAGE OF THE BODY"

1 An interesting project that you may wish to undertake is the invention of your own system of kinegraphs. Begin by taking a particular situation and describing as many movements as you can and then determining whether or not each movement is meaningful. Finally, symbolize the important movements by using the kinegraphs you have invented.

2 Study a short movie while the sound is turned off. Make notes on your observations of proxemics and body language and what you learn from these aspects of behavior. Turn on the sound and make notes on your findings once again. Write a paper which discusses the quantitative and qualitative differences in what you learned from both viewings. Ideally, you should try to determine the relative importance of body language, verbal communication, and proxemics.

3 Devise an experiment that will test the effects on behavior of various arrangements of chairs in a classroom. Use the article and chart on pp. 544–546 as a starting point. You may wish to poll the feelings of members of a number of classes and elicit reasons for their feelings.

4 Play a game that involves body language. For example: Divide players into groups which will act out situations involving body language— a tough cop ticketing a motorist, one person trying to give directions to another but not succeeding, a man trying to be friendly with a woman who really does not wish to be bothered but who also does not wish to be impolite. Performances should be judged by the group

as a whole on the basis of the degree to which performers illustrate a knowledge of body language.

5   *Do a study of printed advertisements for the purpose of determining the degree to which they illustrate principles of body language and proxemics. You should limit your study to advertisements in a particular area (e.g., perfume, stockings, cars, cigarettes, etc.).*

6   *Ray L. Birdwhistell has claimed that a trained observer can tell where a person is from by the body language he uses. Study a foreigner or a person who lives in a part of the country different from your own to see if you can identify characteristics of nonverbal language to support Birdwhistell's statement.*

7   *It has been estimated by Birdwhistell that 65% of communication is extra-verbal, whereas only 35% is verbal. Study a dramatic presentation of a play or a movie made from a novel and test the accuracy of Birdwhistell's claim. For example, locate a specific scene in the written work in which the thoughts and feelings of a character are revealed through an omniscient narrator. Study how these feelings and thoughts are conveyed to you in the dramatic version.*

8   *Body language as a science may be new, but authors as far back in history as Homer were aware of how important the descriptions of characters could be. In his short story "Clay" in Dubliners, James Joyce describes Maria as having witch-like characteristics, the recognition of which is central to the meaning of his story. Joyce does not tell us that Maria is a witch; he shows her to be one, and that method is very effective. Herman Melville in his short story "Bartleby the Scrivener" makes use of his knowledge of proxemics. The story's subtitle is "A Story of Wall Street," and it is indeed a story of walls and the frustrations that they symbolize in Bartleby, the main character. Do a study of a scene from a work of literature for what it tells you through its use of kinesics and proxemics.*

SELECTED BIBLIOGRAPHY

Ardrey, Robert. *The Territorial Imperative.* New York: Atheneum, 1966. (An examination of the concept of territoriality, the relationship of men and animals to space.)

Baker, Stephen. *Visual Persuasion.* New York: McGraw-Hill, 1961. (An analysis of "picture-talk" in modeling, advertising, and corporate business.)

Birdwhistell, Ray L. *Introduction to Kinesics.* Louisville, Kentucky: University of Louisville Press, 1952. (Introduction to the field of kinesics, with kinegraphs and what they symbolize.)

————. "Kinesics." *International Encyclopaedia of Social Sciences.* Ed. David L. Sills. New York: The Macmillan Company and The Free Press, 1968. (A brief but technical introduction.)

————. *Kinesics and Context: Essays on Body Motion Communication.* Philadelphia: University of Pennsylvania Press, 1970. (An interesting collection of Birdwhistell's essays on nonverbal human communication; excellent bibliography.)

Blackmon, Rosemary. "How Much Do You Tell When You Talk?" *Vogue,* July 1961, pp. 40–41, 100–01. (A readable discussion of paralinguistic speech features.)

Chaitanya. "The School of Silence." *Quest,* 59 (Autumn 1968), 48–51. (Gesture, movement, and silence as means of dramatic expression and communication.)

Chase, Stuart. *The Proper Study of Mankind . . .* New York: Harper & Row, 1956. (See pp. 276–89; an informative chapter on the communication sciences, twelve disciplines pursuing communication study.)

Critchley, M. *The Language of Gesture.* London: Arnold, 1939. (A valuable early study.)

Darwin, Charles R. *The Expression of the Emotions in Man and Animals.* London: J. Murray, 1873. (A germinal work.)

Davis, Flora. "The Way We Speak 'Body Language.' " *The New York Times Magazine,* May 31, 1970, Section 6, pp. 8–9, 29, 31–32, 34, 41–42. (An introductory essay on the work of Birdwhistell, Scheflen, Goffman, and Kendon with kinesics; illustrated.)

Fabun, Donald, "The Silent Languages." *Communications: The Transfer of Meaning.* New York: The Macmillan Company, 1968. (An introductory discussion of the languages of time, color, and space.)

Goffman, Erving. *Behavior in Public Places.* New York: The Free Press of Glencoe, 1963. (A psychiatrist's analysis of public behavior.)

————. *The Presentation of Self in Everyday Life.* Edinburgh: University of Edinburgh, Social Sciences Research Center, 1956. (An analysis of an individual's impressions of himself when appearing before others.)

Hall, Edward T. "Proxemics." *Current Anthropology,* 9 (April–June 1968), 83–104. (A good introduction to proxemics with charts, comments by authorities, and bibliography.)

————. *The Hidden Dimension.* New York: Doubleday & Company, 1966. (A fascinating discussion of human and animal use of space.)

Harris, Christie, and Moira Johnston. *Figleafing Through History: The Dynamics of Dress.* New York: Atheneum, 1971. (An entertaining historical discussion of clothes and how they affect the self-conceptions of individuals in different societies.)

Hayes, Francis. "Gestures: A Working Bibliography." *Southern Folklore Quarterly,* 21 (December 1957), 218–317. (Extensive references to books and articles on gestures; annotated.)

Hewes, Gordon W. "World Distribution of Certain Postural Habits." *American Anthropologist,* 57 (April 1955), 231–44. (Distribution and significance of certain standing and sitting positions.)

Mehrabian, Albert. "Communication Without Words." *Psychology Today,* 2 (September 1968), 52–55. (A basic discussion of nonverbal forms of communication.)

Michael, G., and F. N. Willis, Jr. "The Development of Gestures as a Function of Social Class, Education, and Sex." *Psychological Record,* 18 (October 1968), 515–19. (A study of eight groups of children differing in social class, education, and sex.)

Morris, Desmond. *The Human Zoo.* New York: McGraw-Hill, 1969. (A zoologist's analysis of the sociological implications of population clusters.)

Nierenberg, Gerard I. *The Art of Negotiating*. New York: Hawthorn Books, 1968. (Practical application of kinesics to interpersonal relationships.)

————, and Henry H. Calero. *How To Read A Person Like A Book*. New York: Hawthorn Books, 1971. (A profusely illustrated, popular treatment of kinesics and proxemics.)

"Parting Shots: What Are The Politicians Really Saying?—Body Language Tells You." *Life*, October 9, 1970, pp. 82–84. (Selected pictures of politicians with interpretative remarks.)

Pittenger, Robert E., Charles F. Hockett, and John J. Danehy. *The First Five Minutes: A Sample of Microscopic Interview Analysis*. Ithaca, New York: Paul Martineau, Publisher, 1960. (An in-depth analysis with emphasis on paralinguistic features of a five-minute interview between a psychiatrist and a young female patient.)

Ruesch, Jurgen, and Weldon Kees. *Nonverbal Communication: Notes on the Visual Perception of Human Relations*. Berkeley and Los Angeles: University of California Press, 1956. (An investigation of nonverbal forms of communication; dated illustrations.)

Scheflen, A. E. "The Significance of Posture in Communications Systems." *Psychiatry*, 27 (November 1964), 316–31. (A psychiatrist's analysis of the significance of postural activities and markers in interview and group situations; illustrated.)

Smith, Henry Lee, Jr. "Language and the Total System of Communication." *Linguistics Today*. Ed. A. A. Hill. New York: Basic Books, 1968. (An interesting, readable analysis of the totality of communication.)

4 5 6 7 8 9 10 11 12 13 14 15   88 87 86 85 84 83 82 81 80 79 78 77 76 75 74